GERONIMO
AND SITTING BULL

Leaders of the Legendary West

BILL MARKLEY

TWODOT®

Guilford, Connecticut
Helena, Montana

A · TWODOT® · BOOK
An imprint and registered trademark of The Rowman & Littlefield Publishing Group, Inc.
4501 Forbes Blvd., Ste. 200
Lanham, MD 20706
www.rowman.com

Distributed by NATIONAL BOOK NETWORK

Copyright © 2021 by Bill Markley
Illustrations by James Hatzell

All rights reserved. No part of this book may be reproduced in any form or by any electronic or mechanical means, including information storage and retrieval systems, without written permission from the publisher, except by a reviewer who may quote passages in a review.

British Library Cataloguing in Publication Information available

Library of Congress Cataloging-in-Publication Data
Names: Markley, Bill, 1951- author. | Hatzell, Jim, illustrator.
Title: Geronimo and Sitting Bull : leaders of the legendary west / Bill
    Markley ; Jim Hatzell, illustrator.
Description: Guilford, Connecticut : TwoDot, [2021] | Includes
    bibliographical references and index.
Identifiers: LCCN 2020054575 (print) | LCCN 2020054576 (ebook) | ISBN
    9781493048441 (paperback) | ISBN 9781493048458 (epub)
Subjects: LCSH: Geronimo, 1829-1909. | Sitting Bull, 1831-1890. | Indians
    of North America—Biography. | Apache Indians—Wars, 1883-1886. | Apache
    Indians—Kings and rulers—Biography. | Dakota Indians—Kings and
    rulers—Biography. | Dakota Indians—Wars.
Classification: LCC E89 .M375 2021 (print) | LCC E89 (ebook) | DDC
    920.0092/97—dc23
LC record available at https://lccn.loc.gov/2020054575
LC ebook record available at https://lccn.loc.gov/2020054576

♾™ The paper used in this publication meets the minimum requirements of American National Standard for Information Sciences—Permanence of Paper for Printed Library Materials, ANSI/NISO Z39.48-1992

*Dedicated to my parents, Bill and Gloria Markley,
who instilled in me a love of the West.*

Dedicated to the Chiricahua people and the Hunkpapa people.

We will avoid them [the army] if we can. If we cannot, we will fight.
—SITTING BULL

*We thought it more manly to die on the warpath
than to be killed in prison.*
—GERONIMO

Geronimo and Sitting Bull.

Contents

ILLUSTRATIONS LIST

Introduction

Geronimo. Sitting Bull. Most Americans and many people worldwide have heard these two Indian names. Today, most of the general public knows little about the lives of these great leaders. However, during the second half of the nineteenth century when they opposed white intrusion and expansion into their territories, just the mention of their names could spark fear or anger. After they surrendered to the army and lived in captivity, they evoked curiosity and sympathy for the plight of the American Indian.

I'm concerned the current younger generation is losing touch with the past. On a visit to Tucson, Arizona, I entered a large bookstore and approached the counter. A young man on the opposite side of the counter was busy on a computer.

"Excuse me," I said.

"Can I help you?" he answered, looking up.

"Do you have any books on Geronimo?"

He gave me a blank stare, then said, "What's that?"

Shocked, I said, "Geronimo! The great Apache leader!"

Shrugging, he responded, "No idea. Never heard of him."

Fortunately, another employee heard our exchange and led me to the Native American section.

Who were Geronimo and Sitting Bull? How did they emerge as leaders of their people, rising to become world-renowned?

The Apaches of the Southwest fought neighboring tribes, the Spanish, the Mexicans, and later, the Americans. Their tactics were pure guerrilla warfare—raiding for food and supplies and fighting only when it was to their advantage. Geronimo, known for his spiritual gifts, was fierce in his fighting abilities and a master of eluding pursuers.

The Lakotas of the northern plains also fought neighboring tribes as well as the Americans when they began to encroach on their territory. The Lakotas raided for horses and battled for glory and honor. Sitting Bull, through brave deeds and living an honorable life, emerged as a charismatic warrior, holy man, and leader.

In their own ways, what Geronimo and Sitting Bull wanted to do was to protect their people and preserve their ways of life. What would you do if people of a different race invaded your homeland? Told you where you must live? Told you how you must live? Told you your religion was wrong? Took your children far away, raised them in their schools, and punished them if they spoke their native language? What would you do?

It's hard to see the world through Geronimo and Sitting Bull's eyes. Today, many Americans are disconnected from creation. We live in homes filled with conveniences never dreamed of by nineteenth-century Apaches and Lakotas—clean hot and cold running water, and electricity to light up the night, warm homes in the winter and cool them in the summer, and power anything conceivable. Instead of raising crops or hunting for game, we go to a grocery store where we can buy any food item we want. Automobiles, ships, and airplanes transport us anywhere in the world. We communicate with each other at the speed of an electron. The Apaches and Lakotas were more in tune with nature, they were immersed in it—the warmth of the sun, the bite of a frigid wind, the fragrance of growing things, the songs of birds, the calls of animals, the feel of earth and water.

Information about Geronimo and Sitting Bull was written mostly by their enemies. Even when sympathetic whites recorded their words, they may have gotten them wrong. Both men came from traditions and mind-sets different not only from Americans but from each other. The Apache and Lakota languages are different from English, and they are different from each other. Interpreters may have translated wrong, and recorders may have embellished what was said for their own purposes.

I have used the Apache and Lakota accounts as much as possible unless there was clear contradiction with documented white accounts. People recall events differently. There are contradictory remembrances between Apache individuals and between Lakota individuals. However, Apache and Lakota recountings of events were important—especially accounts of battles—and the latter had to be verified by witnesses. I believe Geronimo and Sitting Bull's accounts of their war exploits, because if they made them up or embellished them, others who were there would have challenged them on those stories.

To state the obvious, Geronimo and Sitting Bull were living the American dream—life, liberty, and the pursuit of happiness—in their own ways, but mainstream America contrived to take their dreams away because they did not conform with what the government and the white population—foes as well as friends—believed was best for them. All Geronimo and Sitting Bull wanted to do was to continue to live their lives as their ancestors had done.

Even if we don't want to be judgmental, we are. We cannot fit these people into our concept of how they should have thought or how they should have acted. Some of the things they believed and the actions they took repulse people living today. Maybe the things we do today will be repulsive to future generations.

I am not an Apache or a Lakota, and I realize I do not understand the subtleties of their cultures. In this book I attempt to tell Geronimo and Sitting Bull's stories as straightforwardly as I can, realizing my own limitations and the limitations of the record that has come down to us. I may not be one hundred percent accurate, but I have strived for one hundred percent honesty.

So, are you ready? Let's enter the world of the Apaches and Lakotas in the search for Geronimo and Sitting Bull.

CHAPTER 1

The Early Years, 1829–1845

USSEN, THE CREATOR, FORMED THE EARTH AND THEN CREATED White Painted Woman, sending her to Earth during a time when monsters dominated, said the Dine (the People).[1] White Painted Woman had two sons, Killer of Enemies and Child of the Water, who killed the monsters. Some Dine said they were descended from Killer of Enemies and other Dine said they were descended from Child of the Water.[2]

The Dine traveled from the far north, leaving behind people in current-day Alaska and Canada who speak a similar language, Athabaskan. The Dine roamed south, exploring and hunting along the slopes of the Rocky Mountains. Some Dine ended their migration in what is now northern Arizona and New Mexico, later to become known as Navajo, bitter rivals to their relatives who continued their journey south. These Dine settled in current-day western Texas, southern Arizona, and New Mexico, and the Mexican states of Sonora and Chihuahua. The Zuni people who contested the arrival of the Dine called them "the enemy," or Apache.[3]

As the Apaches spread throughout what would later be called Apacheria, they further divided into subgroups, becoming isolated from each other. They never formed a cohesive alliance for defense or offense. To the east, Apache bands pursued the buffalo, acquiring customs of plains tribes and living in buffalo-hide tepees. No significant buffalo herds roamed to the west, so those Apaches hunted a variety of animals. They lived at higher mountain elevations in rancherias, movable villages, consisting of brush shelters called wickiups.[4]

The Apache way of life centered on a warrior culture. Apaches practiced two types of warfare: raiding to acquire supplies, and revenge.[5]

In 1598, the Spanish began to settle northern New Mexico, where they first encountered Apaches. Later, they entered what would become Arizona, establishing missions and fortified towns called *presidios*, such as Tubac and Tucson. Warfare increased between the Spanish and Apaches, reaching extreme brutality on both sides.[6]

By trade and theft, the Apaches acquired horses from the Spanish. They never had the desire to raise their own, but usually stole them, using the horses until they were worn out or not needed and then slaughtering them for food. The Apaches acquired additional goods from the Spanish, metal for spears and arrowheads, and later firearms, with which they became proficient.[7]

In 1786, the Spanish established a tentative peace with the Apaches, providing them feeding stations where they distributed food and traded goods. More Spanish settlers arrived in Apacheria, but ten years later, the peace ended when the government could no longer finance distributions to the Apaches, and both sides resumed brutal raids.[8]

With Mexico winning its independence from Spain in 1821, the conflict with the Apaches became dysfunctional. One Mexican state would be at peace and trading with Apaches while the other state warred against them. Some governors put a bounty on Apache scalps, paying $100 for an adult male, $50 for an adult female, and $25 for a child.[9]

Into such a world an Apache baby boy was born. His parents named him Goyahkla, One Who Yawns. He would grow up to become known worldwide as Geronimo.

Wakan Tanka, the Big Holy, created and sustains everything in the universe, said the Lakotas. He formed people from the earth and gave them life.[10] White Calf Buffalo Woman came to the Lakotas, giving them a sacred pipe. She instructed them how to use it for the well-being of the people and told them to always select a good man to care for it. When she told the people it was time for her to leave, she walked away singing, then—changing into a white buffalo—she galloped off.[11]

The Lakota people—*Lakota* means "alliance of friends"—once lived in the woodlands of the current states of Ohio and Indiana during the fourteenth century. Pressure from enemy tribes forced them westward with other closely related groups, the Dakotas and the Nakotas, who spoke the same language but with different dialects. By the 1600s, the Dakotas and Nakotas settled in what are now the states of Wisconsin and Minnesota. From there, bands migrated into eastern North Dakota, South Dakota, and Nebraska as the Lakotas continued farther west, crossing the Missouri River into western North Dakota, South Dakota, Nebraska, eastern Colorado, Wyoming, and Montana.[12]

The Chippewas, enemies of the Lakotas, Dakotas, and Nakotas, called them *Naduwessi*, meaning "snakes" or "enemies." When French explorers and fur traders met them in the 1600s, they used a plural variation of *Naduwessi*, creating the word *Naduwessioux*. The word was shortened over the years to *Sioux*, which was picked up by the British and Americans.[13]

The Lakotas gradually acquired horses through trade and theft. They cared for their horses, and through breeding, increased the size of their herds. They obtained metal for arrowheads and spear points, and eventually, firearms. By being mounted on horseback and using improved weapons, the Lakotas became efficient buffalo hunters living in buffalo-hide tepees and following the migrating herds. Through the eighteenth century, the Lakotas continued to acquire more horses and firearms, which in turn provided a consistent food supply. Their population increased and they become a powerhouse on the northern plains.[14]

The Lakotas consisted of seven tribes. Each tribe subdivided itself into seven bands. By common consent, each band would recognize a chief who led by example. The chief followed the wishes of a council of elders who made decisions by consensus. There were warrior societies and from these societies the chief, again, with the consensus of the council, appointed men called *akicita* who acted as enforcers or policemen.[15]

When the bands came together as a tribe, the tribe was governed by a council made up of representatives from each of the band councils. The tribal council was led by older, well-known chiefs. The tribal council appointed four men called praise-worthy men, or shirt wearers, to carry out the council's decisions with the help of the *akicita*. The tribe gave them special shirts to wear. They were to be models to the community—brave, generous, stoic. At any time, they could lose their shirt if they failed the tribe's expectations.[16]

The tribes came together each year in June for a Sun Dance, and on occasion some of the tribes would combine for large buffalo hunts.[17]

The Lakotas fought with most of their neighboring tribes, but there would also be times of peaceful trade with those same tribes. In 1803, the United States bought the Louisiana Territory from France. This territory encompassed much of the land the Lakotas ranged across. The next year, President Thomas Jefferson sent the Corps of Discovery led by Meriwether Lewis and William Clark to explore the territory and locate a route to the Pacific Ocean. As they traveled up the Missouri River and into what is now South Dakota, the Corps of Discovery met the Yankton Nakotas, establishing a good relationship with them, but, farther upriver at the mouth of the Bad River, a confrontation with the Brulé Lakotas almost erupted into violence until cooler heads prevailed. Lewis and Clark were wary of the Lakotas after that. For the next thirty years, the major contact Lakotas would have with whites would be when they encountered occasional American and Canadian fur trappers and traders at isolated trading posts along the Missouri River and its tributaries.

Into such a world a Lakota baby boy was born whose parents would name him Jumping Badger. He would grow up to be known worldwide as *Tatanka Iyotake*—Sitting Bull.

The boy who would become Geronimo said he was born in June 1829.[18] He was born into the Bedonkohe band of the Chiricahua

Apaches who ranged in and around the Mogollon Mountains, the headwaters of the Gila River, which would later be western New Mexico and eastern Arizona.[19]

The boy's father Taklishim, The Gray One, and mother Juana named him Goyahkla, One Who Yawns. He was a middle child out of three brothers and four sisters.[20]

Goyahkla was the grandson of the great chief Mahco, a wise and renowned warrior. Mahco was dead before Goyahkla was born, but his father Taklishim told him about the great feats and wise actions of his grandfather, and Goyahkla would treasure those tales throughout his life. The chieftainship did not pass to Taklishim, and Goyahkla would never be considered a hereditary chief.[21]

Goyahkla's childhood was the same as that of other Apache boys. His father told him tales of raids and battles, warrior bravery, and exciting hunts. His mother taught him about the Earth and sky and to pray to Ussen for strength, health, wisdom, and protection. Goyahkla learned the Chiricahuas' spiritual traditions and ceremonies. His mother taught him about White Painted Woman, Child of the Water, the Mountain Spirits, and other entities. Goyahkla learned that the number four was sacred, and that there were forces called Powers that were given to certain humans, who were called *di-yen*. The Powers were neutral and could be used for good or evil. Those who used their Power for evil were considered witches. The Apaches were concerned about ghosts. They tried not to touch dead bodies and buried the dead as quickly as possible. They either destroyed all the deceased person's belongings or included them in the burial so his or her spirit would not return for them. Thus, the spirit could begin its journey to its place in the afterlife.[22]

Goyahkla and his brothers and sisters played games that would benefit them later in life, including mock battles and hide-and-seek. When they were old enough, they helped in the family's two-acre vegetable patch, planting, caring for, and harvesting corn, beans, melons, and pumpkins. The children were taught to care for the family dogs and horses.[23]

Goyahkla learned about the different wild plants and their uses, whether for food or medicinal purposes. The children accompanied the women to gather berries sometimes far from home, and would take along horses to carry the baskets of berries back to the rancheria. Goyahkla was on one berry-picking trip he would remember for the rest of his life. One of the women, Cho-ko-le, along with her horse and little dog, became separated from the rest of the women and children. As she rode through dense brush, a grizzly bear attacked her and the horse. She was unseated, and the horse ran away. She fought the bear with a knife while her dog attacked the bear's hind feet. Cho-ko-le was able to fend off the bear until it took a swipe at her head, ripping away most of her scalp. She was able to stab the bear four times, after which it left her alone. She managed to bind her scalp back onto her head but was so weak she could not walk. The horse returned to the rancheria without her. After two days of looking, a search party found her and brought her home where *di-yen* used their Powers to heal her.[24]

Along with the other children, Goyahkla learned to make and shoot slingshots and bows and arrows. They shot at targets and at each other. He learned to care for and protect horses. He was taught to ride and to hunt on horseback.[25] Goyahkla hunted game animals—buffalo, elk, deer, antelope, rabbits, and turkeys, as well as predators—eagles, bears, and mountain lions. Ussen forbade Apaches to eat fish, frogs, and snakes.[26] He learned what plants to gather and how to prepare them for various medicinal remedies, and he also learned how to remove arrowheads and bullets—knowledge that he would use in the future.[27]

Goyahkla and the other children were taught to move without being seen or heard. Goyahkla excelled at remaining motionless—so much so that in later life some believed he could actually become invisible. The children were conditioned to increase their stamina, running for as many as four miles with pebbles held in their mouths or mouthfuls of water and told not to swallow, learning to breathe only through their noses as they raced across uneven desert terrain and up and down mountain slopes. In the winter, they were instructed to break through the ice and jump into bone-chilling water and remain there until told they could come out. All of this conditioning was to prepare them for the hardy life of Chiricahua society.[28]

When Goyahkla was ten years old, his father became sick and died. Although she could have remarried immediately since she had children to care for, Goyahkla's mother chose to remain single. From that moment on, Goyahkla helped provide for his mother.[29]

The Nednhis were the southernmost band of Chiricahuas, living in the Sierra Madre Mountains of northern Mexico. A group of Nednhis traveled north to the headwaters of the Gila River to visit with Bedonkohe relatives. Goyahkla became good friends with one of the visitors, a boy about his same age named Juh (pronounced "Hoo"). Their friendship would grow and last a lifetime. Juh was full of mischief. One of his tricks was to trail Goyahkla's sisters and other Bedonkohe girls when they left the rancheria to gather nuts. After the girls had filled their baskets, he and his friends would surprise them and steal their baskets. Goyahkla's grandmother learned of this and had Goyahkla and his friends ambush the ambushers. The prank ended after that. Juh stuttered, and when he became excited, the stutter became severe. Goyahkla learned to understand what Juh was saying, which would become useful to both in later years.[30]

The greatest Chiricahua leader during Goyahkla's early life was the Bedonkohe, Mangas Coloradas (Red Sleeves). Many Chiricahuas admired and followed Mangas Coloradas because he was courageous in warfare. Although Mangas Coloradas hated Mexicans, he tolerated and traded with those in the state of Chihuahua. Many Chiricahua bands, including Goyahkla's Bedonkohe band, accepted Mangas Coloradas as their leader, and Goyahkla grew up modeling himself after him. Goyahkla never saw a white man during his childhood.[31]

—◦—

The boy who would become Sitting Bull was born into the Bad Bow band of the Hunkpapa tribe of the Lakota people, possibly in March 1831.[32] He may have been born on the Grand River in present-day South Dakota.[33] The Lakotas roamed over the vast northern plains bounded by the Missouri River to the east and the Big Horn Mountains to the west, as well as north into Canada and south into Nebraska along the Republican River. In the middle of this territory were the timbered slopes of the Black Hills, which the Lakotas considered sacred.[34]

The boy's father—at the time named Tatanka Iyotake (Sitting Bull)—and mother, Her-Holy-Door, named him Jumping Badger.[35] Jumping Badger had an older sister, Good Feather Woman, and twin younger sisters, Twin Woman and Brown Shawl Woman. The boy was born into a prominent family. His father and two uncles, Four Horns and Looks-for-Him-in-a-Tent, were all chiefs.[36]

Jumping Badger was brought up in a loving family. Parents considered children special gifts from Wakan Tanka. They doted on them, never punishing them. Like all Lakota mothers, Her-Holy-Door would be a major influence on her son until his voice began to change.[37]

His parents taught him about nature, and of the living and the inanimate within it, how everything was interrelated together and with the spirit world through Wakan Tanka. They told him four was a sacred number. There were four directions, four seasons, four stages of life, and above all, four great virtues—bravery, fortitude, generosity, and wisdom. He learned White Buffalo Calf Woman had instructed the people how to pray to Wakan Tanka using sacred pipes. He was told that when the time came, he would go on a vision quest to find what the spirits had in store for him. He saw and learned about Lakota ceremonies such as sweat lodges, and the most important of all, the Sun Dances, performed to ensure the prosperity and increase of the tribe.[38]

Jumping Badger was deliberate. He always thought before acting. The people nicknamed him Hunkesni (Slow Moving), but he was anything but slow, and soon excelled in foot races, beating all the other boys. He became good at long distance running, swimming, and diving.[39] At five years old, he began straddling horses behind his mother, and by ten he was a master horseman. He became an expert in training horses, and his mounts were considered the best.[40]

He loved playing games with the other children. One game he enjoyed was the hoop game where one team using sticks tried to roll a hoop through the opposing team's goal while the opposing team tried to prevent the goal and score their own.[41]

By the age of seven, he had made a bow and arrows. He spent a great deal of time and effort bringing one arrow in particular to perfection. One day, a man considered a master arrow maker held a contest for all the young boys. He told them they were to go on a hunt in the trees along the river and the boy who brought back the prettiest bird would win a bow and quiver full of arrows. The boys entered the timber. Jumping Badger spied an oriole and was about to shoot when along came another boy, considered a bully, who shot at the bird but missed. His favorite arrow had gotten tangled in branches high in a tree.

Jumping Badger said he would help him retrieve it. He shot a blunt arrow at the stuck arrow and knocked it to the ground, but in so doing, he broke the other boy's arrow. The boy became angry, and a fight was about to break out between all the boys, who were now taking sides. To cool the situation, Jumping Badger gave the bully his fine arrow, resolving the tense situation. The boys returned to the village at the end of the day with no beautiful birds, but they told the arrow maker what had happened between Jumping Badger and the bully. The arrow maker was impressed with Jumping Badger's ability to keep the peace and awarded him the prize bow and quiver of arrows. Jumping Badger made friends easily, and many of the boys would remain his lifelong friends.[42]

In accordance with Lakota tradition, when Jumping Badger's father believed he was old enough, he asked the boy's uncle, Four Horns, to begin instructing him in the way of Lakota men and their responsibilities. Four Horns was honored to do so and took Jumping Badger into his home, where he lived from that time on. He would still be close to his family, but in this manner, he would learn what it meant to be a good Lakota.[43]

As Jumping Badger became older, he excelled in archery and throwing a spear through a moving hoop.[44] Four Horns honed Jumping Badger's tracking, stalking, and hunting skills. When Jumping Badger was ten years old, Four Horns took him out to a small buffalo herd to kill his first buffalo. Four Horns pointed out a particular cow on the outside of the herd for Jumping Badger to shoot. He warned him not to enter into the herd where he and his horse might be injured or killed if the herd stampeded. Jumping Badger did not heed his uncle's advice. Charging straight into the herd, he selected a large bull, and shooting his arrows into the animal, killed him. The herd stampeded. Fortunately, Jumping Badger and his horse were not injured.

Four Horns was angry and asked why he had not shot the cow. Jumping Badger said when he'd approached the cow, he saw she had a calf; he knew if he killed the cow, the calf would have no milk. Four Horns marveled at the boy's compassion. Jumping Badger showed further compassion when he shared the best cuts of meat with a widow and her two children.[45]

Since the early 1820s, American fur companies had established trading posts on the Missouri River at the mouth of the Bad River in present-day South Dakota. During Jumping Badger's early life, the Hunkpapas traded buffalo hides and furs with the whites at Fort Pierre, which was Pratte, Chouteau, and Company's main trading center on the Upper Missouri. Situated on the west bank of the

Sitting Bull's first buffalo hunt.

Missouri three miles upriver from the mouth of the Bad River, Fort Pierre would have been where Jumping Badger encountered whites for the first time. The Hunkpapas had a cordial relationship with the traders at the fort and did a brisk business.[46]

The traders purchased on average seventeen thousand buffalo hides a year from the tribes. The price per hide varied based on its quality. In 1843, the price for buffalo robes ranged from $1.50 to $4.00 apiece. The Indians would buy weapons such as Northwest guns, lead, and powder, along with hatchets, knives, and metal spear and arrow points. They bought blankets, coats, shirts, bolts of cloth, beads, salt, pepper, sugar, candy, coffee, and tobacco, as well as metal items such as iron kettles and tin plates and cups. The prices of Northwest guns ranged from $8 to $12, wool blankets from $3 to $7, and coffee, sugar, and flour were $1 per pound. Jumping Badger would grow up knowing white traders and their goods.[47]

Apache Tribes and Lakota, Nakota, and Dakota Tribes

The *Dine* (or *Indeh*) people became known by the Zuni name *Apache*, which means "enemy." They were divided into various tribes and those tribes divided into smaller bands. The Apaches were linked by a common language, similar lifeways, and religion, but they did not join together in any common cause. The Apache groups have been called by a variety of names, sometimes based on the location of their rancherias. Many times, individual members would leave one tribe or band and join another. The Mescalero tribe lived east of the Rio Grande River in New Mexico, and the Lipan tribe lived on the Texas plains. The Plains Apaches, also known as the Kiowa Apaches, lived on the southern plains, hunting buffalo and living in tepees. The Jicarilla tribe lived in northern New Mexico and southern Colorado. The Western Apache tribes, living mostly in Arizona and western New Mexico, were called by a variety of names and are named here by their location: White Mountain, Cibecue, San Carlos, Southern Tonto, and Northern Tonto. The Chiricahuas lived in southeastern Arizona, western New Mexico, and northern Mexico. The Chiricahuas were further divided into Chihenne, Chokonen, Nednhi, and Bedonkohe bands. Geronimo was born into the small Bedonkohe band.[48]

The *Oyate* ("people") are made up of three groups, the Dakota, Nakota, and Lakota (each means "alliance of friends"). The Chippewas called them *Naduwessi*, which means "snakes" or "enemies." The French, who first met them, pluralized the Chippewa word to *Naduwessioux*, which became shortened to Sioux and was picked up by the British and Americans. The Dakotas, Nakotas, and Lakotas share similar religions, customs, and lore. They speak the same language using different dialects, but can understand each other, and they have come together for common causes. In general, the Dakotas lived in Minnesota and Iowa, the Nakotas, in eastern North Dakota and South Dakota, and the Lakotas, in northwestern Nebraska, western North Dakota and South Dakota, and eastern Wyoming and Montana.

Each of the three groups is further divided into tribes. The Dakotas are divided into Mdewakanton, Wahpekute, Wahpeton, and Sisseton. The Nakotas are divided into Yankton and Yanktonai. The Lakotas are divided into Sicangu (Brulé), Oglala, Hunkpapa, Miniconjou, Sihasapa (Blackfeet), Oohenumpa (Two Kettle), and Itazipo (Sans Arc). The Lakotas are also known by the name *Titunwan*, or "to live where they can see," which in English became "Teton." The Lakotas are further known as *Oceti Sakowin* (Seven Fires). Sitting Bull was born into the Bad Bow band of the Hunkpapa tribe.[49]

CHAPTER 2

Warriors, 1845–1851

GOYAHKLA'S FATHER AND MALE MENTORS TAUGHT HIM THERE were two types of Apache warfare—raid and revenge. When on a raid, the goal was to obtain supplies and not to kill people unless confronted. Apaches looked on their victims as resource providers who they could return to in the future for more food, horses, and supplies. When Apaches were out for revenge, the whole point was to kill and kill again.[1]

Mangas Coloradas led the Chiricahuas in a war of revenge against the Mexicans. For Mangas the war started in 1837. The Mexican state of Sonora had had enough of Apache raids and hired the American John Johnson to kill Apaches. The government would pay him and his men a bounty for proof of every Apache they killed. On April 22, 1837, Johnson and his band of seventeen men, pretending to be friendly traders, invited a mixed group of Apaches into their camp in the Animas Mountains in southwest New Mexico. The Apache invitees included Mangas and his wives. Johnson's men loaded their muskets and also loaded a cannon with metal scraps. After the Apaches entered the camp, Johnson's men fired upon their unsuspecting guests, killing twenty of them, including two of Mangas's wives. Johnson and his men cut off their victims' ears along with their scalps and collected their bounties from the Sonoran officials.

Mangas began an unforgiving war of revenge against the Sonorans. In December 1839, the state of Chihuahua followed Sonora's lead and hired the American trader James Kirker to put together a band of killers who efficiently stalked, killed, and scalped

Apaches, collecting their bounties. Mangas and his Chiricahuas wreaked revenge on every Mexican they encountered.[2]

When a Chiricahua boy believed he was ready, he could begin his training as a warrior. A *di-yen* who had Power to locate and defeat enemies and keep the warriors from harm instructed the boys in warrior rituals, as well as what they needed to do, and not do, and what to expect on the warpath or raid. They had to learn over eighty unique words used only on raids. The *di-yen* provided each boy with special clothing meant to protect him while on the raid or in warfare.[3]

When the raiding party left the rancheria, each boy was assigned a mentor to guide him, and in return the boy served the mentor as his attendant. While on the raid, the boys were required to set up camp, fetch water, build and care for the fire, cook, and any other duties assigned. They were urged to show courage, but the warriors usually kept them out of harm's way if there was combat. After being on four raids, if the men determined a boy had done well, he was given the status of a fighting man. He was then in control of his own life, and could marry and join future raids. At some point in his young life, Goyahkla told the adults he wanted to begin his warrior training.[4]

The Chihuahua government grew tired of the constant warfare with the Chiricahuas, and on July 4, 1842, they made peace with them. The Chihuahua government once again began issuing food to the Chiricahuas. The August 13, 1843, rations records in the Chihuahuan town of Corralitos show the name Geronimo.[5]

Mexicans were now calling Goyahkla "Geronimo." Since he was caring for his mother, the Mexicans may have allowed him to receive food supplies for the family. No one knows for sure why he was given the name Geronimo; maybe the Mexicans gave him that name to make it easier for their recordkeeping. The English form of Geronimo is Jerome (the name of an early Christian saint who translated the Bible into Latin).

By 1846, Geronimo was seventeen years old. He had successfully completed his four raids and had been admitted to the council of warriors. He could now do as he pleased, participate in raids and warfare, and marry.[6]

Geronimo bringing horses in payment for his future wife.

Geronimo had been in love with Alope, a fair, slender, delicate girl, and she was in love with him. Now that he was admitted to the council of warriors, he could marry her—what he said was "[p]erhaps the greatest joy to me." However, before he could marry her, he had to pay her father, No-po-so, who demanded a large number of horses Geronimo did not possess. He wondered what No-po-so's game was. Did he not care about their love for one another? Maybe he wanted to keep her with him longer, as she was a dutiful daughter.[7]

Geronimo did not reply to No-po-so's demand, but left the rancheria. After several days of raiding, he returned to No-po-so's wickiup with the required number of horses and left with Alope as his wife.[8]

He and Alope erected their wickiup near his mother's, and Geronimo furnished it with furs and hides. The wickiup was Alope's domain. She decorated it with her beadwork and pictures painted on hides.[9]

Geronimo's boyhood friend Juh courted Geronimo's favorite sister, Ishton, and they married. Juh and Ishton returned south to the Sierra Madre Mountains, where he would become a Nednhi leader.[10]

Geronimo and Alope led a normal Apache life. They would have three children who played and worked as he had done. "We followed the traditions of our fathers and were happy," Geronimo would later say.[11]

Another benefit to being admitted to the council of warriors was the right to participate in raids and warfare. Geronimo said, "I could go on the warpath with my tribe. This would be glorious. I hoped soon to serve my people in battle. I had long desired to fight with our warriors."[12]

Geronimo did not have long to wait. The Mexicans had run out of funds and ended the Chiricahuas' food rations, resulting in increased Chiricahua raids. During the autumn of 1845, the state of Chihuahua reverted to war and hired James Kirker to resume his killing spree.[13]

In early July 1846, a party of Chokonen and Nednhi Chiricahuas agreed to a truce to negotiate a peace treaty in the Chihuahua town of Galeana. The townspeople invited the Chiricahuas to a feast where they proceeded to get them drunk. Early on the morning of July 7, Kirker and his men rode into town and murdered 130 Chiricahua men, women, and children. They attached the Chiricahua scalps to long poles and proceeded to the capital of Chihuahua City where the governor and priests led Kirker and his men in a procession through the streets and then held a fiesta in celebration. The Chiricahuas were now out for revenge against all Mexicans.[14]

Events unknown to the Chiricahuas and beyond their control were occurring that would profoundly alter the course of their existence. In April 1846, war had broken out between Mexico and the United States over boundary disputes. The Americans invaded Mexico on several fronts. The Army of the West under the command of Stephen Watts Kearny took Santa Fe, New Mexico, in August 1846 and then proceeded to march westward to assist in the conquest of California.[15]

On October 18 and 19, Mangas Coloradas and Kearny met. Mangas was happy the Americans were fighting their common enemy, the Mexicans, and pledged "good faith and friendship to all Americans." Kearny needed remounts and Mangas's Bedonkohe Chiricahuas traded a herd of mules stolen from Sonora. Kearny and the Army of the West proceeded toward California, and Mangas gathered his warriors to head south to seek revenge.[16]

A Chihenne Chiricahua chief named Cuchillo Negro formed an alliance of Apaches for a revenge attack on Galeana. Mangas Coloradas and his Bedonkohe warriors, including Geronimo, already renowned as a raider, were part of the alliance. Their number also included Mangas's son-in-law Cochise, a rising leader of the Chokonen Chiricahuas, whose father had been killed in the Galeana massacre.[17]

In November of 1846, 175 Apaches attacked and defeated a force of Mexican soldiers and townsmen outside Galeana. Geronimo's reputation as a warrior grew when he was singled out as one of the fiercest fighters in the attack.[18] Although the record is nonexistent, it's likely that for the next few years, Geronimo continued to raid and war against the Mexicans in Sonora and Chihuahua.

On February 2, 1848, representatives of the United States and Mexico signed the Treaty of Guadalupe Hidalgo, ending the war between the United States and Mexico. Mexico seceded to the United States a vast territory that included most of the present states of New Mexico and Arizona—a large portion of which was Apacheria. Later, in 1853, the United States would acquire roughly an additional thirty thousand square miles of Apacheria from Mexico named the Gadsden Purchase. Relations between the Chiricahuas and the White Eyes—their name for Americans—started out cordial when fighting their mutual enemy, Mexico, but as time went on, the relationship cooled, and each side began to take advantage of the other, trying to get the upper hand.[19]

Geronimo met his first White Eyes in 1851. They were members of the Mexican Boundary Commission sent by the US government to survey the boundary between the United States and Mexico. Geronimo had heard about the White Eyes, and with a few friends

rode to visit their camp. Geronimo and his friends did not understand the White Eyes' speech, but they were able to convey they were
friendly, and shook hands. They traded horses and hides for White
Eyes' shirts and food. Geronimo and his friends hunted game for the
surveyors, who paid them in money. They did not know what it was
until much later when some Navajos told them what it was used for.
Geronimo later said, "They were good men, and we were sorry when
they had gone into the west."[20]

<hr />

Lakota boys went on vision quests to receive spiritual guidance, usually between the ages of ten and fifteen. Each boy first participated
in a sweat lodge with a *Wichasha Wakan*, a holy man, and possibly a
few select adult men. The sweat lodge was a willow-framed domed
structure covered with hides, constructed over a pit. At the center of
the pit were super-heated rocks over which water was poured, creating steam as the holy man prayed and sang. The sweat lodge fortified
and purified the participants.[21]

Alone, the boy found a high place where he fasted for up to four
days. During the quest, spirits would come to him in the form of
animals or humans to give him instructions for his life. After the
boy returned to the village, he participated in another sweat lodge
where he would tell the holy man and any other participants what
the spirits had revealed to him. The holy man would interpret what
the spirits had told or shown the boy, after which the young man was
meant to act on the revelation that gave him power separate from all
others.[22]

There is no record as to when or where Jumping Badger had his
vision quest or what was revealed to him. It was personal, and he
guarded what the spirits told him.[23]

It was 1845, Jumping Badger was fourteen years old, and the
Hunkpapas were camping along the Powder River. A war party was
organized to search for their traditional enemies, the Crows. The
warriors—including Jumping Badger's father, Tatanka Iyotake, and
uncle, Four Horns—rode to the west in search of a fight with their
enemies. Jumping Badger accompanied the war party.[24]

Jumping Badger's father gave him a coup stick used to touch the enemy. It was the greatest of honors to be able to touch or count coup on a living enemy. It was more honorable than killing an enemy. A dead enemy could also be touched, but the honor was not as great. The first person to count coup received the greatest honor. Up to four men could count coup on an enemy. The coup had to be witnessed by other warriors or it did not count. After a battle, the warriors would get together and agree on who had performed what deed. Each warrior with acknowledged accomplishments and honors on the battlefield was given the right to announce these deeds in public. It was his résumé.[25]

On the third day out, the Hunkpapas came upon and surprised a Crow war party. Jumping Badger raced his horse out ahead of the others, chasing after a Crow warrior, who dismounted and drew an arrow in his bow. Before the Crow could shoot, Jumping Badger struck him with his coup stick and rode him down. A following warrior struck and then killed the Crow. The Hunkpapas were victorious, killing several of their enemies and taking horses and plunder.[26]

Sitting Bull's first coup.

Tatanka Iyotake embraced Jumping Badger, saying, "Today you are a warrior. You are now a man." He gave Jumping Badger an eagle tail feather to wear in his hair signifying he had touched an enemy in battle. Before entering the Hunkpapa village, Tatanka Iyotake painted Jumping Badger black and gave him a bay war horse as his own. Jumping Badger sat on the bay as Tatanka Iyotake led it through the village and proudly proclaimed his son was brave and had struck the enemy. Tatanka Iyotake threw a feast in honor of his son and gave away four good horses to those in need. He proclaimed that from then on, his son would be known by his own name, Tatanka Iyotake—Sitting Bull—and that he would take the name "Jumping Bull."[27]

The name *Tatanka Iyotake* means more in Lakota than the English words convey. The name stands for a strong bison bull that when surrounded will sit down on his haunches and courageously fight to the death.[28]

Jumping Bull gave his son a circular buffalo-hide shield painted blue, in the center of which was a black bird-like figure, possibly a thunderbird. On one side of the thunderbird was a red semicircle and on the other, a black semicircle. Four eagle feathers were attached to the rim. This design had appeared to Jumping Bull in a dream. Sitting Bull believed the shield held special powers for success and protection.[29]

In addition, Jumping Bull gave his son Sitting Bull a lance—a seven- to eight-foot ash shaft topped with a notched eight-inch iron blade. Sitting Bull's mother decorated the entire shaft with blue and white beads, and a golden eagle tail feather dangled from it. The lance was Sitting Bull's favorite weapon. He would carry it and the shield throughout his years as a warrior.[30]

A year later, Sitting Bull had another chance to add to his reputation. The Hunkpapas were camped on the Musselshell River in what is now Montana. Scouts reported unknown enemies had been spotted in the hills around the village. Fifteen men, including Sitting Bull, rode out to investigate. They were ambushed by a twenty-man Flathead war party. The Flatheads dismounted and formed a firing line behind their horses. Sitting Bull announced he would attempt to ride the "daring line," which meant riding between two opposing forces, close to the enemy position. Sitting Bull raced his horse between the two lines, sitting upright, not trying to conceal himself alongside his horse. The arrows and musket balls missed him until just at the end when a ball hit his left foot. The fight continued until several were killed and wounded on both sides. The Flatheads rode away, and the Hunkpapas returned to their village where a celebration was held, which included honoring Sitting Bull for his ride along the daring line and receiving a battle wound. This gave him the right to wear a red eagle feather in his hair, signifying he'd been wounded in battle.[31]

One day, Sitting Bull was out hunting by himself along the Grand River. He entered the timber and sat down to rest with his back to a tree. As he began to doze, he saw a small yellowhammer woodpecker on a nearby tree watching him. He fell asleep and dreamt, and in his dream, a grizzly bear approached. He was frightened and could not move. He heard the yellowhammer tap twice against a tree, and then it seemed to say, "Lie still! Lie still!"

Sitting Bull opened his eyes and found his dream was true. A grizzly bear was approaching him. He forced himself to obey the woodpecker's advice, closing his eyes and not moving. He felt and smelled the bear's breath. It brushed against his body as it examined him. After what must have seemed an eternity, the bear ambled away. When he opened his eyes, he saw the yellow woodpecker perched on the tree trunk, watching him. The bird had saved his life. Sitting Bull was so grateful he composed and sang a song to the woodpecker:

> Pretty bird, you saw me and took pity on me;
> You wish me to survive among the people.
> O Bird People, from this day always you shall be my relatives!

From then on, Sitting Bull honored the Bird People, composing and singing songs about them. He studied their ways and referred to them when he talked. People said he understood the language of the birds, especially meadowlarks and magpies. They also said he talked with wolves and buffalo.[32]

Sitting Bull was a song composer and a good singer, and people always requested he sing during social events.[33] Over the next few

The bear, the woodpecker, and Sitting Bull.

years, he continued to hunt, participate with other warriors on raids, and excel in the traditions of the Lakotas.

The Gadsden Purchase, 1853–1854

The United States bought what is now southern Arizona and the southwestern corner of New Mexico, almost thirty thousand square miles, from Mexico in 1854, in what is called the Gadsden Purchase Treaty. After the war with Mexico in 1848, the United States had acquired most of what is now California, Nevada, New Mexico, and Arizona. With the discovery of gold in California in 1849, the US government began planning the construction of a transcontinental railroad to link the East and West Coasts. A Southern route was considered favorable, but it would have to pass through territory owned by Mexico and occupied by Apaches.[34]

In 1852, Secretary of War Jefferson Davis authorized the US ambassador to Mexico, James Gadsden—who was also president of the South Carolina Railroad Company and a transcontinental railroad proponent—to negotiate with the leader of Mexico, Antonio Lopez de Santa Anna, the purchase of land needed for a railroad. The purchase treaty was completed and first ratified by the US Congress and then by the Mexican legislature, taking effect on June 8, 1854. The agreement stipulated that the United States would pay Mexico $7 million upon signing and an additional $3 million after the border between the two countries was surveyed. The Americans and Mexicans worked efficiently together to survey the border, which was completed in 1854.[35]

The treaty was unpopular in both countries. Americans thought it was too much to pay for desolate land, and Mexicans believed Santa Anna had sold too much of their territory and had squandered the money, forcing him into exile.[36]

In 1853, Congress had authorized four teams to survey potential transcontinental routes. When the reports were complete, Secretary Davis recommended the Southern route from New Orleans to San Diego as the best route, with fewer mountains to cross and lesser amounts of snow, but Northern concerns that a Southern railroad would promote slavery and the outbreak of the Civil War put any plans for a Southern transcontinental railroad on hold. However, by 1877, the Southern Pacific Railroad had laid tracks from California into Arizona, and by 1883, the line was linked into Texas so passengers and freight could travel by rail from New Orleans to Los Angeles.[37]

CHAPTER 3

Trade and Conflict, 1851–1860

BY THE BEGINNING OF 1851, SOME CHIRICAHUAS HAD MADE PEACE with the state of Chihuahua, which resumed trading and distributing food rations to them at the town of Janos. However, the followers of Cochise and Mangas Coloradas, including Geronimo, remained aloof and would not commit to peace. They continued raiding and waging war, especially in the neighboring state of Sonora, where in 1850 alone Apaches had killed 111 Sonorans.[1]

In January 1851, two war parties totaling 200 men each invaded Sonora. Cochise and Mangas Coloradas led one of the parties, and most likely Geronimo was with them. Killing and plundering all who were in their way, they rampaged deep into Sonora, almost as far as the city of Hermosillo.[2]

Two small forces of government troops totaling 150 men from Arispe and Bacoachi set out to intercept the invaders on their return north. On January 20, 1851, as Mangas Coloradas and Cochise's war party drove approximately 1,000 head of horses and 350 head of cattle, the Mexican troops ambushed them at Pozo Hediondo (Stinking Springs). At first the Mexicans had the upper hand, but as all the Chiricahuas gathered and joined in the fight, the Mexicans were outnumbered and defeated. Twenty-six soldiers were killed and forty-six wounded. There is no record of how many Apaches were killed.[3]

Fresh Mexican troops gathered to pursue the Chiricahuas, but when they reached the scene of the battle, they found the Chiricahuas had mutilated the Mexican dead. Horrified, they ended the chase. Mangas Coloradas and Cochise returned to their home country, north of the US border, and some of the raiders returned to their rancherias in Chihuahua, north of Janos.[4]

The Mexican federal government sent Mexican War veteran Colonel José María Carrasco to command the troops in Sonora. Carrasco swore "a war to the death and without quarter against all tribes called Apache, excepting only women of all ages and boys fifteen and below." He began to organize his men and waited for the right opportunity.[5]

Mangas Coloradas decided to lead his Bedonkohe Chiricahuas, including women and children, to Janos to negotiate peace and trade with the townspeople. Geronimo and Alope along with their three children and Geronimo's mother went along. The Bedonkohes set up camp near the Chiricahua rancherias, along the river outside Janos. The townspeople welcomed them, holding fiestas and providing liquor to the Chiricahuas.[6]

Learning that seven mules had been stolen from the Sonoran town of Bacerac, Carrasco led four hundred soldiers after the raiders, crossing the Sierra Madre Mountains from Sonora into Chihuahua. Knowing Chiricahuas were camped outside Janos, he sent troops in their direction.[7]

March 5, 1851, began like any other day for the Bedonkohes outside Janos. They left a few men in camp to guard the women and children as well as their horses and possessions. The rest of the men, including Mangas Coloradas and Geronimo, entered the town where they traded, ate, and drank liquor.[8]

Carrasco's troops attacked the Chiricahua rancherias, killing the guards and a number of women and children while capturing those who could not escape. The troops confiscated the horses and weapons and destroyed all the supplies.[9]

As the Bedonkohe men started to return to their camp, they came upon fugitives from Carrasco's attack. Fearing the troops would come after them, they scattered and hid until nightfall. They rendezvoused by the river and then returned to camp where they found the bodies of their loved ones. Geronimo's wife Alope, their three young children,

Geronimo at Janos, Mexico, where his family was attacked.

and his mother were dead. Geronimo, his mind numb, turned away from the carnage and, saying not a word, stared at the river.[10]

When Mangas Coloradas called a council, Geronimo joined it. Eighty warriors were left. They had no weapons or supplies. The US border was far to the north, and they were surrounded by enemies. The decision was made to leave for home immediately. As it was not good to touch the dead, they were left where they lay. Without a sound, the surviving Bedonkohes headed north.[11]

Geronimo's world was shattered. "I stood until all had passed, hardly knowing what I would do," he recalled. "I had no weapon, nor did I hardly wish to fight, neither did I contemplate recovering the bodies of my loved ones, for that was forbidden. I did not pray, nor did I resolve to do anything in particular, for I had no purpose left. I finally followed the tribe silently, keeping just within hearing distance of the soft noise of the feet of the retreating Apaches."[12]

They traveled rapidly for two days and three nights until they crossed the border into the United States, where they then rested for two days. Geronimo finally ate something and began to talk with a few others who had also lost family members. No one else had lost as many loved ones as he had.[13]

A few days later, Geronimo returned home. As was tradition, he burned down his wickiup and that of his mother, along with every belonging of Alope, his three children, and his mother. The only thing Geronimo desired now was retribution—a thirst for revenge that would last a lifetime.[14]

The state of Chihuahua protested to the federal government in Mexico City. It was outraged that a Sonoran army had crossed its borders without informing Chihuahua of its intentions, attacking peaceful Chiricahuas at Janos. Colonel Carrasco defended his actions. He believed the Chiricahuas living outside Janos and Mangas Coloradas's Bedonkohes were the culprits who had been raiding in Sonora, and he found witnesses and evidence they were trading their plunder in Janos. At the end of its investigation, the Mexican government exonerated Carrasco.[15]

Colonel Carrasco's official report stated his troops had killed sixteen men and five women in the Chiricahua camps and taken sixty-two prisoners, mostly women and children, who were sent south to become servants. None of them ever returned.[16]

John Cremony, an American member of the Mexican Boundary Commission, met Carrasco in Fronteras, Sonora. During their discussion, Carrasco brought up his attack on Janos, saying, "We killed a hundred and thirty [Apaches] and took about ninety prisoners, principally women and children."[17] Since he was being investigated for wrongdoing by the Mexican federal government, did he downplay the number of Chiricahuas killed in his official report? The Chiricahuas had no count. Daklugie, Juh's son and Geronimo's nephew, later said, "[N]early all the women and children were killed. My uncle [Geronimo] lost his wife, mother, and three children."[18]

Soon after his return, Geronimo left the rancheria and found a solitary spot to be alone. He sat with his head down, weeping. "Goyahkla!" a spirit voice called four times. "No gun can ever kill you," the voice said. "I will take the bullets from the guns of the Mexicans, so they will have nothing but powder. And I will guide your arrows."[19]

Mangas Coloradas began organizing a revenge war party. Of course, the Bedonkohe warriors would participate, but they wanted to enlist the support of other Chiricahua bands. Since Geronimo had lost more than anyone else, Mangas Coloradas appointed him to visit the Chokonen and Nednhi bands to request their support. He first visited Cochise and his Chokonen warriors, and they agreed. He then traveled into Mexico where he found his brother-in-law, Juh. He and his Nednhi warriors said they would participate. It took a year to organize the war party.[20]

The next summer, warriors from the three bands met on the Mexican border. Mangas Coloradas led the Bedonkohes, Cochise led the Chokonens, and Juh led the Nednhis. They hid their families in the mountains and left their horses behind, traveling on foot through the mountains and along the river bottoms to conceal themselves from the Mexicans.[21]

They arrived at Arispe, Sonora, roughly seventy miles south of the border, and set up camp within view of town. Eight townsmen rode to the Chiricahua camp to parley with the war party, but they were not in the mood to talk. They killed and scalped all eight men, in hopes of luring the soldiers out of the town.[22]

The next day, soldiers advanced from the town to attack the Chiricahuas. The fighting amounted to only general skirmishing until late in the day, when the Chiricahuas captured the troops' supply train.[23]

The next morning, two companies of infantry and two companies of cavalry approached the Chiricahua camp. Geronimo told the three Chiricahua leaders that he recognized the cavalry as those who had massacred the Bedonkohes and his family at Janos. They gave Geronimo the honor of directing the battle, since he had lost more family than anyone else.[24]

Geronimo arranged the warriors in the timber along the river. The Mexican troops deployed, the infantry forming a line of two ranks, with the cavalry at the rear held in reserve. The infantry advanced toward the Chiricahua position and opened fire.[25]

Geronimo sent warriors to the rear of the Mexican troops to harass them from behind while he led a charge from the front.

Knowing these troops were the ones who had murdered his mother, wife, and children enraged Geronimo. He killed many soldiers.[26]

Mexican soldiers began shouting, "Watch out! Watch out! Geronimo!" The Chiricahuas took up the cry, and ever after, he would be known by all as Geronimo.[27]

After two hours of fighting, Geronimo and three other warriors were closest to the soldiers' position. They were out of arrows; their spears were broken off in the bodies of their enemies. Two soldiers came at them and fired, killing two of the men with Geronimo. Geronimo and the other warrior fled toward the timber as the two soldiers drew their sabers and chased them. The one soldier caught the other warrior and killed him with his saber. Geronimo reached his men and grabbed a spear. The soldier who was after Geronimo slashed at him with his saber, but missed. Geronimo lunged at the soldier with his spear and killed him. Geronimo snatched the saber in one hand and held his knife in the other. He fought the remaining soldier, killing him with his knife.[28]

The soldiers had had enough and left the battlefield. The Chiricahuas shouted their war whoops, and Geronimo ordered the scalping of all the dead soldiers. Apaches did not usually take scalps, but when they did, it was meant to insult the dead. After taking them, they simply threw the scalps away.[29]

Geronimo later said, "I could not call back my loved ones, I could not bring back the dead Apaches, but I could rejoice in this revenge."[30]

During this time, Geronimo married a beautiful Bedonkohe girl, Chee-hash-kish, who would become the mother of his son Chappo and his daughter Dohn-say (also called Tozey, or Lulu). Chiricahua culture permitted men to marry more than one wife if they could support them. Geronimo, being an experienced hunter and raider, married a second Bedonkohe girl, Nana-tha-thtith, who bore him one child.[31]

Seeking more revenge on the hated Mexicans, Geronimo convinced two friends to go on a raid with him into Sonora. They traveled south on foot through the Sierra de Antunez Mountains. At their southern end, Geronimo and his friends reached a village where they attempted to steal five horses at daybreak, only to be ambushed.

Geronimo's two friends were killed, and he had to run for his life. The Mexicans were relentless, pursuing him on foot and on horseback. He killed at least two pursuers, but the rest kept after him. After two days, the Mexicans gave up and Geronimo was able to reach the safety of his rancheria, but his two friends were dead, and he had nothing to show for it. People blamed him for his friends' deaths. "Having failed," Geronimo said, "it was only proper that I should remain silent."[32]

Undeterred, Geronimo persuaded two more friends to go with him through the Sierra Madre Mountains into Mexico, several months later. They selected a village to raid near the mountains, set up camp, and went to sleep the night before their planned daybreak attack. Mexican scouts discovered their camp and ambushed them, killing one of the warriors. Geronimo and his remaining friend managed to escape.

Discovering a company of mounted Mexican troops with a pack train advancing from the south, they followed the troops, heading north and crossing the US border. Geronimo and his companion realized the troops were heading toward their rancheria and raced to get there first to warn the people. When they arrived, they found most of the men were away from home. The Chiricahuas began organizing a defense. Three hours later, the Mexican troops arrived and fired into the rancheria, killing three little boys. Geronimo and the other warriors were able to drive the troops out of the mountains by nightfall. They lost two warriors, killing eight soldiers. Four warriors followed the troops who were in full retreat southward and returned to the rancheria to report that the troops had crossed the border back into Mexico.[33]

After the Chiricahua warriors, who had been away, returned to the rancheria, Geronimo led twenty-five of them into Mexico, following the troops' trail. The war party entered the Sierra de Sahuaripa Mountains and on the second day of their trek discovered a cavalry company that had been involved in the attack on their rancheria.[34]

Geronimo believed they could defeat the soldiers and devised a trap. The Chiricahuas found a narrow defile the cavalry would have to ride through as they followed the trail. Armed with spears and bows and arrows, the warriors hid in positions on both sides of the defile.[35] They waited until the cavalry reached the spot where they would be able to surround them and then the signal was given to attack. Knowing they could not ride out of the trap, the troops dismounted and used their horses as breastworks. Geronimo realized the Chiricahuas were running low on arrows and led a charge. Warriors raced in on the troops from all sides. The hand-to-hand fighting was intense. Brandishing a spear, Geronimo charged a trooper, who leveled his gun at him. Geronimo slipped in a pool of blood and slid under the trooper, who smashed him on the head with his gunstock, knocking him out.[36]

The Chiricahuas were victorious, killing all the troopers, but they paid a heavy price with many warrior deaths. They found Geronimo still alive, and after bathing his head with cold water, he regained consciousness. They bandaged his head wound, and even though he was weak from loss of blood and had a severe headache, he was able to walk on his own back to the rancheria. It took months for him to fully recover, and he would have a scar from this wound for the rest of his life.[37]

More and more White Eyes were entering Apache country. Since 1824, small numbers of American trappers had pursued beaver along the Gila River and its tributaries.[38] There were a few prospectors, not in any number for the Apaches to worry about, and some Americans were settling around Tubac and Tucson, but again, not in large numbers. Several military expeditions passed through Apache territory without incident. After gold was discovered in California in 1849, thousands of gold seekers traveled through Chiricahua country.[39]

Even though New Mexico and what would become Arizona were now part of the United States, Apaches still attacked Mexicans living there. They saw no difference between Mexicans living north or south of the border—they were all enemies.[40]

On December 12, 1848, Apaches attacked a detachment of soldiers stationed at Doña Ana, New Mexico, and raided towns along the Rio Grande. In August 1849, Apaches attacked El Paso, Texas, killing citizens and running off a large herd of mules. Pursuing troops

caught them near the Pinos Altos Mountains in Chiricahua territory, destroying their camp and recovering the mules. It is not known
if these raiders were Chiricahuas or if Geronimo might have been
involved.[41]

The army eventually built Fort Webster on the Mimbres River in
1852, hoping to control the Apaches who continued raiding the Rio
Grande settlements. On July 11, Apache leaders, including Mangas
Coloradas, met with John Greiner, acting superintendent of Indian
Affairs, and Colonel Edwin Sumner and signed a peace treaty in
which the federal government would provide regular allotments to
the Apaches.[42]

In 1854, the United States and Mexico concluded the Gadsden
Purchase Treaty in which the United States bought roughly thirty
thousand square miles of Mexican territory, a large portion of which
would form the southern portion of the current state of Arizona and
included the towns of Tubac and Tucson.

Occasional confrontations occurred over the years. In November
1856, Henry Dodge, a popular Navajo agent, was killed. The Navajos
and the White Eyes believed a Mogollon Apache had done it.[43]

In May 1857, Colonel Benjamin Bonneville led the army's Gila
Expedition, which passed through the Bedonkohe homeland, killing
seven Chihenne men, including their leader, Cuchillo Negro, who
were not involved in the agent's death. In another attack, on a Coyotero Apache village, they killed forty warriors who were not con-
nected to the agent's death. However, the army later learned the man
responsible for the murder had been staying with the Coyoteros and
had been killed in the attack. This military invasion was disturbing
to all Apaches, but soon conditions returned to a wary peace.[44] Even
though the army gradually established several forts in New Mexico
Territory, Apaches still considered Mexicans fair game and occasionally would raid White Eyes when it was convenient.

In 1857, John Butterfield won the government contract for coast-
to-coast mail service from St. Louis to San Francisco and started the
Overland Mail Company. The Overland Mail traveled the California
Trail, which ran through Apache country. Its first stagecoach, carrying
mail and passengers, left St. Louis for San Francisco on September

16, 1858. The Bureau of Indian Affairs sent agent Dr. Michael Steck to Apache Pass between the Chiricahua and Dos Cabezas Mountains to confer with Cochise. He met Cochise there along the California Trail at the newly constructed Overland Mail stage station. Cochise agreed to allow the Overland Mail stagecoaches and passengers to pass through Chiricahua territory. Geronimo was at this meeting and had a favorable opinion of Dr. Steck, although later in life he could not remember the name of the leader of the White Eyes. Butterfield built ten stations along the route through Apache territory. Not only did he arm his employees, he also provided the Chiricahuas with gifts to protect his interests. For the next couple of years, Chiricahuas and White Eyes tolerated each other along the Trail.[45]

Since 1803, the Spanish and then Mexicans had sporadically worked the Santa Rita copper mines at the southern edge of the Pinos Altos Mountains in Chiricahua territory. Later, White Eyes used them as a base for further mineral exploration when on May 18, 1860, a party of prospectors discovered gold northwest of the copper mines. By August, the rough-and-tumble gold camp of Pinos Altos had sprung to life as over seven hundred prospectors explored the tributaries of the Gila River—the Bedonkohe homeland. Things were about to change for everyone, and not for the best.[46]

For the Lakotas on the northern Great Plains, war parties were an important part of their lives. Any experienced warrior could lead a war party, and any warrior interested could go along. Much planning went into the war party, and a holy man was consulted to aid in its success. Two objectives for the war party were to win glory and accumulate horses. Horses were considered a sign of wealth and success, so the more horses a war party brought back, the better. In Lakota warfare, not only was the killing of men in a fight honorable, but also that of women and children. Bodies were scalped and parts taken for trophies. The body was mutilated so it would appear that way in the afterlife. The Lakotas knew their enemies would do the same to them.[47]

Sitting Bull was active in battles and raids. During his lifetime, he would count coup sixty-nine times and be wounded in battle at least three times.[48] In the late 1860s, Sitting Bull obtained sheets of paper on which he drew pictographs of his fights and coups. At least twelve of these took place during the 1850s, and each one shows Sitting Bull victorious over his Crow and Assiniboine foes—men and women.[49]

He joined the Kit Fox, the Buffalo, and the Strong Heart societies. The Strong Heart Society was the most prestigious of all. Fifty of the bravest, most compassionate Hunkpapa warriors were members. Their duties were to protect the people and care for the needy and orphans. Two members of the Strong Hearts were designated as sash wearers. Sash wearers rode into battle, dismounted, and staked their sash to the ground. They fought from that position until they won, were released by one of the other Strong Hearts, or were killed. By the age of seventeen, Sitting Bull became one of the two sash wearers.[50]

By his mid-twenties, Sitting Bull had been elected the leader of the Strong Heart Society. Within the Strong Hearts, he and his friends Crow King, Gall, and others formed an inner elite group, the Midnight Strong Heart Society, taking that name because they met during the middle of the night.[51]

Sitting Bull excelled in the use of all weapons, including firearms, but his favorite weapon was the lance. He became known to Lakota enemies, who feared his name. He would taunt them, shouting "Sitting Bull, I am he!" Soon those who rode with him would shout, "We are Sitting Bull's boys!"[52]

Sitting Bull was a skilled hunter as well as an accomplished warrior. He was respectful to animals and killed no more than what was needed, offering a portion of the kill to Wakan Tanka. Loving horses and owning a large herd, he was an excellent horseman and relished participating in and betting on horse races.[53] His nephew White Bull said, "Wherever he was and whatever he did his name was great everywhere."[54]

By the mid-1850s, Sitting Bull had married Light Hair. In accordance with Lakota custom, she owned the tepee and all within it, overseeing everything that concerned the home; he would only help if asked.[55]

Shortly after Sitting Bull and Light Hair were married, they went on a hunting trip together along the Powder River. They were about a half-day's journey from their village when they erected their tepee in a grove of cottonwood trees. They were both inside, Sitting Bull working on new arrows, and Light Hair, boiling bones to render fat. As she was skimming fat from the top of the cooking pot, she saw a reflection in the liquid of the spoon. It was a Crow warrior's face looking down the tepee's smoke hole. He must have climbed a low-hanging branch to spy on the couple. Light Hair quietly warned Sitting Bull, who grabbed his bow and an arrow and shot through the smoke hole. By the time they got outside, the man had disappeared, leaving a bloody trail. The couple hurriedly broke camp and returned to their village.[56]

Sitting Bull was not considered a medicine man, but he did learn healing techniques, what plants were used in treating different illnesses and what ceremonies were to be performed. He did take care of the sick, but it was not one of his major activities.[57]

Sitting Bull was attuned to the spiritual world. He received dreams and visions. Thunderbirds came to him in dreams. This was a high spiritual honor, and those who were visited by the thunderbirds had to perform the *Heyoka* ceremony and react and perform everything contrary, in some cases, acting foolish. If something was funny, the thunderbird dreamer must cry. If it was summer, he must dress as if it was winter. He must walk and ride backwards. During the *Heyoka* ceremony, the dreamer had to put his hands into a pot of boiling water to remove meat. He had to act contrary until the *Heyoka* ceremony was complete, otherwise lightning might strike him. Once the dreamer had participated in the *Heyoka* ceremony, he could return to normal. Only those who dreamed of thunderbirds could paint their faces with lightning bolts, and that is how Sitting Bull painted his face.[58]

In the spring of every year, the Lakota tribes gathered for the Sun Dance. For twelve days they would honor the sun and ask for the well-being of the tribes. It was also a festive social gathering where family and friends who may not have seen each other for long periods of time could enjoy each other's company.[59]

As part of the festival, men who wished to fulfill sacrificial vows first purified themselves in a sweat lodge before dancing and blowing on eagle-bone whistles while staring at the sun. During or after completing the dance, the dancer might have a spiritual experience. There was a wide range of dances a man could perform. The highest form of sacrificial dance was to have skewers inserted through the flesh of the chest and back and then be suspended from the dance pole by ropes tied to the skewers. The dance could also include a buffalo skull attached to the man as a weight. The dancer hung or pulled against the pole until his flesh was ripped, releasing him. This was considered the highest form of self-sacrifice for the tribe. This most-difficult rite was the one a man must perform if he was to be considered a *Wichasha Wakan*, a holy man.[60]

In June of 1856, the Hunkpapas held their Sun Dance on the east side of the Little Missouri River. Twenty-five-year-old Sitting Bull was ready to perform the highest form of the Sun Dance to become a *Wichasha Wakan*. The skewers were inserted into his back and chest and he danced while staring at the sun and blowing on an eagle-bone whistle. He asked for good health and plenty of food for the Hunkpapas. A voice spoke to him: "Wakan Tanka gives you what you ask for. Wakan Tanka will grant your wish." After his Sun Dance, the people considered him a *Wichasha Wakan*, one who could commune with Wakan Tanka. Sitting Bull would participate in the Sun Dance many times during his life.[61]

In the autumn of 1856, Sitting Bull joined a hundred other warriors in a raid to steal horses from the Crows. They traveled westward and found a large Crow camp with plenty of horses north of the Yellowstone River, in present-day Montana. They raided the camp at night and got away with many horses. The next day as they were driving the herd homeward, a large Crow war party caught up with them and charged.[62]

The Hunkpapas formed a line and waited for them. The Crows stopped before reaching the Hunkpapas and formed a line. Three Crow warriors came forward. The first raced his horse in among the

Hunkpapas and counted coup on two warriors. The second charged forward and killed a Hunkpapa.[63]

Sitting Bull rode forward to confront the third warrior, a Crow chief. When Sitting Bull was well out in front of the Hunkpapas, he dismounted and shouted, "Come on! I'll fight you. I am Sitting Bull!" Carrying his shield and a new flintlock trade gun, Sitting Bull ran toward the chief. The Crow chief dismounted with his flintlock gun and ran toward Sitting Bull.[64]

As they got close, the Crow stopped and took aim as Sitting Bull dropped to one knee, placing his shield in front of him and taking aim. The Crow fired first, and then Sitting Bull shot. The Crow's bullet struck Sitting Bull's shield, deflecting the bullet downward so that it plowed through the bottom of Sitting Bull's left foot from toe to heel. Sitting Bull's bullet hit the chief in the stomach, killing him. Sitting Bull limped to the chief, thrust his knife into his heart, and scalped him. Seeing their leader fall, the Crow warriors left. Sitting Bull's foot wound did not heal properly, and he would limp for the rest of his life.[65]

A hundred warriors saw the single combat between Sitting Bull and the Crow chief, and they said it was an excellent display of bravery. The Midnight Strong Hearts elected him their leader, and he was made leader of all the Strong Hearts.[66]

The winter of 1857 brought sadness. Sitting Bull's wife, Light Hair, died in the birth of their son. His mother and other female relatives would help to care for the boy and manage Sitting Bull's home for him. Four years later, disease would claim this son's life. Sitting Bull would then formally adopt his sister's son, One Bull, who was about the same age as his deceased son.[67]

After the death of Light Hair, Sitting Bull joined a raiding party against the Assiniboines. The temperatures were frigid, freezing the Missouri River thick enough for the Hunkpapa warriors to cross on foot east of the confluence of the Yellowstone with the Missouri River in present-day North Dakota.[68]

The warriors were strung out in a line as they crossed the ice, with Sitting Bull toward the rear. Those in front came upon a single Assiniboine tepee on the north bank. The Assiniboine family saw the warriors' approach. The husband and eleven-year-old son attempted to put up a fight while the wife with her baby and young son started running. The warriors in the front easily killed the husband, wife, baby, and little boy. The eleven-year-old had shot his last arrow. The warriors surrounded the boy and four had counted coup on him. It was time for him to die, just as Sitting Bull arrived. The boy saw Sitting Bull, ran to him, threw his arms around him, and cried, "Big Brother, save me!"[69]

Sitting Bull, impressed by the boy's bravery, took pity on him. He threw his arms around the boy and told the others he was taking him to be his brother. Sitting Bull formally adopted the boy, who was so well treated he never wanted to return to the Assiniboines. The Hunkpapas believed Sitting Bull's compassion for the defenseless boy showed he was a great chief.[70]

Later that year, the Hunkpapas gathered near the mouth of the Grand River where it enters the Missouri River. They needed to select a war chief. Four of Sitting Bull's friends, Strikes-the-Kettle, Black Bird, Brave Thunder, and Gall, nominated him at the council meeting. The council agreed with his nomination, presented it to the people, and they concurred. Sitting Bull was now a war chief of the Hunkpapas.[71]

In June 1859, Sitting Bull's band had been camping along the headwaters of the Cannonball River in what is now modern-day North Dakota. They broke camp, and as they headed toward the northwest, the people and animals were strung out in a long line. Two boys were out ahead of everyone.[72]

From a hidden position, fifty Crow warriors swept down on the head of the procession, cutting off the two boys from the rest of the Hunkpapas and killing one of them in front of everyone. Even though the Crow warriors outnumbered the Hunkpapa warriors, the latter quickly and forcefully attacked the Crows and slowly pushed them back. After several Crow warriors were killed, they lost heart and began retreating.[73]

One Crow warrior, holding a musket at the ready, stopped the advancing Hunkpapas. Sitting Bull's father, Jumping Bull, rode up and said to the Hunkpapa warriors, "Leave that Crow to me. Last night I had a terrible toothache, and I wished I was dead. Now my chance has come. I have longed for such a day."[74]

Jumping Bull raced his horse toward the Crow who waited for him. Jumping Bull dismounted and the Crow did the same. They ran toward each other, the Crow with his musket and Jumping Bull with bow and nocked arrow. The Crow shot first, hitting Jumping Bull in the shoulder and forcing him to drop the bow, but the older man continued running toward the Crow, who drew his knife. Jumping Bull fumbled for his, but it had swiveled from his side to his back. Before he could reach it, the Crow stabbed him above the collarbone, then grabbed him by the hair, repeatedly stabbing him.[75]

Sitting Bull was on another part of the battlefield when he was told his father was being killed. He raced his war horse in his father's direction, but he was too late.[76]

Still alive, Jumping Bull had dropped to his knees. The Crow stood over him and drove his knife into the top of Jumping Bull's skull. As he fell over, the knife blade broke away from the handle. The Crow mounted his horse and began to make his escape.[77]

Sitting Bull raced after the Crow and caught up with him. Thrusting his lance, Sitting Bull pierced the Crow's body, killing him. Hunkpapa warriors rode up and shot into the Crow's body. Sitting Bull dismounted, drew his knife, and cut the Crow to pieces.[78]

Sitting Bull and the Hunkpapa warriors pursued the larger Crow war party across the prairie, killing ten of them. Hunkpapa warriors captured three Crow women and an infant left behind. Their captors planned to kill them, but Sitting Bull requested they be allowed to live and be treated kindly. The warriors followed his wishes, and later that summer, the women and infant were sent home on good horses.[79]

After his father's death, Sitting Bull always placed his tepee by his mother's, providing for her care and protection. Sitting Bull gave his father's name to his adopted Assiniboine brother. From then on, the boy would be known as Jumping Bull.[80]

Sitting Bull was kind to everyone—the elderly, children, and animals. People liked him. He was *Wichasha Wakan* and tried to live his life as close to the four Lakota virtues as he could: bravery, fortitude, generosity, and wisdom.[81]

Hunkpapa contact with whites was limited in the 1850s. They did most of their trading at Fort Pierre Chouteau on the Missouri River's west bank, north of the Bad River in present-day South Dakota. On occasion, they would trade at the few other fortified trading posts in the Upper Missouri—Forts Clark, Rice, and Union. However, these posts catered to Hunkpapa enemies such as the Arikaras, Mandans, and Assiniboines. Many times, Hunkpapa warriors visited these forts to attack their enemies, and an occasional white trader would fall victim, too. The Métis were another Hunkpapa contact for white trade goods. The Métis were of mixed Indian and French-Canadian heritage. Based out of the Red River of the North, they transported their trade goods to Indian villages by two-wheeled carts.[82]

Back in 1851, representatives of the US government, Indian superintendent David Mitchell and Indian agent Thomas Fitzpatrick, had invited all the plains tribes to come to Fort Laramie in present-day southeast Wyoming to discuss peace. The conference took place that September east of Fort Laramie, and the resulting treaty was known as the Horse Creek Treaty, or Fort Laramie Treaty. Estimates suggest that between eight thousand and twelve thousand people attended the conference.[83]

The tribes agreed to peace with the whites and peace among themselves. They agreed to allow emigrants to pass through their lands and allow the US government to establish forts. The white men insisted the Sioux have one chief to speak for all of them. Of course, this was unheard of to the Lakotas, Dakotas, and Nakotas. Against the Lakotas' better judgment, Mitchell appointed the Brulé Lakota leader Conquering Bear head chief of all the Sioux. In return, the government would pay the tribes indemnities for damages already done by emigrants and pay annuities for fifty years (later, the US Senate reduced the amount of years to ten). The Hunkpapas, who did not attend the conference and did not sign the treaty, ignored it. Nonetheless, the government expected them to abide by the treaty, and gave them annuities once a year. This began a rift among the Lakotas between those who accepted the annuities and those who did not.[84]

On August 19, 1854, armed conflict erupted between the US Army and the Brulé Lakotas that would eventually affect all Lakotas, including the northern Hunkpapas. A Miniconjou man who was staying in Conquering Bear's Brulé village near Fort Laramie killed and butchered a Mormon emigrant's cow. When its owner reached Fort Laramie, he told the fort's commander of his loss. The commander discovered the cow killer was staying at Conquering Bear's village. He sent Lieutenant John Grattan, commanding twenty-nine soldiers and an interpreter, along with a 12-pounder howitzer and a 12-pounder mountain gun, to arrest the man. Misunderstandings developed between Grattan and Conquering Bear, possibly because of faulty translations. Grattan ordered the guns fired. People were wounded and killed. Conquering Bear was mortally wounded. Infuriated Brulé warriors killed Grattan and all his men.[85]

Many whites were furious over the Grattan massacre. The army ordered Brigadier General William Harney to lead a six-hundred-man command of infantry and dragoons to apprehend the culprits. As the army headed out to find the Lakotas, Harney remarked, "By God, I'm for battle—no peace."[86]

On September 3, 1855, Harney's troops attacked Little Thunder's village on Blue Water Creek at Ash Hollow, Nebraska. Little Thunder was the successor of Conquering Bear. The people ran and the troops pursued, shooting them down. Lieutenant Colonel Philip St. George Cooke, who led the dragoons, said, "There was much slaughter in the pursuit." They captured seventy women and children and killed eighty-five Brulés—many of them women and children.[87]

The army had bought Fort Pierre from Pierre Chouteau Jr. & Company in April 1855. That July, Harney sent 275 troops there to make it ready for military occupation.[88]

Harney marched his troops from Ash Hollow to Fort Laramie, then, on September 29, he marched them cross-country to Fort Pierre, arriving October 19. The fort was in rough shape and had inadequate housing for the troops, who had to endure a harsh winter.[89]

In early March 1856, Harney held a treaty council with nine Lakota tribes; as many as seven thousand people may have been there on the Missouri River floodplain near Fort Pierre.[90] There is no record, but Sitting Bull most likely would have been there with the Hunkpapas.

Harney, whom the Lakotas named Mad Bear, delivered an extensive list of demands, including the provision that Lakotas allow white men to travel the trail he had taken from Fort Laramie to Fort Pierre. Anyone who killed a white person must be handed over to the army, as well as anyone who stole from the whites. All stolen items must be returned. They must make peace with all their enemies. The Lakotas believed Harney's demands were unrealistic, but they humored him anyway.[91]

The Hunkpapa chief Bear's Rib attempted to reason with Harney, but he would not listen. Harney wanted a head chief for every tribe who the government could deal with, and Harney appointed Bear's Rib to that position. Of course, this was completely contrary to the Lakotas' way of doing things. Harney wanted each appointed head chief to designate sub chiefs. Bear's Rib appointed nine, including Sitting Bull's uncle, Four Horns, and his Miniconjou brother-in-law, Makes Room. Congress would never ratify Harney's treaty with the tribes.[92]

Harney was convinced Fort Pierre was unsuitable as a military post. On June 3, 1856, he selected a new site for a fort 150 miles downriver. It would be named Fort Randall. On May 16, 1857, Fort Pierre was officially abandoned, and for the time being, the US Army would be far from the Hunkpapas. Sitting Bull and most of the Hunkpapas ignored the desires of the white men and continued in the traditions of the Hunkpapas—hunting, trading, and fighting their enemies.[93]

CHAPTER 4

The White Eyes' Civil War and Beyond, 1860–1871

MANGAS COLORADAS, BEDONKOHE CHIRICAHUA LEADER AND Geronimo's mentor, had always been friendly toward Americans, but with the invasion of prospectors into the Gila River country and the establishment of the mining town of Pinos Altos in 1860, his goodwill began to diminish. The miners had come to stay, cutting down trees to build their town and tearing up the earth and streams in their relentless search for gold. On top of it all, they held the Apaches in contempt.[1]

Horses and mules went missing around Pinos Altos, and the miners blamed the Apaches. On December 4, 1860, after a mule had been killed and slaughtered, a band of thirty Pinos Altos miners attacked a Chihenne rancheria near Fort Webster on the Mimbres River, killing four people and capturing thirteen women and children. Many Chiricahuas considered this attack unprovoked and saw themselves at war with the White Eyes.[2]

Then in early February 1861, the Chokonen leader Cochise sent a message to Mangas Coloradas and his warriors, including Geronimo, asking them to come to Apache Pass. He needed help.

Back in January, Aravaipa Apaches had raided Johnny Ward's ranch along Sonoita Creek south of modern-day Patagonia, Arizona. The Apaches took Ward's herd of cattle along with his young stepson Felix. Ward went to nearby Fort Buchanan and requested help to recover his stepson and herd. On January 29, 1861, the fort's commander sent a fifty-four-man detachment of Seventh Infantry, Company C, under the command of Lieutenant George Bascom to search for the Apaches and recover the boy. Johnny Ward went along as their interpreter.[3]

The raiders' trail led east toward Apache Pass between the Chiricahua and Dos Cabezas Mountains, home of Cochise's Chokonen Chiricahuas. Based on the route the raiders had taken, Bascom and his men believed Chokonens must have been the ones who had kidnapped Felix Ward. The soldiers arrived at Apache Pass on February 3, 1861, where they met a sergeant and twelve-man detail on their return to Fort Buchanan. Bascom added them to his detachment and made camp near the Overland Mail station. Bascom wrote in his report, "I . . . arrived at Apache Pass . . . feeling confident that they [the Chokonens] had the boy."[4]

James Wallace, the Overland Mail station manager, was friends with Cochise. Bascom asked Wallace to go to Cochise's rancheria two miles away and invite him to come in for a talk. Wallace went to see Cochise and returned saying he would come talk the following day.[5]

Cochise arrived the next day at noon as promised. He brought along his wife, his son Naiche, nephew Chie, his brother Coyuntura, and two other adults.[6]

Lieutenant Bascom invited them for dinner. He and Ward ate with Cochise and Coyuntura in one tent while the other members of Cochise's party ate in a separate tent.[7]

Communication was poor between those meeting in Bascom's tent. Bascom did not speak Apache or Spanish. Ward spoke English and Spanish. Cochise and his brother Coyuntura spoke some Spanish.[8]

When asked about the whereabouts of Felix Ward and the stolen livestock, Cochise said he knew nothing about the boy's kidnapping or the livestock, but he agreed to search for the boy, asking for ten days to locate him, to which Bascom agreed.[9]

Ward then said something in Spanish to Cochise, alarming him. Whether Ward spoke on purpose or Cochise misunderstood Ward's

Spanish, Cochise believed the army was holding him and the others in his party hostage until the boy was returned. Drawing his knife, Cochise jumped up and cut his way out of the tent. Coyuntura did the same but was captured. Ward ran after Cochise, drew his pistol, and fired at Cochise as he ran up a hill. The soldiers had to load their muskets. By the time they could fire, Cochise had scrambled up the hill far enough that the musket fire was ineffective.[10]

Bascom kept Cochise's people as hostages for the return of Felix Ward. Cochise sent messages for help, and Apaches began arriving from every direction as Bascom moved his men to the Overland Mail station for better protection.[11]

Cochise returned to parley for the release of his family and friends, but Bascom refused to release them until the kidnapped boy was returned. Cochise captured James Wallace and the Apaches began firing on the soldiers. Their firepower was limited to bows and arrows and a few firearms.[12]

By February 6, Geronimo had arrived with Mangas Coloradas and his Bedonkohe warriors. Mangas Coloradas learned his daughter and grandson were being held by the White Eyes. Lieutenant Bascom estimated five hundred to six hundred Apaches were surrounding them.[13]

The Apaches were now attacking travelers on the California Trail. While most of them were able to get through to the Apache Pass station, members of the eastbound Montoya wagon train were not so fortunate. They were setting up camp for the night near a grove of oak trees when the Apaches attacked, killing six Mexicans and capturing three White Eyes and two Mexicans. They chained each captive Mexican to a wagon wheel and then set the wheels on fire. They kept the White Eyes alive as bargaining chips. Geronimo, who participated in the attack, later said, "After a few days skirmishing, we attacked a freight train. . . . We killed some of the men and captured the others."[14]

Continued negotiations with Bascom did not proceed the way Cochise wanted. Bascom demanded the release of Wallace and the three other Americans, saying that he would release Cochise's relatives and friends after this was accomplished. Cochise was only willing to release Wallace and not the others. On February 7, Cochise appeared and negotiated further, again without success. On February 8, the Chiricahuas spotted a column of infantry north of the Dos Cabezas Mountains, marching toward El Paso. Believing the soldiers were on their way to attack them, Cochise had Wallace and the three other hostages killed, and the Apaches left.[15]

Assistant Surgeon Colonel Bernard Irwin, led an eleven-man rescue contingent from Fort Buchanan. On February 10, they captured three Coyotero Apache raiders and recovered stolen livestock, arriving at Apache Pass without incident. They passed by the site of the Montoya wagon train where they saw the remains of eight Mexicans. Soon after this, on February 14, Lieutenant Isaiah Moore leading seventy mounted soldiers of the First Dragoons from Fort Breckenridge, north of Tucson, arrived at Apache Pass. They sent out a scouting party that discovered the Apaches had abandoned their camps, leaving behind the punctured, charred remains of Wallace and the other hostages.[16]

The soldiers buried the murdered Mexican teamsters and American hostages. They took the six adult male Apaches, including Cochise's brother, to the graves of the murdered men and hanged them from the nearest trees. The bodies were left dangling for months until they decomposed and fell to the ground. The hangings outraged and horrified the Apaches. The White Eyes' actions at Apache Pass would be remembered by all Apaches for years. For Cochise it was now total war.[17]

Geronimo went into hiding in the mountains, later saying, "After this trouble all the Indians agreed not to be friendly with the white men any more. . . . Sometimes we attacked the white men—sometimes they attacked us . . . this treachery on the part of the soldiers had angered the Indians and revived memories of other wrongs, so that we never again trusted the United States troops."[18]

The troops took Cochise's wife and son to Fort Buchanan where they were released. What about the boy, Felix Ward? Years later, he was found living with Coyotero Apaches and would work as a scout and interpreter for the army. The soldiers would nickname him Mickey Free.[19]

Unknown to the Chiricahuas, the White Eyes had been having a long-standing disagreement over slavery. Disagreements escalated into violence and death, especially in Kansas Territory. On November 6, 1860, Abraham Lincoln won the election for president of the United States. The Republican Lincoln was antislavery, and this convinced Southern slave states to secede from the Union and form their own confederacy.

When Texas seceded from the Union, the Overland Mail Company moved its route to the north, abandoning its stations in Apache territory. Mangas Coloradas and Cochise believed they had forced out the Overland Mail Company. Mangas Coloradas raided livestock around Pinos Altos and even ran off all the livestock from Fort McLane. Soon, all but about one hundred miners had abandoned Pinos Altos.[20]

On April 12, 1861, open warfare erupted between the states when Confederate forces fired on Union-held Fort Sumter, in Charleston Harbor, South Carolina. The Union Army, needing troops in the eastern part of New Mexico Territory to confront advancing Confederate troops, abandoned Forts McLane, Buchanan, and Breckenridge in July. Many civilians left the territory, concerned about Apache attacks. Again, the Apaches believed they had forced the army and civilians to leave.[21]

The Confederacy would hold New Mexico Territory for a while but would soon retreat to Texas after losing several battles to Union troops. Even though the Chiricahuas now considered the White Eyes their enemies, Geronimo's passion for revenge against Mexicans knew no bounds.

In the summer of 1861, Geronimo led twelve Bedonkohe warriors on a raid into Chihuahua, traveling south along the eastern slopes of the Sierra Madre Mountains for four days. They crossed the Sierra de Sahuaripa Mountains into the vicinity of Casas Grandes, where they attacked a mule pack train. The muleskinners fled for their lives, leaving the mules with their packs behind. Two of the mules were loaded with bacon, which the warriors threw away, as Apaches did not eat pork. The warriors took the pack train northwest into Sonora, heading toward their predetermined rendezvous location in the Santa Rita Mountains, in present-day Arizona.[22]

One morning, as they were finishing their breakfast, Mexican cavalry ambushed them. A bullet struck Geronimo below his left eye. He fell to the ground, unconscious. Believing Geronimo was dead, the troops pursued the other warriors into the timber.[23]

Regaining consciousness, Geronimo ran toward the timber. A second company of cavalry spotted him and fired at him. A bullet grazed his side as the troops gave chase. Geronimo scrambled up a canyon where the horses could not go, and the troops ended their pursuit.[24]

Geronimo and the other warriors arrived separately at their Santa Rita Mountains rendezvous. From there, they returned empty-handed to their rancheria. Geronimo was wounded, but not discouraged. Again, people blamed him for the raid's failure, but he said nothing.[25]

It was September, and Geronimo remained at the rancheria, recovering from his wound. His left eye had swelled shut. Most of the men were away; some were hunting, while others had traveled north to trade with the Navajos for blankets. One day, as the women began to prepare breakfast, a barrage of gunfire erupted. Three companies of Mexican troops had surrounded the rancheria and were attacking. Many women and children were killed, including Geronimo's third wife Nana-tha-thtith and their child. Geronimo had no time to prepare a defense. He was able to fire one arrow, hitting an officer before he scrambled away up into the rocks. Four women were captured, and the troops plundered the rancheria. What they did not take, they burned, including all the wickiups.[26]

The deaths of Geronimo's wife Nana-tha-thtith and their child could only have added to Geronimo's hatred for Mexicans. Winter was close at hand, and the Bedonkohes needed to concentrate on survival. Geronimo's revenge would have to wait.

It is not known which attacks Geronimo participated in against American soldiers during this time. He never talked about fighting American soldiers, only Mexicans. Both Mangas Coloradas and Cochise actively attacked travelers and settlers, the town of Pinos

Altos, and army patrols, both Union and Confederate. Geronimo was always closely associated with Mangas Coloradas, Cochise, and Juh. Many historians believe he must have been involved in actions against American soldiers.[27] On the other hand, after Geronimo's wounding sometime in the summer of 1861 and the attack on his rancheria that fall, he may have been too weak to participate in the attacks on the White Eyes for the rest of that year.

In the spring of 1862, the California Column, made up of 2,350 Union infantry and cavalry, entered Arizona and New Mexico from the west and soon forced the Confederate troops to leave.[28]

On June 25, 1862, 140 Union soldiers reached Apache Pass and set up camp at the ruins of the Overland Mail station. Cochise and his warriors took up defensive positions and fired upon the troops. The commanding officer, Lieutenant Colonel Edward Eyre, showed a white flag and negotiated with Cochise until he learned that warriors had killed three of his men as the talks were taking place. The Chiricahua attack resumed through the night and the next morning until the troops continued their march east.[29]

Leaving his slow-moving supply train accompanied by a guard detail to follow behind, Captain Thomas Roberts led a hundred-man detachment of the California Column and a few civilians along with two howitzers westward to Apache Pass on July 15. He intended to replenish their dwindling water supply before crossing and traveling on to Mesilla.[30]

The Chiricahuas were well aware of their approach. Mangas Coloradas and Cochise as well as Juh assembled their warriors, including Geronimo, to prevent the soldiers from reaching the springs.[31]

The Chiricahuas held the high ground and were well protected behind rocks. During the two-day battle, the troops used the howitzers to blast the warriors' positions. Sergeant Albert Fountain, leading a desperate charge, routed the warriors from the high ground, allowing the troops to reach the much-needed water.[32]

Roberts sent six cavalrymen to warn the supply train not to enter Apache Pass. Mangas Coloradas led an attack on the six men. Private John Teal was cut off from the others and kept up a stiff resistance until that evening, when he shot and severely wounded Mangas

Coloradas. Teal managed to rejoin the other cavalrymen at the supply train.[33]

The next day, Roberts reached the supply train and escorted it to Apache Pass, where with his full command he attacked the Chiricahua positions. By 4:00 p.m., the warriors had withdrawn.[34]

Cochise led his followers to Sonora while Mangas Coloradas's followers took him to Janos, Chihuahua, where a Mexican doctor treated his wound, and he soon recovered. Juh would have returned to his homeland in Mexico. Geronimo most likely stayed with Mangas Coloradas.[35]

On July 27, 1862, General James Carleton, commander of the California Column, arrived at Apache Pass. Captain Roberts strongly suggested they establish a post near the springs at Apache Pass; otherwise, future travelers would have to fight every time they stopped for water. Carleton agreed and established Fort Bowie, which would play a prominent role in the Apache Wars, and Geronimo's life.[36]

By mid-August, Mangas Coloradas had healed enough to return with his followers, including Geronimo, to their Bedonkohe homeland in the Mogollon Mountains.[37]

Geronimo was itching to head back to Mexico to raid once again. While it was still summer, he led eight men south, crossing the border and traveling along the west side of the Sierra Madre Mountains for five days before entering the southern part of the Sierra de Sahuaripa Mountains.[38]

There they ambushed a pack train, forcing its four mounted drivers to flee for their lives. The long train was heavily laden with supplies—blankets, cloth, saddles, tin ware, and sugar. They drove the pack train rapidly north and crossed the border with their plunder.[39]

Traveling through the Santa Catalina Mountains, they came upon a White Eye with his pack train. Upon seeing the Bedonkohes, the man raced his horse up a canyon away from them. They let him go and found that his pack train was loaded with cheese.[40]

Two days later, they arrived at their rancheria where Mangas Coloradas gathered all the Bedonkohes together for a celebration. They held a great feast, killing and eating some of the mules, dancing through the night, and dividing the spoils among the people.[41]

Three days after reaching the rancheria, scouts reported that dismounted Mexican cavalry were approaching. Mangas Coloradas divided the warriors, leading one contingent, while Geronimo led the other. They hoped to capture the Mexicans' horses and wipe out the troopers, but after four hours of fighting, their plan did not work. Ten Mexicans and one warrior were killed in the fight. Harassed by thirty warriors, the cavalry retreated across the border.[42]

Mangas Coloradas was tired of the constant warfare with the White Eyes and sought peace. He still trusted them.[43]

Unknown to Mangas Coloradas and other Apaches, General James Carleton had seen firsthand the grisly remains of travelers killed along the road from Tucson to Mesilla, and had issued instructions to attack all Apaches.[44]

On September 19, 1862, Mangas Coloradas sent a message to Carleton, saying that he wanted to live in peace with the Americans. Carleton ignored his overture, writing to his subordinate, Colonel Joseph West, "Mangas Coloradas sends me word he wants peace, but I have no faith in him."[45]

The second week of January 1863, Carleton sent West with 250 men to establish a base of operations at old Fort McLane. Their mission was to attack and subjugate Mangas Coloradas and his Bedonkohes.[46]

Mangas Coloradas still believed he could make peace with the Americans. Earlier, during the fall of 1862, he had met with Captain Jack Swilling, a former Confederate officer, at Pinos Altos. Mangas Coloradas believed he could achieve peace with Swilling's help, even though Swilling had told Mangas Coloradas he was going to kill him for his involvement in the Freeman Thomas fight in Cooke's Canyon, where seven Americans had been massacred and mutilated.[47]

In January 1863, Mangas Coloradas held a council with his warriors and other Chiricahua leaders in either the Mogollon or Peloncillo Mountains. There he told them he was willing to go to Pinos Altos and attempt to make peace. Geronimo and many others told him not to go, but he went anyway.[48]

An advance patrol of West's men led by Captain Edmund Shirland met Swilling and a party of prospectors at the ruins of old Fort

McLane. Swilling believed he could convince Mangas Coloradas to come in to Pinos Altos for talks and then capture him. Shirland and his men as well as Swilling and some of the prospectors rode to Pinos Altos.[49]

On the morning of January 16, 1863, Mangas Coloradas and a party of warriors approached Pinos Altos. The soldiers were hidden in buildings as Swilling went to greet the Bedonkohe leader. Upon reaching Mangas Coloradas, Swilling gave a signal and the troops emerged from the buildings with leveled weapons. Swilling told Mangas Coloradas he had to come with him and to tell his warriors to go away.[50]

Swilling and Shirland took Mangas Coloradas to Fort McLane and turned him over to West, who was now a brigadier general. West said to Mangas Coloradas, "[You have] murdered your last white victim, you old scoundrel." Mangas Coloradas replied he had only fought in self-defense after the miners had arrived.[51]

Mangas Coloradas was placed under guard within the walls of an adobe building's ruins. The night of January 18, 1863, was bitter cold. The only fire that night was where Mangas Coloradas was being held prisoner. West told the guards he wanted Mangas Coloradas dead by morning. The guards tormented Mangas Coloradas, holding heated bayonets to his feet and legs before finally shooting him.[52]

One soldier scalped him, and others threw his blanket-wrapped body into a ravine, covering it with rocks and dirt. A few days later, army surgeon David Sturgeon had Mangas Coloradas's body exhumed and his head cut off. Sturgeon had the head boiled to remove the flesh from the skull and sent it to a New York museum.[53]

When the Chiricahuas learned of Mangas Coloradas's betrayal and death, they were furious. They were even more horrified when they heard what had been done to his body. They believed that whatever was done to the body in this life would be carried over into the afterlife—meaning Mangas Coloradas would appear without his head in the next world.

The Apaches would not trust the Americans after this. Warfare would continue, and they would increase their mutilations of White Eyes.[54]

Geronimo said of Mangas Coloradas's murder and subsequent American troop attacks on the Chiricahuas, "Perhaps the greatest wrong ever done to the Indians was the treatment received by our tribe from the United States troops about 1863."[55]

Geronimo had been left in charge of the Bedonkohes, who had not traveled with Mangas Coloradas. They were staying either in the Mogollon or Peloncillo Mountains when they learned Mangas had been killed and decided to move to the mountains near Apache Pass, Cochise's country.[56]

As they traveled through the mountains, they came upon four men herding cattle. They killed the men and drove the herd to their camp. They were in the process of butchering the animals when mounted American troops attacked. The warriors put up the best resistance they could with spears and bows and arrows—no match for the army's firepower. One warrior, three women, and three children were killed as the Bedonkohes scattered in all directions.[57]

Two days later and fifty miles away, the Bedonkohes reassembled. The same troops attacked them about ten days after they had reassembled. The fight lasted all day until that evening, when the Bedonkohes retreated farther into the mountains. The troops did not pursue them and left the countryside.[58]

Geronimo's Bedonkohes found Cochise's Chokonens and Cochise took leadership of both bands. Shortly after this, American troops attacked, forcing them to retreat. Under Geronimo's leadership, the Bedonkohes separated from Cochise's Chokonens and returned to either the Mogollon or Peloncillo Mountains where they were safe from the army for more than a year.[59]

Over the next few years, Geronimo and his band would sometimes act on their own and other times act under the leadership of Cochise, based in the Chiricahua Mountains, or Juh, based in Mexico.[60]

As the Americans' Civil War continued, the threat of a renewed Confederate invasion of New Mexico was minimal. On February 24, 1863, Congress separated the western half of New Mexico, forming the territory of Arizona. Apaches continued to raid, and US troops were relentless in their pursuits through the duration of and after the Civil War.[61]

In the summer of 1863, Geronimo was ready for another raid into Mexico. He selected three warriors to travel with him to the Sierra de Sahuaripa Mountains in Sonora. They attacked a small village forty miles west of Casas Grandes, what Geronimo called "Crassanas." At noon, the people were off the street. Armed only with spears and bows and arrows, the raiders gave a war whoop and the four of them charged into town. The villagers ran out of the buildings, scattering in all directions. The warriors shot arrows at the fleeing Mexicans, killing one.[62]

They ransacked the town, taking food and supplies from homes and businesses. Finding the town's horses and mules, they loaded them with everything they could carry and herded them north. The townspeople did not attempt to pursue them. When they arrived at the rancheria, they held a feast, distributed gifts, and danced through the night and into the next day. There were enough supplies to last the band for more than a year.[63]

In the fall of 1864, Geronimo once again led a raid into Mexico. He handpicked twenty well-armed warriors and traveled to the Sierra de Antunez Mountains in Sonora where they set up camp. They attacked and plundered several villages and then attacked and captured a mule train, killing one of the drivers, while two others escaped. The warriors discovered the mule train's cargo was bottles of mescal. After setting up camp, Geronimo and his warriors began sampling the liquor. "The Indians began to get drunk and fight each other," Geronimo later said. "I, too, drank enough mescal to feel the effect of it, but I was not drunk." His men began fighting each other. He ordered them to stop, but no one would listen. He was worried Mexican troops could ambush them and ordered men to stand guard, but they would not listen. Finally, his men were so drunk they could do no further harm to each other. Geronimo poured out what was left of the mescal, put out the fires, moved the mules away from the camp, and treated the wounds of two men. He had to cut an arrowhead out of one man's leg and remove a spear point from another man's shoulder. He then stood guard until morning.[64]

The next day, as they headed toward the US border, they captured cattle from a herd and drove the animals ahead of them. They reached their rancheria where they held a feast and dance. The cattle and mules were slaughtered, the meat cured and stored so they would have plenty that winter.[65]

Geronimo's second wife, Chee-hash-kish, gave birth to a son, Chappo, in 1864, and to a daughter, Lulu, in 1865. Sometime after this, Geronimo married a fourth wife, She-gha, a close relative of Cochise. No one actually knows how many wives Geronimo had. Depending on the source, the number ranges between nine and twelve.[66]

By April 1865, the Civil War was coming to an end. Settlers, prospectors, and travelers increased in New Mexico and Arizona. They were easy targets for Apaches to plunder and kill. The government increased its manpower and resources, building forts and sending out patrols to protect citizens and end the Apache threat. No one knows to what extent Geronimo participated in these attacks on Americans. He and his band divided their time between the United States with Cochise and Mexico with Juh.[67]

It was the summer of 1865 and time for Geronimo to raid into Mexico. He took along four mounted warriors. Their plan was to capture more cattle. They rode south to the Sierra de Antunez Mountains in Sonora. From there, they headed southwest to the mouth of the Yaqui River, where they saw the expanse of the Sea of Cortez.[68]

Turning north, they plundered several villages. When they were northwest of Arispe, they stole sixty head of cattle. They crossed the border and arrived at their rancheria with no Mexicans in pursuit. Geronimo and his men gave out presents, the cattle were slaughtered, and the band feasted and danced in celebration.[69]

Geronimo was not satisfied. That fall, he returned to Mexico leading nine warriors on foot to villages south of Casas Grandes, where they collected a large herd of horses and mules. On their return north, they were camped in the mountains near Arispe when they were attacked by Mexican troops, losing all of their animals and plunder. Geronimo and his men made it safely back to their rancheria, but he was determined to return to Mexico for more raiding.[70]

Sometime after 1865, Geronimo married his fifth wife, a Bedonkohe named Shit-sha-she. After that he married a sixth wife, Zi-yeh, who was a Nednhi, but it is not known when they were married.[71] These marriages show Geronimo was a successful provider, able to support a large family.

In early summer of 1866, Geronimo took to raiding again. This time, he led thirty mounted warriors on a wide loop through Mexico, descending through Chihuahua to the Sierra de Sahuaripa Mountains, then sweeping north through Sonora. They killed about fifty Mexicans, acquiring plunder and amassing a large herd of horses, mules, and cattle. Mexican troops never appeared to stop them. On their return to the rancheria, they again gave presents, feasted, and danced.[72]

In 1867, Mangas, the youngest son of Mangas Coloradas, led eight warriors on a raid into Sonora.[73] Geronimo went along, later saying, "I went as a warrior, for I was always glad to fight the Mexicans."[74]

They rode into Sonora south of Arispe where they found a herd of cattle. They killed two vaqueros who had been watching over the herd and drove it north. As they approached Arispe on the second day, Mexican cavalry rapidly approached. The warriors abandoned the cattle and raced toward nearby timber where they dismounted and fought on foot. The troops collected the warriors' horses and the cattle, driving them toward Arispe. Five days later, the empty-handed warriors walked into their rancheria. Everyone considered the results of the raid a disgrace.[75]

Geronimo and five of the warriors were determined to return to Sonora. Mangas had no desire to go, so Geronimo led them on foot to the Sierra de Sahuaripa Mountains where they raided villages. They returned to the rancheria with a large herd of horses loaded with plunder.[76]

In 1868, Mexican cavalry crossed the border and were able to round up all of Geronimo's band's horses and mules. The warriors killed two Mexican scouts near their rancheria, but the troops and horses were long gone before the warriors could stop them.[77]

Geronimo led twenty warriors trailing the troops into Sonora. They found their animals at a ranch not far from the town of Nacozari. The warriors attacked, killing two vaqueros and driving off not only their own animals but also the ranch's livestock.[78]

As the warriors drove the herd north toward the border, Geronimo and three warriors trailed farther behind to intercept anyone who might try to retake the herd. They discovered nine mounted vaqueros following their trail.[79]

Once the vaqueros had bedded down for the night, Geronimo and his men sneaked into their camp and stole the horses from their picket line. The vaqueros never awoke. The band was jubilant when Geronimo and his men returned with their horses and those of the Mexicans. Everyone considered it a good trick to take the Mexicans' horses while they slept.[80]

In the winter of 1869–1870, Ishton, Geronimo's sister and Juh's wife, was pregnant and staying at Geronimo's rancheria while Juh was raiding in Mexico. When it was time for the baby's birth, the delivery became difficult. Everyone feared she would die. Alone, Geronimo climbed a mountain and prayed for four days. On the morning of the fifth day, he faced east and, lifting his hands to the sunrise, Power spoke to him: "The child will be born and your sister will live; and you will never be killed with weapons, but live to an old age." Ishton lived and gave birth to a healthy baby boy who was named Daklugie, meaning "Forced-his-way-through" or "One-who-grabs."[81]

The Chiricahuas soon came to believe that Power came to both Juh and Geronimo to know future events.[82]

As the winter of 1870–1871 began, American troops made a surprise attack on Geronimo's rancheria.[83] They killed five women, seven children, and four warriors, took all their horses, equipment, and supplies, and burned the wickiups and anything not of use.[84]

Geronimo and three warriors trailed the troops, who rode off toward San Carlos, Arizona. Geronimo and his men could not catch up with them and turned back. They came upon a Mexican and a White Eye, shot them off their horses, and took the animals back to the rancheria.[85]

Winter was harsh and game was scarce. Some tribes were receiving US government rations, but Geronimo had never asked for any. He knew that the Chihenne leader, Victorio, living at the sacred Ojo Caliente (Hot Springs) in New Mexico, was at peace with the Americans who were giving him provisions after holding peace talks at the nearby town of Cañada Alamosa, New Mexico. Cochise had briefly visited there and conferred with the Americans, who wanted to move his people east of the Rio Grande to the Mescalero Apache Reservation. Cochise said he was interested in peace but would not leave his homeland. Talks broke off in December 1870, and hostilities continued between Cochise and the White Eyes.[86]

Geronimo led his people to Ojo Caliente, where Victorio welcomed them and shared provisions with them. Geronimo's band stayed with Victorio's people for about a year while they accumulated supplies and recovered. Geronimo later said, "We had perfect peace. We had not the least trouble with Mexicans, white men, or Indians."[87] Geronimo and his band may have had "perfect peace" at Ojo Caliente and its vicinity, but this did not stop Geronimo and his warriors from accompanying their Nednhi friends on raids and in fights.

One of the US Army's most effective and relentless officers in attacking Apaches was Lieutenant Howard Cushing with the Third Cavalry. Fellow officer Lieutenant John Bourke later claimed Cushing had killed more Apaches than anyone else.[88] In February 1871, Cushing led his troops in the destruction of two Apache rancherias, and in April, they destroyed three more rancherias, killing thirty people.[89]

Juh knew of Cushing's attacks and was determined to kill him for the pain and suffering he had caused. Three times Juh's warriors had fought with Cushing's troops.[90]

On April 26, Cushing, with his civilian English friend William Simpson and a detail of seventeen men, was sent on a mission to find Cochise.[91]

Cushing and his men believed they had found the trail of Cochise.[92] On May 5, heading toward the Whetstone Mountains, two miles north of the Babocomari River, they found burning grass and a trail made by a single set of female moccasins leading up a narrow canyon. It was not Cochise but Juh and Geronimo who had set a trap, and Cushing and his men rode into it.[93]

Apache warriors fired from hidden positions in the canyon. Simpson, who carried a Henry repeater rifle, was the first to be killed. A bullet slammed into Cushing's chest. As his men tried to carry the wounded officer away, he was shot in the face. Cushing, Simpson, and two other dead were left on the field as the troopers fought a running battle to save their lives. After a mile-long pursuit, the Apaches let them go.[94] Juh's son Asa Daklugie later said, "Juh wasn't much interested in the troops—just Cushing."[95]

The American president, Ulysses Grant, appointed a new commander for the Department of Arizona, Lieutenant Colonel George Crook. Crook was reluctant to take the appointment, writing that he was "tired of Indian work." However, he always did his duty, and upon arrival in Arizona on June 4, 1871, he rode through the eastern part of the territory with five companies of cavalry, searching for Cochise to fight and subdue, but never found him.[96] Crook wrote that Cochise was "an uncompromising enemy to all mankind" and his Chokonen Chiricahuas were "the worst of all Apaches."[97]

Crook studied the Apaches and came up with two innovative techniques to subdue them. First, he realized his troops needed to move quickly, and supply wagons slowed them down. He switched to pack-mule trains to carry supplies. Second, he found Apaches to act as scouts, leading troops to track down other Apaches.[98]

In the meantime, Cochise was interested in the possibility of peace and accepted an offer of further discussions at Cañada Alamosa in New Mexico, outside of Crook's military department. Arriving there on September 28 with 250 people, he met with government officials in early October. The editors of the *Las Cruces Borderer* interviewed Cochise, and that interview appeared in the November 1, 1871, issue. Cochise said he wanted peace and was willing to settle at Ojo Caliente, and many other bands would, too. However, he had no control over the other bands, and the government should not hold him responsible for them. He specifically mentioned the Nednhis, meaning Juh and Geronimo, would fight "until the last one was killed."[99]

As the decade of the 1860s began, the Hunkpapas probably knew little of the strife the United States was experiencing over slavery, which would lead to open warfare in April 1861. Pierre Chouteau Jr. & Company had built a new Fort Pierre on the west bank of the Missouri River, two miles north of the old fort's site, in 1859. There, Sitting Bull and the Hunkpapas resumed their trade in buffalo hides and furs for the white man's goods. Sitting Bull also worked as a middleman for the Fort Berthold interpreter and trader Pierre Garreau, employee of Pierre Chouteau Jr. & Company. Sitting Bull made good trades, but after two years, he ended the working arrangement when Garreau did not pay him the agreed-upon amount.[100]

The Lakotas were becoming even more distrustful of white men. They wanted the traders to continue business at their posts along the Missouri River, but they were concerned about the US government. Discord continued between those Hunkpapas who took the government annuities and those who refused, believing that by accepting the gifts they were trading away their homeland. Many were concerned the increased riverboat traffic on the Missouri River was bringing in potential settlers who would take their lands. Trespassing hunters were taking their game. Military expeditions were illegally exploring their lands. They were aware of the Dakota tribes' problems and conflicts with settlers entering their lands in what would become the states of Iowa and Minnesota. They were concerned about what had happened in 1858 to the Yankton Nakotas, whom the US government had pressured into selling almost all their land—fourteen million acres between the Big Sioux and the Missouri Rivers, the future southeast portion of South Dakota.[101]

After Light Hair's death, Sitting Bull married a woman named Snow-on-Her. They would have two daughters—Many Horses, born in 1865, and Walks Looking, born in 1868. He was very fond of both daughters. Sitting Bull continued to live his life in the traditional Hunkpapa way—hunting, war parties, and serving as a *Wichasha Wakan* (holy man). His pictographs, thought to depict events from the late 1850s to early 1860s, show him stealing horses from the Crows on three different occasions, counting coup on an Arikara warrior, counting coup on a Crow woman, and wounding a Crow warrior.[102]

In the spring of 1862, an increase in Missouri River steamboat traffic to Montana was disturbing to the tribes. When gold was discovered there later that summer, riverboat traffic would increase even more, causing Lakota hostility.[103]

On May 27, 1862, a steamboat arrived at Fort Pierre with a new Indian agent named Samuel Latta, who would distribute the annual annuities. Bear's Rib, who General Harney had appointed as chief—as well as two thousand to three thousand Nakota and Lakota tribal members, many of them warriors—were there to greet Latta and receive the gifts. The Hunkpapas, including Sitting Bull, were there.[104]

Latta reported the meeting with the tribes was contentious. The various leaders spoke of their grievances. Latta said, "[They] did not at all appreciate the guardianship of the Great Father." Some said they would not take the government annuities anymore. They considered the whites trespassers, and they were going to put a stop to their travel on the Missouri River. Harney had promised them protection from their enemies, and here the whites were supplying firearms and ammunition to their enemies, the Mandans, Hidatsas, and Arikaras. They wanted the white men to stop cutting down all the trees to be used as fuel for the steamboats and killing all the buffalo.[105]

The anti-annuity faction had had enough. On June 5, 1862, 150 Miniconjous and Sans Arcs arrived at Fort Pierre stating that they planned to kill the chiefs Harney had appointed. The next day, two Sans Arcs, Mouse and One-That-Limps, confronted Bear's Rib at the fort. Mouse shot his musket, hitting Bear's Rib in the left arm and chest, as Bear's Rib fired his double-barreled shotgun, hitting Mouse. They both died, and Bear's Rib's warriors killed One-That-Limps.[106]

Six weeks later, ten traditionalist Hunkpapa chiefs signed a letter and handed it to Pierre Garreau to give to Agent Latta. They did not want annuities; they did not want white men traveling through their territory on land or by river, because they might take their land. If the US government did not stop white intruders, the Hunkpapas would. If the government sent soldiers, the Hunkpapas were ready to fight.[107]

For years, the Dakotas of Minnesota had been slowly losing to white encroachment. Year by year they were forced to sell more land as thousands of settlers developed farms. Losing their hunting grounds, the Dakotas were encouraged by the government to farm, but their crops were poor, and they were facing starvation. The Dakotas resented the traders who had been cheating and deceiving them. As the Civil War unfolded, some of the funds set aside for the tribes by treaty were diverted to the war effort, and other funds were lost through theft and mismanagement.[108]

On August 17, four young Wahpetons looking for food murdered five settlers, two of whom were women. The die was cast, and the tribes rose up in rebellion. By the time Governor Alexander Ramsey appointed Henry Sibley as colonel to lead a military response, the Dakotas had killed over 800 Minnesotans. Sibley organized a force of 1,500 men to battle the Dakotas. On September 23, at Wood Lake, Minnesota, Sibley's troops defeated the Dakotas. Many surrendered, but others fled to Dakota Territory.[109]

At the same time, things were heating up along the Missouri River. In August 1862, Lakotas attacked a Missouri River steamboat transporting miners to the Montana goldfields, and on October 10, 1862, Nakota Yanktonais fired on a returning mackinaw boat filled with miners about 150 miles downriver from Fort Berthold. Other travelers heading downriver reported encounters with hostile, taunting Indians.[110]

In response to the Dakota and Lakota hostilities, the federal government created the Department of the Northwest, headquartered in St. Paul, Minnesota. Major General John Pope was assigned to command the department, and under him was Henry Sibley, who was promoted to brigadier general, and Brigadier General Alfred Sully.[111]

It was important to the Union cause that the Montana gold-mining efforts continue, and that those who had participated in the Minnesota uprising and escaped be punished. There were rumors the Dakotas were building up strength to reenter Minnesota and continue their rampage.[112]

Pope and his aides developed a plan of attack for the spring of 1863. Sibley would march a column of infantry westward along the Minnesota River and then northwest to Devil's Lake to confront the Dakotas, and Sully would lead a column of mounted troops along the Missouri River to intimidate the Lakotas into submission. The two columns were to converge in a pincer movement, trapping the hostile tribes.[113]

At the end of June 1863, Sibley's force of 2,000 infantry, 800 cavalry, 150 artillerymen, and a few scouts began their march up the Minnesota River. Sully's troops consisted of 1,200 cavalry, 325 infantrymen, and 8 mountain howitzers. A train of 150 wagons pulled by 500 mules, and 4 steamboats, all loaded with equipment and supplies, were scheduled to accompany the expedition up the Missouri River. On June 23, 1863, Sully's expedition left the frontier town of Yankton, Dakota Territory, marching upriver along the Missouri's east bank.[114]

By mid-July, Sibley reached the James River, forty miles south of Devil's Lake, Dakota Territory, where he established a base camp. His scouts learned there were Dakotas to the west. Marching his troops in their direction, he caught up with them on July 24, at Big Mound, where they fought, and the Dakotas retreated to the west. At Dead Buffalo Lake, Hunkpapa and Blackfeet buffalo hunters had joined the Dakotas when Sibley attacked again. The pursuit continued to Stony Lake, where a battle was fought, and then finally at the mouth of Apple Creek where it entered the Missouri River. The warriors battled the troops until all the women and children escaped to the west bank of the Missouri River. On July 29, the warriors crossed the river, and on July 31, Sibley withdrew. For three days Sibley's scouts looked for Sully's column; not finding it, Sibley began his return to base camp.[115]

It is possible Sitting Bull was one of the Hunkpapa participants in these fights. He was at least at the Apple Creek fight. One of Sitting Bull's pictographs shows bullets flying around him as he counts coup on one of Sibley's muleskinners and steals a saddled mule during the fight.[116]

Sully's troops did not reach the scene of Sibley's battles until late August. His speed had been hampered by the rough terrain his troops had to cross, and low flows on the Missouri River had forced two of the steamboats to turn back. Sully discovered the Dakotas and Lakotas had returned to the east side of the Missouri River to continue their buffalo hunts. His troops made contact with the tribes on September 3 and fought a fierce late-afternoon battle with them at Whitestone Hill. It is not known whether Sitting Bull participated. That night the tribes escaped to the west. Between 150 and 300 warriors were killed, 22 soldiers were dead, and 250 women and children had been captured.[117]

Sully had several more skirmishes with the Dakotas and Lakotas before returning downriver. On the Missouri River's east bank at Farm Island, several miles downriver from Fort Pierre, he had a new fort built—Fort Sully—where he left a garrison. Stationing troops downriver at Fort Randall, Yankton, and Vermillion, Sully spent the winter at army district headquarters in Sioux City, Iowa.[118]

In the autumn of 1863, the Hunkpapas encountered Arikaras who had just harvested a corn crop and were returning to their permanent camp at Fort Berthold. The two tribes negotiated a truce to trade corn for buffalo hides. While members of both tribes visited each other's camps to trade, a group of the men decided to hold horse races—Arikara against Hunkpapa. Rivalries were intense and betting was heavy. One race was very close, and the judges couldn't agree. An Arikara judge struck a Hunkpapa judge and a brawl ensued. Men rushed for their weapons. Fighting broke out and visitors in each village were held hostage.[119]

An Arikara chief rode into the midst of the fighting, signaling for a truce. He then asked for Sitting Bull to come to his village at once. Sitting Bull rode to the Arikara village and allowed his horse to be led in. He negotiated with the Arikara chief. They settled their differences—the hostages on both sides were released and trading resumed. Sitting Bull's reputation as an honorable man was known not only among his own people, but also among his enemies.[120]

By June 1864, General Sully and 2,200 troops were on the march again up the Missouri River, accompanied by three riverboats carrying building material and five companies of the Thirtieth Wisconsin Volunteer Infantry. One of Sully's duties was to establish a new fort on the Upper Missouri. On July 7, he found an appropriate location on the west bank, eight miles north of the mouth of the Cannonball River, where he left the Thirtieth Wisconsin to construct the new Fort Rice.[121]

After being joined by a brigade from Fort Ridgley, Minnesota, Sully proceeded westward along the Cannonball River with almost 3,000 troops on July 19. They were slowed down by an unwanted civilian wagon train they were obligated to protect—250 men, women, and children with their 150 ox-drawn wagons and large cattle herd, bound for the Montana goldfields.[122]

The Lakotas, Dakotas, and Nakotas learned Sully's troops were on their way. They were scattered in small bands but came together, ready for a fight. Possibly as many as 1,600 lodges with 3,000 warriors, including Sitting Bull, assembled and moved to Dakota Territory's Killdeer Mountain, to the east of the Little Missouri River badlands, and waited for Sully's troops.[123]

Leaving troops along the Heart River to protect the emigrants and most of his supplies and equipment, Sully advanced northwest with 2,200 men toward the village. On July 28, warriors rode out five miles from the village to confront the troops. The Indians were confident they would beat the troops. They did not disband the camp and send the women and children away; in fact, they remained and watched the fight unfold. A portion of the cavalry remained mounted while nine companies were ordered to dismount and form a skirmish line.[124]

A Lakota warrior, Long Dog, knew his medicine was strong that day and raced his horse in front of the troops. They shot at him and missed. The soldiers had fired first. Sitting Bull and the other warriors believed the troops had started the fight and the battle was on.[125]

Single warriors rode out seeking individual combat or in small groups to challenge the whites. The troops stayed in formation, firing rifles and artillery when ordered, while the warriors fought as individuals, using trade muskets, lances, and bows and arrows.[126]

The troops slowly and methodically pushed the warriors back toward the village over the five-mile stretch. The artillery wreaked havoc on Indians who had taken cover in a ravine and then commenced firing on the village.[127]

Sitting Bull was in the thick of the fighting all day. As troops were converging on the village from the west, Sitting Bull's uncle, Four Horns, was shot in the back. Sitting Bull with his nephew White Bull guided the still-mounted Four Horns to cover in a thicket where they took care of him. He would later recover from his gunshot wound.[128]

The army won the battle and captured the village. The warriors and their families retreated with what little they could carry. Sully lost two men. The troops counted one hundred dead Indians, but more bodies had probably been carried away. The next day, the troops burned everything they could find: tepees, food, household items, everything—an estimated two hundred tons of material.[129]

The Indian refugees from the destroyed village at Killdeer Mountain traveled southwest and set up camp on the western edge of the Little Missouri River badlands. They were joined by Cheyenne warriors and other Lakota bands who had not been involved in the Killdeer Mountain fight.[130]

From August 7 through August 9, Sully slowly pursued the Indians' trail westward into the badlands. The troops had to construct a road to pass through the deep ravines and jagged cliffs, and all the while, the Indians attempted to ambush them and slow their advance. There was little water or grass for the horses and mules, and they started dying.[131]

The Indians' firepower was ineffective on the advancing troops. Frustrated, Sitting Bull advised, "Let them go, and we will go home." However, the fight continued until the night of August 8. Sitting Bull had a shouted exchange with one of Sully's Indian scouts. The scout wanted to know who they were fighting. Sitting Bull answered, "Hunkpapas, Sans Arcs, Yanktonais, and others. Who are you?"

"Some Indians with the soldiers," the scout replied.

"You have no business with the soldiers," Sitting Bull shouted. "The Indians have no fight with the whites. Why is it the whites come to fight the Indians?"[132]

As Sully's troops reached the Indian camp on August 9, the tribes abandoned it and scattered southeast into the badlands. Sully estimated he had killed three hundred Indians in the badlands, but there was no way to really know. The army lost nine men, and about one hundred were wounded.[133]

Sitting Bull said of the battles with Sully's troops, "The white soldiers do not know how to fight. . . . Also, they seem to have no hearts." Sitting Bull learned white soldiers did not fight as Lakotas did, for personal honor and glory; the white soldiers fought only to kill.[134]

Sully proceeded to the Yellowstone River with the emigrant train in tow. Leaving the wagon train to proceed on its own to the Montana goldfields, he eventually returned to Fort Rice, and later would follow the Missouri downriver and back to Sioux City, Iowa, for the winter.[135]

Sitting Bull's band followed a buffalo herd southeast toward the divide between the Little Missouri tributaries and those of the Grand River. On September 2, they encountered a westward-proceeding wagon train. A forty-man convalescent cavalry escort, led by two officers out of Fort Rice, accompanied the wagon train, which was led by Captain James Liberty Fisk. The wagon train, consisting of eighty ox-drawn wagons and Red River carts and numbering 170 men, women, and children, had originated in Minnesota and was heading toward the Montana goldfields.[136]

They were crossing rough country. One of the wagons overturned as they were crossing a dry draw, Deep Creek. The wagon train continued forward as nine soldiers and three civilians with a second wagon remained behind to aright and fix the wagon.[137]

Unknown to the wagon train, Sitting Bull and a hundred warriors had been stalking them. The warriors waited until the wagon train was about a mile away and then attacked the party working on the wreck.[138]

Sitting Bull, astride a fast horse, reached the rear guard and work party first. He raced up to his target, a mounted soldier. They grappled. Sitting Bull was attempting to unseat the soldier as the man drew his revolver and fired point-blank into Sitting Bull's left hip, the bullet exiting the small of his back. Sitting Bull turned his horse and raced from the fight. White Bull and Jumping Bull dressed his wound and took him back to the village, six miles away.[139]

Even though Sitting Bull was out of action, the fight continued. The Hunkpapas killed everyone in the work party and rear guard before a rescue party could reach them. The wagon train attempted to continue on its westward trek, but the Hunkpapas harassed it so much that it formed a defensive circle and plowed up prairie sod to construct defensive walls. They named it Fort Dilts after their scout who had been killed in the fight on the first day. Constant gunfire and a 12-pounder mountain howitzer Fisk had brought along kept the more than 300 Hunkpapa warriors at bay. Fifteen soldiers volunteered to ride two hundred miles back to Fort Rice for a rescue party. Even though the Hunkpapas were on their trail, they made it safely back to the fort. Sully, who had just reached the fort on his return trip downriver, sent a 900-man relief expedition, which arrived at Fort Dilts on September 20. By then, the Hunkpapas had tired of the siege and left in search of buffalo. Against Fisk's protests, the emigrants believed it was too dangerous to proceed and voted to return to Fort Rice with the relief expedition.[140]

While convalescing in camp, Sitting Bull began to take an interest in the plight of a captive white woman living with Brings Plenty. Her name was Fanny Kelly. Back on July 12, 1864, she had been captured by Oglalas along the Oregon Trail in modern-day Wyoming. The Oglalas had traded her to Brings Plenty. News of her living with the Hunkpapas had reached the whites, and they sent Indians to the Hunkpapas requesting her return, but Brings Plenty was pleased with her work ethic and did not want to give her up.[141]

The Hunkpapas were becoming annoyed with all the visitors attempting to trade for Fanny. Sitting Bull believed her return might restore some goodwill with the whites, perhaps convincing them to leave the Hunkpapas alone. One December day, Sitting Bull's Lakota

Blackfeet friend, Crawler, and three warriors and their wives arrived to trade for Fanny and take her back to the whites. Sitting Bull agreed, and after a confrontation between Crawler and Brings Plenty, they all traveled to Fort Sully to return Fanny.[142]

Concerned the Lakotas would attempt to use her as a ruse to take the fort, Fanny gave a letter of warning to a friend, Jumping Bear, who took it to the fort's commander. On December 9, 1864, over a thousand Lakotas appeared with Fanny outside the fort. Concerned about a possible attack, the soldiers allowed only ten Lakotas to enter the stockade with Fanny. Sitting Bull was one of those excluded from the fort. The Lakotas did not attack the fort, and camped there a few days, doing some trading before moving on. "She is out of our way," Sitting Bull later said. He could tell by the look on Fanny Kelly's face that she was homesick, "So I sent her back."[143]

General Sully had not only built Fort Rice in the middle of Lakota territory, but he had also garrisoned troops at the trading posts of Fort Union and Fort Berthold. During the harsh winter of 1864–1865, the Lakotas would attack lone white men or small parties venturing from the forts. When spring arrived, the Lakotas stepped up their harassment of the troops whenever the opportunity presented itself, with Sitting Bull leading the Hunkpapas.[144]

In early 1865 a Cheyenne delegation from the south arrived in Sitting Bull's camp with news of an atrocity in Colorado. Back on November 29, 1864, Black Kettle's peaceful Southern Cheyenne band had been attacked at Sand Creek by more than 700 men of the Colorado militia, led by Colonel John Chivington. When the massacre was over, 28 men were dead, and 105 women and children killed. All were scalped, and many, including women and children, were mutilated, with militiamen taking body parts as trophies. The Cheyenne delegation asked Sitting Bull and the Hunkpapas to smoke the war pipe with them, which they did.[145]

Many Lakotas had come together for the annual Sun Dance on the headwaters of the Heart River in June of 1865. General Sully was leading his army once again up the Missouri River and would be at Fort Rice in July. He sent messengers to the Sun Dance requesting the Lakotas come to the fort for peace talks. Sitting Bull argued against going, but many were for going to the fort to talk. Some left right away; others, including Sitting Bull's band, were reluctant, but slowly headed in that direction.[146]

Sully reached the east bank of the Missouri River, and on July 13, as he was being ferried across the river, the fort's commander fired his cannons in salute. The Lakotas, who had already arrived at the fort, panicked, believing it was the beginning of another Sand Creek massacre. As people fled, officers tried to calm them down, but rumors of massacre quickly spread to the incoming Lakota bands, including Sitting Bull's.[147]

Sitting Bull organized a 300-man revenge attack on Fort Rice. On the morning of July 28, they killed one soldier and wounded several more while capturing some livestock. Sitting Bull did not accomplish much. He and six warriors made off with two horses. Many Lakotas were hostile, and any peace talks would have to wait.[148]

General Sully wrote on August 8, "A chief (who wishes to lead the war party) called Sitting Bull, hearing this [the alleged massacre] on his return to camp, went through the different villages cutting himself with a knife and crying out that he was just from Fort Rice; that all those that had come in and given themselves up I had killed, and called on the nation to avenge the murder." This was the first time Sitting Bull was mentioned in a report.[149]

For the rest of the summer of 1865, it was relatively peaceful at the Missouri River forts. Sully and his force of over 1,000 men had left Fort Rice on July 23, marching northeast toward Devil's Lake and arriving there on July 29. From there, he marched west to Fort Berthold and, taking along the fort's garrison, returned to Fort Rice on September 5. He returned downriver, never encountering any Indians to fight. Sully did not find any hostile Indians because they had all headed west across the Little Missouri River to the Powder River.[150]

However, American troops were still harassing the Hunkpapas as well as other tribes. Brigadier General Patrick Conner had been given the task to subdue the tribes in eastern Wyoming and western Dakota Territory, as well as reconnoiter for potential roads to the Montana goldfields. Conner's Powder River Expedition consisted of over 2,600 men divided into three columns that would march separately and converge on the Powder River, hoping to trap the tribes between the three prongs.[151]

Two of the columns led by Colonel Nelson Cole and Lieutenant Colonel Samuel Walker joined forces north of the Black Hills in Dakota Territory. They proceeded together toward the Powder River Valley in Wyoming. There, on September 1, they encountered 400 to 500 Lakota warriors who harassed them with hit-and-run tactics. The troops were running low on rations, and the horses and mules were in weakened conditions. On the night of September 2, the temperature plummeted, and an intense rain and sleet storm hit. The next morning, 225 horses and mules were dead, forcing the troops to abandon most of the supply wagons.[152]

On September 5, over 1,000 Lakota warriors attacked, with Sitting Bull leading his Hunkpapas. After repulsing the attacks, the troops continued their march south toward food. Those Lakota bands let them go, but on September 8, Oglala bands and other tribes attacked the troops before they reached the newly constructed Fort Conner in Wyoming on September 20. After this, the Powder River Expedition would soon come to an end.[153]

In October, government peace commissioners met with representatives of the Lakota tribes and signed peace treaties where the Lakotas would receive annuities in exchange for peace with the whites and peace with each other. However, there were many Lakotas, a good portion being Hunkpapas, including Sitting Bull, who would have nothing to do with the peace treaties and continued to raid and wage war.[154]

In 1866, after he had been married to Snow-on-Her for a couple of years, Sitting Bull married Red Woman, which was acceptable to do. He would have a son by Red Woman. Snow-on-Her was not at all happy with this new arrangement, especially as it seemed to her that Sitting Bull was showing preference for Red Woman. It was not a happy home. The women constantly warred with each other until Sitting Bull could stand it no more. Believing the worst of Snow-on-Her, he divorced her by taking her back to her family, but their two daughters stayed with him.[155]

In the spring of 1866, Sitting Bull resumed his attacks on Fort Rice, but soon he would have an even more hated target. That summer, the army began constructing a new fort two miles downriver from the trading post, Fort Union, on the east bank of the Missouri River, and named it Fort Buford. This fort was right in the center of Hunkpapa territory, and Sitting Bull would wage war against it for four years.[156]

The attacks on Fort Buford began in August as Sitting Bull's Hunkpapa warriors attacked anyone working on the fort or traveling through. During the fall and then into the winter of 1866–1867, the fort was under siege. The Hunkpapas twice captured the fort's sawmill and icehouse along the river, and from that position, fired on the fort. Sitting Bull beat on the saw blade and sang a song until he and his warriors were chased out by artillery and infantry. They burned the fort's stockpiled firewood supply and cut off all communication to and from Fort Buford, leading to speculation in the newspapers that everyone in the fort had been massacred.[157]

Upriver, the Hunkpapas and traders at Fort Union still conducted a wary business. Sitting Bull acquired a red shirt and told head trader David Pease to tell the soldiers he would be wearing that shirt and they should aim for him. He planned to kill every last one of them. Pease told the fort's commander who issued orders if they saw a warrior wearing a red shirt to shoot at him. Sitting Bull also sent messages directly to the fort, stating he would destroy Fort Buford.[158]

During that same time, beginning in the summer of 1866, Red Cloud was leading the Oglala Lakotas as well as Cheyenne and Arapaho allies, 3,000 warriors, in war against the whites in Wyoming and Montana. Running along the eastern foothills of the Big Horn Mountains was a new road to the Montana goldfields, the Bozeman Trail. The army built three forts along the trail to help protect emigrants. From south to north the forts were Reno (the renamed Fort Conner), Phil Kearny, and C. F. Smith. Red Cloud maintained a constant siege of these forts, concentrating most of his efforts on destroying Fort Phil Kearny, where, on December 21, 1866, a young warrior, Crazy Horse, started to make a name for himself with the defeat and massacre of Captain William Fetterman and eighty soldiers.[159]

In 1867, the army provided two additional targets for Sitting Bull and his Hunkpapas with the construction of Fort Stevenson on the east bank of the Missouri River, between Forts Rice and Buford, and Fort Totten at Devil's Lake. Along with the Hunkpapa attacks on the forts, travelers and mail carriers risked their lives crossing Hunkpapa territory.[160]

As Sitting Bull's war raged into the spring of 1868, the US government wanted the hostilities to stop and began peace negotiations with the Cheyennes, Arapahos, Oglalas, and other Lakota tribes who had been fighting in Wyoming and Montana. The government agreed to abandon the Bozeman Trail and the forts associated with it. Boundaries were set for the Great Sioux Reservation that included what is now western South Dakota, extending from the Missouri River westward, including the Black Hills. The southern border was the Nebraska state line while the northern boundaries were undefined, and those to the west were the summits of the Big Horn Mountains. The western area in Wyoming and Montana was called "unceded Indian territory." The treaty included annuities for the tribes and established agencies for administration. One clause stated, "They [the Indians] will not in the future object to the construction of railroads, wagon roads, mail stations, or other works of utility or necessity, which may be ordered or permitted by the laws of the United States."[161]

Starting in April 1868, the tribes who had been fighting in what was known as Red Cloud's War all eventually signed what would become known as the Fort Laramie Treaty of 1868. The government wanted the Hunkpapas on the Upper Missouri River to sign the treaty, too, but Sitting Bull was not interested.[162]

In May, Sitting Bull and his warriors killed and mutilated two civilian workers in the hay fields outside Fort Buford. They rode to Fort Stevenson, but the soldiers there were on alert. Sitting Bull and his warriors rode the trail to Fort Totten, killing two mail carriers while allowing two other mail carriers to live when they found they were mixed-race, but still stripping them of everything they had, including their clothes. Sitting Bull gave them a message to deliver:

He refused to meet with any peace commissioners, and would continue to kill white men until they left his country.[163]

The one man all the northern plains tribes respected and the government believed could convince the Hunkpapas to meet and sign the treaty was the Jesuit missionary Pierre-Jean De Smet. The Lakotas called him Black Robe, and he agreed to the mission. Leaving Fort Rice with an escort of eighty Lakota leaders and warriors, he arrived at Sitting Bull's Yellowstone River camp on June 19, 1868.[164]

Sitting Bull welcomed De Smet and insisted he and his interpreters stay in his tepee. He placed guards around the tepee to ensure their protection. On June 20, the tribal council met with 500 people in attendance. Sitting Bull's uncle, Four Horns, opened the proceedings with the sacred pipe ceremony. De Smet made the case for peace and asked that the Hunkpapas meet with the peace commissioners at Fort Rice. Black Moon, one of the major chiefs of the Hunkpapas, then spoke, saying they too wanted peace, but there were many grievances against the whites. Sitting Bull spoke next as war chief. He hoped for peace and said he would be friends with the whites, but he would not agree to selling any part of their country. The whites had to stop cutting down timber along the Missouri River, and the forts had to be abandoned. De Smet later noted that when Sitting Bull had finished his speech, "with cheers from all, he resumed his seat." None of the Hunkpapa leaders believed the peace talks would lead anywhere, but, out of respect for Black Robe, they would send a delegation led by Gall and a few lesser chiefs.[165]

After the council meeting, De Smet told them stories from the Bible, saying that God had sent His Son Jesus to reconcile all people to God. He blessed the children, baptized some of the adults, and gave Sitting Bull a crucifix.[166]

The Hunkpapa delegation arrived at Fort Rice on July 2. They listened as the white peace commissioners read to them and other tribal leaders the provisions of the Fort Laramie Treaty. The whites called for each chief to speak and then sign the treaty. Gall spoke first. He probably did not understand any of what had just been read to him. He said, "The whites ruin our country. If we make peace, the military posts on this river must be removed and the steamboats stopped from coming up here." He said they would not accept annuities, but he did want twenty kegs of gunpowder. He again said the forts had to go and the steamboat traffic had to stop. The other Hunkpapa representatives said the same as Gall. The other chiefs spoke, and then Gall was first to sign the treaty document, which was unchanged.[167]

The white peace commissioners left the meeting pleased the Hunkpapa representatives had signed the treaty—unchanged. They believed those signatures committed Sitting Bull and all the other Hunkpapa leaders to the treaty. It is obvious Gall and the others believed that for peace to occur, the whites had to accept their spoken provisions. A piece of paper with a mark made by them on it did not mean anything to them. Sitting Bull and the other leaders who were not at the meeting would think it ludicrous they would be held to the agreement. Actions to them meant more than words. The steamboats needed to stop and the forts abandoned. Then there would be peace.[168]

Nothing changed. The steamboats still plied the river. The forts remained in place. Gall, Sitting Bull, and the Hunkpapas did not change their way of life; they did not stop their warfare against the whites and their tribal enemies. In September, Sitting Bull led 150 warriors raiding the Fort Buford cattle herd. They killed three soldiers and ran off 250 head.[169]

On January 2, 1869, Frank Grouard, whose father had been an American missionary and his mother, Polynesian, was carrying mail from Fort Hall, Idaho, to the Fort Peck trading post at the mouth of the Milk River on the Missouri River in Montana. It was snowing hard and a cold wind blew the snow directly into his face. Grouard wore a bearskin coat as well as bearskin leggings, hat, and mittens. As he rode, leading a packhorse through a ravine, two Indians attacked. They grabbed his horses, took his gun, and knocked him to the ground. One was trying to remove his coat while the other was trying to shoot him. Grouard held on to the warrior who was trying to take his coat and kept swinging him to keep him between himself and the shooter.[170]

A third Indian rode up, followed by eleven more. The third Indian on the scene said something to the two men attacking Grouard. He

Sitting Bull saves Frank Grouard.

dismounted, and lifting a heavy bow, struck the one with the gun and then struck the one trying to remove Grouard's coat.[171]

The man with the bow was Sitting Bull. He took Grouard to the Hunkpapa village and formally adopted him as his brother, naming him Standing Bear. They gave him the nickname "Grabber" because a bear will reach out and grab its prey and pull it close to its body. Grouard later learned that when Sitting Bull rode up to where the two warriors were fighting him, Sitting Bull thought Grouard was actually a bear. Then when he learned his mistake, he thought it was funny. Grouard would remain in Sitting Bull's village as part of the family until the fall of 1873.[172]

There were quite a number of Lakota leaders who had not signed the white man's treaty. There may have been as many as a third of the Lakota population who refused to abide by the treaty. Sitting Bull's uncle, Four Horns, was one of the most influential Lakota leaders who had not signed the treaty. He was concerned they were not forcing the soldiers out of Lakota territory. They needed a new approach. Four Horns came up with the idea for a supreme chief who all the Lakotas could unite behind—and Sitting Bull was that candidate.[173]

Four Horns conferred with other Hunkpapa leaders and they agreed on the concept of a supreme chief for all the Lakotas, and that Sitting Bull best fit that position. The Hunkpapas called a council of all the tribes on the Powder River, most likely in 1869. Many bands came, such as Crazy Horse's Oglalas, who refused to follow Red Cloud, who had signed the treaty. Bands of Yanktonais and even some Cheyennes attended. All agreed on the new position of supreme chief and approved Sitting Bull for that position.[174]

They held a solemn ceremony conferring the new title on Sitting Bull. Four Horns declared, "For your bravery on the battlefields and as the greatest warrior of our bands, we have elected you as war chief, leader of the entire Sioux nation. When you tell us to fight, we shall fight, when you tell us to make peace, we shall make peace." Sitting Bull took his new position seriously, accepting the responsibility for the well-being of all the Lakota people. He set the example of never visiting an agency or taking annuities. He would fulfill their expectations, holding the coalition of bands together against the US government for the next seven years.[175]

There were Lakota leaders who had signed the Fort Laramie Treaty who did not accept Sitting Bull's leadership of all the Lakota tribes, those principal leaders being Red Cloud and his Oglalas and Spotted Tail of the Brulés.[176]

It was most likely in 1869 that several prominent warriors organized a new twenty-member society called the Silent Eaters, and Sitting Bull became its leader. The Silent Eaters' purpose was the welfare of the tribe. They met late at night and ate together, discussing tribal concerns. They were serious and did not joke and tell stories; neither did they sing and dance as other societies did. The tribal council always considered their advice when making decisions, and they became Sitting Bull's strongest backers.[177]

During the winter of 1869–1870, Sitting Bull's band was camped at the mouth of the Powder River where it joins the Yellowstone River.

It was frigid, and deep snow covered the ground. Two boys were away from camp, hunting on foot. Thirty Crows, only one mounted on a horse, attacked them. One boy was killed, and the other was able to escape back to camp.[178]

Sitting Bull organized a 100-warrior revenge party. They found the boy's scalped and mutilated body in the snow and then followed the Crows' trail that led to a rocky hill where they had taken a defensive position. Sitting Bull was out front well in advance of all the Hunkpapas in a dawn attack. Fighting was intense and lasted all morning. Sitting Bull and the Hunkpapa warriors overran the Crows' natural fortress, killing them all, but not without loss to the Hunkpapas—thirteen dead and seventeen wounded. Among the dead was Sitting Bull's youngest uncle, Looks-for-Him-in-a-Tent, who had received a gunshot to the chest. This was a devastating loss to Sitting Bull and the rest of the family.[179]

During the summer of 1870, the Hunkpapas were camping with bands of the Oglalas, Miniconjous, and Sans Arcs along the Yellowstone River, below the mouth of the Rosebud River. One day, Sitting Bull left a large gathering saying he believed a vision was coming to him. He sang as he walked out of camp. When he came back, he said he had seen a spark of fire come at him but it had vanished before it reached him. He performed the pipe ceremony and saw a vision in the smoke. In two days, they would battle enemy Indians and kill many of them, but some Lakotas would die, too.[180]

Scouts rode out and found a Flathead camp along the Musselshell River. The Flatheads usually lived on the other side of the mountains to the northwest but would venture onto the plains to hunt buffalo. The Lakotas didn't want them hunting in their territory and considered them trespassers.[181]

Sitting Bull organized a 400-member war party and rode to the Flathead camp. They sent decoys to lure the Flathead warriors away from the village after which the main body of Lakotas would ambush them. The decoys worked. The Flathead warriors chased them out to where the Lakotas were waiting and a major battle unfolded.[182]

The fighting seesawed back and forth with casualties on both sides. A Miniconjou chief, Flying-By, called for the Lakotas to end the attack. Many followed him off the field, but Sitting Bull and a few others continued fighting.[183]

A Flathead warrior had dismounted, and Sitting Bull charged him. He wanted to capture his horse. The Flathead aimed his rifle and fired, the bullet hitting Sitting Bull's left forearm. He was assisted back to camp where his wound soon healed. His vision of the enemy camp and battle came true, and the vision of the fiery spark coming at him must have represented the bullet that wounded him.[184]

In August 1870, James Kimball, the post surgeon at Fort Buford, bought a series of drawings from a Yanktonai who claimed Sitting Bull had made them. The drawings show Sitting Bull counting coup, being wounded, killing enemies, and stealing horses. Years later, in December 1881, Sitting Bull would verify they were copies of his drawings made by his uncle, Four Horns. Forty-one of the fifty-five drawings in the packet were of Sitting Bull; the others were of his adopted brother, Jumping Bull. Twelve of the drawings show Sitting Bull counting coup on white men; four show him killing white men; and at least seven show him stealing horses from white men.[185]

On September 25, 1870, Sitting Bull led 200 Hunkpapa, Miniconjou, and Cheyenne warriors on an attack of a party of civilian woodcutters from Fort Buford. They were felling trees two miles upriver from old Fort Union, which had been abandoned in 1867. Charles Teck was driving eight oxen when warriors cut him off from the rest of the party. He went down fighting, shooting five warriors before he was killed and scalped. The Lakotas butchered the oxen and then rode off.[186]

Tragedy struck in 1871 when Sitting Bull's wife Red Woman died of sickness. He now had his two daughters with Snow-on-Her and his infant son with Red Woman to care for. His sister Good Feather—whose son, One Bull, Sitting Bull had adopted—and Sitting Bull's mother, Her-Holy-Door, helped care for the children.[187]

In the autumn of 1871, the Lakotas spotted surveyors guarded by soldiers along the Yellowstone River in the heart of their prime hunting ground. The Hunkpapas sent people to the new government agencies at the mouths of the Grand River and Cheyenne River on the Missouri River to find out from friends what the surveyors were doing. They were told the white men were surveying for a railroad.[188]

Unknown to the Lakotas, Northern Pacific Railroad investors and financial tycoon Jay Cook, nicknamed the "Financier of the Civil War," had signed a contract on January 1, 1870, for the financing and construction of a second transcontinental railroad from Duluth, Minnesota, to Tacoma, Washington Territory, that would follow the Yellowstone River through Lakota lands.[189]

Army escorts protected eastern and western survey teams exploring the Yellowstone River looking for potential routes as part of their surveys. The newspapers and journalists believed Sitting Bull and his followers would contest the surveys along the Yellowstone. The July 8, 1871, edition of the *Army Navy Journal* stated, "The present chief, Sitting Bull, who has for his chief soldier a Sandwich Islander [Frank Grouard], declares he will never make peace with the whites."[190]

Neither survey encountered Indians, leading to the belief future surveys would have no problems with them. They also found a route for the railroad through the Little Missouri River badlands they believed would work. The next, more-detailed phase of surveying the route would begin in 1872. Meanwhile, tracks were being laid westward in Minnesota and would be close to reaching Moorhead by December 31, 1871.[191]

On September 8, 1871, just after nightfall, Sitting Bull arrived outside the walls of Fort Peck and told the head trader that his people wanted to trade. They established a truce, and trade went well between the Lakotas and the fort. On October 12, Sitting Bull returned to Fort Peck and said he was willing to meet with a government agent and make peace. He said he would prevent any warriors from attacking other tribes or whites. He kept his word. At one point, a war party was forming to attack whites and other Lakota enemies. Sitting Bull and his warriors had to resort to violence to stop it. Eight warriors and twenty horses were killed in the incident and the lodges of the rebellious warriors were cut to pieces.[192]

President Ulysses Grant had appointed A. J. Simmons as Special Indian Agent to obtain rights-of-way for the Northern Pacific Railroad through Indian lands. He arrived at Fort Peck on November 4 and for three weeks met fifteen times with the chief Black Moon and other Sitting Bull representatives at Fort Peck. Simmons never rode out to Sitting Bull's village and Sitting Bull himself never came to the fort. Black Moon told Simmons that Sitting Bull was interested in peace, but on these conditions: There could be no railroad along the Yellowstone River because it would destroy the game; Fort Buford needed to be abandoned; the new trading post at the mouth of the Musselshell River in Montana must be abandoned; and all soldiers and other whites had to leave Lakota territory. Simmons told Black Moon those things would not happen. He told him the Lakotas must do what the "Great Father" wanted them to do and cease their hostility, or "[h]e could exterminate the Tetons if he so desired." For some reason Simmons and government leaders had false hopes from these inconclusive negotiations that Sitting Bull would be willing to sign a peace treaty. The truth was the exact opposite—Sitting Bull was ready to fight to protect Lakota lands and the Lakota way of life.[193]

1868 Fort Laramie Treaty

Since June 1866, the Oglala leader Red Cloud and other Lakota, Cheyenne, and Arapaho leaders and their warriors had been waging warfare in Wyoming's Powder River country against travelers and forts along the Bozeman Trail to the Montana goldfields.

In 1867, the US government decided to seek peace with the warring tribes. As a negotiating point, it was willing to abandon the Bozeman Trail and its forts as Montana travelers were now using an alternate, faster route riding the rails to Salt Lake City and then heading north from there. The government also wanted to restrict the warring tribes to reservations and was willing to provide annuities as an incentive. A peace commission made up of Commissioner of Indian Affairs Nathaniel G. Taylor, generals William Tecumseh Sherman, Alfred H. Terry, William H. Harney, and others met with some Brulé and Oglala leaders in April and May of 1868. The Brulé leader Spotted Tail signed the treaty, and after the army abandoned the forts on the Bozeman Trail, Red Cloud also signed the treaty. Commissioners traveled to various locations throughout the summer of 1868 getting signatures of other tribal leaders.[194]

One of the major provisions of the treaty was the establishment of the Great Sioux Reservation. The area encompassed what is now western South Dakota and included the Black Hills. The eastern border was the Missouri River and the southern border was the Nebraska northern state line. The northern and western boundaries were undefined and called "unceded Indian territory," which stretched to the summits of the Big Horn Mountains.[195]

The treaty included annuities for the tribes and established agencies for administration. One clause stated, "They [the Indians] will not in the future object to the construction of railroads, wagon roads, mail stations, or other works of utility or necessity, which may be ordered or permitted by the laws of the United States."[196]

The Indians could hunt buffalo in the unceded territory "so long as the buffalo may range thereon in such numbers as to justify the chase." They also had the right to hunt buffalo north of the North Platte River and on the Republican Fork of the Smoky Hill River. General Sherman did not want this provision but was overruled by the other commissioners. Sherman wrote in a letter to General Phil Sheridan, "I think it would be wise to invite all the sportsmen of England & America there this fall for a Grand Buffalo hunt, and make one grand sweep of them all. Until the Buffaloes & Indians are out from between the [rail] Roads we will have collisions & trouble."[197]

Article XII of the treaty stated any sale of reservation lands had to be approved by three-fourths of the adult male population of the reservation.[198] This would become an important point for the Lakotas when in later years the federal government pressured them to diminish the reservation. Sitting Bull, Crazy Horse, and other Lakota leaders refused to sign the treaty, and possibly up to a third of the Lakota population rejected it.[199]

CHAPTER 5

Struggles to Continue Their Way of Life, 1871–1876

GERONIMO WAS UNKNOWN TO THE WHITE EYES UNTIL THE 1870S. He and his band of Bedonkohes remained independent, at times associating with Juh and his Nednhis in Mexico as well as with Cochise and his Chokonens in Arizona.[1] From the winter of 1870–1871 until the spring of 1872, they recovered from the US Army attack, staying with Victorio and his Chihennes at Ojo Caliente in New Mexico.[2]

Government officials had earlier led Cochise and his Chokonens to believe they could settle at Ojo Caliente. However, the Indian agent, Orlando Piper, and the new military commander for the Department of New Mexico, Colonel Gordon Granger, told Cochise, Victorio, and other leaders that the Chiricahuas must move seventy miles to the northwest to the cold, desolate Tularosa Valley. This infuriated all the Chiricahuas. They believed Tularosa was haunted with evil spirits. At the end of March 1872, Cochise and his Chokonens began their return to Arizona.[3]

Geronimo and his Bedonkohes most likely left at the same time with the Chokonens. Victorio held a four-day feast and dance for the departing Bedonkohes. Geronimo later said, "No one ever treated our tribe more kindly than Victoria [*sic*] and his band. We are still proud to say he and his people were our friends."[4]

By mid-May, the Chokonens and Bedonkohes had left Arizona for Mexico, joining Juh and his Nednhis outside Janos, where they attempted to negotiate a peace treaty and receive rations from the

Chihuahua government. However, Sonoran troops crossed the state line in early July, attacking and destroying Juh's rancheria.[5] This convinced Cochise and most of the Chiricahuas to return to Arizona, where Cochise established his rancheria in the Dragoon Mountains, and from which his warriors resumed their raiding and killing.[6] Geronimo and his Bedonkohes must have joined them at some point that summer.

Many in Arizona, including Crook, doubted Cochise was sincere about desiring peace. Crook had wanted to hunt down all Apaches not on reservations and had sent out notices saying that any Apaches not on their reservations by the middle of February 1872 would be considered hostile, and attacked. However, President Grant took matters out of Crook's hands and ordered him to suspend his attacks. Grant had appointed a commissioner, Brigadier General Oliver Otis Howard, to negotiate peace with the Apaches.[7]

Howard had seen lots of action during the Civil War, losing his right arm in battle. After the war, President Andrew Johnson had appointed him head of the Freedmen's Bureau, tasked with protecting the rights of freed slaves in the South. Howard, a devout Christian, was nicknamed "Christian General."[8]

Howard outranked all other officers in Arizona and New Mexico and was given full power to do whatever was necessary to preserve peace between the government and the tribes and to convince them to go to permanent reservations. Howard believed his main objective needed to be "to make peace with the warlike Chiricahuas under Cochise."[9]

After spending the summer trying to locate Cochise, Howard met with Tom Jeffords at Fort Tularosa, New Mexico, on September 7, 1872. Jeffords, who was Cochise's friend, agreed to take Howard to Cochise, but he told Howard he could not take along an escort of soldiers if he ever wanted to see Cochise.[10]

While Howard was at Fort Tularosa, he met with the Chihenne leaders, Victorio and Loco, who complained about conditions at Tularosa. They wanted their reservation relocated to Cañada Alamosa. Howard agreed to let them return, thinking it would be easier to convince Cochise to go there for his reservation.[11]

It took several days for Jeffords and Howard to select the men to accompany them. By September 19, the party consisted of Jeffords and Howard; Chie and Ponce, both relatives of Cochise; Zebina Streeter, who was closely associated with the Chihennes; Howard's assistant, Lieutenant Joseph Sladen; Jake May, a Spanish interpreter; and J. H. Stone, a cook.[12]

The party met with a Chokonen leader named Nazee, who told them Cochise was in the Dragoon Mountains, and if they wanted to have a chance to meet with him, they needed to reduce their party. So Howard sent Streeter, May, and Stone to Fort Bowie with a note to the commander stating not to send any patrols in the direction of the Dragoon Mountains.[13]

Howard and his party reached Cochise's camp in the Dragoons on September 30. Cochise was not there; however, he did arrive the next day. Cochise was willing to talk, but first he wanted to call in all his leaders for the discussions, and he wanted Howard to go to Fort Bowie to make sure no soldiers would be attacking his men as they traveled to the conference site. Howard rode forty miles to the fort, issued those orders, and returned to Cochise's camp with his entire party and gifts for the Chiricahuas—2,000 pounds of corn, cloth, and sacks of coffee, sugar, and flour.[14]

After most of the leaders and warriors, about fifty, had arrived, the talks got under way. Geronimo acted as Cochise's interpreter, translating from Apache to Spanish.[15]

Howard said the Chiricahuas could have their reservation at Cañada Alamosa. Cochise dropped his bombshell: He wanted his reservation in the Chiricahua Mountains. The discussions went on for a long time; finally Howard gave in and said yes to the Chiricahua Mountains reservation.[16]

On October 11, Cochise insisted that Howard send for Captain Samuel Sumner, commander of Fort Bowie, and his officers so they could be present at the conference, which Howard did. As Sumner and his three officers rode out to the Dragoon Mountains the next day, Howard, Cochise, and his warriors prepared to ride out and meet them.[17]

Howard agreed to ride double with Geronimo. He later wrote, "[A]s I was willing, he [Geronimo] sprang up over my horse's tail and by a second spring came forward, threw his arms around me and so rode many miles on my horse. During that ride we became friends and I think Geronimo trusted me."[18]

After Howard and the Chiricahuas rendezvoused with Sumner and his men, they continued their negotiations at the Dragoon Springs Overland Mail station ruins, and came to an agreement. The reservation boundaries were immense, stretching from the western foothills of the Mule and Dragoon Mountains at the Mexican border north to Dragoon Springs, then northeast to Stein's Peak, then south along the New Mexico border to the Mexican border. Fort Bowie would remain within the reservation boundaries. Cochise also wanted Jeffords to be his agent and Howard agreed, although Jeffords was not too keen on the idea. Cochise made peace with the Americans. He would stay on the reservation and protect the Tucson Road; in return the Americans would give him food and supplies.[19]

Howard told Cochise his people needed to stop raiding into Mexico. In Cochise's mind, he did not make peace with the Mexicans, and since the southern border of his reservation was the Mexican border, the Chiricahuas would continue to raid into Mexico, and Mexicans would continue to chase them into the United States.[20]

Geronimo later said, "He [Howard] always kept his word with us and treated us as brothers." He went on to say, "We could have lived forever at peace with him."[21]

Lieutenant Joseph Sladen had noticed Geronimo was wearing a high-quality shirt, one that would not have been found in a trader's store. He got close enough to Geronimo to see that there was an embroidered name at the bottom of the shirt—"Cushing." Could it be Geronimo was Lieutenant Howard Cushing's killer?[22]

President Grant would issue an executive order on December 14, 1872, officially establishing the Chiricahua Reservation and setting its boundaries. Jeffords went to work immediately establishing the agency in a small building rented from Nick Rogers at his Sulphur Springs Ranch, ten miles east of the Dragoon Mountains. From there, he distributed rations to the Chiricahuas. The agency would remain at Sulphur Springs until August 1873, when it was moved to San Simon, then moved again to Pinery Canyon that November, and finally, on May 14, 1875, to Apache Pass near Fort Bowie.[23]

Jeffords's management style was easygoing compared to other Indian agents at other reservations. Although they were restricted to the reservation, the Apaches could go wherever they wanted within its boundaries, whereas at other reservations, Indians were required to live close to the agency building so the agent could count them daily. Jeffords did not force them to wear identity tags or require that they appear in person to receive their rations. He did make frequent trips to their rancherias to count the members.[24]

Crook agreed with the citizens of Arizona—Cochise's Chiricahuas could not be trusted. They were sure Cochise would soon break the peace. However, he and his warriors did keep the peace—in the United States.[25]

On November 15, 1872, Crook, who would become a brigadier general in 1873, began his offensive against western Arizona Apaches, attacking their rancherias to force them to their reservations. They learned that even though he was relentless in warfare, he was true to his word, and began calling him Nantan Lupan—Chief Gray Wolf.[26]

After Cochise and Howard's peace council, Geronimo returned to Mexico, arriving at his rancheria outside Janos, where Juh's rancheria was also located. Late in November, Geronimo and his Bedonkohes and Juh and his Nednhis, totaling roughly three hundred people, traveled to the Chiricahua Reservation. After meeting with Cochise and Jeffords, they settled there. In late December 1872, there were 1,244 Chiricahuas living in the area—700 at Cochise's reservation, and 544 at Tularosa, New Mexico.[27]

In the spring of 1873, the Chihenne leader Nana, who was married to Geronimo's sister Nah-dos-te, and other Chihenne and Bedonkohe leaders left the Tularosa Reservation with 150 people to visit their relatives and friends on the Chiricahua Reservation. Most set up their rancherias near Geronimo and Juh's in the Chiricahua Mountains. Things were quiet until mid-June 1873, when a combined force of Chiricahuas, including Geronimo and Juh, left on a monthlong raid through Chihuahua and Sonora, Mexico.[28]

Geronimo returned to the Chiricahua Reservation with a captive Mexican boy, Panteleon Rocha. Jeffords learned about the boy and rode to Geronimo's rancheria where he negotiated with Geronimo for Panteleon's release, eventually reuniting him with his parents.[29]

Nana and his people returned to Tularosa at the end of July 1873. Sometime during that period, Mexican troops crossed the border and attacked Geronimo's rancheria, but he and his warriors repelled them.[30]

The Mexican government was pressuring the United States to stop Apache raiding into Mexico. The US government in turn demanded Jeffords put an end to it. He convinced Cochise that if the raids did not stop, the government would remove him as their agent and disband the reservation. In early November 1873, Cochise held a council with all the Chiricahua leaders. He told them he was in charge of the Chiricahua Reservation and that all raids into Mexico must stop. If any of them did not like that, they would have to leave the reservation. Geronimo and Juh would not give up raiding. They led their people off the reservation and into Mexico.[31]

Traveling south along the Sierra Madre Mountains, Geronimo's Bedonkohes would either kill or take prisoner anyone they came upon so no one could tell the Mexican troops their whereabouts. They set up their rancheria in the Sierra Madre Mountains near Nacori in Sonora and from there they began their raids on villages, never having any major encounters with the army. They would remain south of the border for a year.[32]

Meanwhile, back in Arizona, Cochise, who was now about seventy years old, had been sick with stomach ailments. His family believed a Chihenne witch had cursed and poisoned him. He had two sons, Taza and Naiche. Knowing he was going to die, Cochise told the tribal leaders he had selected his older son Taza to take his place. He made Taza and Naiche agree to keep the peace with the White Eyes. On June 8, 1874, Cochise died in the East Stronghold of the Dragoon Mountains.[33]

The prospects for the continuation of the Chiricahua Reservation were dismal. Only about half the Chiricahuas on the reservation accepted Taza as their leader. The Mexican government continued to complain to the US government about Apache raids from the reservation. The US government wanted to consolidate Apaches on fewer reservations. It wanted the Chiricahua Reservation eliminated to open it up for settlement. The government was just waiting for the right excuse.[34]

In September 1874, the government abandoned the Tularosa agency and allowed Victorio and the Chihennes to return to Ojo Caliente and Cañada Alamosa for their reservation. Government administrators believed this would be a good place to consolidate all the Chiricahuas. Jeffords said if the government tried to force his Apaches to move, they would fight.[35]

The government was also interested in moving the Chiricahuas to the northwest, to another Apache reservation: the White Mountain Reservation, with an agency at San Carlos and Fort Apache to the northeast of the agency. On August 8, 1874, twenty-two-year-old John Clum became the agent at San Carlos. Clum began feuding with the army and trained his own Apache police force so he would not have to rely on soldiers. He believed there was only one right way to do things and that was his way. Clum believed the Chiricahuas needed to be moved to San Carlos where he could manage them better than Jeffords did.[36]

Geronimo and his band returned to the Chiricahua Reservation a year after he had left for Mexico, sometime in the fall of 1874. He claimed that he remained in Arizona for about a year.[37]

During 1875, the Indian Office began consolidating reservations in Arizona and New Mexico for administrative efficiency. General Crook was against consolidation, but it did not matter. In March 1875, the army transferred Crook to the northern plains, where he would take command of the Department of the Platte that July. On March 22, 1875, Colonel August Kautz took command of the Department of Arizona.[38]

Then on April 16, 1875, a special commissioner from Washington proposed to move the Chiricahuas from their reservation to the Ojo Caliente Reservation, but the Chiricahua leaders said no. In November 1875, a federal Indian inspector, Edward Kemble, toured the reservations and also recommended the Chiricahua removal to the Ojo Caliente Reservation.[39]

Apache raids in Mexico would continue into the spring of 1876.[40] Geronimo said that after a year in Arizona, he returned to Mexico for a year. However, it would have been less than that, as he was known to be back on the Chiricahua Reservation the first part of June 1876. Juh had returned to the reservation in early April, so this is probably when Geronimo returned, too.[41]

While in Mexico, Geronimo and Juh's people joined together, establishing their rancherias in the Sierra Madre Mountains near Nacori, as before. They were organizing their first raids when their scouts discovered two companies of Mexican cavalry approaching their camps.[42]

Taking sixty warriors, Geronimo and Juh left their rancherias and attacked the troops five miles away. The troops retreated to a hilltop where they dismounted and took up positions, firing on the Chiricahuas. The fighting lasted for hours. No warriors had been hit, but the Mexicans had lost a few men. Geronimo led his men in a charge up the hill, overwhelming the Mexicans and killing them all. That night, Geronimo and Juh moved their rancherias eastward, crossing from Sonora into Chihuahua. The rest of their time in Mexico, they were not attacked by troops.[43] Geronimo most likely returned to the Chiricahua Reservation in early April 1876.

On April 6, Pionsenay, a Chokonen whose half-brother Skinya was an opposition leader to Taza, and a companion rode to Nick Rogers's ranch at Sulphur Springs. They had learned Rogers had a barrel of whiskey and he was selling the liquor. They had been raiding in Mexico and bought several bottles of whiskey for ten dollars' worth of stolen gold dust.[44]

Pionsenay and a nephew returned the next day for more whiskey, which Rogers sold to him. After consuming a large amount of the liquor, Pionsenay picked a fight with Skinya. When two of their sisters tried to stop the fight, Pionsenay shot and killed both of them. He and his nephew returned to Rogers's ranch for more whiskey.

Fred Hughes, one of Tom Jeffords's assistants, later claimed Geronimo was with them. Rogers refused to sell him more. Pionsenay and his nephew shot and killed Rogers and his partner Orisoba Spence on the spot, then ransacked the building, taking all the whiskey, food, and ammunition. They next killed Gideon Lewis and raided along the San Pedro River.[45]

Arizonans were outraged. Tucson newspapers called for slaughtering the Chiricahuas. On May 1, 1876, Congress passed legislation mandating the removal of the Chiricahuas from their reservation to San Carlos at the White Mountain Reservation, and later that year, on October 30, the Chiricahua Reservation would be dissolved by executive order.[46]

On May 3, 1876, John Quincy Smith, commissioner of Indian Affairs, sent a telegram to John Clum telling him to take charge of the Chiricahua Reservation, and, "if practicable," take the Chiricahuas to San Carlos. On June 5, Clum arrived at the Apache Pass Agency near Fort Bowie with fifty-six Apache police and five companies of the Sixth Cavalry to escort the Chiricahuas to San Carlos.[47]

The first thing Clum did was relieve Jeffords of his duties. Clum next met with Taza, telling him the Chiricahuas had to leave. Taza was reluctant and said many of the people would not want to go, but Clum convinced him it was for the best.[48]

When Geronimo and Juh heard that Taza had agreed to the removal to San Carlos, they said Taza, a Chokonen leader, could not speak for them. They said they needed to meet directly with Clum himself. On June 7, Geronimo, Juh, and another Nednhi leader, Nolgee, rode into the Apache Pass Agency. They met with Clum, who insisted they must go with him to San Carlos. Geronimo spoke for the three of them, saying they needed twenty days to gather their people, who were away from the rancherias. Clum was suspicious and gave them only four days; they agreed, and rode away.[49]

The next day, Clum's Apache police paid a visit to Geronimo, Juh, and Nolgee's rancherias. They were deserted. The Bedonkohes and Nednhis were gone, taking only what they could carry. They had killed the dogs so their barking would not give them away, and they had killed any horses left behind so they would not whinny to the departing horses. The Bedonkohe and Nednhi trail led south to Sonora.[50]

On the northern plains, farmers had been rapidly settling southeastern Dakota Territory since 1872. Residents considered Sioux Falls, Dakota Territory, safe from Indian attacks, and stagecoaches were making regular runs to Fort Randall and the new Fort Sully, twenty-three miles upriver from the original Fort Sully. General Phil Sheridan, commander of the Military Division of the Missouri, wrote in his 1872 annual report that he was surprised at the rapid settlement of Dakota Territory, which "only a year or two since was in the possession of the Indians."[51]

The Northern Pacific Railroad planned two more detailed surveys for its proposed route through western Dakota Territory and Montana, as the railroad construction advanced westward by fits and starts toward its proposed Missouri River crossing. The army would again protect the railroad survey teams. One team would leave from Fort Ellis near Bozeman, Montana, and the other team would leave from Fort Rice. The plan was for both to follow the Yellowstone River from opposite directions and meet at the mouth of the Powder River. Neither the railroad nor the army believed Indians would be much of a problem, even as the Indians made threats.[52]

In late March 1872, Sitting Bull sent Spotted Eagle, a Sans Arc chief, to talk with Colonel David Stanley at Fort Sully. Sitting Bull wanted confirmation of rumors the surveyors and the army would be returning to the Yellowstone. When Stanley told him yes, Spotted Eagle calmly replied that he and Sitting Bull had never consented to the building of a railroad, which would drive off the buffalo and be the death of them. Stanley reported that Spotted Eagle said "[h]e would fight railroad people as long as he lived, and would tear up the tracks and kill its builders."[53]

Sitting Bull's personal life was improving. He had married a widow named Seen-by-her-Nation who had a deaf-mute son later called John Sitting Bull. Shortly after this marriage, Sitting Bull married again, this time to his new wife's sister, Four Robes, also widowed, who had a son named Little Soldier. His two sister-wives cared for his children, and Sitting Bull finally achieved harmony and stability in his family.[54]

That June, a new town called Edwinton was being laid out at the future Missouri River railroad crossing. A year later, promotors would rename it Bismarck in honor of German chancellor Otto von Bismarck, in hopes of attracting German investment in the railway and to entice German farmers to settle along the Northern Pacific tracks.[55]

At the same time the promoters were surveying and selling Edwinton lots, the army was demonstrating its commitment to protecting the future railroad by constructing Fort McKeen several miles downriver on the west bank of the Missouri. That November, the army would rename it Fort Abraham Lincoln.[56]

The federal government had been encouraged by the discussions between Special Indian Agent A. J. Simmons and Chief Black Moon back in November of 1871. Congress authorized $500,000 in food and clothing for the Lakotas at Fort Peck. Benjamin Cowen, assistant Secretary of the Interior, arrived at Fort Peck with the provisions, and during August 1872, wanted to meet with Sitting Bull and other Hunkpapa leaders to convince them to go with him to Washington, DC, to meet with the president and settle their differences. Sitting Bull did not go to meet Cowen, but sent his brother-in-law, His-Horse-Looking, who told Cowen that Sitting Bull had told him, "Whenever he found a white man who would tell the truth, to return, and he would go to see him." Apparently, His-Horse-Looking did not find one, and Sitting Bull stayed away.[57]

On July 26, 1872, the eastern railroad survey left Fort Rice for the Yellowstone River. Colonel David Stanley, commanding 586 infantry troops, artillery, and Indian scouts, escorted the survey. Stanley's officers included Lieutenant Lewis Dent Adair, first cousin to Julia Dent Grant, the president's wife.[58]

The western railroad survey left Fort Ellis on July 27, 1872, escorted by Major Eugene Baker's troops. The party of surveyors, cavalry, infantry, and scouts, totaling almost 500 men, included a party of 20 prospectors hoping to find gold deposits.[59]

At midsummer, Sitting Bull's Hunkpapas and other Lakota tribes held a Sun Dance on the Powder River about 125 miles upriver of its mouth on the Yellowstone. They put together a 1,000-man war party to attack the Crows in the Yellowstone valley above the Big Horn River. As they entered Crow territory, Lakota scouts reported there were soldiers on the north bank of the Yellowstone River across from Arrow Creek (also known as Pryor's Creek). It was the western survey party.[60]

On August 12, 1872, the war party approached from the south and established camp for the night. As Sitting Bull, Crazy Horse, and the other leaders sat in council to discuss whether to continue their raid against the Crows or to fight the soldiers, some of the young men sneaked off on their own, swam their horses across the Yellowstone River, and attacked the camp. By their actions, they had made the decision instead of the council.[61]

The fight continued through the night. The Lakotas captured some livestock and ransacked several civilian tents. The warriors took up positions on the bluffs overlooking the survey party's camp. The Hunkpapa warrior Plenty Lice was shot and killed. His body was behind the soldiers' lines, and the warriors could not retrieve it.[62]

The next morning, Sitting Bull and Crazy Horse were directing the attack from the high bluffs. Many of the young warriors were attempting deeds of bravery, including racing their horses in large circles along the daring line. Crazy Horse joined them. A medicine man named Long Holy had convinced some of the young men that he had had a vision they were bulletproof, so they rode again and again along the solders' position. Some were wounded but none were killed. Sitting Bull believed too many were being hurt. They had already proven themselves and did not need to perform any more acts of bravery. He called to end the attack. Long Holy and many warriors protested, contesting his authority.[63]

And then, Sitting Bull did an extraordinary thing. He dismounted from his horse and laid his bow, quiver of arrows, and gun on the ground. He slowly limped away from the Lakota lines toward the soldiers, and when he was midway and in clear view of the soldiers, he sat on the ground facing them. He removed his sacred pipe

Sitting Bull confronts the US Army.

from its pouch, filled the bowl with tobacco, lit it with his flint and steel, and began to smoke. All the while, bullets zipped by and kicked up dust around him.[64]

He called over his shoulder to the Lakota warriors, "Any Indians who want to smoke with me, come on!"[65]

His nephew White Bull, another Lakota named Gets-the-Best-of-Them, and two Cheyenne warriors walked out and sat down in a row with him, facing the troops. Sitting Bull passed the pipe to them and they smoked it until it was done. All the while, bullets continued to whiz around them. Sitting Bull cleaned the bowl with a small sharp stick, buried the ashes, and then returned the pipe to its pouch. He and the others stood and returned to the Lakota lines. Sitting Bull slowly limped while the others raced back.[66]

Sitting Bull picked up his weapons, mounted his horse, and shouted, "That's enough! We must stop! That's enough!"[67]

They all listened to him except Crazy Horse, who said to White Bull, "Let's make one more circle toward the soldier line." So the two raced their horses, circling close to the soldiers, who all fired at them. As they galloped back toward the Lakota lines, Crazy Horse's mount was shot out from under him, but he was able to run out of range of the soldiers' rifles.[68]

That was the end of the attack. A civilian and one soldier were killed and two wounded. The Lakotas captured sixteen head of beef cattle and eight mules and horses. Several warriors were injured and two killed, one of whom was Plenty Lice. The warriors were angered when they saw four soldiers throw his body onto a fire.[69]

The officers and head civilian surveyors were rattled. They made a halfhearted attempt to continue the survey farther down the Yellowstone River, but constantly seeing Indians on the opposite riverbank unnerved them, and the western railroad survey party returned to Fort Ellis, its survey incomplete. Sitting Bull had stopped the western railroad survey in its tracks.[70]

As the war party was disbanding and most of the men returning to their homes, a messenger from Gall arrived in Sitting Bull's camp. Gall was 160 miles downriver with a small war party. On August 16, they had encountered Colonel Stanley's eastern railroad survey on O'Fallon Creek near the Yellowstone River. Gall wanted Sitting Bull to bring a war party to help attack. Sitting Bull gathered all the warriors he could find and rode downriver.[71]

Gall had conducted a dawn raid on the survey camp, but this did not stop Stanley, who continued to proceed to the Yellowstone and then upriver until he had reached the mouth of the Powder River, where he was to meet Baker's western survey party. They erected a rock mound as a marker and fired their 12-pound Napoleon cannon as a message to Baker, but there was no response. Gall's Hunkpapas were on the west bank of the Powder River and Stanley's troops were on the east side. Gall laid down his weapons and walked to the edge of the west bank and had a shouted exchange with Stanley, who had laid down his pistol and walked to the opposite east edge of the river. Gall asked Stanley why they were there. When Stanley told him, Gall replied that if they were going to build a railroad, they had to pay. He then shouted he was bringing more warriors for a big fight. When Stanley turned away, the warriors started shooting again, some of them aiming at but missing the colonel.[72]

Constantly being harassed by Gall's warriors, the eastern railroad survey began its return to Fort Rice, leaving the Yellowstone River and camping again at O'Fallon Creek on the evening of August 21. By this time, Sitting Bull and his warriors had joined Gall. Some of the warriors tried to cut off an Arikara scout. The rest of the scouts gave chase but could not catch the warriors.[73]

The next day, Sitting Bull and his warriors had taken a position on a high, rugged bluff and opened fire on an escort for the engineers who were surveying. Two companies and part of a third company of infantry assaulted the bluff. Sitting Bull stood behind a large rock formation and shouted that he was Sitting Bull, and all the tribes would come together to exterminate the soldiers.[74]

While the troops were occupied attacking Sitting Bull's warriors on the bluff, one hundred mounted warriors charged to within one hundred yards of the circled wagons but were repelled by the Gatling guns and infantry muskets. None of the warriors were hit, and with that, the attack ended for the day.[75]

Sitting Bull, Gall, and the Lakota warriors harassed the eastern railroad survey all the way back to Fort Rice. Stanley had ordered that no one leave the protection of the camp alone. Stephen Harris, Colonel Stanley's black servant, and two officers were killed, one of whom was Lieutenant Lewis Adair, first cousin to the president's wife. Each had disobeyed orders and had been on his own, away from the column, when killed.[76]

The government had been pressuring American traders not to supply firearms and ammunition to non-treaty Indians. Sitting Bull also preferred not to trade with Americans unless he absolutely had to. During the fall of 1872, he traveled to a Métis camp north of the Missouri River in Montana and made an agreement with them whereby they would visit his camp that winter to trade firearms and ammunition for buffalo robes and furs.[77]

In December 1872, the Interior Department established an agency for the Lakotas and Dakotas at Fort Peck. Eight hundred

Lakota tepees, many of them Hunkpapa, were pitched around the fort. Most of the Lakotas reasoned they would take government rations but would still contest the railroad entering their country. The Indian agents believed if the Indians took the government rations, they were agreeing to allow the railroad access. Sitting Bull was not one of those. He continued to refuse government rations and camped at the Big Dry.[78]

During the winter of 1873, the Métis, who Sitting Bull had invited to his camp on the Big Dry, arrived with sleighs loaded with trade goods. Five of those sleighs carried whiskey, and soon the camp was on a drunken spree that lasted a week. There may have been as many as five thousand people in the camp. As whiskey was consumed, arguments erupted; some people were seriously hurt, others killed. There was a faction who wanted to kill Sitting Bull, but his supporters protected him. The Métis traded away all the firearms and ammunition and then left in the middle of the night with what whiskey was left.[79]

That April, Sitting Bull's village was camped on the Rosebud River. A scouting party came upon a Métis rider. Shots were fired and one of the Hunkpapas was killed. Sitting Bull organized a 100-man war party that discovered a camp of 400 Métis at the mouth of the Rosebud, on the Yellowstone River. The Hunkpapas considered the Métis trespassers since they were well within the Hunkpapa hunting grounds. The Métis were ready for an attack. They had circled their wagons and dug an earthen berm around the camp. They were well-armed and even had a cannon.[80]

The Hunkpapas charged the fortification but had to turn away as the Métis firepower was too intense. They then dismounted and shot most of the Métis horses. The Métis sent out a horse as bait and Hunkpapa warrior Cloud Man took it. He raced out on his horse to capture the Métis horse. The Métis shot his horse and then shot and killed him. Sitting Bull raced his horse out to Cloud Man's body and brought it back. The Métis charged and drove off the Hunkpapas' horses. Many brave deeds were done that day. After eight Hunkpapas had been killed, Sitting Bull told his warriors, "We have fought enough; let us go home."[81]

That spring, Sitting Bull had a falling-out with Frank Grouard.[82] The trader at Fort Peck wanted Sitting Bull's business, but Sitting Bull still wanted to deal with the Métis, who had brought the weapons, ammunition, and whiskey to his camp the past winter. Grouard made a deal with the trader and also the Indian agent at Fort Peck to identify the Métis who had sold illegal whiskey to the Hunkpapas. Grouard told Sitting Bull he was going on a horse-stealing raid, and, being trustful of his adopted brother, Sitting Bull gave Grouard his permission. Instead of going on a raid, Grouard went to Fort Peck where he met troops and rode with them to the Métis camp, where he identified one hundred traders who had been to the Hunkpapa camp. The troops confiscated any whiskey they could find along with Métis horses. As the troops arrested the Métis, a group of Santees in camp recognized Grouard.[83]

The commander gave Grouard permission to take three Métis horses. When he returned to Sitting Bull's camp, he told Sitting Bull he had captured them in a raid. Grouard told Sitting Bull to select one of the three horses for his own. Grouard then gave one to Sitting Bull's sister and the other to Sitting Bull's mother. Sitting Bull was pleased with what Grouard had told him he had done and bragged to everyone about his adopted brother's accomplishments.[84]

Ten days later, the Santees who had been in the Métis camp rode into Sitting Bull's camp and told him what Grouard had done. Sitting Bull was furious. Grouard hid in Sitting Bull's sister's tepee where she and Sitting Bull's mother protected Grouard. Otherwise, Grouard later said, Sitting Bull had "told me that he should kill me." After that, Grouard made sure he stayed out of Sitting Bull's way until later that year when he left to live with the Oglalas.[85]

Sitting Bull and the Lakotas had won their fight with the army and railroad during the 1872 season, preventing the surveying of 150 miles of the railroad route, but the Northern Pacific Railroad and federal government were relentless; they wanted it completed in 1873.[86]

The Northern Pacific continued to lay tracks across Dakota Territory. Correspondent for the *St. Paul Daily Pioneer* Mark Kellogg wrote from Bismarck, on May 31, 1873, "The 'end of the track' was twelve miles east of Bismarck, Friday night. It will reach here next Thursday, if the weather permits. The arrival of the track is impatiently waited for by those settled here."[87]

In March 1873, Commanding General of the Army William Tecumseh Sherman had told Congress, "This railroad [the Northern Pacific] is a national enterprise, and we are forced to protect the men during its survey and construction, through, probably, the most warlike nation of Indians on this continent, who will fight for every foot of the line."[88]

Sherman augmented Colonel Stanley's troops by sending to Fort Rice 450 cavalry troopers, 10 companies of the Seventh Cavalry, led by Lieutenant Colonel George Armstrong Custer. Also going along was a member of General Sheridan's staff, Lieutenant Colonel Frederick Dent Grant, the president's son. Fred claimed he planned to avenge the death of his cousin, Louis Adair. Instead of two expeditions, there was one led by Stanley. It had two components; one began surveying westward from Fort Abraham Lincoln on June 17, and the other left Fort Rice on June 20. Both would soon join together. The expedition comprised 1,575 officers and men, 350 civilians, a large number of Indian scouts, two 3-inch Rodman rifled artillery pieces, 300 wagons, 2,300 horses and mules, and a herd of 700 beef cattle. The Lakotas knew of the expedition's movements from the start. In fact, there was an attack almost right away west of Fort Abraham Lincoln, leaving four Lakotas dead.[89]

On August 3, about four hundred lodges of Sitting Bull's Hunkpapas, as well as Miniconjous, Cheyennes, and others, were camped on the north bank of the Yellowstone near the Tongue River when they learned the expedition was approaching from downriver. Sitting Bull ordered the camp to be struck and moved upriver to a river crossing away from the advancing troops.[90]

On August 4, the warriors set a trap to ambush two cavalry companies ten miles in advance of Stanley's expedition. These ninety-one officers and men led by Lieutenant Colonel George Custer were resting their horses in a cottonwood grove. Six Lakota and Cheyenne decoys galloped toward them. Custer ordered the men to mount up while he and his orderly, Private John Tuttle, chased after the decoys until he saw 250 mounted warriors emerge from a large stand of cottonwoods. When they saw he would not advance any further, they charged. Custer and Tuttle raced back toward the troops. His brother, Lieutenant Tom Custer, dismounted twelve men, forming a skirmish line that held off the warriors as Custer galloped back and organized the rest of the men in a defensive position behind a dry streambank in the cottonwood trees along the Yellowstone. They covered Tom and his men as they fell back to the defensive position. For three hours they held off the warriors and then chased them away with a charge while waiting for Stanley's expedition.[91]

At the same time this fight was taking place, the Seventh Cavalry's veterinary surgeon and its sutler left Stanley's column to water their horses at the river. Indians fired upon and killed them. Disobeying orders, two soldiers had left the column to hunt and Indians killed one of them. Custer lost no one in his fight, and it was unknown how many, if any, Indians had been killed or wounded.[92]

As the expedition continued to advance upriver, they came upon the sites of two abandoned Indian camps. Stanley sent Custer forward to locate and attack the Lakotas if possible. He advanced with eight companies of cavalry and all the Indian scouts, approximately 460 men.[93]

Custer reached the north side of the ford that Sitting Bull's people had used to cross the Yellowstone. His men foundered trying to determine how best to cross. In the meantime, Sitting Bull had gathered more warriors from neighboring bands and led a war party to attack Custer's camp at the ford.[94]

On the morning of August 11, 1873, Sitting Bull was on the river bluffs as his warriors opened the attack, firing on the camp from timber on the south bank of the Yellowstone. The troops returned fire and the fight lasted most of the day. Warriors swam their horses across the Yellowstone and attacked. Mounted cavalry counterattacked as the band played Custer's favorite battle tune, the Irish quickstep "Garryowen."[95]

Custer's orderly, Private John Tuttle, was an excellent marksman and had just hit three Indians on the far side of the river when the warriors brought up their best marksman, who shot Tuttle through the forehead.[96]

Stanley arrived and had the artillery trained on the warriors shooting from the south bank. After firing three exploding shells into their positions, the battle was over. Two soldiers had been killed and two wounded. Frank Grouard, who was with the Hunkpapas but did not participate in the fight, said one Indian was killed.[97]

Sitting Bull moved his village south, up the Big Horn River, and that ended his contact with the expedition. The last confrontation was on August 16, when six warriors took potshots at some naked soldiers cooling off in the Yellowstone.[98]

Sitting Bull's defense of the Hunkpapa Yellowstone River hunting grounds and Custer's official report on the fighting frightened Northern Pacific investors. The biggest investor, Jay Cooke's firm, had borrowed large sums of money in support of the railroad. Believing they were going bankrupt, his partners closed the doors to his business on September 18, triggering the Panic of 1873, the second worst depression in American history.[99]

For the next few years there would be no government or business interest in the Hunkpapa hunting grounds in the Yellowstone River valley. The Panic of 1873 put a halt to the Northern Pacific's railroad construction until 1878, and its transcontinental line would not be completed until September 1883.[100] But there were still those who wanted access to the buffalo and other game in the Hunkpapa hunting grounds.

The Crows, who also hunted the Yellowstone River valley, claimed it for their own, so there were constant fights and raids between them and the Lakotas. Whites also wanted access to the abundant herds of buffalo and other game.[101]

In late February of 1874, a 150-member party out of Bozeman, Montana, calling itself the Yellowstone Wagon Road and Prospecting Expedition, headed down the Yellowstone River. One of their objectives was to locate gold deposits. They were heavily armed with repeating rifles and two cannons. Montana Territory governor Benjamin Potts provided them ammunition from the territorial armory. As they made their way downriver past the mouth of the Big Horn

River, Sitting Bull's Hunkpapas, Crazy Horse's Oglalas, and the Miniconjous of Hump, Fly By, and Makes Room learned of their presence.[102]

In April, Sitting Bull had led several hundred warriors in three separate attacks. Each time, "the Boys," as the whites called themselves, had put up a good defense and counterattacked. Sitting Bull's warriors had managed to kill one white and run off some livestock. The Boys were out to kill the Lakotas any way they could. When they abandoned one camp, they left behind food laced with strychnine, but the Lakotas were wary and did not touch it. At another abandoned campsite, the Boys left a false grave booby-trapped with explosives. When the Lakotas investigated, it blew up but did not kill anyone. The constant attacks and bad weather convinced the Boys to return to Bozeman.[103]

In the summer of 1874, Sitting Bull's Lakotas were busy raiding settlements and farms in Montana's Gallatin Valley and attacking anyone encroaching on their hunting grounds.[104] Unknown to Sitting Bull and the Hunkpapas, another military expedition, this time led by Lieutenant Colonel George Custer, was planning to head from Fort Abraham Lincoln to the sacred Black Hills.

According to the 1868 Fort Laramie Treaty, the Black Hills were part of the Great Sioux Reservation and off limits to whites. There had always been rumors of paying quantities of gold in the Black Hills, and early expeditions around them had found a few traces. Prospectors and speculators wanted the Black Hills opened to search for the yellow metal, but the Lakotas opposed any entry.[105]

In the spring of 1874, General Phil Sheridan had directed Custer to explore the Black Hills and determine a site for a future military post as well as survey and map the area, and to record the topography and geology.[106]

Custer based his expedition out of Fort Abraham Lincoln, taking ten companies of the Seventh Cavalry and two infantry units. There were over 1,300 horses and mules, 110 wagons and civilian teamsters, and a herd of 300 beef cattle. A 16-piece mounted military band was part of the expedition. Seventy Indian scouts, including his favorite Arikara scout, Bloody Knife, and white civilian scouts, including Lonesome Charlie Reynolds, were to guide the troops. Lieutenant Colonel Fred Grant, son of President Grant, went along, as well as two of Custer's brothers, Captain Tom Custer and Boston Custer, as civilian forage master. The army assigned Captain William Ludlow with the Corps of Engineers and six enlisted men to survey the topography and create maps of the Black Hills. There were geologists and botanists, a photographer, newspaper reporters, and two experienced miners.[107]

As the band played "The Girl I Left Behind Me," Custer and his troops set out in a southwesterly direction from Fort Abraham Lincoln on July 2, 1874. He had a thousand men consisting of cavalry and infantry, three Gatling guns, and a rifled cannon. The expedition crossed the treeless prairie, arriving at the northern Black Hills and entering them on July 24. They slowly journeyed on a southerly route, finding flower-filled valleys, swift-flowing creeks, and large stands of pines.[108]

On August 2, miners Horatio Ross and William McKay created excitement when they announced that they had panned profitable amounts of gold from French Creek. The next day, Custer sent Lonesome Charlie Reynolds south to Fort Laramie, Wyoming, with his report mentioning they had found gold. The reporters gave Reynolds their dispatches sensationalizing the discovery of gold. Soon newspapers across the country were proclaiming the new find. One of the first announcements was in the August 12, 1874, edition of the *Bismarck Tribune*. Headlined "GOLD!," the article predicted that the Black Hills would "become the El Dorado of America."[109]

The Custer expedition turned north and left the Black Hills on August 15, reaching Fort Abraham Lincoln on August 30. That entire time, they had only one encounter with Lakotas, and that was with a small band in the Black Hills. The encounter was peaceful due to Custer's intervention.[110]

The damage was done. Gold seekers illegally rushed to the Black Hills. The army tried to stop them but could not keep them all out. Sitting Bull and the other non-treaty Lakotas would soon learn of Custer's expedition and the stampede of prospectors to the Black Hills.[111]

In August 1874, Governor Potts had had enough of the Lakota raids on Montana's citizens and wanted the army to go on the offensive against them. He wrote to the superintendent of Indian Affairs: "The lives and property of our people [are] at the mercy of 'Sitting Bull' and his band of murdering robbers." The governor wanted the army to attack Sitting Bull's village and severely punish his people.[112]

For more than a year, Sitting Bull's warriors had regularly raided the Crow Agency on the Yellowstone River. The government agent at Crow Agency was having problems with traders selling illegal whiskey to the Crows. In June 1875, he was in the process of having the agency moved fifteen miles south, away from the river and farther from the protection of Fort Ellis, now ninety miles away. The Lakotas attacked the white construction crew and wagons hauling supplies to the agency. Men were wounded and some lost their lives.[113]

At that year's Sun Dance, the Hunkpapas and the Northern Cheyennes cemented their alliance. As warriors from other Lakota bands watched, Sitting Bull performed a special dance at the Sun Dance lodge to represent their intertribal unity and success in war. Taking a pipe from the Cheyennes and a pipe from the Hunkpapas, he danced with both toward the Sun Dance pole while leading his war horse. After he did this four times, he said, "The Great Spirit has given our enemies to us. We are to destroy them. We do not know who they are. They may be soldiers."[114]

That July, the Lakotas battled a combined force of Crows and Nez Perces along the Yellowstone below the mouth of the Big Horn River. After two days of fighting, the Crows and Nez Perces rode north. The Lakotas pursued and fought them again, killing Long Horse, a major Crow chief.[115]

At the same time the Lakotas were battling the Crows and Nez Perces, Fellows Pease led forty-five white men from Bozeman into the Yellowstone hunting grounds, intending to stay. Pease was a trader and had been an agent for the Crows. He built a trading post on the north bank of the Yellowstone River near the mouth of the Big Horn River. Pease's objective was to provide neutral ground between the Lakotas and Crows where they could trade with him in peace.

That was not going to happen. The Lakotas wanted the trading post gone and attacked. The post would remain under siege into the spring of 1876, during which time six men were killed and eight wounded.[116]

In July 1875, Brigadier General George Crook took over command of the Department of the Platte, which included the Black Hills. Touring the Black Hills, Crook found 1,200 prospectors and ordered them to leave. It's not known how many listened to him.[117]

In August 1875, Young Man Afraid of His Horses, leading a 100-man delegation of Brulés and Oglalas from the Red Cloud Agency in Nebraska, arrived at Sitting Bull's camp on the Tongue River, near the Big Horn Mountains. They came to invite the non-treaty tribes to meet with government commissioners, who wanted them to agree to sell the Black Hills. Along with the delegation were two men of mixed race, Louis Richard and Frank Grouard. Grouard first sought out his friend Crazy Horse, who told Grouard he would not go to meet with the commissioners. When Sitting Bull summoned Grouard to his tepee, Grouard asked Crazy Horse to go with him. Sitting Bull wanted to know why he was in the village. Grouard told him about the commission and that the government wanted to buy the Black Hills. He asked Sitting Bull if he would go to the Red Cloud Agency. Sitting Bull replied that Grouard would hear his response at the next tribal council.[118]

The next day, the council was held in the middle of the village with approximately a thousand warriors in attendance. The delegation told them the federal government wanted to buy the Black Hills. The government commissioners wanted them to come to the Red Cloud Agency to listen to their offer, discuss it, and come to an agreement. About one hundred non-treaty Indians spoke, saying they would not sell the Black Hills. Sitting Bull declared he would not sell his land, he had never been to an agency, and he was no agency Indian. Grouard later said, "[Sitting Bull] told me to go out and tell the white men at Red Cloud that he declared open war, and would fight them wherever he met them from that time on."[119]

There were many in camp who wanted to kill the agency Indians that night, but Crazy Horse shamed them and put an end to it. When Grouard and the agency Indians left to return to the Red Cloud Agency, a large group of non-treaty Indians went with them.[120]

The federal government commission was led by President Grant's good friend, a US senator from Iowa, William Allison. Two additional important members were Brigadier General Alfred Terry, commander of the Department of Dakota, and Reverend S. D. Hinman. Squabbles erupted between the two principal Lakota leaders, Spotted Tail of the Brulés and Red Cloud of the Oglalas, as to who would be in charge of negotiations for all the Lakotas. They even disagreed as to the location of the meeting, finally settling on a site eight miles east of the Red Cloud Agency.[121]

Washington's instructions to the commission were to acquire the entire Black Hills, get the tribes to cede the Big Horn Mountains, and have them grant the government rights-of-way through the unceded territory east of the Big Horns. The commission was not told what amount the government was willing to pay—only that the tribes could be assured they would receive a "fair equivalent." Finally, the tribes needed to understand that anything they agreed to would have to be approved by Congress before it could go into effect.[122]

The commission arrived at the agency on September 4, but the first meeting with the tribes did not start until September 20. It took time for the Lakota representatives to show up, and when they did, many of them were fighting angry. Some staged mock charges on the white men and their cavalry escort. Allison estimated almost five thousand people attended. The wrangling back and forth took days. The tribes could not agree among themselves, and they did not agree to what the commission proposed.[123]

The final commission proposal was that the federal government would lease the Black Hills for $400,000 per year, but if the Indians were willing to sell, the government would pay them $6 million in fifteen annual payments. Congress would have to approve either way, and three-fourths of the adult males in each tribe would have to sign the agreement in accordance with the provisions of the Fort Laramie Treaty.[124]

The tribes' counteroffer was that they would exchange the Black Hills for the government taking care of all tribal members' needs, including the best food, mules and cattle, and wagons, now and for the next seven generations. The commissioners thought the tribal position extravagant and unrealistic.[125]

In the end, nothing came of the meetings. The angry, frustrated commission returned to Washington, DC, and reported to Congress that the government should offer a "fair equivalent" for the Black Hills and tell the Lakotas they must take it.[126]

By the fall of 1875, estimates suggested fifteen thousand whites had entered the Black Hills searching for gold and establishing mining camps.[127]

On November 3, President Grant met secretly with trusted advisors in the White House. Present were General Phil Sheridan, Brigadier General George Crook, Secretary of the Interior Zachariah Chandler, and Commissioner of Indian Affairs Edward Smith. They agreed the government would continue to declare it illegal for whites to enter the Black Hills, but the army would stop evicting trespassers. The non-agency tribes along the Big Horn Mountains and the Yellowstone River must report to and remain at the agencies; if they did not, Sheridan would begin a winter campaign against them.[128]

Six days after the meeting, Indian Bureau inspector Erwin C. Watkins, who had toured the Lakota agencies, filed a report on "Sitting Bull's band and other bands of the Sioux Nation, under-chiefs or 'head-men' of less note, but no less untamable and hostile." He said they had "the best hunting-ground in the United States"; therefore, they did not need government aid. He said they raided white settlements and friendly bands, and their actions drew young warriors to them. He went on to say that all peaceful attempts to reason with these "wild and untamable" Indians had failed, and recommended the government "send troops against them in winter—the sooner the better—and whip them into subjection." Secretary of the Interior Chandler sent the report on to Sheridan. Chandler then instructed his Indian agents "to notify Sitting Bull's band, and other wild and lawless bands of Sioux Indians residing without the bounds of their reservation," to report to the agencies by January 31, 1876, or be forced there by the army.[129]

Sheridan began to prepare for a winter campaign against the Lakotas and Cheyennes. Scouts learned that Sitting Bull's village was on the Little Missouri River, and Sheridan planned to have Custer's Seventh Cavalry march west from Fort Abraham Lincoln to attack them. Colonel John Gibbon's column would march east along the Yellowstone River from Forts Ellis and Shaw. Both columns were in the Department of Dakota, which included Dakota and Montana Territories, and were under the command of Brigadier General Alfred Terry. General Crook, commander of the Department of the Platte, which included Wyoming Territory, would lead a column north from Fort Fetterman to the Powder River. Sheridan did not instruct that the columns had to work together. His main concern was that the troops would not be able to get moving to attack before spring weather, when the bands would scatter and be more difficult to find.[130]

Meanwhile, life continued unchanged for Sitting Bull and his Hunkpapas, raiding, hunting, and living their lives in their traditional way. In 1875 or early 1876, Sitting Bull founded and was the leader of the White Horse Riders warrior society. These warriors acted as police and staged festive parades for the entertainment of the Hunkpapas.[131]

Sitting Bull's band moved westward from the Little Missouri to the mouth of the Powder River, where they encamped for the winter. The agency for the Hunkpapas was at Standing Rock on the Missouri River, halfway between the Cannonball and Grand Rivers.[132]

On December 22, 1875, a directive to Standing Rock's agent arrived, stating that the tribes needed to report to the agency by January 31, 1876, or be considered hostile. Messengers were sent out, but the winter was harsh and Sitting Bull's band was 240 miles away. There is no record of whether a messenger ever reached Sitting Bull's camp or not. Even if a messenger had, Sitting Bull most likely would have ignored it. What's certain is that Sitting Bull did not arrive at the Standing Rock Agency by January 31, in the dead of winter, and was now considered a fair target for the army.[133]

Sitting Bull's warriors continued to surround and harass Fort Pease throughout the winter. The traders gave up and sent a message to Fort Ellis requesting rescue. On March 4, a column of cavalry arrived at Fort Pease and escorted the remaining nineteen men back to Fort Ellis.[134]

Things rarely go according to plan, and that was certainly the case for General Sheridan. On February 7, 1876, Secretary of the Interior Chandler authorized Sheridan to proceed against the tribes that had not reported to the agencies. When Sheridan notified Terry to move against Sitting Bull's people, Terry informed Sheridan the Seventh Cavalry would not be able to head out until spring, severe weather and deep snow making travel impossible for the cavalry. Informants had also alerted Terry that Sitting Bull's band had left the Little Missouri River and traveled west two hundred miles.[135] It is ludicrous to think the federal government would demand Indian families journey through these harsh winter conditions to reach an agency when at the same time the Seventh Cavalry could not leave Fort Abraham Lincoln due to these same conditions.

On March 17, Gibbon's Montana Column began its slog through deep snow downriver along the Yellowstone, establishing its base camp at the mouth of the Big Horn River, near abandoned Fort Pease. From there, Gibbon sent out patrols but found no Indians.[136]

General Crook's column left Fort Fetterman, Wyoming, on March 1. The 900-man column consisted of 10 cavalry companies, 2 infantry companies, and a number of scouts. They marched northward through snowstorms and subzero temperatures to reach the Powder River across the border in Montana on March 16.[137]

One of the scouts ranging far ahead of the column returned, reporting to Crook that he and other scouts had spotted two Indian hunters and believed they were returning to a village.[138]

Crook established camp and sent Colonel Joseph Reynolds with 300 men to find and attack the village. That night, the scout who had spotted the hunters led Reynolds's troops, following the hunters' trail, to a village of about 100 lodges with possibly 700 to 1,000 people. The village was situated in timber beneath the rocky bluffs along a dry riverbed.[139]

On the morning of March 17, the troops attacked the village, surprising the people, most of whom were still in their lodges. The warriors grabbed their weapons and hurried the women and children to the rocky bluffs or to protective cover along the river. From those positions they started firing on the soldiers. The scout who had found the camp believed it was Crazy Horse's village, but it was not. It was a Cheyenne camp with a few Oglala lodges.[140]

The troops captured the village's herd of over 700 horses. They set fire to all the lodges, sparing one that housed a woman who had been shot in the thigh. Some lodges contained kegs of powder that exploded when the flames reached them, hurling tepee poles and their contents in every direction. The troops burned tepee furnishings, supplies, furs, beautifully decorated hides, and all the food—everything.[141]

When the warriors counterattacked, Reynolds panicked and quickly left the village, failing to take with him the bodies of four dead soldiers.[142] In all the shots fired, one warrior had been killed.[143]

That night, Cheyenne and Oglala warriors recovered most of the horses from Reynolds, who had failed to place guards over the herd. When they reached Crook's column and Crook learned what had happened, he was furious. The column returned to Fort Fetterman where Crook filed court-martial charges against Reynolds. Crook would need to regroup and resupply before taking to the field again.[144]

The Cheyennes and Oglalas journeyed four days north down the Powder River until they reached Crazy Horse's village. They did not have enough food for themselves and the refugees from the destroyed camp, so together they traveled north and east for two days to Sitting Bull's camp. Sitting Bull's people took in the refugees, giving them shelter, clothing, and food. The Cheyenne warrior Wooden Leg later said, "I can never forget the generosity of Sitting Bull's Hunkpapa Sioux."[145]

The warriors from the destroyed village told Sitting Bull about the attack. When they mentioned who the scout was who had led the soldiers to their village, Sitting Bull became angry and said, "One time that man should have been killed and I kept him, and now he has joined the soldiers. He is no good and should be killed."

"That man" was Sitting Bull's adopted brother, Standing Bear, nicknamed Grabber—Frank Grouard.[146]

Lakota Sun Dance

The Sun Dance was the Lakotas' most important public religious ceremony. The Lakotas held the *Wiwang Wacipi*, Gazing at the Sun as You Dance, to ensure their prosperity and increase and that of the buffalo as well. Each summer, usually in June, the bands would join to hold the Sun Dance. Lasting twelve days, it was a time of visiting and renewing friendships. The first four days were for socializing, holding a variety of religious ceremonies and meetings of men's societies. The second four days were spent instructing and preparing those who had pledged to participate in the Sun Dance. The last four days were the actual dance itself.[147]

A circle sixty feet in diameter was prepared on level ground for the dance area. A hole was dug in the center of the circle and sharp gravel was scattered within the circle. A *Wichasha Wakan* (holy man) selected and marked a cottonwood tree with a fork in the trunk near the top; this would become the *Wiwang Wacipi* pole to be placed in the middle of the dance area. Warriors went out to find the marked tree and then attacked it as an enemy, counting coup on it.

Next a young, pure woman representing White Buffalo Calf Woman made the first four cuts to the tree for each of the four directions. Those who would be performing the Sun Dance then cut down the tree, making sure it did not touch the ground. The branches were trimmed off except for the fork in the trunk and those at the very top; their leaves were to remain intact. A chokecherry bough was tied to the fork. Offerings and spiritual symbols were tied to the trunk, and at the top was tied an effigy of a man, an effigy of a buffalo, and a buffalo skull. Gifts of dried meat, tobacco, and chokecherry juice were placed in the hole at the center of the dance area and then the tree was placed in the hole and raised.[148]

Each dancer fasted, purified himself in the sweat lodge, and pledged to suffer for the people. Many participants had their chest or upper back pierced by sharpened bones or sticks; leather ropes were attached from these sticks to the *Wiwang Wacipi* pole, or to buffalo skulls. As drummers created a beat, the participants danced and blew on eagle-bone whistles while gazing at the sun and pulling against the pole or skulls, until, ripping their flesh, they broke free. Some could choose to dance and not be skewered; others danced with their arms cut with between ten and two hundred gashes. Some even chose to be skewered and suspended off the ground from the *Wiwang Wacipi* pole. For the participants, the dance lasted until they pulled free or passed out. Some would receive visions during or after their dance. Sitting Bull participated in many Sun Dances, and was pierced many times.[149]

CHAPTER 6

Little Big Horn, Summer 1876

THE NORTHERN PLAINS HUNTING BANDS LIVING IN THE UNCEDED lands believed life would continue as it always had. Sure, there were fights with whites when they entered Lakota and Cheyenne territory, but it was the same as if the Crows or Assiniboines had trespassed. Crook's March 17, 1876, attack on the Cheyenne camp brought them up against the hard reality that things had changed. Soldiers had attacked a camp in frigid conditions just to destroy it. The attack angered Lakotas and Cheyennes, including many who were living at the agencies. Chiefs who had been peaceful now advocated war, and young men bent on fighting left for the unceded territories.[1]

It was the end of March 1876. Sitting Bull's village was located at Chalk Butte on the divide between the Powder River and the Little Missouri River. On April 1, the refugees from the destroyed Cheyenne village and Crazy Horse's Oglala camp arrived at Sitting Bull's village and remained with the Hunkpapas.[2]

The Lakotas and Cheyennes held a council. They believed the soldiers would attack again. If the whites wanted war, so be it; they would give them war. They agreed the best defense for the hunting bands was to stay together. Sitting Bull was reconfirmed as leader of the Lakotas and Dakotas, and the Cheyennes were united under their war chief, Two Moons. They sent messengers to all the hunting bands suggesting they join Sitting Bull and Two Moons for mutual protection. The Lakotas, Dakotas, and Cheyennes all looked to Sitting Bull for leadership. The Cheyenne warrior Wooden Leg said,

"[Sitting Bull] had come now into admiration by all Indians as a man having a kind heart and good judgement as to the best course of conduct."[3]

Sitting Bull left the camp to pray for guidance in locating that spring's Sun Dance site. Crossing the Rosebud and riding northwest several miles, he found an appropriate high point to pray. He set up a buffalo skull as his altar and placed his sacred pipe on it. He brought offerings of tobacco and dried meat. He smoked, prayed, and sang. The evening of the second day, a whirlwind advanced from the north and a second whirlwind approached from the south. The two whirlwinds joined in front of him and in the whirlwinds, he saw a vision of a rock formation with a jagged blue streak through it that looked like a lightning bolt.[4]

The tribes followed the annual migration of the buffalo herds as they moved upriver on the Yellowstone. The village was increasing in size. By mid-April, it had grown to 360 lodges, and each day new families were arriving. The village was moving more often now since its increasing population rapidly exhausted resources at each new location.[5]

War parties went out on the prowl. On May 2, fifty Lakota warriors raided Colonel John Gibbon's camp on the Yellowstone, stealing all thirty-nine horses belonging to Gibbon's Crow scouts.[6]

It was mid-May, and as Brigadier General Alfred Terry was preparing to lead the Dakota Column westward to join with Gibbon on the Yellowstone, he was concerned. His scouts reported that Sitting Bull's camp had now increased to 1,500 lodges, and reports from Fort Laramie stated that 1,400 warriors had left the Red Cloud and Spotted Tail agencies for the Powder River.[7]

President Grant was displeased with Lieutenant Colonel George Custer, and Terry was now leading the Dakota Column—not Custer. Custer had provided information on corruption with sutlers or traders at military facilities to the *New York Herald*. The *Herald* had accused Secretary of War William Belknap of selling the positions of post sutlers and pocketing the money. The president's brother was accused of being part of the scheme.[8]

Custer was called to testify before two Democrat-controlled House committees on corruption in Republican President Grant's administration. Much of Custer's testimony was hearsay and exaggerated. Although he had no direct evidence concerning the president's brother, he still repeated rumors that he was involved in Belknap's scandal.[9]

The president ordered Custer relieved of command of the Dakota Column, and Sheridan replaced him with Terry. Humiliated, Custer wrote a letter to Grant asking to at least be allowed to lead the Seventh Cavalry into the field. Terry and Sheridan both supported Custer's petition, and on May 8, 1876, the president relented. Terry would continue to lead the column, but Custer would command the Seventh Cavalry under Terry.[10]

The Dakota Column totaled close to 1,000 men made up of 12 companies of the Seventh Cavalry, 3 companies of infantry, and 40 scouts—mostly Arikara—including Custer's favorite, Bloody Knife, who hated the Hunkpapas. Bloody Knife's father was Hunkpapa and his mother was Arikara. The Hunkpapas, especially Gall, had humiliated Bloody Knife as a boy, and in return, Bloody Knife had led soldiers to Gall's camp where Gall had been severely bayoneted but survived. One hundred and fifty wagons hauled the Dakota Column's supplies.[11]

As the column of infantry and cavalry marched out of Fort Abraham Lincoln on the morning of May 17, 1876, Custer's wife Libbie rode with him for the day. An early morning mist shrouded the Missouri River valley. Libbie later wrote, "As the sun broke through the mist a mirage appeared, which took up about half the line of cavalry, and thenceforth for a little distance it marched, equally plain to the sight on the earth and in the sky."[12]

From May 21 to 24, Sitting Bull's village camped on the Rosebud River about seven miles from the Yellowstone. Sitting Bull felt an urge to leave the camp and climbed a nearby butte to pray. Praying and meditating, he fell asleep. In a dream, he saw the wind blow a large dust storm rapidly approaching from the east. In the west he saw a white cloud resembling an Indian village with snowcapped mountains behind it. The dust storm rapidly advanced on the cloud village. Behind the dust, he could see a formation of cavalry troops with their weapons charging the village. The dust storm hit the cloud with the crack of thunder, flashes of lightning, and a downpour of rain. When the storm was over, the cloud village remained, and the dust storm was gone.[13]

Sitting Bull returned to the village and told the other leaders his vision. He believed the cloud village represented their village and the dust storm represented soldiers who were going to attack them but be defeated. The leaders sent out scouts to watch for soldiers coming from the east.[14]

On May 29, 1876, General Crook led his column north out of Fort Fetterman. Called the Big Horn and Yellowstone Expedition, it consisted of 15 companies of cavalry, 5 companies of infantry, and several scouts, including Frank Grouard. Later, 176 Crow and 86 Shoshone warriors would join it, swelling its numbers to more than 1,200 men. Over 100 wagons each pulled by 6 mules and hundreds of pack mules hauled the army's supplies.[15]

At the end of May, Sitting Bull's village moved farther up the Rosebud and camped near a cone butte. More and more family groups from the agencies were arriving, as well as single warriors.[16]

The first night in their new camp, Sitting Bull participated in a sweat lodge, and several Cheyenne elders were there as well. He related to them his quest to locate the Sun Dance and his vision of the two whirlwinds and the rock with the blue streak. The Cheyennes knew the place; it was on the Rosebud—Deer Medicine Rocks. They said it was a sacred place with many pictographs etched into its rock. This is where the Sun Dance would be held.[17]

The next morning, Sitting Bull invited his nephew, White Bull, his adopted brother, Jumping Bull, and a son of his cousin, Chief Black Moon, to sit with him while he prayed on top of the cone butte. They smoked the sacred pipe and then Sitting Bull prayed to Wakan Tanka for the people. He asked for enough game animals to last them through the winter, and for peace between all the tribes. At the end he prayed, "If you do this for me, I will sun dance two days and two nights and will give you a whole buffalo."[18]

When he finished his prayer, Sitting Bull wiped his face with sage, descended the hill, and went buffalo-hunting, taking with him White Bull. He shot three buffalo and, choosing the fattest cow, he left it on the prairie positioned on its belly with legs stretched out in four directions, as his offering to Wakan Tanka.[19]

On June 4, the village moved farther up the Rosebud valley, about forty-five miles south of the Yellowstone, and remained there until June 8. At Deer Medicine Rocks they held their Sun Dance. The rocks displayed a wide assortment of petroglyphs created by various tribes. Not only would Sitting Bull dance, but he would fulfill an additional vow to give his flesh in sacrifice. Black Moon was the intercessor conducting the Sun Dance, and Sitting Bull was chief of the dancers.[20]

Sitting Bull first fasted and purified himself in a sweat lodge. As he entered the dance circle wearing only a loincloth, people saw on his back the many scars from his past Sun Dances. He approached the dance pole and sat with his back to it. As Sitting Bull blew on his eagle-bone whistle and called out to Wakan Tanka, Jumping Bull used an awl and a knife to remove one hundred bits of flesh from both of Sitting Bull's arms. He never flinched. Sitting Bull rose, and untethered, began his dance. He danced and danced around the pole, blowing on his eagle-bone whistle, fasting, and gazing at the sun—all that day, through the night, and into the next day. About noon, he stopped and seemed to faint but remained standing as he gazed at the sun. Some of the people lowered him to the ground and doused him with cold water.[21]

Black Moon bent over him. Sitting Bull spoke to him in a quiet voice. His prayers had been heard. His offering had been accepted. He had seen a vision when he had stopped his dance. He told Black Moon the vision and Black Moon relayed it to the people.[22]

A voice had told Sitting Bull to look at an image below the sun. He saw soldiers and horses as numerous as grasshoppers racing toward their village. The soldiers and their horses were upside down—feet pointed to the sky and heads pointed to the earth, and their hats were falling down. The soldiers were falling right into their village. Below, there were some Indians upside down, too. The voice

Sitting Bull explains his vision at Deer Medicine Rocks.

told Sitting Bull, "These soldiers do not possess ears. They are to die, but you are not supposed to take their spoils." The people were joyful and took courage. They knew they would win against the white soldiers.[23]

In early June, a Cheyenne hunting party reported seeing soldiers far to the south. On June 9, the Cheyenne Little Hawk led around a dozen men in an attack on Crook's camp on the Tongue River. They shot into the camp and tried to stampede the soldiers' horses but were unsuccessful.[24]

Sitting Bull's village now knew soldiers were returning to attack the hunting bands. They remembered the attack on the Cheyenne village last March and they were angry. This time, they would be ready for the soldiers, and they were confident they would win. By mid-June, the village had grown to around 460 lodges with an estimated 3,000 people, of which possibly 800 were warriors. On June 15, they migrated out of the Rosebud watershed to Davis Creek in the Big Horn River watershed, in the Wolf Mountains.[25]

Crook asked Frank Grouard where he thought the Sioux camp was, and Grouard told him he believed the camp was on the Rosebud. Crook prepared to get his troops there as quickly as he could.[26]

Little Hawk and his men left Sitting Bull's camp again to spy on the soldiers. On June 16, they discovered the troops had left all of their wagons under a strong guard of soldiers and teamsters at their base camp on Goose Creek, and were rapidly advancing north toward the Rosebud. Little Hawk raced back to Sitting Bull's camp with the news.[27]

The chiefs held a council meeting, and all agreed to leave the soldiers alone unless they came to attack the village. However, many of the young men did not listen and slipped away during the night, maybe as many as five hundred. When they discovered warriors were leaving in droves, Sitting Bull and Crazy Horse determined to go too, and by the early morning light of June 17, they were leading a large group of warriors south to confront the troops. Sitting Bull was now forty-five years old, at which age a man was not expected to fight unless it was in defense of women and children, but still Sitting Bull went.[28]

About 8:00 a.m., after a two-hour march, Crook called a halt along the Rosebud to rest. Crow scouts had reported that they had seen some Sioux to the north and wanted to see what was going on, so Crook sent them back downstream. He ordered the horses unsaddled and picketed. Some men napped and others smoked pipes while Crook played whist with some of his officers as the Crow and Shoshone scouts rode ahead, farther down the valley.[29]

An overwhelming force of Cheyenne and Lakota warriors came upon the Crow and Shoshone scouts. Shouts and fired shots alerted the troops, who quickly prepared for battle as the scouts raced back, shouting "Heap Sioux! Heap Sioux!"[30]

White Bull rode with Sitting Bull along the east side of the attack. Even though Sitting Bull carried his rifle, his arms were swollen from his recent flesh sacrifice. They were useless in a fight, so he rode to the top of a close ridge where he could view the action and shout encouragement to the warriors: "Steady men! Remember how to hold a gun! Brace up, now! Brace up!"[31]

The Cheyennes and Lakotas were angry. These were the same soldiers who had attacked and destroyed the Cheyenne village during the winter.[32]

John Finerty of the *Chicago Times* later reported that "the enemy [were] swarming in crowds upon the higher range of the bluffs in every direction on a line of at least two miles. They were all mounted and fired with wonderful rapidity."[33]

The troops, split into three separate commands, were disciplined for the most part. The Cheyennes and Lakotas had no overall strategy. They surged around the troops, at times completely surrounding them. The troops slowly advanced against the warriors as the fighting became general later in the day, but the warriors were constantly on the offensive.[34]

While the fighting raged, Crook sent Captain Anson Mills with half the cavalry down the valley, thinking that Sitting Bull's village must be six to eight miles downriver. Crook hoped to capture and destroy it, forcing the Indians to surrender, but the village was actually twenty-five miles away. Mills and his men had entered the Rosebud canyon, which looked to them like an excellent place to be ambushed, when they received orders to climb out of the canyon and help Lieutenant Colonel William Royall's cavalry unit, which was being hard-pressed by a large war party. When they reached the top and were on level ground, they saw a mass of warriors attacking Royall's troops. Mills charged and chased them off.[35]

The Cheyennes and Lakotas fought against the Crows and Shoshones in traditional Indian warfare, counting coup on each other. The whites did not fight in that fashion. The warriors cut off some of the soldiers from their comrades, slaughtering them. By mid-afternoon, the fight had lasted six hours. Tired and hungry, the Cheyenne and Lakota warriors decided to end the attack and rode away. It was a good fight, with many coups and deeds of glory.[36]

Ten of Crook's men had been killed and more than 20 wounded, a few not expected to live. His troops had carried 100,000 rounds of ammunition, expending 25,000 rounds. They found 13 Indian bodies and 150 dead horses on the field. There was no telling how many dead and wounded had been carried off.[37]

The Cheyennes and Lakotas stopped Crook's column in its tracks. He ended his advance toward their village and claimed victory, since he had held the field at the end of the day. Returning to base camp, he sent messages stating he needed more men and ammunition. For six weeks, he did not advance but waited while he and his men went hunting and fishing. Crook himself shot plenty of game and one day caught seventy trout. The Crow and most of the Shoshone warriors became disgusted with the lack of action and left.[38]

There had been many acts of valor on both sides. The Cheyennes called the battle "Where the Girl Saved Her Brother." As the Cheyenne warrior Chief Comes in Sight was riding the daring line in front of the soldiers, his horse was shot from under him. His sister Buffalo Calf Road Woman raced her horse to her brother's side as soldiers' bullets whistled all around them. He jumped up behind her and they raced out of range of the guns to safety.[39]

The people of Sitting Bull's village wanted to hold a victory dance, but they could not do so at their current location, where there had been mourning for those killed in the fight. So, at break of day on June 18, they followed Reno Creek downstream and then to the river valley they called Greasy Grass, known to the whites as the Little Big Horn. At their new site, they celebrated their victory for four nights—singing, dancing, and feasting. Adding to the celebration, scouts reported the soldiers had returned to their base camp on the Tongue River. Sitting Bull realized that stopping those soldiers was a great victory, but he also knew it was not what his visions had foretold.[40]

Over the next six days, the size of Sitting Bull's camp more than doubled. The people who had wintered over at the agencies were returning—some to hunt, and others to fight if need be. An estimated 1,000 lodges housed possibly 7,000 people. Numbers of warriors ranged from 800 to 1,800. No one took a head count.[41]

Cheyenne scouts reported large antelope herds to the north and west. The leaders determined that everyone had obtained enough buffalo meat, so they would now hunt the antelope. On June 24, the entire village moved to the north downriver eight miles and established camp along the floodplain on the west bank of the Little Big Horn. Groves of cottonwood trees lined the river and on the east bank rose a series of bluffs intersected by ravines. The village was immense, stretching three miles along the river, with Sitting Bull's Hunkpapas at the upstream end and the Cheyennes at the downstream end, with the rest of the Lakota bands in middle positions.[42]

Sitting Bull's wives set up the family's tepee along the southern end of the Hunkpapa circle with its entrance facing east. Thirteen people were living in the tepee at the time, including his two wives, his children and adopted children, his mother, sister, and, temporarily, Gray Eagle, his wives' brother. His nephew One Bull's wife pitched their tepee next door.[43]

That evening, Sitting Bull asked One Bull to accompany him. They crossed the river and climbed to the top of a high ridge opposite the downriver Cheyenne circle. As the sun dipped behind the Big Horn Mountains, Sitting Bull presented offerings to Wakan Tanka—a buffalo robe, a ceremonial pipe, and tobacco wrapped in buckskin and tied to carved cherry sticks.[44]

He prayed:

Wakan Tanka, pity me. In the name of the tribe I offer you this peace-pipe. Wherever the sun, the moon, the earth, the four points of the wind, there you are always. Father, save the tribe, I beg you. Pity me. We want to live. Guard us against all misfortunes or calamities. Pity me.[45]

Sunday, June 25, 1876, began like any other day in the massive camp along the Little Big Horn River. By midday the temperature was getting hot as people went about their business. Boys were taking horses to the river to drink while others were playing and swimming. Some people had slept in late, as an all-night victory dance had taken place. Several women were starting to take down their lodges as the plans were to continue moving downriver in search of game. Women were outside the village digging wild turnips when a mounted warrior raced toward them, shouting that soldiers were coming. Looking to the east, they saw a cloud of dust raised by advancing soldiers. The women ran to camp, sounding the alarm, surprising the people. Just as the warnings were being given, mounted soldiers approached the eastern end of the Hunkpapa village.[46]

Men rushed to prepare for battle. Some needed to paint their protective symbols on themselves and their horses. Others ran to the herds to get their war horses, and still others gathered their weapons. While some women continued to tear down their lodges, other women along with children and the elderly were running or riding horses to reach the safety of the western bluffs. Older men escorted the women and children to provide protection. No one knew if other soldiers were poised nearby to attack the families. Volleys of bullets from soldiers' carbines were slamming into the village, shredding tepees and shattering poles.[47]

All was mass confusion. Accounts of what happened and time sequences vary from person to person. No one knew who these soldiers were. Were they the same soldiers they had fought just a few days before, or was this a whole new army to contend with? Unknown to the Indians, it was Custer and the Seventh Cavalry.

After the Dakota Column had left Fort Abraham Lincoln on May 17, it had marched west, reaching the mouth of the Powder

River on the Yellowstone on June 8, where the riverboat *Far West* was moored, having brought troops and supplies up the Yellowstone River. On June 9, the *Far West* conveyed Terry upriver to confer with Gibbon. Terry learned that on May 26, Lieutenant James Bradley had traveled eighteen miles up the Rosebud, where he had seen a large Indian camp off in the distance. Neither Terry nor Gibbon had any knowledge as to Crook's whereabouts.[48]

On June 10, Terry had sent Major Marcus Reno, with six companies of the Seventh Cavalry and a Gatling gun, on reconnaissance up the Powder River. His orders stated for Reno to go upriver as far as the Little Powder River, then head west to the Tongue River and descend north to the Yellowstone, where Terry would be waiting for him. Reno went beyond the bounds of his orders, riding farther west into the Rosebud watershed, where he found evidence of a large trail heading upriver and large campsites. Reno returned, and on June 20, he met with Terry and Custer aboard the *Far West*, reporting what he had found.[49]

On Thursday, June 22, Terry sent Custer, leading approximately 660 men of the Seventh Cavalry and scouts, including 6 additional Crow scouts, up the Rosebud to find the Indian village. Terry would lead the rest of the Dakota Column and Gibbon's troops up the Big Horn River and hopefully trap the Indians between Custer, Crook, and Terry's troops. On June 24, Custer followed a large Indian trail that turned toward the Little Big Horn watershed. On Sunday morning, June 25, his scouts reported a large Indian village was fifteen miles away on the Little Big Horn River. Although Custer originally planned to hit the village in a morning attack on June 26, he changed his plans when he received information that Indians had discovered their whereabouts and would most likely warn the village.[50]

To avoid this, he decided to attack that very day. Custer and his men crossed from the Rosebud watershed into the Little Big Horn watershed. They proceeded down what is today called Reno Creek. The pack mules were slowing the advance, so Custer left Company B and a few men from each of the other companies to guard the pack train while the rest of the troops moved out rapidly. Custer divided his men again, sending Captain Frederick Benteen with three companies to reconnoiter the Little Big Horn bluffs off to the left. Custer told Benteen that if he saw Indians, he was to attack; if he did not see anything, he was to rejoin Custer as quickly as possible. Custer assigned Reno three companies to form the left battalion and ride on the left bank of Reno Creek, and Custer commanded the right battalion, consisting of five companies that rode on the right bank of the creek.[51]

Reports came in from the scouts that some Indians were fleeing downstream. Custer ordered Reno to pursue them. Custer would support him, continuing down the right side of Reno Creek and up into the bluffs. Reno crossed the Little Big Horn River and followed the Indians toward the village. As the Indians approached the village, they stopped running and stood their ground. Reno ordered his men into line of battle, then shouted "Charge!," and the battalion advanced at a gallop.[52]

At the first warning shouts and shots, Sitting Bull limped as fast as he could back to his lodge to find and protect his family.[53] His adopted son One Bull and brother-in-law Gray Eagle, who both acted as Sitting Bull's bodyguards, had been watering Sitting Bull's horses at the river; they now brought the animals to his tepee. His wives must have already grabbed the children and were fleeing with the others to the western bluffs, but his mother and sister were still there. Placing them on horseback, he ensured that they were on their way to the bluffs.[54]

Entering his lodge, Sitting Bull grabbed his shield, bow, arrows, and war club. He gave One Bull his treasured war gear, saying, "You will take my place and go out and meet the soldiers that are attacking us. Parley with them, if you can. If they are willing, tell them I will talk peace with them." He sent Good Bear Boy and others with One Bull to attempt to parley with the soldiers. One Bull and the others mounted their horses and galloped toward the troops, where they quickly realized the soldiers were not about to parley.[55]

Sitting Bull did not take the time to paint himself or attach feathers. As he strapped on his cartridge belt, his adopted son Blue Mountain brought him his black stallion war horse.[56] Iron Elk, another bodyguard, handed him a Winchester carbine and revolver.

Bullets whistled through the camp as he mounted his black stallion and shouted encouragement to the warriors: "Brave up. Boys, it will be a hard time—brave up!"[57]

Sitting Bull with his nephew White Bull and other warriors rode to a shallow draw between the village and the troops, who were now dismounted and firing as a skirmish line. Two bullets hit Sitting Bull's horse. He lost all hope of parleying with the soldiers, saying, "Now my best horse is shot. It is like they have shot me. Attack them." He shouted further encouragement to the warriors as he exchanged fire with the soldiers.[58]

As some of the Arikara scouts edged close to the Hunkpapa camp, shooting and killing women and children, the number of mounted Lakota warriors was increasing, and a large number of them were beginning to outflank the soldiers' left. These were Major Marcus Reno's men, and he ordered them to fall back into the timber along the river.[59]

After first preparing for battle, Crazy Horse arrived with a large force of warriors, many mounted and others on foot. The mounted warriors surrounded the soldiers' position in the timber as the dismounted warriors attacked from the east and north.[60]

The soldiers were becoming concerned about their position. Some were running low on ammunition. Reno had no idea where Custer or Benteen were. He learned that Indians were shooting his troopers' horses. He believed he needed to get out of there and find a more-defensible position. He ordered the men to mount up, but not everyone heard the order. The Indians' gunfire increased. Chaos ensued among some of the troops. As a barrage of gunfire swept through the trees, one bullet slammed into the back of Bloody Knife's head, splattering blood and brains on Reno's face and front. Reno yelled, "Any of you men who wish to make your escape, draw your revolvers and follow me." He formed no rear guard and many men were still dismounted as Reno led the troops out of the timber and onto the valley's prairie.[61]

At first the warriors fell back from the troops, but when they realized the cavalry was leaving instead of attacking them, they began to attack the soldiers. Some warriors said it was like a buffalo hunt as they raced alongside the soldiers, killing them. Many of the deaths that occurred in Reno's battalion occurred during his retreat. The soldiers crossed the river and rode up into the bluffs where they took a position on high ground. About ten minutes after establishing their position on the bluff, they saw Benteen's column approaching from the south.[62]

Thirty-two of Reno's men had been killed and twenty were missing. The survivors on top of the ridge could see warriors ransacking and scalping the bodies.[63]

As Sitting Bull rode along the riverbank, he saw One Bull racing after four dismounted soldiers who had been left behind and were now making a mad dash across the river to join the rest of the troops. Sitting Bull called to One Bull, "Let them go! Let them live to tell the truth about this fight." One Bull relented and rode up to Sitting Bull. Sitting Bull saw that One Bull was covered in blood and was concerned he had been seriously wounded. One Bull laughed and said it was Good Bear Boy's blood, who had been wounded and he had helped back to the village.[64]

As Sitting Bull followed the trail of death and destruction made by the retreating soldiers and chasing warriors, he saw several warriors gathered around a black man sitting on the ground. The man had a serious chest wound and was asking the warriors in Lakota not to count coup on him since he was dying. The man was Isaiah Dorman, known to the Lakotas as Teat and married to a Hunkpapa woman. Custer had brought him along as a civilian interpreter. Eight years earlier Teat had been hospitable to Sitting Bull and seven of his warriors, giving them a meal of mush and syrup, a pot of coffee, and some tobacco. Sitting Bull told the warriors, "Don't kill that man. He is a friend of mine." Sitting Bull dismounted and gave Teat water. After he rode away, a woman whose ten-year-old brother had been killed shot Teat in the head, and other women following behind her proceeded to mutilate his body.[65]

Returning to the village, Sitting Bull rode into the Hunkpapa camp where he encouraged the warriors by saying, "A bird, when it is upon its nest, spreads its wings for defense, but it can cackle and try to drive away the enemy. We are here to protect our wives and children, and we must not let the soldiers get them. Make a brave fight!"[66]

Sitting Bull continued riding through the camp along the Little Big Horn until he was opposite Medicine Tail Coulee. There, warriors had stopped a second group of soldiers from crossing the river and advancing on the village. The soldiers fired two volleys and began to withdraw back up the coulee. Plenty of young men remained in the village who had not yet entered the fight, and Sitting Bull encouraged them to attack the soldiers. He crossed the river and rode partway up the coulee until he had reached the waiting warriors, encouraging them to pursue and fight the soldiers.[67]

Sitting Bull had no way of knowing if there was a third group of soldiers that would attack the hundreds of women and children gathered on the western bluffs. So, he rode there, joining the other older men in protecting the women and children. From that vantage point, he could see the fight at what would be called Last Stand Hill. At the time, he had no idea that it was Custer and members of the Seventh Cavalry who were dying there.[68]

Sitting Bull later returned to camp where he treated a wound to White Bull's ankle, and then treated others' wounds. That evening Sitting Bull and White Bull rode to the ridge northeast of the soldiers' position on Reno Hill. They joined in with the warriors who were shooting from that vantage point. Later that night, Sitting Bull returned to the village, where the council of leaders decided they would not break camp as had been planned, but instead remain where they were.[69]

The battle continued into the next day. Sitting Bull returned to the ridge about noon and ordered the warriors to end the siege. "Enough!" he shouted. "Those soldiers are trying to live, so let them live. Let them go. If we kill all of them, a bigger army will march against us." Terry's column was advancing up the Little Big Horn, and it was time to break camp and move the village.[70]

By evening, the people had packed their belongings and were on the move upriver. Two nights later, they established camp far from the battlefield but still in the Little Big Horn valley, where they held a victory dance. Custer and over 260 of his men had been killed.

There is no accurate count of how many Indians had been killed, but it would have been low compared to the number of soldiers killed.[71]

The victory over Custer fulfilled Sitting Bull's Sun Dance vision, but it did not make him happy. "I feel sorry that too many were killed on each side, but when Indians must fight, they must." His other concern was that people had failed to heed his warning not to take anything from the dead soldiers. They had stripped the bodies and mutilated them. "For failure on your part to obey," he told the people, "henceforth you shall always covet white people's belongings."[72]

CHAPTER 7

Geronimo Goes to San Carlos and Sitting Bull Goes to Canada, 1876–1878

JOHN CLUM, SAN CARLOS INDIAN AGENT, WITH FIFTY-SIX APACHE police and five companies of the Sixth Cavalry, arrived at the Apache Pass Agency on June 5, 1876. They were there to escort the Chiricahuas to the San Carlos Agency.[1]

Geronimo, Juh, and Nolgee had no intentions of going to San Carlos, so during the night of June 7, they slipped away, leading the Bedonkohes and Nednhis south toward Sonora. Geronimo's deception angered Clum; from this time on, he would attribute many of the Apache depredations to Geronimo.[2]

On June 12, Clum, his scouts, and the cavalry, with 322 Chiricahuas, many loaded into army wagons, left Apache Pass for San Carlos. Of this group, 42 were men, including Cochise's sons, the Chokonen leaders Taza and Naiche, and Chihuahua, who led a separate band of Chokonens.[3]

The Chiricahuas and their escort arrived at the Gila River on the White Mountain Reservation on June 18. Taza agreed to establish the Chokonen rancheria two miles downriver from the abandoned Fort Goodwin. There was no wood, no game, and the water was unfit to drink. Not only was their new home a hot and dry desert, but the river was a breeding ground for malaria-carrying mosquitoes. Nearby were the forested White Mountains, but they belonged to the White Mountain Apaches.[4]

Tucson's *Arizona Citizen* editorialized in its June 24, 1876, edition, "Henceforth Chiricahua [Reservation] drops out of sight as a nursery for bad Indians . . . the magnificent corner of the Territory known as Chiricahua will chiefly attract attention through the mineral discoveries and agricultural developments of white settlers."[5]

In the meantime, Geronimo, Juh, and Nolgee had crossed the border into Mexico and set up camp in the Sierra Madre Mountains. On July 21, Geronimo returned to the United States, leading forty people to the Ojo Caliente (Warm Springs) Reservation, where they visited family and friends. Some of the Chiricahuas who refused to go to San Carlos were living there as well. Geronimo liked Ojo Caliente, believing it was a good place where he could draw rations and continue to conduct raids. He returned to Mexico and told Juh his findings, but Juh said he would stay in Mexico.[6]

By November 1876, Geronimo and his Bedonkohes had joined a small band of Bedonkohes and Chihennes roaming the Florida and Animas Mountains of New Mexico, close to the Mexican border. From these locations Geronimo continued to raid.[7]

In early December, Bedonkohes, most likely led by Geronimo, ran off a herd of twenty-one horses from a ranch in the Sonoita Valley southeast of Tucson. For weeks, Lieutenant John Rucker, leading seventeen troopers of the Sixth Cavalry, a surgeon, and thirty-four San Carlos Apache scouts led by Chief of Scouts Jack Dunn, followed the raiders' trail. It led to a rancheria near the Animas Mountains.[8]

They attacked at dawn on January 9, 1877, and after a fierce fight where the Chiricahuas forced back the attackers twice, the scouts and troops captured the rancheria, killing ten Chiricahuas and capturing a five-and-a-half-year-old boy who turned out to be a nephew of Geronimo. They burned all the wickiups and captured forty-six horses and mules. It is possible this was Geronimo's rancheria.[9]

Soon after this attack, Geronimo was at Ojo Caliente where he was most likely the instigator in organizing another raid into the Sonoita Valley. Between forty to fifty Chiricahuas rode with him as they picked up more members from Mexico for their war party, including Juh, Pionsenay, and their followers. The raiders split into two parties, and from February 4 to February 8, 1877, they rode through Sonoita Valley, stealing around a hundred head of livestock and killing at least seven men—some reports indicate as many as fifteen—before crossing the border into Sonora.[10]

Blaming inaction on the part of Department of Arizona commander General August Kautz, Arizona governor Anson Safford was outraged over the murders and thefts. However, the only Apaches raiding in Arizona at the time were coming from outside Kautz's jurisdiction—Mexico and Ojo Caliente in New Mexico. Kautz sent Lieutenant Austin Henely to Ojo Caliente to track down the culprits. On March 16, 1877, after meeting with the Ojo Caliente acting agent Walter Whitney, Henely saw Geronimo, who was "indignant because he could not draw rations for the time he was out." Geronimo and others had returned to the agency with a hundred head of stolen horses. Henely believed Geronimo and about fifty Chiricahua warriors had taken part in the last raid through the Sonoita Valley.[11]

Henely reported his findings to Kautz, who informed Governor Safford. Safford in turn telegrammed Commissioner of Indian Affairs Edward Smith in Washington, DC, that the raiders had been found at Ojo Caliente. In addition to arresting the culprits, Safford wanted the reservation shut down or an agent appointed who could control the Apaches. On March 20, 1877, Smith telegrammed San Carlos agent John Clum authorizing him to take his Indian police and arrest the renegade Chiricahuas, return the stolen horses to their rightful owners, and take the perpetrators to San Carlos and hold them for murder and robbery. He was to call upon the army if he needed assistance.[12]

At the end of December 1876, Clum had returned from a disastrous trip. Wanting to travel east to marry his girlfriend, he had asked the Bureau of Indian Affairs to pay for his trip. The bureau said no. He then concocted a scheme to take a troupe of Apaches east for a "Wild Apache" show that would surely pay for his trip. He selected twenty-two Apaches to go with him, including Taza, Cochise's son and Chokonen leader. They left San Carlos on July 27, 1876. Not only was the show a flop, losing money, but while they were visiting Washington, DC, Taza developed pneumonia and died. Commissioner of Indian Affairs Smith agreed to pay for the party's trip home. Clum left the Apaches in the care of one of his white civilian assistants and traveled to Ohio, where he married his sweetheart.[13]

With one hundred Indian police, Clum left Arizona heading eastward after Geronimo. Reaching Fort Bayard, New Mexico, in mid-April 1877, he contacted Major James Wade, who would meet him with three companies of the black Ninth Cavalry at Ojo Caliente on April 21. One of Clum's scouts reported that on April 14, Geronimo and eighty to one hundred followers had received rations at Ojo Caliente.[14]

The next day, Clum telegrammed Commissioner of Indian Affairs Smith, recommending that all the Apaches at Ojo Caliente be removed to San Carlos. Two days later, Smith approved the removal with the caveat the military concur, but Clum never told the military about it.[15]

Clum with twenty-two mounted police arrived at the Ojo Caliente agency the afternoon of April 20. The rest of the police, who were on foot and commanded by Chief of Police Clay Beauford, arrived at 4:00 a.m. on April 21, hiding themselves in the commissary building next to the agency headquarters.[16]

Major Wade had sent a telegram to Clum telling him the cavalry's arrival would be delayed by a day. Clum decided to capture Geronimo and the other leaders before the cavalry arrived, believing their presence would scare away the Apaches.[17]

Clum sent a message to Geronimo's rancheria inviting him and other leaders to come to the agency for a talk. They were coming in anyway since it was ration day, and Geronimo was led to believe it would be a friendly meeting. Geronimo arrived later that morning with about fifty men, women, and children.[18]

Clum with his twenty-two police met Geronimo and his people in front of the agency headquarters. Clum gave a signal, raising his left hand and touching the brim of his hat. Beauford's police came out of the commissary building, surrounding Geronimo and his followers. The scouts disarmed the men as Clum told Geronimo he had broken his promise at Apache Pass last June. Because of that, he would be placed in irons. Calling Clum "the False White Eye" who had broken Cochise, Jeffords, and Howard's peace treaty, Geronimo

John Clum arrests Geronimo.

said he would not believe a word Clum said after sending a false messenger to him declaring peace. "Do not talk to me about breaking treaties," Geronimo said. "You and your sick brain!"[19]

Clum had the agency blacksmith rivet shackles to Geronimo's ankles as well as to the ankles of other leaders, Fatty, Ponce, and Jatu. Before it was over, Clum had arrested thirteen additional leaders and warriors.[20]

Major Wade and his men arrived on April 22, and on April 24, Clum met with Loco, Victorio, Nana, and other Apache leaders, telling them they must relocate to San Carlos. They agreed, really having no other choice given the presence of the police and cavalry. About 150 Chiricahuas slipped away before the guarded and shackled Geronimo and the 16 other prisoners were loaded into army wagons. On May 1, 1877, 453 Chiricahuas began their four-hundred-mile walk to San Carlos. Before they arrived on May 20, 8 of them died from smallpox.[21]

Upon reaching San Carlos Agency, Clum had the still-shackled Geronimo and other prisoners locked in the agency jail. Clum notified the Pima County sheriff in Tucson that he had Geronimo, and the sheriff could come get him.[22]

Clum had been publicly critical of General August Kautz and his handling of the Apaches. In response, Kautz sent Lieutenant Lemuel Abbot and a detachment of soldiers to San Carlos to observe the Apaches and how the agency issued rations. Abbot arrived at San Carlos the day after Clum's return. Clum was indignant that the army was monitoring his actions. In an exchange of telegrams with the Bureau of Indian Affairs, Clum threatened to resign if the troops were not removed. The troops stayed, and Clum was gone by July 1.[23]

Clum kept Geronimo shackled for the two months he remained as agent. Geronimo could not understand why he was a prisoner. Clum had told him he was arrested because he had left Apache Pass. "I do not think that I ever belonged to those soldiers at Apache Pass or that I should have asked them where I might go," Geronimo later said.[24]

The Pima County sheriff never came to get Geronimo, so toward the end of July, Indian inspector William Vandever released Geronimo and the other prisoners. He joined the Chokonens fifteen miles upriver from San Carlos at the site Taza had selected. Taza's younger brother Naiche now led the tribe. Geronimo said after being released from jail, "We had no more trouble with the soldiers, but I never felt at ease any longer at the Post."[25]

For Geronimo and the other Chiricahuas, life at San Carlos was completely different from what they had known. Instead of living freely in mountains with clear water and forests providing game, they had to exist in the desert with brackish water and cacti supporting little game. Adding to their misery, the Apaches who were already living on the White Mountain Reservation resented the influx of Chiricahuas. The Indian Bureau established a subagency near the Chihenne rancheria, and the army built Fort Thomas upriver.[26]

On August 21, 1877, Henry Hart became the new agent at San Carlos. Almost immediately he had problems. Apaches were leaving the reservation without authorization; the whites called them breakouts. Pionsenay had arrived at the reservation, and on September 1, he convinced a few Chokonen warriors and their families to leave with him for Mexico, where he would be killed later that year in a fight with Sonorans.[27]

On September 2, Victorio, Loco, and Nana left the reservation with over three hundred Chihennes for their Ojo Caliente home. After several fights with the army, they surrendered and were told to stay at Ojo Caliente until the government could determine what to do with them. After surrendering, Victorio said their troubles had all begun with "bad Indians," including Geronimo, who had been using Ojo Caliente as a base to carry out raids.[28]

On September 23, Agent Hart met with Geronimo, Naiche, and other Chokonen leaders where he appointed Geronimo a "captain" of the Chiricahuas. Geronimo and the other leaders promised they would remain on the White Mountain Reservation.[29]

Throughout the rest of 1877 and into the summer of 1878, the ration allotments were substandard, late-arriving, and less than adequate for the Apaches living on the White Mountain Reservation. This was due to a combination of Congress not approving full funding as well as contractors and government employees siphoning off supplies for their own use and profit.[30]

Colonel Orlando Willcox replaced Colonel August Kautz as commander of the Department of Arizona on March 5, 1878, as the Chokonen subagent Ezra Hoag worried the dissatisfied Chokonens would break out. Adding to their misery of poor environment and scanty rations, that spring, malaria struck the Chokonens, killing between fifty and sixty of them.[31]

In midsummer 1878, Agent Hart allowed the Chiricahuas and White Mountain Apaches to leave the Gila Valley and enter the Santa Teresa Mountains to gather food, beat the heat, and get away from the malaria. There in the mountains, Geronimo, his family, and some friends obtained corn and brewed the alcoholic drink tiswin. The agents had banned the making of tiswin and strictly enforced the ban by demolishing brewing containers and placing the brewers and consumers in jail.[32]

The night of August 1, 1878, Geronimo's group held a tiswin party. Becoming drunk, Geronimo berated one of his drunken nephews, who, taking the criticism to heart, committed suicide.[33]

Geronimo had been contemplating leaving the reservation. Now the agents would most likely discover that his people had brewed and drank tiswin. The penalty would be back to jail for him. Blaming himself for his nephew's suicide must have been the last straw. After being shackled in irons for months, forced to live in a desert environment, fed inadequate rations, watching fellow Chiricahuas die from the "shaking sickness," or what would later be known as malaria, then being responsible for a nephew's suicide, Geronimo decided to leave the reservation with his three wives and two children the very next day.

To the whites, Geronimo, the Bad Indian, had broken out and was on the run.[34]

<hr />

After repelling Custer's surprise attack on June 25, 1876, Sitting Bull's massive village continued following the buffalo herds. At first, they traveled up the Little Big Horn River to the foothills of the Big Horn Mountains. Small bands and families continued to join as others left based on their individual needs and desires. Some wished to hunt on their own while others began their return to the agencies.[35]

Through July, the village moved eastward to the Rosebud River, then to the Tongue, and then on to the Powder River near the Yellowstone. August saw the splitting up of the massive village since it was not practical for continued hunting. Many people had accumulated the meat and hides they needed and planned to return to their agencies for the winter. Some hunting bands crossed the Yellowstone heading north for the Missouri River; others turned south, following the Powder; while some bands, including Crazy Horse's, traveled south along the Little Missouri River. Sitting Bull led the large village made up of the Hunkpapas, Sans Arcs, and Miniconjous north and downriver on the Little Missouri, toward Killdeer Mountain. From there they traveled southeast to Twin Buttes at the headwaters of the Grand River in Dakota Territory.[36]

Here, probably in late August, Johnny Bruguier, of mixed race, rode into Sitting Bull's village. Bruguier, who was on the run, had been an interpreter at the Hunkpapas' Standing Rock Agency until he and his brother had killed another agency employee during a drunken brawl. Some in camp believed he was an army scout and wanted to kill him, but Sitting Bull thought otherwise, saying, "Well, if you are going to kill this man, kill him, and if you are not, give him a drink of water, something to eat, and a pipe of peace to smoke." He then adopted Bruguier as a brother, invited him to live in his lodge, and gave him a horse. In return, Bruguier gave Sitting Bull a Winchester rifle. The Hunkpapas named him Big Leggings, because he had ridden into camp wearing wing-shaped chaps. Everyone learned to like him, and since he could speak both Lakota and English, Sitting Bull used him as his clerk.[37]

Back on the morning of June 27, 1876, General Terry's Dakota Column had reached the site of the Little Big Horn battle, joining Reno and the rest of the Seventh Cavalry survivors. After burying the dead, most of whom had been stripped and horribly mutilated, the Dakota Column returned to the Yellowstone. They sent the most seriously wounded back to Fort Abraham Lincoln aboard the steamboat *Far West*.[38]

On August 5, after weeks of inaction, Crook's Big Horn and Yellowstone Expedition was on the march. Resupplied by a wagon train and reinforced by seven companies of infantry and ten companies of the Fifth Cavalry, led by Colonel Wesley Merritt, the column now numbered about 2,200 men. Arriving with Merritt as scout was Buffalo Bill Cody.[39]

Merritt's cavalry had been on its way to rendezvous with Crook, when on July 17 they intercepted Cheyenne warriors from Morning Star's band who were leaving the agencies in Nebraska, on their way to join the hunting bands along the Yellowstone. In a skirmish on Warbonnet Creek in Nebraska, Cody killed the warrior Yellow Hair in single combat. Cody then scalped Yellow Hair, shouting, "The first scalp for Custer."[40]

On August 10, Crook's expedition and Terry's Dakota Column met on the Rosebud River about thirty miles upriver of its mouth on the Yellowstone. The two columns then marched east following the massive Indian camp's trail through rain and mud to the Powder River. The columns marched down the Powder River to its mouth on the Yellowstone where they waited for a steamboat to resupply them. It arrived on August 23, and after unloading its cargo, Buffalo Bill Cody left with it. Disgusted with the army's slowness and lack of aggressiveness, Cody had resigned as scout, and so did most of the remaining Indian and white scouts.[41]

Crook disliked being under Terry's command and believed the combined columns of over 4,000 men were too big and moving too slowly to catch the Indians. On August 26, Crook separated from Terry, heading straight east to the Little Missouri badlands as Terry proceeded downriver on the Yellowstone, and eventually back to Fort Abraham Lincoln, leaving Colonel Nelson A. Miles with the Fifth Infantry on the Yellowstone to continue to patrol. As Crook marched eastward, Frank Grouard and the other scouts discovered that Sitting Bull's massive village was breaking up into small bands and scattering in all directions. A few warriors attempted hit-and-run raids from time to time, but usually stayed well away from the troops.[42]

Crook's expedition traversed the Little Missouri badlands, arriving at the headwaters of the Heart River on September 5, low on supplies. His plan had been to continue to march east to Fort Abraham Lincoln, and from there, to cut back southwest to the southern Black Hills, where he had sent his wagon train with its supplies.[43]

With two days of rations left, Crook revised his plans. Instead of heading to Fort Abraham Lincoln, he would march the column to the Black Hills where he believed he could better protect the miners from the Indians. His officers were dubious about this decision. It would take about seven days to get to the Black Hills on their two days' worth of rations. Crook ordered that they would now be on half rations.[44]

The weather was rainy and miserable as the troops slogged south through the mud. Mules and horses began to collapse and were slaughtered for food.[45]

By September 7, men were also collapsing alongside the animals. Crook made the decision to send a detachment to the northern Black

Hills towns to acquire supplies. The detachment was then to return with the supplies, meeting Crook's column along the line of march. Captain Anson Mills was chosen to lead 150 cavalrymen; several scouts, including Frank Grouard; 16 mule packers; and 61 mules. They readied themselves and left that night.[46]

Around 3:00 p.m. the next day, as Mills's detachment approached Slim Buttes to the south, they saw a horse herd in the distance. Upon reconnoitering the area at the base of Slim Buttes' sandstone bluffs, Mills and Grouard discovered an Indian village by a tree-lined winding stream. They returned to the detachment where Mills conferred with his officers. They were all in agreement: They would attack the village at dawn the next morning.[47]

Mills divided his troops into three groups. Two units of dismounted soldiers were stationed on opposite sides of the village. At first light, the horse herd was startled and raced through the village. The third unit of twenty-five mounted troopers followed, shooting into tepees and capturing about half of the four hundred head of horses.[48]

The sleeping families were taken completely by surprise. The dismounted soldiers began firing into the village as people cut their way out of their lodges. Women and children raced south and west to a deep ravine and to the nearby bluffs as the warriors stood and fought a rearguard action, until all who could make it were safe behind them.[49]

Mills sent a message to Crook stating that he needed support while his troopers ransacked the thirty-five lodges. The men found 5,500 pounds of dried meat and other food, stacks of buffalo hides, and a guidon, along with other items that had belonged to members of the Seventh Cavalry.[50]

The Indians were not going away and they continued to shoot at the soldiers. Later, prisoners told the soldiers the village's leader was a Lakota named American Horse, but he also was known by other names—Iron Plume, Black Shield, and Iron Shield.[51]

Sitting Bull's camp was thirty miles away near Twin Buttes, on the Grand River. A messenger arrived there saying soldiers were attacking American Horse's camp. Sitting Bull was in mourning. A few days earlier, a mule had kicked one of his sons in the head, killing him. Nonetheless, Sitting Bull and his warriors prepared themselves to go to the aid of American Horse's people. Mounting a white horse, Sitting Bull led close to a thousand warriors toward Slim Buttes.[52]

Crook arrived at American Horse's village at 11:30 a.m. His column was so strung out that the last troops did not arrive until later in the afternoon.[53]

American Horse and others had been holding out in the deep ravine. After the soldiers fired several concentrated barrages into the ravine, the surviving Lakotas, including the severely wounded American Horse, surrendered. Several dead women and a dead child were found in the ravine, and another child whose foot was shot off later died. That night, American Horse would die from a wound to his abdomen. Fourteen of Crook's men would be wounded during the engagement and two killed, a soldier and a white scout.[54]

At 4:15 p.m., Sitting Bull and his forces arrived and began shooting at Crook's men from the southern and western bluffs. Mounted warriors raced toward the troops' horse herd, located northwest of the village, in an attempt to drive off the herd. The guards repelled them, but they did manage to capture about a dozen cavalry horses.[55]

Crook ordered the troops to advance and hold the high ground. Most of the heaviest fighting took place in the southwestern bluffs. The soldiers pushed the Lakota warriors from their positions, but as the warriors fell back, they continued to fire from new locations. Lots of ammunition was expended on both sides, with few casualties. The fight lasted for an hour, and then the warriors for the most part stopped shooting. Throughout the fight, Sitting Bull on his white horse rode from Lakota position to position, shouting encouragement to the warriors.[56]

Crook's prisoners told him Crazy Horse's and Sitting Bull's camps were both in the vicinity of the Little Missouri River, and that Sitting Bull was heading north toward Antelope Buttes. From this information, Crook believed he was being attacked by Crazy Horse.[57]

A drizzling rain fell during the night. The warriors began firing at the troops again around midnight. The attack died down to a few random shots through the morning fog.[58]

That morning, September 10, Crook released the women and children captives after lecturing them that the government did not make war on women and children, but would "keep pegging away at all Indians in hostility until the last had been killed or made prisoner." A few of the prisoners decided to remain with the troops until they could reach an agency.[59]

Reports varied on how many Lakotas had been killed. The scout and correspondent Captain Jack Crawford wrote the *Omaha Daily Bee* on September 17, stating, "We killed about fifty Indians," but he did not say how many were women and children.[60] Reuben Davenport, correspondent for the *New York Herald*, wrote, "The attacking force of Indians was about 500 in number and their loss about forty-five killed and wounded." Two other reporters had even lower numbers—twenty and four. In Crook's official report to General Sheridan, he gave no numbers of Indian deaths; the only mention is of "killing some Indians."[61]

According to the reporters there were at least two dead children, three dead women, and two dead men brought out of the deep ravine. Frank Grouard said eleven people were killed in the ravine. One of the women prisoners ran to her lodge only to find that her child that she'd left there had been killed. After the bodies had been laid out, unknown to Crook and his officers, the Indian scout Ute John proceeded to scalp the dead women, and a few soldiers followed his example.[62]

Even though Crook had now found the Indians he had been pursuing all these weeks, he made the determination not to stay and fight but to proceed to the northern Black Hills towns to resupply. Crook ordered that any food the expedition could not carry be destroyed, any horses they could not use be killed, and that the village and all its contents be burned. There was so much to destroy that it took a dozen huge bonfires to burn everything. Crook's column left the village's smoking ruins on the morning of September 10, marching east and then south along the eastern edge of Slim Buttes. Sitting Bull and his warriors followed, fighting Crook's rear guard.[63]

After following and fighting the troops for two miles, Sitting Bull called off the attack. They needed to return to American Horse's camp and care for any survivors, and the dead.[64]

Upon entering the devastation that had been American Horse's village, the warriors searched for survivors. They found the prisoners Crook had released. They repeated Crook's message—that he did not make war on women and children, but would be relentless in killing or capturing the hunting bands. One of the released prisoners was five-year-old Little Wound, who had been shot in the foot. He told the warriors he had witnessed his mother being shot dead.[65]

Sitting Bull approached a woman sitting hunched on the ground with a blanket pulled over her head. He asked, "Are you living?" There was no answer. She was dead. He removed the blanket and recognized Red Water Woman, a Miniconjou. Nearby were the bodies of an old man and an old woman. They found a dead mother and infant. In the deep ravine, an old woman was still alive, shot in the back, but two women and the warrior Blue Stem lay dead. They found the pregnant daughter of Little Eagle. She had been wounded, losing her unborn child.[66]

Deeply troubled by the deaths and destruction, Sitting Bull said nothing as they buried the dead and returned to their village with the survivors. Later on, he would learn that his adopted brother Frank Grouard had led the troops to American Horse's camp.[67]

Crook's expedition continued to plod south through the rain and the mud. The men became disorganized and strung out along the line of march. On Saturday, September 16, Crook and an escort left the column, riding sixteen miles ahead to his namesake town, Crook City, where he was welcomed by a joyous crowd. His expedition became known as the Mud March and the Horsemeat March.[68]

Some believed the attack on the Lakota village was a major victory, while others weren't so sure, especially when considering it was 2,000 soldiers against an initial 35 family lodges. Crook failed to take the fight to the very warriors he had been chasing all this time. Many within the army, as well as some outside it, blamed Crook for the lack of success. The attack on a sleeping village alarmed many Lakotas, who left the agencies, some joining Crazy Horse and others joining Sitting Bull.[69]

Sitting Bull and his Hunkpapas as well as the Miniconjous and Sans Arcs headed northwest to the Yellowstone buffalo herds. On October 10, as they crossed to the north bank of the Yellowstone River, scouts brought the good news of large buffalo herds, but also the bad news of soldiers, still present in the Yellowstone country. The scouts had found a westward-bound wagon train hauling supplies and guarded by infantry.[70]

Back in August, when General Terry's Dakota Column had returned to Fort Abraham Lincoln, Terry had left behind Colonel Nelson A. Miles with the Fifth Infantry to continue patrolling the Yellowstone. Miles planned to remain at the mouth of the Tongue River through the winter, and his five hundred men were building a temporary post with cabins to live in. The flows in the river had decreased so steamboats were bringing supplies up the Yellowstone as far as the mouth of Glendive Creek, and then wagons were hauling the supplies from there.[71]

On the morning of October 11, the men of the wagon train were preparing to break camp when Lakota warriors struck. They ran off forty-seven mules and shot so many others, the wagon train had to return to Glendive Creek.[72]

October 15, the supply train again started out for Miles's encampment with eighty-six wagons and a four-company infantry guard of two hundred men. Several hundred warriors harassed the wagon train, but it proceeded on even when the Lakotas set fire to the prairie in front of it.[73]

Sitting Bull's nephew White Bull was in the thick of the fight. He rode to within seventy-five yards of the wagons where he was shot in the upper left arm. He was in shock, but friends took him back to the village to treat his wound, and he would recover.[74]

The next day, as warriors continued to plague the advancing wagon train, the tribal council met and debated whether they should try to talk peace with the soldiers. Sitting Bull had Johnny Bruguier write a message for him in English. He had the message attached to a forked stick and sent a young man to place the message in the trail in front of the wagons, where the soldiers would see it.[75] The message read:

> *Yellowstone.*
> *I want to know what you are doing traveling on this road. You scare all the buffalo away. I want to hunt on the place. I want you to turn back from here. If you don't, I will fight you again. I want you to leave what you have got here, and turn back from here.*
>
> *I am your friend,*
> *SITTING BULL*
> *I mean all the rations you have got and some powder. Wish you would write as soon as you can.[76]*

Lieutenant Colonel Elwell Otis, commanding the four companies of infantry, read the note and sent a scout to inform Sitting Bull that he intended to proceed to the post at the Tongue River, and if Sitting Bull wanted a fight, he would give it to him.[77]

Shortly after this, several Lakotas appeared waving a white cloth and a parley was held between Otis and a few Lakota leaders. The information regarding whether or not Sitting Bull participated in the meeting is contradictory. If he was there, he did not say anything.[78]

The chiefs told Otis he was driving off the buffalo. They were hungry, needed more ammunition, and wanted peace. Otis said they had wasted their ammunition shooting at his men and he had no authority to make peace. In the end, he gave them 150 pounds of hardtack and two sides of bacon. Since Otis gave them a gift, the Lakotas allowed the wagon train to proceed in peace, while they headed north along Cedar Creek to hunt a large buffalo herd.[79]

Colonel Miles had become concerned with the delay of the supply train and headed east with the entire Fifth Infantry. That evening, he came upon the train and met with Otis, who informed him of his encounter with the Lakotas.[80]

Sending the train on to the Tongue River post, Miles led 394 troops of the Fifth Infantry and an ordnance rifle artillery piece north in pursuit of Sitting Bull.[81]

On October 21, Sitting Bull's village was at the headwaters of Cedar Creek. As Miles's troops approached the village in skirmish order, Sitting Bull and his warriors arrayed themselves on top of an intervening ridge. Sitting Bull sent two representatives under a flag of truce to ask for a parley. Miles had no interpreter, but after much back-and-forth, Miles agreed to a parley, with Johnny Bruguier acting as interpreter for both sides, who would not carry weapons.[82]

Unarmed, Sitting Bull, six Lakotas, and Bruguier walked down the slope toward the soldiers. Miles rode out with an officer and six men and then dismounted between the lines. The Lakotas, noting that Miles wore a long coat trimmed in bear fur and a fur cap, called him Bear Coat after that. Miles and the officer carried revolvers on their belts, concealed under their coats.[83]

The Lakotas spread a blanket to sit on. Miles did not want to sit but finally kneeled. They smoked the sacred pipe, but that did not help things go well during the meeting, which lasted for most of the afternoon. Sitting Bull wanted Miles and his soldiers to leave the Yellowstone and the army to abandon Fort Buford. He wanted the Lakotas to be able to deal with white traders and be free to follow the buffalo. Miles wanted the Lakotas' unconditional surrender, and for them to come with him to the Tongue River post, where they would stay until they learned what the government would do with them. Neither man agreed to the other's demands.[84]

During the parley, a young warrior came up behind Sitting Bull. Miles believed he saw the man slip a carbine to Sitting Bull under his buffalo robe as ten to twelve additional warriors slowly drifted in to join Sitting Bull's side. The young man was Sitting Bull's nephew, White Bull, whose left arm was in a sling. He had not taken off his revolver strapped to his hip under his buffalo robe, and that is probably what Miles saw. White Bull had come to warn Sitting Bull that it appeared the soldiers were preparing for battle. Miles became concerned the warriors with Sitting Bull might try to attack him. They could not reach an agreement, so Miles ended the parley, saying they should each think about what had been said and resume talks the next day.[85]

The next morning, the Lakotas saw troops in battle formation advancing toward the village and Miles's artillery piece positioned on a high hill. The women began to take down the tepees and pack as the men took defensive positions. Sitting Bull and more chiefs attended the meeting with Miles, who this time spread a bearskin on the ground for them to sit on.[86]

The positions of both sides were the same as the day before, although the Miniconjou and Sans Arc leaders tried to be more conciliatory, with some even considering the possibility of surrender. Both Sitting Bull and Miles were angry with each other. Sitting Bull was so angry, he was speechless. Miles lost his patience and gave the Lakotas an ultimatum: If they did not immediately surrender unconditionally, he would consider them hostile, and attack. Miles gave Sitting Bull fifteen minutes to surrender. Bruguier probably did not translate the fifteen-minute ultimatum. There would not have been any Lakota words for fifteen minutes at the time. Later, none of the Lakota participants recalled it, and they certainly did not have timepieces of their own.[87]

Both parties returned to their lines, and at the end of fifteen minutes, Miles gave the order to attack. The warriors set fire to the dry grass and slowly retreated, covering the flight of their families as the artillery piece pounded the warriors' position and the infantry advanced. During this action, which would be called the Battle of Cedar Creek, one warrior was killed and two soldiers wounded.[88]

For the next two days, and over the course of forty miles, Miles's troops pursued and pressured Sitting Bull's people as they headed east to the headwaters of Bad Route Creek and descended along that to the Yellowstone. The Lakotas fought back, setting fire to the prairie. At one point, the warriors surrounded Miles's troops and applied so much pressure he ordered the troops to form a hollow square to repel the attack. He had to bring all his reserves into action and use his artillery.[89]

However, the Miniconjous and Sans Arcs were finished. They planned to surrender, but not Sitting Bull. With 30 Hunkpapa lodges—about 400 people—he headed north to the Missouri River to continue to hunt buffalo.[90]

Miles overtook the 400 lodges of the Miniconjous and Sans Arcs. Their chiefs and 2,000 people surrendered to him. Their number included Sitting Bull's nephew, White Bull. Miles held five of the chiefs hostage and sent them under escort to their agencies, and the rest pledged to return on their own to the agencies.[91]

It was the end of October when Sitting Bull's band reached the Big Dry and set up camp about twenty-five miles south of Fort Peck on the Missouri River, where they planned to hunt buffalo and trade with other Lakotas and Métis.[92]

Sitting Bull selected 100 young Hunkpapa men for special duty. They were called Sitting Bull's Soldiers, reporting to him every morning for duties. They were to be always vigilant for attacks on the village. They were to keep their guns and ammunition handy and to have a fast horse ready to mount. When out hunting, they were to kill extra animals and bring back meat for the old and helpless. Every evening they paraded around the camp, and the people were impressed.[93]

Miles returned to his post at the mouth of the Tongue. On November 6, rested and resupplied, he headed north with 434 men in pursuit of Sitting Bull.[94]

Sitting Bull's village had grown to over 100 lodges. Ever watchful, his scouts kept him informed of Miles's movements. As Miles marched his troops north to the Big Dry, Sitting Bull led his Hunkpapas east.[95]

Reaching Fort Peck on November 17, Miles found Johnny Bruguier, who had separated from Sitting Bull. Miles and Bruguier made a deal: Miles would help defend Bruguier in his murder charges if he would help Miles capture Sitting Bull. Miles sent Bruguier out on his own to find Sitting Bull and attempt to persuade him to surrender.[96]

Miles heard rumors that Sitting Bull had moved south again to the Big Dry, and other rumors he was heading west. He sent some troops back to the Big Dry while he marched the rest of his troops west, just as severe winter weather hit. They marched one hundred miles along the north bank of the Missouri River toward the Musselshell, until a messenger reached Miles, informing him that Sitting

Bull had gone in the opposite direction. Having reached the extent of his supplies, Miles marched most of the men southeast, arriving at his post on the Tongue River on December 12.[97]

Crazy Horse, whose village was located on the Powder River, sent Sitting Bull a message. He needed more ammunition, and asked Sitting Bull to trade for more and join him at his village. Sitting Bull obtained fifty boxes of ammunition and was getting ready to join Crazy Horse.[98]

Miles had sent Lieutenant Frank Baldwin and 112 men back down the Missouri River. They reached Fort Peck on December 6, where Baldwin met with Johnny Bruguier.[99]

Bruguier had found Sitting Bull and attempted to get him to surrender, but he had refused. Bruguier told Baldwin that when he'd left Sitting Bull on December 3, Sitting Bull's plan was to head up the Milk River to the mouth of the Porcupine. Baldwin sent Bruguier to Miles to relay the information while he and his troops went after Sitting Bull.[100]

Baldwin's men reached the banks of the Milk River on December 7, marching past Sitting Bull's camp without realizing it. Sitting Bull was able to evacuate his 120-lodge village, crossing the ice on the Missouri River to the south bank. They found a safe place for the women and children to hide while Sitting Bull and his warriors waited at the Missouri River bluffs to contest the soldiers' crossing. Realizing they could be entering a trap, Baldwin pulled back his men from the river.[101]

Sitting Bull's village traveled southeast to the Red Water River. The temperatures were frigid, with two feet of snow on the ground on the morning of December 18, when Sitting Bull's scouts discovered Baldwin's troops had followed them and were advancing in a skirmish line toward the village. Many of the men were out hunting. Those warriors in camp rushed out to defend the village while the women and children fled south. Baldwin had a small howitzer and fired three solid shots that demoralized the warriors, who followed after the women and children. Sitting Bull's people left much behind in their haste—lodges, buffalo robes, tons of dried meat, utensils, and sixty head of horses and mules. What Baldwin's men could not use, they burned, slaughtering unwanted horses and mules.[102]

Baldwin loaded his wagons with food and hundreds of buffalo robes and proceeded on to Miles's post on the Yellowstone. One of the important items Sitting Bull was able to remove from the village before it was looted and destroyed was the fifty boxes of ammunition.[103]

On January 15, 1877, Sitting Bull with about one hundred lodges arrived at Crazy Horse's village at the Tongue River, located in the foothills of the Big Horn Mountains, where most of the Lakota and Cheyenne hunting bands were camped.[104]

Dull Knife was the leader of one of the Cheyenne bands camped on the Tongue River. Back on November 25, 1876, Dull Knife's people had been camped on the Red Fork of the Powder River when Colonel Ranald Mackenzie and ten companies of cavalry, part of General Crook's command, attacked. Their scouts included Sitting Bull's adopted brother, Frank Grouard. The Cheyenne warriors fought a rearguard action, protecting the women and children as they escaped, but more than forty men were killed. In addition, seven hundred horses were captured and two hundred lodges and their contents destroyed, including thousands of pounds of dried buffalo meat.[105]

During the last days of December 1876, some of Crazy Horse's warriors had stolen over a hundred head of beef cattle from Miles's camp at the mouth of the Tongue River. Miles had followed them with four hundred troops. On January 7, 1877, Crazy Horse led his warriors in an attempt to ambush the troops at Wolf Mountain, which failed. Both sides used lots of firepower, with the troops adding artillery rounds. Casualties were light on both sides, and at the end of the day, a blizzard put a stop to the fight. The warriors left and the troops returned to their camp.[106]

These attacks were part of General Sheridan's strategy to subdue the hunting bands and force their surrender. In the summer of 1877, he would establish two forts in the middle of the hostiles' hunting grounds—Fort Keogh on the Tongue River, and Fort Custer on the Big Horn River. He would continue to direct his commanders to attack any Indians not at their agencies. The second part of his strategy was for the military to take over management of the agencies and then confiscate the Indians' guns and horses, which began in the fall of 1876.[107]

By February 1877, Sitting Bull had had enough of the army's constant harassment. He would go where the US Army could not follow. He would go to Canada and take his Hunkpapas and any other bands that wanted to go along. Some Hunkpapa bands including Black Moon's had already crossed the border into Canada. It was estimated that more than 3,000 Lakotas had crossed the border and were living at Wood Mountain in present-day Saskatchewan, Canada.[108]

By mid-March, Sitting Bull and his band had crossed the Missouri upriver from Fort Peck and camped in the river valley. On March 17, an ice jam backing up the Missouri River flow broke, destroying much of the village and wiping out Fort Peck.[109]

Sitting Bull's band numbering around 1,000 people continued to hunt and travel northward. The first part of May 1877, they passed the stone cairns placed at three-mile intervals marking the US and Canada boundary, the Medicine Line. They were now in Canada, Grandmother's Land, where the US Army could not follow them. That same week, believing he would be given an agency in the Powder River country, Crazy Horse and 889 of his people surrendered at Camp Robinson in Nebraska. At the same time, Colonel Miles and his troops attacked Lame Deer's Miniconjou village near the Rosebud. Lame Deer was killed, and his people had to abandon their village, which the army burned to the ground.[110]

No stranger to Canada, Sitting Bull established the Hunkpapa camp on the west side of Wood Mountain near Pinto Horse Butte. Later in May, a small party of North-West Mounted Police led by Major James Walsh, commander of Fort Walsh to the west, rode into Sitting Bull's camp. Sitting Bull and his chiefs held a council with Walsh, who told them they were welcome to remain in Canada as long as they obeyed the rules. Walsh told Sitting Bull and his men that Canadian law applied to all regardless of who they were,

Indian or white. Further, the Lakotas were not permitted to cross the boundary with the United States to kill and steal.[111]

Sitting Bull and his leaders agreed to keep the peace. They witnessed Mountie justice in action and saw that it was fair. The Lakotas gave Walsh the name Long Lance because of the lances the Mounties carried. Walsh and Sitting Bull respected each other, and over the months, that respect would grow into friendship.[112]

The Mounties promised that the US Army would not attack Sitting Bull's people while they remained in Canada. There were abundant buffalo herds to hunt and they could live as they had in the old days.[113] The Mounties allowed the Hunkpapas to buy guns and limited ammunition for hunting. They traded buffalo robes at Jean-Louis Légaré's Wood Mountain trading post. Légaré was an honest and genuinely caring person, and Sitting Bull would come to know him well.[114]

Even though relations between the Lakotas and the Canadian government were cordial, the Canadians wanted the Lakotas to return to the United States, and they worked toward that goal. Tribes previously living in the territory the Lakotas now occupied did not want them there, believing these interlopers were diminishing their Canadian buffalo herds.[115]

Sitting Bull did not want trouble with the Canadian tribes. One of the first things he did was to visit the other tribes and make peace. The Lakotas had always been enemies with the most powerful of these tribes, the Blackfeet. He rode to the village of their leader Crow Foot, where they smoked and made peace. Sitting Bull said, "We will be friends to the end of our lives—my children shall be your children, and yours mine," and Crow Foot agreed. After their council, Sitting Bull renamed one of his young twin sons Crow Foot. There was much feasting and dancing.[116]

The Lakotas' presence was a diplomatic problem for the Canadians, who asked the US government to drop its unconditional-surrender position and allow the Lakotas to return to the United States with their guns and horses, but the Americans refused. US government officials took the position that the Canadians could keep the Lakotas, but must guarantee they not cross the border into the United States.[117]

The US government finally relented to Canadian requests to work for the return of the Lakotas, and on August 14, 1877, President Rutherford B. Hayes authorized a Sitting Bull Indian Commission headed by Brigadier General Alfred Terry to meet with Sitting Bull. Terry and his commission departed St. Paul, Minnesota, on September 15, for Fort Benton, Montana. From there, they would head north to Fort Walsh, Canada.[118]

Trouble had been brewing at the Red Cloud Agency in Nebraska, the week before Terry's departure. The army was worried Crazy Horse and his people would flee north to join Sitting Bull in Canada. General Crook ordered the arrest of Crazy Horse, and ensuing events led to his death at Fort Robinson, Nebraska, on September 5, 1877.[119]

Crazy Horse's followers started to quietly leave for Canada. The first would arrive in Sitting Bull's camp in late November 1877, with more following into the spring of 1878.[120] The news of Crazy Horse's death at the hands of the army would most likely have reached Sitting Bull before Terry's commission did.

Sitting Bull was aware that for four months the US Army had been pursuing and fighting the Lakota enemy, the Nez Perces, who had been friendly with Americans. The US government had been forcing them onto a new smaller reservation, which led to violence and the flight of over 1,000 men, women, and children. General Oliver O. Howard and his troops pursued them for 1,500 miles as other columns converged and attacked the fugitives. On September 30, Colonel Nelson Miles and his troops trapped the Nez Perces at Bear Paw Mountain in northern Montana, forty miles from the Medicine Line, as Howard's column caught up and joined him. A small portion of the band led by White Bird was able to slip away into Canada while the other Nez Perces who were severely wounded or too weak to keep running remained with Chief Joseph, surrendering to Miles on October 5.[121]

Meanwhile, the Canadian government sent Major Walsh to convince Sitting Bull to go to Fort Walsh to meet with Terry's commission. When Walsh arrived in Sitting Bull's camp on October 7,

Sitting Bull was in mourning; his nine-year-old son by Red Water Woman had died from a disease.[122]

Sitting Bull and his chiefs met with Walsh. They told him they did not want to meet with the Americans, who were all liars. They wanted to stay in Grandmother's Land, and nothing the Americans could say would change their minds. They finally agreed to meet with the Americans, but only because Walsh and Grandmother asked them to do so.[123]

As the Lakotas and Walsh prepared to leave for Fort Walsh the next day, the Nez Perce chief White Bird and about fifty men, forty women, and their children arrived in Sitting Bull's camp. They were in bad shape. Walsh wrote, "Many of them were wounded—men, women, and children. Some were shot badly through the body, legs, and arms." Sitting Bull and his people had pity on them and welcomed their former enemies, feeding them, caring for their wounds, and providing shelter. Sitting Bull and his people were angry at how the army had treated these people and now did not want to go to Fort Walsh to meet with Terry's commission.[124]

Walsh spent the rest of the day and into the next trying to convince Sitting Bull and his leaders to go to Fort Walsh. They finally relented, and the next day Sitting Bull, Walsh, and about twenty Lakotas rode west to the fort.[125]

Terry's commission arrived at the fort on October 16. The next afternoon, they met with Sitting Bull, his leaders, and one Lakota woman, with the Mounties in attendance to observe. To the Lakotas, just meeting with Terry was an offense in and of itself. Terry was the commander who had sent Custer to attack their village; he along with Crook had pursued them the summer before; and he was the one who had led the soldiers to confiscate the horses and guns from Lakotas at Standing Rock and Cheyenne River Agencies.[126]

Sitting Bull and his followers greeted the Mounties cordially, shaking hands and saying "How." When they came to the Americans, they would not shake hands. Sitting Bull looked at them with disdain and said "How," very slowly. The Lakotas sat on buffalo robes on the floor and the Americans in chairs behind a table. Sitting Bull asked the Americans to sit on the floor with them. Terry and the other Americans did move their chairs out from behind the table but would not sit on the floor. The Lakotas refrained from opening the meeting with their pipe ceremony.[127]

Terry spoke first, saying the Great Father wanted peace. Sitting Bull and his people could return to the United States; they would be pardoned and given food, clothing, and cattle. They would not be harmed as long as they surrendered their horses and guns, but if they returned and did not give up their horses and guns, "[they] must be treated as enemies of the United States."[128]

Sitting Bull stood and talked. He went through the history of how badly the United States had treated his people, so they had to take refuge in Canada, and they intended to remain there. "You come here to tell us lies, but we don't want to hear them." He ended by saying directly to Terry, "Don't you say two more words. Go back home where you came from."[129]

The others took their turns speaking. The woman, The One That Speaks Once, spoke for the Lakota women, saying, "I wanted to bring up my children there [the United States] but you did not give me time. I came here to raise my family and have a little peace."[130]

As the Lakotas all stood to leave, Terry said, "Shall we say to the president that you refuse the offers he has made to you?"

There was a long silence, and then Sitting Bull replied, "If we told you more, you would have paid no attention. That is all I have to say. This part of the country does not belong to your people. You belong on the other side. This side belongs to us."[131]

Sitting Bull and the other Lakotas shook hands and talked with the Mounties, ignoring the Americans, and then left. Terry requested that the Mounties ask Sitting Bull and the other leaders again for him if they would accept his offer. The Lakota leaders again said no.[132]

Two reporters had accompanied Terry's commission, and Sitting Bull agreed to interviews with each of them. For the first time, the American people would hear Sitting Bull's side of the story. He repeated the injustices committed against his people. The reporters showed him to be true to his heritage and possess unshakable principles and convictions.[133]

Sitting Bull and the other leaders believed they had won a great victory over Terry, whom they had humiliated. They believed his only option was to commit suicide. Terry and the other US government leaders never believed Sitting Bull would accept their terms, so now he was Canada's problem.[134]

There were plenty of buffalo herds, and the Lakotas separated into smaller bands to hunt throughout the winter of 1877–1878 and into the spring and summer of 1878. They replenished their supplies of meat and accumulated hides for trade. Life was good again.[135]

CHAPTER 8

Geronimo's Breakout and Sitting Bull's Surrender, 1878–1881

ON AUGUST 2, 1878, GERONIMO, ALONG WITH HIS THREE WIVES and two children, left the San Carlos Agency for Mexico, where he found Juh and his Nednhis at their rancheria in the Carcay Mountains. Juh's representatives had been negotiating a peace treaty with Chihuahua state government representatives in Janos. Juh's position was simple: The Nednhis would make peace with Sonora and Chihuahua; all they wanted in return was to "live in the country where they were born."[1]

Around September 1, Juh, Nolgee, Geronimo, and other leaders met with Mexican government officials in Janos to discuss peace. The Mexicans said there would be no peace unless the Nednhis relocated to Ojinaga, to the southeast near the Texas border—250 miles away. Juh did not like the terms but asked for time to consider. The Mexicans gave the Chiricahuas until September 25 to agree to their terms; otherwise, they would resume their attacks. The Chiricahuas had no intention of relocating to Ojinaga, and moved their rancheria farther south into the Sierra Madre Mountains.[2]

Chocolate Pass, which slices through the mountains between Casas Grandes to the east and Galeana to the west, was one of Juh's favorite places to ambush Mexicans. On September 26, 1878, the day after the peace deadline, Juh, Geronimo, and the Nednhis attacked a train of freight wagons hauling beans to Silver City, New Mexico. They slaughtered all twenty-five men, women, and children.[3]

November 12, 1878, was a significant day. Geronimo, Juh, and Nolgee had split, leading three separate groups in continued raids. Nolgee and his forty-four people entered Janos to discuss peace. The citizens of Janos threw them a fiesta. While they celebrated, Mexican federal troops surrounded the Nednhis, killing Nolgee, eight men, and twenty-six women and children.[4]

That same day, Sonoran troops had crossed the border into Chihuahua and attacked Geronimo's forty-member rancheria in the mountains south of Casas Grandes, killing twelve of Geronimo's warriors.[5]

As these events were occurring, the US government was forcing the Chihennes living at their Ojo Caliente home to return to San Carlos. Troops were en route, escorting Loco and 172 Chihennes back to San Carlos, but Victorio and about 90 people stayed behind in the mountains, vowing to fight to remain in their home.[6]

During the year 1879, Geronimo and Juh continued to raid, at times together and at other times separate, throughout Chihuahua and Sonora, and possibly across the border into the United States. By September 4, 1879, Victorio and his warriors had joined with Juh in an attack on the Ninth Cavalry's horse herd at Ojo Caliente, killing five soldiers and three civilians and then stealing the herd of sixty-eight horses and mules.[7]

The Ninth Cavalry pursued them across the border into Mexico. On October 27, Victorio and Juh's warriors, with Geronimo joining, fought the troops to a standstill. Heading east, the warriors attacked and killed two parties of Mexicans at Carrizal, Chihuahua. By November, Juh and Geronimo had parted ways with Victorio, who returned to New Mexico.[8]

A year later, Mexican troops would surround and kill Victorio along with sixty-two of his warriors and twenty-six women and children on October 15, 1880, at Tres Castillos, Chihuahua. Nana with a few survivors would escape, killing and raiding across the American Southwest and Mexico.[9]

Leaving Victorio, Juh and Geronimo, along with their warriors, began the 150-mile ride back to their rancheria to the west in the Carcay Mountains near Janos, raiding and killing as they went.[10]

Arriving home about November 25, 1879, they found Gordo and Ah-Dis, Chiricahua messengers, had arrived with messages from friends at San Carlos and from the US Army inviting them to return to San Carlos to live. At first, Juh and Geronimo were skeptical, but after much discussion they decided to go. If they did not like it, they could always leave. However, before traveling to San Carlos, they would need more horses and supplies, so they robbed and murdered to prepare for their journey.[11]

Colonel Orlando Willcox, the commander of the Department of Arizona, wanted Juh and Geronimo's people to live at San Carlos. He believed it was in the best interests of Americans, Mexicans, and Apaches that Juh and Geronimo's people live there. The Indian Bureau had agreed to allow the army to run San Carlos. Captain Adna Chaffee was appointed acting agent, and he set to work cleaning out the rat's nest of corruption and began running an honest, efficient agency.[12]

Back in July 1879, Willcox had appointed Lieutenant Harry Haskell to find Juh and Geronimo and bring them back to San Carlos. It took Haskell time. He met with knowledgeable Americans such as Chief Scout Archie McIntosh and Tom Jeffords, now a civilian prospector, as well as Naiche and other Chiricahua leaders, to determine how best to approach Juh and Geronimo and convince them that life was better at San Carlos.[13]

By early December 1879, Lieutenant Haskell had not heard back from his messengers, Gordo and Ah-Dis, and decided to venture into Mexico with two soldiers and two Apache scouts in search of Juh and Geronimo's people. He met an Indian scout company under the command of Lieutenant Augustus Blocksom, who joined him. Two days into their journey and after crossing the border, they saw smoke signals in the Guadalupe Mountains to the east. Haskell sent his two scouts to learn what the signals meant.[14]

One of the scouts returned the night of December 12 and told Haskell that Juh and Geronimo would see him, but he could not bring any troops. Haskell left immediately with the scout and Blocksom's interpreter.[15]

They arrived at Juh and Geronimo's rancheria the next evening, where eighty Chiricahuas with "most restless and suspicious tempers" met them. Gordo took Haskell to Juh's wickiup where he met with Juh and Geronimo.[16]

Several days earlier, the Chiricahuas had held a council meeting to decide if they should give up the warpath and return to live at San Carlos. Everyone agreed to do so except for one leader, who argued against it. The argument became heated until Geronimo shot—and killed—the dissenter.[17]

Juh and Geronimo's one concern was that they would be put in jail. Haskell assured them they would not go to jail. As long as they lived in peace, the agent would treat them well. Haskell also said he would accompany them to San Carlos and would stay with them until they were comfortable.[18]

Haskell and his men rode with 102 Chiricahuas, crossing the border and then traveling north to Fort Bowie. There, on December 30, 1879, they held a council with Tom Jeffords and others. The Chiricahuas expressed their happiness to see Jeffords. They were told they could keep their weapons and could establish their rancheria at the subagency, with the Chokonens.[19]

On January 7, 1880, Juh's Nednhis along with Geronimo's Bedonkohes arrived at the San Carlos Agency where they established their rancheria near Naiche's Chokonens, on the north bank of the Gila River.[20]

Most members of the four Chiricahua bands were now at San Carlos except for those with Victorio and a small band of Bedonkohes. Those at San Carlos numbered approximately 700 people. Since 1876, the Chiricahua population had decreased by 400 to 450 lives lost.[21]

Juh and Geronimo did not believe they had surrendered to Haskell; they had only agreed to give up fighting and live at San Carlos. They distrusted the White Eyes and were always ready to bolt at the first sign of trouble.[22]

During 1880 and into 1881, the Chiricahuas did not cause any problems on the reservation. They got along with the other Apaches and seemed to be content and happy.[23]

In the summer of 1881, the White Mountain Apaches, the Chiricahuas' neighbors to the north, were following Nakadoklini,[24] a prophet who allegedly could temporarily bring dead leaders back to life and who prophesied the whites would soon vanish. His message was peaceful and did not advocate violence. He taught the people a new dance with him at the center of it. The dance was frightening to White Eyes. Nakadoklini and his new religion created quite a stir with the White Mountain Apaches, but the Chiricahuas did not seem to care about it.[25]

In August 1881, the San Carlos agent, who was now Joseph Tiffany, and Colonel Orlando Willcox received reports that Nakadoklini was plotting an uprising. Tiffany sent a message to Colonel Eugene Carr, commander of Fort Apache, to arrest Nakadoklini. The message read in part, "It would be well to arrest Nakadoklini and send him off or have him killed without arresting."[26]

According to Daklugie, Juh's son and Geronimo's nephew, Juh and Geronimo with their families traveled to Nakadoklini's rancheria and met with him. Although they did not join in his dance, he impressed them, and they believed his message that Apaches should leave revenge to Ussen.[27]

On August 30, Carr arrived at Nakadoklini's Cibecue Creek rancheria with two companies of cavalry, eighty-five men, several civilians, and twenty-three Apache scouts, including thirteen of Nakadoklini's own people. Daklugie later said that Juh and Geronimo were still there when the troops arrived. Accounts are varied, but after the troops arrested Nakadoklini, they shot and killed him. The White Mountain Apaches were furious and attacked the troops. Most of the Apache scouts turned on the soldiers. Possibly eighteen Apaches, including six of Carr's scouts who had turned on the troops, and seven of Carr's soldiers were killed as he beat a hasty retreat back to Fort Apache.[28]

The White Mountain Apaches attacked Fort Apache. They killed any White Eyes they could find. Colonel Willcox, believing he needed more troops to handle the situation, called for reinforcements to be sent to the White Mountain Reservation.[29]

The influx of troops was disturbing to Juh and Geronimo. Willcox ordered the arrest of the White Mountain Apaches involved in the Cibecue fight, which included the leaders, George and Bonito. On September 30, 1881, approximately seventy-five men, women, and children were taken into custody. George and Bonito eluded cavalry sent to apprehend them and raced to the Chiricahua rancherias that night to tell them the soldiers planned to arrest all Apache leaders and shackle them.[30]

The Chiricahua leaders quickly convened a council. Chatto, one of Naiche's Chokonens, was present, and later said, "Geronimo was like a wild animal. Troops made him nervous" and Juh was "very much excited." Geronimo and Juh dominated the council, which came to the consensus that they needed to flee. Geronimo later said, "We thought it more manly to die on the warpath than to be killed in prison."[31]

That night at 10:30 p.m., Geronimo, Juh, Bonito, and Chokonen leaders Naiche, Chatto, and Chihuahua, with over 375 men, women, and children, left San Carlos, their destination—Mexico.[32]

By the fall of 1878, commercial hide hunters and the hunting tribes' continued need for food and robes were reducing the northern plains buffalo herds. Many Canadian tribes blamed the Lakotas for the smaller herd sizes. Lakota hunters began crossing the border into the United States in search of game. Sitting Bull crossed into the United States but remained close to the border.[33]

The Nez Perce chief White Bird who had escaped across the border to join Sitting Bull sought revenge on US troops. The Nez Perces were allies with the Crows, who still lived in the United States and were traditional enemies of the Lakotas. White Bird convinced Sitting Bull to seek peace with the Crows in hopes they would join them in their fight against the US Army. Sitting Bull sent a tobacco peace offering to the Crows. Not only did they reject his offer, but they raided his horse herd, stealing nearly one hundred animals.[34]

Sitting Bull was furious and began gathering a war party to attack the Crows. Learning of Sitting Bull's plans, Major James Walsh paid him a visit in his camp, just south of the Canadian border, on January 23, 1879. Walsh listened to Sitting Bull and the other chiefs' grievances against the Crows and the Americans. He advised them not to retaliate, as it might cause further harm to the Hunkpapas. Sitting Bull listened to Walsh's advice and did not attack the Crows. In a March 23 meeting with Walsh at Wood Mountain, Sitting Bull maintained that he wanted to continue to live in Canada and would not attack anyone, only fighting in self-defense. He said his hunters needed to continue to cross back into the United States only to hunt, and when they had enough food and hides, they would return to Canada. Walsh asked Sitting Bull to allow anyone who wanted to return to the United States and surrender to do so. Sitting Bull agreed to that. In the past, his *akicita* enforcers had prevented people from leaving.[35]

In June, Sitting Bull's village was camped on Rock Creek, south of the border. There, Stanley Huntley, a reporter for the *Chicago Tribune*, interviewed Sitting Bull. He told Huntley, "I am a hunter, and will hunt as long as there is wild game on the prairie." He did not want gifts from the US government, and he refused to farm. Concerning the US Army, he said, "We will avoid them if we can. If we cannot, we will fight."[36]

The US government was finished with the Lakotas entering the country. On June 5, General Alfred Terry ordered Colonel Nelson Miles to attack the Lakotas and force them back into Canada. By mid-July, Miles and his troops were marching north from the site of old Fort Peck. His column consisted of almost 700 infantry and cavalry, as well as artillery. They were joined by 143 Crow, Cheyenne, and Assiniboine warriors.[37]

Sitting Bull's village was following the buffalo herds along the Milk River. One morning, eight of Miles's scouts approached Sitting Bull's village. Five remained on a hill at a distance while three rode into camp. Two were Cheyennes and the third was Sitting Bull's adopted brother, Big Leggings (Johnny Bruguier). Upon reaching the camp, they entered the first tepee they came to, keeping their weapons with them. Later, an angry, unarmed Sitting Bull and two armed warriors entered.[38]

Ignoring the traitor Bruguier, Sitting Bull demanded to know from the Cheyennes if the army was following them to his camp. They said no, but announced they had been sent to offer Sitting Bull and his people peace if they surrendered; otherwise, the army would chase them all over the country. Sitting Bull said he would not surrender—he planned to stay right where he was. Then he sent the scouts away.[39]

On July 17, Sitting Bull's hunters had killed many buffalo along Beaver Creek, a southern tributary of the Milk River. Most of the 600 Hunkpapas headed north, leaving about 120 men, including Sitting Bull, women, and children, to finish their butchering.[40]

Eighty strangers approached from the south. The Hunkpapas saw that the strangers had red handkerchiefs tied to their gun barrels and believed it was a sign that they wanted to parley. But that was not the case. They were Miles's Cheyenne and Crow scouts. The handkerchiefs were displayed so the soldiers could distinguish the scouts from hostile Indians.[41]

Sitting Bull and his people realized their mistake when the scouts opened fire, killing two of them. As the women and children fled toward the main camp, the men fought to keep the scouts from reaching their loved ones.[42]

Carrying a white flag, a Crow rode between the opposing lines. The Hunkpapas stopped firing and a warrior rode out to see what the Crow wanted. A noted Crow warrior named Magpie challenged Sitting Bull to fight in single combat between the lines. Sitting Bull accepted.[43]

The two warriors raced their horses toward each other. Magpie fired his rifle first, missing Sitting Bull. Sitting Bull fired his rifle, blowing off the top of Magpie's head. Sitting Bull dismounted and scalped Magpie, mounted Magpie's prized horse, and slowly rode back to the Hunkpapa lines.[44]

Two companies of mounted troops led by Lieutenant Philo Clark arrived and began to press the Hunkpapas. Clark had been involved in circumstances surrounding Crazy Horse's death. The interpreter

Billy Garnett had claimed General George Crook and Lieutenant Clark had met with Red Cloud and other Oglala leaders, conspiring to have Crazy Horse killed. The man who killed Crazy Horse would be paid $300 and be given Clark's prized racehorse.[45]

Clark's men and scouts advanced toward Sitting Bull and his warriors, who slowly retreated, providing protection for the women and children. The main body of Hunkpapas learned of the attack and sixty warriors raced to assist Sitting Bull. With their new numbers, the Hunkpapas reversed the attack and began surrounding Clark and his men. Clark sent messengers to Miles requesting assistance. As Miles and the main body of troops arrived on the scene, Sitting Bull and his men dropped back.[46]

The Hunkpapas successfully crossed the Milk River but had to leave some possessions and meat behind. Miles's artillery fired a few parting shots at them as they headed toward the border and sanctuary in Canada. Miles proclaimed he had won a great victory over Sitting Bull at the Battle of Milk River.[47]

By 1880, the buffalo herds were becoming scarce. On May 23, Sitting Bull sent One Bull to Fort Buford to negotiate a return to the United States. The government's terms were still the same, and unacceptable to Sitting Bull, but people were becoming hungry and began crossing the border, surrendering.[48]

The Canadian government's policy toward the Lakotas changed. From now on the government would give them no help. They must return to the United States.[49]

Major James Walsh left that spring to plead their case with the Canadian government. In answer, the government reassigned him to Fort Qu'Appelle, 140 miles away from Sitting Bull. Walsh's replacement at the Wood Mountain Post was Inspector Lief Crozier, and Lieutenant Colonel Acheson Irvine replaced Colonel James Macleod at Fort Walsh. Both men's goal was to make Sitting Bull and his people leave Canada.[50]

Ignoring Sitting Bull, Crozier met with other Hunkpapa leaders. By the end of 1880, he, along with an American interpreter named Edward "Fish" Allison, had convinced Spotted Eagle,

Rain-in-the-Face, Gall, Jumping Bull, and other leaders to surrender to the Americans, along with their more than 1,500 followers.[51]

The winter of 1880–1881 was extremely cold. Sitting Bull and his Hunkpapas were back in the United States, camped along the Milk River. General Alfred Terry sent two separate columns of troops to converge on Sitting Bull's camp and capture it between them. He was alerted to their movements and escaped into Canada. But there was no rest for the Lakotas as the Blackfeet and Crees attempted to raid them.[52]

Sitting Bull was dealt another blow in January of 1881 when his trusted lieutenant Crow King defected with 350 people and surrendered. The Mounties' Lieutenant Colonel Irvine continued his attempts to persuade more Lakotas to return to the United States.[53]

Irvine's efforts did not fall on deaf ears. By April of 1881, he had persuaded the Oglala leader Low Dog to surrender to the Americans. He left with 135 people, taking most of the warriors with him. Sitting Bull was now left with mostly old men, women, and children.[54]

Sitting Bull began to talk about the possibility of surrendering, and on April 5, he sent a delegation headed by One Bull to Fort Buford to see how those who had surrendered were being treated. One Bull did not like what he had seen at Fort Buford, and Sitting Bull decided against surrendering. The Canadian Mounted Police became even more unfriendly, trying to force the Lakotas to leave. They would not even help the Lakotas when there was a clear case of horse theft. Cree warriors had stolen Lakota horses. Sitting Bull's men recognized one of the culprits, who took refuge inside the Wood Mountain Post. Inspector Crozier refused to do anything about the theft. It was no secret that some Canadian tribes were now threatening to kill Sitting Bull if they got the opportunity.[55]

On April 19, Sitting Bull moved the Hunkpapa village to Willow Bunch, thirty-five miles to the east of Wood Mountain Post, where his old friend Jean-Louis Légaré had established his new trading post. A few days later, Légaré held a feast for the hungry Hunkpapas and suggested it was time for them to surrender to the Americans.[56]

Légaré offered to lead another delegation to Fort Buford to discuss the possibility of Sitting Bull's surrender and see how those who had surrendered were living. He would also take along any people who wished to surrender. Sitting Bull agreed to Légaré's proposal.[57]

As Légaré's delegation was heading to Fort Buford, Sitting Bull left on April 28 to travel north to Fort Qu'Appelle to see Major Walsh and ask his advice. He took with him between two hundred and four hundred people, leaving sixty lodges of people behind at Willow Bunch.[58]

When Sitting Bull reached Fort Qu'Appelle, he found Walsh was not there. The Minister of the Interior had ordered Walsh to remain in the East.[59]

Sitting Bull and his band caught fish and killed ducks along Lake Qu'Appelle. They traded horses for flour with the local Catholic mission. But it was not enough. They were growing more hungry waiting for Walsh's return.[60]

During Sitting Bull's absence, Légaré and the delegation returned to Willow Bunch with a favorable report on conditions at Fort Buford. Another group of Hunkpapas agreed to travel south and surrender. This group included Many Horses, Sitting Bull's beloved oldest daughter. She was eloping with a man who had asked Sitting Bull for her hand in marriage, and Sitting Bull had refused.[61]

On May 25 and 26, Canadian Indian commissioner Edgar Dewdney met with Sitting Bull at Fort Qu'Appelle. Dewdney told Sitting Bull he needed to surrender to the Americans. Sitting Bull said he wanted to remain in Grandmother's Land. His people were hungry and needed food. Dewdney said that if Sitting Bull and all his people agreed to surrender and began their trip south, he would give them food. No agreement was reached.[62]

On June 16, Sitting Bull's Hunkpapas began heading back to Willow Bunch where he hoped Walsh would come and talk with him. Upon reaching Willow Bunch in early July, Sitting Bull became desperate. The Hunkpapas were out of food and people were hungry. He told Légaré that if he threw a feast for his people, he would do whatever Légaré wanted.[63]

Légaré told Sitting Bull he had spent almost all of his money feeding Sitting Bull's people and it was time for them to surrender. On July 12, Légaré set out for Fort Buford with most of Sitting Bull's people. Sitting Bull did not go with them, and tried to get them to come back. The next day Sitting Bull and the last holdouts gave up and joined the procession south.[64]

Légaré sent a messenger to Major David Brotherton, commander at Fort Buford, to notify him that Sitting Bull's band was coming in to surrender and they needed food. Brotherton sent six wagons of food, which reached Légaré and Sitting Bull's party on July 16, about fifty miles from the fort. The Hunkpapas were fed well.[65]

The next day, Captain Walter Clifford, a sergeant, and five Indian scouts from Fort Buford met Sitting Bull and his party to escort them the rest of the way to the fort. Sitting Bull questioned Clifford about his daughter, Many Horses. He had heard she had been placed in irons at Fort Yates. Clifford told Sitting Bull it was not true, but Sitting Bull did not believe him. He considered the idea that they should make a break for it and hide out along the Tongue River where they could continue to hunt, but he thought better of it and resigned himself to his fate.[66]

Sitting Bull and his Hunkpapas arrived at Fort Buford at noon on July 19, 1881. His followers had been reduced to 44 men and 143 women and children. They only had 14 horses left, and many of the people rode in Légaré's carts. Sitting Bull was dressed in poor clothing and had a large handkerchief bound around his head with the edge pulled down partly over his eyes, which were severely infected. Clifford showed them where they could camp behind the fort's storehouse and gymnasium. Major Brotherton welcomed Sitting Bull and said they could eat and rest. They had to surrender their weapons and horses, but Sitting Bull could keep his Winchester carbine until the next day, July 20, which was set for Sitting Bull's official surrender.[67]

At 11:00 a.m. the next day, Sitting Bull and thirty-two of his men, as well as his five-year-old son, Crow Foot, entered Major Brotherton's office. Brotherton was there, as well as Captain Clifford, two other officers, Légaré, an interpreter, a reporter, and the Canadian Mounted Policeman, Captain Alexander Macdonell, to represent his country. They all sat down. Sitting Bull, his Winchester on the floor between his feet, sat beside Brotherton.[68]

Brotherton spoke first, stating that Sitting Bull and his band were to be sent down the Missouri River to the Standing Rock Agency, where they would join the rest of the Hunkpapas. They would be treated the same as all the others who had surrendered, and they would not be harmed.[69]

Brotherton asked Sitting Bull if he wanted to speak. Staring ahead, Sitting Bull did not say anything for what seemed like five minutes. He then spoke to the Hunkpapas, but what he said was not translated. He gestured to Crow Foot, who picked up Sitting Bull's Winchester and handed it to Brotherton.[70]

Sitting Bull then said to Brotherton:

I surrender this rifle to you through my young son, whom I now desire to teach in this manner that he has become a friend of the Americans. I wish him to learn the habits of the whites and to be educated as their sons are educated. I wish it to be remembered that I was the last man of my tribe to surrender my rifle. This boy has given it to you, and he now wants to know how he is going to make a living.[71]

Sitting Bull continued, saying that he wanted a reservation along the Little Missouri River for his people, and to be able to visit Walsh and his friends in Canada and trade there whenever he wanted. He was concerned about his daughter, Many Horses, and wanted her to be brought to him. "I wish to continue my old life of hunting," he said. But it was not to be.[72]

Sitting Bull surrenders at Fort Buford, Dakota Territory.

CHAPTER 9

Geronimo's Raids and Sitting Bull, Prisoner of War, 1881–1884

THE NIGHT OF SEPTEMBER 30, 1881, CHIRICAHUA LEADERS GERONIMO, Juh, Bonito, Naiche, Chatto, and Chihuahua, with over 375 men, women, and children, broke out of San Carlos, their destination—Mexico. Less than a third of the people had horses to ride. They would need to find more. Fortunately, agency officials had allowed the men and boys to keep their firearms, and they had plenty of ammunition.[1]

They first traveled upriver on the Gila for about twelve miles, then began heading south through the San Pedro Valley. Splitting into four groups, they would later rendezvous at Black Rock in the Santa Teresa Mountains. Geronimo and his Bedonkohes traveled with Juh's Nednhi. Along the way, Geronimo led a raid on a ranch and two freight trains, stealing fifty horses and mules.[2]

On October 2, twenty miles north of Fort Grant, they attacked a freight wagon train bound for San Carlos, killing six men and taking supplies, weapons, ammunition, and over a hundred mules. Following the road south toward Fort Grant, they came upon John Moulds, who was hauling supplies to Cedar Springs station. They killed him and took his supplies and four horses. Twenty minutes later they attacked four soldiers and a civilian telegraph operator repairing a telegraph line, killing them all, wrecking the line, and taking their horses and weapons.[3]

Captain Reuben Bernard—leading a three-company detachment of the First and Sixth Cavalry, made up of one hundred troopers and more than thirty Western Apaches—followed the Chiricahuas. Shortly after discovering the bodies of the five members of the telegraph line detail, they followed the Chiricahuas' trail to the Pinaleno foothills, where they were fired upon. Dismounting, the soldiers fought in a skirmish line. By day's end, they had fired over four thousand rounds at what would be known as the Battle at K-H Butte. A sergeant was killed and three men were wounded during the fight. Bernard and his men rode to Fort Grant where they regrouped and stocked up on more ammunition.[4]

The next day, Geronimo, Juh, and Naiche led a raiding party to Henry Hooker's Sierra Bonita Ranch, making off with 135 horses. They stole 51 horses and mules from another ranch and freight train, and that night, they killed an old rancher named Josh Vance. The Chiricahuas now had more than 500 head of animals and were making good time toward Mexico.[5]

On October 4, Bernard's troops were back in the field. They had traveled by the new railroad to the Dragoon Mountains where they joined forces with two companies of the black Ninth Cavalry, led by Captain Henry Carroll from New Mexico.[6] The combined troops headed up a narrow canyon in the Dragoons, hoping to surprise the Chiricahuas.[7]

The fugitives had made camp in Grapevine Canyon, where they had come upon Mike Noonan's cattle herd. Killing seventy-nine steers, they had finished butchering the carcasses and were in the process of packing the meat. Eager Apache scouts, in advance of the troops, opened fire on the Chiricahuas before the troops could get into position. Some believed the scouts did it to warn the Chiricahuas.[8]

The warriors fought a rearguard action while the women and children escaped south along the eastern foothills of the Dragoons. The battle went on for the entire day. Three soldiers were wounded. Bernard thought one Chiricahua might have been killed. Three children and a woman were captured. Some supplies were left behind, as well as forty head of livestock. The Apache scouts believed the

Chiricahuas were headed in the direction of the new boomtown, Tombstone.[9]

After John Clum had left San Carlos as Indian agent, he went to Tucson and eventually wound up in Tombstone, where he founded a newspaper, *Epitaph*, ran for mayor, and won. On October 4, a rider galloped into town shouting "Geronimo is coming! Geronimo is coming!" The mine whistles blew to alert the townspeople. Determined to go after Geronimo, Mayor Clum formed a thirty-five-man posse that included a few notable characters, such as the Earp brothers, Wyatt, Virgil, and Morgan, as well as Cochise County sheriff Johnny Behan.[10]

"Remember men, no quarter, no prisoners," Clum announced to his posse. "I delivered Geronimo to the army once, in irons. They turned him loose. If we get him this time, we will send him back to the army, nailed up in a long, narrow box, with a paper lily on his chest."[11]

As the posse rode east toward where they suspected the fleeing Chiricahuas would be heading toward Mexico, they were hit by an intense, long-lasting thunderstorm. On the east side of the Dragoon Mountains, they came upon Captain Bernard and his cavalry, who were encamped, waiting for the storm to subside. Clum and his men pressed on and finally took shelter in a cramped line shack for the night. The next day, they followed the fugitives' trail until it crossed the Mexican border. There was no use continuing, so the cold and soaking-wet posse turned around and headed home.[12]

The Apaches had continued raiding ranches for horses and mules, including stealing fourteen horses from Frank McLaury's ranch on October 5.[13]

After traveling 216 miles and successfully fighting the army in three rearguard actions, the Chiricahuas crossed the border on October 7, 1881. The US Army could not follow them without Mexican permission.[14]

Juh led the Chiricahuas toward his sanctuary in Chihuahua's Carcay Mountains, near Janos. Meeting the Chihenne leader and Geronimo's brother-in-law Nana and his people in the mountains, they decided to play a practical joke on Geronimo, who was farther behind, leading a party of warriors. They hid themselves in the rocks and when Geronimo, relaxed and unobservant, rode up to their position, Nana and the others popped out from their hiding positions to surprise him, and joked at Geronimo's expense.

"I knew all the time you were here," Geronimo said.

"You did not," Nana responded. "And you, the sly fox of the Apaches!"[15]

The Chiricahua bands held a warm reunion, feasting and dancing all night. Agreeing to work together under Juh's leadership, the combined bands now numbered over 425 people.[16]

The Chiricahuas traded stolen American livestock for corn and ammunition in Janos while they raided in Sonora and Arizona. Juh had put out peace feelers to the Chihuahua government. On November 9, Juh and Geronimo met with Colonel Joaquin Terrazas, east of Casas Grandes. Terrazas was the brother of the governor. Juh asked for peace and a home in the Carcay Mountains. Terrazas said he would recommend that to his brother. He gave them presents and invited them to town, but they were wary of him and did not go. It was a good thing they did not, as Terrazas had plans to ambush them once they reached town.[17]

The Chiricahuas continued to raid. In December, Geronimo led forty warriors into Sonora, attacking settlements in the Sierra Madre's western foothills. On December 19, they attacked a mule train and then killed two mail carriers. The next day they ambushed a detachment of soldiers who were on their trail, killing five of them. They later fought another group of soldiers, killing three. In three days, Geronimo's raiders had killed fifteen people, wounded five, and captured two children. Two days later, they killed five men at a mescal camp. Troops were sent in pursuit, but Geronimo and his men ambushed them, wounding the leader and four of his men and killing fourteen of their horses, forcing the pursuers to retreat. Returning to their rancheria with their loot, they set off again to attack more targets in Sonora, stealing 139 head of livestock and, after driving off the packers, capturing a mule train.[18]

Believing peace with the Mexicans was futile, the Chiricahuas needed more warriors. Loco, Zele, and Chiva's bands—totaling three hundred people, including fifty warriors—had remained at San Carlos. Juh sent messages to Loco and the San Carlos Chiricahua leaders, inviting them to join him in Mexico. They did not come. The Chiricahuas in Mexico warned them that if they did not come voluntarily, they would come and get them.[19]

General Orlando Willcox learned of the threats by the Chiricahuas in Mexico and sent out patrols along the border, as did the army in New Mexico. The San Carlos Agency police were on alert.[20]

Geronimo volunteered to lead a party to San Carlos to bring the Chihennes to their Mexico stronghold. Sixty-three warriors would go with him, including Naiche, Chatto, Chihuahua, Mangas, Bonito, and Kaytennae, as well as Victorio's sister Lozen, a woman warrior with a special Power—the ability to determine the location of enemies. Standing with outstretched arms and palms pointing up, she would slowly rotate until her palms began tingling and turning colors, indicating the direction of the enemy. The more intense the tingling, the closer the enemy.[21]

Before Geronimo's party left, Colonel Terrazas met with the Chiricahua leaders again, on April 8 and 10, 1882, trying to lure them into Casas Grandes, where he planned to ply them with liquor and kill them. Terrazas refused to talk with Juh; he would only talk with Geronimo, who acted as spokesman for the Chiricahua leaders. Again, they were suspicious and did not fall for Terrazas's bait.[22]

On April 11, Geronimo and his 63 warriors headed north to retrieve the Chihennes at San Carlos. Juh and Nana with about 30 warriors remained in Mexico to protect the 325 women and children. Where Geronimo's party slipped across the border into the United States and what route they took north is up for debate.[23]

George Stevens, the sheriff of Graham County, Arizona, lived in Safford. Twenty miles north of Safford, near Ash Flats, Stevens owned a ranch employing Mexicans and White Mountain Apaches to care for his flock of ten thousand sheep. Stevens's ranch foreman was a Mexican named Victoriano Mestas, whom Geronimo had captured when he was a boy. Geronimo had treated him well, until Mestas was traded to a white rancher. Approximately nine Mexican men, two Mexican women, Richard Bylas and three other White

Mountain Apache men with their families, as well as Mestas, his wife, and their three children were at the ranch when Geronimo's raiders hit. There are four accounts of what took place, all telling the same story but with varying details.[24]

On the afternoon of April 16, a White Mountain Apache galloped onto the ranch property and told Mestas he had seen Chiricahua warriors and believed they were going to raid the ranch. Mestas and Bylas had everyone move to high ground, where they built a fortification. Early the next morning before dawn, a voice called, "It is me, Mestas; it is Geronimo. I have many men and they are hungry. We will not harm you, for I am Geronimo, your friend."[25]

Bylas warned Mestas not to listen to Geronimo, and shouted, "You lie, Geronimo—you want to kill us. Always you are a liar."[26]

The exchange went back and forth. Mestas remembered Geronimo had been kind to him when he was a boy, and allowed him and his warriors into their fortification. The warriors killed sheep, and the ranch women began cooking mutton and tortillas for them. Geronimo did not like mutton and had a pony belonging to the son of George Stevens killed and butchered for his meal.[27]

When the warriors had finished eating, Geronimo gave a signal and his men disarmed the Mexican herders and bound their hands behind them. Mestas was wearing an embroidered Mexican shirt. Geronimo ordered him to take it off because he wanted it, and did not want to get blood on it. He ordered Mestas, his family, and the Mexican women tied up.[28]

Realizing Geronimo was going to kill all the Mexicans, Bylas said, "Why do you want to kill these people after they have fed you and you promised to harm no one?" Naiche and Chatto agreed with Bylas, and added they would have lost many men if they had attacked.[29]

But then Chihuahua said, "These people are Mexicans and they are our enemies. Always the Mexicans have lied to us and killed our people." With that, Geronimo ordered a rope run through the prisoners' bound hands. They were marched up a hill where the warriors shot and stabbed the defenseless men, women, and children. Mestas was tortured until one of the warriors split his skull with a hatchet, and others used rocks to bash in the skulls of his wife and two of their little boys.[30]

The warriors found they had missed nine-year-old Stanislaus Mestas, who Bylas's wife had hidden behind her. "Kill him too," Geronimo said, but one warrior, Jelikine, protected the boy, threatening Geronimo with a spear. Geronimo relented and let the boy live.[31]

As the war party rode away, they took the White Mountain men with them and left two Chiricahuas behind to make sure none of the White Mountain women went for help. Changing his mind again, Geronimo sent men back to the ranch to kill Stanislaus. Bylas's wife begged for his life. They listened to her pleas and said they would tell Geronimo that they had not been able to find the boy.[32]

The raiders stopped near Ash Flats for the rest of the day. Geronimo sang four songs, after which his Power informed him they would safely reach San Carlos. They traveled at night, arriving at the ridges north of the San Carlos subagency, where they hid during the day of April 18.[33]

That night, at approximately 7:00 p.m., the raiders implemented their plan. Geronimo took most of the warriors and rode toward the San Carlos main agency eighteen miles west, where Loco and Zele's rancherias were located. Bonito and several men went to Chiva's rancheria, consisting of four men and thirty women and children, and got them moving. About 9:00 p.m., Chihuahua and seven men rode a half-mile west of the subagency and cut the telegraph line to the main agency.[34]

Three hours later a Western Apache scout arrived at the subagency with the news that Chiricahua warriors were riding toward the main agency. Telegraph operator Ed Pierson tried to send a message to the main agency but realized the line was down. Later that night, he and a few Apache scouts found the cut line and repaired it. He sent the message, but Stumpy Hunter, the operator at the main agency, was sleeping.[35]

Geronimo and his men reached the main agency about 1:00 a.m. on April 19. One man, a Nednhi, went to get Zele at his rancheria while Naiche and Chatto went to Loco's rancheria. After the Nednhi brought Zele to Loco's wickiup, Naiche and Chatto told the two leaders they and their people must leave with them, or they would be killed.[36]

Shortly before sunrise, Loco's rancheria awoke to shouts. Jason Betzinez, who was a young boy at the time, said, "We saw a long line of Apache warriors spread out along the west side of the camp and coming our way with guns in their hands. . . . One of their leaders was shouting, 'Take them all! No one is to be left in camp. Shoot down anyone who refuses to go with us!'" Geronimo had ordered his men to shoot anyone who would not leave.[37]

The people were given little time to pack. Betzinez said they had no time to gather their horses or eat before they started moving. Geronimo and about thirty warriors led the three hundred Chiricahuas from San Carlos east along the Gila River as Chihuahua and others hung back as a rear guard.[38]

Stumpy Hunter finally received the alert from the subagency. He went to Albert Sterling, the chief of the Indian police, and was relaying the message when they heard two shots from Loco's rancheria. Not waiting for the Indian police to catch and saddle their horses, Sterling and an Apache sergeant named Sagotal mounted their horses and raced in the direction of the shots. Chihuahua and his men ambushed them. Sterling's horse was killed, and he was shot in the hand. As he tried to make his escape on foot, he was shot twice and killed. Sagotal raced back to the main agency.[39]

When Sagotal reached the agency, he found the Indian police were ready to ride, and Sterling's friend Charles Connell agreed to lead them. When they arrived at the ambush site, they found Sterling's body mutilated, with his head cut off. Chihuahua's men were still there. They shouted to Sagotal to go away; they did not want to fight fellow Apaches. But the police stayed. The Chiricahua warriors opened fire. Connell took cover behind Sterling's headless body. The fight ended when a bullet slammed into Sagotal's head, killing him. The Indian police withdrew, and the Chiricahua rear guard followed the reluctant fugitives and their rescuers.[40]

As Geronimo led the people northeast along the Gila River, they stole twenty-three horses and two mules from a contractor's herd and ransacked a freight wagon train filled with liquor and clothing, taking the horses and burning the wagons. Knowing the cavalry would soon follow, they turned north, entering the Gila Mountains, and then continued east. Ten miles east of the subagency, at Green Hill, their advance guard came upon three prospectors and killed them. Geronimo sent a raiding party to George Stevens's ranch to steal sheep.[41]

Jason Betzinez said, "Geronimo was pretty much the main leader. . . . Geronimo seemed to be the most intelligent and resourceful as well as the most vigorous and farsighted. In times of danger he was the man to be relied upon."[42]

After traveling twenty-four hours, they came to Ash Flats, twenty miles north of Fort Thomas, where they rested. The Stevens ranch raiding party arrived with a flock of several hundred sheep to feed the people.[43]

From there they separated into smaller groups and would rendezvous later. One group skirmished with troops at Ash Creek but got away. Chiricahua warriors killed five men at Gold Gulch and nine men at Church's Smelter. Four Mexicans were killed at the Coronado ranch, and later, three Americans. Felix Knox ran into the Chiricahuas and fought them, buying time for his family and their Mexican employee to escape before he was killed. Naiche respected Knox's courage, and instead of mutilating his body, covered it with a blanket. By the end of the day on April 22, more than fifty people had been killed by the marauders as the army mobilized to search for them.[44]

Warriors had been attacking Hill's ranch to steal more horses. The main body of fugitives waited out of sight behind a hill as an Apache girl began her first menstruation. This was a most important event in a girl's life, marking her entry into womanhood, and it was vital the traditional Apache ceremony be held for her. It was normally a four-day event, but since the warriors were in a hurry to get the people to Mexico, they held a shortened version of the ceremony.[45]

As the sun set on April 22, the warriors who had been attacking the ranch returned to the main group with several more horses and mules. The leaders decided the people would continue to travel south that night, through the upper San Simon Valley along the foothills of the Peloncillo Mountains, to reach the rendezvous location at Horseshoe Canyon, four miles north of Stein's Peak. During the moonless night, twenty-eight members of Loco's band, who did not want to go to Mexico, slipped away and headed north to Navajo country, reaching Fort Wingate on May 10.[46]

The Chiricahuas turned east, heading into the Peloncillos and arriving at their rendezvous location, Horseshoe Canyon, by daybreak on April 23. There they rested and began cooking their meals.[47]

Troops throughout Arizona and western New Mexico were searching for the Chiricahua raiders. Lieutenant Colonel George Forsyth with five companies of the Fourth Cavalry and a contingent of Indian scouts was using a train on the east-to-west-running Southern Pacific Railroad in his search. Forsyth had been on General Phil Sheridan's staff during the Civil War and was one of the heroes of the 1868 Beecher's Island fight against Cheyenne warriors.[48]

Forsyth sent a small detachment of six Indian scouts and one enlisted man led by Lieutenant David McDonald to investigate the Stein's Peak area for any signs of the Chiricahuas. At 8:00 a.m. on April 23, the scouts found the trail of twelve warriors headed into Doubtful Canyon. As they followed the trail, the Chiricahuas ambushed them, killing four of the scouts. McDonald and his men retreated until they were joined by six Yavapai scouts. After sending a messenger back to Forsyth, McDonald returned to the scene of the ambush, where he saw Chiricahua warriors dancing and celebrating over the bodies of his scouts. McDonald shot and killed one of them as the rest took cover.[49]

Forsyth and his five companies arrived shortly after noon. The warriors had taken positions along the south and west rims of Horseshoe Canyon while the women and children were higher up on the mountainside. The troops opened fire at 1:00 p.m. The fight lasted for two and a half hours. As the troops advanced in skirmish order, the warriors retreated to new positions. Two of Forsyth's men were killed and four wounded. None of the warriors were killed.[50]

Even though he estimated the warriors to be between sixty and one hundred, Forsyth did not believe these warriors were the San Carlos raiders. He broke off the fight and marched his troops north toward the Gila River.[51]

That night, Geronimo led the people from the western end of Doubtful Canyon into the San Simon Valley. Traveling south, they crossed the railroad tracks. Following along the eastern side of the Chiricahua Mountains, they reached the north side of Blue Mountain, where they found water late on the morning of April 24. Most of them rested while raiding parties went out, killing and plundering.[52]

The Chiricahuas continued south that afternoon. For the next thirty-six hours, the leaders pushed the people southward along the Chiricahua Mountains and through the Guadalupe Mountains, taking only a few rest breaks. South of Cloverdale, New Mexico, they crossed the border into Mexico on the morning of April 26.[53]

They continued seventeen miles south of the border to a valley on the eastern slopes of the Espuelas Mountains, where they set up camp to rest and celebrate. Believing they were safe from attack, they did not post guards.[54]

Unknown to the Chiricahuas, US troops had illegally crossed the border into Mexico as they followed their trail. Captain Tullius Tupper led two companies of the Sixth Cavalry as well as a contingent of Indian scouts under the leadership of Chief of Scouts Al Sieber. Sieber and some of his scouts found the camp of the celebrating Chiricahuas the night of April 27. After hearing Sieber's report, Tupper worked out a plan of attack with Captain William Rafferty where they would attack the camp from two sides. The Indian scouts would be on one side and the cavalry on the other. Once everyone was in position, the scouts would open fire first, and then the cavalry would open fire.[55]

The cavalry was still riding to get to their position on the morning of April 28 when some of the scouts spotted people walking toward a mescal roasting pit. Seeking revenge for the death of his brother, Sagotal, one of the scouts shot and killed a young woman. The shots alerted the camp. Men rushed to grab their weapons as the women and children ran for cover. The cavalry charged and then dismounted to exchange fire with the Chiricahuas.[56]

Geronimo and several warriors led the Chiricahua defense. The fight lasted most of the morning, until Tupper's men began to run low on ammunition. Taking seventy-nine captured horses with them, the cavalry withdrew back across the border. In the end, the Chiricahuas killed one soldier and wounded two others while the army killed at least three women and five men, including Loco's son.[57]

Concerned American troops might attack again, that night, the Chiricahuas continued their trek southward toward the safety of Juh's sanctuary in the Carcay Mountains. By 5:00 a.m. on April 29, they had separated into three groups as they followed Alisos Creek southeast near the Sierra Madre foothills. Naiche, Chatto, and Kaytennae led a fifteen-warrior advance guard about an hour ahead of the main body of people, who were strung out in a long line consisting mostly of walking women and children guarded by a few men. About two miles behind them, Geronimo and Chihuahua led thirty-two warriors who were ready to fight any pursuing American troops.[58]

Unknown to the Chiricahuas, 250 troops of the Sixth Mexican Infantry knew they were coming, and their commander, Lieutenant Colonel Lorenzo García, planned an ambush along Alisos Creek. The troops remained hidden as Naiche and Chatto's advance guard rode past. It was 5:00 a.m. when the main body arrived. García sprung his trap.[59]

The troops fired a volley into the women and children before they charged, shooting and bayoneting people. Men, women, and children scattered in every direction.[60]

Hearing the gunfire, shouts, and screams, Geronimo, Chihuahua, and their men raced forward to the scene of carnage. Geronimo led the men in a countercharge that pushed the troops back. He shouted to the warriors to gather around him to make a stand to protect the remaining women and children. Geronimo and his warriors led them to an arroyo where they took a defensive position against the troops.[61]

At approximately 10:00 a.m. García sent a detachment of infantry commanded by Captain Antonio Rada on a bayonet charge to rout the Chiricahuas. The men cursed and shouted "Geronimo, this is your last day!" as they charged. The warriors fired into the oncoming soldiers, who only made it halfway to their objective before Rada was shot and killed. Geronimo claimed that he killed an officer during the fight.[62]

Several Chihenne detractors said Geronimo acted cowardly by hiding with the women during this fight, but they are at odds with others who said he acted bravely. The fighting continued sporadically throughout the afternoon. Both sides ran low on ammunition. Naiche, Chatto, and Kaytennae's men, who were a mile in advance of the main party, had stopped to rest and smoke, never returning to help in the fight.[63]

In the evening, the Chiricahua leaders decided they needed to make a run for it to the foothills of the Carcay Mountains.[64] The prairie grass was set on fire, either by the Chiricahuas to provide a distraction, or by the Mexicans to try to force the defenders out of the arroyo. Fearing the little children might make noise during their escape and give away their location, there was talk about killing them. At least one mother choked her child to death because she did not want her baby to be a Mexican slave. Geronimo, along with most of the warriors, women, and children, slipped out of the arroyo while his cousin Fun and a few other warriors remained to cover the retreat.[65]

By the end of the day, the Chiricahuas had killed two officers and nineteen of García's men, wounding an additional thirteen. García's men counted seventy-eight dead Chiricahua men, women, and children, and he had captured thirty-three women and children. The captives included Loco's sixteen-year-old daughter, who was never heard from again.[66]

The survivors met at their prearranged rendezvous location. The next morning, they looked from their high vantage point to see off in the distance the Mexican troops meeting more troops—they were Americans. The Chiricahuas expected to see a fight between the Mexicans and Americans but were disappointed.[67]

The American troops were those led by Lieutenant Colonel George Forsyth. He had realized his mistake riding north to the Gila River and had turned south, following Geronimo's trail into Mexico, where García and his men met him. García told Forsyth he was illegally in Mexico. Forsyth explained that he had been following the renegade Chiricahuas. García said they had destroyed most of them and showed Forsyth the battlefield where unburied bodies still remained. Forsyth's doctors gave García's wounded soldiers medical attention as Forsyth headed back north.[68]

On the morning of May 1, Geronimo led the survivors south toward Juh's stronghold, forty miles away. He sent out a raiding party that returned with cattle, which the people slaughtered and ate. Knowing they were worn out, Geronimo allowed them to rest for two days. They continued on, arriving at Juh's rancheria on May 5, 1882. With the arrival of Geronimo and the survivors from San Carlos, the remnants of the four Chiricahua bands were now all together, totaling 650 people. Although he had Chihenne detractors, Geronimo was considered co-leader with Juh.[69]

Geronimo and Juh decided to try to make a treaty again with Mexicans in Chihuahua. Jason Betzinez believed Geronimo was interested in acquiring whiskey. About May 18, Juh and Geronimo met with Colonel Joaquin Terrazas and Casas Grandes officials, who welcomed the Chiricahuas to their town to trade.[70]

Between 200 and 250 Chiricahuas set up camp along the San Miguel River, three miles southwest of Casas Grandes. Men and women entered the town and traded with the citizens.[71]

The Chiricahuas had no idea that Terrazas was planning to massacre them in town. He had 560 troops waiting nearby, but kept delaying the attack, waiting for more Chiricahuas to become comfortable and enter the town. On May 24, however, the Chiricahuas started to become suspicious and stayed away. Terrazas changed his plans, deciding to surround and attack their camp on the morning of May 25.[72]

That same morning, the Casas Grandes officials sent the Chiricahuas a wagonload of bottled mescal and a second wagon filled with corn they could use to make tiswin. While many of the people drank throughout the afternoon and into the evening, Terrazas led his men to the camp and began to surround it.[73]

The troops to the southwest were still not in position when, just before dawn, other troops began firing prematurely. Alerted to the attack, Geronimo and Juh led many of the people out of the camp to high ground in the southwest, where the troops had not yet taken position. There they would make their stand.[74]

The soldiers entered the camp, slitting the throats of men too drunk to escape. For some reason, Terrazas did not have his troops attack the Chiricahuas on the hill, who were able to fade away and escape.[75]

Terrazas's troops killed ten Chiricahuas and captured thirty-seven men and women. A few days later, Lieutenant Colonel Lorenzo García and his troops arrived in town. Knowing that many of these Chiricahuas had been in the fight at Alisos Creek, Terrazas turned over twenty-five prisoners to García, whose troops told them to run and then shot them all. One of the captured women who was not turned over to García was Geronimo's second wife, Chee-hash-kish. They had been married since 1852, and she was the mother of Chappo and Lulu. She was sent south and later married another captive Chiricahua, never to see Geronimo again.[76]

In late June 1882, Juh remained in his Sierra Madre sanctuary with most of the people while Geronimo took Chihuahua and Kaytennae and thirty men and their families on brutal raids into Sonora. Anyone caught by Geronimo was tortured, killed, and mutilated. Geronimo knew no mercy for Mexicans, or, for that matter, any Americans he caught south of the border.[77]

The evening of August 27, Geronimo's warriors entered the Castillo ranch house as the family was eating supper. A Castillo cousin watched from a hiding place as the warriors shot and killed the grandparents, parents, and five children. The warriors cheered and then mutilated the bodies. When they were finished, they burned the buildings and rode away.[78]

Sometime during 1882, Geronimo's sixth wife, Zi-yeh, gave birth to a boy, Fenton. However, tragedy struck when Geronimo's sister Ishton, Juh's wife, was shot and killed during an attack by Mexican troops. In the same attack, their daughter was shot in the leg. It did not heal properly, and a year later it would be amputated at San Carlos.[79]

Back in the United States, events were taking place that would affect the lives of the Chiricahuas. The deaths of the Apache prophet Nakadoklini and others at Cibecue Creek; the White Mountain Apache attacks; Geronimo's breakout, and his forceful rescue of Loco and the Chihennes, had resulted in government officials blaming each other for what had gone wrong. In his attempt to lay the blame on others, General Orlando Willcox, commander of the Department of Arizona, disputed with General in Chief William Sherman, eventually going over Sherman's head by sending a letter directly to President Chester A. Arthur. In July 1882, Willcox received notice that he was being relieved of command of the Department of Arizona.[80]

General George Crook took command on September 4, 1882, and went to work hiring more Apache scouts to track down Apache raiders and using pack mules to haul field supplies rather than wagons, giving greater mobility to troops chasing Apaches. Crook put two trusted, competent officers in charge of the Apache scouts—Captain Emmet Crawford and Lieutenant Charles Gatewood. Crawford had been with Crook on his Big Horn and Yellowstone Expedition against Sitting Bull's village, and had been one of the leaders in the attack on American Horse's village at Slim Buttes. Gatewood had led Apache scouts in the fight against Victorio. His scouts liked and trusted him.[81]

During Geronimo's 1882 summer raids through Sonora, troops were constantly on the hunt for his warriors. Occasionally, they would catch up with them and skirmish. One night in September, Geronimo said they would be attacked by Mexican troops the next day, and told the warriors where and at what moment they would appear. He had predicted correctly. The women and children were sent to hide in high mountain slopes while Geronimo and his men watched the troop movements. They followed the soldiers and attacked them later that day, capturing all of their horses.[82]

By early October, Geronimo and his band had rejoined Juh in his stronghold. After sending out two successful raiding parties throughout Chihuahua, killing many people and stealing a large amount of livestock, Juh and Geronimo led the people north and set up their rancheria thirty miles from the town of Galeana.[83]

One of their reasons for moving was revenge. Juan Mata Ortíz, one of the leaders of the attack at Casas Grandes, owned a nearby ranch. Juh and Geronimo began sending out raiding parties hoping to lure Mexicans into Chocolate Pass where they could ambush them, but no one would take the bait and enter the pass.[84]

On November 12, 1882, Chiricahua raiders attacked Ortíz's ranch, killing a vaquero and stealing livestock. The next day, Ortíz led twenty-one men from Galeana and followed the raiders' trail into Chocolate Pass.[85]

Geronimo and Juh were waiting for them with between 130 and 140 warriors divided into two groups. Their hope was that when the first volley was fired into the Mexicans, they would ride forward and be trapped between the two groups. This did not happen.[86]

The first volley killed several Mexicans and horses. Ortíz led his men to the top of a high hill where they made a stand. Geronimo, Juh, and other older warriors provided covering fire while the young men charged up the hill and overwhelmed the Mexicans in hand-to-hand combat.[87]

One Mexican mounted a horse and started to race away. "Let him go!" Geronimo shouted. "He will tell the rest of the soldiers in town what has happened whereupon more Mexicans will come out to the rescue. In that way we can kill other soldiers."[88]

Two Chiricahua warriors were killed, along with all the Mexicans. It was reported they captured Ortíz and burned him at the stake. His body was found mutilated and partially burned.[89]

Geronimo and Chihuahua led 250 people to the Bugatseka stronghold in Sonora while Juh led the rest of the people into more rugged country. For the first six months of 1883, Geronimo and his warriors conducted successful raids from Bugatseka to the west, into Sonora.[90]

However, Juh was not so fortunate. Mexican troops had located his camp, and on January 23, 1883, they attacked at dawn. Juh and the warriors were able to regroup outside camp and defend the survivors, but fourteen people had been killed, including one of Juh's wives and a son-in-law and Bonito's wife and child. Among the thirty-seven captives were two of Geronimo's wives, one who called herself Mañanita, and the other, fifth wife Shit-sha-she, and two of his children, as well as Chatto's wife and two children.[91]

Juh and the survivors went to Bugatseka where Geronimo's people took them in. Juh had fallen from favor for allowing a surprise attack to happen on his rancheria. The people now looked to Geronimo for leadership. Geronimo and his warriors continued to brutally raid in Sonora to replenish food, horses, and supplies. The estimates of men, women, and children killed in Geronimo's raids ranged from 93 to 115. One report claimed that 27 of these were Americans killed south of the border.[92]

Geronimo's people needed more cartridges for their guns. Since the guns were manufactured in America, it made sense to the Chiricahuas to raid into the United States. Chatto and Bonito led twenty-six men on a raid into Arizona and New Mexico to gather weapons and more cartridges. In six days, they traveled four hundred miles across the Southwest, killing eleven White Eyes and stealing large amounts of livestock, guns, and ammunition. One warrior was killed during the raid and another deserted and returned to the White Mountain Reservation. He was a White Mountain Apache named Tazoe, or, as the White Eyes called him, Peaches, whose Chiricahua wife and their children had been killed in the attack by García.[93]

Toward the end of the raid, Chatto, Bonito, and their men came upon Judge Hamilton McComas, his wife Juniata, and their six-year-old son Charley, who were traveling from Silver City to Lordsburg, New Mexico, and had stopped to picnic along the road. The family jumped in their wagon and tried to outrun the raiders, who easily caught up with them, shooting the judge dead and bashing in Juniata's skull. Bonito took Charley as his captive.[94]

Adding to the outrage felt by the citizens of Arizona and New Mexico over Chatto and Bonito's raid and murders across the Southwest, the murders of Judge McComas and his wife and the capture of young Charley made them furious. They wanted Charley recovered.[95]

In July 1882, the United States and Mexico had signed an agreement that each country's troops could cross the border into the other country if they were in close pursuit of marauding Indians. General Crook had met with the governors of Chihuahua and Sonora and Mexican military officers, and they all welcomed him to cross the border to pursue the Chiricahuas.[96]

General Sherman issued orders for Crook to pursue the Chiricahuas into Mexico. Crook stationed cavalry units at key points along the border to prevent further raids into the United States. He put together an expedition to enter Mexico, consisting of 42 cavalry troopers under the command of Captain Adna Chaffee, and 193 Apache scouts under the command of Captain Crawford and Lieutenant Gatewood. In addition, he had a pack train of 350 mules managed by 76 packers. Other notable characters who were part of the expedition were Crook's aide de camp, Lieutenant John Bourke; Chief of Scouts Al Sieber; Archie McIntosh; Sam Bowman; and interpreter Mickey Free.[97] Crook also had a scout who could help him find Chiricahua strongholds—the White Mountain Apache Tazoe, or Peaches, who had deserted from Chatto and Bonito's raid.[98]

Crook's expedition gathered at John Slaughter's San Bernardino Ranch on the Arizona side of the border and crossed into Mexico on May 1, 1883. They followed the rivers south and then on May 7, Peaches led them eastward, climbing into the Sierra Madre Mountains toward Bugatseka, Geronimo's stronghold.[99]

On May 15, Crook's scouts came upon the rancheria at Bugatseka and charged in, catching the Chiricahuas by surprise. Most of the warriors were away and the scouts easily captured the village, killing seven men and at least one old woman trying to surrender, while capturing two boys, a girl, and a young woman, who was Bonito's daughter.[100]

Bonito's daughter told Crook her father had recently returned from a raid with a white boy, and Bonito wanted to surrender and return to San Carlos. Crook released her and said he would be camped at the headwaters of the Bavispe River, where he would wait for the leaders to come to him to talk peace.[101]

On May 18, Chihuahua, brandishing a lance, galloped into Crook's camp and reined his horse to a stop in front of Crook at his tent. As Chihuahua spoke, the translators told Crook the old woman the scouts had killed was Chihuahua's aunt. Chihuahua did not see that as a gesture of friendship. They gave him tobacco and food, and later he began negotiations for his followers' return to San Carlos. Other Chiricahuas entered the camp over the next few days, wishing to return to San Carlos. Many were disheartened that fellow Apaches were working with US troops to track them down. By May 19, around one hundred Chiricahuas had surrendered, most of them Chokonens.[102]

When Crook asked about the boy, Charley McComas, the Chiricahuas said he had run off. Years later, Chihuahua's daughter told Jason Betzinez what had happened to Charley. When Crook's scouts killed the old woman at Bugatseka, her son was so enraged that he had killed Charley, crushing him with rocks.[103]

At the time Crook's scouts attacked Bugatseka, Geronimo and his people were 120 miles away in Chihuahua. Geronimo led a raiding party, leaving the women and children behind in camp. His objective was not to kill, but to capture Mexicans to exchange for his family and other people captured at Casas Grandes and at Juh's rancheria. On May 9, they captured six wives of Mexican soldiers stationed at Casas Grandes, on the main road southeast of Galeana. Geronimo told the women, one of whom had a nursing baby, not to be afraid; they would not be harmed. He sent an old woman to Casas Grandes to let the soldiers know he wanted to exchange captives.[104]

On May 15, the evening of Crook's scouts' attack on Bugatseka, Geronimo's warriors were eating their meal. Jason Betzinez sat beside Geronimo, who held a knife in one hand and a piece of beef in the other. He suddenly dropped the knife and said, "Men, our people whom we left at our base camp are now in the hands of US troops! What shall we do?" His Power had revealed this to him. Geronimo and his men had no idea that American troops had crossed the border. The warriors believed what Geronimo said and responded that they wanted to return immediately.[105]

Leaving that night, their travel was slowed by the Mexican women, who were not used to moving as swiftly as Chiricahuas.[106]

Beside their trail, they left the bodies of two Mexican men they had captured. Geronimo had first tortured them; then the other warriors had speared and clubbed them to death, after which they mutilated the bodies, cutting off the head of one. Along with the bodies, they left a note saying they would bring the women prisoners to Casas Grandes in fifteen days.[107]

The women and children of Geronimo's camp had started moving toward Bugatseka when the raiding party caught up with them a few days later. That evening, Geronimo and the warriors held a council where Geronimo announced another prophecy: "Tomorrow afternoon as we march along the north side of the mountains we will see a man standing on a hill to our left. He will howl to us and tell us that the troops have captured our base camp."[108]

The next afternoon, they were about fifteen miles from Bugatseka when an Apache standing on a hilltop to their left began to howl. He came down and told them that General Crook and his troops had taken Bugatseka, and now all the Chiricahuas were in his custody. Once again Geronimo's Power had predicted what would happen.[109]

Geronimo and the men held a council on the evening of May 19 and decided they would withhold any action until they had determined what the situation was at Bugatseka. Early the next morning, they found Crook's camp, and from on top of a ridge they saw Chiricahuas were camping with the soldiers and scouts. Before taking all the people down to the camp, Geronimo positioned warriors to shoot into camp if need be.[110]

It was around 9:00 a.m. when Geronimo's warriors were spotted on rock ledges about a thousand feet above camp. The scouts grabbed their weapons and took cover as some of the women shouted to Geronimo and Kaytennae to come down. Crook wanted peace. Geronimo sent two older men into camp to find out if it was true. If they did not come back by a certain time, Geronimo and his warriors would attack. The two men soon returned halfway up the mountainside and called for everyone to come in.[111]

Alone, Crook had walked off with his shotgun, bird hunting. Fishing and hunting were his passions, and several times he had gone hunting alone while the expedition was in the Sierra Madres. He was in a field of tall yellow grass and had shot a couple of birds when Geronimo and the other Chiricahua leaders suddenly surrounded him. They took his shotgun and birds and then sent for Mickey Free and Si-biyana to translate. The leaders said Crook had been shooting in their direction. They all sat on the ground and talked for a couple of hours and then walked into camp with Crook.[112]

Geronimo and his men capture General George Crook.

That was the Apaches' story, and versions of it were printed in US newspapers. Crook and Lieutenant Bourke never mentioned this incident in their writings.[113]

Crook and Bourke's version was that throughout the day, Chiricahua men had begun visiting the camp. Early that evening, Geronimo and other leaders entered the camp. Crook was eating his supper by the campfire when Geronimo sat down on a log near him. Other leaders joined Geronimo, sitting beside him. Geronimo then moved and sat beside Crook, and through Mickey Free, asked to talk. At first, Crook did not answer and just kept eating. He then pointed to all the people who had surrendered and said, "Choose peace or war as you please." Geronimo left Crook's side and went back to the log he had been sitting on. About an hour later, Geronimo approached Crook again and said he wanted to go back to San Carlos. Crook ended the conversation by saying Geronimo needed to surrender unconditionally or fight.[114]

That night the Chiricahuas held a victory dance, and some of the White Mountain scouts participated.[115]

The next morning, Crook invited Geronimo, Naiche, Chatto, and Jelikine to breakfast. Geronimo believed Crook was very powerful to have been able to cross the border into Mexico and find him. Crook told them he had come as a friend to take them back to San Carlos, but if they chose to fight, he would fight them. Crook then said, "I am not going to take your arms from you because I am not afraid of you."[116]

"We give up," Geronimo said. "Do with us as you please." He again said he wanted to return to San Carlos.[117]

By the end of the day, 229 Chiricahuas had surrendered, and more would arrive the next day. Crook sent the freed Mexican women to Casas Grandes.[118]

The Chiricahuas were holding another victory dance that evening and invited Crook's scouts. Geronimo and other leaders were angry and plotted revenge on the Apache scouts who had led Crook and his men to their stronghold and attacked, killing their own people. Once the scouts began to dance with the Chiricahua young women, a signal would be given for the warriors to attack and kill them. There was much opposition to the plan, as many were friends or relatives of the scouts. The dance went as planned, but at the last minute Chief of Scouts Sieber would not allow the scouts to attend.[119]

Crook was running low on supplies and began the slow return to San Carlos on May 30, 1883. Geronimo left Crook on June 1, telling Crook he was looking for more people who were still scattered in the Sierra Madre Mountains. He had earlier brought in 116 people, along with Chatto, Kaytennae, and Chihuahua. Without committing to a date, Geronimo assured Crook he would follow as soon as he found the rest of his people. Also staying behind were Chiricahua leaders Chatto, Naiche, Kaytennae, Chihuahua, and Juh, as well as approximately 200 people, of which 60 were men.[120]

On June 11, 1883, Crook crossed the border back into the United States with 325 Chiricahuas—52 men and 273 women and children. Accompanying Crook were the Chiricahua leaders Loco, Nana, and Bonito.[121]

Crook soon learned he had another problem: The Interior Department had refused to accept the Chiricahuas' return to San Carlos. The Indian agent at San Carlos, Philip Wilcox, who was good friends with Secretary of the Interior Henry Teller, did not want them, and said the other Apaches on the reservation also did not want them there.[122]

Crook left for Washington, DC, and on July 7, met with Teller, Secretary of War Robert Todd Lincoln,[123] and Commissioner of Indian Affairs Hiram Price. They reached an agreement that the army would have all responsibility for the Chiricahuas, including feeding them. The army would also be responsible for all police duties on the reservation. The Interior Department would be responsible for feeding and supplying all non-Chiricahua Apaches. Crook would settle the Chiricahuas on the White Mountain Reservation anywhere he chose, except at San Carlos Agency.[124]

Crook's officers established their headquarters at San Carlos Agency. They were not impressed, and soon named it "Hell's Forty Acres." The army temporarily settled the Chiricahuas at Loco's old rancheria site east of San Carlos, where they were completely dependent on the army for food, as there was no game and no agave plants.[125]

Meanwhile, back in Mexico, the Chiricahuas raided the Mexicans to replenish horses and supplies taken by Crook's scouts when they had attacked the Bugatseka rancheria. Geronimo raided and murdered throughout Sonora for the rest of June and all of July 1883. The Chiricahua leaders agreed they would try to recover their captive relatives before heading to San Carlos.[126]

One of Geronimo's wives, who called herself Mañanita, had escaped from her Mexican captors in Chihuahua City and after a forty-four-day journey found Geronimo's rancheria in the Sierra Madres. She said thirty-five other Chiricahuas, including Geronimo's wife Shit-sha-she, another unnamed wife of his, Chatto's wife and two children, and Chihuahua's brother, were being held captive there.[127]

Near the end of August, the Chiricahuas were camped fifteen miles from Casas Grandes. They began holding peace talks with Mexican army officers outside town. Geronimo spoke for the Chiricahuas, stating they wanted the return of their people. The Mexicans stalled into September, holding two additional talks and plying the men with bottles of mescal, hoping to catch all the leaders in one place with their guard down in order to kill them. In particular, they wanted to capture Geronimo and execute him. Meanwhile, they allowed small groups of Chiricahuas into town to trade.[128]

Tragedy struck on September 21, 1883. Juh was on a drinking spree, and while riding a steep trail along the Casas Grandes River, he ran his horse off the trail and fell to his death in the river.[129]

A third talk was arranged in early October. The Mexican officers put into position about sixty soldiers dressed as civilians with hidden firearms. The plan was to surround and attack the Chiricahua leaders, but Geronimo became suspicious when the Mexican "civilians" began to gather near them. Geronimo said, "We might as well go back, there are too many soldiers." He told the Mexican officers they had to leave but would be back in ten days. They never returned.[130]

When Geronimo and his men returned to their rancheria, they found Bonito and a companion had arrived. Crook had authorized Captain Crawford to send them to find the Chiricahuas and ask why they were not returning to San Carlos.[131]

Naiche, Chihuahua, Kaytennae, and about a hundred men, women, and children agreed to return with Bonito. Instead of going with them, Geronimo sent his eighteen-year-old son Chappo to investigate the conditions at San Carlos. He wanted to be assured he would not be put in jail as John Clum had done to him.[132]

After they left, Geronimo continued to lead raiding parties into Sonora, stealing horses and cattle to take to San Carlos.[133]

It appeared Geronimo wasn't coming in. Arizonans scorned Crook, believing he had allowed Geronimo to fool him. On December 11, 1883, Crawford sent Chappo and Chihuahua into Mexico to find Geronimo and report to him what they had found at San Carlos. They did just that, and assured him he would be treated well at San Carlos.[134]

Geronimo and his followers, ten men and twenty-two women and children, along with Chappo and Chihuahua, left Bugatseka on January 26, 1884. They leisurely headed north driving their stolen livestock, 100 horses and mules and 133 head of cattle, at a not-too-fast pace, wanting to keep them fattened.[135]

On February 25, 1884, Geronimo and his band crossed the border into Arizona and camped at Skeleton Canyon. The next day they met Second Lieutenant Britton Davis and his Apache scouts who would escort them to San Carlos. Since Geronimo had brought along livestock, they had to travel more slowly and use routes where there would be pasture and water.[136]

On March 4, they reached Sulphur Springs Ranch where they made camp and met Lieutenant William "Bo" Blake and a fifteen-man cavalry detachment assigned to help escort Geronimo and his people to San Carlos. Davis and Blake had been classmates and friends at West Point.[137]

Two government inspectors arrived in camp—John Clark, deputy collector of customs, and William Howard, special inspector of customs. They claimed since Geronimo had brought cattle across the border without paying duty, they were seizing the cattle. They had no official documents to back up their claim. Davis told the inspectors Geronimo would fight before he gave up the cattle. They countered by saying they would get a posse from the town of Willcox to take the cattle. Davis asked them to wait until the next day, as he was sending a man to Willcox to telegraph a message to Crook, asking for instructions. The men agreed to that. Davis and Blake conferred separately and reasoned that if they tried to take Geronimo's cattle from him, there would be a fight.[138]

That evening, Blake brought out a nearly full bottle of Scotch whisky and shared it with the inspectors, who had an enjoyable time draining the bottle before turning in for the night. Davis and Blake along with their interpreter Mickey Free went to Geronimo and explained the situation, suggesting he and his people sneak off with the cattle into the night. At first, Geronimo was angry and said he would stay and fight, but they convinced him it would be a great joke if he could pull it off.[139]

When the inspectors woke the next morning, Geronimo's people, Blake's detachment, and the cattle were gone. Davis and his men were still there. When the inspectors asked where the Apaches and livestock had gone, Davis said he didn't know. Of course, they did not believe him but admitted it was a good trick. After the inspectors left, Davis and his scouts caught up with the cavalcade heading toward San Carlos.[140]

On March 16, 1884, Geronimo and his band drove the herds of horses and cattle to San Carlos Agency on the White Mountain Reservation, which they would call home once again.[141]

—◦—

Sitting Bull had formally surrendered on July 20, 1881, at Fort Buford, ironically the fort he had fought to remove from Hunkpapa territory. A reporter told Sitting Bull his daughter Many Horses was safe and happily living at Standing Rock, but he was still not willing to believe a white man. Major Brotherton sent a telegram to General Terry telling him the good news—that Sitting Bull had surrendered. He sent a second telegram to Crow King and Low Dog at Standing Rock Agency, giving them the same information.[142]

Thirty-five Hunkpapa families were still in Canada. Légaré left to bring them to Fort Buford. Sitting Bull wanted to remain there until they arrived, but on July 26, Brotherton received orders that

Sitting Bull and his people were to be sent to Standing Rock Agency aboard the steamboat *General Sherman* when it arrived from Coal Banks, Montana.[143]

The *General Sherman* arrived on July 28, and the next morning Sitting Bull and 187 of his people, escorted by Captain Clifford and 70 infantrymen, steamed down the Missouri River. Sitting Bull, wearing goggles to protect his infected eyes, and his Hunkpapas lined the decks of the steamboat as it arrived at Bismarck, Dakota Territory, on Sunday morning, July 31. A large crowd waited at the landing to get a glimpse of Sitting Bull.[144]

The Hunkpapas were allowed off the boat to collect two days' worth of rations. Sitting Bull, his sister Good Feather, and a few of his leaders were taken to a reception in his honor at Bismarck's prestigious Sheridan House, where many asked Sitting Bull for his autograph. He had learned how to write his name in English when he lived in Canada. They were taken from the Sheridan House to the Merchants Hotel where a banquet was held in their honor. The whites were amazed to see that Sitting Bull and the other Hunkpapas knew how to handle knives, forks, and spoons. The Hunkpapas were equally amazed when they ate ice cream for the first time.[145]

They returned to the steamboat, which pulled away from the landing at 6:00 p.m. as the crowd watched and a band played.[146]

As the *General Sherman* approached Fort Yates at noon, August 1, 1881, Sitting Bull and his Hunkpapas lined the rails. They flew a yellow flag depicting a deer in the center. A large crowd led by Gall had gathered onshore, kept back from the riverbank by soldiers holding rifles with fixed bayonets. People shouted "How!" from the boat and from the riverbank when they spotted friends and loved ones. The people on the boat chanted and then went silent as the boat came alongside the landing. It was an emotional reunion for all, with Sitting Bull wiping tears from his face.[147]

After they were escorted off the boat and shown where to set up their camp, Sitting Bull's daughter Many Horses was brought to him. Sitting Bull was so happy to see her, and relieved to learn that she had left her husband and was rejoining the family.[148]

During Sitting Bull's time at Fort Yates and Standing Rock, reporters constantly asked him what he wanted. His answer was consistent—all he wanted was to be left alone in peace to hunt and trade.[149]

Most of the Hunkpapas and other Lakotas still considered Sitting Bull their leader. This was a concern of Secretary of the Interior Samuel Kirkwood and Secretary of War Robert Todd Lincoln. Both believed Sitting Bull and his band were a bad influence on the other Hunkpapas and needed to be removed from Standing Rock. Sitting Bull and his people were designated prisoners of war and were to be sent downriver to Fort Randall.[150]

On September 6, 1881, Colonel Charles Gilbert, the commander at Fort Yates, informed Sitting Bull that he and his band would be removed in a few days when the *General Sherman* arrived. Sitting Bull was furious. The white man had lied to him again. He was powerless. There was nothing he could do. No one could tell him what their fate would be. There was no plan. Every white man he had ever talked with had lied to him—American soldiers, Canadians, and translators.[151]

Gall, Crow King, and all the Hunkpapas were upset. Gilbert ordered a full alert and had the artillery loaded and in position for possible use. Troops were sent to Sitting Bull's camp where they ordered the Hunkpapas to dismantle it and move to the riverbank.[152]

The *General Sherman* arrived on September 10 and Sitting Bull and his people were ordered to get on the boat. The people milled about on the riverbank—angry and in despair. Women wailed. Children cried. One mother drove a knife into her baby, killing it. She then turned the knife on herself, but others were able to stop her before she killed herself. Troops with fixed bayonets slowly herded the angry, frightened people onto the boat. Some were separated from their loved ones, who were away from the camp at the time. A rifle butt slammed into One Bull's back, shoving him onto the boat. It was reported they had to bind Sitting Bull and carry him on board.[153]

The steamboat carrying Sitting Bull and his 165 men, women, and children, guarded by a company of infantry, left for Fort Randall that afternoon. The four-hundred-mile trip took a week to complete. As they passed the Cheyenne River Agency, the Lakotas there demonstrated their grief and anger over this injustice to their leader. The only bright spot on the trip was the birth of a baby girl to Sitting Bull's wife, Four Robes.[154]

The *General Sherman* arrived at Fort Randall on the evening of September 17, 1881. Sitting Bull and his band would be there for twenty months of almost continuous inaction. Along with the boredom, there would be no answer to their questions: How long would they be there? What was to happen to them?[155]

The troops initially guarding them were companies of the black Twenty-fifth Infantry, later to be replaced, in November 1882, by companies of the white Fifteenth Infantry. The officers of both units grew to like Sitting Bull and his people, and some of them would become their advocates for better treatment.[156]

The Hunkpapas set up their camp of thirty tepees in the traditional manner a half-mile west of the fort on level ground. Sitting Bull was allowed to run the camp in the Hunkpapa manner. Military guards were posted around the perimeter of the camp, but people could come and go as they pleased.[157]

Many people, both Lakota and white, visited Sitting Bull and his camp. Lakota leaders came from all parts of the Great Sioux Reservation to pay their respects and confer with their leader. However, General Phil Sheridan downplayed Sitting Bull's importance, saying, "[Sitting Bull] is not a chief and never was, and his influence—if he has any—arises more from the notoriety that has been given him than from any talent for leadership that he has ever displayed."[158]

In October 1881, Rudolf Cronau, who wrote and created illustrations for a German magazine, arrived at Fort Randall and quickly made friends with Sitting Bull and other members of the band. Sitting Bull allowed Cronau to paint his portrait, and as Sitting Bull sat and Cronau painted, they tried to teach each other Lakota and German. Sitting Bull was interested in learning new painting techniques and Cronau worked with him. Sitting Bull created new pictographs that showed Cronau's European influence. Sitting Bull also signed them in English.[159]

As winter approached, the Hunkpapas needed clothing and supplies. A list of needed items was submitted to the army in October 1881. What they were wearing was becoming threadbare and their tepees were becoming worn. New supplies did not arrive. Sitting Bull's people were caught in a bureaucratic quagmire. The army claimed it did not have the funds to supply clothing and supplies to the Hunkpapas. The Interior Department said since Sitting Bull's people were considered prisoners of war and were under the control of the army, the army had to pay for their clothing and tepee coverings. Finally, the army said it would find the funds for the supplies, which arrived at Fort Randall toward the end of February 1882.[160]

In January 1882, a smallpox epidemic had broken out in the United States. Sitting Bull and his leaders met in council and allowed the post surgeon to vaccinate everyone at the end of February.[161]

Sitting Bull had become friends with the Presbyterian minister John Williamson, who spoke fluent Lakota and never pressured him to become a Christian. The Catholic Church, represented by Bishop Martin Marty, and the Episcopal Church, represented by Bishop William Hare, vied for Sitting Bull's favor. Hare won because of his offer to educate Lakota children. Sitting Bull was an advocate for educating the children so they could better understand the whites and be on an equal footing. The Hunkpapas selected three boys and two girls to attend Hare's school at the Yankton Indian Agency across the Missouri River. One of the boys was Sitting Bull's adopted son Little Soldier.[162]

In the summer of 1882, the federal government insisted ten children from Sitting Bull's band must attend the Carlisle Indian Industrial School in Pennsylvania for the three- to four-year program. The school had been established to educate and train Indian boys and girls and to remove the "Indianness" from them.[163]

Sitting Bull and his people had most likely heard about the treatment of children at the school—that it was run in a military style. The children wore uniforms, their hair was cut short, and they were not allowed to speak their own languages. Most disturbing of all was the physical punishments, and the fact that some children had died of illness. The Brulé leader Spotted Tail had visited Carlisle and, not liking the physical punishment of children, had removed his children from the school. Sitting Bull and his band refused to send their children, and by October the government dropped the demand.[164]

Colonel George Andrews, commander at Fort Randall, wrote about Sitting Bull and his band in his annual report on September 5, 1882:

> *They have caused but very little trouble and thus far, their conduct has been commendable. The restrictions, necessarily imposed upon their freedom of movements, together with the uncertainty of their future, are to them a source of annoyance and anxiety.*[165]

Andrews went on to write that twelve Hunkpapas had died since their arrival. The living worried they would all die there. Sitting Bull's family was not spared the sorrow of death. His daughter, who was born on the steamboat a year earlier, became ill. She went into convulsions and died. Sitting Bull, grief-stricken, wept.[166]

Ever since he and his people had been sent to Fort Randall, Sitting Bull had asked army officers and civilians why he was there as a prisoner of war. Their letters supporting him were sent to Washington, but there was never any response. In December 1882, the Reverend John Williamson wrote a letter for the Yankton chief Strikes-the-Ree in support of Sitting Bull's release and sent it to Secretary of War Robert Lincoln. Lincoln concurred with the letter and sent it on to the secretary of Interior and the commissioner of Indian Affairs, stating he believed Sitting Bull and his people should be turned over to the Bureau of Indian Affairs.[167]

In January 1883, James McLaughlin, the Standing Rock agent, visited with officials in Washington, DC, and followed up with a letter expressing his support to release Sitting Bull and his band to his care at Standing Rock. By mid-March 1883, after much back-and-forth between government departments, Lincoln informed Henry Teller, commissioner of Indian Affairs, that the army would transfer Sitting Bull and his people to the care of the Bureau of Indian Affairs.[168]

Lieutenant Colonel Peter Swaine, commander at Fort Randall, received the order for Sitting Bull's transfer on March 26. There is no record, but he probably would have told Sitting Bull the good news at that time.[169]

On April 28, 1883, Sitting Bull and 151 members of his band boarded the *W. J. Behan* and steamed up the Missouri River to Standing Rock Agency. The steamboat stopped in the towns of Chamberlain and Pierre where crowds greeted the Hunkpapas. Sitting Bull signed his autograph for admirers, and while in Pierre sat for his photograph, wearing a hat with a butterfly pinned to it.[170]

The *W. J. Behan* steamed up to the Fort Yates landing on May 10 at 3:00 p.m. A throng of Lakotas and whites happily shouted for Sitting Bull, but a reporter for the *Yankton Daily Press and Dakotan* noted in the May 14 edition that Gall and Crow King did not appear enthusiastic about his arrival. They may have looked upon Sitting Bull as competition for the leadership Agent McLaughlin had given them.[171]

The *Yankton Daily Press and Dakotan* held a lengthy interview with Sitting Bull. "We were taught to live on the buffalo, but I am told they are nearly all killed," he said. "I would like that killing stopped if I could. I hear some talk of my going to Grand River to farm, thirty-five miles distant. That would suit me very well. My heart is pleased."[172]

Agent James McLaughlin was forty-three years old when Sitting Bull arrived at Fort Yates. McLaughlin, born in Canada, had arrived in St. Paul, Minnesota, in 1863. He had an eighth-grade education and was trained as a blacksmith. His wife Marie Louise's father was French-Canadian, and her mother was Mdewakanton Dakota. A staunch supporter of the Catholic Church, McLaughlin had been an Indian agent for twelve years and had been stationed at Standing Rock since 1881. He was authoritarian and paternalistic, and believed it was his duty to civilize the Indian.[173]

Agent McLaughlin did not meet Sitting Bull and the other Hunkpapas on their arrival, but sent a message for them to come to his office the next afternoon. At 3:00 p.m. the next day, Sitting Bull and about twenty of his men entered McLaughlin's office. The agent was not there, as he was visiting the agency school, so they waited for his return.[174]

Upon McLaughlin's arrival, Sitting Bull and his men introduced themselves and McLaughlin introduced himself and his wife. They smoked the pipe and then McLaughlin invited Sitting Bull to speak. Sitting Bull's speech, which lasted about an hour, covered his leadership of the Hunkpapas and how he planned to manage the tribe at Standing Rock. It was God's will that he was chief of all the Lakotas, and he should be named first on the agency rolls. He wanted all the people gathered together so he could control the young men and keep the peace. He did not want individuals to draw their own rations, but rather wanted them given to him so he could distribute the rations to the people, which had always been the way of the chiefs. He would now farm but needed the animals and implements to do so. He was willing to dress in white man's clothing. He wanted to observe how to farm, and would wait until next year to plant and raise crops. He wanted to go to Washington and see "the great chief" and talk with him about the government commissioners who had come to the reservation while he was a prisoner at Fort Randall and attempted to take Lakota lands. He objected to the whites killing game on the reservation. He wanted to be rich so he could keep his people straight. He produced a list of men he wanted named chiefs under him.[175]

McLaughlin thought Sitting Bull's speech was "utter nonsense." When Sitting Bull finished, McLaughlin said he was going to speak frankly and honestly with him, part of which was, "You will not be the biggest chief. You will be treated just like any other Indian at Standing Rock. You will receive rations individually as does everyone else. You will follow regulations. And you will farm the land assigned to you."[176]

McLaughlin's response was a disheartening surprise to Sitting Bull. McLaughlin pulled out his watch and signaled the meeting was over.[177]

Within days, McLaughlin had twelve acres plowed for Sitting Bull's band to farm. Later, McLaughlin inspected the plot and found Sitting Bull working with a hoe. He asked Sitting Bull if farming was difficult and Sitting Bull responded, "No." He told McLaughlin he was determined to become a farmer.[178]

McLaughlin formed a dislike for Sitting Bull that would remain well after Sitting Bull's death. In his August 15, 1883, report to the commissioner of Indian Affairs, he wrote, "Sitting Bull is an Indian of very mediocre ability, rather dull, and much inferior to Gall and others of his lieutenants in intelligence.... He is pompous, vain, and boastful, and considers himself a very important personage."[179]

Back in 1882, while Sitting Bull was held prisoner at Fort Randall, Secretary of the Interior Henry Teller had formed the Sioux Land Commission, led by a former governor of Dakota Territory, Newton Edmunds. The commission's objective was to get the Lakotas to agree to the division of the Great Sioux Reservation into six separate, smaller reservations, as well as the sale of almost half the reservation land to be opened up to white settlement. The commission had visited the Lakota tribes, coercing and bullying tribal leaders into signing an agreement for the breakup of the reservation and the sale of the land. Agent McLaughlin and Bishop Martin Marty both worked to persuade Lakota leaders to sign. The Fort Laramie Treaty of 1868 stipulated that any diminishing of the reservation needed approval of three-fourths of the adult male Lakota population. Although the reservation's adult male population at the time was roughly 5,000, the commission's agreement had only 384 signatures.[180]

The Senate refused to ratify the agreement, and in 1883 it sent a select committee to investigate conditions on the Great Sioux Reservation and in Montana. The committee made up of five senators was headed by Senator Henry Dawes of Massachusetts.[181]

The committee first visited Pine Ridge Agency in August, meeting with the Oglalas. Chief Red Cloud angrily denounced the Sioux Land Commission's efforts to divide the reservation and sell off land. The Dawes committee's meeting had allowed Red Cloud to reassert his leadership against Indian Agent Valentine McGillycuddy's control, and the committee did not want something like that to happen again.[182]

When the committee arrived at Standing Rock in late August, they first met with Agent McLaughlin. He recommended they not talk to Sitting Bull, "He is a habitual liar and schemer." McLaughlin recommended the reservation be broken up and allotments of food and clothing be phased out quickly so the Indians would be forced to become self-sufficient farmers.[183]

The committee members sat behind a table as the meeting room filled with Lakota men, including Sitting Bull, who remained in the back. The committee seemed to ignore the concerns of the first two speakers, Lakota leaders Running Antelope and John Grass. "Those men [the Sioux Land Commission] fairly made my head dizzy, and my signing was an accident," John Grass said. "The white men talked in a threatening way."[184]

Sitting Bull saw that the committee members seemed disinterested in what the speakers had to say. When Red Fish, an older respected man, started to speak his grievances, an Indian policeman told him he looked like he had been drinking, and to sit down. The committee members did not interfere. Sitting Bull became concerned the committee was there to take advantage of the Lakotas. The committee members saw men were murmuring in the back around Sitting Bull.[185]

"Ask Sitting Bull if he has anything to say to the committee," Senator Dawes said.

"Of course I will speak if you desire me to do so," Sitting Bull replied. "I suppose it is only such men as you desire to speak who must say anything."

As Sitting Bull came forward, Dawes said, "We suppose the Indians would select men to speak for them. But any man who desires to speak, or any man the Indians here desire shall talk for them, we will be glad to hear if he has anything to say."

"Do you know who I am, that you speak as you do?" Sitting Bull asked.

"I know that you are Sitting Bull, and if you have anything to say, we will be glad to hear you."

"Do you recognize me? Do you know who I am?" Sitting Bull asked again.

"I know you are Sitting Bull," Dawes replied.

"You say you know I am Sitting Bull, but do you know what position I hold?"

"I do not know any difference between you and the other Indians at this agency."

"I am here by the will of the Great Spirit, and by His will I am chief . . . you men come here to talk with us, and you say you do not know who I am. I want to tell you that if the Great Spirit has chosen anyone to be the chief of this country, it is myself."

"In whatever capacity you may be here today, if you desire to say anything to us, we will listen to you; otherwise we will dismiss the council," Dawes said.

"Yes, that is all right," Sitting Bull said. "You have conducted yourselves as men who have been drinking whiskey, and I came here to give you some advice."

With that, Sitting Bull waved his hand and all the Lakota men walked out of the meeting.[186]

The senators were furious. McLaughlin initiated damage control by asking Running Antelope to speak with Sitting Bull. McLaughlin asked the friendly Yanktonais to come back to the meeting, which they did. Running Antelope and others convinced Sitting Bull that these men were not out to steal their land or harm them, and that he should apologize. He agreed and returned to the meeting.[187]

Sitting Bull began: "I came in with a glad heart to shake hands with you, my friends, for I feel I have displeased you; and I am here to apologize to you for my bad conduct and to take back what I said." He then launched into a long speech, once again apologizing, telling the history of his leadership and the wrongs whites had committed against the Lakota people. Sitting Bull said that his people had tried to follow the white man's way. They didn't want to sell any land, but rather wanted the land back that had always been theirs, including the Black Hills and Powder River country. He said, "I look around and see my people starving." They needed more food and clothing, not less. If they were to live like white people, he said, they needed horses and wagons, cattle, oxen, pigs, and sheep, and farm implements. He ended by asking for clothing for his people before winter arrived.[188]

As Sitting Bull finished, Senator John Logan of Illinois, whom the Lakotas named High Hat because of the hat he wore, rose and demanded that before Sitting Bull sat down, he would have his say. He did not accept Sitting Bull's apology and blasted him for insulting the committee by saying they were drunk. He said Sitting Bull was "not a great chief," and he "had no following, no power, no control, and no right to any control." He said Sitting Bull should be grateful the government was taking care of the Lakotas, and he should be thankful the committee was there. Logan ended by saying that if Sitting Bull ever disrespected them again, he would have him thrown into the guardhouse.[189]

"I wish to say a word about my not being a chief, [that I] have no authority, am proud, and consider myself a great man in general," Sitting Bull said.

"We do not care to talk any more with you tonight," Logan said.

"I would like to speak," Sitting Bull said. "I have grown to be a very independent man, and consider myself a very great man."

"You have made your speech," Logan responded. "And we do not care to have you continue any further."

"I have just one more word to say," Sitting Bull said. "Of course, if a man is a chief, and has authority, he should be proud, and consider himself a great man."[190]

This confrontation reinforced McLaughlin's efforts to curb Sitting Bull's power by working with Gall and John Grass in leadership roles as well as selecting the men to be on the Indian police force.[191]

Bismarck became the new capital of Dakota Territory, and it just so happened that the Northern Pacific Railroad that Sitting Bull had contested back in the early 1870s was about to be completed in Montana, with the last celebratory spike being driven by dignitaries. The railroad guests were going to be in Bismarck, and promoters believed they should hold a dual celebration in early September. Railroad and government dignitaries including former president Ulysses Grant were going to be on hand for the laying of the new capitol building's cornerstone. The promoters wanted Indians there, and most of all, they wanted Sitting Bull.[192]

An invitation was sent to Sitting Bull through McLaughlin. Even though he disliked Sitting Bull, McLaughlin believed it would be good for him to attend, and it could only benefit McLaughlin, as well. At first Sitting Bull declined, but after further persuasion, he relented.[193]

Sitting Bull experienced his first railroad ride from Mandan across the Missouri River to Bismarck. He led the parade carrying the American flag. He was asked to speak at the cornerstone ceremony, which he did. Sitting Bull scolded the crowd in Lakota, calling them thieves and liars for taking Lakota land and forcing them onto the reservation. The horrified translator made up a false translation, speaking favorably about the progress Sitting Bull saw in Bismarck.[194]

Sitting Bull had learned he could make money by selling his autograph, charging $1.50 and $2.00. The money would come in handy to buy things he wanted. He took a nice plug hat from one man in exchange for his autograph and wore the hat in the parade.[195]

During the year 1884, Sitting Bull's mother Her-Holy-Door died. She had lived in Sitting Bull's lodge ever since his father had been killed by the Crows, twenty-six years earlier. She would be missed. She had been one of his closest advisors.[196]

In March 1884, Sitting Bull got to travel again. McLaughlin had business in St. Paul, Minnesota. Sitting Bull learned about the trip and wanted to go along to see more of the white man's world. McLaughlin thought it was a good idea and might help civilize Sitting Bull. The railroad provided passes for Sitting Bull, one of his wives, and One Bull. McLaughlin's wife also went along. They stayed two weeks at the Merchants Hotel in St. Paul and toured all aspects of the big city—government institutions, banks, grocery stores, and factories. The highlight for Sitting Bull was watching the city fire department in action with its teams of horses harnessed to the fire engines, extension ladders and fire hoses in operation.[197]

That spring, McLaughlin gave permission for Sitting Bull to move his family south to the Grand River. His brother-in-law Gray Eagle gave him a cabin on the north side of the river, a horse, and some cattle. Several miles downriver, Running Antelope had established a settlement with a store. Some of Sitting Bull's followers and family joined him, farming along the river. Over the years, with the assistance of a district farmer who helped the Lakotas, Sitting Bull prospered as he improved his farm, growing oats, corn, and potatoes. He acquired twenty horses, forty-five head of cattle, and a flock of eighty chickens.[198]

Sitting Bull's eyes were still bothering him, and he hoped living along the Grand River would help to alleviate the problem. He chose to stay away from the agency as much as possible and only went there to receive rations. Sitting Bull asked McLaughlin for a subagency on the Grand River, but that was denied. He asked for a day school, to which McLaughlin agreed. By living forty miles from Standing Rock Agency and McLaughlin, Sitting Bull was freer. McLaughlin liked the distance between them, too, thinking Sitting Bull could do little harm there.[199]

Apache Sunrise Ceremony

The Sunrise Ceremony, also known as the Sunrise Dance, is a ceremony of life and is the most important and elaborate ceremony in Apache culture. It is also the most important ceremony in the life of an Apache female. The Sunrise Ceremony begins at the first sign of menarche, a girl's first menstruation, and is a series of private and public rituals that take place over the course of four days. Throughout the four-day ceremony, the girl becomes sacred and is transformed into the Apache heroine, White Painted Woman.[200]

Ussen, the Creator, formed the Earth and then created White Painted Woman, sending her to Earth during a time when monsters dominated. White Painted Woman had two sons, Killer of Enemies and Child of the Water, who killed the monsters. The Chiricahuas believed they were descended from Child of the Water.[201]

White Painted Woman gave the Sunrise Ceremony to the Apaches, saying the girls needed a puberty rite. She said each girl should have a feast. There should be songs and dancing along with visits from the Mountain Spirits. The Mountain Spirits would bring good fortune, but if they were disrespected, they would bring misfortune, sickness, and even death.[202]

The four days of the Sunrise Ceremony represents how the girl should live out her life. She is to exhibit self-control and good character during the ceremony so it will become her character for life.[203]

The girl's family provides everything for the Sunrise Ceremony, and since it affects the whole band, others might help to contribute to the festivities. The women members of the family make and have blessed special beautiful buckskin clothing for the girl to wear during the ceremony. During the four days, an older woman stays with the girl and acts as her attendant and advisor. Another important person is a male singer who acts as master of ceremonies throughout the four days.[204]

Each evening before that night's festivities begin, masked dancers representing the Mountain Spirits appear and dance. A clown wearing a mask with a long nose or big ears might appear with the masked dancers to make fun of people and perform humorous antics. The first evening, the girl's attendant, marked with pollen on her face, offers pollen to the four directions. Pollen is a symbol of life and renewal. The attendant then paints pollen on the girl's face. The people form a line to the south, and as they walk past the girl, they paint pollen on her face and in turn, she paints pollen on their faces, through which they all receive blessings.[205]

By the end of the Sunrise Ceremony, the girl is changed into White Painted Woman and receives all her desirable qualities. The girl shares blessings with the other participants in the ceremony, and the girl herself receives a greater sense of her purpose and identity as she is now an Apache woman, seeking to pattern her life after White Painted Woman.[206]

CHAPTER 10

The Wild West, 1884–1885

ON JUNE 1, 1883, GERONIMO HAD PROMISED GENERAL GEORGE Crook he would follow him across the border into the United States and return to San Carlos, but first, he needed to locate the rest of the Chiricahuas scattered throughout the Sierra Madre Mountains. Geronimo made good on his promise, although it was months later when he arrived at San Carlos on March 16, 1884, leading a small band of 10 men and 22 women and children, herding 100 head of horses and mules and 133 head of cattle.[1]

Captain Emmet Crawford, Crook's man in charge of the Chiricahuas at San Carlos, met Geronimo and his band and had them camp along the Gila River where Loco had had his rancheria.[2]

Acting under orders from Crook, Crawford immediately confiscated Geronimo's cattle herd. Geronimo protested. They were his cattle that he had taken from Mexicans, not Americans. He wanted to use the animals to begin raising a herd for the Chiricahuas. Crawford told Geronimo he could keep the horses and mules, but the cattle had to be sold. The herd would be sold at auction on June 26, 1884, bringing $1,762.50. The proceeds were sent to the Mexican government to help cover Mexican cattle owners' claims. Geronimo never forgave Crook or Crawford for this act.[3]

Five days after reaching San Carlos, Geronimo met again with Captain Crawford. Geronimo praised Crook and hoped Crook would be able to free the Chiricahuas being held captive by the Mexicans.

He told Crawford to watch out for bad Indians of other tribes, and if they talked about him, not to believe them.[4]

Geronimo said Crook had told him he could have anything he wanted and live wherever he wanted, which was at Eagle Creek—off the reservation. Geronimo emphasized Crook had told him he and his people could live at Eagle Creek. Crawford replied Eagle Creek was now owned by white people. Geronimo responded the government could buy the land from them for his people. Crawford said the government had decided to relocate the Chiricahuas to Turkey Creek, which was seventeen miles south of Fort Apache. Geronimo replied there was no game there, and not enough land for all of them to plant melons, corn, and other crops. "There is no mescal to bake around Fort Apache," Geronimo said. "We will starve to death." He said if they couldn't go to Eagle Creek, what about looking at Ash Creek to see if that would be an appropriate place to live. Crawford agreed to allow Chiricahua leaders to inspect Ash Creek. Geronimo said, "We want to be alone and have no Indians but Chiricahuas with us."[5]

After examining the locations and holding extensive discussions, the Chiricahua leaders decided on relocating to Turkey Creek, against Geronimo's objections. It would be a good place for the Chiricahuas to live. At almost 8,000 feet in elevation, it was more to Chiricahua liking, with good water, grass, and timber, as well as opportunities for hunting and gathering wild berries, nuts, and vegetables.[6]

In early May, 512 Chiricahuas set off for their new home. Along the way, they were joined by General Crook and his escort. The Chiricahuas were happy to see him. Crook held a council meeting with the leaders, who told him of their loved ones being held captive by the Mexicans. The captives included one of Geronimo's wives and one of his children. Crook promised them he would do what he could.[7]

On May 9, 1884, the Chiricahuas reached Turkey Creek. They were happy to be away from the other Apaches at San Carlos Agency who had not been friendly to them. Since they were now closer to Fort Apache than to San Carlos Agency, Lieutenant Britton Davis served as their army agent, and Lieutenant Charles Gatewood at Fort Apache was the military agent for the nearby White Mountain Apaches.[8]

The Chiricahuas went right to work setting up their rancherias, developing their fields, and planting crops. Geronimo's plot of land was alongside Jason Betzinez's plot. Betzinez said that first year they "did real well" raising corn and potatoes. Crook believed the Chiricahuas were content, stating Geronimo and Chatto had the best-maintained fields, but Davis did not believe Geronimo and the other leaders were content.[9]

Davis found people to spy for him, including Chiricahua leader Chatto, the interpreter, Mickey Free, the scout, Peaches, and a woman. Chihuahua developed suspicions about possible spies, so one night he lay near Davis's tent. He heard a pebble hit the tent's canvas and then saw Chatto entering the tent. Another pebble hit the tent and Mikey Free entered. Two more pebbles hit the tent announcing the entrance of the woman spy and a third man. He overheard them telling Davis that Geronimo and Kaytennae were planning an uprising and that he, Chihuahua, planned to kill Davis.[10]

The next morning, Chihuahua, who Davis had earlier made a scout, confronted Davis about the spies and their lies. Right then and there, Chihuahua quit as a scout. After this incident, the Chiricahuas did not trust the people acting as Davis's spies.[11]

Trouble came to a head in June 1884. Crook had forbidden two Apache practices: the brewing of the corn beer, tiswin, and a husband's right to beat his wife, both of which Davis attempted to enforce. The Chiricahuas said when they met with Crook in Mexico and agreed to return to the United States, they had never agreed to give up these two practices. They thought it ironic that Davis told them they could not drink tiswin when he himself drank alcohol.[12]

Mickey Free and the woman spy told Davis, while he was out turkey hunting near Kaytennae's rancheria, that Kaytennae was on a tiswin spree. Kaytennae learned that Davis was approaching his camp and believed he was on his way to put an end to the party. Kaytennae prepared to ambush Davis, but at the last minute, Davis heard a turkey call in the opposite direction and took another route, saving his life. Other Chiricahuas insisted Mickey Free and Chatto, who was a rival of Kaytennae's, made up the story.[13]

Davis sent a message to Fort Apache for troops and had Kaytennae arrested. He was taken to San Carlos where Captain Emmet Crawford had him placed in irons and jailed. He was tried on June 27 for inciting a rebellion. The jury, made up of White Mountain Apache leaders, declared he was guilty and Crawford, who acted as judge, sentenced him to three years' hard labor at the military prison on Alcatraz Island. Kaytennae's arrest and imprisonment at Alcatraz alarmed and angered Geronimo and Naiche.[14]

On July 1, 1884, Davis enlisted Chatto in the Apache scouts and appointed him a first sergeant. Chatto and Geronimo were now on bad terms. Geronimo believed Chatto and Mickey Free were telling Davis lies about him. He and the other Chiricahua leaders believed what had happened to Kaytennae could happen to any of them. Whenever Chatto or Mickey Free saw Geronimo or another Chiricahua leader, they would draw their hands across their throats, signifying his head was to be cut off.[15]

The army learned that the Chiricahuas held four Hispanic captives from New Mexico. All four boys were eventually released, with Geronimo being instrumental in helping release three of them. When Crook paid a visit to Fort Apache that fall, Geronimo and the other leaders asked him about their relatives being held captive in Mexico. He told them he had asked the War Department to investigate their situation for him.[16]

By November 1884, the temperature was dropping below freezing and snow had begun to fall. Davis moved the Chiricahuas from Turkey Creek to lower elevations along the White River, three miles upstream from Fort Apache. There was not much to do during the winter. The number of tiswin parties increased and the Fort Apache jail had lots of inmates.[17]

Lieutenant Davis had a low opinion of Geronimo, stating he was "a thoroughly vicious, intractable, and treacherous man." Lieutenant James Parker, who was stationed at Fort Apache, held the opposite view, writing, "Geronimo we saw constantly; he was friendly and good natured."[18]

In the spring of 1885, the Chiricahuas planted crops along the White River near Fort Apache. Geronimo invited Davis to inspect his farm. The next day Davis arrived to find Geronimo sitting under the shade of a tree as one wife fanned him and the other two wives hoed the field. The Chiricahuas would soon be moving back to Turkey Creek, but the army would allow them to return to tend their fields along the White River.[19]

Meanwhile, Crook had been pressing the State Department to get Mexico to release the captive Chiricahuas. Mexico denied it held any Chiricahua captives. The State Department asked Crook for a list of the captives' names, with details on each. Crook tasked Lieutenant Davis to compile a list of names including sex, age, and details of their capture. Davis listed ninety-five people and Crook sent the information to the adjutant general's office in Washington, DC, on April 7, 1885. On April 29, Crook wrote a letter to the governor of Chihuahua asking about Chiricahua captives. On May 2, the governor wrote back, stating that thirteen Chiricahua women had been released. It was wonderful news for their families, but traveling by foot, it would take them months to return to the US border.[20]

The first part of May 1885, Captain Francis Pierce, who had replaced Captain Emmet Crawford at San Carlos, accompanied by Lieutenant Davis, arrived at Fort Apache with a pack train loaded with ten thousand pounds of annuities for the Chiricahuas and the White Mountain Apaches. On May 10, they issued the annuities at Fort Apache and the Chiricahuas held a dance that night at their White River farms.[21]

Geronimo had been concerned; he thought the annuities should have been issued at Turkey Creek, not Fort Apache. He also worried that if Gatewood had been replaced, Crook may have been replaced, too, meaning his agreement with Crook would not be honored by others. Davis assured Geronimo that Crook was still in command, but Geronimo still worried.[22]

At some point, Davis added to Geronimo's worries by informing the Chiricahua leaders that the US Congress had recently passed the Major Crimes Act, which stated crimes committed by Indians would be tried not by tribal courts but by the courts in the state or territory the crime was committed. Therefore, Arizona Territory would have jurisdiction over the Chiricahuas whenever they committed a major crime: murder, manslaughter, rape, assault with intent to kill, arson, burglary, and larceny.[23]

On the early morning of May 12, Pierce and Davis accompanied the Chiricahuas back to Turkey Creek. The Chiricahuas were happy and held a celebration that afternoon. Pierce made a speech telling the Chiricahuas how impressed he was with their good behavior, saying that he would pass that information along to General Crook. Naiche and Geronimo each gave speeches about the benefits of living in peace. Pierce wrote that the Chiricahuas were "cheerful and contented. All indications [are] that they will remain quiet."[24]

The following day, as Pierce headed back to San Carlos and Davis returned to his camp three miles from Fort Apache, the Chiricahua women began to brew tiswin for another celebration. One of them, Mangas's wife Huera, was considered an expert brewer. Mangas and Geronimo nursed grudges against Davis and Chatto. In the past, Davis—with Chatto's assistance—had thrown some of Geronimo's people in jail for drinking tiswin. During the tiswin drinking party that took place on the night of May 14, Mangas and Geronimo convinced the other Chiricahua leaders to confront Davis concerning their rights to drink tiswin and beat their wives.[25]

The morning of May 15, Davis awoke to find Geronimo and other leaders standing in a line outside his tent. Behind them stood more men, totaling over thirty Chiricahuas. Chatto and the Apache scouts, armed with Springfield rifles, gathered nearby. Geronimo and the leaders wanted to talk.[26]

Davis invited the leaders into his tent where they squatted in a semicircle. Loco, Nana, Zele, and Bonito were hungover. Mangas, Naiche, Chihuahua, and Geronimo were drunk. Mickey Free acted as interpreter.[27]

When Davis realized they had been drinking tiswin, he threatened to report them to General Crook. The leaders were belligerent as they told Davis they would treat their wives as they saw fit, and they had never agreed to stop brewing and drinking tiswin. Davis stalled for time. He said he would send a telegram to General Crook informing him of their concerns and would let them know of Crook's response. That satisfied the Chiricahua leaders and they returned to their rancherias.[28]

Davis rode to Fort Apache where he telegrammed Captain Pierce at San Carlos about the confrontation. Believing Pierce would forward the message to Crook in Prescott, Davis waited for instructions.[29]

When Pierce received Davis's telegram, he did not know what to do. Davis assumed Pierce would forward the telegram to Crook, since part of the message read, "Have told the Indians that I would lay the matter before the General." Instead of forwarding it to Crook, however, Pierce woke Chief of Scouts Al Sieber, who himself was recovering from a drunk. Sieber looked at the message and said it was just another tiswin drunk, and Davis would handle it. With that, Pierce let it go, never forwarding the message to Crook or responding to Davis. Not until months later would Crook and Davis learn about the telegram, and by then it would be too late.[30]

As Geronimo and the other Chiricahuas waited for a response, they became anxious. Geronimo and Mangas began to believe Davis and Chatto and maybe even Crook were planning to arrest them. Mickey Free had been telling Geronimo about Arizona newspaper articles that had been violently critical of him. Their fears were stoked by Mangas's wife Huera, who disliked Americans and who passed along rumors.[31]

By May 16, the lack of any response from Davis was maddening for Geronimo and Mangas. They worried they were to be arrested, placed in irons, and sent off to Alcatraz, as had happened to Kaytennae.[32]

That day, Nadiskay, an Eastern White Mountain Apache married to a Chiricahua, arrived from Fort Apache. He told Geronimo that he heard Crook had ordered Davis and his scouts to arrest Mangas and him, and if they resisted, Davis was to kill them. Huera, who was not only an expert tiswin brewer but also recognized as having Power, backed up Nadiskay's claim, adding, "If you are warriors you will take to the warpath and the Gray Fox [Crook] must catch you before you are punished."[33]

That did it. Geronimo and Mangas decided to flee to Mexico before they were arrested, but they could not convince Naiche and Chihuahua. Only fifteen men agreed to join them. They needed more men than that if they wanted to live by raiding in Mexico again.[34]

Geronimo developed a plan that would force the other Chiricahuas to leave. Two of his cousins, Fun and Tisna, were members of the Apache scouts. Geronimo instructed them to kill Davis and Chatto. Naiche and Chihuahua would have no choice but to flee. Fun and Tisna agreed to do the killing and headed to Davis's camp.[35]

Geronimo told the other Chiricahua leaders that Fun and Tisna had already killed Davis and Chatto. Most believed him and felt they now had no choice but to run. By dusk on May 17, 1885, 144 Chiricahuas were leaving the reservation led by Geronimo, Mangas, Naiche, Chihuahua, and Nana. However, 400 Chiricahuas remained, including the leaders Chatto, Zele, Bonito, and Loco.[36]

For whatever reason, Geronimo's cousins failed to kill Davis and Chatto, but they convinced two other scouts to join them in Geronimo's breakout. Their failure to kill Davis and Chatto would not be known by Chihuahua and other Chiricahuas until later.[37]

Still waiting for instructions at Fort Apache, Lieutenant Davis was umpiring a Sunday-afternoon baseball game when Mickey Free and Chatto arrived at the fort to tell him they had learned the Chiricahuas were breaking out for Mexico. Davis attempted to send a telegram to Pierce, but the Chiricahuas had cut the wires. Working with Lieutenant Gatewood, they gathered twenty-one Apache scouts along with two companies of the Fourth Cavalry, over one hundred men led by Captain Allen Smith, and by 7:00 p.m., they were riding toward Turkey Creek to arrest Geronimo and Mangas. Six miles from camp, they met a Chiricahua who told them Geronimo and Mangas had left with a large number of Chiricahuas. They were on their way back to Mexico.[38]

<hr />

When Sitting Bull visited St. Paul, Minnesota, with Agent James McLaughlin in March 1884, they stayed at the Merchants Hotel. Alvaren Allen, the hotel's owner, saw the crowds of people wanting to see Sitting Bull. Allen was not only a hotel owner, he was also a showman. He met privately with McLaughlin and they both agreed a show featuring Sitting Bull was bound to make lots of money. However, Sitting Bull would need to be closely supervised, McLaughlin said. Before returning to Standing Rock, the two men agreed to work together to make the show happen.[39]

Allen sent a letter to Senator D. M. Sabin asking him to request that the Indian Office allow Sitting Bull to go on tour. At the same time, McLaughlin worked to turn away requests from others who wanted Sitting Bull as part of their show. The most prominent of these showmen was William F. Cody—Buffalo Bill.[40]

Cody asked that Sitting Bull tour with his Wild West, but in April, McLaughlin sent him a letter stating, "I cannot now entertain any such proposition at the present time," and "I would prefer to have them [Sitting Bull and other Indians] in your troupe to any other now organized that I have knowledge of."[41]

Meanwhile, McLaughlin received approval to take Sitting Bull on tour. McLaughlin wrote Allen concerning Sitting Bull, saying "the old fool" had to be "manipulated and managed as you would eggs" in order to get him to go on the tour. Finally Sitting Bull agreed after being told he would tour Eastern cities and have the opportunity to meet the president.[42]

The show's first performance was in St. Paul, Minnesota, on September 15, 1884. It was called the "Sitting Bull Combination" and featured Sitting Bull; several other men, including his brother-in-law, Gray Eagle; some of their wives; and children. Also along on the tour as interpreter was one of McLaughlin's men, Louis Primeau, as well as McLaughlin's wife Marie Louise and son Harry, to assist.[43]

The show consisted of a tepee erected onstage and the Lakotas dressed in their finest traditional clothing. As the men smoked and the women prepared food, a lecturer told the audience about the Sioux lifestyle. Sitting Bull would address the crowd in Lakota, and after he was finished the interpreter would translate what he had said for the audience. The Sitting Bull Combination was scheduled to tour fifteen Eastern cities.[44]

While the show was still in St. Paul, Sitting Bull went to a theater to see a shooting performance by markswoman Annie Oakley. He was impressed with Annie's performance. When Annie's husband Frank Butler held a cigarette between his lips and she shot off its tip, Sitting Bull stood and shouted in Lakota, "Little Sure Shot," which became her title. They exchanged photographs and later met. With Annie's permission, he made her a member of the Hunkpapa tribe and adopted her as his daughter."[45]

When the Sitting Bull Combination reached New York City, almost six thousand people attended the first matinee and evening show. The house was packed for the next two weeks.[46]

Luther Standing Bear was a young Lakota from the Rosebud Agency.[47] He had graduated from the Carlisle Indian School and was working in John Wanamaker's department store in Philadelphia. Learning that Sitting Bull and others were to appear in a Philadelphia theater, Standing Bear bought a ticket for the show.[48]

Sitting Bull and others sat on the stage as a white man introduced Sitting Bull as the man who had killed Custer. Of course, Sitting Bull and the other Lakotas had no idea what the man said. Sitting Bull stood and addressed the crowd in Lakota. He called the audience his friends and told them that he and the other Lakotas were on their way to see the president of the United States. He planned to tell the president that the Lakota children needed to be educated to do the same things as white people do. "There is no use fighting," Sitting Bull said. "The buffalo are all gone, as well as the rest of the game . . . I am going to shake the hand of the Great Father at Washington, and I am going to tell him all these things."[49]

The white man stood and said he would interpret what Sitting Bull said, but instead he told the story of the "Custer massacre" and how the Sioux had overrun Custer and wiped out his soldiers. Standing Bear smiled as the translator told his lies. Two Lakota women sitting onstage spied Standing Bear and kept looking at him. At the end of the show, the interpreter said anyone who wanted to could come up onstage and shake hands with the man who had killed Custer.[50]

Standing Bear went up onstage with the rest of the crowd. One of the Lakota women grabbed him by the hand and said in Lakota,

"How many winters are you here?" When he replied in Lakota, she was overjoyed, and learning his father was Standing Bear, she said he was a relative and called to the others. As Sitting Bull and the other Lakotas happily gathered around Standing Bear, the white crowd had no idea what was happening. The white translator came over and wanted to know what was going on. Standing Bear translated for Sitting Bull to the man that Sitting Bull wanted him to go to the hotel with them to eat with them.[51]

At the hotel, Sitting Bull continued to quiz Standing Bear as to how far away Washington was, and in what direction. When Standing Bear told him, Sitting Bull was surprised and said, "Why, we must have passed the place." When the white "translator" entered the room, Sitting Bull used Standing Bear as his translator, asking the man when they were going to see the president and when they were going home. The man answered, "You are soon going home, and on the way, you may see the president." With the white man in the room, Standing Bear did not get a chance to tell Sitting Bull about the white man's lies. Sitting Bull and the Lakotas never got to see the president, and returned to Standing Rock in late October.[52]

McLaughlin was disappointed with Sitting Bull's trip to the East. Instead of sending Sitting Bull as part of the Dakota exhibit at the 1884–1885 World's Industrial and Cotton Centennial Exposition in New Orleans, McLaughlin sent Gall.[53]

Buffalo Bill Cody learned that Sitting Bull had appeared in Alvaren Allen's show. He contacted McLaughlin again, requesting that Sitting Bull be allowed to tour with his Buffalo Bill's Wild West. After some back-and-forth, McLaughlin finally relented and said he would not stand in the way of Sitting Bull going, but Cody would have to get permission from Secretary of the Interior Lucius Lamar.[54]

Cody worked to get endorsements from Generals Terry, Crook, Miles, and Sheridan. On April 29, 1885, he telegrammed Secretary Lamar requesting Sitting Bull be allowed to tour with his Wild West. Cody would take custody of Sitting Bull and be responsible for him. Lamar responded by writing no and underlining it three times. Commissioner of Indian Affairs John Atkins told Cody he and Secretary Lamar considered Sitting Bull a war criminal and were opposed to Cody's plan.[55]

Cody was not done. He received endorsements from General William Sherman and Colonel Eugene Carr, with whom he had served. He said while Sitting Bull was with him, he would receive the best of care. Lamar relented and said Sitting Bull was allowed to go.[56] Now Cody just had to convince Sitting Bull.

On June 6, Cody's publicity manager Major John Burke[57] was en route from Chicago to Standing Rock to convince Sitting Bull to join Buffalo Bill's Wild West for the season. At first Sitting Bull was cool toward the idea, but as Burke was showing Sitting Bull his publicity material, Sitting Bull spied a picture of Annie Oakley. She had signed on that year to tour with the Wild West. If Little Sure Shot was involved, then Sitting Bull would join.[58]

The contract, which would be in effect for four months, stated Sitting Bull would receive $50 per week, included a $125 signing bonus, and gave him exclusive rights for the sale of his photographs and autographs. He also insisted on his own translator, William Halsey, whom he trusted.[59]

A number of Hunkpapa men, women, and children, including Sitting Bull's wives and children, were hired to participate in the show. On June 8, they loaded the belongings they would need for the next four months and headed toward Bismarck, where they caught an eastbound train.[60]

On June 12, 1885, Major Burke arrived with Sitting Bull and the other Hunkpapas in Buffalo, New York. As they stepped off the train, Sitting Bull was dressed in his finest Lakota clothing and wore a full eagle-feather headdress. The Hunkpapas were escorted to waiting carriages that took them to Buffalo's Driving Park, where Buffalo Bill's Wild West was already under way.[61]

When they arrived at the park, Cody was on horseback demonstrating his shooting skills before a crowd of twelve thousand people. Sitting Bull and the rest of the Hunkpapas observed the performances of Indians on horseback attacking a stagecoach, horse races, and an attack on a cabin. They watched as Annie Oakley performed her shooting skills to thunderous applause.[62]

As members of the show gathered around Sitting Bull to get their first look at him, Annie Oakley stepped forward. Sitting Bull was happy to see her. She asked him about a red silk handkerchief and coins she had sent him.[63]

"I got them," Sitting Bull said. "But I left them at home for safety. I am very glad to see you. I have not forgotten you, and feel pleased that you want to remember me."[64]

Toward the end of the show, Cody indicated it was time to introduce Sitting Bull. Cody stood in front of the grandstand. The crowd cheered as Sitting Bull's carriage arrived and stopped near Cody. Sitting Bull and Burke got out of the carriage and walked toward Cody, who walked toward them. Cody held out his hand and Sitting Bull clasped it. Burke pointed at Cody and said in Lakota, "This is the white chief." Then, gesturing to Sitting Bull, he said in Lakota, "The Great Dakota Sioux King." Sitting Bull smiled and looked at the crowd as Cody launched into a long speech recounting both their deeds of war. Cody ended by saying, "He, from his standpoint, fought for what he believed was right, and made a name for himself to be known forever. The man I now introduce to you is Sitting Bull, the Napoleon of the red race, who has journeyed thousands of miles to be present with us today."[65]

After the show, Cody escorted Sitting Bull and the Hunkpapas to a clubhouse for refreshments and then to their camp for a dinner of steak, potatoes, bread, and coffee.[66]

Cody already had other Indians performing in the show, most of whom were Pawnees, traditional enemies of Lakotas. At first there was a little tension, but after they smoked the pipe together, tensions were reduced.[67]

For the next four months they toured over forty major cities of the Northeast, Midwest, and Canada. The 1885 advertisements, posters, and billboards for Buffalo Bill's Wild West were changed to include the phrases, "Larger and Greater than Ever" and "the renowned Sioux Chief Sitting Bull."[68]

When the show arrived in a new city, the performers would parade down the main street. Buffalo Bill rode first, and then right behind him rode Sitting Bull, wearing his eagle-feather headdress.[69]

At the beginning of the performance, Frank Richmond, the announcer, informed the crowd, "Here he comes! The Napoleon of the Plains! Chief Sitting Bull, ladies and gentlemen!" as Sitting Bull, again wearing his eagle-feather headdress, buckskin clothing, and paint, entered and rode around the ring once, either on horseback or in a carriage looking straight ahead, not interacting with the crowd, which shouted a mixture of cheers and boos. That was extent of his involvement with the show.[70]

Even though the performances reenacted violent encounters between white men and Indians, Cody promoted reconciliation, using himself and Sitting Bull as the focal point, his promotional material proclaiming "Foes in '76—Friends in '85."[71]

After the show, Sitting Bull sold his photographs, autographs, and personal possessions in the replica Indian village. People began to see Sitting Bull not as a fiendish caricature but a loving husband and father, surrounded by his family. He made himself available to meet with people. Reporters requested interviews and Sitting Bull usually granted them. Of course, the question that always came up was, What happened at the Little Big Horn?[72]

When not performing, Sitting Bull liked to dress in fine clothing—a print shirt with the tail hanging out over black flowered pants, beaded moccasins with rubber soles, a brocade waistcoat, a scarlet tie, and jewelry, including a crucifix. On his head, he wore a beaver-felt top hat. He enjoyed walking the streets of American cities after everyone had gone indoors for the night.[73]

Sitting Bull was generous. "The contents of his pockets were often emptied into the hands of small, ragged little boys," Annie Oakley said. "Nor could he understand how so much wealth could go brushing by, unmindful of the poor." He concluded that if white people would not take care of their own, they certainly weren't going to take care of the Indians. "The white man knows how to make everything," Sitting Bull said, "but he does not know how to distribute it."[74]

Cody became a true advocate for the Lakotas, telling the newspapers, "The defeat of Custer was not a massacre. The Indians were being pursued by skilled fighters with orders to kill. . . . They had

Sitting Bull gives money to poor children during Buffalo Bill's Wild West.

their wives and little ones to protect and they were fighting for their existence."[75]

Sitting Bull had made Annie Oakley a member of the Hunkpapa tribe and adopted her as his daughter. He gave her a pair of moccasins one of his daughters had made that he had worn during the Battle of the Little Big Horn. Sometimes, he would sit in Annie's tent and watch as she crocheted and sewed her costumes or listen as she read from the Bible. They took comfort in each other's company.[76]

Buffalo Bill's Wild West began playing in Washington, DC, on June 22. This was Sitting Bull's first time in the capital. One of his top reasons for joining the Wild West was to meet the president and speak for his people. Cody had his staff help Sitting Bull draft a letter to President Grover Cleveland, and later, Sitting Bull had the opportunity to meet briefly with him.[77]

He also met with Interior Secretary Lucius Lamar, who issued a decree that Sitting Bull and his party could continue traveling with Cody throughout the country to view its population and resources. After that, Sitting Bull and his Hunkpapas met General Phil Sheridan, who had replaced General William Sherman as commanding general of the US Army. As they entered his offices, the fifteen Hunkpapas admired Sherman's paintings of Western scenes while Sitting Bull ignored the general who had at one time denied Sitting Bull even existed.[78]

In Philadelphia, the Indian Rights Association wanted to talk with Sitting Bull. The association stressed that Indians needed to lose their tribal identities and become the same as all other Americans. During the meeting, the association members began discussing the Little Big Horn fight. One member turned to the interpreter and said, "Ask Sitting Bull if he ever had any regret for his share in the Custer massacre," adding that he must "flee from the wrath to come" for murdering an American hero. Sitting Bull jumped to his feet and pointed his fingers in the questioner's face. "Tell this fool that I did not murder Custer," Sitting Bull shouted. "It was a fight in open day. He would have killed me if he could. I have answered to my people for the dead on my side. Let Custer's friends answer for the dead on his side."[79]

Before Buffalo Bill's Wild West reached Boston, the July 20, 1885, edition of the *Boston Post* said that "arrangements [have] been made to illuminate the grounds by electricity" for the performance. While in town, Sergeant John Ryan, who had been at the Little Big Horn with Major Marcus Reno's battalion, showed Sitting Bull a Seventh Cavalry guidon that had been captured by the Indians, and they discussed the fight and how Ryan had recovered the guidon.[80]

Buffalo Bill's company entered Canada, and after a performance in Toronto, the *Globe* printed an interview with Cody and Sitting Bull in its August 23, 1885, edition in which Sitting Bull spoke fondly of his old Mounted Police friend, Major James Walsh. If the two ever met while Sitting Bull was in Canada, there is no record of it.[81]

Later that month they were performing in Montreal to enthusiastic crowds. While in town, Cody and Sitting Bull visited the studio of world-renowned photographer William Notman. Both men had had their photographs taken separately, but this was the first time they had their photograph taken together. Both were dressed in the clothing they wore in the Wild West performance. Cody held a Winchester rifle as they stood and looked to their left. It became an iconic photo, titled "Foes in '76—Friends in '85"——and it was used for the rest of that season and into the following seasons to promote the Wild West.[82]

It was raining as the show season ended in St. Louis on October 11, 1885. Sitting Bull was asked what he thought of the tour through the country. "The wigwam is a better place for the red man," he was quoted as saying. "He is sick of the houses and the noises and the multitudes of men."[83]

He walked to Annie Oakley's tent and gave her a quiver of fine arrows, beaded moccasins, and a feather headdress. During the performers' final meal together, the band played "Auld Lang Syne," and Cody's partner Nate Salsbury thanked them on behalf of Cody and himself for a successful season, saying he would see them all in the spring.[84]

Before Sitting Bull left, he and Cody exchanged gifts. Sitting Bull gave Cody a bear-claw necklace, representing might and strength, as the bear was the ally of the greatest warriors. Cody gave

Sitting Bull the light gray horse he had been riding for the last four months. Sitting Bull had become attached to the horse, which was trained to do tricks such as sitting back on its haunches as it raised a front leg and hoof.[85]

Cody also gave Sitting Bull a white sombrero, size eight. Sitting Bull attached a small American flag to the hatband and was very proud of it. Sitting Bull gave his beaver-felt top hat to an employee at a St. Louis hotel. Later on, Sitting Bull caught one of his relatives wearing his sombrero and in anger said, "My friend Long Hair [Cody] gave me this hat. I value it very highly, for the hand that placed it upon my head had a friendly feeling for me." After that no one touched his hat.[86]

At the end of the 1885 season, Buffalo Bill's Wild West was a success, grossing over $1 million, with a profit of $100,000. Attendance was estimated at more than a million people throughout the season.[87]

Buffalo Bill Cody and Sitting Bull had many conversations. At the end of one particular exchange, Sitting Bull told Cody:

We are not as many as the White Man. But we know this land is our land. And while we live and can fight, we will fight for it. If the White Man does not want us to fight, why does he take our land? If we come and build our lodges on the White Man's land, the White Man drives us away or kills us. Have we not the same rights as the White Man?[88]

CHAPTER 11

Geronimo on the Run, 1885–1886

It was dusk on May 17, 1885, as Geronimo, Mangas, Naiche, Chihuahua, and Nana led 144 Chiricahuas off the White Mountain Reservation. Thinking General George Crook had ordered Mangas's and his arrest for tiswin brewing, Geronimo believed they had to escape the reservation and head for Mexico. Needing a substantial number of warriors to survive in Mexico, Geronimo thought the only way to convince Naiche, Chihuahua, and other leaders, along with their warriors, to leave with him was to have Lieutenant Britton Davis and the Chiricahua scout Chatto killed. Their murders would convince the others they had no choice but to flee. So Geronimo told them Davis and Chatto were already dead without checking to make sure they had actually been killed. When Geronimo discovered the assassins had failed to carry out their deeds, he decided not to tell Chihuahua and the others.[1]

Knowing the Apache scouts would soon be on their trail, the Chiricahuas raced southeast through the night of May 17. They glimpsed pursuers before crossing Eagle Creek and climbing into the rugged mountains beyond on May 18. The next day, the women and children scattered from the men and would later rejoin them. The men took difficult mountain paths, forcing their pursuers to go slowly.[2]

The warriors killed anyone they came upon, taking their weapons and ammunition. They burned ranch houses, stole horses and mules, and killed cattle. They split into two main groups, one headed by

Geronimo and the other headed by Chihuahua. Smaller raiding parties prowled the countryside.[3]

Separated by some distance, Geronimo's group and Chihuahua's group stopped to rest on May 21, possibly along the San Francisco River. A raiding party arrived with one of the deserter Apache scouts at Chihuahua's camp. The scout told Chihuahua that Lieutenant Davis and Chatto were still alive. Chihuahua was furious, believing Geronimo had duped him, and he vowed to kill Geronimo.[4]

Someone must have rushed to Geronimo's camp and warned him Chihuahua was coming to kill him. He quickly got his people moving east and then south to Devil's Creek.[5]

By the time Chihuahua, his brother Ulzana, and the deserter scout reached Geronimo's camp, they were long gone. Chihuahua decided to head north along the San Francisco River and lay low before heading south.[6]

On May 22, Lieutenant Britton Davis left Fort Apache in pursuit of Geronimo and the Chiricahua fugitives. Interpreter Mickey Free and fifty-eight Apache scouts wearing red headbands rode with him—thirty-two White Mountain Apaches, four San Carlos Apaches, and twenty-two Chiricahuas led by Chatto. Crook had telegrammed Davis to let the Chiricahua scouts know that if the fleeing Chiricahuas reached Mexico and started terrorizing again, the Mexicans would not release their captive relatives. This was incentive enough for many, and for others, who disliked Geronimo, whom they believed had brought all their troubles upon them. It was now Chiricahuas hunting Chiricahuas. It would be friend against friend, relative against relative.[7]

Captain Allen Smith with one hundred men of the Fourth Cavalry and a dozen White Mountain Apache scouts under the command of Lieutenant Charles Gatewood had been pursuing the Chiricahuas from Fort Apache since May 17. On the same day Davis left Fort Apache, Smith and his men were following Geronimo's trail along Devil's Creek, into Devil's Canyon.[8]

Smith called a halt for a noon break in the deep, narrow canyon, leaving Lieutenant James Parker in charge while he and Lieutenant James Lockett went bathing in the creek.[9]

Geronimo's camp was on a plateau about five hundred yards from the rim of the canyon. They knew Smith and his men were down below. Geronimo, Mangas, and Naiche positioned the twenty warriors they had with them around the canyon rim, so they had the troops and scouts surrounded.[10]

Gatewood sent the Apache scouts to climb the east side of the canyon to look for signs of the fugitives. As the scouts closed in on the Chiricahuas' hidden position, Geronimo fired the first shot, severely wounding a scout. The rest of the warriors opened fire, sending the scouts scrambling back down the slope. Parker and Lieutenant Leighton Finley ordered troops to follow them as they made their way up the steep eastern canyon slopes and rock ledges, dodging bullets all the way. Parker, who had been on friendly terms with Geronimo, was now trying not to be hit by one of his bullets.[11]

Parker and Finley with seventeen men reached the top of the canyon as the warriors dropped back, forming a rear guard for the women and children who had already broken camp and were on the move. Gatewood had rallied the scouts and brought them to the top, followed later by Captain Smith, dressed in his drawers and boots. After a halfhearted chase, Smith determined they could not overtake the fugitives and ended their pursuit for the day. A scout and two troopers had been wounded in the fight.[12]

General George Crook and the commander of the District of New Mexico, Colonel Luther Bradley, were sending all the troops and Apache scouts they could muster into the field, searching for, trailing, and trying to cut off the fleeing Chiricahuas. The fugitives eluded their pursuers as they continued to murder, loot, and destroy anyone and anything in their path, reaching New Mexico and speeding south. Arizona citizens were in an uproar as newspapers printed stories of Chiricahua outrages, some real and others not so real—all pointing to Geronimo and his band. By June 4, Crook would estimate the Chiricahuas had killed seventeen citizens.[13]

On May 24, 1885, Geronimo, Mangas, and Nana decided to explore the possibilities of either finding refuge on the Mescalero Apache Reservation in New Mexico or convincing the Mescaleros to join them in their fight against the White Eyes. Mangas led about forty people southeast toward Kingston, New Mexico, where he would wait for Geronimo, who headed northeast to the Rio Grande with six men and two women. The plan was for Geronimo's fourth wife, She-gha, along with their three-year-old daughter and another woman, to approach the Mescaleros and find out if they would be willing to help. Geronimo and the others would wait at prearranged meeting locations for the women's return.[14]

As Geronimo's group traveled eastward, they came upon three White Eyes at Antelope Springs and killed them. Stripping the bodies of everything useful and taking the livestock, they proceeded on their way. Crossing the Rio Grande, they entered the Caballo Mountains, where the women left on their mission. Geronimo and his men returned west to Emory Pass in the Black Range.[15]

On May 26, a White Eye discovered Mangas's band several miles east of Kingston and alerted the army. The band scattered before the army could reach them and led the soldiers on a merry chase. Warriors diverted the troops from the women and children, who crossed the Mimbres Mountains, and ten miles north of Fort Cummings, they rendezvoused with Geronimo's party. By May 29, the reunited band crossed the border into Mexico.[16]

Geronimo had left two men behind to wait for the return of She-gha and the other woman. They never appeared. The two women didn't have a chance to make their case. The Mescalero Indian police immediately seized them when they appeared at the agency. The Mescaleros had no intention of wrecking their good relations with the White Eyes. In fact, they had vowed to "fight Geronimo." The women were turned over to the agent, who handed them over to the army, which held them prisoner at Fort Stanton, New Mexico. When questioned, they said Geronimo planned to wait in the San Andres Mountains for any Mescaleros who wanted to join him. From there he planned to raid along the east side of the Rio Grande River.[17]

By June 10, Geronimo and the other scattered Chiricahua bands had all crossed the border into Mexico, not losing a single person. Geronimo, Mangas, Naiche, and their people settled in at their old stronghold at Bugatseka in Sonora, while Chihuahua set up his rancheria on a ridge north of Oputo, also in Sonora. The Chiricahuas believed they were safe in their mountain strongholds and relaxed their guard.[18]

Crook and Bradley were not done. They stationed troops along the border with Mexico to intercept any Chiricahua raiding parties that might try to cross. Crook sent two detachments into Mexico's Sierra Madre Mountains in search of the Chiricahuas.[19]

Captain Emmet Crawford, leading a forty-man detachment of A Company of the Sixth Cavalry and a pack train, joined Lieutenant Britton Davis and his Apache scouts on June 9, at Skeleton Canyon, where Crawford took command of Davis and his scouts, who now numbered 130. Chief of Scouts Al Sieber joined them with a second pack train, and they crossed the border into Mexico on June 11, 1885.[20]

Chatto, leading thirty of Crawford's scouts, discovered Chihuahua's rancheria at dawn on June 23 during an intense rainstorm. They attacked, but Chihuahua and fourteen men, women, and children escaped. The scouts killed a woman and then discovered a cave where fifteen women and children were hiding. They captured them all, including Chihuahua's son Eugene and daughter Ramona and the wife and two children of Chihuahua's brother Ulzana. Crawford sent the prisoners with an officer, ten troopers, and ten Apache scouts to Fort Bowie. Chihuahua and Ulzana were furious over Chatto's attack and were out for revenge.[21]

On July 7, Captain Wirt Davis left Fort Bowie with the second detachment consisting of two companies of the Fourth Cavalry and 102 White Mountain and San Carlos Apache scouts wearing white headbands and led by Lieutenant Matthias Day. Most of the scouts were White Mountain and San Carlos Apaches, along with sixteen Chiricahuas Gatewood had recruited. One of the White Mountain scout leaders was Bylas, who was out for revenge. Bylas had been at the Stevens ranch when Geronimo and his raiders had killed all the Mexicans living there. Davis's destination was also the Sierra Madre Mountains, south of the border.[22]

On August 7, Bylas found Geronimo's rancheria at Bugatseka. Early that afternoon, Lieutenant Matthias Day and Chief of Scouts

Charlie Roberts led eighty-six Apache scouts in the attack. Day was hoping to encircle the village, but a braying mule gave them away.[23]

As the scouts fired into the village, Geronimo initially tried to rally the warriors to protect the women and children. The scouts recognized Geronimo and shot at him. Grabbing his baby boy, he began running, but the shots pouring in at him were so hot, he dropped his son as he dodged and weaved in his escape. The scouts thought they had hit him at the moment he dropped his son. All those who escaped had to leap from a steep bluff.[24]

The scouts killed two women and one boy. They captured almost all the women and children, totaling fifteen. Among the captives were two of Geronimo's wives and five of his children, one of whom was wounded.[25] The captives included Mangas's wife Huera, one of the instigators in the breakout.[26]

When Day returned with the scouts and prisoners to Davis's camp, he found Lieutenant Crawford's detachment had arrived. Crawford had Geronimo's wives brought to his tent where he instructed Chatto and Mickey Free to question them. Geronimo's wives told Crawford they believed Naiche and his people were somewhere on the western slopes of the Sierra Madre Mountains, but they had no idea of Chihuahua's whereabouts, and they said they did not know Geronimo's plans. Believing Geronimo's wives were lying, an enraged Crawford drew his pistol and threatened to shoot them if they didn't tell the truth. Mickey Free said they were not lying. Crawford relented, ordering everyone out of his tent.[27]

Geronimo gathered his scattered band now consisting of about forty people and headed southeast into Chihuahua. His brother-in-law Nana was still with him, but Mangas left with a small group. Only a few women remained, including the female warrior Lozen.[28]

The attack on their rancheria was a devastating loss for Geronimo's band. They could easily replace food, horses, weapons, and supplies through raids, but their loved ones were now in the hands of the Americans. The loss of their wives severely hampered the remaining warriors' way of life. In Apache culture certain duties were performed by men and other duties, such as food preparation and making and repairing clothing, were performed by women.[29]

The army's search for Geronimo continued. The prisoners from Geronimo's rancheria were sent to Fort Bowie. General Crook wanted all captured Chiricahuas to be held there as potential bargaining chips for the surrender of Geronimo and the others.[30]

Captain Emmet Crawford decided to split his detachment, sending Lieutenant Britton Davis, Al Sieber, Mickey Free, Chatto, and forty-one scouts ahead of the main column. Davis was to act independently and follow Geronimo wherever he went. On August 13, during heavy rain that lasted five days, Davis's detachment advanced east into the rugged Sierra Madres in search of Geronimo. Many Chiricahuas on both sides believed Geronimo's Power had caused the rain. He had been known to bring the rain after sitting down and singing for an hour.[31]

Captain Wirt Davis took his command to the western slopes of the Sierra Madre Mountains in the search for Chihuahua and Naiche. A Mexican army led by General Diego Guerra had been pursuing Chihuahua, and one of his detachments had been bloodied by Chihuahua's fifteen-man band. Throughout the summer months Chihuahua and Naiche raided jointly or singly, rampaging through Sonora and into Arizona. On September 22, Captain Davis's scouts caught up with Chihuahua and Naiche in the El Tigre Mountains. The Chiricahuas fought a rearguard action, killing and mutilating a Western Apache scout, cutting off his nose and leaving a butcher knife protruding from where his nose had been. The firefight was intense, bringing the scouts to a standstill and allowing Naiche's women and children to escape.[32]

Meanwhile, Crawford's men ran into an unexpected delay as they trailed Geronimo. Lieutenant Britton Davis and his scouts, who were far in advance of the rest of the detachment, ran low on supplies. Davis authorized the scouts to shoot a beef cow. The shots notified not only Geronimo to the close proximity of Davis and his scouts, but also Mexican troops in the area. Crawford had not heard from Davis for some time and sent Lieutenant Charles Elliott with eight Apache scouts, two packers, and six mules with rations for Davis's men. Elliott and his men were captured after Mexican troops shot at them. They were taken to San Buenaventura where they were paraded down the main street and then jailed. Davis learned of the arrests of Elliott and the scouts. He arrived in town and after meeting with the army commander, he was able to explain the situation and negotiate their release.[33]

It was not until noon the following day that Davis and his men could extract themselves from the Mexicans, who had now become their hosts. For the next three days, Davis and his scouts followed Geronimo's trail to the southeast. Davis later wrote about what happened on August 28: "We came out upon the crest of a small range of mountains to see, fifteen or eighteen miles ahead of us, small dots on the plain which the scouts pronounced Geronimo's band heading north."[34]

Geronimo's people had raided the Santa Clara ranch of General Luis Terrazas, where they had stolen horses and were now heading north toward the US border. Davis reasoned he would never be able to catch them, but if he remained on their trail, he might be able to apply enough pressure that they might make a mistake and run into another detachment.[35]

Geronimo had decided to head back to the United States to rescue his wives and children. He mistakenly believed they were at Fort Apache, but Crook was holding them at Fort Bowie. Nana with five men and ten women and children remained behind in the mountains, northwest of Janos. Geronimo took with him five men, one of whom was his son Chappo, and four or five women.[36]

For three days, Lieutenant Britton Davis and his men followed Geronimo's trail, covering 125 miles on foot. During the third day, after trudging through a torrential rain, Mexican troops overtook them. The commander told Davis they were taking over the pursuit of Geronimo. According to the agreement between the United States and Mexico, Davis had to give up pursuit, which he did. He began marching toward El Paso, Texas, the nearest border point. They had to cross a shallow alkali lake and then traverse a waterless desert, running out of food before they reached their destination.[37]

On September 5, 1885, Davis reached Fort Bliss at El Paso, Texas, immediately wiring Crook that Geronimo was headed toward

New Mexico. However, Geronimo had most likely already crossed the border ten miles east of Palomas Lake.[38]

Davis was amused to learn that because no one had heard from him, it was believed his Apache scouts had murdered him; his obituary had even been printed in the New York newspapers. Davis ran into an old friend of his father who offered to hire him to manage his ranch and mining interests in northwestern Chihuahua. He accepted the position and resigned from the army.[39]

There were no sightings of Geronimo's raiders until September 9, when four Mexican men and women arrived at Fort Cummings, New Mexico, reporting that they had spotted eight Apaches east of Mule Springs. No one could figure out what Geronimo was up to. Crook believed Geronimo was raiding for plunder and to recruit more warriors.[40]

On September 10, rancher Brady Pollock was searching for stray horses on Macho Creek when Geronimo ambushed him, firing two bullets into his body. Geronimo's warriors smashed in Pollock's skull and rode off with thirteen horses. Heading north, they stole sixteen horses from another ranch and spent the night in the foothills of the Mimbres Mountains.[41]

The next day, Avaristo Abeyta was cutting poles when the raiders attacked. Trying to outrun them on his horse, they shot it out from under him and then killed him. An hour later, they killed George Horn in Gallinas Canyon.[42]

In the same canyon, seventeen-year-old Martin McKinn and his eleven-year-old brother Santiago were herding their father's cattle about two miles north of their ranch. Around 11:00 a.m., the boys had stopped for their lunch break. Martin was reading a book while Santiago played in the rocks along the creek. Santiago heard a gunshot and saw Martin lying on the ground. An Indian, who he later learned was Geronimo, ran up to Martin and smashed in his head. Santiago tried to hide, but the raiders found him and brought him back to where Martin's body lay as Geronimo stripped off Martin's coat and shirt and put them on. They allowed Santiago to live and took him with them, along with the horse and mule the boys had been riding.[43]

At 11:30 a.m., the raiders entered Noonday Canyon where they ransacked and then set fire to miners' cabins, rounded up the livestock, and shot at four White Eyes three hundred yards away, nicking one in the ear. The raiders rode west, crossing the Mimbres River. Santiago observed that Geronimo and his five warriors rode at the front while the women and he rode in the rear. That night they camped in a canyon somewhere north of Georgetown, New Mexico.[44]

The next day, Geronimo and his raiders came upon two woodcutters. They killed one, but the other managed to escape. Following the Upper Mimbres River, they came upon the Allen ranch where Mrs. Allen was alone with her three children. Seeing the raiders approaching, she and the children made a run for it. A large Indian, possibly Geronimo, came after them, but the family dog lunged at him, giving them time to escape. The raiders did not pursue the Allen family, who walked eight miles to the Fort Bayard sawmill.[45]

By now, the countryside was on the alert. Cavalry from Fort Bayard, state militia from Hillsboro, and a group of ranchers that included John McKinn, Santiago's father, followed the raiders' trail.[46]

Geronimo's group spent the night at the headwaters of Sapillo Creek. The next few days they moved rapidly into the Gila wilderness. Their pursuers gave up the chase. John McKinn was concerned that if they got too close, the raiders would kill Santiago.[47]

On September 15, the raiders reached the sanctuary of Teepee Canyon, northeast of Mogollon Peak, remote from settlements and well hidden. Here they rested a few days, making themselves known again the evening of September 18 when they stole three horses from two ranches near the San Francisco River. The next morning, they appeared along the Blue River in Arizona where they shot William Raspberry through the mouth, killing him. Traveling rapidly, they headed toward the White Mountain Reservation.[48]

Leaving the horses behind with one warrior, the women, and Santiago, Geronimo and four warriors traveled on foot, entering the White Mountain Reservation from the east. Easily slipping past the Apache scout patrols Lieutenant Gatewood had posted, Geronimo reached the east fork of the White River after midnight on September 22. There, he expected to find the Chiricahuas at their farms, but instead there was only a White Mountain woman guarding her crops.[49]

The woman told Geronimo that Gatewood had moved the Chiricahua rancherias closer to Fort Apache. She also said their families who had been captured at Bugatseka were not there, but Geronimo's wife She-gha and daughter were there. Geronimo had the woman lead them to the Chiricahua rancheria and show him She-gha's wickiup.[50]

Reunited with his wife and daughter, Geronimo learned that She-gha's companion Bi-ya-neta Tse-dah-dilth-thlith, who had been with her at the Mescalero Reservation, was also there, and she left with them, too.[51]

The raiders silently slipped out of the rancheria, stole White Mountain Apache horses, and rode east to rejoin the rest of their party. They rode hard, creating as much distance as they could before the soldiers and scouts learned of their visit.[52]

The next morning, Gatewood sent White Mountain scouts after Geronimo's raiders, but they were long gone. Gatewood telegrammed Crook to tell him the news of Geronimo's raid, and they had a rapid exchange back and forth. At one point, Crook messaged, "Kill Geronimo and his entire party," but later modified his demands, stating that capturing Geronimo was preferable to letting him escape back to Mexico.[53]

Geronimo and his band had disappeared. No one could find their trail. Then on the evening of September 27, Geronimo struck again. A. L. Sabourne was driving a wagonload of goods to Cooney City, New Mexico, and was at Cactus Flat when a single shot hit him in the chest, killing him. Geronimo's people ransacked the wagon. Finding a large amount of candy, they immediately ate it all. The next day, everyone was sick—too much sugar. They spent the next few days resting and feasting on the food from Sabourne's wagon. Santiago believed the warriors spent time gambling to see if he lived or died. Fortunately, those in favor of him living won.[54]

General Crook was frustrated that Geronimo and his raiders were not being caught or killed. He had a telegram sent to Gatewood to deliver to the Apache scouts: "The general will give $100 for each head of a hostile Chiricahua buck brought in by an Indian scout or volunteer. Tell the White Mountain Indians that the general . . . is getting tired of doing all their work for them."[55]

Geronimo's band rode south, raiding through New Mexico on their return to Mexico. One day they came upon three Mescalero Apache women, one with a baby and another with a small boy, who would later be known as Charlie Smith. The women had been gathering piñon nuts. Geronimo's band took them all. The third woman, who would be called Ih-tedda (or Young Girl) became Geronimo's wife, some believe his seventh.[56]

Traveling by night, Geronimo's raiders reached the Animas Valley on October 9, 1885, where they stole thirty horses before crossing the border into Mexico. During the same time Geronimo was on his raid to Fort Apache, Chihuahua and his brother Ulzana had been raiding in Arizona, as well as Naiche, all returning unscathed to Mexico about the same time Geronimo did.[57]

At some point, Geronimo's raiders reunited with Nana and the rest of the band and headed south toward Casas Grandes. On October 11, they shot at a pack train, hurting no one. Later that day, they attacked fourteen vaqueros, killing one. They traveled toward Carretas, then headed south to their stronghold at Bent-ci-iye, where they met Naiche and Chihuahua and their bands. They had not been all together since their split on May 19. Chihuahua must have had enough time to calm down following Geronimo's ruse, as there is no record of any violence between the two. The leaders conferred as to what their next plan of action would be. Chihuahua and Ulzana would take some warriors and head north across the border, seeking to free relatives and take revenge. Geronimo, Naiche, and Nana would remain in Mexico with a dozen warriors and boys guarding sixty women and children, while raiding to restock supplies.[58]

In late October, Chihuahua and Ulzana crossed the border on separate raids. While Chihuahua raided and killed in southwestern New Mexico, Ulzana with twelve warriors dashed toward Fort Apache, seeking to free captured relatives and kill Chatto and Mickey Free. Not finding their relatives, Chatto, or Mickey Free, Ulzana's raiders took vengeance on the White Mountain Apaches, killing twenty-one people while losing one of their own. By the end of December, Ulzana had re-crossed the border into Mexico. During his raid through the Southwest, Ulzana's raiders had traveled 1,200 miles, killing 38 people and stealing roughly 250 horses and mules.[59]

As Geronimo, Chihuahua, and Ulzana were raiding that fall, the federal government's internal disagreements over how to handle the Chiricahua raids in the Southwest came to a head. Citizens of New Mexico and Arizona voiced their outrage in the newspapers and to the president and Congress, believing General Crook was mismanaging the situation. On November 29, 1885, Lieutenant General Phil Sheridan—bringing along Colonel Luther Bradley, commander of the District of New Mexico, and three Washington staff officers—arrived at Fort Bowie to meet with General George Crook and devise a plan to protect the citizens of the United States and stop the Chiricahua raids.[60]

With Democrat Grover Cleveland elected as president in 1884, General William Sherman had retired as head of the army and Sheridan was appointed in his place. Sheridan knew nothing about Apaches and relied on his old West Point classmate and fellow Civil War officer General George Crook as to how to fight Apaches. Sheridan was skeptical about using Apache scouts but deferred to Crook's judgment.[61]

Since September 4, 1882, Crook had been commander of the Department of Arizona within the Division of the Pacific. He was busy during the summer of 1885. He met with Luis Torres, the governor of Sonora, who supported Crook's military efforts in his state. He had petitioned Washington officials to end the dual management of the White Mountain Reservation by the Department of the Interior and the army, with its agency at San Carlos. By mid-August the entire reservation's management was under Crook's control. Crook was disappointed with Colonel Bradley's response to the Chiricahua raiders in New Mexico, but was powerless to do anything more than make suggestions.[62]

Nelson A. Miles was now a general and the commander of the Department of Missouri. Colonel Bradley's District of New Mexico was part of his command. Miles, a competitor to Crook, despised

Crook's use of Indian scouts and was vocal about it. Crook resented the younger, know-it-all Miles.[63]

Crook suggested the District of New Mexico be placed under his control so he could better coordinate efforts against the Chiricahuas. Miles believed he could do a better job at that than Crook and had the backing of the governor of New Mexico.[64]

On another matter, Crook was concerned with the federal Major Crimes Act, which required any Chiricahuas who had committed crimes who surrendered were to be turned over to state and local authorities in the jurisdictions where the crimes had been committed. Crook became convinced Chiricahua warriors would never agree to surrender and be turned over to state and local justice. They would also want specific conditions as to what would happen to them. The alternative was to hunt them down and kill them all, which would take years. After conferring with several lawyers, Crook proposed that the Chiricahua fighters be designated prisoners of war and relocated outside Arizona. He also planned to continue sending columns of Apache scouts and troops into Mexico to force the Chiricahuas to surrender.[65]

When Sheridan arrived at Fort Bowie to meet with Crook, there were several issues to resolve. First, Sheridan would give Crook temporary command of the District of New Mexico to better coordinate efforts against the Chiricahuas. Second, although he disagreed with the concept, Sheridan would allow Crook to continue to use Apache scouts. Third, Sheridan agreed to treat the Chiricahuas as prisoners of war and not turn them over to state and local authorities.[66]

Then Sheridan dropped a bombshell: They would not only remove the Chiricahuas who were on the warpath, but all Chiricahuas, including those who had remained peaceful and those who acted as scouts for the army. The plan was to send them to Fort Marion, Florida, where they would remain permanently.[67]

Crook was against the mass removal. Captain Crawford had arrived at Fort Bowie, and Crook brought him into the meeting to voice his opinion. Crawford believed that if the Chiricahua scouts learned their families were being deported to Florida, it would have a disastrous effect on the scouts' performance. Sheridan dropped the idea—for the time being.[68]

When Sheridan left Fort Bowie on November 29, Crook had everything he wanted to force the Chiricahuas to surrender. Miles believed the removal of New Mexico from his department was a personal slap in the face, done to make him look bad. Crook had better now produce results.[69]

Geronimo and Naiche were staying busy down in Mexico. In mid-October 1885, they killed three men during a raid near Temosachic in Chihuahua. On October 27, they attacked and occupied part of the mining town of Dolores, killing three men there. The band settled into the rugged mountain wilderness between the Sátachi and Aros Rivers, just across the border in Sonora. The wilderness was called Espinosa del Diablo—the Devil's Backbone. There, Chihuahua joined them after his New Mexico raid, bringing the rancheria's total population to roughly eighty—twenty-four of whom were warriors and adolescent boys.[70]

Reports of Chiricahua atrocities continued to pour into the Mexican government. On November 14, 1885, twenty Chiricahua warriors attacked three men at El Soquete, Sonora, killing Jose Jayme; November 23, Geronimo and Naiche led an attack killing two men in the District of Ures, Sonora. On November 25, Geronimo and Naiche's warriors killed Francisco Munguia, Antonio Lopez, and Trinidad Vega at La Parida, Sonora. The pursuing troops found only two of their bodies. On or about December 9, in two separate attacks, Chiricahuas killed Paulino Guttierez and Pedro Barron while wounding two other men near Sahuaripa, Sonora. Around December 25, Chiricahuas killed Francisco Lavandera and Jose Moreno in the vicinity of Granados, Sonora.[71]

Captain Wirt Davis left Guadalupe Canyon in Arizona on November 21, 1885, crossing into Chihuahua, Mexico. He led a new contingent of one hundred San Carlos Apache scouts, none of whom were Chiricahuas; George Wratten, as chief of scouts; a company of the Fourth Cavalry; and three pack trains. For two months they scoured the Sierra Madres' eastern slopes searching for the Chiricahua bands, with no success. The detachment became worn down and

Davis's health deteriorated. In early January 1886, General Crook authorized their return to Fort Bowie.[72]

On December 11, 1885, Captain Emmet Crawford crossed the border into Sonora, Mexico, at Agua Prieta. His command consisted of 5 officers; a hospital steward; 2 chiefs of scouts, Tom Horn and William Harrison; an interpreter, Concepcion; 100 new White Mountain and Chiricahua Apache scouts; and 3 pack trains with 12 civilian packers—a total of 121 men. Chatto was not with the scouts this time, being replaced by Geronimo's second cousin Noche as sergeant major. Crawford's command headed south following the Bavispe River along the western slopes of the Sierra Madres.[73]

On December 25, Tom Horn, along with a detachment of ten scouts, including Noche, left the column on foot, searching for the Chiricahua camp. As the days passed, they discovered a promising trail leading into Espinosa del Diablo. They began finding cattle carcasses, and then the scouts smelled smoke from mescal roasting pits. After two weeks, they had found the Chiricahua rancheria located on a well-protected high point.[74]

Having left the pack trains behind, Captain Crawford followed rapidly behind Horn, and after a twelve-hour march through rough terrain, they caught up with the advance scouts northeast of the rancheria before dawn on January 10. Crawford decided to surround and attack the Chiricahuas right away. He divided the men into three detachments, one led by Horn and the other two led by Lieutenants Marion Maus and William Shipp.[75]

As they were getting into their positions, some of which were in the heights above the rancheria, burros in the Chihuahuas' livestock herd began braying, sensing the presence of the newcomers. Three men left their wickiups to check on the herd about four hundred yards from the rancheria.[76]

Spotting the three men, White Mountain scouts opened fire, seeking revenge for their relatives' murders by Ulzana's raiders near Fort Apache. The Chiricahuas fired back as people emerged from their wickiups. Geronimo shouted, "Scatter and go as you can!" Horn raced toward the sound of Geronimo's voice. Horn claimed Crawford had given him a direct order to kill Geronimo. He stopped his pursuit when he realized that none of the scouts were following him. Geronimo organized the warriors fighting a rearguard action as their families ran toward the river.[77]

The scouts soon broke off the fight. The White Mountain scouts were not enthusiastic about attacking wide-awake, well-armed Chiricahua warriors, and the Chiricahua scouts were concerned about harming family and friends. No one on either side had been injured in the morning's half-light. Crawford's Apache scouts had captured thirty head of horses and mules and everything in the rancheria. They remained there while the Chiricahuas regrouped along the river.[78]

That afternoon, Lozen, the female warrior, and her friend Dahteste approached the rancheria. Lozen had a message from Geronimo, Naiche, and Chihuahua: They were willing to talk about a return to San Carlos. Crawford gave her food and said he would meet with them the next day on a flat along the river, a mile from the rancheria.[79]

Crawford had camp set up a hundred yards from the rancheria and ordered everything burned that was not of use to them. The men sat around large bonfires that provided some warmth from the bitter cold.[80]

Crawford set out sentries that night. One group of six on a hill east of the camp became drowsy and most of them fell asleep. The Chihenne scout Eskin-zion believed Geronimo was using his Power to cause them to fall asleep. Eskin-zion used his own Power to counteract Geronimo's. He sang and sang until they all were awake. When Geronimo realized Eskin-zion had thwarted his spell, he yelled at him from out of the darkness.[81]

Early on January 11, scouts spotted men advancing from out of the heavy morning fog and alerted the camp. At first, Tom Horn and Lieutenants Maus and Shipp thought they were Captain Wirt Davis's Apache scouts—until the unknown men fired, wounding three of Crawford's scouts.[82]

The scouts started shooting back until Crawford arrived and told them to cease firing. The scouts who held the position at this side of the camp were all Chiricahuas. After about fifteen minutes, the other side stopped firing. Crawford learned the attackers were Mexican troops, 128 Tarahumara Indians from Chihuahua led by Major Mauricio Corredor, who it was said had shot and killed Victorio.[83]

The Mexicans didn't care if Crawford's men were an American force. They had no peaceful intentions. Believing the Americans and Apache scouts were low on ammunition and that they could easily overwhelm them, they were eager to take Apache scalps and collect the bounties.[84]

With a break in the shooting, Crawford, waving a white handkerchief, Maus, and Horn walked out unarmed to meet Corredor and nine men all armed. Horn walked ahead of the others by about one hundred feet. He greeted Corredor in Spanish, but Corredor ignored him, walking past with four other men toward Crawford and Maus.[85]

Geronimo and the other Chiricahuas were watching what was taking place from the bluffs on the opposite side of the Aros River.[86]

The two groups stopped about six feet from each other. Crawford did not speak Spanish but Maus did. Maus said to Corredor, "Don't you see we are American soldiers. Look at my uniform and the captain's." He explained they had fought with the Chiricahuas and captured their rancheria. Corredor appeared sorry, saying they had believed the Apache scouts were hostiles.[87]

Maus could hear the scouts reloading their weapons and he saw Mexican troops advancing on his left to a higher position from which they could shoot down upon them. The Chiricahuas and the Tarahumaras had long been enemies, and now traded taunts and insults.[88]

Corredor became nervous and started backing toward Horn. Crawford said to Maus, "For God's sake, don't let them fire."[89]

"*No tiros*," Corredor said to the Americans, meaning, "Don't fire."[90]

"No," Maus responded to Corredor, telling him not to let his men fire.[91]

Maus turned toward the scouts, ordering them not to shoot. Crawford climbed a five-foot-high rock and stood on top waving his white handkerchief. One of Corredor's nine men took a position behind a little tree twenty-five yards from Crawford. Taking aim at Crawford, he pulled the trigger, shooting him in the forehead.

Crawford tumbled from the rock, his brains oozing from the entry hole. He still lived but was unconscious.[92]

Both sides blazed away at each other. Corredor turned and as he ran past Horn, smiled at him and fired a shot, wounding Horn in the arm. The Mexicans were all shooting at the Americans. Unhurt, Maus raced to cover. A Chiricahua scout grabbed Lieutenant Shipp and pulled him to safety.[93]

The Chiricahua scouts targeted and killed or wounded nine of the ten men in Corredor's party. A Bedonkohe scout named Binday shot Corredor through the heart. Dutchy, a Chokonen who was Crawford's orderly, shot and killed the man who had shot Crawford. Corredor's second in command, Lieutenant Juan de la Cruz, was riddled by thirteen bullets. Maus saw two other Mexicans take cover behind a tree who were shot and killed.[94]

From the bluffs across the river, Geronimo laughed at seeing the Mexicans and Apache scouts shooting at each other.[95]

All the Mexican officers were killed. With Crawford appearing mortally wounded, Lieutenant Maus was now in command of the American contingent. After a two-hour gun battle, Horn and Maus negotiated a cease-fire with Sergeant Santa Ana Perez. Maus estimated his men had fired between four thousand and five thousand rounds and were running low on ammunition. Through the rest of that day and into the next, there were tense moments between the two armed camps. At one point, the Mexicans tricked Maus during negotiations and held him hostage in exchange for the American mules and rations. When the Chiricahua scouts learned of this, they stripped, preparing for battle, and shouted to the Mexicans that Geronimo and his warriors were ready to join them in the fight. This news was disheartening to the Mexicans, who promptly released Maus.[96]

As a steady rain fell on January 13, Maus and his men broke camp and began their march to the west toward Nacori Chico, carrying Crawford by hand in a litter and a seriously wounded scout mounted on a mule.[97]

That night, Geronimo sent Lozen and Dahteste to Maus saying he wanted to meet the following morning. Maus and his party were to come unarmed. When Maus arrived at the meeting location the next morning, Geronimo and the other leaders were not there. Two Chiricahua warriors met him and said Geronimo and the others would meet them the following morning. Again, they told Maus to come unarmed.[98]

Early on the morning of January 15, Maus, Horn, Concepcion, and several scouts, all unarmed, arrived at the meeting location. Geronimo, Naiche, Chihuahua, Nana, and fourteen men arrived, all heavily armed. After they had all sat in a circle, Geronimo stared at Maus directly in the eyes and asked, "Why did you come down here?"

"I came to capture or destroy you and your band," Maus replied. Geronimo stood, walked over to Maus, and shook his hand, telling Maus he trusted him.[99]

Geronimo recounted their grievances at the reservation. Maus told Geronimo if they did not surrender, the Mexican and US armies would continue to pursue them. Geronimo said they were willing to meet with General Crook south of the border near San Bernardino in two moons and talk about surrendering. To show their sincerity, the next day, January 16, Nana and another warrior—along with seven women and children, including Geronimo's wife Ih-tedda and one of his daughters, as well as Naiche's wife and son, and Geronimo's sister and wife to Nana—arrived at Maus's camp and said they would go with Maus. If the Chiricahuas were detained and could not make the meeting in two moons, Geronimo promised his cousin Noche he would get word to him about the delay.[100]

Maus later learned the Apache scouts and the Chiricahua warriors were in contact with each other. The warriors had money and the scouts had cartridges. The warriors had bought cartridges from the scouts for a dollar apiece.[101]

On January 17, Maus was sitting with Crawford, who opened his eyes. Maus talked to him. Crawford could not speak but comprehended what Maus was saying. After five minutes, Crawford lost consciousness, never to awaken again. He died the next day. They continued their march to Nacori Chico, where they buried Crawford's body.[102]

Leaving Nacori Chico, Maus and his scouts headed north along the Bavispe River. After traversing more than one thousand miles, they crossed the border on February 1, 1886, and returned to Fort Bowie with Nana and the other hostages. Learning of Crawford's death, Crook refused to meet with Maus and went hunting for several days. He ordered Maus and his men to return south of the border at John Slaughter's San Bernardino Ranch and wait for Geronimo's arrival. He was not to negotiate with Geronimo, but to notify Crook of his arrival and then hold him there until Crook could arrive. Maus camped about ten miles south of the border along the San Bernardino River and waited for Geronimo's smoke signals.[103]

Crook's plan was to offer Geronimo and the other Chiricahuas in Mexico two years' exile in the East and then a possible return to the White Mountain Reservation. He had arranged the early release of Kaytennae from Alcatraz, and Crook hoped Kaytennae would help convince Geronimo to surrender. However, Arizona and New Mexico citizens were still outraged and wanted Geronimo handed over to them so they could inflict their own justice. They let their demands be known to President Cleveland, who demanded that something be done. Sheridan, who was feeling the pressure from all angles, wanted Geronimo turned over to state and local authorities, stating, "If he cannot be dealt with summarily, the Dry Tortugas would be a good reservation for him." He told Crook that Geronimo would not be allowed to return to Arizona. However, Sheridan added that he was "not to make any promises to the hostiles unless it is necessary to secure their surrender."[104]

For the next two months, throughout Sonora, the Chiricahuas killed and raided for food, horses and mules, weapons, and ammunition. They wanted to be well stocked for when they returned to their old haunts at Fort Apache on the White Mountain Reservation.[105]

Chihuahua and five to six warriors left the main band in search of Ulzana and his raiders who had crossed the border back into Sonora on December 31, 1885. The brothers reunited around January 22 in the region of the Teras and El Tigre Mountains, and together resumed raiding and killing.[106]

Geronimo and Naiche's band did the same throughout Sonora, murdering and acquiring livestock and provisions. In the early morning of March 8, 1886, twenty-two Chiricahua warriors led by Geronimo and Naiche attempted to steal livestock from John Hohstadt's ranch at Mababi on the eastern slopes of the Ajos Mountains. One of Hohstadt's vaqueros spotted the approaching warriors and alerted Hohstadt and others at the ranch. They ambushed the warriors. Hohstadt shot the Chiricahua warrior Chinche in the forehead, killing him. The firing from the rancher and his men was so hot that the warriors were only able to steal two horses, and had to leave Chinche's body behind. Hohstadt and his men scalped Chinche, cut off his ears, stripped the body, and then threw it on a bonfire.[107]

The Chiricahuas were now out for revenge. It didn't have to be taken on the men who had killed Chinche; it could be anyone. That afternoon, four men and Felipa Andrada, who was pregnant, and her two children, aged three and one, stopped at Capulin, a spring about a half-mile from Mababi. Geronimo, Naiche, and their men ambushed the party, killing three of the men. The fourth man was able to escape on foot. They brutally murdered Felipa and her two children. Cutting open her womb, they placed the unborn child in her lifeless arms. About 5:00 p.m. that same day, Refugio Frederico came upon the bodies. The Chiricahuas shot at him, wounding him and his horse, but he managed to escape.[108]

On March 15, Maus saw Geronimo's smoke signal on top of a high point twenty miles to the south. He sent word to Crook, and then along with four to five scouts, he rode to the smoke signal where they found messengers from Geronimo and Naiche who told them the Chiricahua band was forty miles away in the mountains, near Fronteras. Maus sent them back to Geronimo with the message that Mexican troops were in hot pursuit, looking for them, and for their own protection, they should come right away to his camp.[109]

Geronimo and his band arrived at Maus's camp on March 19 with a herd of stolen livestock. Maus tried to convince Geronimo that since the Mexican troops were looking for his band, it would be safer for them to cross the border and go to Fort Bowie, but he refused and said they were ready to fight any Mexican troops. Instead, they established their camp at a strong defensive position in the lava fields of Cañon de los Embudos (Canyon of the Funnels), eighteen miles below the border. Geronimo said Crook could meet with them there. Maus set up his camp a half-mile from the Chiricahuas.[110]

Maus kept sending messages to Crook with no response from the general. As the days passed with no sign of Crook, the Chiricahuas became more nervous. Each day, Geronimo came to Maus's camp and asked if Crook had arrived.[111]

Meanwhile, Crook organized a fifty-six-mule pack train and on March 22 sent it on ahead of him to Maus's camp. Accompanying the pack train were Kaytennae, who Crook had released from Alcatraz, Nana, Naiche's mother, and the White Mountain Apache scout Alchesay, whom Crook would use to help persuade Geronimo and his band to surrender.[112]

Crook and his aides, Captain John Bourke and Captain Cyrus Roberts, who had his twelve-year-old son along, left Fort Bowie on March 23. The next day, they joined Captain Allen Smith with two companies of the Fourth Cavalry, as well as several civilians who tagged along, including Camillus S. Fly, a photographer from Tombstone.[113]

While waiting for Crook to arrive, Maus's scouts had introduced Geronimo and his warriors to beef contractors and brothers, Charles, Siegfried, Godfrey, and Robert Tribolet, who had set up a mescal camp, selling that alcohol and whiskey to the Apache scouts. Now they were selling to Geronimo and his warriors. When Maus and his officers had tried to stop the Tribolets from selling liquor, one brother responded they were in Mexico and the US Army had no authority over them. They had moved below the border to get away from the law. Crook's delay with no word, combined with the consumption of liquor, put Geronimo and the other warriors in a foul mood.[114]

On March 25, as Crook and his entourage approached Cañon de los Embudos, he and Captain Roberts took off after an antelope and shot it. Geronimo, Naiche, and several warriors suddenly appeared, greeted them, and escorted them to Maus's camp. Crook went straight to the mule packers' camp for lunch.[115]

Geronimo, Naiche, and twenty-four warriors entered the packers' camp in small groups. They were heavily armed, and Crook thought they looked "fierce as so many tigers." Crook selected a spot to meet under the shade of a cottonwood and a sycamore tree. He sat on a small ledge that gave him a higher position than the others. His officers and some warriors gathered around as Geronimo sat on the ground across from Crook, and Nana sat beside him.[116]

As the meeting was about to begin, riders driving a herd of horses approached. It was Chihuahua and Ulzana accompanied by six warriors. Chihuahua warmly greeted Crook, and they joined the meeting. Fly asked them all to pose for a photograph, to which they complied.[117]

Geronimo and Naiche first conferred, and then Crook said to Geronimo, "What have you to say? I have come all the way down from Bowie." Geronimo answered, stating he had been living peacefully at White Mountain until Chatto, Mickey Free, and Lieutenant Britton Davis had begun to speak badly about him. He did not know why they did this. "I hadn't killed a horse or a man, American or Indian," Geronimo said. He heard rumors from an Indian, Wodiskay [Nadiskay], and then from Huera, Mangas's wife, that he was going to be seized and placed in the guardhouse. "I learned from the American and Apache soldiers, from Chatto, and Mickey Free, that the Americans were going to arrest me and hang me, and so I left," Geronimo said. He went on to say he had been living exactly the way General Crook had told him to live and he wanted to know who had ordered his arrest. "I want to do right," Geronimo continued. "Very often there are stories put in the newspapers that I am to be hanged. I don't want that anymore."[118]

Geronimo's speech went on for a long time, during which Crook stared at the ground, refusing to look at Geronimo.[119]

"What is the matter that you don't speak to me?" Geronimo asked Crook. He continued to talk and again asked, "Why don't you look at me and smile at me?" Geronimo continued on with his speech. He and Crook then got into an exchange. Crook asked him why he had killed innocent people. Geronimo did not answer that question but asked his own, about who had ordered his arrest. They were both talking past each other.[120]

"Everything you did on the reservation is known," Crook said. "There is no use for you to try and talk nonsense. I am no child. You must make up your own mind whether you will stay on the warpath or surrender unconditionally. If you stay out, I'll keep after you and kill the last one, if it takes fifty years." Crook said he had brought back Kaytennae from Alcatraz, and that originally Geronimo did not want him to come back, but now he was happy to see him.[121]

"I am a man of my word," Geronimo said. "I am telling the truth, and why I left the reservation."

"You told me the same thing in the Sierra Madre," Crook replied. "But you lied."

"Then how do you want me to talk to you?" Geronimo asked. "I have but one mouth; I can't talk with my ears."

"Your mouth talks too many ways."

"If you think I am not telling the truth, then I don't think you came down here in good faith."

The exchange continued on for some time until Crook finally ended it by saying, "I have said all I have to say. You had better think it over tonight and let me know in the morning."

"All right, we'll talk tomorrow," Geronimo said, "I may want to ask you some questions, too, as you have asked me some."[122]

That night Crook sent Kaytennae and Alchesay to the Chiricahua camp to tell the leaders if they all surrendered, they would go into exile in the East for two years and then be allowed to return to the White Mountain Reservation. They found Geronimo and the Chiricahuas angry over the way Crook had treated Geronimo, and Geronimo was ready to leave.[123]

As Crook's two emissaries talked to them, the Chiricahuas calmed down. The talks went on through the night. The next morning, Kaytennae and Alchesay returned to Crook, saying that Geronimo, Naiche, and Chihuahua were willing to talk with him again.[124]

In the meantime, the photographer Fly, his assistant, and Captain Bourke visited the Chiricahua camp. They found Geronimo very cooperative, allowing them to take multiple photographs. While they were in the camp, they saw Santiago McKinn, who had been captured by Geronimo six months earlier.[125]

That afternoon, Crook met privately with Geronimo, Naiche, Chihuahua, and others. None of them would agree to the unconditional surrender, but when Crook offered the two-year exile in the East and then the return to the White Mountain Reservation, they thought this more acceptable. Crook believed he could deviate from the unconditional surrender based on Sheridan's words in his February 1, 1886, letter that told him to do what needed to be done, "if necessary to secure their surrender."[126]

At noon on March 27, 1886, the Chiricahua leaders met with Crook to formally surrender. Geronimo sat cross-legged by the streambank under a mulberry tree. He had blackened his face with powder from the mineral galena. Chihuahua surrendered first, then Naiche. Geronimo was last to surrender, saying, "Two or three words are enough. I surrender myself to you." He then shook Crook's hand. "We are all comrades, all one family, all one band. What the others say I say. I give myself up to you. Do with me what you please. I surrender. Once I moved like the wind. Now I surrender to you and that is all." Geronimo again shook Crook's hand. He continued talking, asking that his wife and daughter be brought to him at Fort Bowie or Silver Creek. Crook responded, saying, "They can meet you on the road somewhere. I can't tell where." Geronimo ended his talk by asking if Kaytennae and Alchesay wanted to say something. There was no discussion about the Chiricahuas surrendering their weapons.[127]

That night, the Chiricahuas visited Charles Tribolet's liquor camp. Tribolet sold them three five-gallon demijohns of whiskey. They took the whiskey back to camp where they held a rip-roaring party—yelling and shooting in the air. Occasional shots were sent in the direction of the packers' camp and army tents. The next morning before daylight, Kaytennae and Alchesay reported to Crook that many Chiricahuas were drunk, Naiche the worst, having passed out.[128]

At 6:45 a.m. on March 28, Crook began his return to Fort Bowie. Leaving Maus in charge of bringing the Chiricahuas to the fort, Crook explained that he needed to be in communication with

General Sheridan. Several miles north of the camp, Crook and his men came upon Geronimo and four other warriors riding two mules. Bourke wrote that they were "all drunk as lords."[129]

Maus sent the pack train north to his old camp ten miles below the border. It wasn't until noon that he was able to get the Chiricahuas moving north. Later that afternoon, Maus met Geronimo and his warriors, many of whom were drunk. Geronimo said they would follow but warned him away, saying he would not be responsible for Maus's life.[130]

The Chiricahuas set up their camp about a half-mile from Maus's camp. When Maus visited their camp, he found they were all drinking heavily. He learned that Naiche, who was still drunk, had believed his wife was flirting with another man and had shot her in the leg.[131]

Maus ordered Lieutenant Shipp to take a detail and destroy all the liquor at Tribolet's camp. The next day, March 29, the Chiricahuas traveled only seven to eight miles when they suddenly decided to stop for the day, only two miles south of the border. They told Maus their livestock were worn out and needed to rest. The Chiricahuas split into two camps. Chihuahua and fifty-one people camped separately from Geronimo and Naiche, with forty-one.[132]

That same day General Crook reached Fort Bowie around 3:00 p.m., and sent a telegram to General Sheridan. The telegram was a follow-up to an earlier one he had sent by courier to the fort for telegramming, telling Sheridan the Chiricahuas were coming in. However, the surrender was not unconditional—the kind he had been told to obtain. Crook had negotiated with the Chiricahuas that they could return to the White Mountain Reservation after two years. Again, he believed he had room to negotiate away from unconditional surrender based on Sheridan's words in his February 1, 1886, letter, telling him to do what needed to be done "if necessary to secure their surrender."[133]

On the morning of March 30, Maus was awakened and told that Geronimo and Naiche with eighteen warriors and twenty-two women and children had slipped away into the night. Maus sent a courier to Crook with the news of Geronimo's departure and ordered Lieutenant Samson Faison to escort Chihuahua and the remaining

Chiricahuas with a sufficient detail to Fort Bowie while he and the rest of the command followed Geronimo's trail to the west and south into rough terrain, where they eventually had to give up.[134]

Meanwhile, Crook received a telegram from Sheridan stating that the president did not agree to the conditional surrender. It had to be unconditional. The Chiricahuas were only guaranteed their lives. Crook was told to renegotiate the surrender and take every precaution to ensure that the Chiricahuas did not escape. Sheridan ended his message by stating, "You must make at once such disposition of your troops as will insure against further hostilities by completing the destruction of the hostiles unless these terms are accepted."[135]

Later that day, Maus's courier arrived at Fort Bowie with the message that Geronimo and Naiche had escaped. Crook immediately telegrammed the information to Sheridan, who replied, "Your dispatch . . . has occasioned great disappointment."[136]

They exchanged further messages as to what to do next. Sheridan wanted Crook to rely on regular troops and not scouts. Crook wanted to continue with his scouts. On April 1, Crook ended his telegram to Sheridan: "It may be, however, that I am too much wedded to my own views in this matter, and as I have spent nearly eight years of the hardest work in my life in this department, I respectfully request that I may now be relieved from its command."[137]

April 2 was a busy day. Sheridan sent Crook a telegram relieving him of his duties and assigning General Nelson A. Miles in his place to command the Department of Arizona. Crook was being reassigned to command of the Department of the Platte. However, until Miles arrived on the scene, Crook would still command.[138]

At noon, the officers and soldiers at Fort Bowie were holding a ceremony for Captain Emmet Crawford. His body had been exhumed from Nácori Chico and was being sent to Kearney, Nebraska. During the ceremony, Lieutenant Faison arrived with Chihuahua's band, which included the boy, Santiago McKinn, who would eventually be returned to his father. Chihuahua and his followers were happily reunited with family members.[139]

Cochise County sheriff Robert Hatch arrived that afternoon with a warrant for the arrest of Chihuahua, Nana, and the other warriors who had surrendered. Crook told Hatch he would only hand them over if directed by the secretary of war.[140]

Crook later met with Chihuahua, who blamed Geronimo for the breakout. Geronimo had "dragged him off the reservation with lies." He said Geronimo "would never come in now." Crook did not tell Chihuahua that President Cleveland had rejected their deal. The Chiricahuas would not be returning to the White Mountain Reservation after two years.[141]

Crook telegrammed Sheridan that the Chiricahuas should be sent East immediately. The next day, April 3, Sheridan ordered Crook to send them to Fort Marion, Florida, "as soon as practicable." The two generals agreed not to tell the Chiricahuas the president had rejected their return in two years. If Geronimo and Naiche ever found out, they would never surrender.[142]

On April 7, 1886, Crook and the Apache scouts escorted the Chihuahua prisoners of war to the Fort Bowie train station. The combined group numbered seventy-seven people—fifteen men, twenty-nine women, and thirty-three children. Among them were two wives and three children of Geronimo, two wives and two children of Naiche, and Huera, wife of Mangas. Before boarding the special train with its army escort, Crook had the Apache scouts disarm the warriors. The train pulled out of the Bowie station, and six days later, April 13, they reached Fort Marion, Florida. Only two of those men would ever return to the Southwest.[143]

On April 11, 1886, General Miles arrived at Fort Bowie and Crook formally transferred the Department of Arizona to him. Things would be different now. Miles would rely less on Apache scouts and more on regular army troops.[144]

Why had Geronimo and Naiche, along with eighteen warriors and twenty-two women and children, turned their backs on surrendering and fled in the middle of the night of March 30? There is no indication that Geronimo had a premonition Crook's agreement was worthless. There is no record that he learned the government would not return them to the White Mountain Reservation after a two-year exile. However, Geronimo did say he had a bad feeling about Crook. He thought Crook had treated him shabbily. Crook never answered

Geronimo's question to his satisfaction about who had ordered his perceived arrest when living near Fort Apache. Years later, Geronimo said, "It was hard for me to believe him [Crook] at the time. Now I know what he said was untrue, and I firmly believe that he did issue the orders for me to be put in prison, or to be killed in case I offered resistance."[145]

Geronimo continued, "We started with our whole tribe to go with General Crook back to the United States, but I feared treachery and decided to remain in Mexico ... [W]hen we became suspicious, we turned back."[146]

Captain John Bourke believed the liquor seller Charles Tribolet had filled Geronimo and others' heads with lies. Tribolet told Geronimo and the others they would be killed when they crossed the border into the United States. Bourke said the army should "have justified the hanging of the wretch Tribollet [sic] as a foe to human society."[147]

Geronimo and Naiche led eighteen warriors, fifteen women, including Lozen, and seven children west into rough mountainous terrain. They split up and scattered using every trick in the book, including stepping only on rocks and backtracking to confuse and throw off their pursuers, who eventually gave up near Fronteras, Sonora.[148]

On April 2, the Chiricahuas headed west toward the Magdalena River in Sonora, raiding for livestock. Then on April 20, they began killing again, murdering five Mexican men and women.[149] On April 21, they killed one man and wounded another at Alisos. On April 22, they attacked three men who were fishing in the Casita Mountains, killing two. The third man was never found.[150] On April 23, they killed three men at the Casita ranch but allowed the ranch owner's wife and small child to escape and take shelter in their hacienda. Vaqueros rode to the nearby town of Imuris to sound the alarm. Ten soldiers rode to the ranch where the warriors ambushed them, killing two.[151]

The Chiricahuas entered the Pinito Mountains twenty miles southeast of Nogales where the warriors left the women and children with a few men. On April 26, 1886, they rode to the Buena Vista ranch on the border, ten miles east of Nogales. There, they killed and bashed in the heads of three Mexicans and an American before crossing into Arizona. That same day, outside the small settlement of Calabasas, they attacked two Mexicans, killing one.[152]

Early the next morning, Chiricahua raiders rode into town and helped themselves to six horses. A seven-man posse went after them but was repulsed in a small canyon and chased back to town.[153]

About 9:00 a.m. that day, they rode onto a ranch owned by Artisan L. Peck, eight miles northwest of Nogales. Petra Peck, the pregnant wife of Artisan, heard their dogs barking and sent her ten-year-old niece Trinidad Verdin to investigate. Trinidad returned, telling Petra an Apache was sitting near a corner of the corral. Holding her two-year-old son in her arms, Petra ran out to the corral. The man shot and killed her, picked up the boy by the legs, and smashed his head against an adobe wall.[154]

Trinidad ran to the house and hid under a bed. By now, fifteen warriors had ridden up to the house and begun ransacking. One warrior found Trinidad under the bed, pulled her out by the ankles, and was about to kill her when Geronimo entered and prevented her murder. He placed Trinidad on a horse behind his son Chappo. They set fire to the blacksmith shop and rode off with twelve horses and a variety of weapons.[155]

Two miles west of the ranch house, the warriors spotted Artisan Peck and his neighbor Charlie Owens, who had dismounted their horses to doctor some cattle. The warriors shot at and chased after the two ranchers, who, unarmed, ran to their horses, trying to escape. One shot hit Owens in the neck, killing him. Another shot hit Peck's horse, throwing him to the ground. Stunned, Peck was struck by the warriors and stripped of his clothes, down to his red flannel underwear. Then they stopped.[156]

They took Peck to the top of a knoll and surrounded him. A young man who spoke English introduced Peck to Geronimo. Geronimo said "Mangas Coloradas," meaning Red Sleeves. Peck used to work at Sonoran mines with rolled-up shirtsleeves, revealing red flannel underwear. The Indians had liked him and named him Mangas Coloradas. The English speaker told Peck not to talk to Trinidad, but, sobbing, she still told Peck what had happened. Geronimo said to

Peck that he was a good man, so he was sparing his life. When they rode off, they told Peck not to return to his ranch house or he would be killed. He went anyway and found his murdered wife and child.[157]

The next day, ten miles west of the Peck ranch, the warriors attacked the Bartlett ranch, wounding John Shanahan, who died the following day. They also wounded John "Yank" Bartlett while stealing fifty head of horses. By May 2, they had made their way back into Sonora where they rejoined the women and children in the Pinito Mountains.[158]

They had become aware American troops were following them. Captain Thomas Lebo, leading Company K of the black Tenth Cavalry, was a day's march behind the warriors, and had been following them since their attack on Calabasas.[159]

On May 3, along the east slopes of the Pinito Mountains, the troops followed the Chiricahuas' trail into what is known today as Cajón de los Negros, in their honor. Around mid-afternoon they came upon the Chiricahua warriors positioned about three hundred yards ahead of them on top of a semicircular cliff and behind strong natural defenses.[160]

Lebo ordered the men into a skirmish line. Every fourth man remained behind holding four horses. As they advanced toward the warriors' position Corporal Edward Scott fired, setting off an intense volley from the warriors. One bullet smashed Scott's kneecap, and another bullet killed Private Joseph Hollis.[161]

The battle raged for an hour. The warriors tried to steal the cavalry horses but were thwarted in their attempt. Geronimo and Naiche with sixteen men and two teenagers held off the troops until nightfall and then slipped away. Reinforced by an additional company of the Fourth Cavalry, Lebo continued following the Chiricahuas' trail over treacherous terrain. In one stretch, three mules fell from the cliffs to their deaths. The troops lost the Chiricahuas' trail five days later and turned back.[162]

During the next week, Geronimo and Naiche continued their rampage, killing at least three Mexicans and two Americans.[163]

On the morning of May 11, Geronimo and Naiche's warriors ambushed Mexican National Guard troops from Magdalena at

Pinalta, north of the Huscomes Mountains. They killed three men and wounded two more before the troops retreated. That afternoon a second force consisting of 150 Mexicans and Papago Indians arrived. When the Chiricahuas opened fire, the troops fled, leaving behind their supplies and thirty-three horses.[164]

Three days later, the Chiricahuas were spotted thirty-five miles to the east. A vaquero with that information rode to the camp of Captain Charles Hatfield's Company D of the Fourth Cavalry. Hatfield's camp was three miles south of the border on the San Pedro River. Hatfield and his thirty-four troopers and two Mexican scouts were soon on the Chiricahuas' trail that led into the Cuitaco Mountains, to the east of Santa Cruz.[165]

About 9:00 a.m. on May 15, one of the scouts found the Chiricahua camp, but at the same time, the Chihuahuas spotted the troops. They formed a rear guard, holding off the soldiers who were on the high ground while the women and children escaped. The Mexican scouts identified Geronimo and Naiche, who were using field glasses to spot the troops' positions. The fight was brief. The troops took the camp, capturing supplies and twenty-one horses.[166]

Hatfield decided to continue to Santa Cruz. It was about noon when his troops reached a spring in a narrow gorge. Geronimo and Naiche sprung a trap, killing two men, wounding two more, and recovering all their supplies and livestock, as well as four of the troopers' horses, including Hatfield's.[167]

The next day, Company I of the Fourth Cavalry came upon the Chiricahuas, who were resting in an arroyo west of the Cananea Mountains. They attacked and took five horses, two of which belonged to Hatfield's Company D, as well as a few rifles and ammunition. That night the Chiricahuas stole twenty-five horses from the town of Santa Cruz.[168]

Naiche sent five warriors east to the San Jose Mountains and then into Arizona, raiding as they traveled to the Dragoon Mountains, while he and Geronimo along with the rest of the band traveled west toward Nogales. Continuing west for the next two days, they killed three Mexicans and two Americans before crossing into Arizona through the Pajarito Mountains.[169]

Here, probably around May 18, Naiche and Geronimo decided to split for the time being. Geronimo wanted to stay in Mexico and Naiche wanted to go to Fort Apache. It's possible he believed his two wives and two children, whom he had sent with Crook, would be there, as well as family members of other warriors in the band. Geronimo turned back south to Sonora with two men, two women, one child, and Trinidad Verdin, while Naiche raced north with eight men and nineteen women and children.[170]

General Miles had patrols out trying to track down the elusive Chiricahuas. He was furious they weren't being caught and offered a $2,000 reward (valued at more than $53,000 in 2020 currency) for Geronimo, dead or alive.[171]

Naiche's band traveled toward Fort Apache, raiding and killing thirteen people along the way. Later when he was asked why they killed innocent people, Naiche explained, "It was war. Anyone who saw us would kill us, and we did the same thing."[172]

During the night of May 25, Naiche and seven warriors visited the Chiricahua rancheria near Fort Apache, where they learned that many of their family members had been sent East with Chihuahua. Naiche and his band continued to raid and kill as they headed south. Before disappearing into Sonora, they killed Henry Baston and took his two horses outside Arivaca, Arizona, and then stole another twenty horses from the town on the night of June 9.[173]

After separating from Naiche, Geronimo and his small band traveled southwest and then cut east into the Pinito Mountains. From there they journeyed southeast to the Azul Mountains. Geronimo and his wife cared for Trinidad Verdin. Sometimes the women would hit her if she did not understand what they were telling her, but the men never hit her. However, the men did scold her if she forgot to step only on rocks or grass and left a footprint in the dirt.[174]

Naiche's band met them at their rendezvous site in the Azul Mountains, where they stayed for two days; then, together again, they moved to the Madera Mountains. Around June 11, they separated into three smaller groups. Geronimo's band was composed of six Chiricahuas and Trinidad. The three groups' plan was to reunite later where the Aros and Yaqui Rivers join north of Sahuaripa.[175]

Patricio Valenzuela owned a ranch eight miles east of Cucurpe, Sonora. On the evening of June 16, Valenzuela's vaqueros found a cow and an ox slaughtered by Apaches. Valenzuela gathered a force of thirty men and followed the raiders' trail. On the afternoon of June 17, Valenzuela's men entered El Gusano Canyon where they ran into and surprised Geronimo's band.[176]

Geronimo shouted for everyone to scatter. Valenzuela's men fired at the Chiricahuas who were fleeing farther into the box canyon. Geronimo's wife had mounted her horse as a bullet hit her. She dismounted, pulled a revolver, and shot at the Mexicans, who riddled her with bullets and afterwards scalped her.[177]

Mounting his horse, Geronimo pulled Trinidad up behind him and raced farther into the canyon. His horse stumbled and fell, throwing both Geronimo and Trinidad. Trinidad believed Geronimo had been hit by a bullet. Racing up the slope, he called for her to follow, but she saw this as her chance to escape and ran to the safety of Valenzuela's men.[178]

Geronimo scrambled up into the rocks where he found a cave to hunker down in. Valenzuela told his men to be careful as they tried to outflank and kill Geronimo. By the time Valenzuela had called off the attack at dusk, Geronimo had killed three men, shooting them in the head, and wounding a fourth. He easily escaped during the night, rejoining the rest of his band.[179]

The next day, Valenzuela's men saw Indians advancing toward them and retreated, almost firing on them, until they discovered the Indians were scouts for Captain Henry Lawton with the Fourth Cavalry. Lawton's men had been on the trail of the Chiricahuas since May 5. When Lawton's command reached El Gusano Canyon, it was composed of forty troopers, a pack train, and twenty Apache scouts, none of whom were Chiricahuas, led by Chief of Scouts Tom Horn and Lieutenant Leighton Finley. Also along were Lieutenant Robert Walsh and Assistant Surgeon Leonard Wood. Lawton took his command to Valenzuela's ranch where they waited for additional troops and fresh information on the Chiricahuas' whereabouts.[180]

On June 30, General Nelson Miles arrived at Fort Apache to visit the Chiricahua rancheria, hiring Tom Jeffords to advise him in his decision-making and to act as his liaison with Jeffords's old friends. Miles believed the four hundred Chiricahuas must leave Arizona. He was distrustful of Chiricahua scouts, dismissing most of them. He was also concerned the Chiricahuas were still armed and still had their horses. He said the Chiricahuas were a "troublesome, disparate, disreputable band of human beings I had never seen before and hope never to see again." Miles developed two concurrent plans for the Chiricahuas.[181]

His first plan was to send a delegation of Chiricahua leaders to Washington, DC, to meet with federal officials and the president. He wanted the delegation first to visit the Wichita Mountains near Fort Sill, which he hoped they would like and would want to move to. Miles selected ten men and three women for the delegation, which included Chatto, Noche, Loco, and Kaytennae, as well as Mickey Free and Sam Bowman as interpreters. As Miles sent them off to Washington, their visit to Indian Territory was disapproved. No one in government other than Miles wanted them relocated to Indian Territory. The Chiricahuas themselves did not want to leave their Arizona homes. On July 3, Miles suggested to Sheridan that all Chiricahuas should be removed from Arizona; even though they remained at peace and were starting to farm and ranch, the citizens of Arizona and other tribes disliked them.[182]

By mid-July, Miles had developed his second plan, which was to send a Chiricahua delegation to Geronimo and Naiche to convince them to surrender with the condition they would be sent to Florida, but the president had the final say in their disposition. Miles selected Lieutenant Charles Gatewood to lead the delegation of two men who had ridden with Geronimo in the past and who had relatives currently with Geronimo and Naiche. They were Kayitah and Martine. Gatewood could speak Apache, but he wanted someone with him who was fluent, so he hired young George Wratten, a former trader at San Carlos. He also hired Frank Huston to handle three pack mules, and later, rancher Tex Whaley to act as a courier.[183]

After the attack at El Gusano Canyon, Geronimo's band headed east and then south down the Sonora River. Somewhere along the way, the three Chiricahua groups rendezvoused and formed one band

GERONIMO ON THE RUN, 1885–1886

again, traveling south. Geronimo later said about their time in Mexico, "We attacked every Mexican found, even if for no other reason than to kill. We believed they had asked the United States troops to come down to Mexico to fight us."[184]

Traveling southeast through mountainous country cut by deep canyons, Geronimo and Naiche's band reached the Yaqui River six miles below its confluence with the Aros River, where they established their rancheria between two buttes.[185]

Captain Henry Lawton's command had moved to Sinoquipe and was joined by nineteen infantrymen from Fort Huachuca and thirty Apache scouts led by Lieutenant Robert Brown. The infantry did not have a commanding officer, so Lawton put Assistant Surgeon Leonard Wood in charge of them. From Sinoquipe, Lawton marched his men to Cumpas where they encamped.[186]

On July 2, they learned Chiricahuas had killed a man near Tepache the day before. Lawton was determined to find their trail. He decided to leave the cavalry behind and left on July 6 with Wood and the nineteen infantrymen, Brown and the thirty Apache scouts, and a pack train. That same day, a messenger caught up with Lawton to tell him a man had been wounded by Chiricahuas at Tonibabi, a ranch eight miles east of Moctezuma. They changed course, marching to the ranch and finding a Chiricahua trail heading south. On July 9, they were joined by two Mexicans who knew the rough terrain well and would act as guides.[187]

At noon on July 13, two scouts returned to Lawton's camp to tell him they had found the Chiricahua rancheria. Lawton immediately set out to attack and capture the band. He sent Brown and his scouts to the opposite side of the camp, hoping to drive the people toward Wood and his waiting infantry.[188]

One of the Chiricahuas was out hunting and came across Lawton's troops' trail. He raced back to the rancheria, sounding the alarm. Everyone dropped what they were doing and vanished into an upriver canebrake. Rainstorms washed away the Chiricahuas' trail. Disheartened, worn out, and with some of the men ill, Lawton and his command would remain in the vicinity of the Aros River for three weeks as Lawton's scouts were sent out looking for any signs of the

Chiricahuas. Lawton wrote to his wife on July 31 that he planned to continue on in Mexico "until Geronimo is killed or surrenders."[189]

Leaving Fort Bowie on July 16, Lieutenant Charles Gatewood and his party traveled to Cloverdale, New Mexico, on July 18, and crossed the border into Chihuahua, reaching Carretas on July 21. There he met Lieutenant James Parker with the Fourth Cavalry who was to escort Gatewood in his search for the Chiricahuas. Gatewood had been in poor health and his condition worsened, with rheumatism and dysentery. He remained at Carretas for six days to regain his health.[190]

On July 27, Gatewood and his party, escorted by Parker and a mixed detachment of cavalry and infantry numbering not more than forty men, set off to find either Geronimo or Lawton's command. On August 3, after traveling 250 miles, they arrived at Lawton's camp along the Aros River in the Sierra Madre Mountains.[191]

Lawton was not pleased when he learned about Gatewood's peace mission, telling Parker, "I get my orders from President Cleveland direct. I am ordered to hunt Geronimo down and kill him."[192]

Both Gatewood and Parker believed Gatewood had a better chance of finding Geronimo if he was with Lawton, who had scouts and was better supplied than Parker. After Parker and Gatewood further explained the situation, Lawton reluctantly agreed to place Gatewood under his command, with the agreement, Gatewood later wrote, "that whenever he approached the hostiles, & circumstances permitted, I should be allowed to execute my mission."[193]

Before Parker left, Lawton told him, "I refuse to have anything to do with this plan to treat with him [Geronimo]—if Gatewood wants to treat with him he can do it on his own hook."[194]

Meanwhile, the Chiricahua delegation had reached Washington, DC, on July 17, 1886. Captain John Bourke met them and showed them the sights of the city. A week after their arrival, Secretary of the Interior Lucius Lamar met with them, telling them the benefits of moving to the East. Loco replied that they were happy living in Arizona. The next day, July 26, they met with Secretary of War William Endicott. Chatto told him they were happy living at Fort Apache and asked Endicott if his family had been rescued from the Mexicans.

Endicott assured Chatto the government was doing everything possible to return his family. However, Chatto would never see them again.[195]

On July 27, the delegation's escort Captain Joseph Dorst and Bourke took them to meet President Grover Cleveland. The Chiricahuas were told not to speak to the president unless he spoke to them. Cleveland shook their hands and said they did not need to make any speeches to him because what they had already said to Secretary Lamar had been written down and he had read it. "I will give the matter very careful attention," the president promised them.[196]

On July 30, General Sheridan read a letter General Miles had written on July 7 and sent through military channels. In the letter, Miles recommended the removal of the Chiricahuas from Arizona to Indian Territory and provided his reasons why: The Chiricahuas at Fort Apache were "in better fighting condition today than ever before," and the sons of the Fort Apache Chiricahuas will be the "Geronimos of tomorrow." It seemed not to matter that the majority of the Chiricahuas were peacefully attempting to farm, and that some of them had served as scouts for the army. Congress would need to authorize the settlement of the Chiricahuas in Indian Territory, and this was not going to happen anytime soon. Sheridan immediately recommended to President Cleveland that all Chiricahua adult males be sent to Fort Marion, Florida.[197]

The next day, July 31, President Cleveland met with the two department secretaries, as well as Dorst and Bourke. He expanded on Sheridan's proposal, stating that he wanted all Chiricahuas—men, women, and children—sent to Fort Marion, Florida. Bourke argued that most of the Chiricahuas had been peaceful and some had provided valuable service as scouts, but his argument carried no weight. As for the Chiricahua delegation, it never returned to Arizona, but its members were eventually sent to Fort Marion as prisoners of war.[198]

After Lawton's attack on Geronimo and Naiche's rancheria, they left their possessions behind, traveling up the Yaqui River and then following the Aros River. They then turned west, leaving the Sierra Madre Mountains and entering the Mazatan Mountains. On July 23, they ambushed a sixty-mule pack train hauling goods to the town of

Ures, Sonora. They killed five men while one man and two women escaped. It was a much-needed windfall for the band. They packed what they wanted on fifteen mules and slit the throats of the remaining forty-five animals.[199]

The Chiricahuas stole horses from ranches outside Nácori Grande. The following week, they reached the mountains east of Baviacora and from there proceeded north into the Teras Mountains south of Batepito, Sonora, raiding and killing as they went. On August 8, they killed two men at the San Luis mines near Cumpas. The next day they ambushed a courier to Lawton, killing his horse, but the man managed to escape. On August 11, six Americans from the Santa Rosa mines were pursuing the Chiricahuas, who ambushed their pursuers. It was an intense fight. Naiche and an American fired simultaneously at each other. Naiche missed the American, whose shot wounded Naiche. Naiche killed the American with his second shot. Geronimo received a gunshot to an arm. When it was over, three Americans were dead and two wounded. The warriors left with the dead Americans' horses and weapons.[200]

On August 13, Geronimo called from a ridgetop to three vaqueros, saying he wanted a truce. The vaqueros took the message to Sonoran authorities and by August 15, the Distrito of Arispe prefect Jesus Aguirre was meeting with Geronimo and the other Chiricahua leaders. Aguirre said he was in touch with Governor Torres about the peace proposal, and they all agreed to wait eight days for his response.[201]

Geronimo selected a steep ridge in the Teras Mountains overlooking the great bend of the Bavispe River for the location of the Chiricahua rancheria. Not trusting the Mexicans, who had a reputation for massacring Apaches in their towns, Geronimo kept the people away from Fronteras, but they did want more supplies, so he sent Lozen and Dahteste with mules into Fronteras, where the two women bartered for coffee, sugar, ammunition, and mescal liquor.[202]

Geronimo was right not to trust Prefect Aguirre. He and Governor Torres had secretly assembled two hundred troops in town hoping to ambush the Chiricahuas, either capturing them all and sending them to prison or massacring them. Lozen and Dahteste were allowed to do their business unmolested. Aguirre hoped to lull Geronimo into believing it was safe to enter Fronteras.[203]

Lieutenant Wilber Wilder with the Fourth US Cavalry was visiting Fronteras, his command camped about six miles west of town. He learned of the two Chiricahua women and met with them the evening of August 20. Wilder talked with them about the Chiricahuas surrendering to the Americans. They said there might be interest in surrendering if the terms were acceptable. The women invited Wilder to Geronimo's rancheria, but said he could only bring along one other man. Wilder said he was willing, but first he wanted them to return with Geronimo's guarantee of safe passage.[204]

On August 18, Lawton's command was seventy-five miles southeast of Fronteras when they met a pack train from the north. The Mexican packers told them Geronimo was in the vicinity of that town. Lawton directed Gatewood to go at once ahead of the command, try to contact Geronimo, and open negotiations. Gatewood was ill and so slow in heading out that Lawton became indignant. Wood had to talk him out of replacing Gatewood, who finally left camp with his party and a six-man escort at 2:00 a.m. on August 19.[205]

Gatewood rode into Fronteras on August 20 but did not learn about the Chiricahua women until after they had left. Prefect Aguirre became upset when he found out there were so many American troops in the vicinity of Fronteras. Learning Gatewood's mission was to convince Geronimo to surrender to the Americans, Aguirre told him not to follow the women's trail as it would interfere with his own plans.[206]

On August 21, Lawton's command encamped to the south of Fronteras and learned Gatewood was in the Fronteras area and not out on the trail looking for Geronimo. The next day, Lawton, Wood, and Lieutenant Thomas Clay left camp and rode into Fronteras, where they found out Gatewood was at Lieutenant Wilder's encampment. Angry, Lawton sent for Gatewood. While Lawton waited in a saloon, Aguirre plied him with strong alcohol. When Gatewood arrived, Lawton was drunk, and in his place, Wood ordered Gatewood to hit the trail.[207]

Late in the afternoon of August 22, Gatewood and his party, which had now grown to include two additional interpreters, Tom Horn and Jose Yeskes, and an escort of six to eight soldiers from Wilder's command, headed south in the direction of Lawton's camp. When they were well out of town and away from any ranches, Gatewood's party headed up an arroyo to the east and began circling to the north.[208]

Early on the morning of August 23, they found the Chiricahua women's trail and followed it eastward. About noon on August 24, they arrived at the confluence of the Bavispe and San Bernardino Rivers at the foot of the Teras Mountains. Martine and Kayitah believed Geronimo's rancheria would be about four miles away. Gatewood's party remained there while Martine and Kayitah tied a white cloth to the end of a long century plant stem and proceeded in the direction of the rancheria.[209]

Kanseah, at the time a youth, later said he was standing watch at the Chiricahua rancheria. Using field glasses, he spotted two men slowly climbing the slopes to the rancheria. He called to Geronimo that someone was coming. Geronimo and the other warriors joined him and watched as the men approached the camp.[210] When Kanseah could see their faces, he told everyone they were Martine and Kayitah.

"It does not matter who they are," Geronimo said. "If they come any closer they are to be shot."

Yanosha and Geronimo's cousin Fun argued against killing them and said they would shoot anyone who tried to kill Martine and Kayitah. Geronimo backed off and said, "Let them come."[211]

The two men were told to approach the camp. No one would hurt them. They sat with the warriors and had a long discussion about their circumstances and surrender. Martine and Kayitah said many Mexican and American troops were out looking for them. They told them Chihuahua and their family members had been sent to Florida. They said if Geronimo's band surrendered, they would not go to prison but be sent to Florida to join their families. After much back-and-forth, Geronimo agreed to meet with Gatewood to hear what he had to say.[212]

Kayitah stayed with the Chiricahuas for the night, while Martine returned to Gatewood's camp to tell him the good news. The Chiricahuas would talk to him, and Naiche said he would not be harmed. Gatewood had been sending messages back to Lawton informing him of his whereabouts and progress. That evening, Lieutenant Brown with twenty of his Apache scouts arrived at Gatewood's camp.[213]

The next morning, August 25, three warriors met Gatewood, telling him to leave the Apache scouts behind. They directed Gatewood and his party to a glade along the river where Geronimo and Naiche would meet them.[214]

After Gatewood's party reached the spot, warriors began trickling in from various directions. Last to arrive was Geronimo, who laid down his rifle and shook Gatewood's hand, followed by Naiche, who also shook Gatewood's hand. Geronimo was concerned about Gatewood's thinness and asked about his health as he sat close beside him. Gatewood distributed tobacco to the warriors. Women arrived, and along with Gatewood's cook, prepared a common breakfast for everyone as they engaged in small talk. Gatewood asked Geronimo why they were negotiating with the Mexicans. Geronimo replied that they were talking peace with the Mexicans to buy time while acquiring food and mescal. After the meal, they got down to business with the entire band present.[215]

Geronimo sat on a log next to Gatewood, so close that Gatewood could feel Geronimo's six-shooter against his hip. Geronimo began by saying they were all present and would listen to what Gatewood had to say with open ears.[216]

Gatewood gave the ultimatum, "Surrender and you will be sent to join the rest of your people in Florida, there to await the decision of the President of the United States as to your final disposition. Accept these terms or fight it out to the bitter end."[217]

No one spoke. They all stared at Gatewood's eyes for the longest time, and Geronimo's stare was the most intense. Then Geronimo passed a hand down across his eyes. He then extended both arms forward and shook his hands, saying they had been on a three-day drunk. They knew the Mexicans were trying to trick them into going to Fronteras so they could get them drunk and kill them. Geronimo knew the Mexicans and Americans had been drinking together in Fronteras, saying, "Now, in Fronteras there is plenty of wine and mescal, and the Mexicans and Americans are having a good time. We thought perhaps you had brought some with you."[218]

Gatewood replied that they had left so fast, they had failed to bring any along.[219]

Geronimo became serious. He said that the night before, after they had held a council and made medicine, they had developed their own peace proposal. They would stop fighting if they were allowed to return to the White Mountain Reservation and their farms, be provided rations, clothing, and supplies, and be exempt from any punishment for what they had done.[220]

Gatewood responded by saying General Miles had not authorized him to negotiate; all he could do was present the government's proposition with no modifications. The discussion continued for two hours. Geronimo listed the injustices the White Eyes had committed ever since they had invaded the Chiricahuas' country. They were willing to divide the country, but not give it up.[221]

The Chiricahuas broke off the meeting and held their own private conference for over an hour. When they had finished, everyone ate some lunch, drank coffee, and then resumed the discussion. Geronimo said they were willing to give up the entire Southwest, but they would not give up the White Mountain Reservation. Geronimo looked Gatewood square in the eye, saying, "Take us to the reservation or fight."[222]

Naiche added that as long as Gatewood and his men had come in peace, they were in no danger unless they started the fight first.[223]

What Gatewood said next was a lie. He told them all the Chiricahuas at Fort Apache had been sent to Florida. They now had no friends, only enemies at Fort Apache. The removal had not happened yet; in fact, unknown to Gatewood, just the day before, President Cleveland had made it official: All Chiricahuas—men, women, and children—were to be sent to Fort Marion, Florida, and their removal was to proceed at once.[224]

Staring into Gatewood's eyes, trying to determine if he was lying, Geronimo asked a multitude of questions. Was this some kind of trick to get them to surrender? Where did Gatewood get his information? How had the removal been accomplished? Gatewood must have lied well. The Chiricahuas withdrew again to have their own discussion, lasting an hour.[225]

After reconvening, Geronimo said they would not change their position and went into more detail concerning the White Eyes' wrongs against the Chiricahuas. He told Gatewood to go to General Miles and tell him of their concerns.[226]

Gatewood declined, making excuses. He didn't know where General Miles was; besides, General Miles had made up his mind and it could not be changed. Finally, Gatewood said he was too sick.[227]

The meeting continued late into the afternoon. Geronimo asked questions about Miles. What kind of a man was he? How old was he? What did he look like, including hair and eye color? Did he look you in the eye or down to the ground when he talked? Did the soldiers and officers like him? Gatewood tried to answer as truthfully as he could.[228]

When he was done asking questions, Geronimo said, "He must be a good man, since the Great Father sent him from Washington, and he sent you all this distance to us."[229]

It was getting close to sundown when Gatewood learned that Lawton's command had arrived at his camp. He wanted to end the discussion for the night, but the Chiricahuas wanted him to stay a few more minutes.

"We want your advice," Geronimo said. "Consider yourself one of us and not a white man. Remember all that has been said today, and as an Apache, what would you advise us to do under the circumstances. Should [we] surrender, or should [we] fight it out?"

"I would trust General Miles and take him at his word," Gatewood said.[230]

Geronimo said they would hold another council and make more medicine that night. He would let Gatewood know their decision in the morning. They all shook hands and then Gatewood started to ride back to his camp.[231]

Chappo, Geronimo's son, overtook Gatewood and said he wanted to spend the night with him. Gatewood said no. He was concerned the Apache scouts might do him harm. Chappo reluctantly turned back, but Gatewood's actions had a positive effect on the Chiricahuas.[232]

Gatewood met with Lawton, reported all that had happened, and then turned in for the night.[233]

The next morning, Geronimo and four or five of his warriors arrived a few hundred yards from Gatewood's camp. When Gatewood went out to meet them, they dismounted, unsaddled their horses, and laid their weapons on their saddles—except Geronimo, who still had his pistol strapped to his hip. Geronimo shook hands with Gatewood and asked him to repeat his message from Miles and his description of Miles.[234]

Geronimo said they were willing to talk to General Miles and surrender to him in person. They wanted Gatewood to travel with them and they wanted Lawton's command to protect them from Mexican and American troops. They also would keep their weapons until they had formally surrendered to General Miles.[235]

When Gatewood introduced Geronimo to Lawton, Geronimo gave Lawton a hug. The Chiricahuas moved their camp down alongside the army camp. A message was sent to General Miles concerning the arrangements. It was agreed they would meet him across the border at Skeleton Canyon in Arizona.[236]

On August 27, Geronimo and Naiche's band, numbering thirty-eight people, accompanied by Lawton's command, began their journey north. They traveled in two separate groups, with Lawton on the left of the Chiricahuas.[237]

At the end of their trek on the second day, they were going into camp when the Distrito of Arispe prefect Jesus Aguirre arrived from the west with 180 Mexican troops. The Chiricahuas quickly repacked their gear, preparing to flee. Geronimo told Gatewood he was suspicious of treachery on the part of the Americans and Mexicans. Gatewood said that was not the case, and he would run with the Chiricahuas north toward the border while Lawton prevented the Mexicans from following, even if it meant fighting them.[238]

The Chiricahuas and Gatewood took off racing north with an advance guard, flankers, and rear guard to protect the women and children. After putting ten miles' distance between themselves and the Mexican troops, the Chiricahuas stopped to wait for word from Lawton.[239]

Assistant Surgeon Leonard Wood rode to the Chiricahua position. He said the Mexican commander Aguirre was not going to attack but would not be satisfied until he heard directly from Geronimo that the Chiricahuas intended to surrender to the United States.[240]

Lawton brought his troops up and camped near the Chiricahuas while the Mexicans encamped a mile away. It was arranged that Aguirre and seven of his men and Geronimo and seven of his men, all armed, would meet in the American camp to discuss Geronimo's surrender to the Americans.[241]

Aguirre and his men arrived first and then Geronimo and his men rode up and dismounted. Dragging his Winchester rifle by the muzzle in his left hand and wearing his revolver holstered in front of his left hip, Geronimo walked into camp along with Naiche and the other warriors, with revolvers and rifles.[242]

The Mexicans, who had been sitting under a large cottonwood tree with Lawton and Wood, stood when the Chiricahuas arrived. Gatewood introduced Geronimo to Aguirre. The two men shook hands. Aguirre swiveled his holstered pistol to his front. Geronimo put his right hand on his revolver, pulling it halfway out of the holster. The Mexican officers brought their holstered pistols to the front. The warriors leveled their rifles at the Mexicans. Lawton, Clay, and Wood stepped between the two groups. Gatewood stood beside a Mexican soldier ready to wrestle his rifle from him. Realizing the Chiricahuas had him outgunned, Aguirre put his hands behind his back. Geronimo holstered his revolver and dropped his right hand to his side. The situation had been defused.[243]

Aguirre asked Geronimo why he did not surrender to them in Fronteras. Geronimo said he was not a fool. He knew if they surrendered to the Mexicans they would be killed. Aguirre asked Geronimo if he was going to surrender to the Americans, and he replied yes. Aguirre said he was going along to make sure Geronimo surrendered. Geronimo would have none of that. They finally agreed one of Aguirre's men would go along with Lawton and Geronimo to witness the surrender and report back to Aguirre that it had actually happened.[244]

Geronimo and Naiche still feared treachery. Were the Americans and Mexicans going to join forces against them? In order to satisfy them that the Americans meant them no harm, Gatewood first convinced Geronimo and then Lawton that the Chiricahuas should make a run for the border that night and Lawton's command would follow in the morning. Gatewood would remain with the Chiricahuas. Everyone agreed to the plan. Lawton, along with Wood, Lieutenant Clay, and their orderlies, would leave the command in charge of Lieutenant Abiel Smith and join the Chiricahuas later along the trail.[245]

The race for the border began that night of August 28. Over the next few days, the main command lost the Chiricahua trail but eventually caught up. On August 31, 1886, the Chiricahuas and Lawton's command crossed the border into the United States and paused for a rest in Guadalupe Canyon, Arizona.[246]

Leaving Lieutenant Smith in charge of the troops, Lawton left for John Slaughter's San Bernardino Ranch to communicate with General Miles by heliograph, a signaling device using sunlight and mirrors. As Lawton and Miles communicated back and forth, Lawton informed Miles that Geronimo and Naiche wanted to surrender only to General Miles. Miles was preoccupied with making sure the peaceful Chiricahuas at Fort Apache were disarmed and held prisoner, to be shipped off later to Fort Marion, Florida. Miles messaged Lawton that he, Lawton, could accept Geronimo and Naiche's surrender at any time. Miles was not interested in meeting them. In several of his messages, Miles wrote that Geronimo and Naiche should be tricked, forced to lay down their weapons, and seized.[247]

Miles finally sent this message: To demonstrate that they were indeed serious in surrendering, the Chiricahuas needed to guarantee it by sending a hostage to Fort Bowie to show their good faith.[248]

Meanwhile, back at Guadalupe Canyon, Lieutenant Smith began talking with Wood and other officers about taking revenge on the Chiricahuas right then and there. Chiricahuas had killed

American troops in that canyon months earlier. Some Chiricahuas learned about Smith's talk and they all fled the camp.[249]

Gatewood confronted Smith, his superior officer, saying he knew Smith intended murder. Gatewood "threatened to blow the head off the first man if they didn't stop." Wood relented and Smith backed down. Wood sent a message to Lawton that the situation in camp was bad and he needed to hurry back.[250]

Gatewood followed after the Chiricahuas and caught up with Geronimo and Naiche. He told them he would stay with them to prevent any attack, and Naiche told Gatewood to stay close to them, so no warriors did him harm.[251]

Lawton raced his horse back to camp. He was annoyed that the Chiricahuas might escape. Lawton and Wood rode out to the Chiricahua camp, reaching it by 8:00 p.m. Lawton spent a long time reassuring them, and they invited him to supper and to spend the night with them, which he did.[252]

Still worried about the American troops attacking them, Geronimo and Naiche proposed to Gatewood that the people run away from the troops and go into the mountains near Fort Bowie. They would remain there while Gatewood went to arrange their surrender with General Miles. Gatewood believed it was a poor plan and talked them out of it.[253]

Gatewood, tired of the whole affair, told Lawton he believed he had done his duty by contacting Geronimo, and now he wanted to be reassigned elsewhere. Lawton said no, he needed to stay; he was essential for the completion of the mission.[254]

Lawton told Geronimo that General Miles wanted a hostage sent to Fort Bowie so he would know they were serious about surrendering. Geronimo designated Perico, his cousin, as the one to go. Perico left early the next morning, September 1.[255]

Lawton notified General Miles that the hostage was on his way and again stated Geronimo and Naiche wanted to surrender to him personally. Lawton was uneasy about the general's lack of concern, writing his wife on September 2: "I cannot get Miles to come out and the Indians are getting uneasy about it." However, General Miles and his escort finally left Fort Bowie for Skeleton Canyon that same day.

He had forebodings it would not turn out well and was reluctant to go, but at Lawton's insistence, he went.[256]

Geronimo and Naiche's band with their army escort arrived at Skeleton Canyon on the west side of the Peloncillo Mountains the afternoon of September 2. Additional army units had already arrived in the canyon and General Miles was not there to greet them, making the Chiricahuas even more nervous.[257]

Geronimo selected his camp farther back in the canyon on a high rocky defensive position, away from the troops, where he could look down and keep an eye on them and look out into the San Bernardino Valley. Gatewood remained with Geronimo while Naiche and his followers moved farther back into the mountains.[258]

At 3:00 p.m. on September 3, 1886, General Miles finally arrived at Skeleton Canyon. Geronimo had Gatewood take him immediately to meet the general. Geronimo walked right up to Miles and shook his hand. The interpreter introduced Miles to Geronimo as his friend. "I have been in need of friends," Geronimo responded. "Why has he not been with me?" That broke the ice. The officers laughed, and they had a good conversation after that.[259]

General Miles was impressed with Geronimo, writing, "He was one of the brightest, most resolute, determined-looking men that I had ever encountered. He had the clearest, sharpest dark eyes I think I have ever seen. . . . Every movement indicated power, energy and determination. In everything he did, he had a purpose."[260]

Geronimo explained to Miles why he had left the reservation. He believed Chatto and Mickey Free had plotted to kill him. He wanted to return to Fort Apache and live as he had in the past.[261]

Miles told Geronimo the same thing Gatewood and Lawton had: He could not go back to Fort Apache; in fact, the Chiricahuas had all been sent away to join Chihuahua in Florida. Miles said they were going to move all the Chiricahuas so they could all be together in one place. Geronimo heard Miles say that if they surrendered, they would see their families in five days. Geronimo and his people had to surrender unconditionally as prisoners of war. Only the president of the United States had the authority to determine their final disposition.[262]

Geronimo expressed his concern that once they surrendered, the troops would massacre them.[263]

Miles replied if they surrendered to him, they would not be killed, but he would treat them justly. Miles then said the president had control over the Indians, and he was a just and kind man.[264]

Miles drew a line in the dirt, saying, "This represents the ocean." He placed a stone beside the line and said, "This represents the place where Chihuahua is with his band." He picked up two more stones and, placing one some distance from the line and the first stone, said, "This represents you, Geronimo." Then, placing the next stone in the same area as the Geronimo stone, Miles said, "This represents the Indians at Camp Apache." He picked up the Geronimo stone and the Indians at Camp Apache stone and placed them with the Chihuahua stone, saying, "This is what the President wants to do—get all of you together."[265]

At one point in the conversation, Geronimo turned to Gatewood, who was sitting behind him, smiled, and said, in Apache, "Good; you told the truth."[266]

At the end of the meeting, Geronimo shook hands with Miles and said he would go with him no matter what the others did.[267]

Naiche had not been at Geronimo and Miles's meeting. The next day, Geronimo convinced him to come in and talk with Miles. After doing so, Naiche and his people also agreed to surrender.[268]

Geronimo and Miles stood between the troops on one side and the Chiricahua warriors on the other. The two of them placed a large stone on a blanket before them. Geronimo later said, "Our treaty was made by this stone, and it was to last until the stone should crumble to dust; so we made the treaty, and bound each other with an oath."[269]

After the ceremony, Captain Lawton and some of his men gathered rocks and erected a monument on the spot, ten feet across and six feet high.[270]

On the morning of September 5, Miles speeded on his way back to Fort Bowie in an ambulance that also held Geronimo, Naiche, three other men, and a woman. The rest of the band and their army escort would follow along at a slower pace. The general assured Geronimo and the others that their past activities would be forgotten and wiped out. When they reached Fort Bowie that night, Geronimo, Naiche, and the others were disarmed and placed in the guardhouse.

Geronimo's raiding and warfare had finally come to an end.[271]

After Buffalo Bill's Wild West had ended for the season in October 1885, Sitting Bull returned to his settlement on the Grand River. He continued in the ways of a traditional Hunkpapa chief.

Agent James McLaughlin began to think he had made the wrong decision allowing Sitting Bull to travel with Buffalo Bill Cody. "He is inflated with the public attention he received," McLaughlin wrote. "And has not profited by what he has seen, but tells the most astounding falsehoods to the Indians." McLaughlin did not believe Sitting Bull's claim that he had met with President Grover Cleveland, or that the president had told him he was the greatest living Indian and made him head chief of all the Sioux. McLaughlin disapproved of Sitting Bull using his money to provide feasts for the people, and wrote, "I may be obliged to arrest him and confine him to the Guard-house."[272]

In April 1886, Cody sent Major John Burke to Standing Rock to have Sitting Bull sign up for a second season of Buffalo Bill's Wild West. When Burke met with McLaughlin on April 16, McLaughlin told him traveling with Cody's show had had a negative effect on Sitting Bull. "He is such a consummate liar and too vain and obstinate to be benefitted [sic] by what he sees, and makes no good use of the money he thus earns," McLaughlin said. "For the good of the other Indians and the best interests of the Service I am forced to the conclusion that it would be unwise to have him go out this season." Sitting Bull would never have the opportunity to participate in a show again.[273]

Sitting Bull quietly spent that summer with his family at his Grand River settlement. He visited friends and relatives to the south near the Cheyenne River Agency—his brother-in-law Chief Makes Room and nephew White Bull, as well as good friends Hump and Spotted Elk, who now went by the name Big Foot.[274]

Plenty Coups, chief of the Crows, invited Sitting Bull and his Hunkpapas to visit their reservation near the Little Big Horn battle-field in Montana, to make peace between the two tribes. As part of the reconciliation the Crows were offering horses as gifts. The letter was read aloud at a dance and many others outside Sitting Bull's band wanted to go too. Horses were still scarce from when the army had confiscated them all.[275]

A hundred Lakotas from Standing Rock and Cheyenne River Agencies signed petitions to the Indian Office to be allowed to go. It was approved over the objections of the Crow agent, and in early September, Sitting Bull, with a large group of Lakotas, set out for the Crow Reservation.[276]

One of those going along was the metal breast Bull Head. The Lakotas called the Indian police "metal breasts" because of the metal police badges they wore. Agent McLaughlin selected all the metal breasts and they owed allegiance to him, not Sitting Bull.[277]

Bull Head was a Yanktonai and had been a metal breast since 1878. By 1886, he held the rank of lieutenant and was one of three judges in the Court of Indian Offenses. Bull Head lived on the Grand River upriver from Sitting Bull and one of his duties was to keep an eye on Sitting Bull for McLaughlin, and Sitting Bull knew it.[278]

Another member of the group traveling to the Crow Reservation was the Hunkpapa Catch-the-Bear, a good friend of Sitting Bull's and one of his bodyguards.[279]

On their way to the Crow Agency, they stopped to draw rations at Lame Deer Agency on the Northern Cheyenne Reservation in Montana. Two white clerks were working behind the counter. Bull Head asked one of the clerks for an empty flour sack to put his rations in. The clerk laid a sack on the counter. Bull Head left the sack on the counter to look for the items he needed.[280]

Catch-the-Bear had gathered together the goods he needed and also asked for a sack. The second clerk saw the sack on the counter and gave it to Catch-the-Bear, not knowing the first clerk had already given it to Bull Head. Catch-the-Bear put his items in the sack and left the building.[281]

Bull Head returned to the counter with his items and saw that his sack was gone. He learned that Catch-the-Bear had taken the sack and went after him. Bull Head demanded the sack. "This sack is mine," Catch-the-Bear said. "The white man gave it to me." Still demanding the sack, Bull Head jerked it out of Catch-the-Bear's hand and dumped his rations on the ground. When Catch-the-Bear protested, Bull Head hit him on the back and walked off.[282]

Catch-the-Bear called after him, "Today you have insulted me; you have struck me. We have always been friends. But now you have made me angry. Look out in [the] future; I am going to get you."[283]

Other members of the party tried to reconcile the two, but Catch-the-Bear would never forget Bull Head had struck him. Sitting Bull learned of the incident but said nothing.[284]

For two weeks the Crows hosted the Lakotas near the site of the Little Big Horn battle. They feasted, danced, and declared peace. Sitting Bull learned that government agents were signing up individual Crows for land allotments. He did not believe it was a good idea and swayed several Crow chiefs to oppose it.[285]

The Crows had not yet presented the promised horses. At the final and largest gathering, the Crows began bragging and taunting their Lakota guests. Individual warriors stood and recounted their coups and deeds in war against the Lakotas. Sitting Bull and the older Lakotas sat impassive, smoking their pipes. The younger men, including Bull Head and Shave Head, another metal breast, became indignant with the Crows' behavior.[286]

Then a Crow warrior, Crazy Head, ripped off his breechcloth and walked over to where Sitting Bull sat peacefully smoking his pipe. Standing in front of Sitting Bull, Crazy Head thrust his genitals toward Sitting Bull's face. Sitting Bull maintained his calm, slowly puffing on his pipe. If the Crows could anger Sitting Bull and make him break the peace, they would not have to give the promised horses. Sitting Bull defeated the Crows in their attempt.[287]

Afterwards, Crazy Head presented thirty fine horses to Sitting Bull. They were Sitting Bull's to distribute as he saw fit. Bull Head went ahead and roped a beautiful black-and-white-spotted horse. Sitting Bull saw what he had done and called to Catch-the-Bear,

"Throw your rope on that black-and-white-spotted horse, friend. That one that Bull Head has ahold of. That is yours." Bull Head did not want to give up the horse, but Sitting Bull insisted. Sitting Bull then gave Bull Head a fine little buckskin. Through this action, Sitting Bull rebuked Bull Head for his treatment of Catch-the-Bear, but Bull Head would not forget.[288]

CHAPTER 12

Geronimo, Prisoner of War, and Sitting Bull on the Reservation, 1886–1890

GERONIMO AND NAICHE HAD SURRENDERED TO GENERAL NELSON Miles, and on September 5, 1886, they arrived at Fort Bowie where they waited for the rest of the Chiricahua band to arrive. During the day, they were allowed to roam about the fort, buying new clothes in the fort's store and posing for a few photos.[1]

Miles considered Geronimo, Naiche, and their followers as federal prisoners of war and was not about to hand them over to civil authorities. He spoke of Geronimo and Naiche as "brave men" who had surrendered to "brave men." Placing a strong guard outside the fort to keep civilian officials from attempting to arrest the Chiricahuas, Miles wrote to his wife, "We were honor bound not to give them up to a mob or the mockery of a justice where they could never have received an impartial trial."[2]

Miles continued to reassure Geronimo and Naiche. One time, he held out his open hand toward them and traced the lines in his palm, saying, "This represents the past; it is all covered with ridges and hollows." He rubbed his hands together, saying, "This represents the wiping out of the past, which will be considered smooth and forgotten." Another time, he smoothed the dirt with the back of his hand, saying, "Everything you have done up to this time will be wiped out like that and forgotten, and you will begin a new life." He told them, "Leave your horses here, maybe they will be sent to you; you will have a separate reservation with your tribe, with horses and wagons, and no one will harm you." Geronimo and Naiche believed him.[3]

On September 7, General Sheridan sent Miles a telegram stating Miles should hold the Chiricahua men as "close prisoners" in Arizona, "subject to such trial and punishment as may be awarded them by the civil authorities of the Territories of Arizona and New Mexico. The women and children of his party should go to Fort Marion." President Cleveland held the same views as Sheridan.[4]

Miles responded, "Everything is arranged to move them and I earnestly request permission to move them out of this mountain country, at least as far as Fort Bliss, Union, or Fort Marion."[5]

The evening of September 7, Lawton, escorting the rest of Geronimo and Naiche's band, stopped to camp six miles out of Fort Bowie. Earlier that day the march had stopped as Chappo's wife gave birth to their baby. An hour after the birth, Chappo's wife was ready and they continued on.[6]

Early in the morning of September 8, Lieutenant Robert Ames left Fort Bowie for the camp of the Chiricahuas and their escort. Before anyone was awake, he galloped his horse through the camp. Alarmed, the Chiricahuas scattered. Wood said of Ames's actions, "Nothing more idiotic could be imagined." When Lawton's men were able to gather the Chiricahuas back together, two men, a teenage boy, three women, and a child were missing. They later turned up back in Sonora where they continued to raid for the next ten years.[7]

Captain Lawton and his men escorting the Chiricahua band arrived at Fort Bowie later that morning. The men were disarmed. Geronimo, Naiche, and the rest of the band were loaded in wagons that would take them to the Bowie railroad train station. It was about 11:00 a.m. when General Miles, riding along with Captain Lawton and his troops, escorted the captive Chiricahuas out of Fort Bowie as the Fourth Cavalry band played "Auld Lang Syne."[8]

The wagons were driven at a rapid pace. A special train had been waiting at the station for the Chiricahuas. Miles would accompany them for part of the journey as he was headed to Albuquerque, New

Geronimo waits to board the train at Bowie, Arizona.

Mexico. Also accompanying the band was George Wratten, who would continue to act as their interpreter. Two men were added to the group of captives, Kayitah and Martine, the men who had gone on the peace mission to convince Geronimo and Naiche to surrender—captivity their only reward.[9]

Miles, the captives, and their escort reached the train station at 1:30 p.m., and the train pulled out at 2:55 p.m. The Chiricahua passengers totaled twenty-seven—fifteen men, nine women, and three children. None of these people had ever ridden on a railroad train. It must have been a troubling experience. Their journey would take them through El Paso, San Antonio, New Orleans, and finally, Florida.[10]

Another telegram from Washington arrived instructing Miles to keep Geronimo and Naiche's band in Arizona. Miles claimed he never saw it. It might have been a telegram that Acting Assistant Adjutant General William Thompson told Leonard Wood he was not going to give Miles until after he and the Chiricahuas had left on the train.[11]

The telegram was from Adjutant General Hugh Drum, who quoted President Cleveland, writing, "Geronimo and the rest of the hostiles should be immediately sent to the nearest fort or prison where they can be securely confined."[12]

As the train carrying Geronimo, Naiche, and their followers sped through New Mexico and into Texas, telegrams concerning them flew back and forth across the country. General Sheridan and President Cleveland wanted the Chiricahuas held in Arizona so they could be tried in civil courts for murder. Washington officials wanted to know why Miles was sending the Chiricahuas out of Arizona when he had been told to keep them there. Miles responded that there were no military facilities or prisons secure enough to hold them. He had based his movement of the Chiricahuas on a September 4 message stating that the band should be sent to Fort Marion. No one could find that telegram. Further in the exchange on September 9, Miles said he was only carrying out the president's orders by sending the band to the most secure place to hold them, which was at Fort Marion, Florida. By now, President Cleveland had realized that Miles had gone beyond his orders of unconditional surrender and had offered conditions to the Chiricahuas, but he could not get a clear answer from Miles.[13]

On September 10, Cleveland ordered the commander of the Department of Texas, Brigadier General David Stanley, to detain the train with Geronimo and Naiche's band, remove them from the train, and place them in San Antonio's quartermaster's corral. Stanley followed orders and removed them from the train. Cleveland directed Stanley to question Geronimo and Naiche to find out what they understood of the promises Miles had made them.[14]

The quartermaster's corral had high walls and iron gates. Tents were erected within it for the Chiricahuas while they were detained there. The Chiricahuas soon learned they were not in Florida.[15]

The citizens of San Antonio heard of the Chiricahuas' arrival almost immediately. A mob clamored to get into the corral to view them. The Chiricahuas had never seen such a large gathering of white people. Once the crowd had settled down, the army escorted small groups in to visit.[16]

Geronimo told George Wratten he was worried some of the warriors might be killed. He was not concerned about himself; Ussen had told him he would live to be an old man and die a natural death.[17]

Meanwhile, on September 13, at Holbrook, Arizona, the army placed the peaceful Chiricahuas from Fort Apache onto a special Florida-bound train. Traveling cross-country under tight security, 381 people, numbering 278 adults and 103 children, reached Fort Marion on September 20, 1886, where Chihuahua's people lived. Chatto and Loco's Washington delegation arrived about the same time.[18]

Back in San Antonio, the questioning of Geronimo and Naiche did not begin until September 29. General Stanley, with other officers present and George Wratten translating, questioned Geronimo and Naiche separately.[19]

Both Geronimo and Naiche, with Wratten verifying, said they had not thought of surrendering until Lieutenant Gatewood had approached them. General Miles had promised that if they surrendered, their lives would be spared; they would be sent to Florida and reunited with their families; they would have a separate reservation with horses and wagons. No one would hurt them, and their past actions would be wiped away and forgotten.[20]

Stanley sent his findings to Washington, DC. The president and his officials were in a quandary as to what to do. Their desire was to hand over Geronimo, Naiche, and their warriors to civil authorities in Arizona to be tried for murder. However, since General Miles had promised them their lives, that they would be reunited with their families in Florida and receive their own reservation, should the government be bound by Miles's agreement?[21]

President Cleveland finally made a compromise decision supported by the Interior and War Departments. On October 19, Secretary of War William Endicott informed General Sheridan that Geronimo, Naiche, and their adult warriors were to be sent to Fort Pickens, at Pensacola, Florida, "[t]here to be kept in close custody until further orders." The women, children, and the two scouts, Kayitah and Martine, were to be sent to St. Augustine, Florida, to join Chihuahua at Fort Marion.[22]

When General Stanley told Geronimo and Naiche what was going to happen, they protested, saying Miles had promised they would be reunited with their families. Stanley sent their protest along with his own endorsement that the warriors be allowed to join their families through army channels to General Sheridan. Their request was marked "Disapproved." On October 22, the prisoners heading to Fort Pickens were escorted to one railroad car while the prisoners going to Fort Marion were directed to a second car, and then the train pulled out of the San Antonio station.[23]

On October 25 at 2:00 a.m., the fifteen Chiricahua men arrived in Pensacola, Florida. George Wratten remained with them as their interpreter. At 8:30 a.m., a crowd watched as the prisoners boarded a steamboat that ferried them across the bay to Santa Rosa Island, the location of Fort Pickens. Pensacola promoters viewed their arrival as wonderful news that promised to increase tourism.[24]

Back in Arizona, Mangas and his small band had quietly entered the United States and tried to meld in with the White Mountain Apaches at Fort Apache, but they had to surrender on October 18, and were sent East. On November 6, 1886, Mangas and another warrior arrived at Fort Pickens, while the eight women and children were sent to Fort Marion.[25]

Fort Marion's commander had written that at 160 people, Fort Marion was overcrowded. Ignoring that fact, General Sheridan had all but Geronimo and Naiche's warriors sent there. With over 480 Chiricahuas being crammed in and around the fort, conditions were horrible. People died from disease. The army cut their rations twice, resulting in additional people dying from malnutrition. Back in August 1886, Geronimo's four-year-old daughter had died, and by the end of 1886, eighteen more people would die there.[26]

Eligible children were being sent to the Carlisle Indian School in Pennsylvania. By December 8, 1886, forty-four had been sent to the school.[27]

Conditions at Fort Pickens were more spacious for Geronimo and the other warriors. It had been abandoned since the Civil War and was in disrepair, so the fort's temporary commander, Lieutenant Colonel Loomis Langdon, put the prisoners to work six hours a day for five days a week, improving their living quarters and the fort's grounds. They had Saturdays and Sundays off, where they could attend to their own business, including washing and mending their clothes.[28]

The prisoners were neat and orderly, causing no problems, but Langdon wrote his superiors that they were becoming malnourished and needed their rations increased. The original plan was for the prisoners to supplement their diet by fishing, but Chiricahuas would not eat fish. Sheridan issued an order to increase their rations.[29]

Tourists became a large part of the lives of Geronimo and the other prisoners. Hundreds of people flocked to the fort to see them. On one day 459 sightseers arrived. Geronimo and the others manufactured souvenirs to sell. Wratten taught Geronimo how to print his name and he sold many autographs. The Fort Pickens prisoners made a little money, but their main desire was to be reunited with their families.[30]

Through the winter of 1886 into 1887, news of the poor living conditions at Fort Marion and the separation of families started to become known to the general public. In March 1887, Secretary of War William Endicott gave permission for Herbert Welsh, the leader of the influential Indian Rights Association, accompanied by Captain John Bourke, to visit Fort Marion. Not only did they find atrocious living conditions, but the loyal Chiricahua scouts who had provided faithful service to the US government were being treated as prisoners of war.[31]

When Welsh published his report, the public was outraged, but President Cleveland was unmoved, saying that when the Chiricahuas were first transported to Florida, it was not possible to separate the guilty from the innocent. He didn't believe the living conditions at Fort Marion posed a health risk.[32]

General Sheridan asked to have the scouts at Fort Marion counted. It was reported that out of 82 men, 65 had served as government scouts; 4 of the remainder were considered friendly but had been too old to serve; and of the 365 women and children, 284 were family members of the scouts.[33]

Sheridan decided the prisoners had to be moved from Fort Marion. He sent Captain Bourke to inspect the Mount Vernon Barracks thirty miles north of Mobile, Alabama, to see if it would be suitable for the Chiricahuas. On April 13, Bourke sent a telegram to Sheridan saying it had a healthy environment but was not conducive to farming. That was good enough for Sheridan, who on April 18 ordered the Chiricahuas held at Fort Marion to be moved to Mount Vernon Barracks, eligible children to Carlisle Indian School, and the families of Geronimo, Naiche, and their warriors to Fort Pickens.[34]

On April 27, 1887, the moves were made. Mount Vernon Barracks would be the Chiricahuas' home for the next seven years. The arrival of the Fort Pickens prisoners' families, twenty women and eleven children, had to delight Geronimo, Naiche, and the other warriors. Geronimo was reunited with his three wives—She-gha; Zi-yeh, with six-year-old Fenton; and the Mescalero, Ih-tedda, with their baby daughter Lenna. Unfortunately, She-gha died on September 28, 1887. She had been sick at Fort Marion and may have had pneumonia or tuberculosis.[35]

Back on April 17, not knowing that a decision would soon be made to send their families to Fort Pickens, Geronimo, Naiche, and

Mangas had worked with George Wratten to write a letter to General Miles requesting they be brought together with their families and the rest of the Chiricahuas as he had promised. "Put us all together on some reservation . . . and you will soon see what an Indian can do when treated right." Wratten wrote his own letter to Miles, saying the Chiricahuas were easy to handle and worked without complaint. He believed they should be given a chance. They thought of Miles all the time and believed he would do as he said. Miles never responded.[36]

The Fort Pickens prisoners asked Wratten to talk to Lieutenant Colonel Loomis Langdon for them. They wanted to be sent to a place where they could farm. Langdon replied they had acted badly in the past. They should be quiet and let the government forget about them, or they might still receive punishment for their crimes. In October, the prisoners asked Wratten to write to General Miles again. They wanted Miles to know they were behaving well and desired to be given land to farm as he had promised them. Miles never responded.[37]

On November 8, 1887, the citizens of Arizona presented General Miles with an ornamental sword, as Miles later wrote, "in token of their appreciation of my services in ridding their country of the Apaches." They held a street parade in his honor, then a grand reception and ball at Tucson's San Xavier Hotel.[38]

The Fort Pickens prisoners asked Wratten to write a letter to General Stanley in San Antonio. Maybe he would listen to them. They stated the same things they had told Miles. They were behaving well and desired to be given land to farm, as they had been promised. Stanley sat on the letter for three months and then sent it to General Sheridan with his recommendation that the Fort Pickens prisoners be reunited with their people at Mount Vernon Barracks. He believed the government needed to fix this problem and deal with the Chiricahuas in good faith. Four days after receiving the letters, General Sheridan endorsed them and sent them to the adjutant general.[39]

On May 10, 1888, the War Department directed that the Fort Pickens prisoners be transferred to the Mount Vernon Barracks. On May 13, a train carrying Geronimo and the other Fort Pickens prisoners and their families, 46 people, arrived at the train platform two miles away from Mount Vernon Barracks. No one was there to meet them. They carried their belongings to the Chiricahua village. At first, not one of the 343 people came out to greet them. Finally, a woman, possibly a relative, left one of the dwellings, walked up to Geronimo, and cried as she hugged him. Others emerged from their homes, some to greet the newcomers, some just to observe. There is no explanation for the frosty greeting. Maybe they blamed Geronimo and the others for their prisoner-of-war situation. Maybe they had had no knowledge the Fort Pickens prisoners were arriving. At any rate, the Fort Pickens prisoners were soon a part of the Mount Vernon Barracks Chiricahua community, which now numbered 389.[40]

Geronimo and his family were assigned a two-room cabin in the center of the village. His twenty-two-year-old son Chappo had been sent to Carlisle Indian School; however, Chappo's wife and child were living in the village.[41]

A small infantry unit was stationed at Mount Vernon Barracks. The commander was Major William Sinclair and he was also in charge of the Chiricahuas. George Wratten had stayed with Geronimo and the other Fort Pickens prisoners and was now not only interpreter, but also superintendent of Chiricahua activities. He became a valuable asset to the Chiricahuas and to the army.[42]

Tourism flourished. Sightseers rode the train from Mobile to visit the Chiricahuas. Sinclair enjoyed guiding and dining with important visitors. The Chiricahuas manufactured bows and arrows and other handicrafts to sell. Wratten showed Geronimo how to make walking sticks and carve his name in them, which he sold for a dollar apiece. The Chiricahuas soon learned that anything Geronimo sold brought a higher price, so many of them would give him the things they made and he would sell the items for them at the higher price.[43]

Time was up for General Phil Sheridan. His influence on what would happen to the Chiricahuas and other Indian tribes ended when he died of heart failure on August 5, 1888, at his seaside cottage at Nonquitt, Massachusetts.[44]

Captain Bourke had believed Mount Vernon Barracks had a healthy environment, but the Chiricahuas found out otherwise. The land was swampy and infested with mosquitoes. It was hot, humid, and seemed like it was always raining. The Mount Vernon Barracks doctor, Walter Reed, credited with showing mosquitoes carry malaria and yellow fever, reported that the Chiricahuas suffered from diarrhea and chronic lung diseases.[45]

The Massachusetts Indian Association raised money for a school at Mount Vernon Barracks for Chiricahua children and sent two young sisters, Sophie and Sylvia Shepard, to teach. School opened in February 1889 and continued for as long as the Chiricahuas were at Mount Vernon Barracks. They taught eighty children who enjoyed school and loved their teachers.[46]

Geronimo enthusiastically supported the school. He knew the children had to learn the White Eyes' ways so they would not be taken advantage of and could stand up for their rights and prosper. Geronimo remained in the classroom and acted as a strict disciplinarian to the boys.[47]

The Mescalero Apaches in New Mexico had learned that some of their people had been sent East along with the Chiricahuas. They had petitioned the War Department to allow their people to return to their reservation, to which the government consented. Geronimo's wife Ih-tedda, who was pregnant, belonged to the Mescalero tribe. Geronimo and Ih-tedda loved each other, but Geronimo saw this as an opportunity for Ih-tedda and their daughter Lenna to escape the unhealthy environment of Mount Vernon Barracks. She wanted to stay with him, but he divorced her, allowing her to go. In February 1889, twelve people returned to the Mescalero Reservation. There, Geronimo and Ih-tedda's baby boy would be born later that year and named Robert.[48]

General Oliver O. Howard was now the commander of the Division of the Atlantic. In April, he arrived at Mount Vernon to inspect the Chiricahuas' living conditions.[49]

Stepping off the train at the Mount Vernon station, the first person Howard met was Geronimo, who was there to sell his canes to tourists. Geronimo ran to Howard and hugged him twice, speaking in Apache and repeatedly saying "Geronimo." Geronimo found an interpreter and told Howard, "I am a school superintendent now. We have fine lady teachers. All the children go to their school. I make them. I want them to be white children." The Chiricahuas had been allowed to form two fifty-man companies of soldiers. Geronimo told Howard he was very proud of them and worked with them to keep their uniforms and weapons clean.[50]

Geronimo explained to Howard that the Chiricahuas were getting sick at Mount Vernon, saying, "[A]ir bad and water bad." They were homesick for Arizona. He begged Howard to talk to the president, now Benjamin Harrison, about sending them back to Arizona. Howard said the Arizonans and Mexicans did not want them to return.[51]

Howard told Dr. Walter Reed that President Harrison had authorized him to find the Chiricahuas a home. Concerned about the health issues at Mount Vernon Barracks, Howard would send his son and aide-de-camp Lieutenant Guy Howard to investigate.[52]

Ever since Captain Richard Pratt had taken more than 100 of their children to the Carlisle Indian School in Pennsylvania, the Chiricahuas had mourned the absence of their children. In July 1889, Reed compiled statistics on the Chiricahua children sent to Carlisle and found that out of the 112 children sent there, 27—nearly one-third—had died. Of those 27, all but 2 had died of tuberculosis, or as the Chiricahuas called it, the "coughing sickness." Deaths from the coughing sickness were not restricted to Carlisle; many also died from it at Mount Vernon, including the warrior woman, Lozen.[53]

One happy note in all this tragedy: Geronimo's wife Zi-yeh gave birth to a healthy baby girl named Eva. She would be the last of Geronimo's children, and he was devoted to her.[54]

In November 1889, Reed wrote that the climate at Mount Vernon Barracks was killing the Chiricahuas. They needed to be moved, and not anywhere near the Atlantic or Gulf coasts. They needed dry mountain air.[55]

On December 23, 1889, Guy Howard released his report on his findings at Mount Vernon Barracks. Of the 498 Chiricahuas imprisoned, 119, nearly 25 percent, had died in three and a half years. While the death rate of "civilized" people was less than 2 percent a year, the Chiricahua death rate was 6.8 percent. Howard's report concluded that the people needed to be moved to suitable land where they could build homes and farm "by the first of March. Another year's delay would be criminal."[56]

General Howard concurred, sending the report on to army head-quarters with the concluding statement, "I hope, in the interest of justice, as well as of humanity, that speedy action be taken." Army commander Major General J. M. Schofield endorsed the report.[57]

Concurrently, Secretary of War Redfield Proctor sent General George Crook to look for suitable land in North Carolina to settle the Chiricahuas. Crook was impressed by what he found. He then decided to visit the Mount Vernon Barracks.[58]

Arriving unannounced in early January, Crook went straight to Major William Sinclair's quarters where he was spotted by a young Chiricahua. Soon the whole village was aware of his visit.[59]

Crook, Sinclair, and their staffs went to the village where they held a council with the leaders, all of whom were glad to see Crook. As was his custom, Geronimo rose to speak first, but Crook told Wratten to translate the following: "I don't want to hear anything from Geronimo. He is such a liar that I can't believe a word he says." The Chiricahua leaders didn't appreciate Crook's rude behavior toward Geronimo, who was trying to be friendly. Crook's disrespect of Geronimo put a damper on the Chiricahuas' mood.[60]

Crook quizzed the Chiricahuas on their surrender to Miles and whether Apache scouts had been a part of it. He listened to their concerns about the poor environment, their health issues, and their desire to have land where they could build homes and farm. Crook sent his report to Secretary Proctor. Crook wrote about the Chirica-huas' sickness and death rate, recommending their removal to either Indian Territory or North Carolina.[61]

On January 13, 1890, Proctor sent Howard's report and Crook's report to President Harrison, recommending that "those Indians be transferred to Fort Sill in the Indian Territory." A week later, President Harrison recommended to Congress "that provision be made by law for locating these Indians upon lands in Indian Territory." Delegates from Arizona and New Mexico Territories were opposed to moving the Chiricahuas closer to their territories; in addition, advocates for opening up Indian Territory for white settlement also had strong voices in Congress, so ultimately, the president's recom-mendation went nowhere.[62]

On March 21, 1890, General George Crook died of a heart attack in his Chicago home. Geronimo said, "I think that General Crook's death was sent by the Almighty as a punishment for the many evil deeds he committed."[63]

In June 1890, First Lieutenant William Wotherspoon and his family arrived at Mount Vernon Barracks. The army had assigned Wotherspoon to be in charge of the Chiricahua prisoners of war. Wotherspoon was energetic and took his position seriously. He agreed with the previous assessment as to the condition of the Chiricahuas, writing, "They are in a most depressed condition. Hope seems to have been crushed out by the long delays in the many promises made for their improvement."[64]

The Chiricahuas had been working hard but not receiving any compensation. Wotherspoon asked Secretary of War Proctor to set up a fund out of which to pay them something for their efforts, noting that it just might lift their spirits a little. Proctor agreed and set up the fund. The Chiricahuas were happy with being paid, although some of them spent it in saloons, which Wotherspoon then had to combat.[65]

The Chiricahuas tried to maintain their traditions. At night, they would sit around campfires and tell the children of their history. They would prepare the boys and girls for adulthood, and they continued the Sunrise Ceremony and other traditions.[66]

Geronimo continued to restore his prestige by being the disciplinarian at school while introducing the team sports of baseball and football.[67]

By the autumn of 1886, Sitting Bull's old way of life of chasing buffalo and raiding enemy tribes was gone, but he kept to Lakota traditions as well as working to improve his land and livestock along the Grand River on the reservation. He was not averse to trying white men's ways if they fit his wants and needs.

Sitting Bull was a devoted family man. He continued to live with his two wives, Seen-by-her-Nation and Four Robes, and doted on five of his children who still lived at home—two sets of twin boys and one girl. The first set of twins was born in 1876, the daughter was born in 1878, and the second set of twins was born in 1880. Sitting Bull's family would grow with an additional son in 1887 and a daughter in 1888. Not only did he love his own children, but he enjoyed the company of all the children living along the Grand River.[68]

Family members One Bull and Jumping Bull lived nearby, as well as many friends and followers. However, he was not on the best of terms with his brother-in-law Gray Eagle, who lived a little way upriver and on the opposite riverbank.[69]

Every other Saturday, the people traveled to Standing Rock Agency to draw their rations. It was an opportunity to meet friends and socialize and a chance to relive a bit of the old days. Designated cattle were herded into a corral where marksmen shot the animals; then the women would enter the corral and butcher the meat and prepare it for a communal feast.[70]

Sitting Bull became friends with Mary Collins, a Congregationalist teacher and nurse. Collins had established a mission in December 1885 at nearby Little Eagle on the Grand River, ten miles downriver from Sitting Bull's cabin. She had learned the Lakota language and was well liked. She was given the name *Wenonah*, or Princess. She and Sitting Bull became friends and he adopted her as a Hunkpapa.[71]

Although Collins and Sitting Bull discussed Christianity, he continued in his traditional beliefs. She said of Sitting Bull, "He had some indefinable power which could not be resisted by his own people or even others who came in contact with him. [Sitting Bull] was always so tender, gracious and invariably sweet."[72]

Trouble loomed in Washington, DC, where Indian rights activist Senator Henry Dawes of Massachusetts and many others believed the best thing for Indians was to be assimilated into the general population. They felt one of the ways to do this was to make Indians into farmers by allotting each individual acreage.[73]

There had been failed attempts in the past to diminish the twenty-two-million-acre Great Sioux Reservation by dividing it into six smaller reservations. Dawes introduced an act that Congress passed, and the president signed into law, called the Dawes Severalty Act of 1887. The Dawes Act provided 160-acre allotments to

Indian heads of households, 80 acres to single individuals, and 40 acres to each minor living on the reservations. It also provided for the surveying of Western reservation boundaries and the selling of surplus lands to whites. An Indian man could apply for a patent on his 160 acres of land. The federal government then held it in trust for twenty-five years, after which the title would be transferred to the Indian or his heirs. Citizenship would be granted after the process was completed, or if the Indian decided to live off the reservation and live as a white person.[74]

The Dawes Act recognized there were provisions in certain treaties that had to be met before lands could be allotted and surplus property sold. This was the case with the Fort Laramie Treaty, which stated that before the Great Sioux Reservation could be diminished, three-fourths of all adult males would have to agree to it.[75]

On April 30, 1888, Congress passed the Sioux Act of 1888. The act established six smaller reservations carved out of the Great Sioux Reservation and authorized the sale of nine million excess acres to the United States. Congress directed the Secretary of the Interior to appoint a commission to convince the Lakotas to accept the provisions of the two acts. Chairman of the commission was Captain Richard Pratt, the self-righteous superintendent of the Carlisle Indian School. The two other commission members were the president's cousin, Reverend William Cleveland, and Judge John Wright from Tennessee.[76]

On July 21, 1888, the commission arrived at the Standing Rock Agency, the first stop on the commission's mission to the reservation. The Secretary of the Interior had directed agent James McLaughlin to assist in getting the tribal members' signatures.[77]

McLaughlin invited all the men of the Standing Rock Agency to a meeting with the commission, on July 23. Sitting Bull was there but said nothing in public. McLaughlin opened by welcoming the commission. Running Antelope addressed the men, saying they should listen to what the commissioners had to say.[78]

The commissioners explained the division of the reservation into six smaller reservations and the selling of excess land. The government would pay fifty cents an acre as settlers bought the land. The money would be placed in a fund. The interest from the fund would pay for education and agriculture, with the government deducting administrative expenses. They would also give the Lakotas 1,000 bulls and 25,000 cows. The commission handed out copies of the agreement written in English. A few took them.[79]

No one liked the proposal—not even McLaughlin, who admitted it to some of the men when he was away from the commissioners. However, he told them he had to act in favor of it when he was with the commissioners.[80]

On the second day of the meeting, Commissioner Wright threatened the Lakotas, saying it was time they started earning their own living instead of taking government handouts. If they didn't sign the agreement, the government might stop taking care of them.[81]

Most likely it was during the commission's meetings that Sitting Bull and twelve leaders from different parts of the reservation visited Mary Collins. They discussed many things with her and were all pleased when she spoke honestly about the government's offers—the benefits as well as the drawbacks, which government officials never discussed.[82]

Sitting Bull met with the Silent Eaters, the twenty-member society that had focused on tribal welfare since the late 1860s. "The commissioners bring a paper containing what they wish already written out," Sitting Bull said. "It is not what the Indians want, but what the commissioners want. All they have to do is get the signatures of the Indians. Sometimes the commissioners *say* they compromise, but they never change the document." The Silent Eaters agreed to stand together in opposition to signing the agreement.[83]

As days turned into weeks, the commissioners pleaded and threatened the Lakota leaders and men. Sitting Bull acted in a conciliatory manner. All the Lakota leaders reasoned that the commissioners would finally tire and go home. John Grass told the commissioners the price for the land was not enough; besides, the government still owed them for land previously taken. He then listed the promises the government had never kept. Gall stated, "[The] Great Father was guilty of lying and stealing."[84]

Commissioner Pratt said the Lakotas needed to look to the future, not the past, and McLaughlin agreed with him. John Grass said the commissioners were talking too much, but Pratt would not stop. He came up with a plan whereby the men could mark a black ballot for yes and a red ballot for no. The Lakota men were suspicious and very few used a ballot.[85]

Sitting Bull was finally starting to lose patience, saying to the commissioners, "I want to know how many months you expect us to stay here, and by what time you will call a decision."[86]

By August 21, after a month of meetings, the Lakotas had had enough. Gall stood and spoke for everyone, saying they had listened in good humor to what the commissioners had to say, but no thank you. They had things to do and were going home. Commissioner Cleveland would not let them have the last word, saying, "We have come to the conclusion it is better for you to go home and attend to your crops now, and we ourselves will wait here until we get instructions from the Great Father as to what he wishes us to say further to you."[87]

The commission left Standing Rock with twenty-two ballots in favor of the agreement. They traveled to Crow Creek and Lower Brulé Agencies but received only negative results. Deciding to not even go to Cheyenne River, Rosebud, and Pine Ridge Agencies, the commission returned to Washington, DC, recommending that the government force the allotment on the Lakotas. The commission's recommendation was ignored, but a new plan was developed to bring a Lakota delegation to Washington, DC, and convince them of the plan in the nation's capital.[88]

At midnight on Friday, October 12, 1888, a train carrying Sitting Bull and sixty other Lakota chiefs along with their agents and interpreters steamed into Washington, DC. They were given rooms at the Belvedere Hotel. Captain Richard Pratt had excluded Red Cloud from Pine Ridge Agency. Pratt and Red Cloud had had a heated argument over the treatment of children at the Carlisle Indian School. By excluding Red Cloud, the government hoped to diminish his status as a tribal leader.[89]

On the trip to Washington, DC, some Standing Rock delegates had become disheartened, but Sitting Bull remained positive they could stand up to the government officials. He composed and sang a song to lift their spirits:

> Friends, what are you saying?
> The Black Hills belong to me.
> Saying this, I take fresh courage.[90]

The very next day after arriving in Washington, Saturday, October 13, the delegation was taken to the Interior Department where after brief introductions, Secretary William Vilas began talking about the benefits of the Dawes Act and 1888 Sioux Act for the Lakota people. Swift Bird with the Cheyenne River Agency asked that the meeting be postponed, saying they "had been on the train so long that their brains were rocking, and they were like drunken men." Vilas responded that he was a busy man. The Lakotas would not give in. An impatient Vilas dismissed them, saying they better be prepared when they came back Monday morning.[91]

Over the weekend, the Lakota delegation met to develop their response. Some were ready to accept the government's proposal; others did not want to agree to any offer whatsoever. Sitting Bull talked for two hours. He proposed setting a higher price for the land than the offer of fifty cents an acre. Sitting Bull said they should ask for $1.25 per acre, which was the same price at which the federal government had sold its land. In addition, the government should pay them the money up front and right away, and not wait for homesteaders to file claims. Sitting Bull was attempting to keep those who wanted to sell in control, and by setting a higher price, he probably believed the government would not accept it and they could go home with the reservation intact. The delegates accepted Sitting Bull's proposal.[92]

With their meeting completed, the delegates were shown the sights of Washington, DC, including the Smithsonian Institution, where they viewed George Catlin's Indian paintings, and the National Zoo, where Gray Eagle was fascinated by the monkeys and wanted to buy one. They tried a new fad sweeping Washington at the time—smoking cigarettes—although Sitting Bull settled for a good cigar. That Sunday, members of the delegation were invited to various churches, and many went.[93]

On Monday, October 15, the delegation was brought back to the Interior Department where the commissioner of Indian Affairs, members of the House and Senate Committees on Indian Affairs, and the three members of Pratt's commission joined Secretary Vilas.[94]

Vilas again tried to convince the Lakota delegation that the government proposal was good. Sitting Bull was the first delegate to speak. He was cheerful as he addressed the government officials, saying, "My Kinsmen, I am now one of your people . . . I have plenty that I could say myself, but I wish the other men here to speak for me."[95]

John Grass and Gall spoke, as well as American Horse from Pine Ridge. The men told of their grievances against the US government. John Grass said, "Look at our people; we are poor and we ought not to be poor. We ought to be rich. You are the cause of our being poor." The speakers told Vilas that fifty cents an acre was an insult. The government was trying to take advantage of them again.[96]

Vilas made a new offer. He would ask Congress for $1.00 per acre for the first three years. After that the price would drop to seventy-five cents for the following two years, and after that, to fifty cents. Vilas told the delegation he wanted their response in writing. They asked for Agent McLaughlin's help with writing down their proposal.[97]

That same day, all wearing dark suits like those worn by white men, the Lakota delegation, the commissioner of Indian Affairs, the Pratt commission, and other government officials went to the steps of the Capitol building where their picture was taken. Sitting Bull stands conspicuous, slightly to the left of the entire group, at the third row. In his right hand he holds what appears to be a broad-brimmed hat. It's interesting to speculate whether it might be the hat Buffalo Bill gave him.[98]

Forty-seven members of the delegation held firm with their $1.25 price. Fourteen believed they should take Vilas's proposal. McLaughlin wrote down the majority and minority proposals. The delegates signed them, Sitting Bull and all the Hunkpapa delegates signing the majority proposal. They submitted them to Vilas on Wednesday, October 17. He was not pleased, saying only that he needed to review the majority proposal with the president. On Friday, October 19, Vilas rejected the Lakota counteroffer. He said they were to go home immediately. Those delegates who did not want to sell the land were pleased.[99]

McLaughlin insisted one last thing needed to be done before the Lakota delegates left town. They had been promised they would meet President Cleveland. McLaughlin had to convince the government officials to keep that promise. He told them if they didn't, the Lakota leaders would feel slighted and be even harder to work with. The Lakotas were given a brief audience with President Cleveland before boarding a westbound train. Sitting Bull was in good humor; he had beaten the white man at his own game, and his influence with the other Lakota leaders was high.[100]

The presidential election was held in November 1888, with Democrat incumbent Grover Cleveland being defeated by the Republican challenger, Benjamin Harrison. Harrison would be sworn into office on March 4, 1889. For years, the citizens of Dakota Territory had been lobbying the federal government for statehood, and land speculators called "Boomers" continued to press the federal government to open up the Great Sioux Reservation for settlement. The Republicans, who had won a majority in both the House of Representatives and the Senate, were in favor of dividing the territory into two states, and on February 22, 1889, Congress passed the enabling act, creating South Dakota and North Dakota.[101]

Incoming president Benjamin Harrison was in favor of breaking up the Great Sioux Reservation and selling off the excess land. His staff, working alongside the outgoing Interior Department staff, concluded that the best way to move forward was to accept the Lakota proposal of $1.25 per acre. Senator Dawes developed new legislation, the Sioux Act of 1889, with the new dollar amount in it and a few additional modifications. It rapidly moved through both houses and was signed into law on March 2, 1889, by outgoing President Cleveland.[102]

The price would begin at $1.25 for the first three years, but after that, similar to what Vilas had proposed earlier, the price would drop to seventy-five cents for the next two years, and then drop after that to fifty cents per acre. Incentives included $3 million to be placed in trust for education, and government expenses would not be charged off against the Lakotas' money. Congress increased the 160 acres for each head of household or individual to 320 acres. Congress also provided an appropriation of $25,000 to be used to ensure that the Lakotas signed off on the breakup of the reservation and sale of the excess land.[103]

On May 19, President Harrison appointed a new commission to obtain the consent from three-fourths of the Lakota adult males. The chairman was former Ohio governor Charles Foster. The other commission members were former Missouri congressman William Warner and the experienced General George Crook, now the commander of the Division of the Missouri and based out of Chicago. Even though Foster was the chairman, Crook ran the commission.[104]

The commission decided not to go to Standing Rock first, but went to Rosebud, Cheyenne River, and Lower Brulé. In his writings, Crook revealed that the commission had to work behind the scenes to get the needed signatures. Crook learned that Lakota leaders had already reviewed the breakup and sale conditions and had decided in their tribal councils not to agree. When the commission met with the Lakotas together as a group, they supported each other in rejecting the proposal.[105]

Crook used the appropriated $25,000 to provide dinners for tribal members where he could talk about the benefits of the sale. He hired white men married to Lakota women to convince their Lakota friends. The agents had banned Lakota dances, but now Crook allowed them again. When persuasion did not work, the commissioners and their agents reverted to subtle intimidation.[106]

The commission first went to the Rosebud Agency where the Lakotas shouted down the commissioners, but the commissioners threw them feasts. Crook and the other commissioners implied that those who did not sign would miss out on the benefits received by those who did sign. After visiting the other agencies, except Pine

Ridge and Standing Rock, and getting as many signatures as they could, the commission traveled to Pine Ridge, where Red Cloud and other leaders actively resisted. Crook wrote that he offered a $200 bribe to Red Cloud and to each of the other leaders if they would tell the people to vote for the allotment. Red Cloud and the others refused. The commissioners were able to get 684 out of 1,306 adult male signatures from Pine Ridge. In order to get the required three-fourths, they needed to go all out at the last agency on their list—Standing Rock.[107]

People kept Sitting Bull informed as to the commission's progress at the other agencies, but he couldn't do anything to confront it. He had been very ill—possibly with pneumonia. Newspapers speculated he had been so ill he was probably already dead, but he confounded their dire predictions and was slowly recovering.[108]

After Sitting Bull had returned home from the Washington, DC, visit, Catherine Weldon from Brooklyn, New York, began sending him and other Lakota leaders letters containing information on the latest commission news, current fair market value for Dakota land, and maps proposing how the federal government should carve up the reservation.[109]

Weldon was a middle-aged widow with a teenage son in boarding school. She was an artist with a passion to help Indians maintain their ways of life. She belonged to the National Indian Defense Association, the only Indian advocate organization that did not believe in assimilation. The association believed traditional Indian life had value and should be preserved.[110]

Weldon went one step beyond writing letters: She traveled to Standing Rock to meet Sitting Bull and offer her assistance. Her plan was to take a message from him to the Lakota leaders at the other agencies to resist signing in favor of the allotment. She arrived at the Parkin Ranch, a small settlement on the north bank of the Cannonball River, where she had Indian friends she had met on a previous trip. To proceed onto the reservation, she first needed permission from agent James McLaughlin. Weldon had sent Sitting Bull a letter, saying she would like to meet with him at the agency. She had heard nothing back—because McLaughlin had intercepted her letter.[111]

D. F. Barry, a photographer, was traveling to visit Sitting Bull. His guide was McLaughlin's oldest son, Harry. Weldon met them and asked them to tell Sitting Bull she would like to meet with him.[112]

The June 15, 1889, edition of the *Bismarck Weekly Tribune* reported that when Barry met Sitting Bull at his home on the Grand River, he was recovering from his illness. Sitting Bull still planned to fight the breakup of the reservation and allotment, stating, "The white is wise in books. He can read and write and we cannot. We know nothing about books, and the whites have fooled us. Now we are approached with another treaty, but us old men will not sign it. We are not able to deal with your people, but in a few years our young men will know how to handle papers. They are going to school and will soon know how to trade with the government."[113]

Sitting Bull dictated a letter of welcome to Weldon and gave it to Harry McLaughlin to give to her. Weldon never received the letter. Harry gave it to his father. Sitting Bull sent another letter, also intercepted—although she did eventually receive it, five days later than she should have. Sitting Bull sent a messenger who gave Weldon a verbal message that he did want to speak with her, but he was too sick to travel, and she would have to wait.[114]

In the meantime, Agent McLaughlin rode to Parkin Ranch to meet Catherine Weldon. It was a small settlement, and McLaughlin and Weldon were able to recognize each other as he rode in and dismounted. McLaughlin got right down to business, stating Sitting Bull was a coward and selfish. He thought of himself as a great chief, but he was not. He was a backslider and an obstructionist. Weldon was surprised to find out that McLaughlin knew a lot about her, although she didn't know how. He knew she was a member of the National Indian Defense Association and said it had no influence at Standing Rock. McLaughlin ended by telling Weldon she was welcome to stay at Parkin Ranch and that she was allowed to visit the agency as long as she didn't make trouble. Weldon traveled to Standing Rock Agency to try to find out more about Sitting Bull's health and if he could meet with her.[115]

A reporter visiting Sitting Bull told him Lakotas at the other agencies were signing the agreement to break up the reservation and sell the land. He didn't believe it. He said he had people reporting to him telling him the opposite. He believed it was a ploy on the part of the commissioners to scare the people at Standing Rock into signing.[116]

Still recovering from his illness, Sitting Bull drove his wagon to Fort Yates to meet Weldon. She explained to him that she was there representing the National Indian Defense Association and was willing to work with him to stop the commission's breakup of the reservation. She told him she intended to travel through the reservation on her way to the Yankton Agency. Sitting Bull said he would be willing to drive her in his wagon along with his family as far as the Cheyenne River Agency. He was camping near Standing Rock Agency and returned there to begin preparations for the trip.[117]

Weldon went to McLaughlin to request a pass for Sitting Bull to leave and permission for her to travel through the reservation. McLaughlin refused both requests, stating that since the commission would soon be there, Sitting Bull could not go.[118]

Weldon wrote to Red Cloud on July 3: "I asked him [McLaughlin] if he was afraid of a woman & of a woman's influence & threatened to report him to Washington. High words passed between us both & I rose indignantly & left his office." Weldon sent a message to Sitting Bull that the trip was off. He returned to Standing Rock Agency where Weldon further explained the situation. The next morning, angry and indignant, he went to McLaughlin's office. The agent refused to see him. One of McLaughlin's people, Louis Faribault, walked Sitting Bull to the guardhouse. There he accused Sitting Bull of having intentions of carrying off Weldon. Faribault hinted he would be sent to the penitentiary. Sitting Bull was indignant and said he looked upon Weldon as a daughter and would have shielded and protected her from harm. Pained and frustrated, Weldon had Sitting Bull drive her to the Missouri River where she took a ferry and crossed to the east bank, arranging transportation to Yankton Agency from there.[119]

That was not the end of the story, however. Sitting Bull's polite attention to Weldon and her words of friendship to him became the stuff of newspaper gossip. "She Loves Sitting Bull" headlined a story in the July 5, 1889, edition of the *Bismarck Weekly Tribune.* The sub-head proclaimed, "A New Jersey [*sic*] Widow Falls Victim to Sitting Bull's Charms." The story covered why she was there and her argument with McLaughlin when he denied Sitting Bull's travel request. "So abusive and threatening was her language that the agent politely ordered her to leave the reservation." The story went on to say, "She is a great admirer of Sitting Bull and it is gossip among the people in the vicinity of the agency that she is actually in love with the cunning old warrior. Agent McLaughlin's position in the matter is unquestionably right, especially at this time, as Sitting Bull would surely prove a disturbing element at the lower agencies during the conference of the commission on the question of opening the reservation to settlement." The story was picked up by other newspapers across the country.[120]

Weldon's letter was intercepted and never reached Red Cloud. W. J. Godfrey, the Pine Ridge postmaster, opened and read it. On July 11, he forwarded it to a Major Roberts, Sioux Commission, Standing Rock Agency, writing, "I herewith inclose [*sic*] you a fair specimen of a letter from a female crank." The letter wound up in McLaughlin's possession, and he most likely had it available for the commissioners to read when they arrived. At the end of Weldon's Red Cloud letter, she wrote, "Sitting Bull . . . says he will never sign nor will his followers, but that he is afraid some of the other chiefs may sign in order to become popular."[121]

McLaughlin had been against the 1888 proposal, but he believed this new one was good for the Lakotas. He knew the Lakota leaders were solidly against it, so he began working to convince them otherwise.[122]

However, Sitting Bull worked with the same four chiefs McLaughlin had appointed—Gall, John Grass, Mad Bear, and Big Head—and they held firm on not supporting the breakup of the reservation or the allotment. Sitting Bull recruited schoolboys who could understand, read, and write English to attend the commission meetings and record what was being said.[123]

On Thursday, July 25, 1889, the commission's steamboat arrived at Standing Rock. It was their last agency visit. General Crook met with Agent McLaughlin and told him they needed six hundred Lakota signatures to ratify the agreement. The commissioners were relying on McLaughlin to use his influence to get those signatures. The Lakotas knew how important this was, and many had already arrived and pitched their tents outside the agency in anticipation of the meetings.[124]

The next day, the commissioners held their public council meeting outside the agency warehouse. The commissioners and other officials sat behind a table on a raised platform in front of the building as they explained the provisions of the agreement. The Lakotas said they needed time to hold their own councils and discuss what they had just learned, so the council meeting was adjourned until Monday.[125]

The Silent Eaters met and asked Sitting Bull to speak. In a lengthy address he said the government always promised many things for their land. "We are dying off in expectation of getting things promised us." He said the commissioners arrived with well-worded papers that have only what the government wants, never what the Lakotas want. He said he was opposed to the latest agreement and that they must reject it for the sake of their children and grandchildren. He continued, "The Great Father has proven himself an *unktomi* (trickster) in our past dealings." He recounted how the Black Hills had been guaranteed them by treaty, but the government took them anyway. He concluded, "Therefore, I do not wish to consider any proposition to cede any portion of our tribal holdings to the Great Father. If I agree to dispose of any part of our land to the white people I would feel guilty of taking food away from our children's mouths, and I do not wish to be that mean. There are things they tell us [that] sound good to hear, but when they have accomplished their purpose they will go home and will not try to fulfill our agreements with them. My friends and relatives, let us stand as one family, as we did before the white people led us astray."[126]

Sunday evening, McLaughlin met at Fort Yates with Crook and the commissioners, along with a few officers. McLaughlin proposed that if they added a few more incentives, he believed the Lakotas would change their position and sign in favor of the breakup and allotment. He proposed an appropriation of $200,000 compensation for horses the federal government had confiscated from the Lakotas at Standing Rock and Cheyenne River Agencies in 1876. The funds would go to support reservation schools. Crook and the other commissioners agreed to personally support the proposals and get them to Congress. When the time was right, McLaughlin would present the promises to the Lakota leaders—promises that carried no weight unless the Harrison administration supported them and Congress decided to approve them.[127]

On Monday, July 29, the commission resumed holding its public council meeting. For three days, the Lakota leaders Gall, Mad Bear, Big Head, John Grass, and others spoke against the reservation breakup and land sale while the commissioners listened.[128]

During the meetings, the Lakotas' major concern was whether the federal government would cut their beef rations once they had signed the agreement. Crook guaranteed the government would not cut their rations.[129]

On the third day, McLaughlin decided it was time to convince the Lakota leaders to switch their points of view. That evening, the McLaughlins held a reception for the commission with the Fort Yates officers and their wives. McLaughlin slipped away from the festivities and with his interpreter Louis Primeau drove five miles to the home of Nick Cadotte, who was John Grass's brother-in-law. McLaughlin had arranged to secretly meet Grass there. Grass was worried they might be seen together, so they entered a vacant building.[130]

McLaughlin told Grass he needed to change his position to be in favor of signing the agreement. He talked about the concessions the commission would agree to. McLaughlin said that if the Lakotas did not agree to the breakup and allotment, Congress might pass legislation that would still open the reservation without the Lakotas' consent and without any concessions. Grass agreed to change his position. McLaughlin worked with Grass to prepare his speech. McLaughlin then met separately with Gall, Mad Bear, and Big Head, also convincing them to change their positions to be in favor of the agreement.[131]

At 3:00 p.m. on August 3, McLaughlin and the commissioners held a final meeting that included signing the rolls agreeing to the breakup and land sale. McLaughlin did not tell Sitting Bull of this meeting, fearing he and his followers would attempt to dissuade the people from signing. McLaughlin stationed his metal breasts—the Indian police, led by Lieutenant Bull Head—in a four-column formation at the warehouse council area. McLaughlin also had loyal Lower Yanktonai chief Two Bears and his men form a protective semicircle around the commissioners' platform to prevent any trouble from Sitting Bull and his followers.[132]

John Grass spoke first, saying he would change his position on signing the agreement if concessions could be made. He presented the concessions McLaughlin had given him. The commission answered that the concessions would be made. After that, Gall, then Mad Bear and Big Head, all spoke in favor of signing the agreement.[133]

The council area was set up so each signer would approach the commissioners' table, sign the agreement rolls, enter the warehouse when finished, and file out the other side of the building. John Grass, who was to be the first to sign, made a final speech.[134]

Crook then spoke: "Now we have understood that there have been some threats made against the Indians who sign this bill. You need not be alarmed, because no one will be allowed to interfere with you. And if any damage or injury is done [to] those who have signed, we will ask to have it paid for from the rations of those who do not sign. So there must be no trouble. Now the tables will be moved down here and those who want to sign can do so."[135]

Sitting Bull and the Silent Eaters had just arrived in time to hear Crook's speech. He pushed his way through the metal breasts and the crowd, up to the commissioners' table. Up until this time, Sitting Bull had not spoken directly to the commissioners.[136]

Now he said, "I would like to say something unless you object to my speaking. If you do, I will not speak. No one told us of the council today, and we just got here."

Looking at McLaughlin, Crook asked, "Did Sitting Bull know we were going to hold a council?"

"Yes, sir," McLaughlin answered. "Everybody knew it."[137]

With that, John Grass led the others forward to sign the rolls to break up the reservation.

Furious, Sitting Bull turned and left.[138]

John Grass signed, followed by Mad Bear. Gall was to sign third, a position of honor. McLaughlin's wife called out a warning as Sitting Bull and twenty mounted Silent Eaters charged into the men waiting to sign, scattering them. McLaughlin scooped up the rolls so they wouldn't be damaged as Bull Head's metal breasts forced the Silent Eaters away.[139]

They set up for signing again. Before Gall was ready to sign at the third position of honor, Big Head signed at that position. Sitting Bull and his men charged again, but again were repulsed. Gall never got around to signing until position 416 out of 806 signers.[140]

Sitting Bull failed to stop the signers, which included some of his friends and relatives, even his adopted son One Bull.[141]

A reporter caught Sitting Bull before he rode from the council area. He asked Sitting Bull what the Indians thought of giving up their land.

"Indians!" Sitting Bull shouted. "There are no Indians left but me!"[142]

That night Crook wrote in his journal, "Sitting Bull tried to speak after the signing commenced, but I stopped him. Then he tried twice to stampede the Indians away from signing, but his efforts failed, and he flattened out, his wind bag punctured, and several of his followers have deserted him."

In the end, the commission got 5,678 signatures, enough to fulfill the requirements to break up the Great Sioux Reservation and sell off the excess land. Sitting Bull and his supporters had lost.[143]

Two weeks after the commission left the Great Sioux Reservation, the agents received orders to cut the beef issues by 20 percent, what amounted to several million pounds. Crook had assured the Lakotas at every agency that a cut would not happen—something the commission could not promise, but did anyway. The cut had come from Congress. In fact, Congress had authorized the cut even before the commission had left Washington to get the signatures for the breakup of the reservation. Did the commissioners know this ahead of time?[144]

When Sitting Bull had returned home to the Grand River, Agent John McLaughlin sent Sitting Bull's brother-in-law Gray Eagle to confront him. Gray Eagle told Sitting Bull that he needed to start doing what the government wanted or he might get himself killed. Sitting Bull said, "You go ahead and follow the white man's road, and do as he says. But for me, leave me alone."[145]

That August of 1889, Sitting Bull predicted the severe drought that the countryside was experiencing would continue. In fact, there would be very little precipitation until June 1890.[146]

After South and North Dakota citizens ratified their state constitutions and elected state officials, President Benjamin Harrison signed the documents admitting the states of South Dakota and North Dakota into the Union on November 2, 1889.[147]

The winter of 1889–1890 was a bad one for the Lakotas. With the reduction of their beef rations and poor to nonexistent crops, people were hungry. To add to their misery, disease swept through Lakota communities—measles, influenza, whooping cough. Many people sickened and died.[148]

On February 10, 1890, President Harrison declared the Agreement of 1889 was formally accepted and announced the ceded land was open for settlement. However, the concessions and money the commission had promised were nonexistent. The government had not surveyed any of the six new reservations' boundaries or individual allotments. Homesteaders knew about the reduction in price per acre after three to five years and were in no hurry to make the higher payments, so there was no money from land sales. By March 21, Crook was out of the picture, dying of a heart attack. The Lakotas believed the government had duped them.[149]

In May 1890, Catherine Weldon returned to Parkin Ranch in North Dakota on the northern border of what was now Standing Rock Reservation. She wanted to continue to help the Lakota people and live among them. She had been corresponding with Sitting Bull and had sent a letter to Agent McLaughlin expressing her desire to return to the reservation for a short stay, to assist Sitting Bull. McLaughlin had not responded to her letter, but she went anyway.[150]

Weldon's fourteen-year-old son Christie joined her when school was out. Sitting Bull paid several visits to Mrs. Weldon during the spring and then invited her and Christie to his Grand River settlement.[151]

Weldon asked McLaughlin for permission to go to Sitting Bull's settlement and teach children there. McLaughlin did not prevent her from going, but said she would not be allowed to do any teaching.[152]

Early that summer, Mrs. Weldon and Christie traveled to Sitting Bull's home where they would stay for the summer. Sitting Bull and his family lived in two substantial cabins with wood floors. Canvas covered the interior walls to help with insulation and keep the cabins clean. Each cabin had a stove in the center for heating and kerosene lamps for lighting. People slept on low wood platforms.[153]

Sitting Bull lived in the larger cabin with his wife Four Robes, their youngest child, and fourteen-year-old Crow Foot. His younger wife, Seen-by-her-Nation, and her children lived in the nearby, smaller cabin. There was plenty of room for additional guests to stay with the Sitting Bull family. His lodge was always open to anyone, which was the custom of a chief. Many people came to visit every day.[154]

Mrs. Weldon and her son may have stayed at Seen-by-her-Nation's cabin, where later one of her portraits of Sitting Bull would hang in a gilt frame. The Lakotas had strict privacy codes that would have been followed even in crowded living conditions. Sitting Bull's wives were quiet and patient. Seen-by-her-Nation was known to be a jolly person. Mrs. Weldon and her son would not be staying in the wives' home without their approval.[155]

Weldon didn't freeload off the Sitting Bull family. She paid for supplies and provided funds from time to time for the family to hold feasts. She helped out with chores and showed Sitting Bull's wives whites' techniques for housekeeping. She talked with Sitting Bull about white culture and how best to work to preserve the Lakota way of life. Letters arrived for Sitting Bull from around the world. Weldon translated the English, French, and German for him, wrote his responses, and found the time to paint four portraits of him. Sitting Bull named her Woman-Walking-Ahead.[156]

There was no sexual contact of any kind between Sitting Bull and Mrs. Weldon, but that didn't stop the whites at Standing Rock Agency and Fort Yates from denouncing her, saying she was a disgrace. They gossiped that she had become Sitting Bull's wife and was pregnant. Of course, the newspapers picked up on the gossip and ran with it. Weldon was furious about the gossip and insisted to McLaughlin that she was a lady.[157]

Sitting Bull appreciated her abilities, and at some point, he asked her to marry him. Outraged, Weldon said no. She saw the two of them as friends—nothing more. Besides, he had two wives already and she hated polygamy. They argued about it, and that was it. She continued to live there, helping him with the white world and his wives with the chores, writing in her journal, "I think of myself just as great as Sitting Bull."[158]

Back in the summer of 1889, the Lakotas had begun hearing rumors of a new religion sweeping through the tribes that claimed God would restore everything to the way it was before the white man came. A Nevada Paiute named Wovoka spread this message, and many claimed he was a prophet or Messiah.

Several Lakota tribes sent a delegation to see this Messiah for themselves and report back. The delegation included a Miniconjou from the Cheyenne River Reservation, Kicking Bear, who was a nephew of Sitting Bull's wives. The Hunkpapas sent no one, having no interest at the time.[159]

The Lakotas met Wovoka and were convinced his message was true. He taught them that God was going to destroy the world and replace it with a fresh new one. The whites would disappear, the Indian dead would live again, and the old ways would return. For this to happen, the Indians needed to dance the Ghost Dance.[160]

Wovoka taught the Lakotas the Ghost Dance and gave them sacred paint. When they danced, they experienced visions of the new land to come. On his way home from listening to Wovoka preach, Kicking Bear visited the Arapahos and witnessed their Ghost Dance. Dancers fell to the ground as if dead and said they visited heaven, where they were given "water, fire, and wind with which to kill all the whites." He said they made Ghost Shirts that bullets would not pass through. Kicking Bear believed them and introduced the Ghost Shirts to the Lakotas, along with the new Ghost Dance religion.[161]

By the summer of 1890, the Ghost Dance had spread throughout the Lakota reservations, except for Standing Rock. The dancers believed the new world would be coming in the spring of 1891. In the meantime, they would keep dancing into the fall and through the winter until it happened. The white people in surrounding areas didn't understand the Ghost Dance and were getting nervous, thinking the Lakotas were planning a breakout.[162]

The commissioner of Indian Affairs asked the Indian agents to investigate whether the Lakotas were planning violence. All the agents including James McLaughlin agreed the scare was an idle rumor. However, McLaughlin couldn't help himself, adding in his report dated June 18, 1890, "There are, however, a few malcontents . . . who cling to the old Indian ways . . . and . . . whose influence is exerted in the wrong direction." The "removal" of this group of individuals that included Sitting Bull "would end all trouble and uneasiness in the future."[163]

At the time, Sitting Bull's settlement was made up of no more than two hundred men, women, and children. Possibly fifty of the men were of fighting age. After being defeated by the Crook Commission the previous August, Sitting Bull was leading a quiet life on the Grand River.[164]

Many people were participating in the Ghost Dance on the Cheyenne River Reservation. Sitting Bull's Miniconjou friends Hump and Big Foot's people held Ghost Dances.[165]

Sitting Bull was inquisitive and wanted to learn more about the Ghost Dance. He asked McLaughlin several times for permission to go to the Cheyenne River Reservation to investigate it, but McLaughlin refused to let him travel. If Sitting Bull couldn't go to see the Ghost Dance, he would bring it to the Grand River. He sent six young men to Cheyenne River to invite Kicking Bear to come and explain the Ghost Dance. Kicking Bear along with a few followers arrived on October 9. He addressed a large crowd, explaining his journey west to visit the prophet, telling what he had seen and experienced, and relating the prophecies of things to come. He began his speech with, "My brothers, I bring to you the promise of a day in which there will be no white man to lay his hand on the bridle of the Indian's horse." Kicking Bear's revelations inspired the people, giving them hope. Sitting Bull was in favor of holding the ceremony, so they prepared for a Ghost Dance of their own.[166]

Many people including Sitting Bull danced the Ghost Dance. He hoped he would see one of his daughters who had recently died, but it was not to be. He did not go into a trance. He saw nothing. He experienced nothing. Others did, however, talking about what they had seen and composing songs about it. Sitting Bull listened and allowed the dance to continue, even sponsoring the dancers, even though he had become skeptical.[167]

The Ghost Dance was intricate, requiring much preparation. Everything had to be done in the proper way or it would not be *wakan*, or holy. A sacred pole was erected in the middle of the dance area. The dance leaders fasted, and men purified themselves in sweat lodges. A holy man painted the dancers' faces. Both men and women dancers needed to wear eagle feathers in their hair. The people wore sacred shirts and dresses upon which images of the sacred spotted eagle were painted and spotted eagle feathers attached. The dance was unusual in that it was for all people, male and female, young and old. After the beginning ceremonies and prayers, the people formed a circle facing the sacred pole. Each person held the hand of the person on either side of him or her. As the people held hands, they began to sing. Dancing a sidestep, the circle of people rotated. There were no drums or other musical instruments. There were no bonfires within the circle. When someone fell to the ground, unconscious, the other dancers stepped over the person, continuing to sing and dance. When those who had collapsed came to, many were ecstatic, telling of visiting heaven and seeing their departed loved ones.[168]

Sitting Bull's nephew and adopted son One Bull had become a metal breast. He reported to McLaughlin all that Kicking Bear had said, and on the Ghost Dance being held in Sitting Bull's community. McLaughlin later wrote, "It was the appeal that the leaders of the ghost-dance made to the superstitions of the people that I feared most."[169]

On October 13, Agent McLaughlin sent thirteen metal breasts under the command of Captain Crazy Walking to arrest Kicking Bear and expel him from the reservation.[170]

Kicking Bear was preaching to the people when Crazy Walking and his men arrived at Sitting Bull's community. They listened to Kicking Bear and listened to the stories of those who had been dancing and what they had seen in their visions. Sitting Bull told Crazy Walking that Kicking Bear would be leaving the next day, saying, "The education of my children is uppermost. I have a school in my locality. This dance is not the most important undertaking. They will, eventually, stop."

On October 14, Crazy Walking reported this information to McLaughlin.[171]

McLaughlin wanted Kicking Bear escorted off the reservation, immediately. He sent Lieutenant Chatka, who McLaughlin believed had a firm character, along with two other metal breasts handpicked by Chatka. Chatka and his men arrived at Sitting Bull's settlement on October 15 as a dance was in progress. Chatka informed Kicking Bear and his six followers that they needed to leave immediately and escorted them back to the border with the Cheyenne River Reservation. Sitting Bull was insulted by the metal breasts' disrespect shown his guests.[172]

On October 17, McLaughlin sent a letter to the commissioner of Indian Affairs, outlining "a history of the ghost-dancing craze on Standing Rock Reservation." He wrote that he had given One Bull a message for Sitting Bull, saying he wanted to see him at the agency. He believed he could "put a stop to this absurd craze." He ended by writing, "I would respectfully recommend the removal from the reservation and confinement in some military prison at a distance from the Sioux country, of Sitting Bull and the parties named in my letter of June 18 last."[173]

The white settlers were becoming fearful as they began hearing distorted rumors of the Ghost Dance. Newspapers fueled the flames, saying an Indian Messiah was coming to kill them all.[174]

Catherine Weldon was not a Christian and did not believe in the resurrection. She did not believe in the new Ghost Dance and its focus on resurrection. She wanted Sitting Bull to stop the dance. He would not do so. She worried McLaughlin would use the dance to get rid of Sitting Bull. They disagreed over the dance and finally, she decided she would leave the reservation. She had earlier traveled to the Parkin Ranch and left Christie there, returning to Sitting Bull's community to try to stop the Ghost Dance.[175]

On October 22, 1890, Sitting Bull hitched the gray horse Buffalo Bill had given him to his wagon and drove Mrs. Weldon to Fort Yates. He believed the army might seize him when he reached the fort, but the officers were friendly and shook his hand. As Sitting Bull and Weldon said good-bye, they shook hands. Her plans were to stay at the Parkin Ranch, maybe even through the winter. They both believed they would see each other again.[176]

Mrs. Weldon traveled from Fort Yates back to the Parkin Ranch where she remained for several weeks before deciding to head back East. While at the ranch, Christie had stepped on a rusty nail and developed tetanus. On the riverboat trip down the Missouri River, he died at Pierre, South Dakota, on November 19, 1890. Weldon later wrote to Sitting Bull of Christie's death and her sorrow.[177]

After parting with Catherine Weldon, Sitting Bull remained in the vicinity of Fort Yates until October 25, ration day. One Bull found him at the agency that day and gave him Agent McLaughlin's message to see him about the Ghost Dance. Thinking it might be a trap, Sitting Bull picked up his supplies and drove home without visiting McLaughlin.[178]

On October 29, Robert Belt, acting commissioner of Indian Affairs, responded to McLaughlin's letter of concern about the Ghost Dance and Sitting Bull's participation. Belt wrote McLaughlin that he was "to notify Sitting Bull and the other malcontents that the Secretary of the Interior was greatly displeased with their conduct," and Sitting Bull would be held accountable for the conduct of his followers.[179]

As the Oglalas at Pine Ridge held their Ghost Dances, they alarmed the whites in Nebraska, who believed there was going to be an uprising. On November 12, Daniel Royer, the Pine Ridge agent, panicked. He sent a telegram to the Indian Office in Washington, stating, "The police force are overpowered and disheartened," and, "We have no protection, [and] are at the mercy of these crazy dancers."[180]

The next day, November 13, Secretary of the Interior John Noble discussed the situation with President Benjamin Harrison, who told Secretary of War Redfield Proctor to "assume responsibility for any threatened outbreak." That same day, Agent McLaughlin sent a follow-up letter to the commissioner of Indian Affairs, stating that somehow his October letter to Belt outlining his Ghost Dance concerns and recommendation that Sitting Bull and others be locked up in prison had been leaked to the newspapers and printed, and had been read by Standing Rock Lakotas, who now knew of his concerns and recommended actions. It was "causing unnecessary alarm."[181]

On November 14, Acting Commissioner Belt sent Agent McLaughlin and the other Sioux agents a telegram, telling them, "The President has directed the Secretary of War to assume a military responsibility for the suppression of any threatened outbreak among the Sioux Indians."[182]

The next day, Pine Ridge agent Royer telegrammed another urgent appeal for help. That did it. Troops were ordered to Pine Ridge to restore order by none other than Major General Nelson A. Miles, who was now commander of the Department of Missouri, based out of Chicago.[183]

McLaughlin feared the army's involvement, believing "a military demonstration would precipitate a collision and bloodshed." McLaughlin and the commander of Fort Yates, Lieutenant Colonel William Drum, were on the same page, believing they needed to quietly remove Sitting Bull and his Ghost Dance leaders from the reservation.[184]

On November 17, McLaughlin learned a big Ghost Dance was being held at Sitting Bull's settlement. McLaughlin drove his wagon down to the Grand River, taking along his interpreter, Louis Primeau. When they arrived at Sitting Bull's settlement at 3:00 p.m., a dance was in progress with around two hundred onlookers.[185]

Sitting Bull sat inside a tepee erected near the dance area. A middle-aged female dancer swooned. Two men brought her to Sitting

Bull, and when she was revived, he asked her what she had experienced. The dance stopped so all could hear what she said.[186]

McLaughlin reasoned that it was not a good time to have a conversation with Sitting Bull. He and Primeau drove three miles upriver to Bull Head's house where they spent the night.[187]

The next morning at 6:00 a.m., they returned to Sitting Bull's settlement. Lieutenant Bull Head came with them. They met Sitting Bull as he came out of a sweat lodge wearing only a breechcloth and moccasins. They said "How" to each other and shook hands. Someone handed Sitting Bull a blanket, which he draped over his shoulders as they walked over to McLaughlin's wagon.[188]

"Look here, Sitting Bull," McLaughlin began, "I want to know what you mean by your present conduct and utter disregard for department orders. Your preaching and practicing of this absurd Messiah doctrine is causing a great deal of uneasiness among the Indians of the reservation, and you should stop it at once." McLaughlin launched into a lengthy recounting of all the good things he had done for Sitting Bull over the years. Sitting Bull quietly listened and thanked McLaughlin. A crowd had gathered around them. At one point, one of the onlookers raised his voice in protest, interrupting McLaughlin. Sitting Bull ordered the man to be silent.[189]

Sitting Bull then spoke of the new religion and how he believed it could bring good to his people. McLaughlin cut him off, saying it would only bring his people trouble, and he knew it was rubbish. McLaughlin thought Sitting Bull "grew a little defiant" as he said that McLaughlin knew nothing about it.[190]

"Father, I will make you a proposition which will settle this question," Sitting Bull said. "You go with me to the agencies to the West, and let me seek for the men who saw the Messiah; and when we find them, I will demand that they show him to us, and if they cannot do so I will return and tell my people it is a lie."[191]

McLaughlin thought this was a ridiculous idea and refused to go. He counteroffered, saying Sitting Bull should spend a night with him at the agency, where he would convince him the Ghost Dance was wrong. Sitting Bull said he thought that might be good; however, he could not leave without the consent of the people. He would talk it over in council that night, and if they thought it was the right thing to do, he would come to the agency that Saturday.[192]

By now the crowd around them had grown, and McLaughlin thought the people "threatening and sneering." They had spent an hour in discussion and McLaughlin believed he could get no further with Sitting Bull. As McLaughlin, Primeau, and Bull Head were leaving, Sitting Bull dropped the blanket and with upraised arms kept the crowd at bay until McLaughlin and his men had left.[193]

On November 19, McLaughlin reported to the department about his meeting with Sitting Bull. He recommended all Lakotas living along the Grand River who wished to receive their rations needed to renounce the Ghost Dance religion and report to the agency during the next few weeks to enroll. Anyone who did not come in would not receive their rations. The government never officially adopted McLaughlin's recommendation.[194]

McLaughlin held a meeting with the metal breasts and told them they might have to arrest Sitting Bull. It did not go well. The Indian police force rebelled. Captain Crazy Walking and many other officers resigned. Many believed there would be bloodshed, and they did not want to fight their own relatives. McLaughlin discharged One Bull, not trusting him because everyone knew he loved his uncle, Sitting Bull. All metal breasts from Sitting Bull's community resigned.[195]

Lieutenant Bull Head was now in charge of the police force, and McLaughlin let him select his own men. McLaughlin promised the new men pensions if they were killed or wounded in any fight with Sitting Bull's followers. One of the new men, Bob-Tail-Bull, was a friend of Sitting Bull, and his job was to keep an eye on the Ghost Dancers and report back. Bob-Tail-Bull later said, "I never saw him [Sitting Bull] dance. There were a lot of people dancing for a while . . . I know that Sitting Bull tried to stop the dance but they were too many and too firm believers. . . . Father Bernard [a Catholic priest at Standing Rock] had talked with him and assured him the dead would not come back, Sitting Bull publicly announced he did not believe in the Messiah. He told them to quit, but they had no ears."[196]

Reporters rushed to the agencies and filed reports of the latest war rumors. The newspapers continued to print wild stories of the

Sioux on the warpath and of massacres of whites, none of which were true. At least twenty-one reporters and the renowned Western artist Frederic Remington, sent by *Harper's Weekly*, were wandering around Pine Ridge looking for a story—any story.[197]

On November 20, troops suddenly converged on the Pine Ridge and Rosebud Agencies. They did not attack. It was a show of force. Many Ghost Dance followers from both agencies fled to the protection of South Dakota's Badlands where they encamped on a naturally fortified plateau called Cuny Table, which would become known as the Stronghold.[198]

That same day, Acting Commissioner Belt sent McLaughlin a telegram stating if any of the "leaders of excitement or fomenters of disturbance" needed to be arrested, to telegraph their names at once. McLaughlin wired back Sitting Bull's name along with other instigators. He added that he did not recommend making any arrests at that time, but again suggested the Grand River people be told to report to the agency. He believed if Sitting Bull came to the agency for his rations, he could easily be arrested. In the meantime, Lieutenant Bull Head, who lived three miles upriver from Sitting Bull, continued to keep him under surveillance.[199]

On November 21, McLaughlin sent a letter to Jack Carignan carried by Take the Hat. Carignan taught school along the Grand River about a mile from Sitting Bull's settlement. In the letter, McLaughlin wrote that there were rumors of fighting between US troops and Indians at the Rosebud Agency. McLaughlin wanted Carignan and other white people to come to Fort Yates.[200]

On Saturday, November 22, ration day, Sitting Bull sent word to McLaughlin that one of his children was ill and he couldn't come to the agency for their meeting. Twenty other heads of households did not show for their rations but sent their wives instead. McLaughlin refused to give the women their rations, telling them the men needed to come get the supplies themselves, or they could all go hungry.[201]

Schoolteacher Jack Carignan sent McLaughlin a letter on November 27, reporting on the status of the people living along the Grand River. Carignan was invited to a council held by the principal leaders of the Ghost Dance. Sitting Bull was not in attendance.

They were hearing reports that soldiers were coming to the Grand River to stop the dancing—that they "[were] badly frightened" and ready to run. Carignan tried to reassure them that no troops were heading their way and what they had heard were all lies. He further wrote, "I am positive that *no trouble need be apprehended from Sitting Bull and his followers, unless they are forced to defend themselves*, and I think it would be advisable to keep all strangers, other than employees who have business amongst the Indians, away from here, as Sitting Bull has lost all confidence in the whites since Mrs. Weldon has left him."[202]

Newspapers continued to print rumors and fan the flames of war. At least a few newspapers saw through it all, such as South Dakota's *Sturgis Weekly Record*. Its November 28, 1890, edition stated, "This ghost dance has been worked up into a very wonderful and exciting manner by pinhead 'war correspondents' and other irresponsible parties until they have succeeded in massing nearly half of the United States Army to be spectators to an Indian pow wow [*sic*]."[203]

Meanwhile, in Chicago, General Nelson Miles had reviewed McLaughlin's list of those who should be arrested, which included Sitting Bull. Miles believed if he sent troops to arrest Sitting Bull, it might spark a fight. He thought up an alternate plan. He was friends with Buffalo Bill Cody, and he knew Cody and Sitting Bull were friends. If Cody went to visit Sitting Bull, maybe he would peacefully surrender to Cody.[204]

Cody had just returned from his Wild West tour of Europe under a cloud. Several Indians had died while on tour. Acting Commissioner of Indian Affairs Robert V. Belt issued an order to all Indian agents that Indians were not allowed to join any wild west shows. If they did, it would be considered an act of defiance of the US government. Belt had just investigated Cody's Wild West, formally questioning Cody's seventy-nine Indian performers, who all said they were happy with the way Buffalo Bill had been treating, and paying, them. When Belt was done, Cody was exonerated of abusing the Indians.[205]

Miles met with Cody in Chicago, and he agreed to try and bring in Sitting Bull peacefully. Cody said he had to first visit his sisters at his ranch in Nebraska. On November 24, General Miles issued orders for Cody to "secure the person of Sitting Bull."[206]

Two days later, Cody stepped off the train in Bismarck, North Dakota. Accompanying him were two old sidekicks, "Pony" Bob Haslam and Dr. Frank "White Beaver" Powell. On November 28, Cody and his friends, who now also included Steve Burke and "Bully" White, arrived at McLaughlin's office at Standing Rock Agency and presented General Miles's orders.[207]

Concerned that Cody was wrecking his plans to arrest Sitting Bull, McLaughlin met with Colonel Drum, who was on board with McLaughlin's plan to use Indian police. McLaughlin would send a telegram to Belt to stop Cody, while Drum would distract Cody and slow him down.[208]

McLaughlin fired off a telegram to Belt stating that Cody was at the agency to arrest Sitting Bull, and he thought the action unwise, ending with: "I have matters well in hand, and when proper time arrives can arrest Sitting Bull by Indian Police without bloodshed. I ask attention to my letter of November 19. Request General Miles's order to Cody be rescinded and request immediate answer."[209]

In the meantime, Colonel Drum and his officers invited Cody and his friends to the Fort Yates officers' club where they proceeded to entertain him even as Cody entertained them. Cody's ability to hold his liquor was legendary, so the officers formed teams to keep him well liquored and try to drink him under the table.[210]

The next morning, Cody and his men were up and loading a wagon with presents for Sitting Bull and his family. The presents included a large amount of candy Sitting Bull was partial to. By 11:00 a.m., they were ready to go.[211]

In the meantime, Belt met with President Harrison and showed him McLaughlin's telegram. Harrison agreed to have Cody recalled from his mission.[212]

Armed with only presents and candy, Cody and his men along with an entourage of eight reporters were ten miles south of Standing Rock Agency when they were overtaken by a messenger with an order from President Harrison, canceling his mission. Although Cody was furious, there was nothing he could do but obey.[213]

Cody would say later that Sitting Bull would have come back with him, and in so doing the chain reaction of death and destruction leading to Wounded Knee could have been prevented. Cody claimed that when he later talked to President Harrison about the whole affair, Harrison said he regretted recalling Cody. McLaughlin, on the other hand, would later write, "My telegram saved to the world that day a royal good fellow and most excellent showman."[214]

Cody would have been in no danger from his friend Sitting Bull. The same day Cody had arrived at Standing Rock Agency, Sam Clover, a Chicago newspaperman, was with Jack Carignan at Sitting Bull's settlement and took a photograph of the Ghost Dance. No one bothered him.[215]

The third week of November, Agent McLaughlin had strongly suggested that white people on the Standing Rock Reservation come to Fort Yates in case of trouble. Mary Collins had been at the fort when McLaughlin's warning went out and she was detained there. When the Lakotas learned Collins was not leaving the fort, they were concerned there would be war. Collins wanted to return to her house and school, and finally convinced McLaughlin and the commander of Fort Yates, Lieutenant Colonel William Drum, that she would be safe. The Lakotas were delighted with her return.[216]

The Sunday following her return, Mary Collins along with her helper, a little old man with the last name of Grindstone, rode to Sitting Bull's settlement to see him. She said "thousands" of people were there. Collins and Grindstone along with their Congregationalist converts held a church service alongside the Ghost Dance. Each side competed with the other when singing. Afterwards, Collins would write, "I never hear 'Nearer My God to Thee' but I think of that dreadful time."[217]

Sitting Bull had a tepee set up near the dance area. After concluding the church service, Collins walked to his tepee, stood outside, and asked an attendant if she could talk to Sitting Bull. He sent out a message that he would not see her at this time. Undaunted, she sent back a message saying she earnestly needed to talk with him. After a long wait, he sent a message back inviting her inside.[218]

When she entered, Sitting Bull directed her to walk toward the left, indicating certain places not to step, then told her where to sit. He performed certain ceremonies and then it was time for her to talk.[219]

Collins began, "Sitting Bull, you know you do not believe these things." She said he knew Indians, buffalo, and other animals had not been raised from the dead. He needed to end the Ghost Dances, go to Fort Yates, and tell the authorities it was over. "Otherwise the soldiers will come and kill all your people." She concluded if that happened, he would be held responsible.[220]

Sitting Bull, always gracious and with his winning personality, tried to compromise with her. He was very thankful she was teaching the people. He said she needed to let the people know it was all right to dance the traditional Lakota dances, but she would not agree to that. She left his tent not having convinced him to end the dances.[221]

On December 1, Acting Secretary Belt sent McLaughlin a telegram confirming that if there was any outbreak, it was the army's job to suppress it by force. McLaughlin was to "cooperate and obey the orders of the military officers commanding on the reservation in your charge." McLaughlin believed he knew better than his superiors and the army. His Indian police could arrest Sitting Bull without bloodshed.[222]

McLaughlin would just not stop. On December 6 he sent Belt a telegram: "Am I authorized to arrest Sitting Bull and other fomenters of mischief when I think best?" Belt got right back to him: "Replying to your telegram of this date, Secretary directs that you make no arrests whatever, except under orders of the military, or upon an order from the Secretary of the Interior."[223]

One December evening, a man arrived with a message for Sitting Bull from Short Bull, one of the original Lakota delegates who had gone to see the Nevada Paiute, Wovoka. Short Bull had a revelation from Wakan Tanka that the Messiah was coming down from heaven to the dancers at the Stronghold in the Badlands. Short Bull was leading a large number of people to meet him, and he wanted to know if Sitting Bull wanted to be there.[224]

With the weather getting colder, fewer people were gathering to dance the Ghost Dance. Agent McLaughlin wanted Sitting Bull arrested no matter what, and came up with more reasons, which he expressed in the December 10, 1890, edition of Minnesota's *St. Paul Pioneer Press*: "There is no reason why Sitting Bull should not be arrested as soon as he comes within reach of the agency. He has broken his promise to send his children to school, and he did not come in last ration day as ordered. I expect him on Saturday, and we may get him before that time."[225]

It was December 11. Sitting Bull had been thinking about Short Bull's message for several days when the metal breast Running Hawk brought him a letter from Agent McLaughlin. Sitting Bull got his son-in-law, Andrew Fox, who had been educated at the Carlisle Indian School, to read the letter to him. The letter ordered the Ghost Dancers to go home to their farms. Running Hawk warned Sitting Bull that the authorities planned to take the Ghost Dancers' weapons and horses. Separately, Running Hawk told Andrew Fox that he better camp near the agency, because "a fire was to be started in Sitting Bull's camp."[226]

That night Sitting Bull held a council meeting in his house with the Silent Eaters to discuss what to do about McLaughlin's letter, what Running Hawk had said, and whether he should go to meet the Messiah at the Stronghold. They all agreed he should go. Sitting Bull had Andrew Fox write a letter to Agent McLaughlin requesting a pass to go to Pine Ridge. In the letter, Sitting Bull said God made both the whites and the Indians. God has helped the whites and now he was helping the Indians. The Indians were just trying to find the good road to follow. The Indians did not say anything bad about McLaughlin's religion, and he should not say anything bad about theirs. He said he knew McLaughlin thought he was a fool and didn't like him. McLaughlin thought the Indians who followed him were fools, and if he was gone, they would become civilized. Sitting Bull said he had seen it in all the newspapers, but he overlooked it. He said when McLaughlin was in his camp, he had good words about his prayers, but now McLaughlin was taking back those words. The letter concluded with, "Also I want to tell you something. I got to go to Pine Ridge Agency, and to know this pray. So I let you know that and the policeman told me that you [are] going to take all our ponies, guns too. So I want to let you know this. I want answer back soon."[227]

On Friday, December 12, 1880, Brigadier General Thomas Ruger, commander of the Department of Dakota, had a coded telegram sent from St. Paul, Minnesota, to the Fort Yates commander, Colonel William Drum. The telegram read, "The Division commander has directed that you make it your special duty to secure the person of Sitting Bull. Call on Indian agent to cooperate and render such assistance as will best promote the purpose in view. Acknowledge receipt and, if not perfectly clear, repeat back." Earlier, on December 10, General Miles had ordered Ruger to have Sitting Bull arrested.[228]

Miles and Ruger had no intention to pass the duty on to McLaughlin and his Indian police. It was to be strictly a military operation. McLaughlin was to "cooperate and render such assistance" to achieve the arrest. Drum showed the message to McLaughlin. McLaughlin believed the message gave him enough wiggle room to use his Indian police to make the arrest on behalf of the army. Drum agreed with his plan. McLaughlin was confident his Indian police could make the arrest. Without notifying Ruger or Miles, McLaughlin and Drum reversed their roles. They would arrest Sitting Bull on December 20, ration day. Sitting Bull would probably not come to the agency, but most of his people would. Then the Indian police could enter his settlement and arrest him. In the meantime, they would have Lieutenant Bull Head, who lived upriver from Sitting Bull, keep watch to make sure he didn't leave.[229]

At 6:00 p.m. on December 12, Bull Ghost, a Strong Heart and a Sitting Bull bodyguard, delivered Sitting Bull's message to Agent McLaughlin, requesting permission to travel to Pine Ridge Agency. McLaughlin now realized Sitting Bull might leave for Pine Ridge, and he did not want that to happen. He talked with Louis Primeau, who was now the acting police chief, and directed him to send a message to Lieutenant Bull Head.[230]

In the letter, Primeau told Bull Head that Sitting Bull might try to leave the reservation and he needed to watch him closely. Primeau said Bull Head was to gather his policemen together and if asked why, say they were getting ready to build a shelter on Oak Creek. Primeau wrote, "If he [Sitting Bull] should [try to leave] you must stop him, and if he does not listen to you, do as you see fit." Primeau gave the letter to a courier who set off for Bull Head's home on the Grand River.[231]

On Saturday, December 13, McLaughlin gave Bull Ghost a letter for Sitting Bull, which he delivered to him later that day. In the letter, McLaughlin said he was Sitting Bull's friend. He continued by saying Sitting Bull needed to send the Ghost Dancers home, and he was not approving Sitting Bull's request to travel to Pine Ridge, saying, "Therefore, my friend, listen to this advice—do not attempt to visit any other agency at present."[232]

That same day, Sitting Bull held another council in his house. Bull Head had two spies in Sitting Bull's settlement who reported to him they believed Sitting Bull and his party were going to leave for Pine Ridge on Monday, December 15. They said there was talk of shooting any Indian policemen who might try to interfere. Later, some of Sitting Bull's followers said this was not the case. Whatever the truth, Bull Head went to Jack Carignan's school. By this time, he had received Louis Primeau's letter.[233]

At 12:30 a.m. Carignan wrote Bull Head's message to McLaughlin that Sitting Bull planned to travel to Pine Ridge, and that "Bull Head would like to arrest him at once before he has the chance of giving them the slip, as he thinks that if he gets the start it will be impossible to catch him."[234]

On Sunday, December 14, at 4:00 p.m., Indian policeman Hawk Man delivered Bull Head's letter to Agent McLaughlin and Colonel Drum. With Sitting Bull making plans to leave for Pine Ridge, they could not wait to enact their original plan of arresting him on ration day, December 20. They had to act now.[235]

They would have the Indian police arrest Sitting Bull. Drum would position troops far enough south to lend support to the police if the need arose, but at the same time, stay far enough away from Sitting Bull's settlement so they would not alarm the people.[236]

McLaughlin sent a message to Lieutenant Bull Head and Sergeant Shave Head, reading, "I believe the time has arrived for the arrest of Sitting Bull and that it can be made by Indian Police without much risk. I therefore want you to make the arrest before daylight tomorrow morning. . . . The Cavalry will leave tonight and will reach the Sitting Bull crossing of Oak Creek before daylight tomorrow morning [Monday] . . . I have ordered the police at Oak Creek to proceed to Carignan's school to await your orders. This gives you a force of forty-two policemen for the arrest." McLaughlin added a postscript, "You must not let him escape under any circumstances."[237]

At 5:30 p.m., the Yanktonai policeman Red Tomahawk left the agency with the message, racing his horse toward Bull Head's place on the Grand River. He reached Bull Head's home at 10:00 p.m. Bull Head had gathered twenty-nine of his hand-selected policemen from among the Yanktonais, Blackfeet, and a few Hunkpapas.[238]

Meanwhile, Colonel Drum had ordered Captain E. G. Fechet to proceed to the Oak Creek Crossing with Troops F and G of the Eighth Cavalry, totaling 109 men, along with a Hotchkiss gun and a Gatling gun. They were to wait at the crossing unless they learned the police were fighting and needed assistance. At midnight, just before moving out, Drum said to Fechet, "Captain, after you leave here use your own discretion. You know the object of the movement. Do your best to make it a success."[239]

Fechet's column reached Oak Creek Crossing, twenty miles south of the agency, at 3:30 a.m. on December 15. McLaughlin had told him a courier from Bull Head would be waiting there. There was none. Using his own discretion, Fechet decided to press on toward Sitting Bull's settlement. At a fast trot, it would take them three hours to get there.[240]

At 4:00 a.m., Bull Head led his twenty-nine policemen downriver two miles to Sitting Bull's brother-in-law Gray Eagle's house, where they were joined by ten more police. A sad Gray Eagle believed Sitting Bull was on the wrong path and needed to be removed from the reservation for the good of the people. He and three other volunteers joined Bull Head's force. They mounted their horses and removed their hats, as Bull Head prayed to Jesus for help in accomplishing their mission without the shedding of blood.[241]

It was 4:30 a.m. when they rode downriver toward Sitting Bull's settlement. A coyote howled on a ridge. An owl hooted in the trees along the Grand River—not a good omen. Hooting owls warned of impending death.[242]

Rumors had reached Sitting Bull's settlement that the metal breasts planned to arrest him. Catch-the-Bear, leader of Sitting Bull's bodyguards and enemy of Bull Head, made sure his men were prepared and armed in case the metal breasts arrived.[243]

One morning earlier that autumn, Sitting Bull had been walking in the Grand River breaks to retrieve the horse Buffalo Bill had given him. As he climbed through the hills, he heard a meadowlark singing. Its song—"The Lakota will kill you."[244]

The Ghost Dance

In the 1880s, Wovoka, a Paiute also known as Jack Wilson, who lived in Mason Valley, Nevada, not far from Lake Tahoe, had a vision in which God showed him heaven and said if people were good, they would go there. Wovoka preached this message and performed what many Paiutes believed were several weather-related miracles.[245]

Earlier, Wovoka's father Tavibo had also had visions from God about heaven and a new world coming. He taught the Paiute people a sacred dance called the Dance of the Departed Souls, or Ghost Dance, which needed to be performed if the new world was to come.[246]

On New Year's Day 1889, there was an eclipse of the sun. The Paiutes called it "the Day the Sun died." At the time, Wovoka was in bed with a high fever. When the Sun died, Wovoka "died" and went to heaven. God told him the world would be destroyed and replaced with a new fresh world and all the vanished wildlife would return. The whites would disappear and the Indian dead would live again forever, the old ways would return, and everyone would be happy. In order for this to happen, the Indians needed to dance the Ghost Dance.[247]

God gave Wovoka the power to destroy the old Earth and create the new Earth, as well as the power to decide when to do it. However, God also told him to first summon all the tribes and give them the message. He was to instruct them how to perform the Ghost Dance. Every three months they were to purify themselves and then dance the Ghost Dance for five days. They were to continue to work, and they were not to fight among themselves or with the whites. To prove what Wovoka said was true, God gave him the power over rain and snow.[248]

There was a drought in the Paiute country and people approached Wovoka and asked him to make it rain. He said it would rain on a particular day and a downpour did happen on the day he predicted. While the Paiutes believed in him, the whites said it was merely a lucky call.[249]

Wovoka was now considered a prophet and called the Messiah. His fame and message spread rapidly through the tribes to the Bannocks, Shoshones, Crows, Arapahos, Cheyennes, and finally, the Lakotas. Several Lakota tribes appointed a delegation to go to Nevada and see this Messiah for themselves and report back their findings. Included in the delegation were the Oglalas Broken Arm, Flat Iron, Good Thunder, and Yellow Breast; the Miniconjou Kicking Bear; the Brulé Short Bull; and another unidentified man.[250]

They met the Messiah and experienced visions of the new land to come. Wovoka taught them the Ghost Dance and gave them sacred paint. They returned to their tribes as believers. However, they interpreted Wovoka's message in a slightly different way: They did not teach to continue to work for the whites.

On his way home from seeing the Messiah, Kicking Bear visited the Arapahos and saw their Ghost Dance. Dancers fell to the ground as if dead and later said they visited heaven where they were given "water, fire, and wind with which to kill all the whites." He said they made holy shirts and dresses out of white muslin. On the back of each garment was painted an eagle along with blue and yellow stripes. Eagle feathers were tied to each shoulder and sleeve. "They said bullets will not go through these shirts and dresses." Kicking Bear introduced these Ghost Shirts to the Lakotas along with the new religion.[251]

The Ghost Dance spread rapidly through the Lakota tribes. Many who fainted during the dance said they visited heaven and met their departed relatives and friends. The Ghost Dance renewed hope in the Lakota people. One of the many songs performed during these dances spoke of their hope:

The father says so, the father says so.
Over the whole Earth they are coming.
The buffalo are coming, the buffalo are coming.
The father says so, the father says so.[252]

CHAPTER 13

The Killing of Sitting Bull, December 1890

IT WAS AROUND 5:00 A.M. ON MONDAY, DECEMBER 15, 1890. Dogs barked as hoofbeats hammered the earth and came to a stop in Sitting Bull's settlement. No one stirred. There had been a big Ghost Dance the day before. Sitting Bull had not participated but remained quietly at home.[1]

Pounding on their cabin door awoke Sitting Bull and his family. He called out, "Yes, come in the house!"[2]

Lieutenant Bull Head and several Indian police entered. Sitting Bull, who always slept naked, was in bed with his wife Seen-by-her-Nation along with one of their small children. As he sat up, the police grabbed him. Someone lit a lamp as the police found his carbine and knife.[3]

Also in the cabin were his fourteen-year-old son Crow Foot, One Bull's wife Red Whirlwind, and two elderly men who were guests for the night. The rest of the family was sleeping in the smaller cabin to the north.[4]

Two policemen pulled Sitting Bull out of bed and held him by the arms while Lieutenant Bull Head put his hand on Sitting Bull's shoulder and said, "I am holding you."

"Brother," Sergeant Shave Head said, "we have come for you."

"If you fight," Red Tomahawk said, throwing his arms around Sitting Bull from behind, "you will be killed here."

"Yes," Sitting Bull responded.

"What are you jealous people doing here?" Seen-by-her-Nation asked the police. She left to get Sitting Bull's good clothes from the other cabin and called for someone to saddle Buffalo Bill's gift horse for him to ride.[5]

Unnoticed, the two guests and Red Whirlwind slipped out of the cabin. When Seen-by-her-Nation returned with Sitting Bull's good clothes, the police rushed him to get dressed. They tried pushing him through the door, but he braced himself in the doorframe, saying, "Let me go—I'll go without assistance." Sitting Bull was indignant over this treatment, but he was not afraid.[6]

Bull Head held Sitting Bull's right arm, Shave Head held his left arm, and, pointing a revolver at him with one hand and encircling his waist with his other arm, Red Tomahawk stood behind him. Sitting Bull's horse had not arrived. Men were at the corral in the process of catching his horse to saddle it.[7]

While the police waited, an angry crowd grew around Sitting Bull's cabin. The policemen encircled Sitting Bull. It was still dark, but the Indian police could be identified by the white mufflers they wore. One policeman continued to prod Sitting Bull from behind with his revolver. Sitting Bull said to the man, "Yes, yes, you have come for me. I have to go—I am going." But the police shouted back, "Shut up! Be quiet! Do just as we say!" Sitting Bull's supporters were shouting as one of Sitting Bull's wives shrieked and other women began to cry. Children wailed. Dogs barked.[8]

One of Sitting Bull's wives began to chant, "Sitting Bull, you have always been a brave man. What is going to happen now?"[9]

White Bird brought up Sitting Bull's saddled horse. The police began to make their way through the crowd, escorting Sitting Bull to his horse. The crowd continued to grow in size and anger. The police attempted to calm things down but failed.[10]

Gray Eagle pushed his way through the crowd to Sitting Bull and said, "Brother-in-law, do as the agent says. Go with the police."

"No!" Sitting Bull said to him. "I'm not going! Get away! Get away!" Sitting Bull had changed his mind. He would not go with the police.

"All right," Gray Eagle said. "I'm through. I have tried to save you." And with that, he pushed his way out of the crowd.[11]

All the while Lieutenant Bull Head stood close to Sitting Bull, facing him and covering him with his gun. Now Bull Head shouted to the crowd, "Nobody will be killed. We came after Sitting Bull. White Hair [the Lakotas' name for McLaughlin], the agent, wants him. White Hair is going to build the chief a house near the agency, so that whenever any of his people need anything, the Chief can get it for them right away."[12]

Then it was quiet, and no one moved as Catch-the-Bear holding his Winchester pushed his way through the crowd, looking into the face of each policeman as he said, "Where is Bull Head? Bull Head, come here!"

"Here I am!" Bull Head answered.[13]

"I am not going!" Sitting Bull shouted. "Do with me as you like. I am not going. Come on! Come on! Take action! Let's go!"

Catch-the-Bear brought up his rifle and fired a shot at Bull Head, the bullet slamming into his right side. As Bull Head fell, he twisted toward Sitting Bull and shot his gun upwards. The bullet struck Sitting Bull in the chest. Red Tomahawk fired his revolver into the back of Sitting Bull's head. Sitting Bull was dead.[14]

Strikes-the-Kettle shot Shave Head in the stomach as Lone Man charged Catch-the-Bear, who shot at him. It was a misfire. Lone Man grabbed the Winchester from Catch-the-Bear and shot, killing him with his own weapon. The fighting was fierce. Five more of Sitting Bull's followers died, including his adopted brother Jumping Bull.[15]

Three more bullets hit Bull Head, but he still lived. Four Indian police were dead. Red Tomahawk was now in command.[16]

The story is told that as the fighting raged, Sitting Bull's gray horse, the one Buffalo Bill had given him, began to perform as it had when it was in the show, sitting back on its haunches and raising a front leg and hoof. No bullets hit the horse.[17]

The fighting was intense but lasted only a few minutes. Sitting Bull's followers retreated into the trees along the river.[18]

Red Tomahawk had police officers drag the wounded Bull Head, Shave Head, and Middle into Sitting Bull's cabin. Both Bull Head

The death of Sitting Bull.

and Shave Head were mortally wounded. The rest of the Indian police took defensive positions around Sitting Bull's cabins and farm buildings.[19]

The police realized Crow Foot was there, inside Sitting Bull's cabin. They asked Bull Head what they should do with him. Bull Head, with four bullets in him, said, "Do what you like with him. He is one of them that has caused this trouble."

Lone Man struck Crow Foot on the forehead with his rifle butt, sending him out the door where other police shot and killed him.[20]

At 7:30 a.m., Captain Fechet's cavalry arrived on a ridge overlooking Sitting Bull's settlement. They unlimbered the Hotchkiss gun and shot at Sitting Bull's followers in the trees along the river and on a hilltop, driving them away. The cavalry then descended to the settlement and assisted the Indian police. None of Sitting Bull's followers had any desire to fight the army; their fight was with the Indian police. One lone warrior wearing a Ghost Shirt did ride within rifle range and he was shot at but not hit. He was probably testing to see if his shirt's protection worked.[21]

Captain Fechet rode up to Sitting Bull's house and counted eight dead bodies and another four dead bodies inside, with three wounded men—two mortally. Sitting Bull's wives were in the smaller cabin, wailing for their dead husband.[22]

Relatives of one of the dead policemen, Strong Arm, lived close by and arrived on the scene. In his grief and anger, Strong Arm's brother, Holy Medicine, picked up a neck yoke and smashed it down on Sitting Bull's face. First Sergeant James Hanaghan quickly placed a guard over Sitting Bull's body so there would be no further mutilation.[23]

Fechet had issued orders there was to be no ransacking or destruction of Sitting Bull's property, but that didn't stop the soldiers and Indian police. One policeman entered Sitting Bull's smaller cabin where one of Catherine Weldon's portraits of Sitting Bull hung. The man smashed the gilt frame and slashed the canvas before he could be stopped.[24]

The mission had been only to bring Sitting Bull back to the agency. Fechet sent Lakota women out to Sitting Bull's people to let them know the cavalry was not coming after them and was returning to the fort.[25]

Sitting Bull's seven dead followers were left in a cabin. The wounded Indian police were placed in Fechet's ambulance. Red Tomahawk followed through with the original mission, which was to bring back Sitting Bull. The Indian police threw his body into the back of a wagon and then laid their four dead on top of him and drove the wagon to the Standing Rock Agency.[26]

James McLaughlin should never have sent the Indian police to arrest Sitting Bull. Sitting Bull had done no harm. All he wanted to do was travel to Pine Ridge to investigate the Ghost Dance— to "know this pray." If James McLaughlin and other white leaders would have let Sitting Bull go investigate, much death and misery could have been avoided.

Sitting Bull's Graves

After Sitting Bull was killed at his cabin on the Grand River, the morning of December 15, 1890, his sixteen-year-old nephew Clarence Gray Eagle watched as the metal breasts threw Sitting Bull's body into a wagon and laid their own four dead on top of him. The metal breasts and cavalry escorted the bodies north across the new border dividing the states of South Dakota and North Dakota to Fort Yates.[27]

Soldiers wrapped Sitting Bull's body in canvas and then placed it in a wooden coffin. Four military prisoners dug a grave in the fort's cemetery, lowered Sitting Bull's coffin into the hole, and covered it over as Agent James McLaughlin and three army officers watched. There was no memorial service. Gray Eagle said one of Sitting Bull's wives came and sat at his grave, attempting to mourn. "But she was chased away because her mourning was too noisy."[28]

Private J. F. Waggoner, who was detailed to work in the Fort Yates carpenter shop, said he built Sitting Bull's coffin. Waggoner claimed he and another soldier were told to pour quicklime and muriatic acid over Sitting Bull's body. One rumor alleged his body was not buried but had been dissected. Still another story maintained Sitting Bull's body was disinterred and reburied at a secret location. Two youths claimed they dug into the grave, removing two bones. A few years later, Sitting Bull's remains were disinterred, placed in a new wooden box, and reburied in the same spot with a thin slab of concrete poured over the top.[29]

In 1903, the federal government closed Fort Yates, removing all the military graves, leaving Sitting Bull's remains behind. No headstone was placed at the grave. No one tended it. Over the years, Clarence Gray Eagle brooded over the disrespect shown his uncle, Sitting Bull. He had petitioned North Dakota officials to do something about the poor condition of the grave. They promised to do something, but nothing was done.[30]

Gray Eagle worked with a few white men from Mobridge, South Dakota, on the east bank of the Missouri River, across from the Standing Rock Sioux Tribe Reservation. They planned to provide a new resting place for Sitting Bull's remains on the west bank, where he could properly be honored. Mobridge businessmen also saw it as an opportunity to lure visitors to the Mobridge area. Three of Sitting Bull's granddaughters gave Gray Eagle the power of attorney to disinter Sitting Bull's remains and move them to the new location. Walter Tuntland, president of the Mobridge Chamber of Commerce, visited Korczak Ziolkowski, who was carving a mountain monument to Crazy Horse in the Black Hills. Tuntland asked him to carve a bust of Sitting Bull to be placed over the new gravesite, and Ziolkowski agreed, selecting a piece of granite from the Crazy Horse monument to carve the bust.[31]

In 1953, Gray Eagle met with North Dakota state officials who told him he could not disinter Sitting Bull from North Dakota and move him to South Dakota. News of North Dakota's refusal sparked a newspaper war between the two states. Even Montana newspapers jumped into the fray, stating that Sitting Bull should be buried at the Little Big Horn Battlefield on the Crow Reservation.[32]

The Standing Rock Tribal Council passed two resolutions stating Sitting Bull's next of kin had the right to rebury Sitting Bull's remains wherever they wanted as long as it was on the reservation. Standing Rock tribal chairman David Blackhoop stated, "North Dakota officials had no right to thwart the wishes of Sitting Bull's next of kin in this matter. The council demands that Indian rights be recognized, and it vigorously protests the arbitrary action of the North Dakota authorities."[33]

Gray Eagle and his team were undaunted. Realizing North Dakota had no authority over Standing Rock Reservation lands, they contacted the US Interior Department, which responded that it did not care if they disinterred Sitting Bull's body as long as the next of kin approved.[34]

On the night of April 8, 1953, Gray Eagle and Mobridge citizens including Al Miles, a mortician registered in both South Dakota and North Dakota, drove through a snowstorm to Fort Yates. There they met Standing Rock superintendent Charles Spencer, and with his help, they removed the concrete slab and dug through the soil until they reached the bones. They carefully removed large bones, sifted the soil to recover smaller bones, and then refilled the hole. Placing the remains in a bone box, they returned to South Dakota, making sure they traveled on reservation land.[35]

They had a grave waiting for Sitting Bull's remains on a western bluff overlooking the Missouri River. Placing the bone box inside a steel vault, they lowered it into the grave and poured twenty tons of concrete overtop it.[36]

North Dakotans were outraged. "South Dakota Ghouls Steal Sitting Bull's Bones" headlined the *Bismarck Tribune*. "North Dakota had done nothing to honor our great leader," Gray Eagle responded in South Dakota's *Rapid City Journal*. "So we went and got him."[37]

On April 11, 1953, after more than sixty-two years, a memorial service was held for Sitting Bull attended by Gray Eagle, Sitting Bull's three granddaughters, and a crowd of several hundred Lakotas and whites. On September 2 of that year, Ziolkowski's bust of Sitting Bull was dedicated at the site, with Sitting Bull's relatives and an estimated crowd of five thousand Indians and whites in attendance.[38]

North Dakotans wanted Sitting Bull's remains returned. Some said the South Dakota raiders had stolen the wrong bones. Sitting Bull's North Dakota gravesite was restored, and a beautiful headstone erected.[39]

In the late 1950s the US Army Corps of Engineers built the Oahe Reservoir, damming up the Missouri River. The bridge from Mobridge across the Missouri became unstable and had to be abandoned and rerouted upriver, along with the road that ran past Sitting Bull's burial site, so today, Sitting Bull's second grave is located at a remote site.[40]

CHAPTER 14

The Life and Death of Geronimo, 1890–February 17, 1909

SINCE MAY 1888, GERONIMO AND THE ENTIRE CAPTIVE CHIRICAHUA tribe had been living at the Mount Vernon Barracks in Alabama. They were peaceful and industrious, trying to behave the way the federal government wanted them to behave.

In March 1891, President Benjamin Harrison approved the enlistment of Indians in the army. Each regiment stationed in the West was increased by one company composed of Indians, including the Twelfth Infantry stationed at Mount Vernon. In late spring, First Lieutenant William Wotherspoon, in charge of the Chiricahua prisoners, recruited them for Company I. Geronimo wanted to enlist, but Wotherspoon believed he was too old and rejected him. This offended Geronimo.[1]

Lieutenant Wotherspoon placated Geronimo by appointing him justice of the peace for the Chiricahuas, judging misdemeanor cases. After learning his responsibilities, Geronimo did a good job. Wotherspoon believed Geronimo's decisions were wise and he had an excellent influence over the Chiricahuas. He wore a military uniform and received a salary of $10.50 per month. The Chiricahuas considered Geronimo a leader, and white people saw him as friendly and civilized.[2]

In February 1894, Wotherspoon, promoted to captain, left Mount Vernon Barracks to act as aide-de-camp to General O. O.

Howard, and Lieutenant Charles Ballou was now in charge of the Chiricahua prisoners of war. Geronimo had become dissatisfied with George Wratten and wanted him dismissed from his duties as interpreter and superintendent of the Chiricahuas. This most likely came from an earlier event where Geronimo had become drunk and Wotherspoon had Wratten arrest him, making him serve five days at hard labor.[3]

Major George Russell, commander at Mount Vernon Barracks, investigated Geronimo's complaint that Wratten had refused to listen to him when he told him some of the Indian soldiers were misbehaving. In addition, Geronimo complained Wratten was rude and brutal to Chiricahua men and women, telling them to shut up when they were talking. Wratten rebutted Geronimo's accusations in writing. Russell interviewed Geronimo's witnesses using a young interpreter of Geronimo's choosing. Russell reported no one supported Geronimo's accusations. One of them did say they saw Wratten kick a drunken woman, but Wratten said he did not. Russell submitted his findings to Secretary of War Daniel Lamont, who, on May 14, 1894, determined Geronimo's complaints were frivolous and that Wratten would continue to serve the Chiricahuas and the federal government, including his role as interpreter for Geronimo and the Chiricahuas.[4]

Geronimo's son Chappo had been sent to the Carlisle Indian School. He was now thirty years old and had developed tuberculosis. On August 7, 1894, the school superintendent, Captain Richard Pratt, sent him back to Mount Vernon Barracks to die. On September 9, Chappo breathed his last; his wife and their child also died at that time.[5]

"We are vanishing from the earth," Geronimo said. "Yet I cannot think we are useless or Ussen would not have created us."[6]

The issue of moving the Chiricahuas from Mount Vernon Barracks emerged again in 1894. Army officers including Generals Howard and Miles supported relocating the Chiricahuas to Fort Sill, Oklahoma Territory. Arizona and Oklahoma officials fought that proposal, but on August 6, 1894, Congress enacted legislation allowing the Chiricahuas to move to Fort Sill, and President Grover Cleveland, now in his second term, signed it into law.[7]

Fort Sill's commander was angry the Chiricahuas were to be sent to his fort and planned to build a palisade to imprison them. Lieutenant Hugh Scott learned of the commander's plans. Scott believed if the Chiricahuas knew they were to be imprisoned, they would make a run for it and new fighting would break out. Scott went over his commander's head and informed General Nelson Miles. Fort Sill was under Miles's jurisdiction and he agreed with Scott, removing the commander from Fort Sill and placing Scott in charge of the Chiricahuas.[8]

The Chiricahuas, numbering 296 men, women, and children, boarded a special train that took them through New Orleans and Fort Worth to their final destination of Rush Springs, Oklahoma.[9] Along the way, newspapers wrote about them, crowds gathered at their stops to cheer them, and orators gave ovations. Still, there were some who did not feel positive about the move, and believed Geronimo in particular should have been hanged years ago.[10]

When the Chiricahuas detrained at Rush Springs on October 4, 1894, teams of horses and wagons were stationed to take them the last thirty miles west to Fort Sill. Waiting at the fort was a crowd of Comanches and Kiowas wishing to welcome the Chiricahuas. They used plains sign language, but the Chiricahuas had no understanding of it. Finally, they found English-speaking boys in both groups and the welcome proceeded.[11]

The Chiricahuas had few belongings with them. Most of their possessions were on a separate freight train that was destroyed in a New Orleans train shed fire. It was too late in the season to build houses, so they erected wickiups covered with canvas provided by the army and worked to cut timber to be later used for homes and fences.[12]

Lieutenant Scott was sympathetic to the Chiricahuas. He had a reputation for being fair to the Comanches and Kiowas and learned their ways, including sign language. Scott respected the Chiricahuas and worked with them to learn farming and ranching techniques, while allowing them to continue their traditions and celebrations.[13]

Many in the general public were concerned the Chiricahuas might break out and head to Arizona or Mexico. Scott worked with a Mescalero Apache living with the Comanches who marked on a map all the trails and watering holes between Fort Sill and the Mescalero Agency. Scott sent a copy of the map to General Miles and maintained a twenty-day supply of rations and pack mules, ready for the chase. He warned the Chiricahua prisoners of war that the Comanches were his friends and were expert trackers who would help him hunt them down.[14]

Congress appropriated funds to buy Texas cattle to start up a herd for the Chiricahuas. When the cattle arrived at Fort Sill, there were no fenced pastures to hold them, so Scott found soldiers who had worked as cowboys to teach the Chiricahuas how to herd and care for the cattle. Later in 1895, Asa Daklugie arrived from Carlisle Indian School where he had learned animal husbandry. Scott put Daklugie in charge of the herd, and under his management, the herd grew and improved. Geronimo was most likely shown how to herd cattle, as Scott had photographs of him on horseback dressed as a cowboy with his horse and saddle rigged for working cattle.[15]

In the spring of 1895, the Chiricahuas organized themselves into twelve small villages along Cache Creek and Medicine Bluff Creek, west of the fort. Each village was within easy walking distance of the other villages. Lieutenant Scott appointed Chiricahua leaders including Geronimo to the positions of headmen for each of the new villages. Each headman was enlisted in the army, issued a uniform, and paid as a scout. Geronimo was proud of his uniform and loved to wear it.[16]

Men who had learned carpentry at Mount Vernon Barracks built houses for the people, consisting of two rooms separated by a breezeway with a common roof. The Chiricahuas were given land for communal farming and each family was allotted a ten-acre plot for their own garden. Scott found mules for them to plow the land and plant crops. The first year they harvested 250,000 melons and cantaloupes. What they could not eat, they sold.[17]

Geronimo enjoyed raising melons, corn, sweet potatoes, and other vegetables. What his family did not use, he sold to the army. He enjoyed eating watermelons. Every once in a while, he would sit under his arbor, slice pieces from a watermelon, and call to the boys to share it with them.[18]

The Chiricahuas continued to be concerned about their captive family members in Mexico. Wratten wrote a letter to the federal government for them, listing forty-two relatives they believed were being held captive in Chihuahua City. The list included family members of Geronimo, Chatto, Mangas, and Kaytennae. The State Department sent the information to the Mexican government, which replied that the state of Chihuahua had no Chiricahua prisoners.[19]

In 1897, Chicago artist Eldridge Burbank received permission from Lieutenant Scott and Geronimo to paint Geronimo's portrait. Burbank soon realized Geronimo was not a bloodthirsty savage, and Geronimo learned Burbank was not out to take advantage of him, so they became friendly during Burbank's painting sessions. Burbank saw a side of Geronimo that few outside the Chiricahuas saw. "As we worked day after day," Burbank said, "my idea of Geronimo, the Apache, changed. I became so attracted to the old Indian that eventually I painted seven portraits of him."[20]

Geronimo composed songs and sang in a rich, deep voice. He was always ready to lend money to those in need. He had trained his horses to come to him when he whistled. He always put a saucer of milk on the floor for his cat when he left his house. For some reason, he kept the cat's whiskers trimmed.[21]

A magazine editor asked Burbank to have Geronimo tell him his life story. Geronimo agreed to do so, using a boy who understood English to translate. Geronimo lay on his bed as he began his story. When he reached the part where the Mexicans massacred his family, he became agitated, jumped to his feet, and was in such a fury, he could not continue. The boy said to Burbank, "He's telling you the truth. My father tells me the same story." Burbank never finished Geronimo's life story.[22]

Burbank accompanied Geronimo to a large celebration at Fort Sill. Geronimo displayed his gambling ability, dealing at the game of monte and whooping every time he won. Geronimo was also involved in racing his horses. A cowboy offered him a $10 bet to race his horse against the cowboy's. Geronimo searched the fairgrounds for the boy he wanted to be the jockey for his horse. Geronimo found the boy in a baseball game. As Geronimo approached, the boy hit a home run, and as he ran the bases, Geronimo chased after the boy, thinking he was trying to run away from him. The boy jockeyed for Geronimo and narrowly won the race. Geronimo was ecstatic.[23]

That same year, Indian Rights officer Francis Leupp had been in Arizona where people labeled Geronimo an "Apache arch-fiend," proclaiming that if he ever returned to Arizona he would be hanged without benefit of a trial. Leupp then visited the Chiricahua villages where he was impressed to find Geronimo "putting in his honest eight hours of work daily as a farmer in the fields, and at intervals donning his uniform as a United States scout and presenting himself with the other scouts for inspection."[24]

After a mysterious explosion sank the USS *Maine* in the harbor of Havana, Cuba, the United States and Spain declared war on each other in April 1898. The Chiricahuas volunteered to go fight the Spanish, but the army turned them down.[25]

The Chiricahuas and other tribes were peaceful, and all but twenty soldiers had left Fort Sill for the war. The Chiricahua leaders held a council and decided to hold a dance with Mountain Spirit dancers and clowns to request Ussen's protection while the soldiers were gone. Some of the younger people who had returned from Carlisle Indian School misinterpreted the dances, believing they were war dances. George Wratten investigated and reported to the military that he thought there might be an "attempt to escape to Arizona." The army became concerned to the point that all the women and children at Fort Sill were sent to the guardhouse for protection. Soldiers raced back to the fort to confront the impending attack. There was no attack. There was no breakout. All was peaceful in the Chiricahua villages.[26]

When a cavalry captain questioned Geronimo and the other Chiricahua leaders about a possible attack and breakout, they were sad at being mistrusted and said they were innocent. "I am a US soldier," Geronimo said. "I wear the uniform, and it makes my heart sore to be thus suspected."[27]

The 1898 Trans-Mississippi and International Exposition opened in Omaha, Nebraska. Promoters invited representatives from various Indian tribes to attend the exposition's Indian Congress. Over five hundred Indians from thirty-five tribes arrived. Geronimo and Naiche headed a twenty-two-member Chiricahua delegation over the objections of Lieutenant Francis Beach, who was now in charge of them. The Chiricahuas attended from September 9 through October 30.[28]

At every train stop along the way to Omaha, crowds gathered to see Geronimo. He sold buttons from his coat for twenty-five cents and his hat for five dollars. As the train pulled out of each station, Geronimo sewed new buttons on his coat and pulled another hat out of a box to sell at the next station.[29]

People wanted to see Indians dressed in their traditional attire and camping in tents, which they did. Since the Chiricahuas were prisoners of war, soldiers constantly guarded them. They performed traditional dances and sold their handicrafts. Geronimo was the star attraction. One reporter wrote, "Whenever he appears in the procession, the beholders cheer him wildly."[30]

The interpreter for the San Carlos Apaches at the exposition was Jimmie Stevens, who also acted as interpreter for the Chiricahua prisoners of war. Stevens's father George owned the sheep ranch at Ash Flats where in 1882, Geronimo and his men had massacred the Mexican workers and Geronimo had eaten Jimmie's pet pony. Stevens wanted Geronimo to pay him fifty dollars for the loss of his pony, which he did not receive.[31]

On October 12, 1898, President William McKinley and other government officials including General Nelson Miles arrived at the exposition for President's Day. McKinley and other dignitaries gave speeches and toured various exhibits. They were taken to the "Indian colony" where they viewed a sham battle between the Indians. Newspapers reported, "General Miles from the reviewing stand saw face to face his old New Mexican enemy Geronimo."[32]

The *Omaha Evening Bee* reported, "Geronimo looked up into the thousands of faces, apparently trying to locate a familiar one. . . . Suddenly he turned his eyes toward the place where General Miles was sitting. . . . He brushed aside the crowd with his hands and was soon at the side of General Miles. Mustering the best English at his command, he extended his hand and exclaimed: 'Now general, I am glad to see you.' The general reached for the extended hand, but suddenly it was withdrawn and instantly Geronimo clasped the white warrior in his embrace and hugged him as affectionately as would a father who had not seen his son for years."[33]

Exposition promotors arranged for Miles to meet with Geronimo. Miles learned of Jimmie Stevens and had him act as interpreter. Geronimo asked Miles why he had lied to him. Miles smiled and said, "Yes, I lied to you Geronimo. But I learned to lie from the great nantan [chief] of all liars—from you, Geronimo. You lied to Mexicans, Americans, and to your own Apaches for thirty years. White men only lied to you once, and I did it." Geronimo gave a lengthy speech asking that he and the Chiricahuas be allowed to return to Arizona. Mocking his request, Miles said no, and Geronimo walked away, ending the meeting.[34]

Promoters saw the large crowds Geronimo drew and wanted him to participate in their own events. Since he was a prisoner of war, he needed the army's permission to participate, and he was constantly under guard when on the road. He participated in the Pan-American Exposition in Buffalo, New York, from May to October 1901. The promoters paid him $45 a month. He supplemented his income by selling souvenirs and allowing himself to be photographed for a price. President William McKinley attended the exposition. While visiting the Temple of Music on September 6, an assassin shot him twice in the stomach. McKinley died on September 14, and Vice President Theodore Roosevelt became president.[35]

Offers continued to pour in for Geronimo to participate in shows and events. Gordon Lillie invited Geronimo to tour with his Pawnee Bill's Wild West Show for seven months. Geronimo agreed, but the army refused to allow him to participate.[36]

Geronimo participated in events throughout Oklahoma Territory, riding in Lawton's 1902 Fourth of July parade, a parade later that year in Oklahoma City, and Anadarko's 1903 Fourth of July parade.[37]

Christian missionaries had been working with the Chiricahuas, and by 1903, many had become Christians. Noche, Chatto, Chihuahua, and Naiche had joined the Dutch Reformed Church. In 1890,

Geronimo's wife Zi-yeh and their daughter Eva had been baptized into the Catholic Church at Mount Vernon. Geronimo at first worked against Christianity, but by the summer of 1902, he had softened, publicly saying at a camp meeting that his wife supported, the Jesus road was best, adding, "Now we begin to think the Christian white people love us."[38]

A year later, in July 1903, the missionaries held their camp meeting in an oak grove at Medicine Bluff Creek. While riding Zi-yeh's pony, it threw Geronimo, severely injuring him. He slowly rode up to the meeting and entered the tent. Naiche sat down beside him. Geronimo spoke and Benedict Jozhe interpreted for the missionaries: "He [Geronimo] says that he is in the dark. He knows he is not on the right road and he wants to find Jesus." Naiche's face lit up with joy. At the end of the camp meeting, Geronimo said, "I am full of sins, and I walk alone in the dark. I see that you missionaries have got a way to get sin out of the heart, and I want to take that better road and hold it till I die."[39]

Geronimo was baptized the following week. Naiche and others were overjoyed that he was now a Christian. Geronimo had always been religious and viewed Christianity as a supplement to his established beliefs, which he continued to practice. He later said, "I have always prayed, and I believe that the Almighty has always protected me." He said it was good to associate with Christians to improve character and recommended all Chiricahuas become Christians because it would help them live the right way. Geronimo said, "I am not ashamed to be a Christian." He was later expelled from the church for his love of gambling. He continued to practice the Apache religion along with accepting the Christian religion.[40]

In 1904, the army allowed Geronimo to attend the Louisiana Purchase Exposition in St. Louis, Missouri. He was still constantly guarded. People invited him to their homes, but the guards refused to let him go. Geronimo and 150 other Indians were invited to a theater where they watched a motion picture. He enjoyed the experience and liked the scenes of cattle and wildlife the best.[41]

For Geronimo, the most important part of attending this exposition was the opportunity to reunite with his daughter Lenna. He had not seen her since he had sent her mother Ih-tedda back to the Mescalero Reservation. Lenna was now seventeen years old. She told Geronimo about his son, her younger brother Robert. Ih-tedda had been pregnant with Robert when she had left Geronimo. Both Geronimo and Lenna were delighted with their reunion.[42]

Geronimo made lots of money at the exposition. According to S. M. McCowan, who was in charge of the exposition's Indian exhibit, "He [Geronimo] really has endeared himself to whites and Indians alike. . . . He was gentle, kind, and courteous."[43]

Theodore Roosevelt, who had become president after William McKinley died in 1901, ran for president in 1904 and won. His inaugural parade was held in Washington, DC, on March 4, 1905. Thirty-five thousand people participated in the parade comprising West Point cadets, marching bands, and army regiments, including the Seventh Cavalry. Richard Pratt's Carlisle Indian School was represented by 350 uniformed students accompanied by their marching band.[44]

Six mounted Indian leaders rode abreast. Geronimo was one of them. Three rode on white horses, Geronimo and two others on dark horses. Geronimo, wearing traditional Apache headgear and dark clothing, carried a lance. His dark horse was flanked by two white ones, and the riders on each side of him wore eagle-feather bonnets, making him stand out.[45]

Roosevelt stood in the presidential review stand in front of the White House as the mounted Indian leaders approached, riding down Pennsylvania Avenue. "Geronimo!" the crowd cheered. "Hooray for Geronimo!" Walter Harris, a reporter for the *Richmond Times Dispatch*, wrote, "The Indians appeared to interest the President as greatly as any other feature of the parade, with the exception of the cowboys, and when old Geronimo, as if carried away by the cheers which he and his companions received, brandished his spear and gave a wild whoop, the President acknowledged it by waving his hat."[46]

Woodworth Clum was the son of John Clum, the San Carlos agent who had captured Geronimo in 1877. Woodworth, working as a newspaper correspondent, sat near Roosevelt in the presidential review stand. He asked Roosevelt, "Why did you select Geronimo

Geronimo salutes President Theodore Roosevelt at his 1904 inauguration.

to march in your parade, Mr. President? He is the greatest single-handed murderer in American history."

"I wanted to give the people a good show," Roosevelt responded.[47]

On March 9, Virginia's *Alexandria Gazette* reported Geronimo and the other Indian leaders met with President Roosevelt in the White House. After introductions and greetings, a tearful Geronimo requested Roosevelt "take the ropes from the hands" of the Chiricahuas. He continued, "The ropes have been on my hands for many years and we want to go back to our home in Arizona."

"When you lived in Arizona you had a bad heart and killed many of my people," Roosevelt responded. "I have appointed Mr. Leupp the Indian Commissioner to watch you. I cannot grant the request you make for yet awhile. We will have to wait and see how you act."

As the Indian leaders left the president's office, Geronimo wanted to go back and "speak again to the father." Leupp said no. Anything Geronimo had to say to the president would need to be submitted in writing.[48]

In the summer of 1905, Geronimo met Stephen Barrett, superintendent of the school in nearby Lawton, Oklahoma, when he was asked to translate Geronimo's Spanish and a buyer's English to help in the sale of one of Geronimo's headdresses. After that, Geronimo was friendly to Barrett. When Geronimo learned a Mexican had wounded Barrett, he expressed his distaste for Mexicans to Barrett. Geronimo became very cordial after that, telling Barrett tales of his life adventures.[49]

Barrett believed Geronimo's life story should be written and published. He asked Geronimo if he could publish his story, and Geronimo agreed, so long as Barrett paid him. Next Barrett had to get permission from the army. First Lieutenant George Purington was now in charge of the Chiricahuas. Purington disliked them and refused Barrett's request, stating the Chiricahuas had committed many depredations and it had cost the government a great amount of money to subdue them. Barrett wrote that Purington said, "The old Apache [Geronimo] deserved to be hanged rather than spoiled by so much attention by civilians."[50]

After Purington's rejection, Barrett went right to the top, sending a letter to President Roosevelt requesting permission to write Geronimo's life story. Roosevelt responded in writing, saying Barrett could go ahead with Geronimo's story and instructing the army to allow him to proceed. The only stipulation was that the army was to review the manuscript before it was published.[51]

Geronimo wanted Asa Daklugie as his interpreter, and Barrett agreed. Daklugie was an excellent choice. Juh's son and Geronimo's nephew, he had studied at Carlisle Indian School and knew both Apache and English. Even though he was educated in the white man's ways, he was also dedicated to Chiricahua traditions, and trusted Geronimo would not say anything to get them in trouble.[52]

They began the writing process in October. Geronimo refused to talk in front of a stenographer. As Geronimo talked, Daklugie translated, and Barrett rapidly took down notes. Geronimo would not stop and give them time to catch up or ask questions, saying, "Write what I have spoken." However, after Barrett had written each portion and Daklugie read it to Geronimo in Apache, Geronimo would answer their questions or add material to make it more understandable.[53]

Geronimo and Daklugie were careful in what they told Barrett and what they left out. The Chiricahuas were still prisoners of war subject to the control of the army. Geronimo and Daklugie worried Barrett might be a spy, trying to get information the federal government could use against them. Chiricahuas were insecure, believing the army would still execute them if it found evidence of crimes they had committed. When some of Geronimo's former warriors learned he was telling Barrett his story, they became distrustful of him, worried he would tell about their past deeds.[54]

When the draft manuscript was complete, Barrett had the Fort Sill commander, Major Charles Taylor, review it. Taylor developed additional questions to ask Geronimo for clarification. Geronimo answered most of the questions, but there were a few he refused to answer.[55]

Barrett sent the manuscript to President Roosevelt, who wrote back, "This is a very interesting volume which you have in manuscript, but I would advise that you disclaim responsibility in all cases where the reputation of an individual is assailed." Barrett followed Roosevelt's suggestion and footnoted Geronimo's detractions of individuals, clarifying that they were solely Geronimo's opinions.[56]

On June 2, 1906, Barrett sent the manuscript to the War Department. Six weeks later, the War Department sent its concerns to the president. The War Department would not approve the manuscript, but it did not prevent Barrett from publishing it that same year. He did so, including in the Introductory the War Department's memorandum to the president and listing its objections to specific statements by Geronimo, especially his criticism of Generals Crook and Miles.[57]

Barrett's book, *Geronimo: His Own Story*, is flawed. Some parts are garbled—understandable when considering Geronimo spoke in Apache, Daklugie translated into English, and then Barrett wrote it down using his own words, with possible embellishments. As an example, Barrett refers to Geronimo as chief. Later in life, Daklugie told author Eve Ball, "Well, Geronimo never told him that. Neither did I. It was Barrett who made a chief of my uncle." In places, Geronimo's chronology of events does not follow the known historical record, but it still reveals valuable insight into his thoughts and actions.[58]

In his old age Geronimo still hated Mexicans, saying in his book, "I have no love for Mexicans. With me they were always treacherous and malicious. I am old now and shall never go on the warpath again, but if I were young, and followed the warpath, it would lead into Old Mexico."[59]

In the final chapter of the book, Geronimo thanked President Roosevelt for allowing his story to be told. He believed the Chiricahuas had learned the ways of the white people and were now ready to return to their God-given homeland in Arizona that General Miles had promised them. Geronimo concluded his story:

I know that if my people were placed in that mountainous region lying around the headwaters of the Gila River they would live in peace and act according to the will of the President. . . . Could I but see this accomplished I think I could forget all the wrongs that

I have ever received, and die a contented and happy old man. . . .
If I must die in bondage—I hope that the remnant of the Apache
tribe may, when I am gone, be granted the one privilege which
they request—to return to Arizona.[60]

Geronimo's wife Zi-yeh had died of tubular lupus in 1904 and was buried in the Fort Sill Cemetery. On December 25, 1905, Geronimo married Sousche, also known as Mrs. Mary Loto, a widow with a grown son. They soon realized they were not happy living together, and she divorced him by leaving.[61]

It may have been after this that Geronimo married Eugene Chihuahua's aunt, Francesca. She had been captured by Mexicans and sold into slavery in the state of Chihuahua. Five to six years after her capture, Francesca and three other women escaped and began their trek north. During their journey, Francesca was mauled by a mountain lion. Her scalp was nearly torn from her head and her face was so disfigured, she always hid it by wearing a scarf as a veil. No one would marry her, but Geronimo did when they were at Fort Sill. Eugene Chihuahua remembered, "Geronimo said that she deserved a good husband because she was the bravest of Apache women."[62]

In 1907, Geronimo married Azul, also known as Sunsetso and Old Lady Yellow. Mexicans had captured her as a child, but she had escaped. She had been married but widowed by 1906. She was Geronimo's last wife, and they apparently had a happy marriage. There is no good count of how many wives and children Geronimo had. The number of wives ranges from nine to twelve, depending on the researcher.[63]

Geronimo had outlived many of his fellow warriors and family. Some Chiricahuas suspected he was using his Power not for the benefit of the tribe, but at the expense of his family, trading their deaths to prolong his own life. They believed he was a witch.[64]

Geronimo enjoyed drinking. Jason Betzinez wrote, "By any standard his greatest weakness was liquor.[65]

February 11, 1909, was a cold day. Geronimo rode his horse into Lawton where he sold some of his bows and arrows. He wanted whiskey, but being an Indian, he was not allowed to buy it. He gave his proceeds to Eugene Chihuahua, who had a soldier buy the whiskey for Geronimo.[66]

It was after dark. Geronimo was drunk when he mounted his horse to begin the ride back to his home. Along the way, he fell from his horse, landing partially in a creek. He lay in the creek and on the cold ground all night. The next morning, Mrs. Jozhe saw Geronimo's saddled horse by the creek bank, and when she walked up to it, she saw Geronimo on the ground.[67]

Geronimo was taken to his house where he was cared for, but he had developed a severe cold, which steadily grew worse. One of the scouts reported Geronimo's condition to the Fort Sill surgeon, who sent an ambulance to bring Geronimo to the post's Apache hospital. The Chiricahuas did not like to go there. So many of their people had died there that they called it "the death house." Ten women surrounded Geronimo and would not allow the ambulance detail to remove him. The surgeon reported the incident to Lieutenant George Purington, who sent a scout along with the ambulance detail to bring Geronimo to the fort.[68]

By February 15, Geronimo was critically ill with pneumonia. He was told he did not have long to live. He wanted to see his son Robert and daughter Eva one last time before he died. They were attending the Chilocco Indian School, more than two hundred miles away. Instead of sending a telegram to the children, Lieutenant Purington sent a letter.[69]

As Geronimo willed himself to hang on until his children arrived, Eugene Chihuahua sat with him by day, and Asa Daklugie stayed with him at night. Time and time again, he told Daklugie he regretted surrendering. He wished he had died fighting his enemies like Victorio had done.[70]

Geronimo's grandson Thomas Dahkeya had died when he was eighteen years old in March 1908. Thomas's good friend Nat Kayitah had died of pneumonia at the Mescalero Reservation on February 10, 1909. Geronimo said the two youths appeared to him and urged him to become a Christian, but he refused, saying he was unable to follow that path. He asked them why they hadn't come earlier, and they replied he should have listened to the missionaries.[71]

Toward the end, Daklugie held Geronimo's hand. Geronimo's fingers gripped his and Geronimo opened his eyes, saying, "My nephew, promise me that you and Ramona will take my daughter, Eva, into your home and care for her as you do your own children. Promise me that you will not let her marry. If you do, she will die. The women of our family have great difficulty, as Ishton [Daklugie's mother] had. Do not let this happen to Eva!"

Geronimo closed his eyes and slept fitfully. When he awoke, he said, "I want your promise."

"Ramona and I will take your daughter and love her as our own," Daklugie said. "But how can I prevent her from marrying?"

"She will obey you," Geronimo replied. "She has been taught to obey. See that she does."[72]

As soon as Geronimo's children Robert and Eva received Purington's letter and learned of Geronimo's condition, they rushed to be by his side, but the letter did not reach them in time. They were too late. On February 17, 1909, at 6:15 a.m., Geronimo died—still a prisoner of war.[73]

Geronimo's Skull

Geronimo died of pneumonia in the Apache hospital at Fort Sill the morning of February 17, 1909. The funeral was held February 18, after his son Robert and daughter Eva arrived. The funeral procession was nearly a mile long with Apaches, residents of the nearby town of Lawton, and the soldiers from Fort Sill participating. His grave was dug next to his wife Zi-yeh's in the Apache prisoner-of-war cemetery located three miles from the fort.[74]

One Apache custom was to kill a deceased warrior's favorite horse so he could ride it into the afterlife. Geronimo's wife Azul planned to kill his racehorse but was stopped from doing so. However, his nephew Asa Daklugie said, "We could not bury his best war horse with him, but I saw that he had it for the journey." A graveside Christian funeral service was held and then he was buried with his greatest treasures, including jewelry, blankets, and weapons.[75]

For months Chiricahua warriors, two at a time, took turns guarding Geronimo's grave each night. The Chiricahuas were concerned grave robbers would attempt to take his treasure and head just as Mangas Coloradas's head had been taken. As time went on and there were no attempts to rob his grave, the guard was reduced to twice a week.[76]

There was another report that two Apaches had dug into Geronimo's grave, taking his valuable possessions, and decapitating and removing his head. Daklugie said the Chiricahuas watched those two men for years, but if they had taken Geronimo's things and his head, the Chiricahuas never found any evidence of the theft.[77]

In 1931, Fort Sill's Field Artillery School covered Geronimo's grave with a slab of concrete and built a rock monument topped by a stone eagle at the head of the grave.[78]

Rumors began circulating that back in 1918, Geronimo's grave had been robbed and his skull and several bones taken by members of a secret society at Yale University in New Haven, Connecticut. The society is called the Order of Skull and Bones, and the members, called Bonesmen, hold their meetings in a windowless house they call The Tomb. The story goes that six Bonesmen army officers broke into Geronimo's grave, stealing his skull, femur bones, and artifacts. One of those officers was Prescott Bush, the father of former president George H. W. Bush and grandfather of former president George W. Bush, both of whom were also Bonesmen.[79]

In 1930, Skull and Bones produced a publication titled "Continuation of the History of Our Order for the Century Celebration," commemorating its hundredth anniversary. In the document it says that the six army officers had to be careful in planning their robbery of Geronimo's grave. If they were caught, it would not look good in the newspapers.[80]

The publication went on to say, "The ring of pick on stone and thud of earth on earth alone disturbs the peace of the prairie. An axe pried open the iron door of the tomb, and Pat Bush entered and started to dig." Bonesmen referred to each other as Pat, which was short for Patriarch. The robbers removed the skull and bones and took them to one of their rooms to clean them.[81]

In 2005, author Marc Wortman was in Yale's archives researching the experiences of Yale army officer aviators during World War I when he found a letter referring to the theft of Geronimo's skull and bones. The letter from Winter Meade, Class of 1919, in part reads, "The skull of the worthy Geronimo the Terrible, exhumed from its tomb at Fort Sill by your club and Knight Haffuer, is now safe inside the T[omb]—together with his well worn femurs, bit and saddle horn."[82]

In 2009, a descendant of Geronimo brought a lawsuit against the Order of Skull and Bones to return Geronimo's skull and bones. Attorney Ramsey Clark, who formerly served as US attorney general, represented the plaintiff in the case. Skull and Bones said it did not have Geronimo's bones, and they won the case in US District Court. The judge held that the law under which Skull and Bones was sued, the Native American Graves Protection and Repatriation Act, only applied to grave robberies that took place after its enactment in 1990.[83]

What Marc Wortman and others believe is that the Bonesmen did steal a skull and bones, but they robbed the wrong grave, because the 1930 Skull and Bones publication states: "An axe pried open the iron door of the tomb." Geronimo was not in a tomb, but in a grave, and there was no iron door at his grave.[84]

The evidence is inconclusive. Is Geronimo's skull in his grave or is it somewhere else?

CHAPTER 15

The End of the Trail

WE ALL DIE, BUT THE DEATHS OF SITTING BULL AND GERONIMO should never have happened the way they did.

In the case of Sitting Bull, what crime was he accused of committing? What were the charges to arrest him? There was no crime. There were no charges. He was not fomenting a rebellion against the United States. All he wanted to do was investigate the Messiah and Ghost Dance to see if they were real or fake. Agent James McLaughlin had been looking for any excuse to arrest Sitting Bull and found it with Sitting Bull's alleged planned trip to Pine Ridge to investigate the Ghost Dance. If Sitting Bull had to be brought in, why did McLaughlin interfere with General Miles's plan to have Buffalo Bill Cody bring him in? I believe if Cody had been allowed to proceed on to Sitting Bull's settlement, Sitting Bull would have accompanied him back to the agency. The tragedy of Sitting Bull's death and the deaths of the Indian police and Sitting Bull's followers should never have happened. I believe Agent James McLaughlin's ego caused the tragedy.

In the case of Geronimo, why did Lieutenant George Purington send a letter to Geronimo's children instead of a telegram to let them know of their father's imminent death? They could have left soon after receiving a telegram instead of incurring a two-day delay that had them arrive at Fort Sill the day after their father died. Was Purington's dislike of Geronimo so great that he would deprive Geronimo's children from seeing him before he died? I believe Lieutenant

George Purington's dislike of Geronimo prevented Geronimo from seeing his children one last time.

❦

After the death of Sitting Bull, some of the people from Sitting Bull's community and some Ghost Dancers fled south to Big Foot's Miniconjou band on the Cheyenne River Reservation. Learning of Sitting Bull's death, 350 men, women, and children fled south toward the Pine Ridge Agency where they believed they would be safe. The army caught up with them at Wounded Knee, and on December 29, 1890, misunderstandings flared into shots fired. When the fighting was over, at least 146 men, women, and children of Big Foot's band had been killed, along with 30 soldiers and 1 scout.[1]

In June 1891, Sitting Bull's wife Seen-by-her-Nation said a spirit visited her. The spirit told her that in order to preserve Sitting Bull's heritage and bloodline, she and the rest of Sitting Bull's family needed to leave Standing Rock immediately and that a guide would be provided. The next morning, Sitting Bull's wives Seen-by-her-Nation and Four Robes and their children, along with about two hundred Hunkpapas, stole away from the reservation. Led by a meadowlark, they traveled southwest to Red Shirt Table in the South Dakota Badlands where they lived undetected for a year. In the spring of 1892, the Pine Ridge agent discovered the Hunkpapas at Red Shirt Table and enrolled them as members of the Pine Ridge Reservation. To this day, Sitting Bull's descendants from Seen-by-her-Nation and Four Robes are enrolled members of Pine Ridge.[2]

❦

After the death of Geronimo, Congress passed a law on August 24, 1912, releasing the Chiricahuas from their prisoner-of-war status. They were given the choice to either remain and settle at Fort Sill or relocate to the Mescalero Reservation in New Mexico. In April 1913, out of 261 remaining Chiricahuas, 183 chose to go to the Mescalero Reservation and 78 decided to stay in the Fort Sill area.[3]

Asa Daklugie and his wife Ramona took Geronimo's daughter Eva into their household and treated her as their own daughter. She soon decided to marry fellow classmate Fred Godeley, from the Chilocco school. Asa and Ramona attempted to dissuade Eva from marrying Fred to carry out Geronimo's last wish that Eva not marry. She would not listen to them and married him. They soon had a daughter, Evaline, who was born on June 21, 1910, and died two months later. Tuberculosis took Eva's life a little over a year later, on August 10, 1911.[4]

Geronimo's children by Ih-tedda, Lenna and Robert, were members of the Mescalero tribe. They each married, and their descendants are members of the Mescalero tribe today.[5]

Soon after Sitting Bull's death, books were published that struggled with the right and wrong of his death.

In 1891, W. Fletcher Johnson wrote *Life of Sitting Bull and History of the Indian War of 1890–'91*. "Thus died Sitting Bull," Fletcher wrote. "Thus the world was rid of a troubler. But what made him a troubler? Wrongs, injustice, outrage. . . . The real cause of Indian troubles, wars, massacres, is and has been the incredibly and inexpressibly base treatment of the Indians by the white men, in which the Government has often, if not always been *particeps criminis*. There were those who raised a cry of exultation at the death of Sitting Bull. There were many who regarded it with relief. But the real mind and heart of the American people felt sad and ashamed, with a sadness and shame too deep for words. Perhaps it was necessary to kill him. But the circumstances, a century old, that made it necessary to kill him, that made him a being whom it was necessary to kill, are only to be regarded with national humiliation."[6]

In 1910, James McLaughlin, who was no friend of Sitting Bull, published *My Friend the Indian*. McLaughlin wrote much about Sitting Bull. In one passage he said, "Crafty, avaricious, mendacious, and ambitious, Sitting Bull possessed all of the faults of an Indian and none of the nobler attributes which have gone far to redeem some of his people from their deeds of guilt."[7]

Hamlin Garland was one of the first sympathetic authors to write about Sitting Bull and the Hunkpapas. At the end of the nineteenth century and beginning of the twentieth, Garland visited many Indian tribes and reservations throughout the West, meeting and talking with tribe members about the old days and present conditions.

In July 1897, Garland first visited the Hunkpapas at Standing Rock Sioux Reservation. Over the course of several years he returned to interview people who knew Sitting Bull, and a more truthful story emerged from the false story that had portrayed Sitting Bull as a weak leader, not much more than a coward. One example of the misinformation that had been published was an article titled "Three Noted Chiefs of the Sioux" in the December 20, 1890, issue of *Harper's Weekly*. It stated, "This famous chief [Sitting Bull] is a man of mediocre ability, not noted for bravery as a warrior, and inferior as a commander and in intelligence to some of his lieutenants. . . . Personally he is pompous, vain, boastful, licentious, and untrustworthy."[8]

A collection of Garland's fictional stories based on current and historical people and events was published in his *The Book of the American Indian* in 1923. His novella "The Silent Eaters" makes up a large portion of the book. After interviewing many who knew Sitting Bull, Garland wrote "The Silent Eaters," portraying Sitting Bull as a statesman who would only fight when he had to in order to protect his people. " 'The Silent Eaters,' " Garland said, "[was] a brief prose epic of the Sioux, a special pleading from the standpoint of a young educated red man, to whom Sitting Bull was a kind of Themistocles. Though based on accurate information, I intended it to be not so much a history as an interpretation."[9]

The next major work on Sitting Bull to appear was Stanley Vestal's *Sitting Bull: Champion of the Sioux*. Vestal first published it in 1932 and revised it with additional information in 1957.

Stanley Vestal was the pen name for Walter Stanley Campbell. Campbell traveled to the Lakota reservations in South Dakota and North Dakota where he met and became friends with Sitting Bull's nephews, White Bull and One Bull. Campbell interviewed them and other people who had personally known Sitting Bull. The interviews were recorded in Lakota and then translated into English. Based on those interviews and other extensive research Campbell conducted, he crafted his biography of Sitting Bull that became the standard for years.

Campbell's biography paints a romantic word picture of Sitting Bull's life, but it reveals a truer nature than the image created by James McLaughlin and others. All modern histories of Sitting Bull rely on the interviews Campbell conducted with Sitting Bull's contemporaries.

Robert Utley's *The Lance and the Shield: The Life and Times of Sitting Bull*, published in 1993, is the gold standard of biographies on Sitting Bull. Utley stripped away the romance and told Sitting Bull's story as factually as possible. Utley relied on Campbell's research and biography, writing, "I salute Stanley Vestal [Walter Campbell] for his research and for rescuing Sitting Bull's memory from the ignominy that tainted it for a generation after his death."[10]

In 2009, Ernie LaPointe, the great-grandson of Sitting Bull, published *Sitting Bull: His Life and Legacy*. This important book reveals additional details of Sitting Bull's life, passed down through his family.

The first film with a Sitting Bull character was the silent movie *Sitting Bull—The Hostile Sioux Indian Chief* (1914).[11] Through the years he was portrayed in a variety of films, many of them bad, and almost all fictionalized. Some of the more recent films he has been portrayed in are *Buffalo Bill and the Indians, or Sitting Bull's History Lesson* (1976), *Buffalo Girls* (1995 miniseries), *Into the West* (2005 miniseries), *Bury My Heart at Wounded Knee* (2007), *Sitting Bull: A Stone in My Heart* (2008 documentary), and *Woman Walks Ahead* (2017).[12]

Geronimo had his detractors in contemporary newspapers and magazines. However, in 1906 Stephen Barrett published *Geronimo: His Own Story*, which is unique in that it provides Geronimo's version of his life and actions.

In the first part of the twentieth century, Geronimo was used in novels. Edgar Rice Burroughs, creator of Tarzan, wrote two novels with Geronimo as one of the main characters, *The War Chief* (1927) and *Apache Devil* (1933). While serving with the Seventh Cavalry, Burroughs had been stationed at Fort Grant, Arizona, in 1896. He participated in the fruitless search for the Apache Kid and became familiar with the Apaches and sympathetic with their situation. Burroughs wrote in *The War Chief*, "Fewer men died at the hands of the six tribes of the Apaches than fell in a single day of many an offensive movement during a recent war [World War I] between cultured nations."[13]

Woodworth Clum, son of John Clum, the Indian agent at San Carlos, published a biography of his father, *Apache Agent: The Story of John P. Clum*, in 1936. Clum was no fan of Geronimo and used every opportunity to cast him in a poor light. At the end of his book, Clum wrote, "Geronimo died at Fort Sill, Oklahoma, unpunished for his sins, hailed by the newspapers as the 'famous Apache chief,' looked upon less as a robber and murderer than as a hero."[14]

In 1976, after countless hours of research and interviews, Angie Debo published an excellent account of Geronimo's life, *Geronimo: The Man, His Time, His Place*. Debo's landmark book was followed by three well-written twenty-first-century books that deal with Geronimo: Edwin Sweeney's *From Cochise to Geronimo: The Chiricahua Apaches, 1874–1889*, Robert Utley's *Geronimo*, and Paul Andrew Hutton's *The Apache Wars*.

In 1904, Geronimo attended the Louisiana Purchase Exposition in St. Louis, Missouri, where he saw his first motion picture.[15] In the film *Geronimo: The Story of a Great Enemy* (1939), he was portrayed by Chief Thundercloud (aka Victor Daniels).[16] It's interesting to note that Chief Thundercloud also portrayed Sitting Bull in *Annie Oakley* (1935). In the 1950 film *Broken Arrow*, Geronimo is played by Jay Silverheels. This film portrayed Indians in a more favorable light than previous films. It was nominated for three Academy Awards and won a Golden Globe Award.[17] In 1963 Chuck Connors portrayed Geronimo in *Geronimo*. Three decades later, in 1993, two films were released on Geronimo. The first, a feature film, *Geronimo: An American Legend*, was about Geronimo's arrest. Native American actor Wes Studi portrayed Geronimo. The second film was a TNT television movie, *Geronimo*, about his life, with Native American actor Joseph Runningfox portraying a young Geronimo and First Nations actor Jimmy Herman portraying an older Geronimo.[18]

Pop artist Andy Warhol was fascinated with the West and included both Geronimo and Sitting Bull in his "Cowboys and Indians Suite."[19] *True West Magazine* executive editor Bob Boze Bell in his book *The Illustrated Life and Times of Geronimo* has created an excellent collection of color illustrations depicting Geronimo's life and times.

Geronimo's name may be the best known of any Indian leader due to a fun-loving army recruit. In August 1940, volunteers from the Twenty-ninth Infantry Regiment were going to test how best to jump en masse out of an airplane and parachute to the ground at Fort Benning, Georgia. They were instructed to shout their names as they jumped from the airplane. Some of the guys gave Private Aubrey Eberhardt a hard time, saying that he would forget his name when he jumped from the plane. The night before their first scheduled jump, some of the soldiers went to a movie theater to see *Geronimo* (1939), starring Chief Thundercloud in the lead role. The next morning, when the airplane reached the proper altitude and position, the men were given the go-ahead to jump one at a time through the open door. When it was Eberhardt's turn, instead of shouting his name, he shouted "Geronimo!" The men all thought it was fun and shouted "Geronimo!" as they jumped. It became a tradition, spreading throughout the army. The 501st Parachute Infantry Regiment put Geronimo's name on their patch in 1942. Today, many people still shout "Geronimo!" when they make a jump. [20]

America's expanding population and its government forced the Chiricahuas and Hunkpapas to transition from their traditional lifestyles to new, unknown ways of living. Both Geronimo and Sitting Bull forcefully resisted this transition as long as they could. When they no longer could resist, they attempted to make their way through uncharted territory, trying to hold on to as much of their culture as they could.

No one can condone any of the degradations, injuries, and deaths committed by Americans, Mexicans, Apaches, and Lakotas. The murders of Geronimo's family members scarred him for life. Sitting

Bull distrusted Americans, believing most were dishonest. It's easy to look back and say the Americans could have handled it better. What if instead of forcing the Lakotas, Cheyennes, and other northern plains tribes to report to the agencies on the Great Sioux Reservation, the federal government had allowed them to hunt buffalo until such time as there were not enough to feed them, and they would have had to come in on their own volition? What if instead of forcing the removal of the Chiricahuas from their Chiricahua Reservation to San Carlos Agency, the federal government had allowed them to remain on their reservation? Of course, we will never know, but there is a chance that many lives could have been saved.

It wasn't until June 2, 1924, that Congress granted citizenship to all Indians born in the United States. One lesson for all Americans is that we must guard our individual rights. Before Congress granted Indians citizenship, the federal government had unrestricted power over those individuals' lives. Indians were at the mercy of federal agents, military officers, and commissioners. Sure, they could appeal to higher officials, all the way up to the president, but usually government officials sided with those who had made the initial decisions.

Until the end of their lives, Geronimo and Sitting Bull continued to have their people's well-being first in their hearts.

Toward the end of his autobiography, Geronimo said, "It [Arizona] is my land, my home, my fathers' land, to which I now ask to be allowed to return. I want to spend my last days there, and be buried among those mountains. If this could be I might die in peace, feeling that my people, placed in their native homes, would increase in numbers, rather than diminish as at present, and that our name would not become extinct."[21]

As part of Sitting Bull's speech before the Senate Select Committee in 1883, he said, "I am looking into the future for my children [the Lakotas], and that is what I mean when I say I want my country taken care of for me. My children will grow up here, and I am looking ahead for their benefit, and for the benefit of my children's children, too; and even beyond that."[22]

NOTES

CHAPTER 1: THE EARLY YEARS, 1829–1845

1 The People, *Dine*, is also spelled *Indeh*.

2 Carol A. Markstrom, *Empowerment of North American Indian Girls: Ritual Expressions at Puberty* (Lincoln: University of Nebraska Press, 2008), 197–98; W. Michael Farmer, *Apacheria: True Stories of the Apache Culture 1860–1920* (Guilford, CT: TwoDot, 2017), xvi.

3 Paul Andrew Hutton, *The Apache Wars: The Hunt for Geronimo, the Apache Kid, and the Captive Boy Who Started the Longest War in American History* (New York: Broadway Books, 2016), 8, 9.

4 W. Michael Farmer, *Apacheria*, xiii–xiv; Paul Andrew Hutton, *The Apache Wars*, 13.

5 Paul Andrew Hutton, *The Apache Wars*, 11–12.

6 Paul Andrew Hutton, *The Apache Wars*, 10, 11.

7 W. Michael Farmer, *Apacheria*, 2; Paul Andrew Hutton, *The Apache Wars*, 10, 13.

8 Paul Andrew Hutton, *The Apache Wars*, 14.

9 Paul Andrew Hutton, *The Apache Wars*, 14–15.

10 Vine Deloria Jr., *The World We Used to Live In: Remembering the Powers of the Medicine Men* (Golden, CO: Fulcrum Publishing, 2006), xxvi; John G. Neihardt, *Black Elk Speaks: Being the Life Story of a Holy Man of the Oglala Sioux* (Lincoln: University of Nebraska Press, 1932), 5; Josephine Waggoner, *Witness: A Hunkpapha Historian's Strong-Heart Song of the Lakotas* (Lincoln: University of Nebraska Press, 2013), 15.

11 John G. Neihardt, *Black Elk Speaks*, 3–5; Editors of Time-Life Books, *The Spirit World*, The American Indians Series (Alexandria, VA: Time-Life Books, 1992), 59.

12 Joseph M. Marshall III, *The Journey of Crazy Horse: A Lakota History* (New York: Penguin Books, 2004), xxiii; Editors of Time-Life Books, *The Buffalo Hunters*, The American Indians Series (Alexandria, VA: Time-Life Books, 1993), 18–19; Raymond J. DeMallie, volume editor, *Plains*, Handbook of North American Indians, vol. 13, part 2 (Washington, DC: Smithsonian Institution, 2001), 718–33.

13 James Crutchfield, Candy Moulton, Terry Del Bene, eds., *The Settlement of America: Encyclopedia of Western Expansion from Jamestown to the Closing of the Frontier*, vol. 2 (Armonk, NY: M. E. Sharp, Inc., 2011), 435.

14 Pekka Hämäläinen, *Lakota America: A New History of Indigenous Power* (New Haven: Yale University Press, 2019), 84, 85; James Crutchfield et al., *The Settlement of America*, vol. 2, 435.

15 Raymond J. DeMallie, *Plains*, 801–02; Robert M. Utley, *The Lance and the Shield: The Life and Times of Sitting Bull* (New York: Ballantine Books, 1994), 9.

16 Raymond J. DeMallie, *Plains*, 802; Robert M. Utley, *The Lance and the Shield*, 9.

17 Ibid.

18 Geronimo says in his biography that he was born in June 1829. Robert M. Utley in his book *Geronimo* believes Geronimo was born in 1823, stating on page 6, "[T]he year 1823 fits with other known events." Although no one really knows for sure, I chose to use the one Geronimo stated was his birth year.

19 S. M. Barrett, ed., *Geronimo: His Own Story* (New York: Ballantine Books, 1970), 69; Robert M. Utley, *Geronimo* (New Haven: Yale University Press, 2012), 6.

20 Robert M. Utley, *Geronimo*, 6; S. M. Barrett, ed., *Geronimo*, 69; Robert Utley in *Geronimo*, page 7, states that six of Geronimo's seven brothers and sisters were actually his cousins. I chose to use Geronimo's recollection.

21 Robert M. Utley, *Geronimo*, 6–7; S. M. Barrett, ed., *Geronimo*, 81.

22 Alfonzo Ortiz, volume editor, *Southwest*, Handbook of North American Indians, vol. 10 (Washington, DC: Smithsonian Institution, 1983), 415–16; Doug Hocking, *The Black Legend: George Bascom, Cochise, and the Start of the Apache Wars* (Guilford, CT: TwoDot, 2019), 137; S. M. Barrett, ed., *Geronimo*, 70; Robert M. Utley, *Geronimo*, 10–11; W. Michael Farmer, *Apacheria*, xvii.

23 S. M. Barrett, ed., *Geronimo*, 70–71.

24 S. M. Barrett, ed., *Geronimo*, 72–73.

25 David Roberts, *Once They Moved Like the Wind: Cochise, Geronimo, and the Apache Wars* (New York: Simon & Schuster, 1993), 107; Robert M. Utley, *Geronimo*, 12.

26 S. M. Barrett, ed., *Geronimo*, 78–80.

27 S. M. Barrett, ed., *Geronimo*, 73–74.

28 David Roberts, *Once They Moved Like the Wind*, 106–07; Robert M. Utley, *Geronimo*, 12; W. Michael Farmer, *Apacheria*, xxii.

29 S. M. Barrett, ed., *Geronimo*, 81–82; Robert M. Utley, *Geronimo*, 12, 279n11.

30 David Roberts, *Once They Moved Like the Wind*, 62–63, 107; Robert M. Utley, *Geronimo*, 15, 16, 85.

31 Robert M. Utley, *Geronimo*, 7, 9–10; S. M. Barrett, ed., *Geronimo*, 80.

32 Other accounts indicate that Sitting Bull may have been born in 1832, 1834, or 1837. Robert M. Utley, *The Lance and the Shield*, 3, 335n2.

33 Other accounts state that Sitting Bull may have been born on Willow Creek west of Fort Pierre, South Dakota. Robert M. Utley, *The Lance and the Shield*, 3; Ernie LaPointe, great-grandson of Sitting Bull, says he was born along the Yellowstone River in Montana. Ernie LaPointe, *Sitting Bull: His Life and Legacy* (Layton, UT: Gibbs Smith, 2009), 21.

34 Stanley Vestal, *Sitting Bull: Champion of the Sioux* (Norman: University of Oklahoma Press, 1932), 3; Robert M. Utley, *The Lance and the Shield*, 3, 4; Ernie LaPointe, *Sitting Bull*, 21.

35 When Jumping Badger was born his father's name was Returns Again. When the boy was older, Returns Again took the name Sitting Bull, Ernie LaPointe, *Sitting Bull*, 21, 26–27.

36 Ernie LaPointe, *Sitting Bull*, 21; Robert M. Utley, *The Lance and the Shield*, 6.

37 Robert M. Utley, *The Lance and the Shield*, 7.

38 Joseph M. Marshall III, *The Power of Four: Leadership Lessons of Crazy Horse* (New York: Sterling Publishing Company, Inc., 2009), 15; Raymond J. DeMallie, *Plains*, 806–07.

39 Josephine Waggoner, *Witness*, 397; Ernie LaPointe, *Sitting Bull*, 22; Robert M. Utley, *The Lance and the Shield*, 10.

40 Stanley Vestal, *Sitting Bull: Champion of the Sioux*, 4; Josephine Waggoner, *Witness*, 397.

41 Robert M. Utley, *The Lance and the Shield*, 10.

42 Ernie LaPointe, *Sitting Bull*, 23–24; Robert M. Utley, *The Lance and the Shield*, 10–11.

43 Ernie LaPointe, *Sitting Bull*, 22–23.

44 Josephine Waggoner, *Witness*, 397.

45 Ernie LaPointe, *Sitting Bull*, 24–25.

46 Harold H. Schuler, *Fort Pierre Chouteau* (Vermillion: University of South Dakota Press, 1990), 15; Robert G. Athearn, *Forts of the Upper Missouri* (Lincoln: University of Nebraska Press, 1967), 23.

47 Harold H. Schuler, *Fort Pierre Chouteau*, 114–15, 121–22; Robert M. Utley, *The Lance and the Shield*, 38–40.

SIDEBAR: APACHE TRIBES AND LAKOTA, NAKOTA, DAKOTA TRIBES

48 W. Michael Farmer, *Apacheria*, xii–xiii, xvi; Paul Andrew Hutton, *The Apache Wars*, 8, 9; Robert M. Utley, *Geronimo*, 7, 9; Raymond J. DeMallie, *Plains*, 926, 927.

49 James Crutchfield et al., *The Settlement of America*, vol. 2, 434–35; Ernie LaPointe, *Sitting Bull*, 21; Raymond J. DeMallie, *Plains*, 719; Michael Crummett, *Tataka-Iyotanka: A Biography of Sitting Bull* (Tucson, AZ: Western National Parks Association, 2002), 5.

CHAPTER 2: WARRIORS, 1845–1851

1 Doug Hocking, *The Black Legend*, 136–37, 206–07.

2 Robert M. Utley, *Geronimo*, 18; Paul Andrew Hutton, *The Apache Wars*, 15–16.

3 Robert M. Utley, *Geronimo*, 13.

4 Robert M. Utley, *Geronimo*, 14.

5 Robert M. Utley, *Geronimo*, 18.

6 S. M. Barrett, ed., *Geronimo*, 82.

7 S. M. Barrett, ed., *Geronimo*, 83.

8 Ibid.

9 S. M. Barrett, ed., *Geronimo*, 83–84.

10 Robert M. Utley, *Geronimo*, 16.

11 S. M. Barrett, ed., *Geronimo*, 84.

12 S. M. Barrett, ed., *Geronimo*, 83.

13 Robert M. Utley, *Geronimo*, 20.

14 Robert M. Utley, *Geronimo*, 20; Paul Andrew Hutton, *The Apache Wars*, 20–21.

15 James Crutchfield et al., *The Settlement of America*, vol. 2, 332.

16 Paul Andrew Hutton, *The Apache Wars*, 23–24.

17 Paul Andrew Hutton, *The Apache Wars*, 40.

18 Robert M. Utley, *Geronimo*, 20–21.

19 James Crutchfield et al., *The Settlement of America*, vol. 1, 224, 244–45; Paul Andrew Hutton, *The Apache Wars*, 25–27; David Roberts, *Once They Moved Like the Wind*, 22.

20 David Roberts, *Once They Moved Like the Wind*, 115–16; James Crutchfield et al., *The Settlement of America*, vol. 2, 329–30; S. M. Barrett, ed., *Geronimo*, 129–30.

21 Vine Deloria Jr., *The World We Used to Live In*, 23; Raymond J. DeMallie, *Plains*, 807.

22 Vine Deloria Jr., *The World We Used to Live In*, 17, 19; Raymond J. DeMallie, *Plains*, 807.

23 Robert M. Utley, *The Lance and the Shield*, 28.

24 Ernie LaPointe, *Sitting Bull*, 27; Stanley Vestal, *Sitting Bull: Champion of the Sioux*, 8.

25 Stanley Vestal, *Sitting Bull: Champion of the Sioux*, 9, 10.

26 M. W. Stirling, *Three Pictographic Autobiographies of Sitting Bull*, Smithsonian Miscellaneous Collection, vol. 97, no. 5 (Washington, DC: Smithsonian Institution, 1938), 8; Stanley Vestal, *Sitting Bull: Champion of the Sioux*, 11–12; Robert M. Utley, *The Lance and the Shield*, 14; Ernie LaPointe, *Sitting Bull*, 27.

27 Ernie LaPointe, *Sitting Bull*, 28, 29; Stanley Vestal, *Sitting Bull: Champion of the Sioux*, 12–13.

28 Stanley Vestal, *Sitting Bull: Champion of the Sioux*, 18–19; Robert M. Utley, *The Lance and the Shield*, 15.

29 Stanley Vestal, *New Sources of Indian History 1850–1891: The Ghost Dance, the Prairie Sioux, a Miscellany* (Norman: University of Oklahoma Press, 1934), 153–56; Ernie LaPointe, *Sitting Bull*, 28; Robert M. Utley, *The Lance and the Shield*, 15.

30 Stanley Vestal, *New Sources of Indian History*, 153; Robert M. Utley, *The Lance and the Shield*, xi, 19.

31 Ernie LaPointe, *Sitting Bull*, 29; Robert M. Utley, *The Lance and the Shield*, 15–16.

32 Stanley Vestal, *Sitting Bull: Champion of the Sioux*, 20–21; Robert M. Utley, *The Lance and the Shield*, 30.

33 Stanley Vestal, *Sitting Bull: Champion of the Sioux*, 21–22.

SIDEBAR: THE GADSDEN PURCHASE, 1853–1854

35 Frank N. Schubert, *Vanguard of Expansion: Army Engineers in the Trans-Mississippi West 1819–1879* (Washington, DC: Office of the Chief of Engineers, 1980), 62; James Crutchfield et al., *The Settlement of America*, 224.

35 Walter R. Borneman, *Rival Rails: The Race to Build America's Greatest Transcontinental Railroad* (New York: Random House, 2010), 8–9; Frank N. Schubert, *Vanguard of Expansion*, 62; James Crutchfield et al., *The Settlement of America*, 224, 562; "Gadsden Purchase," Wikipedia, accessed January 4, 2020, https://en.wikipedia.org/wiki/Gadsden_Purchase.

36 James Crutchfield et al., *The Settlement of America*, 224.

37 James Crutchfield et al., *The Settlement of America*, 224; Stephen E. Ambrose, *Nothing Like It in the World: The Men Who Built the Transcontinental Railroad, 1863–1869* (New York: Simon & Schuster, 2000), 31.

CHAPTER 3: TRADE AND CONFLICT, 1851–1860

1 Robert M. Utley, *Geronimo*, 23; Edwin R. Sweeney, " 'I had lost all': Geronimo and the Carrasco Massacre of 1851," *Journal of Arizona History*, vol. 27, no. 1, Tucson: Arizona Historical Society (Spring 1986), 36–39.

2 Robert M. Utley, *Geronimo*, 24; Edwin R. Sweeney, " 'I had lost all': Geronimo and the Carrasco Massacre of 1851," 42.

3 Robert M. Utley, *Geronimo*, 24–25; Edwin R. Sweeney, " 'I had lost all': Geronimo and the Carrasco Massacre of 1851," 42. On pages 43–44 of Sweeney's article of 1851, Sweeney states that this battle is the same as the one described in Geronimo's autobiography, *Geronimo* (edited by S. M. Barrett, pages 90–95), which Geronimo says happened on March 5, 1851, after the attack at Janos. Robert Utley agrees with Sweeney's beliefs. I have chosen to show them as two separate actions, as the descriptions differ greatly.

4 Robert M. Utley, *Geronimo*, 26; Edwin R. Sweeney, " 'I had lost all': Geronimo and the Carrasco Massacre of 1851," 44.

5 Robert M. Utley, *Geronimo*, 24; Edwin R. Sweeney, " 'I had lost all': Geronimo and the Carrasco Massacre of 1851," 42.

6 S. M. Barrett, ed., *Geronimo*, 87–88; Robert M. Utley, *Geronimo*, 26–27.

7 Edwin R. Sweeney, " 'I had lost all': Geronimo and the Carrasco Massacre of 1851," 45; David Roberts, *Once They Moved Like the Wind*, 109.

8 S. M. Barrett, ed., *Geronimo*, 87–88; David Roberts, *Once They Moved Like the Wind*, 109. Geronimo says in his autobiography that they were at Janos in the summer of 1858, but most historians agree that the incident took place on March 5, 1851.

9 S. M. Barrett, ed., *Geronimo*, 88. David Roberts, *Once They Moved Like the Wind*, 109.

10 S. M. Barrett, ed., *Geronimo*, 88.

11 S. M. Barrett, ed., *Geronimo*, 88–89.

12 S. M. Barrett, ed., *Geronimo*, 89.

13 S. M. Barrett, ed., *Geronimo*, 89.

14 S. M. Barrett, ed., *Geronimo*, 89–90.

15 Edwin R. Sweeney, " 'I had lost all': Geronimo and the Carrasco Massacre of 1851," 46–47; David Roberts, *Once They Moved Like the Wind*, 109.

16 Edwin R. Sweeney, " 'I had lost all': Geronimo and the Carrasco Massacre of 1851," 46; David Roberts, *Once They Moved Like the Wind*, 109–10.

17 John C. Cremony, *Life Among the Apaches* (San Francisco: A. Roman & Company, 1868), 39.

18 Eve Ball, *Indeh: An Apache Odyssey* (Norman: University of Oklahoma Press, 1980), 80.

19 Angie Debo, *Geronimo: The Man, His Time, His Place* (Norman: University of Oklahoma Press, 1976), 38.

20 S. M. Barrett, ed., *Geronimo*, 90–91.

21 S. M. Barrett, ed., *Geronimo*, 91–92.

22 S. M. Barrett, ed., *Geronimo*, 92–93.

23 S. M. Barrett, ed., *Geronimo*, 93.

24 Ibid.

25 Ibid.

26 S. M. Barrett, ed., *Geronimo*, 93–94.

27 David Roberts, *Once They Moved Like the Wind*, 113.

28 S. M. Barrett, ed., *Geronimo*, 93–94.

29 S. M. Barrett, ed., *Geronimo*, 95; Doug Hocking, *The Black Legend*, 136.

30 S. M. Barrett, ed., *Geronimo*, 95.

31 Angie Debo, *Geronimo*, 47–48; Alfonzo Ortiz, volume editor, *Southwest*, Handbook of North American Indians, vol. 10, 415.

32 S. M. Barrett, ed., *Geronimo*, 96–97.

33 S. M. Barrett, ed., *Geronimo*, 98–99.

34 S. M. Barrett, ed., *Geronimo*, 99.

35 S. M. Barrett, ed., *Geronimo*, 99.

36 Ibid.

37 S. M. Barrett, ed., *Geronimo*, 99–100.

38 Marshall Trimble, *Roadside History of Arizona* (Missoula, MT: Mountain Press Publishing Company, 2004), 16.

39 Doug Hocking, personal communication, November 22, 2019.

40 Robert M. Utley, *Geronimo*, 30.

41 Ibid.

42 Robert M. Utley, *Geronimo*, 31.

43 Doug Hocking, personal communication, November 22, 2019.

44 Robert M. Utley, *Frontiersmen in Blue: The United States Army and the Indian, 1848–1865* (Lincoln: University of Nebraska Press, 1967), 155–57; Robert M. Utley, *Geronimo*, 34; Angie Debo, *Geronimo*, 55.

45 Doug Hocking, *The Black Legend*, 80, 122–23; S. M. Barrett, ed., *Geronimo*, 131–32; Angie Debo, *Geronimo*, 56.

46 Robert M. Utley, *Geronimo*, 29, 36.

47 Robert M. Utley, *The Lance and the Shield*, 16.

48 Ernie LaPointe, *Sitting Bull*, 29–30. Frank Grouard stated that he heard Sitting Bull recount his coups in battle totaling sixty-three; Joe De Barthe, *The Life and Adventures of Frank Grouard* (St. Joseph, MO: Combe Printing Company, 1894), 105. Grouard was captured by the Lakotas sometime during the late 1860s to early 1870s; Robert M. Utley, *The Lance and the Shield*, 94.

49 M. W. Stirling, *Three Pictographic Autobiographies of Sitting Bull*, 3, 7; Robert M. Utley, *The Lance and the Shield*, 18.

50 Robert M. Utley, *The Lance and the Shield*, 18, 29; Ernie LaPointe, *Sitting Bull*, 31–32.

51 Robert M. Utley, *The Lance and the Shield*, 18; Ernie LaPointe, *Sitting Bull*, 33.

52 Robert M. Utley, *The Lance and the Shield*, 19.

53 Stanley Vestal, *Sitting Bull: Champion of the Sioux*, 32–33; Robert M. Utley, *The Lance and the Shield*, 18–19.

54 Robert M. Utley, *The Lance and the Shield*, 19.

55 Ernie LaPointe, *Sitting Bull*, 39–40.

56 Robert M. Utley, *The Lance and the Shield*, 20–21.

57 Robert M. Utley, *The Lance and the Shield*, 28.

58 Robert M. Utley, *The Lance and the Shield*, 29.

59 Robert M. Utley, *The Lance and the Shield*, 31.

60 Robert M. Utley, *The Lance and the Shield*, 28, 32–33; Ernie LaPointe, *Sitting Bull*, 46.

61 Robert M. Utley, *The Lance and the Shield*, 32, 33.

62 Stanley Vestal, *Sitting Bull: Champion of the Sioux*, 26–27.

63 Stanley Vestal, *Sitting Bull: Champion of the Sioux*, 28.

64 Stanley Vestal, *Sitting Bull: Champion of the Sioux*, 28–29.

65 Stanley Vestal, *Sitting Bull: Champion of the Sioux*, 29–30; Robert M. Utley, *The Lance and the Shield*, 21.

66 Stanley Vestal, *Sitting Bull: Champion of the Sioux*, 30, 31.

67 Robert M. Utley, *The Lance and the Shield*, 22–23; Ernie LaPointe, *Sitting Bull*, 40.

68 Stanley Vestal, *Sitting Bull: Champion of the Sioux*, 34.

69 Ernie LaPointe, *Sitting Bull*, 34; Stanley Vestal, *Sitting Bull: Champion of the Sioux*, 34–36.

70 Robert M. Utley, *The Lance and the Shield*, 23–24; Stanley Vestal, *Sitting Bull: Champion of the Sioux*, 37–38.

71 Robert M. Utley, *The Lance and the Shield*, 22.

72 Stanley Vestal, *Sitting Bull: Champion of the Sioux*, 41–42.

73 Stanley Vestal, *Sitting Bull: Champion of the Sioux*, 44, 45.

74 Stanley Vestal, *Sitting Bull: Champion of the Sioux*, 46.

75 Ibid.

76 Ibid.

77 Ibid.

78 Ibid.

79 Stanley Vestal, *Sitting Bull: Champion of the Sioux*, 47, 48–49.

80 Ernie LaPointe, *Sitting Bull*, 41; Robert M. Utley, *The Lance and the Shield*, 25.

81 Robert M. Utley, *The Lance and the Shield*, 35.

82 Doreen Chaky, *Terrible Justice: Sioux Chiefs and U.S. Soldiers on the Upper Missouri, 1854–1868* (Norman: University of Oklahoma Press, 2012), 29; Robert M. Utley, *The Lance and the Shield*, 38, 39–40.

83 Doreen Chaky, *Terrible Justice*, 26.

84 Doreen Chaky, *Terrible Justice*, 27–28.

85 Doreen Chaky, *Terrible Justice*, 30–31; Robert M. Utley, *Frontiersmen in Blue*, 114.

86 Robert M. Utley, *Frontiersmen in Blue*, 114, 115; Robert G. Athearn, *Forts of the Upper Missouri*, 38.

87 Robert M. Utley, *Frontiersmen in Blue*, 117; Robert G. Athearn, *Forts of the Upper Missouri*, 38.

88 Harold H. Schuler, *Fort Pierre Chouteau*, 133.

89 Harold H. Schuler, *Fort Pierre Chouteau*, 133, 134–35.

90 Harold H. Schuler, *Fort Pierre Chouteau*, 135.

91 Robert G. Athearn, *Forts of the Upper Missouri*, 48; Doreen Chaky, *Terrible Justice*, 58–59; Robert M. Utley, *The Lance and the Shield*, 46.

92 Robert M. Utley, *The Lance and the Shield*, 46; Harold H. Schuler, *Fort Pierre Chouteau*, 136.

93 Harold H. Schuler, *Fort Pierre Chouteau*, 136; Robert M. Utley, *The Lance and the Shield*, 46.

CHAPTER 4: THE WHITE EYES' CIVIL WAR AND BEYOND, 1860–1871

1 Edwin R. Sweeney, *Mangas Coloradas: Chief of the Chiricahua Apaches* (Norman: University of Oklahoma Press, 1998), 391.

2 Edwin R. Sweeney, *Mangas Coloradas*, 395, 397–98.

3 Doug Hocking, *The Black Legend*, 4, 5, 152; Paul Andrew Hutton, *The Apache Wars*, 1–2.

4 Doug Hocking, *The Black Legend*, 4, 152, 157, 161, 163.

5 Doug Hocking, *The Black Legend*, 161.

6 Doug Hocking, *The Black Legend*, 162.

7 Ibid.

8 Ibid.

9 Doug Hocking, *The Black Legend*, 162, 261–62.

10 Doug Hocking, *The Black Legend*, 163–64, 308.

11 Doug Hocking, *The Black Legend*, 165–66.

12 Doug Hocking, *The Black Legend*, 168–70.

13 Doug Hocking, *The Black Legend*, 171; Edwin R. Sweeney, *Mangas Coloradas*, 399.

14 Doug Hocking, *The Black Legend*, 172; S. M. Barrett, ed., *Geronimo*, 132.

15 Doug Hocking, *The Black Legend*, 174, 176, 183, 195.

16 Doug Hocking, *The Black Legend*, 184–86, 187, 192, 196–97.

17 Doug Hocking, *The Black Legend*, 198, 201–03; Angie Debo, *Geronimo*, 64.

18 S. M. Barrett, ed., *Geronimo*, 132–33.

19 Angie Debo, *Geronimo*, 63; Doug Hocking, *The Black Legend*, 293.

20 Edwin R. Sweeney, *Mangas Coloradas*, 408, 409, 410.

21 Robert M. Utley, *Frontiersmen in Blue*, 149–50; Edwin R. Sweeney, *Mangas Coloradas*, 410.

22 S. M. Barrett, ed., *Geronimo*, 100–101.

23 S. M. Barrett, ed., *Geronimo*, 101.

24 Ibid.

25 S. M. Barrett, ed., *Geronimo*, 101–02.

26 S. M. Barrett, ed., *Geronimo*, 102, 104; Robert M. Utley, *Geronimo*, 45.

27 Robert M. Utley, *Geronimo*, 48.

28 Edwin R. Sweeney, *Mangas Coloradas*, 428.

29 Berndt Kühn, *Chronicles of War: Apache and Yavapai Resistance in the Southwestern United States and Northern Mexico, 1821–1937* (Tucson: Arizona Historical Society, 2014), 94; Robert M. Utley, *Geronimo*, 47.

30 Edwin R. Sweeney, *Mangas Coloradas*, 430–31.

31 Edwin R. Sweeney, *Mangas Coloradas*, 432; Robert M. Utley, *Geronimo*, 48; Angie Debo, *Geronimo*, 68.

32 Edwin R. Sweeney, *Mangas Coloradas*, 432–37.

33 Edwin R. Sweeney, *Mangas Coloradas*, 438–39.

34 Edwin R. Sweeney, *Mangas Coloradas*, 439–40.

35 Edwin R. Sweeney, *Mangas Coloradas*, 440.

36 Robert M. Utley, *Geronimo*, 50–51; Edwin R. Sweeney, *Mangas Coloradas*, 441.

37 Edwin R. Sweeney, *Mangas Coloradas*, 440; Robert M. Utley, *Geronimo*, 51.

38 S. M. Barrett, ed., *Geronimo*, 105.

39 Ibid.

40 S. M. Barrett, ed., *Geronimo*, 105–06.

41 S. M. Barrett, ed., *Geronimo*, 106.

42 Ibid.

43 Edwin R. Sweeney, *Mangas Coloradas*, 444.

44 Edwin R. Sweeney, *Mangas Coloradas*, 441, 443.

45 Edwin R. Sweeney, *Mangas Coloradas*, 445.

46 Edwin R. Sweeney, *Mangas Coloradas*, 447.

47 Edwin R. Sweeney, *Mangas Coloradas*, 446.

48 S. M. Barrett, ed., *Geronimo*, 135; Edwin R. Sweeney, *Mangas Coloradas*, 446.

49 Edwin R. Sweeney, *Mangas Coloradas*, 447–48.

50 Edwin R. Sweeney, *Mangas Coloradas*, 448–50.

51 Edwin R. Sweeney, *Mangas Coloradas*, 453, 454.

52 Edwin R. Sweeney, *Mangas Coloradas*, 455–57.

53 Edwin R. Sweeney, *Mangas Coloradas*, 460.

54 Edwin R. Sweeney, *Mangas Coloradas*, 461–63; Eve Ball, *Indeh: An Apache Odyssey*, 83.

55 S. M. Barrett, ed., *Geronimo*, 134.

56 S. M. Barrett, ed., *Geronimo*, 135; Edwin R. Sweeney, *Mangas Coloradas*, 446.

57 S. M. Barrett, ed., *Geronimo*, 135–36.

58 S. M. Barrett, ed., *Geronimo*, 136.

59 S. M. Barrett, ed., *Geronimo*, 137–38. For the location that Geronimo's people returned to, see Edwin R. Sweeney, *Mangas Coloradas*, 446.

60 Robert M. Utley, *Geronimo*, 55, 57.

61 Angie Debo, *Geronimo*, 73; Robert M. Utley, *Geronimo*, 56.

62 S. M. Barrett, ed., *Geronimo*, 106–07.

63 S. M. Barrett, ed., *Geronimo*, 107–08.

64 S. M. Barrett, ed., *Geronimo*, 108–09.

65 S. M. Barrett, ed., *Geronimo*, 110.

66 Michael Farmer, *Apacheria*, 66, 68; Robert M. Utley, *Geronimo*, 56.

67 Robert M. Utley, *Geronimo*, 57–58.

68 S. M. Barrett, ed., *Geronimo*, 110.

69 S. M. Barrett, ed., *Geronimo*, 110–11.

70 S. M. Barrett, ed., *Geronimo*, 112–13.

71 Robert M. Utley, *Geronimo*, 57.

72 S. M. Barrett, ed., *Geronimo*, 113.

73 In *Geronimo: His Own Story*, Geronimo uses the name "Mangas Coloradas," but he had been killed in 1863. His youngest son was named Mangas and this is who Geronimo most likely meant led the raid. There is the possibility that either Geronimo or S. M. Barrett, ed., the editor, got the date wrong, and the incident

happened before Mangas Coloradas's death, but I believe it was the son based on how Geronimo relates the story.

74 S. M. Barrett, ed., *Geronimo*, 113; Edwin R. Sweeney, *Mangas Coloradas*, 91–92.

75 S. M. Barrett, ed., *Geronimo*, 113–14.

76 S. M. Barrett, ed., *Geronimo*, 114–15.

77 S. M. Barrett, ed., *Geronimo*, 115.

78 Ibid.

79 Ibid.

80 S. M. Barrett, ed., *Geronimo*, 115–16.

81 Angie Debo, *Geronimo*, 76–77.

82 Eve Ball, *Indeh: An Apache Odyssey*, 61, 87.

83 In *Geronimo: His Own Story*, Geronimo does not give a specific date, only that "[i]t was more than a year after I had been made Tribal Chief." After the attack, he and his band visited Victorio and his band for help, which would indicate they were attacked in late 1870 or early 1871. Edwin R. Sweeney in his book *From Cochise to Geronimo*, pages 76–77, and Robert M. Utley in his book *Geronimo*, page 87, suggest this attack might have been one led by Lieutenant John Rucker on a Chiricahua rancheria that took place on January 9, 1877.

84 S. M. Barrett, ed., *Geronimo*, 138.

85 S. M. Barrett, ed., *Geronimo*, 138–39.

86 S. M. Barrett, ed., *Geronimo*, 139; Robert M. Utley, *Geronimo*, 58–59.

87 S. M. Barrett, ed., *Geronimo*, 139–40.

88 John G. Bourke, *On the Border with Crook* (New York: Skyhorse Publishing, 2014), 29.

89 Paul Andrew Hutton, *The Apache Wars*, 127.

90 Eve Ball, *Indeh: An Apache Odyssey*, 26.

91 Paul Andrew Hutton, *The Apache Wars*, 127.

92 John G. Bourke, *On the Border with Crook*, 105.

93 Paul Andrew Hutton, *The Apache Wars*, 128–29; David Roberts, *Once They Moved Like the Wind*, 60; Robert M. Utley, *Geronimo*, 69.

94 David Roberts, *Once They Moved Like the Wind*, 61; Paul Andrew Hutton, *The Apache Wars*, 129.

95 Eve Ball, *Indeh: An Apache Odyssey*, 27.

96 Edwin R. Sweeney, *Cochise, Chiricahua Apache Chief* (Norman: University of Oklahoma Press, 1991), 319; Robert M. Utley, *Geronimo*, 66; David Roberts, *Once They Moved Like the Wind*, 76–77.

97 David Roberts, *Once They Moved Like the Wind*, 87.

98 David Roberts, *Once They Moved Like the Wind*, 82–83.

99 Edwin R. Sweeney, *Cochise*, 328–29; Robert M. Utley, *Geronimo*, 59–60.

100 Harold H. Schuler, *Fort Pierre Chouteau*, 146; Robert M. Utley, *The Lance and the Shield*, 48.

101 Doreen Chaky, *Terrible Justice*, 82, 94–95, 107.

102 Ernie LaPointe, *Sitting Bull*, 41; Stanley Vestal, *Sitting Bull: Champion of the Sioux*, 317–18; M. W. Stirling, *Three Pictographic Autobiographies of Sitting Bull*, 9, 11, 12.

103 Doreen Chaky, *Terrible Justice*, 115.

104 Doreen Chaky, *Terrible Justice*, 115; Robert M. Utley, *The Lance and the Shield*, 48.

105 Doreen Chaky, *Terrible Justice*, 115–17.

106 Robert M. Utley, *The Lance and the Shield*, 49. There are several slightly different versions of the story of the deaths of these three men.

107 Doreen Chaky, *Terrible Justice*, 119–20.

108 James Crutchfield et al., *The Settlement of America*, vol. 2, 423; Doreen Chaky, *Terrible Justice*, 131; Robert M. Utley, *Frontiersmen in Blue*, 264.

109 Doreen Chaky, *Terrible Justice*, 132, 133; Robert M. Utley, *Frontiersmen in Blue*, 264–65, 268–69.

110 Doreen Chaky, *Terrible Justice*, 143–44; Robert G. Athearn, *Forts of the Upper Missouri*, 95; Robert M. Utley, *The Lance and the Shield*, 51.

111 Robert M. Utley, *Frontiersmen in Blue*, 270; Doreen Chaky, *Terrible Justice*, 136–37.

112 Robert M. Utley, *Frontiersmen in Blue*, 271.

113 Robert M. Utley, *Frontiersmen in Blue*, 271; Robert G. Athearn, *Forts of the Upper Missouri*, 103.

114 Robert G. Athearn, *Forts of the Upper Missouri*, 107; Harold H. Schuler, *Fort Sully: Guns at Sunset* (Vermillion: University of South Dakota Press, 1992), 27.

115 Robert M. Utley, *Frontiersmen in Blue*, 272–73; Robert M. Utley, *The Lance and the Shield*, 53; Dakota Wind (Goodhouse), "The Apple Creek Conflict, 150 Years Later," *Bismarck Tribune*, August 18, 2013, accessed August 22, 2019, bismarcktribune.com/news/local/bismarck/the-apple-creek-conflict-years-later/article_56cc0e3e-0687-11e3-9bf7-001a4bcf887a.html.

116 Stanley Vestal, *Sitting Bull: Champion of the Sioux*, 318; M. W. Stirling, *Three Pictographic Autobiographies of Sitting Bull*, 19.

117 Robert M. Utley, *Frontiersmen in Blue*, 273–74; Harold H. Schuler, *Fort Sully*, 28; Doreen Chaky, *Terrible Justice*, 173–75.

118 Harold H. Schuler, *Fort Sully*, 28–29.

119 Robert M. Utley, *The Lance and the Shield*, 53.

120 Robert M. Utley, *The Lance and the Shield*, 53–54.

121 Harold H. Schuler, *Fort Sully*, 29–30; Robert G. Athearn, *Forts of the Upper Missouri*, 133.

122 Kurt D. Bergemann, *Brackett's Battalion: Minnesota Cavalry in the Civil War and Dakota War* (St. Paul: Minnesota Historical Society Press, 2004), 102–03, 106; Robert M. Utley, *The Lance and the Shield*, 54.

123 Robert M. Utley, *The Lance and the Shield*, 55; Kurt D. Bergemann, *Brackett's Battalion*, 107.

124 Kurt D. Bergemann, *Brackett's Battalion*, 107, 108–09, 111; Robert M. Utley, *The Lance and the Shield*, 55.

125 Kurt D. Bergemann, *Brackett's Battalion*, 110–11; Stanley Vestal, *Sitting Bull: Champion of the Sioux*, 52–53.

126 Robert M. Utley, *The Lance and the Shield*, 56; Kurt D. Bergemann, *Brackett's Battalion*, 109, 111.

127 Kurt D. Bergemann, *Brackett's Battalion*, 111, 115; Robert M. Utley, *The Lance and the Shield*, 56.

128 Stanley Vestal, *Sitting Bull: Champion of the Sioux*, 55–56; Robert M. Utley, *The Lance and the Shield*, 57.

129 Robert M. Utley, *The Lance and the Shield*, 57; Kurt D. Bergemann, *Brackett's Battalion*, 117.

130 Robert M. Utley, *The Lance and the Shield*, 58.

131 Robert M. Utley, *The Lance and the Shield*, 58; Stanley Vestal, *Sitting Bull: Champion of the Sioux*, 58.

132 Robert M. Utley, *The Lance and the Shield*, 58–59; Stanley Vestal, *Sitting Bull: Champion of the Sioux*, 59.

133 Robert M. Utley, *The Lance and the Shield*, 59; Kurt D. Bergemann, *Brackett's Battalion*, 125.

134 Stanley Vestal, *Sitting Bull: Champion of the Sioux*, 61; Ernie LaPointe, *Sitting Bull*, 49.

135 Kurt D. Bergemann, *Brackett's Battalion*, 125–30.

136 Kurt D. Bergemann, *Brackett's Battalion*, 131, 133, 134, 135; Robert M. Utley, *The Lance and the Shield*, 59.

137 Robert M. Utley, *The Lance and the Shield*, 60.

138 Ibid.

139 Ibid.

140 Bill Markley, "Fort Dilts and Fanny's Bid for Freedom," *Wild West Magazine* (April 2014), 52–59.

141 Fanny Kelly, *Narrative of My Captivity Among the Sioux Indians* (New York: Barnes & Noble, 1994), 272; Stanley Vestal, *Sitting Bull: Champion of the Sioux*, 64.

142 Stanley Vestal, *Sitting Bull: Champion of the Sioux*, 64; Doreen Chaky, *Terrible Justice*, 238–39.

143 Fanny Kelly, *Narrative of My Captivity Among the Sioux Indians*, 191–92, 200–02, 273; Bill Markley, "Fort Dilts and Fanny's Bid for Freedom," 52–59; Stanley Vestal, *Sitting Bull: Champion of the Sioux*, 63; Robert M. Utley, *The Lance and the Shield*, 63.

144 Doreen Chaky, *Terrible Justice*, 257–58, 260; Robert G. Athearn, *Forts of the Upper Missouri*, 145–46; Robert M. Utley, *The Lance and the Shield*, 62, 65.

145 Dee Brown, *Bury My Heart at Wounded Knee: An Indian History of the American West* (New York: Henry Holt and Company, 1970), 90, 91; Stanley Vestal, *Sitting Bull: Champion of the Sioux*, 69; Robert M. Utley, *The Lance and the Shield*, 66.

146 Stanley Vestal, *Sitting Bull: Champion of the Sioux*, 72–73; Robert M. Utley, *The Lance and the Shield*, 66–67.

147 Robert M. Utley, *The Lance and the Shield*, 67; Stanley Vestal, *Sitting Bull: Champion of the Sioux*, 73.

148 Robert M. Utley, *The Lance and the Shield*, 68.

149 Robert M. Utley, *The Lance and the Shield*, 67–68; Stanley Vestal, *Sitting Bull: Champion of the Sioux*, 73–74.

150 Robert G. Athearn, *Forts of the Upper Missouri*, 191, 192; Robert M. Utley, *The Lance and the Shield*, 68.

151 Robert M. Utley, *Frontiersmen in Blue*, 308, 323–24.

152 Robert M. Utley, *The Lance and the Shield*, 69; Robert M. Utley, *Frontiersmen in Blue*, 328–29.

153 Robert M. Utley, *The Lance and the Shield*, 69; Robert M. Utley, *Frontiersmen in Blue*, 329–30.

154 Robert M. Utley, *The Lance and the Shield*, 71.

155 Robert M. Utley, *The Lance and the Shield*, 70, 100; Ernie LaPointe, *Sitting Bull*, 41.

156 Robert G. Athearn, *Forts of the Upper Missouri*, 227–28; Robert M. Utley, *The Lance and the Shield*, 71.

157 Robert G. Athearn, *Forts of the Upper Missouri*, 233–34; Robert M. Utley, *The Lance and the Shield*, 71–72.

158 Robert M. Utley, *The Lance and the Shield*, 72, 73.

159 James Crutchfield et al., *The Settlement of America*, vols. 1 and 2, 148, 405–06.

160 Robert M. Utley, *The Lance and the Shield*, 73; Robert G. Athearn, *Forts of the Upper Missouri*, 147, 238.

161 James Crutchfield et al., *The Settlement of America*, vol. 1, 202–03; "Transcript of Treaty of Fort Laramie (1868)," Our Documents, accessed August 25, 2019, https://www.ourdocuments.gov/doc.php?flash=false&doc=42&page=transcript.

162 James Crutchfield et al., *The Settlement of America*, vol. 1, 202–03; Robert M. Utley, *The Lance and the Shield*, 78.

163 Robert M. Utley, *The Lance and the Shield*, 78.

164 Robert M. Utley, *The Lance and the Shield*, 76, 79; Stanley Vestal, *Sitting Bull: Champion of the Sioux*, 98–100.

165 Robert M. Utley, *The Lance and the Shield*, 80–81; Stanley Vestal, *Sitting Bull: Champion of the Sioux*, 101, 105–108.

166 Stanley Vestal, *Sitting Bull: Champion of the Sioux*, 109.

167 Robert W. Larson, *Gall: Lakota War Chief* (Norman: University of Oklahoma Press, 2007), 70–71; Robert M. Utley, *The Lance and the Shield*, 81, 83–84.

168 Robert W. Larson, *Gall: Lakota War Chief*, 71–72.

169 Robert M. Utley, *The Lance and the Shield*, 84.

170 Joe De Barthe, *The Life and Adventures of Frank Grouard* (St. Joseph, MO: Combe Printing Company, 1894), 21–22, 75–76; Stanley Vestal, *Sitting Bull: Champion of the Sioux*, 111.

171 Joe De Barthe, *The Life and Adventures of Frank Grouard*, 77.

172 Joe De Barthe, *The Life and Adventures of Frank Grouard*, 77, 82–83, 93–94; Robert M. Utley, *The Lance and the Shield*, 124.

173 Robert M. Utley, *The Lance and the Shield*, 85, 86–87.

174 Stanley Vestal, *Sitting Bull: Champion of the Sioux*, 91; Ernie LaPointe, *Sitting Bull*, 50; Robert M. Utley, *The Lance and the Shield*, 87.

175 Robert M. Utley, *The Lance and the Shield*, 87, 88; Ernie LaPointe, *Sitting Bull*, 52.

176 Stanley Vestal, *Sitting Bull: Champion of the Sioux*, 92.

177 Stanley Vestal, *New Sources of Indian History*, 231–33; Robert M. Utley, *The Lance and the Shield*, 101.

178 Robert M. Utley, *The Lance and the Shield*, 98; Stanley Vestal, *Sitting Bull: Champion of the Sioux*, 113–14.

179 Joe De Barthe, *The Life and Adventures of Frank Grouard*, 94; Robert M. Utley, *The Lance and the Shield*, 98, 99; Stanley Vestal, *Sitting Bull: Champion of the Sioux*, 114–16.

180 Robert M. Utley, *The Lance and the Shield*, 99; Stanley Vestal, *Sitting Bull: Champion of the Sioux*, 118–19.

181 Robert M. Utley, *The Lance and the Shield*, 99; Stanley Vestal, *Sitting Bull: Champion of the Sioux*, 118.

182 Stanley Vestal, *Sitting Bull: Champion of the Sioux*, 120–23; Robert M. Utley, *The Lance and the Shield*, 99.

183 Stanley Vestal, *Sitting Bull: Champion of the Sioux*, 123; Robert M. Utley, *The Lance and the Shield*, 99–100.

184 Robert M. Utley, *The Lance and the Shield*, 100.

185 M. W. Stirling, *Three Pictographic Autobiographies of Sitting Bull*, 4–7, 12–26, 33; Robert M. Utley, *The Lance and the Shield*, 243; Stanley Vestal, *Sitting Bull: Champion of the Sioux*, 316–20.

186 Robert M. Utley, *The Lance and the Shield*, 90–91.

187 Ernie LaPointe, *Sitting Bull*, 42; Robert M. Utley, *The Lance and the Shield*, 100.

188 Robert M. Utley, *The Lance and the Shield*, 106.

189 M. John Lubetkin, *Road to War: The 1871 Yellowstone Surveys* (Norman: University of Oklahoma Press, 2016), 18, 21, 24.

190 M. John Lubetkin, *Road to War*, 124.

191 M. John Lubetkin, *Road to War*, 268–69.

192 M. John Lubetkin, *Road to War*, 216–17.

193 M. John Lubetkin, *Road to War*, 215, 216, 223–24; Robert M. Utley, *The Lance and the Shield*, 95.

SIDEBAR: 1868 FORT LARAMIE TREATY

194 John D. McDermott, *Red Cloud's War: The Bozeman Trail, 1866–1868*, vol. 2 (Norman: University of Oklahoma Press, 2010), 497, 499; Douglas McChristian, *Fort Laramie: Military Bastion of the High Plains* (Norman: University of Oklahoma Press, 2008), 305; James Crutchfield et al., *The Settlement of America*, vol. 1, 202–03.

195 James Crutchfield et al., *The Settlement of America*, vol. 1, 202–03; "Transcript of Treaty of Fort Laramie (1868)."

196 Ibid.

197 James Crutchfield et al., *The Settlement of America*, vol. 2, 570–71; John D. McDermott, *Red Cloud's War*, 497–98.

198 James Crutchfield et al., *The Settlement of America*, vol. 2, 571; John D. McDermott, *Red Cloud's War*, 498.

199 Robert M. Utley, *The Lance and the Shield*, 84, 85, 87.

CHAPTER 5: STRUGGLES TO CONTINUE
THEIR WAY OF LIFE, 1871–1876

1 Robert M. Utley, *Geronimo*, 57.

2 S. M. Barrett, ed., *Geronimo*, 139–40.

3 Doug Hocking, *Tom Jeffords, Friend of Cochise* (Guilford, CT: TwoDot, 2017), 101; Robert M. Utley, *Geronimo*, 60.

4 S. M. Barrett, ed., *Geronimo*, 140.

5 Robert M. Utley, *Geronimo*, 60; Edwin R. Sweeney, *Cochise*, 343–44.

6 Edwin R. Sweeney, *Cochise*, 344–46.

7 Edwin R. Sweeney, *Cochise*, 346; Paul Andrew Hutton, *The Apache Wars*, 152–53.

8 Paul Andrew Hutton, *The Apache Wars*, 154–55.

9 Edwin R. Sweeney, *Cochise*, 348.

10 Edwin R. Sweeney, *Cochise*, 352; Doug Hocking, *Tom Jeffords, Friend of Cochise*, 102–03.

11 Edwin R. Sweeney, *Cochise*, 352–53.

12 Edwin R. Sweeney, *Cochise*, 349, 352, 354, 455–456n10.

13 Edwin R. Sweeney, *Cochise*, 355.

14 Edwin R. Sweeney, *Cochise*, 356, 358, 359.

15 Oliver Otis Howard, *My Life and Experiences Among Our Hostile Indians* (Hartford, CT: A. D. Worthington & Company, 1907), 220; Oliver Otis Howard, *Famous Indian Chiefs I Have Known* (New York: The Century Co., 1908), 357. In *My Life and Experiences Among Our Hostile Indians*, Howard identifies the man who rides behind him to meet Sumner as Cochise's Indian interpreter, and in *Famous Indian Chiefs I Have Known*, Howard identifies him as Geronimo. It's interesting to speculate that Geronimo spoke and understood Spanish better than Cochise when considering the misunderstanding that led to the incident with Lieutenant George Bascom at Apache Pass in 1861.

16 Edwin R. Sweeney, *Cochise*, 357–62.

17 Edwin R. Sweeney, *Cochise*, 363–64; Oliver Otis Howard, *My Life and Experiences Among Our Hostile Indians*, 220; Oliver Otis Howard, *Famous Indian Chiefs I Have Known*, 357.

18 Oliver Otis Howard, *Famous Indian Chiefs I Have Known*, 357.

19 Edwin R. Sweeney, *Cochise*, 364–65; Doug Hocking, *Tom Jeffords, Friend of Cochise*, 107–08; Paul Andrew Hutton, *The Apache Wars*, 185.

20 Edwin R. Sweeney, *Cochise*, 366; Doug Hocking, *Tom Jeffords, Friend of Cochise*, 108.

21 S. M. Barrett, ed., *Geronimo*, 140.

22 Robert M. Utley, *Geronimo*, 69; Paul Andrew Hutton, *The Apache Wars*, 185–86.

23 David Roberts, *Once They Moved Like the Wind*, 136; Robert M. Utley, *Geronimo*, 75, 77, 288n5; Doug Hocking, *Tom Jeffords, Friend of Cochise*, 78; Edwin R. Sweeney, *Cochise*, 369.

24 Robert M. Utley, *Geronimo*, 72; Doug Hocking, *Tom Jeffords, Friend of Cochise*, 111.

25 Doug Hocking, *Tom Jeffords, Friend of Cochise*, 109, 111.

26 Angie Debo, *Geronimo*, 89, 90.

27 Robert M. Utley, *Geronimo*, 72; Edwin R. Sweeney, *From Cochise to Geronimo: The Chiricahua Apaches, 1874–1886* (Norman: University of Oklahoma Press, 2010), 16.

28 Robert M. Utley, *Geronimo*, 48, 73; Edwin R. Sweeney, *From Cochise to Geronimo*, 23, 24.

29 Edwin R. Sweeney, *From Cochise to Geronimo*, 24.

30 Edwin R. Sweeney, *From Cochise to Geronimo*, 25; S. M. Barrett, ed., *Geronimo*, 117.

31 Robert M. Utley, *Geronimo*, 74; Edwin R. Sweeney, *From Cochise to Geronimo*, 29.

32 S. M. Barrett, ed., *Geronimo*, 117–18.

33 Angie Debo, *Geronimo*, 91; Edwin R. Sweeney, *Cochise*, 395; Eve Ball, *Indeh: An Apache Odyssey*, 23; Robert M. Utley, *Geronimo*, 76; Edwin R. Sweeney, *From Cochise to Geronimo*, 30.

34 Robert M. Utley, *Geronimo*, 76–77; Edwin R. Sweeney, *From Cochise to Geronimo*, 33.

35 Robert M. Utley, *Geronimo*, 77; Paul Andrew Hutton, *The Apache Wars*, 214; Edwin R. Sweeney, *From Cochise to Geronimo*, 29–30, 33.

36 Robert M. Utley, *Geronimo*, 78; Angie Debo, *Geronimo*, 92; Paul Andrew Hutton, *The Apache Wars*, 212.

37 S. M. Barrett, ed., *Geronimo*, 118.

38 Angie Debo, *Geronimo*, 95; Robert W. Larson, *Red Cloud: Warrior-Statesman of the Lakota Sioux* (Norman: University of Oklahoma Press, 1997), 186.

39 Robert M. Utley, *Geronimo*, 77; Edwin R. Sweeney, *From Cochise to Geronimo*, 42–44.

40 Robert M. Utley, *Geronimo*, 79.

41 S. M. Barrett, ed., *Geronimo*, 118; Robert M. Utley, *Geronimo*, 85; Edwin R. Sweeney, *From Cochise to Geronimo*, 47.

42 S. M. Barrett, ed., *Geronimo*, 118.

43 S. M. Barrett, ed., *Geronimo*, 118–19.

44 Robert M. Utley, *Geronimo*, 78–79.

45 Robert M. Utley, *Geronimo*, 79; Doug Hocking, *Tom Jeffords, Friend of Cochise*, 78, 124, 125; Fred G. Hughes, "Geronimo: Some Facts Concerning the Wily Old Apache Chief," *Arizona Daily Star*, March 8, 1890.

46 Robert M. Utley, *Geronimo*, 79, 80.

47 Edwin R. Sweeney, *From Cochise to Geronimo*, 52; Robert M. Utley, *Geronimo*, 80; Woodworth Clum, *Apache Agent: The Story of John P. Clum* (Lincoln: University of Nebraska Press, 1963), 177; Paul Andrew Hutton, *The Apache Wars*, 217.

48 Woodworth Clum, *Apache Agent*, 180; Paul Andrew Hutton, *The Apache Wars*, 217; Robert M. Utley, *Geronimo*, 85.

49 Robert M. Utley, *Geronimo*, 85; Edwin R. Sweeney, *From Cochise to Geronimo*, 58.

50 Edwin R. Sweeney, *From Cochise to Geronimo*, 58–59, 180; Paul Andrew Hutton, *The Apache Wars*, 218; Woodworth Clum, *Apache Agent*, 180.

51 Robert G. Athearn, *Forts of the Upper Missouri*, 261, 277; Harold H. Schuler, *Fort Sully*, 31.

52 M. John Lubetkin, *Before Custer: Surveying the Yellowstone, 1872* (Norman: University of Oklahoma Press, 2015), 22, 23–24.

53 M. John Lubetkin, *Before Custer*, 25, 35, 37–38.

54 Ernie LaPointe, *Sitting Bull*, 42.

55 M. John Lubetkin, *Before Custer*, 22, 60–61; Keith Wheeler, *The Railroaders* (New York: Time-Life Books, 1973), 218.

56 Robert G. Athearn, *Forts of the Upper Missouri*, 282–83.

57 Robert M. Utley, *The Lance and the Shield*, 95–96.

58 M. John Lubetkin, *Before Custer*, 42, 65, 66, 196.

59 M. John Lubetkin, *Before Custer*, 78–79, 80; Robert M. Utley, *The Lance and the Shield*, 107.

60 M. John Lubetkin, *Before Custer*, 105; Robert M. Utley, *The Lance and the Shield*, 107.

61 Ibid.

62 M. John Lubetkin, *Before Custer*, 134; Robert M. Utley, *The Lance and the Shield*, 108.

63 Stanley Vestal, *Sitting Bull: Champion of the Sioux*, 126–27; Ernie LaPointe, *Sitting Bull*, 55; Robert M. Utley, *The Lance and the Shield*, 108.

64 Stanley Vestal, *Sitting Bull: Champion of the Sioux*, 128; Ernie LaPointe, *Sitting Bull*, 56; Robert M. Utley, *The Lance and the Shield*, 108.

65 Stanley Vestal, *Sitting Bull: Champion of the Sioux*, 128.

66 Stanley Vestal, *Sitting Bull: Champion of the Sioux*, 128–29; Ernie LaPointe, *Sitting Bull*, 56.

67 Stanley Vestal, *Sitting Bull: Champion of the Sioux*, 129.

68 Stanley Vestal, *Sitting Bull: Champion of the Sioux*, 130; Robert M. Utley, *The Lance and the Shield*, 109.

69 M. John Lubetkin, *Before Custer*, 136; Robert M. Utley, *The Lance and the Shield*, 109.

70 M. John Lubetkin, *Before Custer*, 108, 138.

71 Robert W. Larson, *Gall: Lakota War Chief*, 84.

72 Robert W. Larson, *Gall: Lakota War Chief*, 83–84; M. John Lubetkin, *Before Custer*, 125–26.

73 M. John Lubetkin, *Before Custer*, 126.

74 Ibid.

75 M. John Lubetkin, *Before Custer*, 107–08, 117, 131.

76 M. John Lubetkin, *Before Custer*, 196, 236–37; Robert M. Utley, *The Lance and the Shield*, 111.

77 Joe De Barthe, *The Life and Adventures of Frank Grouard*, 106; Robert M. Utley, *The Lance and the Shield*, 102.

78 Robert M. Utley, *The Lance and the Shield*, 96–97.

79 Joe De Barthe, *The Life and Adventures of Frank Grouard*, 106–07; Robert M. Utley, *The Lance and the Shield*, 102–03.

80 Robert M. Utley, *The Lance and the Shield*, 103.

81 Robert M. Utley, *The Lance and the Shield*, 104.

82 There is no information as to whether this happened before or after the fight with the Métis.

83 Joe De Barthe, *The Life and Adventures of Frank Grouard*, 109–11.

84 Joe De Barthe, *The Life and Adventures of Frank Grouard*, 112.

85 Joe De Barthe, *The Life and Adventures of Frank Grouard*, 112–13, 117.

86 M. John Lubetkin, *Custer and the 1873 Yellowstone Survey: A Documentary History* (Norman: University of Oklahoma Press, 2013), 27.

87 M. John Lubetkin, *Custer and the 1873 Yellowstone Survey*, 71–72.

88 Robert M. Utley, *The Lance and the Shield*, 111.

89 M. John Lubetkin, *Custer and the 1873 Yellowstone Survey*, 29, 30, 75, 106, 108, 115; Jeffery D. Wert, *Custer: The Controversial Life of George Armstrong Custer* (New York: Simon & Schuster, 1996), 303.

90 Robert M. Utley, *The Lance and the Shield*, 112; M. John Lubetkin, *Custer and the 1873 Yellowstone Survey*, 219.

91 M. John Lubetkin, *Custer and the 1873 Yellowstone Survey*, 219, 225–30; Robert M. Utley, *The Lance and the Shield*, 112.

92 M. John Lubetkin, *Custer and the 1873 Yellowstone Survey*, 230–32, 234.

93 M. John Lubetkin, *Custer and the 1873 Yellowstone Survey*, 237.

94 Robert M. Utley, *The Lance and the Shield*, 112.

95 Robert M. Utley, *The Lance and the Shield*, 113–14.

96 M. John Lubetkin, *Custer and the 1873 Yellowstone Survey*, 250.

97 M. John Lubetkin, *Custer and the 1873 Yellowstone Survey*, 255–56, 259; Joe De Barthe, *The Life and Adventures of Frank Grouard*, 115–16.

98 Robert M. Utley, *The Lance and the Shield*, 114.

99 M. John Lubetkin, *Before Custer*, 23, 281–82; M. John Lubetkin, *Custer and the 1873 Yellowstone Survey*, 16, 314.

100 M. John Lubetkin, *Custer and the 1873 Yellowstone Survey*, 315.

101 Robert M. Utley, *The Lance and the Shield*, 116.

102 Robert M. Utley, *The Lance and the Shield*, 118.

103 Robert M. Utley, *The Lance and the Shield*, 118, 119.

104 Robert M. Utley, *The Lance and the Shield*, 117.

105 James Crutchfield et al., *The Settlement of America*, vol. 1, 158–59; Bill Markley, "Custer's Gold," *True West Magazine* (April 2018), 70.

106 Ibid.

107 Paul Horsted, Ernest Grafe, and Jon Nelson, *Crossing the Plains with Custer* (Custer, SD: Golden Valley Press, 2009), 12, 21; James Crutchfield et al., *The Settlement of America*, vol. 1, 158–59.

108 James Crutchfield et al., *The Settlement of America*, vol. 1, 158–59; Paul Horsted et al., *Crossing the Plains with Custer*, 24, 146; Paul Horsted and Ernest Grafe, *Exploring with Custer: The 1874 Black Hills Expedition* (Custer, SD: Golden Valley Press, 2002), 30.

109 Herbert Krause and Gary D. Olson, *Prelude to Glory: A Newspaper Accounting of Custer's 1874 Expedition to the Black Hills* (Sioux Falls, SD: Brevet Press, 1974), 26; James Crutchfield et al., *The Settlement of America*, vol. 1, 158–59; Paul Horsted et al., *Exploring with Custer*, 87–89.

110 James Crutchfield et al., *The Settlement of America*, vol. 1, 158–59; Bill Markley, "Custer's Gold," 74.

111 James Crutchfield et al., *The Settlement of America*, vol. 1, 158–59; Robert M. Utley, *The Lance and the Shield*, 116.

112 Robert M. Utley, *The Lance and the Shield*, 118.

113 Robert M. Utley, *The Lance and the Shield*, 117.

114 Robert M. Utley, *The Lance and the Shield*, 122–23.

115 Robert M. Utley, *The Lance and the Shield*, 119.

116 Robert M. Utley, *The Lance and the Shield*, 119–20.

117 Robert W. Larson, *Red Cloud*, 186.

118 Joe De Barthe, *The Life and Adventures of Frank Grouard*, 172–73; Thomas Powers, *The Killing of Crazy Horse* (New York: Alfred A. Knopf, 2010), 90–92; Robert M. Utley, *The Lance and the Shield*, 124.

119 Joe De Barthe, *The Life and Adventures of Frank Grouard*, 174.

120 Joe De Barthe, *The Life and Adventures of Frank Grouard*, 175.

121 Robert W. Larson, *Red Cloud*, 186–87.

122 Robert W. Larson, *Red Cloud*, 188.

123 Robert W. Larson, *Red Cloud*, 188–89, 190–91.

124 Robert W. Larson, *Red Cloud*, 193.

125 Robert W. Larson, *Red Cloud*, 191–92.

126 Robert W. Larson, *Red Cloud*, 194.

127 Robert W. Larson, *Red Cloud*, 195.

128 Paul Andrew Hutton, *Phil Sheridan and His Army* (Norman: University of Oklahoma Press, 1985), 298–99.

129 Paul Andrew Hutton, *Phil Sheridan and His Army*, 300.

130 Paul Andrew Hutton, *Phil Sheridan and His Army*, 301.

131 Stanley Vestal, *New Sources of Indian History*, 183; Robert M. Utley, *The Lance and the Shield*, 101.

132 Paul Andrew Hutton, *Phil Sheridan and His Army*, 302; Robert M. Utley, *The Lance and the Shield*, 128.

133 Stanley Vestal, *Sitting Bull: Champion of the Sioux*, 139.

134 Robert M. Utley, *The Lance and the Shield*, 128.

135 Paul Andrew Hutton, *Phil Sheridan and His Army*, 302.

136 Paul Andrew Hutton, *Phil Sheridan and His Army*, 302; Robert M. Utley, *The Lance and the Shield*, 135.

137 Paul Andrew Hutton, *Phil Sheridan and His Army*, 303.

138 Joe De Barthe, *The Life and Adventures of Frank Grouard*, 185–87.

139 Joe De Barthe, *The Life and Adventures of Frank Grouard*, 189–90; Paul Andrew Hutton, *Phil Sheridan and His Army*, 303.

140 John G. Bourke, *On the Border with Crook*, 273, 274; Joe De Barthe, *The Life and Adventures of Frank Grouard*, 192; Paul Andrew Hutton, *Phil Sheridan and His Army*, 303; Thomas Powers, *The Killing of Crazy Horse*, 147.

141 John G. Bourke, *On the Border with Crook*, 275, 276–78; Paul Andrew Hutton, *Phil Sheridan and His Army*, 303.

142 John G. Bourke, *On the Border with Crook*, 278–79, states: "As was whispered among the men, one of our poor soldiers fell alive into the enemy's hands and was cut limb from limb. I do not state this fact of my own knowledge, and I can only say that I believe it to be true."

143 John G. Bourke, *On the Border with Crook*, 278; Paul Andrew Hutton, *Phil Sheridan and His Army*, 303; Thomas Powers, *The Killing of Crazy Horse*, 148.

144 John G. Bourke, *On the Border with Crook*, 279, 280; Paul Andrew Hutton, *Phil Sheridan and His Army*, 303.

145 Thomas Powers, *The Killing of Crazy Horse*, 149–50.

146 Thomas Powers, *The Killing of Crazy Horse*, 150.

SIDEBAR: LAKOTA SUN DANCE

147 Raymond J. DeMallie, *Plains*, 807; Ernie LaPointe, *Sitting Bull*, 44; Robert M. Utley, *The Lance and the Shield*, 8, 31–32.

148 Ernie LaPointe, *Sitting Bull*, 44–45; Editors of Time-Life Books, *The Buffalo Hunters* (Alexandria, VA: Time-Life Books, 1993), 169, 170.

149 Editors of Time-Life Books, *The Buffalo Hunters*, 172; Ernie LaPointe, *Sitting Bull*, 46; Robert M. Utley, *The Lance and the Shield*, 32, 33.

CHAPTER 6: LITTLE BIGHORN, SUMMER 1876

1 Robert M. Utley, *The Lance and the Shield*, 130.

2 Robert M. Utley, *The Lance and the Shield*, 132.

3 Stanley Vestal, *Sitting Bull: Champion of the Sioux*, 143; Robert M. Utley, *The Lance and the Shield*, 133.

4 Ernie LaPointe, *Sitting Bull*, 61–62.

5 Robert M. Utley, *The Lance and the Shield*, 133, 134.

6 Robert M. Utley, *The Lance and the Shield*, 135.

7 Paul Andrew Hutton, *Phil Sheridan and His Army*, 305, 311.

8 Paul Andrew Hutton, *Phil Sheridan and His Army*, 306.

9 Paul Andrew Hutton, *Phil Sheridan and His Army*, 306, 308.

10 Paul Andrew Hutton, *Phil Sheridan and His Army*, 310, 311.

11 James Donovan, *A Terrible Glory: Custer and the Little Bighorn: The Last Great Battle of the American West* (New York: Little, Brown & Company, 2008), 117–18; Paul Andrew Hutton, *Phil Sheridan and His Army*, 311; Robert M. Utley, *The Lance and the Shield*, 311.

12 Elizabeth B. Custer, *"Boots and Saddles," or, Life in Dakota with General Custer* (Norman: University of Oklahoma Press, 1961), 218.

13 Robert M. Utley, *The Lance and the Shield*, 136.

14 Ibid.

15 John G. Bourke, *On the Border with Crook*, 290–91; Thomas Powers, *The Killing of Crazy Horse*, 163, 193; Paul Andrew Hutton, *Phil Sheridan and His Army*, 312.

16 Stanley Vestal, *Sitting Bull: Champion of the Sioux*, 141–42, 145; Robert M. Utley, *The Lance and the Shield*, 134; Ernie LaPointe, *Sitting Bull*, 62.

17 Ernie LaPointe, *Sitting Bull*, 62.

18 Stanley Vestal, *Sitting Bull: Champion of the Sioux*, 148; Robert M. Utley, *The Lance and the Shield*, 137.

19 Stanley Vestal, *Sitting Bull: Champion of the Sioux*, 149.

20 Robert M. Utley, *The Lance and the Shield*, 137; Stanley Vestal, *Sitting Bull: Champion of the Sioux*, 149.

21 Ernie LaPointe, *Sitting Bull*, 63, 64; Stanley Vestal, *Sitting Bull: Champion of the Sioux*, 150; Robert M. Utley, *The Lance and the Shield*, 137, 138.

22 Robert M. Utley, *The Lance and the Shield*, 138; Stanley Vestal, *Sitting Bull: Champion of the Sioux*, 150; Ernie LaPointe, *Sitting Bull*, 64.

23 Robert M. Utley, *The Lance and the Shield*, 138.

24 John G. Bourke, *On the Border with Crook*, 296; Robert M. Utley, *The Lance and the Shield*, 135.

25 Robert M. Utley, *The Lance and the Shield*, 134, 136, 139, 147.

26 Joe De Barthe, *The Life and Adventures of Frank Grouard*, 223.

27 Robert M. Utley, *The Lance and the Shield*, 139–40; John G. Bourke, *On the Border with Crook*, 303, 305; James Donovan, *A Terrible Glory*, 146.

28 James Donovan, *A Terrible Glory*, 147, 149; Robert M. Utley, *The Lance and the Shield*, 140.

29 Oliver Knight, *Following the Indian Wars: The Story of the Newspaper Correspondents Among the Indian Campaigners* (Norman: University of Oklahoma Press, 1960), 184; Paul L. Hedren, *Rosebud, June 17, 1876: Prelude to the Little Big Horn* (Norman: University of Oklahoma Press, 2019), 161–64; James Donovan, *A Terrible Glory*, 149–50. *1876*

30 James Donovan, *A Terrible Glory*, 150; Paul L. Hedren, *Rosebud, June 17, 1876*, 165.

31 Paul L. Hedren, *Rosebud, June 17, 1876*, 275, 277; Stanley Vestal, *Sitting Bull: Champion of the Sioux*, 153.

32 Robert M. Utley, *The Lance and the Shield*, 141.

33 Paul L. Hedren, *Rosebud, June 17, 1876*, 186.

34 Thomas Powers, *The Killing of Crazy Horse*, 184–85; Robert M. Utley, *The Lance and the Shield*, 141; Paul L. Hedren, *Rosebud, June 17, 1876*, 213–14.

35 Thomas Powers, *The Killing of Crazy Horse*, 184–85, 187, 188; James Donovan, *A Terrible Glory*, 150; Paul L. Hedren, *Rosebud, June 17, 1876*, 220–21.

36 James Donovan, *A Terrible Glory*, 150, 152.

37 Thomas Powers, *The Killing of Crazy Horse*, 185, 189.

38 Robert M. Utley, *The Lance and the Shield*, 141, 142–43; Paul Andrew Hutton, *Phil Sheridan and His Army*, 313; James Donovan, *A Terrible Glory*, 153; Thomas Powers, *The Killing of Crazy Horse*, 192; John G. Bourke, *On the Border with Crook*, 325, 327, 329.

39 Paul L. Hedren, *Rosebud, June 17, 1876*, 279–80; James Donovan, *A Terrible Glory*, 151.

40 Paul L. Hedren, *Rosebud, June 17, 1876*, 345; Robert M. Utley, *The Lance and the Shield*, 142.

41 Robert M. Utley, *The Lance and the Shield*, 142.

42 Paul L. Hedren, *Rosebud, June 17, 1876*, 347; Robert M. Utley, *The Lance and the Shield*, 143; Stanley Vestal, *Sitting Bull: Champion of the Sioux*, 154.

43 Stanley Vestal, *Sitting Bull: Champion of the Sioux*, 156; Robert M. Utley, *The Lance and the Shield*, 143–44.

44 Robert M. Utley, *The Lance and the Shield*, 144; Ernie LaPointe, *Sitting Bull*, 67.

45 Robert M. Utley, *The Lance and the Shield*, 144.

46 Gregory F. Michno, *Lakota Noon: The Indian Narrative of Custer's Defeat* (Missoula, MT: Mountain Press Publishing Company, 1997), 20, 23, 24, 31, 32.

47 Robert M. Utley, *The Lance and the Shield*, 148.

48 Alfred H. Terry, *The Field Diary of General Alfred H. Terry: The Yellowstone Expedition—1876*, 2nd ed. (Bellevue, NE: Old Army Press, 1970), 15, 21; James Donovan, *A Terrible Glory*, 160.

49 James Donovan, *A Terrible Glory*, 161, 162, 168.

50 Alfred H. Terry, *The Field Diary of General Alfred H. Terry*, 23; Bill Markley and Kellen Cutsforth, *Old West Showdown: Two Authors Wrangle over the Truth about the Mythic Old West* (Guilford, CT: TwoDot, 2018), 65, 67; James Donovan, *A Terrible Glory*, 181, 190.

51 Bill Markley and Kellen Cutsforth, *Old West Showdown*, 67–68.

52 Bill Markley and Kellen Cutsforth, *Old West Showdown*, 68.

53 There are varying accounts as to what Sitting Bull did or did not do during the fight. Gregory Michno in his *Lakota Noon* shows there were plenty of eyewitnesses placing Sitting Bull in the thick of the action, and for the most part, I follow their narratives of his actions.

54 David Humphreys Miller, *Custer's Fall: The Indian Side of the Story* (Lincoln: University of Nebraska Press, 1957), 88–89; Gregory F. Michno, *Lakota Noon*, 39, 46, 48, 57–59; Robert M. Utley, *The Lance and the Shield*, 150; Stanley Vestal, *Sitting Bull: Champion of the Sioux*, 161.

55 Gregory F. Michno, *Lakota Noon*, 39–40, 41, 57; David Humphreys Miller, *Custer's Fall*, 89; Robert M. Utley, *The Lance and the Shield*, 150.

56 Blue Mountain was the son of Sitting Bull's wife Seen-by-her-Nation, who had been a widow before marrying Sitting Bull; Robert M. Utley, *The Lance and the Shield*, 100.

57 Gregory F. Michno, *Lakota Noon*, 39, 46; David Humphreys Miller, *Custer's Fall*, 89–90; Robert M. Utley, *The Lance and the Shield*, 100–101, 151.

58 James Donovan, *A Terrible Glory*, 235; David Humphreys Miller, *Custer's Fall*, 40–41; Stanley Vestal, *Sitting Bull: Champion of the Sioux*, 162, 163.

59 James Donovan, *A Terrible Glory*, 235, 236; Gregory F. Michno, *Lakota Noon*, 51.

60 James Donovan, *A Terrible Glory*, 137.

61 James Donovan, *A Terrible Glory*, 237, 238, 240–41.

62 Stanley Vestal, *Sitting Bull: Champion of the Sioux*, 164; James Donovan, *A Terrible Glory*, 240–41, 242, 246–49.

63 James Donovan, *A Terrible Glory*, 248.

64 Gregory F. Michno, *Lakota Noon*, 84–85.

65 Lewis F. Crawford, *Rekindling Camp Fires* (Bismarck, ND: Capital Books, 1926), 155; James Donovan, *A Terrible Glory*, 243–44.

66 Gregory F. Michno, *Lakota Noon*, 89, 127.

67 James Donovan, *A Terrible Glory*, 263; Gregory F. Michno, *Lakota Noon*, 106.

68 James Donovan, *A Terrible Glory*, 263; Gregory F. Michno, *Lakota Noon*, 105.

69 David Humphreys Miller, *Custer's Fall*, 159–60; Robert M. Utley, *The Lance and the Shield*, 159; Stanley Vestal, *Sitting Bull: Champion of the Sioux*, 173.

70 David Humphreys Miller, *Custer's Fall*, 189; Stanley Vestal, *Sitting Bull: Champion of the Sioux*, 176; Robert M. Utley, *The Lance and the Shield*, 160; James Donovan, *A Terrible Glory*, 301–04.

71 Robert M. Utley, *The Lance and the Shield*, 160, 161.

72 Robert M. Utley, *The Lance and the Shield*, 161; Gregory F. Michno, *Lakota Noon*, 148; David Humphreys Miller, *Custer's Fall*, 176.

CHAPTER 7: GERONIMO GOES TO SAN CARLOS AND SITTING BULL GOES TO CANADA, 1876–1878

1 Edwin R. Sweeney, *From Cochise to Geronimo*, 52; Robert M. Utley, *Geronimo*, 80; Woodworth Clum, *Apache Agent*, 177; Paul Andrew Hutton, *The Apache Wars*, 217.

2 Edwin R. Sweeney, *From Cochise to Geronimo*, 58–59, 180; Paul Andrew Hutton, *The Apache Wars*, 218; Angie Debo, *Geronimo*, 99.

3 Edwin R. Sweeney, *From Cochise to Geronimo*, 59; Robert M. Utley, *Geronimo*, 85.

4 Robert M. Utley, *Geronimo*, 86; Edwin R. Sweeney, *From Cochise to Geronimo*, 59, 66.

5 Editorial, "San Carlos," *Arizona Citizen*, June 24, 1876.

6 Angie Debo, *Geronimo*, 98–99; Robert M. Utley, *Geronimo*, 86.

7 Robert M. Utley, *Geronimo*, 86.

8 Edwin R. Sweeney, *From Cochise to Geronimo*, 75, 76; Robert M. Utley, *Geronimo*, 86–87.

9 Edwin R. Sweeney, *From Cochise to Geronimo*, 78; Robert M. Utley, *Geronimo*, 87.

10 Berndt Kühn, *Chronicles of War*, 210–11; Edwin R. Sweeney, *From Cochise to Geronimo*, 79.

11 Edwin R. Sweeney, *From Cochise to Geronimo*, 79, 81.

12 Edwin R. Sweeney, *From Cochise to Geronimo*, 81.

13 Edwin R. Sweeney, *From Cochise to Geronimo*, 67–68.

14 Woodworth Clum, *Apache Agent*, 210, 215; Edwin R. Sweeney, *From Cochise to Geronimo*, 82.

15 Edwin R. Sweeney, *From Cochise to Geronimo*, 82.

16 Woodworth Clum, *Apache Agent*, 215, 216; Edwin R. Sweeney, *From Cochise to Geronimo*, 82.

17 Woodworth Clum, *Apache Agent*, 215; Edwin R. Sweeney, *From Cochise to Geronimo*, 82.

18 S. M. Barrett, ed., *Geronimo*, 143; Edwin R. Sweeney, *From Cochise to Geronimo*, 83.

19 Woodworth Clum, *Apache Agent*, 218–19, 223–24; David Roberts, *Once They Moved Like the Wind*, 165–66; Paul Andrew Hutton, *The Apache Wars*, 223.

20 Woodworth Clum, *Apache Agent*, 227; Edwin R. Sweeney, *From Cochise to Geronimo*, 83, 84.

21 Paul Andrew Hutton, *The Apache Wars*, 224; Robert M. Utley, *Geronimo*, 91; Edwin R. Sweeney, *From Cochise to Geronimo*, 83–84.

22 Woodworth Clum, *Apache Agent*, 249, 250.

23 Paul Andrew Hutton, *The Apache Wars*, 224; Edwin R. Sweeney, *From Cochise to Geronimo*, 86–87.

24 Woodworth Clum, *Apache Agent*, 228; S. M. Barrett, ed., *Geronimo*, 144.

25 Robert M. Utley, *Geronimo*, 92–94; S. M. Barrett, ed., *Geronimo*, 144.

26 Jason Betzinez, *I Fought with Geronimo* (Lincoln: University of Nebraska Press, 1959), 46; Robert M. Utley, *Geronimo*, 95.

27 Edwin R. Sweeney, *From Cochise to Geronimo*, 93–94, 105; Robert M. Utley, *Geronimo*, 94–95.

28 Edwin R. Sweeney, *From Cochise to Geronimo*, 95, 98; Robert M. Utley, *Geronimo*, 94, 95.

29 Robert M. Utley, *Geronimo*, 95–96.

30 Robert M. Utley, *Geronimo*, 96; Edwin R. Sweeney, *From Cochise to Geronimo*, 91–92.

31 Edwin R. Sweeney, *From Cochise to Geronimo*, 68, 113, 117–18; Jason Betzinez, *I Fought with Geronimo*, 47; Robert M. Utley, *Geronimo*, 96.

32 Edwin R. Sweeney, *From Cochise to Geronimo*, 117–18.

33 Jason Betzinez, *I Fought with Geronimo*, 47–48; Robert M. Utley, *Geronimo*, 97; Paul Andrew Hutton, *The Apache Wars*, 234; Edwin R. Sweeney, *From Cochise to Geronimo*, 118–19.

34 Jason Betzinez, *I Fought with Geronimo*, 47; Robert M. Utley, *Geronimo*, 96–97; Edwin R. Sweeney, *From Cochise to Geronimo*, 119.

35 Gregory F. Michno, *Lakota Noon*, 301; Robert M. Utley, *The Lance and the Shield*, 165.

36 Gregory F. Michno, *Lakota Noon*, 301; Robert M. Utley, *The Lance and the Shield*, 165–66; Stanley Vestal, *Sitting Bull: Champion of the Sioux*, 184.

37 John S. Gray, "What Made Johnnie Bruguier Run?" *Montana: The Magazine of Western History*, vol. 14, no. 2 (Spring 1964), 42–43; Stanley Vestal, *Sitting Bull: Champion of the Sioux*, 183; Robert M. Utley, *The Lance and the Shield*, 168–69.

38 James Donovan, *A Terrible Glory*, 306, 308–11, 312–13.

39 Jerome A. Green, *Slim Buttes, 1876: An Episode of the Great Sioux War* (Norman: University of Oklahoma Press, 1982), 12–13, 15, 20, 25.

40 Paul L. Hedren, *First Scalp for Custer* (Lincoln: Nebraska State Historical Society, 2005), 25, 28.

41 John G. Bourke, *On the Border with Crook*, 350–51; Jerome A. Green, *Slim Buttes, 1876*, 27, 28–29, 30–31.

42 Jerome A. Green, *Slim Buttes, 1876*, 28, 31, 34; Robert M. Utley, *The Lance and the Shield*, 166.

43 Jerome A. Green, *Slim Buttes, 1876*, 32, 35.

44 Jerome A. Green, *Slim Buttes, 1876*, 35–37.

45 Jerome A. Green, *Slim Buttes, 1876*, 42, 45.

46 Jerome A. Green, *Slim Buttes, 1876*, 46, 48.

47 Jerome A. Green, *Slim Buttes, 1876*, 51, 54.

48 Oliver Knight, *Following the Indian Wars*, 274; Jerome A. Green, *Slim Buttes, 1876*, 60.

49 Oliver Knight, *Following the Indian Wars*, 273, 274; Jerome A. Green, *Slim Buttes, 1876*, 60, 63.

50 Oliver Knight, *Following the Indian Wars*, 275–76; Thomas Powers, *The Killing of Crazy Horse*, 213; Jerome A. Green, *Slim Buttes, 1876*, 134.

51 Oliver Knight, *Following the Indian Wars*, 274–75; Thomas Powers, *The Killing of Crazy Horse*, 212; Jerome A. Green, *Slim Buttes, 1876*, 61, 63, 68.

52 Stanley Vestal, *Sitting Bull: Champion of the Sioux*, 183–85; Robert M. Utley, *The Lance and the Shield*, 166, 170, 365n3. The name of this son of Sitting Bull and who his mother was are unknown.

53 Jerome A. Green, *Slim Buttes, 1876*, 70.

54 John G. Bourke, *On the Border with Crook*, 375; Thomas Powers, *The Killing of Crazy Horse*, 213; Jerome A. Green, *Slim Buttes, 1876*, 128–29.

55 Jerome A. Green, *Slim Buttes, 1876*, 81, 82; Stanley Vestal, *Sitting Bull: Champion of the Sioux*, 186.

56 Jerome A. Green, *Slim Buttes, 1876*, 86–87; Stanley Vestal, *Sitting Bull: Champion of the Sioux*, 187.

57 Jerome A. Green, *Slim Buttes, 1876*, 90, 131. In Joe De Barthe's book *The Life and Times of Frank Grouard*, Grouard never identified the attackers at Slim Buttes. After the battle of the Rosebud, John Finerty, correspondent for the *Chicago Times*, later wrote that he saw an Indian signaling with a mirror during the fight and felt sure it was Crazy Horse. At the Slim Buttes fight, Finerty claimed he saw "Crazy Horse" again. For two hours, he saw an Indian on a white horse leading and encouraging the warriors. Finerty wrote that it was "doubtless Crazy Horse himself." Tom Powers, *The Killing of Crazy Horse*, 185, 214.

58 Jerome A. Green, *Slim Buttes, 1876*, 90, 92.

59 Mac H. Abrams, *Sioux War Dispatches: Reports from the Field, 1876–1877* (Yardley, PA: Westholme Publishing, 2012), 247; John G. Bourke, *On the Border with Crook*, 375; Jerome A. Green, *Slim Buttes, 1876*, 92.

60 Paul L. Hedren, *Ho! For the Black Hills: Captain Jack Crawford Reports the Black Hills Gold Rush and the Great Sioux War* (Pierre: South Dakota State Historical Society Press, 2011), 213.

61 Mac H. Abrams, *Sioux War Dispatches*, 251; Jerome A. Green, *Slim Buttes, 1876*, 130.

62 Mac H. Abrams, *Sioux War Dispatches*, 247–48, 389n68; Joe De Barthe, *The Life and Adventures of Frank Grouard*, 310.

63 Tom Powers, *The Killing of Crazy Horse*, 215–16; Jerome A. Green, *Slim Buttes, 1876*, 96, 134; Mac H. Abrams, *Sioux War Dispatches*, 249; Stanley Vestal, *Sitting Bull: Champion of the Sioux*, 187.

64 Jerome A. Green, *Slim Buttes, 1876*, 96; Stanley Vestal, *Sitting Bull: Champion of the Sioux*, 187.

65 Stanley Vestal, *Sitting Bull: Champion of the Sioux*, 188.

66 Stanley Vestal, *Sitting Bull: Champion of the Sioux*, 187–88.

67 Stanley Vestal, *Sitting Bull: Champion of the Sioux*, 189.

68 Jerome A. Green, *Slim Buttes, 1876*, 108; Paul Andrew Hutton, *Phil Sheridan and His Army*, 323.

69 Jerome A. Green, *Slim Buttes, 1876*, 111–13, 115.

70 Robert M. Utley, *The Lance and the Shield*, 168, 169.

71 Jerome A. Green, *Slim Buttes, 1876*, 31; Cyrus Townsend Brady, *Indian Fights and Fighters* (Lincoln: University of Nebraska Press, 1971), 319.

72 Stanley Vestal, *Sitting Bull: Champion of the Sioux*, 190; Robert M. Utley, *The Lance and the Shield*, 169.

73 Robert M. Utley, *The Lance and the Shield*, 169.

74 Stanley Vestal, *Sitting Bull: Champion of the Sioux*, 191.

75 Robert M. Utley, *The Lance and the Shield*, 169.

76 Cyrus Townsend Brady, *Indian Fights and Fighters*, 321.

77 Cyrus Townsend Brady, *Indian Fights and Fighters*, 322.

78 Robert M. Utley, *The Lance and the Shield*, 170.

79 Cyrus Townsend Brady, *Indian Fights and Fighters*, 322; Robert M. Utley, *The Lance and the Shield*, 170.

80 Cyrus Townsend Brady, *Indian Fights and Fighters*, 322.

81 R. Eli Paul, ed., *The Frontier Army: Episodes from Dakota and the West* (Pierre: South Dakota Historical Society Press, 2019), 59; Robert M. Utley, *The Lance and the Shield*, 171; Cyrus Townsend Brady, *Indian Fights and Fighters*, 322.

82 Nelson Appleton Miles, *Personal Recollections and Observations of General Nelson A. Miles* (Chicago: Werner, 1896), 225; Robert M. Utley, *The Lance and the Shield*, 170–71.

83 Nelson Appleton Miles, *Personal Recollections*, 225, 227; Robert M. Utley, *The Lance and the Shield*, 171; Stanley Vestal, *Sitting Bull: Champion of the Sioux*, 195.

84 Robert M. Utley, *The Lance and the Shield*, 171–72.

85 Nelson Appleton Miles, *Personal Recollections*, 227; Robert M. Utley, *The Lance and the Shield*, 171–72; Stanley Vestal, *Sitting Bull: Champion of the Sioux*, 200–01.

86 R. Eli Paul, ed., *The Frontier Army*, 59; Robert M. Utley, *The Lance and the Shield*, 172.

87 Nelson Appleton Miles, *Personal Recollections*, 227; Robert M. Utley, *The Lance and the Shield*, 172; Stanley Vestal, *Sitting Bull: Champion of the Sioux*, 201.

88 Nelson Appleton Miles, *Personal Recollections*, 227; R. Eli Paul, ed., *The Frontier Army*, 60; Robert M. Utley, *The Lance and the Shield*, 172.

89 Nelson Appleton Miles, *Personal Recollections*, 227, 228; Robert M. Utley, *The Lance and the Shield*, 173.

90 Nelson Appleton Miles, *Personal Recollections*, 228; Robert M. Utley, *The Lance and the Shield*, 173; R. Eli Paul, ed., *The Frontier Army*, 60.

91 Nelson Appleton Miles, *Personal Recollections*, 228; Robert M. Utley, *The Lance and the Shield*, 173.

92 John S. Gray, "What Made Johnnie Bruguier Run?," 44; Robert M. Utley, *The Lance and the Shield*, 176.

93 Stanley Vestal, *Sitting Bull: Champion of the Sioux*, 209.

94 Nelson Appleton Miles, *Personal Recollections*, 228; Robert M. Utley, *The Lance and the Shield*, 177.

95 Robert M. Utley, *The Lance and the Shield*, 177.

96 John S. Gray, "What Made Johnnie Bruguier Run?," 45; Robert M. Utley, *The Lance and the Shield*, 177.

97 Nelson Appleton Miles, *Personal Recollections*, 228, 231; John S. Gray, "What Made Johnnie Bruguier Run?," 45; Robert M. Utley, *The Lance and the Shield*, 177.

98 Robert M. Utley, *The Lance and the Shield*, 178.

99 John S. Gray, "What Made Johnnie Bruguier Run?," 45; Robert M. Utley, *The Lance and the Shield*, 177.

100 John S. Gray, "What Made Johnnie Bruguier Run?," 45.

101 Robert M. Utley, *The Lance and the Shield*, 178.

102 Stanley Vestal, *Sitting Bull: Champion of the Sioux*, 207; Robert M. Utley, *The Lance and the Shield*, 179.

103 Robert M. Utley, *The Lance and the Shield*, 179.

104 Ibid.

105 Paul Andrew Hutton, *Phil Sheridan and His Army*, 326; Tom Powers, *The Killing of Crazy Horse*, 236–38.

106 Tom Powers, *The Killing of Crazy Horse*, 247–49; Robert M. Utley, *The Lance and the Shield*, 179, 180.

107 Paul Andrew Hutton, *Phil Sheridan and His Army*, 321–24.

108 Robert M. Utley, *The Lance and the Shield*, 180, 181.

109 Robert M. Utley, *The Lance and the Shield*, 181, 203.

110 Paul L. Hedren, *After Custer: Loss and Transformation in Sioux Country* (Norman: University of Oklahoma Press, 2011), 154, 156; Robert M. Utley, *The Lance and the Shield*, 182.

111 Robert M. Utley, *The Lance and the Shield*, 184, 185.

112 Ernie LaPointe, *Sitting Bull*, 75; Robert M. Utley, *The Lance and the Shield*, 185, 186.

113 Robert M. Utley, *The Lance and the Shield*, 189.

114 Paul L. Hedren, *After Custer*, 155; Robert M. Utley, *The Lance and the Shield*, 190.

115 Robert M. Utley, *The Lance and the Shield*, 191.

116 Stanley Vestal, *New Sources of Indian History*, 236, 237.

117 Paul L. Hedren, *After Custer*, 155; Robert M. Utley, *The Lance and the Shield*, 191.

118 Paul L. Hedren, *After Custer*, 155, 156; Robert M. Utley, *The Lance and the Shield*, 191.

119 Jesse M. Lee, "The Capture and Death of an Indian Chieftain," *Journal of the Military Service Institution of the United States* (May–June 1914), 326, 327; Thomas Powers, *The Killing of Crazy Horse*, 370; Bill Markley and Kellen Cutsforth, *Old West Showdown*, 99–100.

120 Thomas Powers, *The Killing of Crazy Horse*, 431; Robert M. Utley, *The Lance and the Shield*, 200.

121 James Crutchfield et al., *The Settlement of America*, vol. 2, 352–53; Paul Andrew Hutton, *Phil Sheridan and His Army*, 332–33; Robert M. Utley, *The Lance and the Shield*, 193.

122 Robert M. Utley, *The Lance and the Shield*, 192–93.

123 Ibid.

124 Stanley Vestal, *New Sources of Indian History*, 242; Robert M. Utley, *The Lance and the Shield*, 193–94, 198.

125 Robert M. Utley, *The Lance and the Shield*, 194.

126 Robert M. Utley, *The Lance and the Shield*, 194, 195.

127 Robert M. Utley, *The Lance and the Shield*, 195.

128 Stanley Vestal, *Sitting Bull: Champion of the Sioux*, 216; Robert M. Utley, *The Lance and the Shield*, 196.

129 Robert M. Utley, *The Lance and the Shield*, 196.

130 Stanley Vestal, *Sitting Bull: Champion of the Sioux*, 217.

131 Stanley Vestal, *Sitting Bull: Champion of the Sioux*, 218; Robert M. Utley, *The Lance and the Shield*, 196.

132 Robert M. Utley, *The Lance and the Shield*, 197.

133 Ibid.

134 Robert M. Utley, *The Lance and the Shield*, 197–98.

135 Robert M. Utley, *The Lance and the Shield*, 201.

CHAPTER 8: GERONIMO'S BREAKOUT AND SITTING BULL'S SURRENDER, 1878–1881

1 Edwin R. Sweeney, *From Cochise to Geronimo*, 119–20; Robert M. Utley, *Geronimo*, 97.

2 Edwin R. Sweeney, *From Cochise to Geronimo*, 120; Robert M. Utley, *Geronimo*, 98.

3 Edwin R. Sweeney, *From Cochise to Geronimo*, 120–21.

4 Edwin R. Sweeney, *From Cochise to Geronimo*, 122–23; Robert M. Utley, *Geronimo*, 99.

5 Edwin R. Sweeney, *From Cochise to Geronimo*, 123; Robert M. Utley, *Geronimo*, 99; S. M. Barrett, ed., *Geronimo*, 119–20. Geronimo said this attack took place "about 1880," but Robert Utley and Edwin Sweeney both believe it was the November 12, 1878, attack.

6 Edwin R. Sweeney, *From Cochise to Geronimo*, 124–26; Robert M. Utley, *Geronimo*, 100.

7 Berndt Kühn, *Chronicles of War*, 221, 223; Edwin R. Sweeney, *From Cochise to Geronimo*, 135, 136, 139, 140; Robert M. Utley, *Geronimo*, 100.

8 Robert M. Utley, *Geronimo*, 100; Edwin R. Sweeney, *From Cochise to Geronimo*, 142.

9 Angie Debo, *Geronimo*, 124; Robert M. Utley, *Geronimo*, 100.

10 Edwin R. Sweeney, *From Cochise to Geronimo*, 132; Robert M. Utley, *Geronimo*, 100.

11 Edwin R. Sweeney, *From Cochise to Geronimo*, 142, 143; Robert M. Utley, *Geronimo*, 101.

12 Robert M. Utley, *Geronimo*, 102.

13 Robert M. Utley, *Geronimo*, 101–02.

14 Edwin R. Sweeney, *From Cochise to Geronimo*, 142–43.

15 Edwin R. Sweeney, *From Cochise to Geronimo*, 143; Robert M. Utley, *Geronimo*, 102.

16 Edwin R. Sweeney, *From Cochise to Geronimo*, 143.

17 Ibid.

18 Edwin R. Sweeney, *From Cochise to Geronimo*, 145.

19 Edwin R. Sweeney, *From Cochise to Geronimo*, 144.

20 Robert M. Utley, *Geronimo*, 103, 104; Edwin R. Sweeney, *From Cochise to Geronimo*, 145.

21 Edwin R. Sweeney, *From Cochise to Geronimo*, 145–46.

22 Robert M. Utley, *Geronimo*, 108.

23 Ibid.

24 There are several variations to the spelling of *Nakadoklini.*

25 Angie Debo, *Geronimo*, 127–28; Robert M. Utley, *Geronimo*, 108; David Roberts, *Once They Moved Like the Wind*, 197; Dan L. Thrapp, *The Conquest of Apacheria* (Norman: University of Oklahoma Press, 1967), 220.

26 Robert M. Utley, *Geronimo*, 108; David Roberts, *Once They Moved Like the Wind*, 197; Edwin R. Sweeney, *From Cochise to Geronimo*, 177

27 Eve Ball, *Indeh: An Apache Odyssey*, 54.

28 Robert M. Utley, *Geronimo*, 109; Angie Debo, *Geronimo*, 129–30; David Roberts, *Once They Moved Like the Wind*, 199; Eve Ball, *Indeh: An Apache Odyssey*, 54; Paul Andrew Hutton, *The Apache Wars*, 273, 275, 280–81.

29 Angie Debo, *Geronimo*, 130; Robert M. Utley, *Geronimo*, 109.

30 Edwin R. Sweeney, *From Cochise to Geronimo*, 181; Robert M. Utley, *Geronimo*, 109.

31 S. M. Barrett, ed., *Geronimo*, 144–45; Edwin R. Sweeney, *From Cochise to Geronimo*, 182; Robert M. Utley, *Geronimo*, 110.

32 Paul Andrew Hutton, *The Apache Wars*, 284; Robert M. Utley, *Geronimo*, 110.

33 Robert M. Utley, *The Lance and the Shield*, 201–02.

34 Robert M. Utley, *The Lance and the Shield*, 204–05.

35 Robert M. Utley, *The Lance and the Shield*, 205–06.

36 Robert M. Utley, *The Lance and the Shield*, 207.

37 Robert M. Utley, *The Lance and the Shield*, 206–07.

38 Stanley Vestal, *Sitting Bull: Champion of the Sioux*, 220–21.

39 Stanley Vestal, *Sitting Bull: Champion of the Sioux*, 221–23.

40 Mark J. Nelson, *White Hat: The Military Career of Captain William Philo Clark* (Norman: University of Oklahoma Press, 2018), 150; Robert M. Utley, *The Lance and the Shield*, 208.

41 Robert M. Utley, *The Lance and the Shield*, 208.

42 Ibid.

43 Ibid.

44 Ibid.

45 Mark J. Nelson, *White Hat*, 84; Tom Powers, *The Killing of Crazy Horse*, 377–80.

46 Mark J. Nelson, *White Hat*, 150–51.

47 Mark J. Nelson, *White Hat*, 151; Robert M. Utley, *The Lance and the Shield*, 209.

48 Robert M. Utley, *The Lance and the Shield*, 212.

49 Robert M. Utley, *The Lance and the Shield*, 213.

50 Robert M. Utley, *The Lance and the Shield*, 214–15.

51 Robert M. Utley, *The Lance and the Shield*, 215–17.

52 Robert M. Utley, *The Lance and the Shield*, 218, 220, 222.

53 Robert M. Utley, *The Lance and the Shield*, 220, 221–22.

54 Robert M. Utley, *The Lance and the Shield*, 222.

55 Robert M. Utley, *The Lance and the Shield*, 223.

56 Robert M. Utley, *The Lance and the Shield*, 225.

57 Ibid.

58 Robert M. Utley, *The Lance and the Shield*, 226.

59 Robert M. Utley, *The Lance and the Shield*, 229.

60 Robert M. Utley, *The Lance and the Shield*, 227.

61 Robert M. Utley, *The Lance and the Shield*, 226.

62 Robert M. Utley, *The Lance and the Shield*, 227–28.

63 Robert M. Utley, *The Lance and the Shield*, 229.

64 Ibid.

65 Ibid.

66 Robert M. Utley, *The Lance and the Shield*, 230.

67 Dennis C. Pope, *Sitting Bull, Prisoner of War* (Pierre: South Dakota State Historical Society Press, 2010), 8; Robert M. Utley, *The Lance and the Shield*, 230–32.

68 Dennis C. Pope, *Sitting Bull, Prisoner of War*, 11; Robert M. Utley, *The Lance and the Shield*, 232.

69 Robert M. Utley, *The Lance and the Shield*, 232.

70 Ibid.

71 Dennis C. Pope, *Sitting Bull, Prisoner of War*, 12; Robert M. Utley, *The Lance and the Shield*, 232.

72 Dennis C. Pope, *Sitting Bull, Prisoner of War*, 12–13; Robert M. Utley, *The Lance and the Shield*, 233.

CHAPTER 9: GERONIMO'S RAIDS AND SITTING BULL PRISONER OF WAR, 1881–1884

1 Robert M. Utley, *Geronimo*, 110; Paul Andrew Hutton, *The Apache Wars*, 284; Edwin R. Sweeney, *From Cochise to Geronimo*, 185.

2 Robert M. Utley, *Geronimo*, 110; Paul Andrew Hutton, *The Apache Wars*, 284.

3 Berndt Kühn, *Chronicles of War*, 249; Paul Andrew Hutton, *The Apache Wars*, 284; Edwin R. Sweeney, *From Cochise to Geronimo*, 187.

4 Berndt Kühn, *Chronicles of War*, 249; Paul Andrew Hutton, *The Apache Wars*, 284; Edwin R. Sweeney, *From Cochise to Geronimo*, 188.

5 Berndt Kühn, *Chronicles of War*, 249; Paul Andrew Hutton, *The Apache Wars*, 284–85; Edwin R. Sweeney, *From Cochise to Geronimo*, 188.

6 Berndt Kühn, *Chronicles of War*, 250; Paul Andrew Hutton, *The Apache Wars*, 285.

7 Paul Andrew Hutton, *The Apache Wars*, 285.

8 Edwin R. Sweeney, *From Cochise to Geronimo*, 189; Paul Andrew Hutton, *The Apache Wars*, 285.

9 Edwin R. Sweeney, *From Cochise to Geronimo*, 189; Berndt Kühn, *Chronicles of War*, 250; Paul Andrew Hutton, *The Apache Wars*, 285, 286.

10 Paul Andrew Hutton, *The Apache Wars*, 286–87; Woodworth Clum, *Apache Agent*, 265–66.

11 Woodworth Clum, *Apache Agent*, 265.

12 Woodworth Clum, *Apache Agent*, 266–67; Paul Andrew Hutton, *The Apache Wars*, 287.

13 Berndt Kühn, *Chronicles of War*, 250. Less than two weeks later, on October 26, 1881, Frank McLaury and his brother Tom, along with Billy Clanton, would be shot and killed by the Earp brothers and Doc Holliday behind the O.K. Corral in Tombstone.

14 Edwin R. Sweeney, *From Cochise to Geronimo*, 190.

15 Angie Debo, *Geronimo*, 134–35.

16 Robert M. Utley, *Geronimo*, 113; Edwin R. Sweeney, *From Cochise to Geronimo*, 191.

17 Paul Andrew Hutton, *The Apache Wars*, 290–91.

18 Edwin R. Sweeney, *From Cochise to Geronimo*, 197, 198.

19 Edwin R. Sweeney, *From Cochise to Geronimo*, 195; Paul Andrew Hutton, *The Apache Wars*, 291; Angie Debo, *Geronimo*, 138.

20 Angie Debo, *Geronimo*, 138.

21 Paul Andrew Hutton, *The Apache Wars*, 291; W. Michael Farmer, *Apacheria*, 3–4.

22 Edwin R. Sweeney, *From Cochise to Geronimo*, 205.

23 Edwin R. Sweeney, *From Cochise to Geronimo*, 205, 206, 207.

24 Angie Debo, *Geronimo*, 139–40.

25 Edwin R. Sweeney, *From Cochise to Geronimo*, 208.

26 Ibid.

27 Angie Debo, *Geronimo*, 140–41; Edwin R. Sweeney, *From Cochise to Geronimo*, 208.

28 Angie Debo, *Geronimo*, 141; Edwin R. Sweeney, *From Cochise to Geronimo*, 208.

29 Edwin R. Sweeney, *From Cochise to Geronimo*, 208–09.

30 Dan L. Thrapp, *The Conquest of Apacheria*, 238; Edwin R. Sweeney, *From Cochise to Geronimo*, 209.

31 Dan L. Thrapp, *The Conquest of Apacheria*, 238; Edwin R. Sweeney, *From Cochise to Geronimo*, 209–10.

32 Dan L. Thrapp, *The Conquest of Apacheria*, 238; Edwin R. Sweeney, *From Cochise to Geronimo*, 210; Angie Debo, *Geronimo*, 141.

33 Edwin R. Sweeney, *From Cochise to Geronimo*, 210.

34 Ibid.

35 Edwin R. Sweeney, *From Cochise to Geronimo*, 210–11.

36 Jason Betzinez, *I Fought with Geronimo*, 55; Edwin R. Sweeney, *From Cochise to Geronimo*, 211.

37 Jason Betzinez, *I Fought with Geronimo*, 56; Edwin R. Sweeney, *From Cochise to Geronimo*, 211.

38 Ibid.

39 Edwin R. Sweeney, *From Cochise to Geronimo*, 212.

40 Edwin R. Sweeney, *From Cochise to Geronimo*, 213.

41 Jason Betzinez, *I Fought with Geronimo*, 56; Berndt Kühn, *Chronicles of War*, 253; Edwin R. Sweeney, *From Cochise to Geronimo*, 213, 214.

42 Jason Betzinez, *I Fought with Geronimo*, 58.

43 Jason Betzinez, *I Fought with Geronimo*, 58; Edwin R. Sweeney, *From Cochise to Geronimo*, 214.

44 Edwin R. Sweeney, *From Cochise to Geronimo*, 214–15; Angie Debo, *Geronimo*, 144.

45 Jason Betzinez, *I Fought with Geronimo*, 60–61; Edwin R. Sweeney, *From Cochise to Geronimo*, 215.

46 Jason Betzinez, *I Fought with Geronimo*, 62; Edwin R. Sweeney, *From Cochise to Geronimo*, 215.

47 Edwin R. Sweeney, *From Cochise to Geronimo*, 215–16.

48 Paul Andrew Hutton, *The Apache Wars*, 295.

49 Edwin R. Sweeney, *From Cochise to Geronimo*, 216; Berndt Kühn, *Chronicles of War*, 255.

50 Jason Betzinez, *I Fought with Geronimo*, 63; Edwin R. Sweeney, *From Cochise to Geronimo*, 217.

51 Edwin R. Sweeney, *From Cochise to Geronimo*, 217; Robert M. Utley, *Geronimo*, 117.

52 Edwin R. Sweeney, *From Cochise to Geronimo*, 217.

53 Ibid.

54 Robert M. Utley, *Geronimo*, 118.

55 Robert M. Utley, *Geronimo*, 122; Berndt Kühn, *Chronicles of War*, 256.

56 Edwin R. Sweeney, *From Cochise to Geronimo*, 220; Robert M. Utley, *Geronimo*, 122–23.

57 Robert M. Utley, *Geronimo*, 118–19, 123; Berndt Kühn, *Chronicles of War*, 256; Edwin R. Sweeney, *From Cochise to Geronimo*, 221, 222.

58 Robert M. Utley, *Geronimo*, 119, 120; Edwin R. Sweeney, *From Cochise to Geronimo*, 222, 223.

59 Edwin R. Sweeney, *From Cochise to Geronimo*, 222, 224; Robert M. Utley, *Geronimo*, 123.

60 Jason Betzinez, *I Fought with Geronimo*, 72; Edwin R. Sweeney, *From Cochise to Geronimo*, 224.

61 Jason Betzinez, *I Fought with Geronimo*, 72; Edwin R. Sweeney, *From Cochise to Geronimo*, 224–25.

62 Jason Betzinez, *I Fought with Geronimo*, 74; S. M. Barrett, ed., *Geronimo*, 124; Edwin R. Sweeney, *From Cochise to Geronimo*, 225.

63 Edwin R. Sweeney, *From Cochise to Geronimo*, 227, 228.

64 Talbot Gooday—a Chihenne who disliked Geronimo for forcefully removing him and his family from San Carlos, resulting in the deaths of some of his relatives—said Geronimo told the warriors to abandon the women and children so they could escape. Geronimo's cousin Fun raised his rifle and said he would shoot him if he said that again. With that, Geronimo climbed over the edge of the arroyo and disappeared. Angie Debo, *Geronimo*, 151–52. I don't believe this story. If Geronimo had done this, I don't believe anyone would have followed him afterward.

65 Edwin R. Sweeney, *From Cochise to Geronimo*, 226, 227.

66 Edwin R. Sweeney, *From Cochise to Geronimo*, 232; Berndt Kühn, *Chronicles of War*, 256; Robert M. Utley, *Geronimo*, 123.

67 Jason Betzinez, *I Fought with Geronimo*, 74; Edwin R. Sweeney, *From Cochise to Geronimo*, 232.

68 Edwin R. Sweeney, *From Cochise to Geronimo*, 231; Robert M. Utley, *Geronimo*, 123.

69 Edwin R. Sweeney, *From Cochise to Geronimo*, 232–33; Robert M. Utley, *Geronimo*, 121, 125.

70 Jason Betzinez, *I Fought with Geronimo*, 77; Edwin R. Sweeney, *From Cochise to Geronimo*, 233–34.

71 Edwin R. Sweeney, *From Cochise to Geronimo*, 234.

72 Ibid.

73 Edwin R. Sweeney, *From Cochise to Geronimo*, 234, 235.

74 Edwin R. Sweeney, *From Cochise to Geronimo*, 235.

75 Ibid.

76 Edwin R. Sweeney, *From Cochise to Geronimo*, 236–37; Robert M. Utley, *Geronimo*, 123.

77 Edwin R. Sweeney, *From Cochise to Geronimo*, 239–40; Robert M. Utley, *Geronimo*, 130.

78 Edwin R. Sweeney, *From Cochise to Geronimo*, 245.

79 Robert M. Utley, *Geronimo*, 125; David Roberts, *Once They Moved Like the Wind*, 214–15.

80 Robert M. Utley, *Geronimo*, 124, 134.

81 Edwin R. Sweeney, *From Cochise to Geronimo*, 280; Robert M. Utley, *Geronimo*, 134, 135; Jerome A. Green, *Slim Buttes, 1876*, 59–60.

82 Jason Betzinez, *I Fought with Geronimo*, 90; Robert M. Utley, *Geronimo*, 130.

83 Robert M. Utley, *Geronimo*, 131; Edwin R. Sweeney, *From Cochise to Geronimo*, 247, 249.

84 Edwin R. Sweeney, *From Cochise to Geronimo*, 235, 251.

85 Edwin R. Sweeney, *From Cochise to Geronimo*, 251, 252.

86 Edwin R. Sweeney, *From Cochise to Geronimo*, 250, 252.

87 Jason Betzinez, *I Fought with Geronimo*, 94–95.

88 Jason Betzinez, *I Fought with Geronimo*, 95.

89 Edwin R. Sweeney, *From Cochise to Geronimo*, 253.

90 Robert M. Utley, *Geronimo*, 132.

91 Robert M. Utley, *Geronimo*, 132, 133.

92 Edwin R. Sweeney, *From Cochise to Geronimo*, 288, 298; Robert M. Utley, *Geronimo*, 133.

93 Robert M. Utley, *Geronimo*, 133, 136; Edwin R. Sweeney, *From Cochise to Geronimo*, 290.

94 Edwin R. Sweeney, *From Cochise to Geronimo*, 294–95; Robert M. Utley, *Geronimo*, 136.

95 Robert M. Utley, *Geronimo*, 136.

96 Rachel St. John, *Line in the Sand: A History of the Western U.S.–Mexico Border* (Princeton, NJ: Princeton University Press, 2012), 59; Robert M. Utley, *Geronimo*, 136.

97 Mickey Free was the boy Felix Ward, whose capture by Apaches had set off the trouble between the army and Cochise. Years later, Felix was found living with Coyotero Apaches.

98 Robert M. Utley, *Geronimo*, 136–37.

99 Edwin R. Sweeney, *From Cochise to Geronimo*, 305, 306; Robert M. Utley, *Geronimo*, 137.

100 Robert M. Utley, *Geronimo*, 138–39.

101 Robert M. Utley, *Geronimo*, 138.

102 Edwin R. Sweeney, *From Cochise to Geronimo*, 307; Robert M. Utley, *Geronimo*, 138–39.

103 Jason Betzinez, *I Fought with Geronimo*, 118, 120.

104 Jason Betzinez, *I Fought with Geronimo*, 112–13, 114; Robert M. Utley, *Geronimo*, 138; Edwin R. Sweeney, *From Cochise to Geronimo*, 308, 310.

105 Jason Betzinez, *I Fought with Geronimo*, 113–14.

106 Jason Betzinez, *I Fought with Geronimo*, 114.

107 Edwin R. Sweeney, *From Cochise to Geronimo*, 309, 624n39.

108 Jason Betzinez, *I Fought with Geronimo*, 115.

109 Ibid.

110 Jason Betzinez, *I Fought with Geronimo*, 116.

111 Edwin R. Sweeney, *From Cochise to Geronimo*, 309; Jason Betzinez, *I Fought with Geronimo*, 116.

112 Grenville Goodwin, "Experiences of an Indian Scout: Excerpts from the Life of John Rope, an Old-Timer of the White Mountain Apaches," part 2, *Arizona Historical Review*, vol. 7 (April 1936), 67, accessed December 10, 2019, https://repository.arizona.edu/bitstream/handle/10150/623772/azu_h9791_a72_h6_07_02_art4_w.pdf?sequence=1&isAllowed=y; David Roberts, *Once They Moved Like the Wind*, 235, 236; Paul Andrew Hutton, *The Apache Wars*, 329; Eve Ball, *Indeh: An Apache Odyssey*, 154.

113 David Roberts, *Once They Moved Like the Wind*, 236.

114 Edwin R. Sweeney, *From Cochise to Geronimo*, 309; Robert M. Utley, *Geronimo*, 140.

115 Edwin R. Sweeney, *From Cochise to Geronimo*, 309.

116 Ibid.

117 Robert M. Utley, *Geronimo*, 140.

118 Edwin R. Sweeney, *From Cochise to Geronimo*, 310; Jason Betzinez, *I Fought with Geronimo*, 121.

119 Grenville Goodwin, "Experiences of an Indian Scout," 68–69; Paul Andrew Hutton, *The Apache Wars*, 330–31; Edwin R. Sweeney, *From Cochise to Geronimo*, 309, 310.

120 Edwin R. Sweeney, *From Cochise to Geronimo*, 311; Robert M. Utley, *Geronimo*, 141.

121 Robert M. Utley, *Geronimo*, 141.

122 Ibid.

123 Robert Todd Lincoln was the son of President Abraham Lincoln and Mary Todd Lincoln.

124 Edwin R. Sweeney, *From Cochise to Geronimo*, 319, 320; Robert M. Utley, *Geronimo*, 142.

125 Edwin R. Sweeney, *From Cochise to Geronimo*, 320.

126 Robert M. Utley, *Geronimo*, 143–44.

127 Robert M. Utley, *Geronimo*, 144; Edwin R. Sweeney, *From Cochise to Geronimo*, 329.

128 Edwin R. Sweeney, *From Cochise to Geronimo*, 330; Robert M. Utley, *Geronimo*, 144.

129 Edwin R. Sweeney, *From Cochise to Geronimo*, 331; Robert M. Utley, *Geronimo*, 144–45.

130 Robert M. Utley, *Geronimo*, 145; Edwin R. Sweeney, *From Cochise to Geronimo*, 335.

131 Robert M. Utley, *Geronimo*, 145.

132 Robert M. Utley, *Geronimo*, 145, 147; Edwin R. Sweeney, *From Cochise to Geronimo*, 336.

133 Robert M. Utley, *Geronimo*, 146.

134 Robert M. Utley, *Geronimo*, 146–47.

135 Robert M. Utley, *Geronimo*, 147.

136 Britton Davis, *The Truth About Geronimo* (Lincoln: University of Nebraska Press, 1929), 84–85; Edwin R. Sweeney, *From Cochise to Geronimo*, 355; Robert M. Utley, *Geronimo*, 147.

137 Britton Davis, *The Truth About Geronimo*, 92–93; Robert M. Utley, *Geronimo*, 147.

138 Edwin R. Sweeney, *From Cochise to Geronimo*, 356; Robert M. Utley, *Geronimo*, 147, 148.

139 Britton Davis, *The Truth About Geronimo*, 94–95, 96–98; Robert M. Utley, *Geronimo*, 148.

140 Britton Davis, *The Truth About Geronimo*, 99–101; Robert M. Utley, *Geronimo*, 148.

141 Robert M. Utley, *Geronimo*, 148.

142 Dennis C. Pope, *Sitting Bull, Prisoner of War*, 9.

143 Dennis C. Pope, *Sitting Bull, Prisoner of War*, 14.

144 Dennis C. Pope, *Sitting Bull, Prisoner of War*, 15, 17.

145 Dennis C. Pope, *Sitting Bull, Prisoner of War*, 19.

146 Dennis C. Pope, *Sitting Bull, Prisoner of War*, 20.

147 Dennis C. Pope, *Sitting Bull, Prisoner of War*, 23–24.

148 Dennis C. Pope, *Sitting Bull, Prisoner of War*, 25.

149 Dennis C. Pope, *Sitting Bull, Prisoner of War*, 29, 31.

150 Dennis C. Pope, *Sitting Bull, Prisoner of War*, 37–38.

151 Dennis C. Pope, *Sitting Bull, Prisoner of War*, 39.

152 Dennis C. Pope, *Sitting Bull, Prisoner of War*, 40.

153 Dennis C. Pope, *Sitting Bull, Prisoner of War*, 41, 148n15.

154 Dennis C. Pope, *Sitting Bull, Prisoner of War*, 41, 42.

155 Robert M. Utley, *The Lance and the Shield*, 241; Dennis C. Pope, *Sitting Bull, Prisoner of War*, 43.

156 Dennis C. Pope, *Sitting Bull, Prisoner of War*, 44–45, 112.

157 Dennis C. Pope, *Sitting Bull, Prisoner of War*, 44, 45.

158 Dennis C. Pope, *Sitting Bull, Prisoner of War*, 50, 52, 109, 114.

159 Robert M. Utley, *The Lance and the Shield*, 242, 244.

160 Dennis C. Pope, *Sitting Bull, Prisoner of War*, 81–83.

161 Dennis C. Pope, *Sitting Bull, Prisoner of War*, 83–84.

162 Dennis C. Pope, *Sitting Bull, Prisoner of War*, 55, 69, 78, 86–87; Robert M. Utley, *The Lance and the Shield*, 244.

163 Dennis C. Pope, *Sitting Bull, Prisoner of War*, 102–03.

164 Richmond L. Clow, *Spotted Tail: Warrior and Statesman* (Pierre: South Dakota Historical Society Press, 2019), 227–28; Dennis C. Pope, *Sitting Bull, Prisoner of War*, 102, 105.

165 Dennis C. Pope, *Sitting Bull, Prisoner of War*, 107.

166 Dennis C. Pope, *Sitting Bull, Prisoner of War*, 107, 110.

167 Dennis C. Pope, *Sitting Bull, Prisoner of War*, 122, 123–24.

168 Dennis C. Pope, *Sitting Bull, Prisoner of War*, 124–25, 126.

169 Dennis C. Pope, *Sitting Bull, Prisoner of War*, 126.

170 Dennis C. Pope, *Sitting Bull, Prisoner of War*, 128, 129–30.

171 Dennis C. Pope, *Sitting Bull, Prisoner of War*, 130–31, 167n25.

172 Dennis C. Pope, *Sitting Bull, Prisoner of War*, 131.

173 Norman E. Matteoni, *Prairie Man: The Struggle Between Sitting Bull and Indian Agent James McLaughlin* (Guilford, CT: TwoDot, 2015), 27–28; Robert M. Utley, *The Lance and the Shield*, 249.

174 Norman E. Matteoni, *Prairie Man*, 167; Dennis C. Pope, *Sitting Bull, Prisoner of War*, 132.

175 Norman E. Matteoni, *Prairie Man*, 168; Dennis C. Pope, *Sitting Bull, Prisoner of War*, 132–33.

176 Norman E. Matteoni, *Prairie Man*, 169.

177 Stanley Vestal, *New Sources of Indian History*, 295; Dennis C. Pope, *Sitting Bull, Prisoner of War*, 134; Norman E. Matteoni, *Prairie Man*, 169.

178 Stanley Vestal, *New Sources of Indian History*, 295–96.

179 Norman E. Matteoni, *Prairie Man*, 170; Stanley Vestal, *New Sources of Indian History*, 296–97.

180 Dennis C. Pope, *Sitting Bull, Prisoner of War*, 117–18; Robert M. Utley, *The Lance and the Shield*, 257.

181 Robert M. Utley, *The Lance and the Shield*, 257.

182 Robert W. Larson, *Red Cloud*, 239; Norman E. Matteoni, *Prairie Man*, 171.

183 Norman E. Matteoni, *Prairie Man*, 171–72.

184 Stanley Vestal, *Sitting Bull: Champion of the Sioux*, 239–40.

185 Ibid.

186 Stanley Vestal, *Sitting Bull: Champion of the Sioux*, 240–42.

187 Stanley Vestal, *Sitting Bull: Champion of the Sioux*, 242.

188 Stanley Vestal, *Sitting Bull: Champion of the Sioux*, 242–45.

189 Stanley Vestal, *Sitting Bull: Champion of the Sioux*, 246–47.

190 Stanley Vestal, *Sitting Bull: Champion of the Sioux*, 247.

191 Stanley Vestal, *Sitting Bull: Champion of the Sioux*, 249.

192 Robert M. Utley, *The Lance and the Shield*, 260–61.

193 Norman E. Matteoni, *Prairie Man*, 181.

194 Dee Brown, *Bury My Heart at Wounded Knee*, 426–27; Stanley Vestal, *Sitting Bull: Champion of the Sioux*, 250; Norman E. Matteoni, *Prairie Man*, 181.

195 Robert M. Utley, *The Lance and the Shield*, 261.

196 Robert M. Utley, *The Lance and the Shield*, 252.

197 Robert M. Utley, *The Lance and the Shield*, 261–62.

198 Robert M. Utley, *The Lance and the Shield*, 254–55; Norman E. Matteoni, *Prairie Man*, 185.

199 Norman E. Matteoni, *Prairie Man*, 185, 186.

SIDEBAR: APACHE SUNRISE CEREMONY

200 Carol A. Markstrom, *Empowerment of North American Indian Girls*, 192–93, 194.

201 Carol A. Markstrom, *Empowerment of North American Indian Girls*, 197–98; W. Michael Farmer, *Apacheria*, xvi; Morris Edward Opler, *Myths and Tales of the Chiricahua Apache Indians* (Lincoln: University of Nebraska Press, 1942), 14.

202 Morris Edward Opler, *An Apache Life-Way: The Economic, Social, and Religious Institutions of the Chiricahua Indians* (Lincoln: University of Nebraska Press, 1941), 267–68; Morris Edward Opler, *Myths and Tales of the Chiricahua Apache Indians*, 15.

203 Carol A. Markstrom, *Empowerment of North American Indian Girls*, 194, 264.

204 Morris Edward Opler, *An Apache Life-Way*, 83, 84, 85.

205 Morris Edward Opler, *An Apache Life-Way*, 97, 105–06, 260.

206 Carol A. Markstrom, *Empowerment of North American Indian Girls*, 193, 194.

CHAPTER 10: THE WILD WEST, 1884–1885

1 Robert M. Utley, *Geronimo*, 141, 147, 148.

2 Paul Andrew Hutton, *The Apache Wars*, 336.

3 Paul Andrew Hutton, *The Apache Wars*, 336–37; Edwin R. Sweeney, *From Cochise to Geronimo*, 358; S. M. Barrett, ed., *Geronimo*, 146.

4 Robert M. Utley, *Geronimo*, 149–50; Edwin R. Sweeney, *From Cochise to Geronimo*, 358.

5 Edwin R. Sweeney, *From Cochise to Geronimo*, 363, 365.

6 Edwin R. Sweeney, *From Cochise to Geronimo*, 365, 369.

7 Edwin R. Sweeney, *From Cochise to Geronimo*, 368; Jason Betzinez, *I Fought with Geronimo*, 123–24.

8 Edwin R. Sweeney, *From Cochise to Geronimo*, 369; Jason Betzinez, *I Fought with Geronimo*, 123; Robert M. Utley, *Geronimo*, 150.

9 Jason Betzinez, *I Fought with Geronimo*, 125; Robert M. Utley, *Geronimo*, 151.

10 Eve Ball, *In the Days of Victorio: Recollections of a Warm Springs Apache* (Tucson: University of Arizona Press, 1970), 156, 162–63; David Roberts, *Once They Moved Like the Wind*, 251; Edwin R. Sweeney, *From Cochise to Geronimo*, 373; Eve Ball, *Indeh: An Apache Odyssey*, 49–50.

11 Eve Ball, *In the Days of Victorio*, 163; David Roberts, *Once They Moved Like the Wind*, 251.

12 David Roberts, *Once They Moved Like the Wind*, 252; Edwin R. Sweeney, *From Cochise to Geronimo*, 372.

13 Britton Davis, *The Truth About Geronimo*, 124–25; David Roberts, *Once They Moved Like the Wind*, 252.

14 Paul Andrew Hutton, *The Apache Wars*, 339; Jason Betzinez, *I Fought with Geronimo*, 126.

15 Eve Ball, *In the Days of Victorio*, 166, 168; Edwin R. Sweeney, *From Cochise to Geronimo*, 380; Robert M. Utley, *Geronimo*, 152.

16 Edwin R. Sweeney, *From Cochise to Geronimo*, 380–81, 383.

17 Robert M. Utley, *Geronimo*, 154; Edwin R. Sweeney, *From Cochise to Geronimo*, 385–86.

18 Britton Davis, *The Truth About Geronimo*, 142; Robert M. Utley, *Geronimo*, 155; Edwin R. Sweeney, *From Cochise to Geronimo*, 391.

19 Robert M. Utley, *Geronimo*, 154, 155.

20 Edwin R. Sweeney, *From Cochise to Geronimo*, 393.

21 Edwin R. Sweeney, *From Cochise to Geronimo*, 394, 395.

22 Edwin R. Sweeney, *From Cochise to Geronimo*, 394.

23 Edwin R. Sweeney, *From Cochise to Geronimo*, 405; "Major Crimes Act," *Wikipedia*, accessed December 14, 2019, en.wikipedia.org/wiki/Major_Crimes_Act.

24 Robert M. Utley, *Geronimo*, 155, 156; Edwin R. Sweeney, *From Cochise to Geronimo*, 396.

25 Edwin R. Sweeney, *From Cochise to Geronimo*, 397–98; Robert M. Utley, *Geronimo*, 156.

26 Britton Davis, *The Truth About Geronimo*, 144; Robert M. Utley, *Geronimo*, 156; Edwin R. Sweeney, *From Cochise to Geronimo*, 398.

27 Britton Davis, *The Truth About Geronimo*, 144–45; Robert M. Utley, *Geronimo*, 157.

28 Britton Davis, *The Truth About Geronimo*, 144–47; Jason Betzinez, *I Fought with Geronimo*, 129; Robert M. Utley, *Geronimo*, 157.

29 Robert M. Utley, *Geronimo*, 157.

30 Dan L. Thrapp, *The Conquest of Apacheria*, 313; Robert M. Utley, *Geronimo*, 159; Edwin R. Sweeney, *From Cochise to Geronimo*, 400.

31 Jason Betzinez, *I Fought with Geronimo*, 129; Robert M. Utley, *Geronimo*, 157.

32 Jason Betzinez, *I Fought with Geronimo*, 129.

33 Edwin R. Sweeney, *From Cochise to Geronimo*, 401, 402.

34 Robert M. Utley, *Geronimo*, 158.

35 Ibid.

36 Ibid.

37 Robert M. Utley, *Geronimo*, 158, 161.

38 Britton Davis, *The Truth About Geronimo*, 149; Edwin R. Sweeney, *From Cochise to Geronimo*, 403, 408; Robert M. Utley, *Geronimo*, 158.

39 Norman E. Matteoni, *Prairie Man*, 184; Robert M. Utley, *The Lance and the Shield*, 262.

40 Robert M. Utley, *The Lance and the Shield*, 262–63, 388n3.

41 Robert M. Utley, *The Lance and the Shield*, 263.

42 Norman E. Matteoni, *Prairie Man*, 186; Robert M. Utley, *The Lance and the Shield*, 262.

43 Robert M. Utley, *The Lance and the Shield*, 263; Stanley Vestal, *Sitting Bull: Champion of the Sioux*, 250; Luther Standing Bear, *My People the Sioux* (Lincoln: University of Nebraska Press, 1975), 185.

44 Robert M. Utley, *The Lance and the Shield*, 263; Norman E. Matteoni, *Prairie Man*, 186; Luther Standing Bear, *My People the Sioux*, 185.

45 Courtney Ryley Cooper, *Annie Oakley: Woman at Arms* (New York: Konecky & Konecky, 1927), 75–78; Louis S. Warren, *Buffalo Bill's America: William Cody and the Wild West Show* (New York: Random House, 2005), 253; Bobby Bridger, *Buffalo Bill and Sitting Bull: Inventing the West* (Austin: University of Texas Press, 2002),

315; Deanne Stillman, *Blood Brothers: The Story of the Strange Friendship Between Sitting Bull and Buffalo Bill* (New York: Simon & Schuster, 2017), 172.

46 Robert M. Utley, *The Lance and the Shield*, 263.

47 Spotted Tail's agency in Nebraska had moved north across the border onto the Great Sioux Reservation in July 1878 and was named Rosebud.

48 Luther Standing Bear, *My People the Sioux*, 184–85.

49 Luther Standing Bear, *My People the Sioux*, 185.

50 Luther Standing Bear, *My People the Sioux*, 186.

51 Ibid.

52 Luther Standing Bear, *My People the Sioux*, 187; Robert M. Utley, *The Lance and the Shield*, 264.

53 Robert M. Utley, *The Lance and the Shield*, 264.

54 Deanne Stillman, *Blood Brothers*, 93; Bobby Bridger, *Buffalo Bill and Sitting Bull*, 315.

55 Bobby Bridger, *Buffalo Bill and Sitting Bull*, 315.

56 Bobby Bridger, *Buffalo Bill and Sitting Bull*, 315–16.

57 Burke was never an army major; it was a honorific title he gave himself.

58 Steve Friesen, *Buffalo Bill: Scout, Showman, Visionary* (Golden, CO: Fulcrum Publishing, Inc., 2010), 53; Bobby Bridger, *Buffalo Bill and Sitting Bull*, 315; Robert M. Utley, *The Lance and the Shield*, 264.

59 Deanne Stillman, *Blood Brothers*, 100; Norman E. Matteoni, *Prairie Man*, 188.

60 Louis S. Warren, *Buffalo Bill's America*, 254, 255; Deanne Stillman, *Blood Brothers*, 101.

61 Deanne Stillman, *Blood Brothers*, 116, 123.

62 Deanne Stillman, *Blood Brothers*, 123, 138.

63 Deanne Stillman, *Blood Brothers*, 123–24.

64 Deanne Stillman, *Blood Brothers*, 124.

65 Deanne Stillman, *Blood Brothers*, 139, 140.

66 Deanne Stillman, *Blood Brothers*, 140.

67 Ibid.

68 Bobby Bridger, *Buffalo Bill and Sitting Bull*, 318; Deanne Stillman, *Blood Brothers*, 142, 143.

69 Deanne Stillman, *Blood Brothers*, 145.

70 Louis S. Warren, *Buffalo Bill's America*, 254; Deanne Stillman, *Blood Brothers*, 144–45, 155.

71 Bobby Bridger, *Buffalo Bill and Sitting Bull*, 318.

72 Louis S. Warren, *Buffalo Bill's America*, 254; Deanne Stillman, *Blood Brothers*, 145, 156, 181; Bobby Bridger, *Buffalo Bill and Sitting Bull*, 319; Stanley Vestal, *Sitting Bull: Champion of the Sioux*, 250.

73 Ernie LaPointe, *Sitting Bull*, 88, 89; Bobby Bridger, *Buffalo Bill and Sitting Bull*, 317, 318.

74 Courtney Ryley Cooper, *Annie Oakley*, 124; Stanley Vestal, *Sitting Bull: Champion of the Sioux*, 250–51.

75 Bobby Bridger, *Buffalo Bill and Sitting Bull*, 319.

76 Deanne Stillman, *Blood Brothers*, 172.

77 Bobby Bridger, *Buffalo Bill and Sitting Bull*, 318; Deanne Stillman, *Blood Brothers*, 172, 173; Stanley Vestal, *Sitting Bull: Champion of the Sioux*, 250; Robert M. Utley, *The Lance and the Shield*, 388n14; Steve Friesen, *Buffalo Bill*, 56.

78 Deanne Stillman, *Blood Brothers*, 172–173; Robert M. Utley, *The Lance and the Shield*, 265.

79 Deanne Stillman, *Blood Brothers*, 174–75.

80 Deanne Stillman, *Blood Brothers*, 164–65.

81 Deanne Stillman, *Blood Brothers*, 146, 176.

82 Deanne Stillman, *Blood Brothers*, 146, 147, 177–80.

83 Deanne Stillman, *Blood Brothers*, 182.

84 Ibid.

85 Deanne Stillman, *Blood Brothers*, 183; Stanley Vestal, *Sitting Bull: Champion of the Sioux*, 251; Donovin Arleigh Sprague, *Images of America Standing Rock* (Charleston, SC: Arcadia Publishing, 2004), 61.

86 Ernie LaPointe, *Sitting Bull*, 88, 89; Stanley Vestal, *Sitting Bull: Champion of the Sioux*, 251.

87 Bobby Bridger, *Buffalo Bill and Sitting Bull*, 320.

88 William F. Cody, *Buffalo Bill's Life Story: An Autobiography* (New York: Cosmopolitan Book Corporation, 1920), 300–01.

CHAPTER 11: GERONIMO ON THE RUN, 1885–1886

1 Edwin R. Sweeney, *From Cochise to Geronimo*, 401; Robert M. Utley, *Geronimo*, 158, 161.

2 Robert M. Utley, *Geronimo*, 161; Edwin R. Sweeney, *From Cochise to Geronimo*, 408.

3 Robert M. Utley, *Geronimo*, 161; Edwin R. Sweeney, *From Cochise to Geronimo*, 410.

4 Ibid.

5 Robert M. Utley, *Geronimo*, 161; Britton Davis, *The Truth About Geronimo*, 152.

6 Ibid.

7 Edwin R. Sweeney, *From Cochise to Geronimo*, 413–14, 416; Britton Davis, *The Truth About Geronimo*, 153; Paul Andrew Hutton, *The Apache Wars*, 348.

8 Edwin R. Sweeney, *From Cochise to Geronimo*, 408, 416; Louis Kraft, ed., *Lt. Charles Gatewood & His Apache Wars Memoir* (Lincoln: University of Nebraska Press, 2005), 64.

9 Louis Kraft, ed., *Lt. Charles Gatewood & His Apache Wars Memoir*, 64.

10 Louis Kraft, ed., *Lt. Charles Gatewood & His Apache Wars Memoir*, 65; Edwin R. Sweeney, *From Cochise to Geronimo*, 416.

11 Louis Kraft, ed., *Lt. Charles Gatewood & His Apache Wars Memoir*, 64; Edwin R. Sweeney, *From Cochise to Geronimo*, 417.

12 Louis Kraft, ed., *Lt. Charles Gatewood & His Apache Wars Memoir*, 65; Edwin R. Sweeney, *From Cochise to Geronimo*, 417, 418.

13 Dan L. Thrapp, *The Conquest of Apacheria*, 319–20, 323; Paul Andrew Hutton, *The Apache Wars*, 346; Robert M. Utley, *Geronimo*, 162–63.

14 Edwin R. Sweeney, *From Cochise to Geronimo*, 418–19.

15 Ibid.

16 Edwin R. Sweeney, *From Cochise to Geronimo*, 419–20.

17 Edwin R. Sweeney, *From Cochise to Geronimo*, 420–21.

18 Robert M. Utley, *Geronimo*, 163.

19 Dan L. Thrapp, *The Conquest of Apacheria*, 326–27; Angie Debo, *Geronimo*, 243; Paul Andrew Hutton, *The Apache Wars*, 346.

20 Britton Davis, *The Truth About Geronimo*, 153–54; Angie Debo, *Geronimo*, 243–44; Paul Andrew Hutton, *The Apache Wars*, 347; Edwin R. Sweeney, *From Cochise to Geronimo*, 432.

21 Paul Andrew Hutton, *The Apache Wars*, 348; Angie Debo, *Geronimo*, 244; Edwin R. Sweeney, *From Cochise to Geronimo*, 435–36.

22 Paul Andrew Hutton, *The Apache Wars*, 348; Angie Debo, *Geronimo*, 243–44; Edwin R. Sweeney, *From Cochise to Geronimo*, 440.

23 Paul Andrew Hutton, *The Apache Wars*, 348, 349; Edwin R. Sweeney, *From Cochise to Geronimo*, 444.

24 Paul Andrew Hutton, *The Apache Wars*, 349; Edwin R. Sweeney, *From Cochise to Geronimo*, 445.

25 There were at least two of Geronimo's wives among the captives, with the possibility of a third.

26 Paul Andrew Hutton, *The Apache Wars*, 348–49; Edwin R. Sweeney, *From Cochise to Geronimo*, 444.

27 Paul Andrew Hutton, *The Apache Wars*, 349; Edwin R. Sweeney, *From Cochise to Geronimo*, 445.

28 Paul Andrew Hutton, *The Apache Wars*, 350; Edwin R. Sweeney, *From Cochise to Geronimo*, 445.

29 Angie Debo, *Geronimo*, 245.

30 Robert M. Utley, *Geronimo*, 166; Edwin R. Sweeney, *From Cochise to Geronimo*, 446.

31 Paul Andrew Hutton, *The Apache Wars*, 350; Edwin R. Sweeney, *From Cochise to Geronimo*, 446, 454–55; Dan L. Thrapp, *The Conquest of Apacheria*, 332.

32 Edwin R. Sweeney, *From Cochise to Geronimo*, 446–50.

33 Britton Davis, *The Truth About Geronimo*, 183–88; Edwin R. Sweeney, *From Cochise to Geronimo*, 455–59.

34 Britton Davis, *The Truth About Geronimo*, 188–89.

35 Britton Davis, *The Truth About Geronimo*, 189.

36 Edwin R. Sweeney, *From Cochise to Geronimo*, 461.

37 Britton Davis, *The Truth About Geronimo*, 189, 191–92.

38 Edwin R. Sweeney, *From Cochise to Geronimo*, 460, 461.

39 Britton Davis, *The Truth About Geronimo*, 194.

40 Edwin R. Sweeney, *From Cochise to Geronimo*, 461, 462.

41 Edwin R. Sweeney, *From Cochise to Geronimo*, 462; Berndt Kühn, *Chronicles of War*, 277.

42 Ibid.

43 Edwin R. Sweeney, *From Cochise to Geronimo*, 462–63; Berndt Kühn, *Chronicles of War*, 277–78.

44 Edwin R. Sweeney, *From Cochise to Geronimo*, 463.

45 Ibid.

46 Edwin R. Sweeney, *From Cochise to Geronimo*, 464.

47 Ibid.

48 Edwin R. Sweeney, *From Cochise to Geronimo*, 465, 469; Berndt Kühn, *Chronicles of War*, 278.

49 Edwin R. Sweeney, *From Cochise to Geronimo*, 469; Angie Debo, *Geronimo*, 246.

50 Edwin R. Sweeney, *From Cochise to Geronimo*, 469.

51 Perico, Geronimo's cousin—whom he referred to as brother—was along on the raid, hoping to recover his family. He and Bi-ya-neta Tse-dah-dilth-thlith would marry and remain married for the rest of their lives. Angie Debo, *Geronimo*, 125, 246.

52 Edwin R. Sweeney, *From Cochise to Geronimo*, 469–70; Angie Debo, *Geronimo*, 125, 246.

53 Edwin R. Sweeney, *From Cochise to Geronimo*, 470.

54 Edwin R. Sweeney, *From Cochise to Geronimo*, 471.

55 Edwin R. Sweeney, *From Cochise to Geronimo*, 473.

56 Eve Ball, *Indeh: An Apache Odyssey*, 56; Angie Debo, *Geronimo*, 246–47. Again, there is no real good count on how many wives he had.

57 Edwin R. Sweeney, *From Cochise to Geronimo*, 477, 478.

58 Edwin R. Sweeney, *From Cochise to Geronimo*, 477–79; Berndt Kühn, *Chronicles of War*, 280.

59 Paul Andrew Hutton, *The Apache Wars*, 353; Dan L. Thrapp, *The Conquest of Apacheria*, 339.

60 Robert M. Utley, *Geronimo*, 175–76; Paul Andrew Hutton, *The Apache Wars*, 354.

61 Robert M. Utley, *Geronimo*, 165.

62 Edwin R. Sweeney, *From Cochise to Geronimo*, 464–65, 467; Robert M. Utley, *Geronimo*, 134, 189.

63 Edwin R. Sweeney, *From Cochise to Geronimo*, 464–66.

64 Paul Andrew Hutton, *The Apache Wars*, 354; Robert M. Utley, *Geronimo*, 175; Edwin R. Sweeney, *From Cochise to Geronimo*, 466.

65 Edwin R. Sweeney, *From Cochise to Geronimo*, 466, 467; Robert M. Utley, *Geronimo*, 174.

66 Paul Andrew Hutton, *The Apache Wars*, 355; Robert M. Utley, *Geronimo*, 176.

67 Robert M. Utley, *Geronimo*, 175–76; Paul Andrew Hutton, *The Apache Wars*, 354; Edwin R. Sweeney, *From Cochise to Geronimo*, 467–68, 491.

68 Robert M. Utley, *Geronimo*, 176; Paul Andrew Hutton, *The Apache Wars*, 354–55; Edwin R. Sweeney, *From Cochise to Geronimo*, 491.

69 Edwin R. Sweeney, *From Cochise to Geronimo*, 491; Robert M. Utley, *Geronimo*, 177.

70 Edwin R. Sweeney, *From Cochise to Geronimo*, 493, 495; Robert M. Utley, *Geronimo*, 178; Paul Andrew Hutton, *The Apache Wars*, 358.

71 Berndt Kühn, *Chronicles of War*, 281, 282, 283.

72 Robert M. Utley, *Geronimo*, 175, 177; Edwin R. Sweeney, *From Cochise to Geronimo*, 486–87.

73 Paul Andrew Hutton, *The Apache Wars*, 354, 355; Edwin R. Sweeney, *From Cochise to Geronimo*, 380, 486–87; Robert M. Utley, *Geronimo*, 175, 178.

74 Nelson Appleton Miles, *Personal Recollections*, 455; Paul Andrew Hutton, *The Apache Wars*, 357; Edwin R. Sweeney, *From Cochise to Geronimo*, 494.

75 Paul Andrew Hutton, *The Apache Wars*, 357, 358; Edwin R. Sweeney, *From Cochise to Geronimo*, 497.

76 Nelson Appleton Miles, *Personal Recollections*, 456; Paul Andrew Hutton, *The Apache Wars*, 358; Edwin R. Sweeney, *From Cochise to Geronimo*, 497–98; Robert M. Utley, *Geronimo*, 178.

77 Nelson Appleton Miles, *Personal Recollections*, 456; Paul Andrew Hutton, *The Apache Wars*, 358; Edwin R. Sweeney, *From Cochise to Geronimo*, 498; Robert M. Utley, *Geronimo*, 178; Tom Horn, *Life of Tom Horn, Government Scout and Interpreter* (Scotts Valley, CA: CreateSpace, 2016), 108.

78 Nelson Appleton Miles, *Personal Recollections*, 456; Paul Andrew Hutton, *The Apache Wars*, 358; Edwin R. Sweeney, *From Cochise to Geronimo*, 498.

79 Paul Andrew Hutton, *The Apache Wars*, 358–59; Edwin R. Sweeney, *From Cochise to Geronimo*, 498–99; Nelson Appleton Miles, *Personal Recollections*, 456–57; Sherry Robinson, *Apache Voices: Their Stories of Survival as Told to Eve Ball* (Albuquerque: University of New Mexico Press, 2000), 12.

80 Edwin R. Sweeney, *From Cochise to Geronimo*, 499.

81 Ibid.

82 Nelson Appleton Miles, *Personal Recollections*, 457–58.

83 Nelson Appleton Miles, *Personal Recollections*, 458; Edwin R. Sweeney, *From Cochise to Geronimo*, 500–01; Paul Andrew Hutton, *The Apache Wars*, 257.

84 Nelson Appleton Miles, *Personal Recollections*, 458; Edwin R. Sweeney, *From Cochise to Geronimo*, 501.

85 Ibid.

86 Edwin R. Sweeney, *From Cochise to Geronimo*, 504.

87 Nelson Appleton Miles, *Personal Recollections*, 458; Edwin R. Sweeney, *From Cochise to Geronimo*, 501.

88 Nelson Appleton Miles, *Personal Recollections*, 458; Edwin R. Sweeney, *From Cochise to Geronimo*, 501–02.

89 Edwin R. Sweeney, *From Cochise to Geronimo*, 502; Nelson Appleton Miles, *Personal Recollections*, 458.

90 Nelson Appleton Miles, *Personal Recollections*, 458.

91 Ibid.

92 Nelson Appleton Miles, *Personal Recollections*, 458; Edwin R. Sweeney, *From Cochise to Geronimo*, 502–03.

93 Edwin R. Sweeney, *From Cochise to Geronimo*, 503.

94 Edwin R. Sweeney, *From Cochise to Geronimo*, 503; Nelson Appleton Miles, *Personal Recollections*, 458–59.

95 Angie Debo, *Geronimo*, 250.

96 Nelson Appleton Miles, *Personal Recollections*, 459; Edwin R. Sweeney, *From Cochise to Geronimo*, 505; Paul Andrew Hutton, *The Apache Wars*, 361.

97 Nelson Appleton Miles, *Personal Recollections*, 464; Edwin R. Sweeney, *From Cochise to Geronimo*, 505.

98 Nelson Appleton Miles, *Personal Recollections*, 465; Paul Andrew Hutton, *The Apache Wars*, 361. Sherry Robinson, *Apache Voices*, 12.

99 Nelson Appleton Miles, *Personal Recollections*, 465; Paul Andrew Hutton, *The Apache Wars*, 362; Edwin R. Sweeney, *From Cochise to Geronimo*, 505.

100 Nelson Appleton Miles, *Personal Recollections*, 465; Edwin R. Sweeney, *From Cochise to Geronimo*, 505; Angie Debo, *Geronimo*, 251.

101 Nelson Appleton Miles, *Personal Recollections*, 465.

102 Nelson Appleton Miles, *Personal Recollections*, 466.

103 Nelson Appleton Miles, *Personal Recollections*, 467; Paul Andrew Hutton, *The Apache Wars*, 363; Edwin R. Sweeney, *From Cochise to Geronimo*, 513–14.

104 Paul Andrew Hutton, *The Apache Wars*, 363; Edwin R. Sweeney, *From Cochise to Geronimo*, 514.

105 Robert M. Utley, *Geronimo*, 181; Edwin R. Sweeney, *From Cochise to Geronimo*, 516.

106 Edwin R. Sweeney, *From Cochise to Geronimo*, 507, 511, 512, 516–17.

107 Robert M. Utley, *Geronimo*, 181; Edwin R. Sweeney, *From Cochise to Geronimo*, 517; Berndt Kühn, *Chronicles of War*, 285.

108 Edwin R. Sweeney, *From Cochise to Geronimo*, 517–18; Berndt Kühn, *Chronicles of War*, 285.

109 Nelson Appleton Miles, *Personal Recollections*, 467.

110 Edwin R. Sweeney, *From Cochise to Geronimo*, 519, 520; Nelson Appleton Miles, *Personal Recollections*, 467; Angie Debo, *Geronimo*, 253.

111 Edwin R. Sweeney, *From Cochise to Geronimo*, 520; Angie Debo, *Geronimo*, 253.

112 Edwin R. Sweeney, *From Cochise to Geronimo*, 520–21.

113 Edwin R. Sweeney, *From Cochise to Geronimo*, 521.

114 Edwin R. Sweeney, *From Cochise to Geronimo*, 515, 521.

115 Paul Andrew Hutton, *The Apache Wars*, 364.

116 John G. Bourke, *On the Border with Crook*, 474; Paul Andrew Hutton, *The Apache Wars*, 365; Edwin R. Sweeney, *From Cochise to Geronimo*, 521.

117 Paul Andrew Hutton, *The Apache Wars*, 365; Robert M. Utley, *Geronimo*, 184.

118 Britton Davis, *The Truth About Geronimo*, 200, 201–02; Edwin R. Sweeney, *From Cochise to Geronimo*, 522.

119 Paul Andrew Hutton, *The Apache Wars*, 366.

120 Britton Davis, *The Truth About Geronimo*, 204–05.

121 Britton Davis, *The Truth About Geronimo*, 205.

122 Britton Davis, *The Truth About Geronimo*, 205–07.

123 Paul Andrew Hutton, *The Apache Wars*, 366; Robert M. Utley, *Geronimo*, 185.

124 Robert M. Utley, *Geronimo*, 185.

125 Edwin R. Sweeney, *From Cochise to Geronimo*, 523.

126 Ibid.

127 David Roberts, *Once They Moved Like the Wind*, 271; Britton Davis, *The Truth About Geronimo*, 207, 209, 210.

128 John G. Bourke, *On the Border with Crook*, 480; Edwin R. Sweeney, *From Cochise to Geronimo*, 524.

129 Ibid.

130 Nelson Appleton Miles, *Personal Recollections*, 468.

131 Nelson Appleton Miles, *Personal Recollections*, 468; Edwin R. Sweeney, *From Cochise to Geronimo*, 525.

132 Ibid.

133 Edwin R. Sweeney, *From Cochise to Geronimo*, 523, 528.

134 Nelson Appleton Miles, *Personal Recollections*, 468–70; Edwin R. Sweeney, *From Cochise to Geronimo*, 526.

135 Nelson Appleton Miles, *Personal Recollections*, 472.

136 Edwin R. Sweeney, *From Cochise to Geronimo*, 529; Nelson Appleton Miles, *Personal Recollections*, 472.

137 Nelson Appleton Miles, *Personal Recollections*, 474–75.

138 Nelson Appleton Miles, *Personal Recollections*, 475; Edwin R. Sweeney, *From Cochise to Geronimo*, 530.

139 Edwin R. Sweeney, *From Cochise to Geronimo*, 530, 531.

140 Edwin R. Sweeney, *From Cochise to Geronimo*, 531.

141 Edwin R. Sweeney, *From Cochise to Geronimo*, 530.

142 Edwin R. Sweeney, *From Cochise to Geronimo*, 531.

143 Edwin R. Sweeney, *From Cochise to Geronimo*, 532–33.

144 Edwin R. Sweeney, *From Cochise to Geronimo*, 533.

145 S. M. Barrett, ed., *Geronimo*, 148.

146 S. M. Barrett, ed., *Geronimo*, 149.

147 John G. Bourke, *On the Border with Crook*, 480–81; Dan L. Thrapp, *The Conquest of Apacheria*, 364.

148 Nelson Appleton Miles, *Personal Recollections*, 468–69; Paul Andrew Hutton, *The Apache Wars*, 369.

149 Berndt Kühn in *Chronicles of War* on page 285 says three men and two women were killed, and Edwin R. Sweeney in *From Cochise to Geronimo* on page 536 says two men and three women were killed.

150 Berndt Kühn, *Chronicles of War*, 285, 286; Robert M. Utley, *Geronimo*, 193; Edwin R. Sweeney, *From Cochise to Geronimo*, 536.

151 Edwin R. Sweeney, *From Cochise to Geronimo*, 536.

152 Edwin R. Sweeney, *From Cochise to Geronimo*, 536–37.

153 Edwin R. Sweeney, *From Cochise to Geronimo*, 537.

154 Kieran McCarty and C. L. Sonnichsen, "Trini Verdin and the Truth of History," *Journal of Arizona History*, vol. 14, no. 2 (Summer 1973), 149; Edwin R. Sweeney, *From Cochise to Geronimo*, 537.

155 Edwin R. Sweeney, *From Cochise to Geronimo*, 537.

156 McCarty and Sonnichsen, "Trini Verdin and the Truth of History," 151; Edwin R. Sweeney, *From Cochise to Geronimo*, 537.

157 McCarty and Sonnichsen, "Trini Verdin and the Truth of History," 151; Edwin R. Sweeney, *From Cochise to Geronimo*, 537–38.

158 Berndt Kühn, *Chronicles of War*, 287; Edwin R. Sweeney, *From Cochise to Geronimo*, 538.

159 Edwin R. Sweeney, *From Cochise to Geronimo*, 538.

160 Edwin R. Sweeney, *From Cochise to Geronimo*, 538–39.

161 Edwin R. Sweeney, *From Cochise to Geronimo*, 539.

162 Edwin R. Sweeney, *From Cochise to Geronimo*, 539; Paul Andrew Hutton, *The Apache Wars*, 375; Robert M. Utley, *Geronimo*, 197; Nelson Appleton Miles, *Personal Recollections*, 489–90.

163 Edwin R. Sweeney, *From Cochise to Geronimo*, 539.

164 Edwin R. Sweeney, *From Cochise to Geronimo*, 540.

165 Edwin R. Sweeney, *From Cochise to Geronimo*, 540; Berndt Kühn, *Chronicles of War*, 287.

166 Edwin R. Sweeney, *From Cochise to Geronimo*, 541.

167 Ibid.

168 Ibid.

169 Edwin R. Sweeney, *From Cochise to Geronimo*, 541–42.

170 Paul Andrew Hutton, *The Apache Wars*, 375; Edwin R. Sweeney, *From Cochise to Geronimo*, 543.

171 Paul Andrew Hutton, *The Apache Wars*, 375. Melissa Hayes personal communication, October 12, 2020.

172 Ibid.

173 Paul Andrew Hutton, *The Apache Wars*, 376; Berndt Kühn, *Chronicles of War*, 290.

174 Edwin R. Sweeney, *From Cochise to Geronimo*, 548; McCarty and Sonnichsen, "Trini Verdin and the Truth of History," 152, 161.

175 Edwin R. Sweeney, *From Cochise to Geronimo*, 549.

176 Edwin R. Sweeney, *From Cochise to Geronimo*, 549–50.

177 Edwin R. Sweeney, *From Cochise to Geronimo*, 550; McCarty and Sonnichsen, "Trini Verdin and the Truth of History," 161.

178 Ibid.

179 Bob Boze Bell, *The Illustrated Life and Times of Geronimo* (Cave Creek, AZ: Two Roads West, 2020), 70; Edwin R. Sweeney, *From Cochise to Geronimo*, 550.

180 Jack C. Lane, ed., *Chasing Geronimo: The Journal of Leonard Wood, May–September 1886* (Lincoln: University of Nebraska Press, 1970), 27, 37, 55; Edwin R. Sweeney, *From Cochise to Geronimo*, 549, 550, 552; Robert M. Utley, *Geronimo*, 198; Paul Andrew Hutton, *The Apache Wars*, 373.

181 Doug Hocking, *Tom Jeffords, Friend of Cochise*, 147; Paul Andrew Hutton, *The Apache Wars*, 377; Edwin R. Sweeney, *From Cochise to Geronimo*, 556; Nelson Appleton Miles, *Personal Recollections*, 495–96.

182 Angie Debo, *Geronimo*, 271, 272–73; Nelson Appleton Miles, *Personal Recollections*, 497; Paul Andrew Hutton, *The Apache Wars*, 378.

183 Louis Kraft, ed., *Lt. Charles Gatewood & His Apache Wars Memoir*, 123–24; Paul Andrew Hutton, *The Apache Wars*, 377–78; Dan L. Thrapp, *The Conquest of Apacheria*, 353.

184 S. M. Barrett, ed., *Geronimo*, 150.

185 Edwin R. Sweeney, *From Cochise to Geronimo*, 553–54.

186 Edwin R. Sweeney, *From Cochise to Geronimo*, 552.

187 Edwin R. Sweeney, *From Cochise to Geronimo*, 553.

188 Edwin R. Sweeney, *From Cochise to Geronimo*, 554.

189 Edwin R. Sweeney, *From Cochise to Geronimo*, 554, 555; Louis Kraft, ed., *Lt. Charles Gatewood & His Apache Wars Memoir*, 124.

190 Louis Kraft, ed., *Lt. Charles Gatewood & His Apache Wars Memoir*, 124, 125, 126.

191 Louis Kraft, ed., *Lt. Charles Gatewood & His Apache Wars Memoir*, 126–27; Dan L. Thrapp, *The Conquest of Apacheria*, 354.

192 Louis Kraft, ed., *Lt. Charles Gatewood & His Apache Wars Memoir*, 126.

193 Louis Kraft, ed., *Lt. Charles Gatewood & His Apache Wars Memoir*, 127.

194 Louis Kraft, ed., *Lt. Charles Gatewood & His Apache Wars Memoir*, 126.

195 Paul Andrew Hutton, *The Apache Wars*, 379; Edwin R. Sweeney, *From Cochise to Geronimo*, 565.

196 Paul Andrew Hutton, *The Apache Wars*, 380.

197 Edwin R. Sweeney, *From Cochise to Geronimo*, 565.

198 Paul Andrew Hutton, *The Apache Wars*, 380, 381; Edwin R. Sweeney, *From Cochise to Geronimo*, 567.

199 Robert M. Utley, *Geronimo*, 199; Edwin R. Sweeney, *From Cochise to Geronimo*, 559.

200 Edwin R. Sweeney, *From Cochise to Geronimo*, 559–60.

201 Edwin R. Sweeney, *From Cochise to Geronimo*, 560.

202 Sherry Robinson, *Apache Voices*, 12; Robert M. Utley, *Geronimo*, 208.

203 Louis Kraft, ed., *Lt. Charles Gatewood & His Apache Wars Memoir*, 130; Edwin Sweeney in *From Cochise to Geronimo*, page 561, believes the two women's names were Tah-das-te and Dejonah.

204 Louis Kraft, ed., *Lt. Charles Gatewood & His Apache Wars Memoir*, 130; Edwin R. Sweeney, *From Cochise to Geronimo*, 561.

205 Jack C. Lane, ed., *Chasing Geronimo: The Journal of Leonard Wood*, 98; Louis Kraft, ed., *Lt. Charles Gatewood & His Apache Wars Memoir*, 130.

206 Edwin R. Sweeney, *From Cochise to Geronimo*, 561; Louis Kraft, ed., *Lt. Charles Gatewood & His Apache Wars Memoir*, 131.

207 Jack C. Lane, ed., *Chasing Geronimo: The Journal of Leonard Wood*, 99, 136n17.

208 Edwin R. Sweeney, *From Cochise to Geronimo*, 561; Louis Kraft, ed., *Lt. Charles Gatewood & His Apache Wars Memoir*, 131.

209 Louis Kraft, ed., *Lt. Charles Gatewood & His Apache Wars Memoir*, 132; Edwin R. Sweeney, *From Cochise to Geronimo*, 562.

210 Eve Ball, *In the Days of Victorio*, 185.

211 Eve Ball, *In the Days of Victorio*, 185, 187.

212 Eve Ball, *In the Days of Victorio*, 187.

213 Louis Kraft, ed., *Lt. Charles Gatewood & His Apache Wars Memoir*, 133, 134.

214 Louis Kraft, ed., *Lt. Charles Gatewood & His Apache Wars Memoir*, 134–35; Edwin R. Sweeney, *From Cochise to Geronimo*, 562–63.

215 Louis Kraft, ed., *Lt. Charles Gatewood & His Apache Wars Memoir*, 136, 138; Edwin R. Sweeney, *From Cochise to Geronimo*, 563.

216 Louis Kraft, ed., *Lt. Charles Gatewood & His Apache Wars Memoir*, 138.

217 Ibid.

218 Ibid.

219 Ibid.

220 Louis Kraft, ed., *Lt. Charles Gatewood & His Apache Wars Memoir*, 138–39.

221 Louis Kraft, ed., *Lt. Charles Gatewood & His Apache Wars Memoir*, 139.

222 Ibid.

223 Louis Kraft, ed., *Lt. Charles Gatewood & His Apache Wars Memoir*, 140.

224 Louis Kraft, ed., *Lt. Charles Gatewood & His Apache Wars Memoir*, 140; Robert M. Utley, *Geronimo*, 204.

225 Louis Kraft, ed., *Lt. Charles Gatewood & His Apache Wars Memoir*, 140–41.

226 Louis Kraft, ed., *Lt. Charles Gatewood & His Apache Wars Memoir*, 141.

227 Ibid.

228 Louis Kraft, ed., *Lt. Charles Gatewood & His Apache Wars Memoir*, 141–42.

229 Louis Kraft, ed., *Lt. Charles Gatewood & His Apache Wars Memoir*, 142.

230 Ibid.

231 Louis Kraft, ed., *Lt. Charles Gatewood & His Apache Wars Memoir*, 142–43.

232 Louis Kraft, ed., *Lt. Charles Gatewood & His Apache Wars Memoir*, 143.

233 Ibid.

234 Louis Kraft, ed., *Lt. Charles Gatewood & His Apache Wars Memoir*, 144.

235 Louis Kraft, ed., *Lt. Charles Gatewood & His Apache Wars Memoir*, 144; Edwin R. Sweeney, *From Cochise to Geronimo*, 564.

236 Louis Kraft, ed., *Lt. Charles Gatewood & His Apache Wars Memoir*, 144.

237 Edwin R. Sweeney, *From Cochise to Geronimo*, 570.

238 Louis Kraft, ed., *Lt. Charles Gatewood & His Apache Wars Memoir*, 145; Edwin R. Sweeney, *From Cochise to Geronimo*, 570.

239 Louis Kraft, ed., *Lt. Charles Gatewood & His Apache Wars Memoir*, 145–46.

240 Louis Kraft, ed., *Lt. Charles Gatewood & His Apache Wars Memoir*, 146.

241 Ibid.

242 Louis Kraft, ed., *Lt. Charles Gatewood & His Apache Wars Memoir*, 146; Jack C. Lane, ed., *Chasing Geronimo: The Journal of Leonard Wood*, 106–07.

243 Louis Kraft, ed., *Lt. Charles Gatewood & His Apache Wars Memoir*, 146–47; Jack C. Lane, ed., *Chasing Geronimo: The Journal of Leonard Wood*, 106–07.

244 Louis Kraft, ed., *Lt. Charles Gatewood & His Apache Wars Memoir*, 147.

245 Ibid.

246 Robert M. Utley, *Geronimo*, 215; Louis Kraft, ed., *Lt. Charles Gatewood & His Apache Wars Memoir*, 147–48.

247 Jack C. Lane, ed., *Chasing Geronimo: The Journal of Leonard Wood*, 108; Edwin R. Sweeney, *From Cochise to Geronimo*, 571.

248 Nelson Appleton Miles, *Personal Recollections*, 519–20.

249 Louis Kraft, ed., *Lt. Charles Gatewood & His Apache Wars Memoir*, 150.

250 Robert M. Utley, *Geronimo*, 216; Jack C. Lane, ed., *Chasing Geronimo: The Journal of Leonard Wood*, 108.

251 Louis Kraft, ed., *Lt. Charles Gatewood & His Apache Wars Memoir*, 150.

252 Jack C. Lane, ed., *Chasing Geronimo: The Journal of Leonard Wood*, 108–09; Louis Kraft, ed., *Lt. Charles Gatewood & His Apache Wars Memoir*, 151.

253 Louis Kraft, ed., *Lt. Charles Gatewood & His Apache Wars Memoir*, 151–52.

254 Louis Kraft, ed., *Lt. Charles Gatewood & His Apache Wars Memoir*, 152.

255 Edwin R. Sweeney, *From Cochise to Geronimo*, 571; Nelson Appleton Miles, *Personal Recollections*, 520.

256 Edwin R. Sweeney, *From Cochise to Geronimo*, 572; Nelson Appleton Miles, *Personal Recollections*, 520.

257 Robert M. Utley, *Geronimo*, 217.

258 Louis Kraft, ed., *Lt. Charles Gatewood & His Apache Wars Memoir*, 152.

259 Edwin R. Sweeney, *From Cochise to Geronimo*, 572; Robert M. Utley, *Geronimo*, 217; Angie Debo, *Geronimo*, 291.

260 Nelson Appleton Miles, *Personal Recollections*, 520–21.

261 Angie Debo, *Geronimo*, 294; Paul Andrew Hutton, *The Apache Wars*, 385–86.

262 S. M. Barrett, ed., *Geronimo*, 154; Nelson Appleton Miles, *Personal Recollections*, 521.

263 Nelson Appleton Miles, *Personal Recollections*, 521.

264 Nelson Appleton Miles, *Personal Recollections*, 522.

265 Angie Debo, *Geronimo*, 292.

266 Louis Kraft, ed., *Lt. Charles Gatewood & His Apache Wars Memoir*, 153.

267 Ibid.

268 Edwin R. Sweeney, *From Cochise to Geronimo*, 573.

269 S. M. Barrett, ed., *Geronimo*, 154.

270 Angie Debo, *Geronimo*, 293. Note: Years later, cowboys tore the monument apart and found a bottle with a paper inside it with the names of the officers present at the ceremony (Angie Debo, *Geronimo*, 293).

271 Edwin R. Sweeney, *From Cochise to Geronimo*, 573.

272 Robert M. Utley, *The Lance and the Shield*, 265, 266.

273 Bobby Bridger, *Buffalo Bill and Sitting Bull*, 320–21; Robert M. Utley, *The Lance and the Shield*, 266.

274 Robert M. Utley, *The Lance and the Shield*, 266.

275 Josephine Waggoner, *Witness*, 174; Robert M. Utley, *The Lance and the Shield*, 266; Norman E. Matteoni, *Prairie Man*, 194; Stanley Vestal, *Sitting Bull: Champion of the Sioux*, 251.

276 Robert M. Utley, *The Lance and the Shield*, 266.

277 Norman E. Matteoni, *Prairie Man*, 194; Stanley Vestal, *Sitting Bull: Champion of the Sioux*, 252.

278 Ibid.

279 Stanley Vestal, *Sitting Bull: Champion of the Sioux*, 252.

280 Norman E. Matteoni, *Prairie Man*, 194; Stanley Vestal, *Sitting Bull: Champion of the Sioux*, 251–52.

281 Stanley Vestal, *Sitting Bull: Champion of the Sioux*, 252.

282 Ibid.

283 Stanley Vestal, *Sitting Bull: Champion of the Sioux*, 252–53.

284 Stanley Vestal, *Sitting Bull: Champion of the Sioux*, 253.

285 Robert M. Utley, *The Lance and the Shield*, 266–67.

286 Stanley Vestal, *Sitting Bull: Champion of the Sioux*, 253.

287 Ibid.

288 Stanley Vestal, *Sitting Bull: Champion of the Sioux*, 254.

CHAPTER 12: GERONIMO, PRISONER OF WAR, AND SITTING BULL ON THE RESERVATION, 1886–1890

1 Angie Debo, *Geronimo*, 296.

2 Nelson Appleton Miles, *Personal Recollections*, 527; Edwin R. Sweeney, *From Cochise to Geronimo*, 573; Angie Debo, *Geronimo*, 296.

3 Angie Debo, *Geronimo*, 295.

4 Angie Debo, *Geronimo*, 295–96; Edwin R. Sweeney, *From Cochise to Geronimo*, 573.

5 Edwin R. Sweeney, *From Cochise to Geronimo*, 573.

6 Edwin R. Sweeney, *From Cochise to Geronimo*, 573; Jack C. Lane, ed., *Chasing Geronimo: The Journal of Leonard Wood*, 111.

7 Jack C. Lane, ed., *Chasing Geronimo: The Journal of Leonard Wood*, 111; Edwin R. Sweeney, *From Cochise to Geronimo*, 573.

8 Nelson Appleton Miles, *Personal Recollections*, 527; Jack C. Lane, ed., *Chasing Geronimo: The Journal of Leonard Wood*, 111.

9 Jack C. Lane, ed., *Chasing Geronimo: The Journal of Leonard Wood*, 112; Nelson Appleton Miles, *Personal Recollections*, 528; Angie Debo, *Geronimo*, 298.

10 Robert M. Utley, *Geronimo*, 219; Angie Debo, *Geronimo*, 298, 300; Edwin R. Sweeney, *From Cochise to Geronimo*, 574.

11 Nelson Appleton Miles, *Personal Recollections*, 528; Jack C. Lane, ed., *Chasing Geronimo: The Journal of Leonard Wood*, 112.

12 Jack C. Lane, ed., *Chasing Geronimo: The Journal of Leonard Wood*, 114.

13 Robert M. Utley, *Geronimo*, 225, 226.

14 Robert M. Utley, *Geronimo*, 226; Angie Debo, *Geronimo*, 301.

15 Robert M. Utley, *Geronimo*, 223.

16 Ibid.

17 Ibid.

18 Edwin R. Sweeney, *From Cochise to Geronimo*, 574–75; Angie Debo, *Geronimo*, 301.

19 Angie Debo, *Geronimo*, 303; Robert M. Utley, *Geronimo*, 223.

20 W. Michael Farmer, *Geronimo: Prisoner of Lies: Twenty-Three Years as a Prisoner of War, 1886–1909* (Guilford, CT: TwoDot, 2019), 30; Robert M. Utley, *Geronimo*, 223.

21 Angie Debo, *Geronimo*, 308.

22 Ibid.

23 Angie Debo, *Geronimo*, 308–09.

24 Angie Debo, *Geronimo*, 309, 110, 321; W. Michael Farmer, *Geronimo: Prisoner of Lies*, 54.

25 Edwin R. Sweeney, *From Cochise to Geronimo*, 575, 576.

26 W. Michael Farmer, *Geronimo: Prisoner of Lies*, 37, 41; Angie Debo, *Geronimo*, 316.

27 Angie Debo, *Geronimo*, 319.

28 Angie Debo, *Geronimo*, 321.

29 W. Michael Farmer, *Geronimo: Prisoner of Lies*, 56.

30 Robert M. Utley, *Geronimo*, 227–28.

31 Robert M. Utley, *Geronimo*, 231.

32 Ibid.

33 Ibid.

34 Robert M. Utley, *Geronimo*, 233; W. Michael Farmer, *Geronimo: Prisoner of Lies*, 43.

35 W. Michael Farmer, *Geronimo: Prisoner of Lies*, 43, 57, 61, 68; Robert M. Utley, *Geronimo*, 233; Angie Debo, *Geronimo*, 326, 333–34.

36 Robert M. Utley, *Geronimo*, 232.

37 Robert M. Utley, *Geronimo*, 234; Angie Debo, *Geronimo*, 328.

38 Nelson Appleton Miles, *Personal Recollections*, 532.

39 Angie Debo, *Geronimo*, 328; Robert M. Utley, *Geronimo*, 234.

40 Robert M. Utley, *Geronimo*, 234, 235, 236.

41 Robert M. Utley, *Geronimo*, 236.

42 Angie Debo, *Geronimo*, 336; Robert M. Utley, *Geronimo*, 237, 238.

43 Eve Ball, *Indeh: An Apache Odyssey*, 153; Robert M. Utley, *Geronimo*, 238.

44 Paul Andrew Hutton, *Phil Sheridan and His Army*, 372.

45 Robert M. Utley, *Geronimo*, 237, 239; W. Michael Farmer, *Geronimo: Prisoner of Lies*, 49.

46 W. Michael Farmer, *Geronimo: Prisoner of Lies*, 74; Angie Debo, *Geronimo*, 341.

47 Eve Ball, *Indeh: An Apache Odyssey*, 154.

48 S. M. Barrett, ed., *Geronimo*, 157; Angie Debo, *Geronimo*, 342.

49 Robert M. Utley, *Geronimo*, 240.

50 Oliver Otis Howard, *Famous Indian Chiefs I Have Known*, 358, 361.

51 Oliver Otis Howard, *Famous Indian Chiefs I Have Known*, 361–62.

52 Angie Debo, *Geronimo*, 344; Robert M. Utley, *Geronimo*, 241.

53 W. Michael Farmer, *Geronimo: Prisoner of Lies*, 49; Eve Ball, *Indeh: An Apache Odyssey*, 154.

54 W. Michael Farmer, *Geronimo: Prisoner of Lies*, 154.

55 Robert M. Utley, *Geronimo*, 241.

56 Eve Ball, *Indeh: An Apache Odyssey*, 158; Robert M. Utley, *Geronimo*, 241.

57 Eve Ball, *Indeh: An Apache Odyssey*, 158.

58 Ibid.

59 Angie Debo, *Geronimo*, 344.

60 Eve Ball, *Indeh: An Apache Odyssey*, 154.

61 Angie Debo, *Geronimo*, 374; Eve Ball, *Indeh: An Apache Odyssey*, 158.

62 Eve Ball, *Indeh: An Apache Odyssey*, 159; Robert M. Utley, *Geronimo*, 241–42.

63 Paul Andrew Hutton, *The Apache Wars*, 417; S. M. Barrett, ed., *Geronimo*, 149.

64 Robert M. Utley, *Geronimo*, 242.

65 Ibid.

66 Eve Ball, *Indeh: An Apache Odyssey*, 154.

67 Robert M. Utley, *Geronimo*, 242.

68 Robert M. Utley, *The Lance and the Shield*, 270.

69 Robert M. Utley, *The Lance and the Shield*, 270, 271.

70 Robert M. Utley, *The Lance and the Shield*, 271.

71 Stanley Vestal, *New Sources of Indian History*, 61–63; *Mary Collins Collection*, South Dakota State Historical Society, Manuscript Collection, accessed February 5, 2020, https://history.sd.gov/archives/manuscripts.aspx.

72 Robert M. Utley, *The Lance and the Shield*, 255; Stanley Vestal, *New Sources of Indian History*, 64.

73 Norman E. Matteoni, *Prairie Man*, 164.

74 Paul L. Hedren, *After Custer*, 166, 167; Robert W. Larson, *Red Cloud*, 251; Norman E. Matteoni, *Prairie Man*, 201–02.

75 Paul L. Hedren, *After Custer*, 167; Norman E. Matteoni, *Prairie Man*, 203.

76 Paul L. Hedren, *After Custer*, 167; Norman E. Matteoni, *Prairie Man*, 203, 204.

77 James McLaughlin, *My Friend the Indian* (Lincoln: University of Nebraska Press, 1989), 274; Norman E. Matteoni, *Prairie Man*, 205.

78 James McLaughlin, *My Friend the Indian*, 274; Norman E. Matteoni, *Prairie Man*, 205.

79 Norman E. Matteoni, *Prairie Man*, 205.

80 James McLaughlin, *My Friend the Indian*, 274; Norman E. Matteoni, *Prairie Man*, 205.

81 Norman E. Matteoni, *Prairie Man*, 206.

82 Stanley Vestal, *New Sources of Indian History*, 63–64.

83 Stanley Vestal, *New Sources of Indian History*, 301, 303.

84 Robert M. Utley, *The Lance and the Shield*, 274; Norman E. Matteoni, *Prairie Man*, 206.

85 Robert M. Utley, *The Lance and the Shield*, 274; Norman E. Matteoni, *Prairie Man*, 206–07.

86 Robert M. Utley, *The Lance and the Shield*, 274.

87 Norman E. Matteoni, *Prairie Man*, 207.

88 Norman E. Matteoni, *Prairie Man*, 208; Robert W. Larson, *Red Cloud*, 254.

89 Robert M. Utley, *The Lance and the Shield*, 275; Norman E. Matteoni, *Prairie Man*, 208–09; Robert W. Larson, *Red Cloud*, 228, 254–55.

90 Stanley Vestal, *New Sources of Indian History*, 302.

91 Norman E. Matteoni, *Prairie Man*, 210–11; James McLaughlin, *My Friend the Indian*, 278.

92 Robert M. Utley, *The Lance and the Shield*, 276; Norman E. Matteoni, *Prairie Man*, 211.

93 Robert M. Utley, *The Lance and the Shield*, 275; Norman E. Matteoni, *Prairie Man*, 209; James McLaughlin, *My Friend the Indian*, 278.

94 James McLaughlin, *My Friend the Indian*, 279.

95 Stanley Vestal, *New Sources of Indian History*, 302.

96 Norman E. Matteoni, *Prairie Man*, 211, 212; Stanley Vestal, *New Sources of Indian History*, 302.

97 James McLaughlin, *My Friend the Indian*, 279; Norman E. Matteoni, *Prairie Man*, 212.

98 US Commissioners and Delegations of Sioux Chiefs Visiting Washington, October 15, 1888, Photograph, US Library of Congress, accessed February 5, 2020, www.loc.gov/item/93514650; Norman E. Matteoni, *Prairie Man*, 212–13.

99 James McLaughlin, *My Friend the Indian*, 279; Norman E. Matteoni, *Prairie Man*, 212.

100 Stanley Vestal, *New Sources of Indian History*, 302; Stanley Vestal, *Sitting Bull: Champion of the Sioux*, 258; James McLaughlin, *My Friend the Indian*, 280.

101 Ralph V. Hunkins and John Clark Lindsey, *South Dakota: Its Past, Present, and Future* (New York: Macmillan, 1932), 117; J. Leonard Jennewein and Jane

Boorman, eds., *Dakota Panorama* (Freeman, SD: Brevet Press, 1973), 372; Paul L. Hedren, *After Custer*, 167.

102 Norman E. Matteoni, *Prairie Man*, 214.

103 Norman E. Matteoni, *Prairie Man*, 214–15.

104 Norman E. Matteoni, *Prairie Man*, 215.

105 Norman E. Matteoni, *Prairie Man*, 216.

106 Norman E. Matteoni, *Prairie Man*, 216; Robert M. Utley, *The Lance and the Shield*, 277.

107 Eileen Pollack, *Woman Walking Ahead: In Search of Catherine Weldon and Sitting Bull* (Albuquerque: University of New Mexico Press, 2002), 27; Robert W. Larson, *Red Cloud*, 258, 259.

108 Eileen Pollack, *Woman Walking Ahead*, 25.

109 Eileen Pollack, *Woman Walking Ahead*, 21.

110 Norman E. Matteoni, *Prairie Man*, 216.

111 Eileen Pollack, *Woman Walking Ahead*, 22, 24–25; Stanley Vestal, *Sitting Bull: Champion of the Sioux*, 264.

112 Eileen Pollack, *Woman Walking Ahead*, 25.

113 Ibid.

114 Eileen Pollack, *Woman Walking Ahead*, 25; Stanley Vestal, *New Sources of Indian History*, 93.

115 Eileen Pollack, *Woman Walking Ahead*, 26.

116 Eileen Pollack, *Woman Walking Ahead*, 27.

117 Stanley Vestal, *New Sources of Indian History*, 94; Norman E. Matteoni, *Prairie Man*, 219.

118 Stanley Vestal, *New Sources of Indian History*, 94.

119 Stanley Vestal, *New Sources of Indian History*, 94, 95.

120 "She Loves Sitting Bull," *Bismarck Weekly Tribune* (Bismarck, North Dakota), July 5, 1889, page 7, Newspapers.com, accessed February 7, 2020, www.newspapers.com/image/81382767/?terms=Bismarck%2BTribune%2BSitting%2BBull; Stanley Vestal, *New Sources of Indian History*, 99.

121 Stanley Vestal, *New Sources of Indian History*, 95–96; Eileen Pollack, *Woman Walking Ahead*, 49.

122 James McLaughlin, *My Friend the Indian*, 280–81.

123 Stanley Vestal, *Sitting Bull: Champion of the Sioux*, 257; Stanley Vestal, *New Sources of Indian History*, 306.

124 James McLaughlin, *My Friend the Indian*, 280–81.

125 James McLaughlin, *My Friend the Indian*, 282; Robert M. Utley, *The Lance and the Shield*, 278; Norman E. Matteoni, *Prairie Man*, 221.

126 Stanley Vestal, *New Sources of Indian History*, 303–04.

127 James McLaughlin, *My Friend the Indian*, 283.

128 James McLaughlin, *My Friend the Indian*, 284.

129 Norman E. Matteoni, *Prairie Man*, 228.

130 James McLaughlin, *My Friend the Indian*, 284.

131 James McLaughlin, *My Friend the Indian*, 284–85.

132 Robert W. Larson, *Gall: Lakota War Chief*, 208; Dee Brown, *Bury My Heart at Wounded Knee*, 431; Robert M. Utley, *The Lance and the Shield*, 278, 279; Norman E. Matteoni, *Prairie Man*, 225.

133 James McLaughlin, *My Friend the Indian*, 286.

134 Dee Brown, *Bury My Heart at Wounded Knee*, 431; Norman E. Matteoni, *Prairie Man*, 225; Robert M. Utley, *The Lance and the Shield*, 278.

135 Stanley Vestal, *Sitting Bull: Champion of the Sioux*, 261.

136 Dee Brown, *Bury My Heart at Wounded Knee*, 431; Stanley Vestal, *Sitting Bull: Champion of the Sioux*, 261.

137 Stanley Vestal, *Sitting Bull: Champion of the Sioux*, 261.

138 Dee Brown, *Bury My Heart at Wounded Knee*, 431; Robert M. Utley, *The Lance and the Shield*, 278.

139 Robert M. Utley, *The Lance and the Shield*, 278–79; Stanley Vestal, *Sitting Bull: Champion of the Sioux*, 261–62.

140 Robert W. Larson, *Gall: Lakota War Chief*, 208; Robert M. Utley, *The Lance and the Shield*, 279.

141 Robert M. Utley, *The Lance and the Shield*, 279.

142 Dee Brown, *Bury My Heart at Wounded Knee*, 431.

143 Robert W. Larson, *Gall: Lakota War Chief*, 208–09; Robert M. Utley, *The Lance and the Shield*, 279.

144 Robert M. Utley, *The Lance and the Shield*, 279; Norman E. Matteoni, *Prairie Man*, 228; Stanley Vestal, *Sitting Bull: Champion of the Sioux*, 262.

145 Stanley Vestal, *Sitting Bull: Champion of the Sioux*, 263.

146 Stanley Vestal, *Sitting Bull: Champion of the Sioux*, 264.

147 Hunkins and Lindsey, *South Dakota: Its Past, Present, and Future*, 117–18; Jennewein and Boorman, eds., *Dakota Panorama*, 373.

148 Robert M. Utley, *The Lance and the Shield*, 280.

149 Norman E. Matteoni, *Prairie Man*, 228; Robert M. Utley, *The Lance and the Shield*, 280; Stanley Vestal, *Sitting Bull: Champion of the Sioux*, 268; Paul Andrew Hutton, *The Apache Wars*, 417.

150 Norman E. Matteoni, *Prairie Man*, 243.

151 Norman E. Matteoni, *Prairie Man*, 243; Eileen Pollack, *Woman Walking Ahead*, 94–95.

152 Norman E. Matteoni, *Prairie Man*, 243.

153 Eileen Pollack, *Woman Walking Ahead*, 103–04; Robert M. Utley, *The Lance and the Shield*, 299.

154 Robert M. Utley, *The Lance and the Shield*, 299; Eileen Pollack, *Woman Walking Ahead*, 101, 102; Stanley Vestal, *New Sources of Indian History*, 55, 56.

155 Eileen Pollack, *Woman Walking Ahead*, 101, 104, 109; Stanley Vestal, *New Sources of Indian History*, 56.

156 Eileen Pollack, *Woman Walking Ahead*, 100, 102, 107.

157 Eileen Pollack, *Woman Walking Ahead*, 101, 102; Robert M. Utley, *The Lance and the Shield*, 283.

158 Eileen Pollack, *Woman Walking Ahead*, 111, 112, 113.

159 Rex Alan Smith, *Moon of the Popping Trees: The Tragedy at Wounded Knee and the End of the Indian Wars* (Lincoln: University of Nebraska Press, 1975), 70, 71; Eileen Pollack, *Woman Walking Ahead*, 123.

160 Roger L. Di Silvestro, *In the Shadow of Wounded Knee: The Untold Final Story of the Indian Wars* (New York: Walker & Company, 2007), 64; Rex Alan Smith, *Moon of the Popping Trees*, 68.

161 Rex Alan Smith, *Moon of the Popping Trees*, 72–73, 75.

162 Robert M. Utley, *The Lance and the Shield*, 284; Stanley Vestal, *Sitting Bull: Champion of the Sioux*, 269.

163 James McLaughlin, *My Friend the Indian*, 196–97.

164 Stanley Vestal, *Sitting Bull: Champion of the Sioux*, 270; Robert M. Utley, *The Lance and the Shield*, 282.

165 Rex Alan Smith, *Moon of the Popping Trees*, 88–89.

166 James McLaughlin, *My Friend the Indian*, 184, 185; Rex Alan Smith, *Moon of the Popping Trees*, 103.

167 Stanley Vestal, *Sitting Bull: Champion of the Sioux*, 272–73; Roger L. Di Silvestro, *In the Shadow of Wounded Knee*, 70; James McLaughlin, *My Friend the Indian*, 190.

168 Rex Alan Smith, *Moon of the Popping Trees*, 83, 84, 87.

169 James McLaughlin, *My Friend the Indian*, 185.

170 James McLaughlin, *My Friend the Indian*, 191.

171 James McLaughlin, *My Friend the Indian*, 191; Robert M. Utley, *The Lance and the Shield*, 284; Stanley Vestal, *New Sources of Indian History*, 341.

172 James McLaughlin, *My Friend the Indian*, 191; Eileen Pollack, *Woman Walking Ahead*, 116.

173 James McLaughlin, *My Friend the Indian*, 191, 200; Robert M. Utley, *The Lance and the Shield*, 285.

174 Eileen Pollack, *Woman Walking Ahead*, 116–17.

175 Eileen Pollack, *Woman Walking Ahead*, 117, 123, 132.

176 Eileen Pollack, *Woman Walking Ahead*, 136–37.

177 Eileen Pollack, *Woman Walking Ahead*, 262, 264.

178 Eileen Pollack, *Woman Walking Ahead*, 138.

179 James McLaughlin, *My Friend the Indian*, 200.

180 Robert M. Utley, *The Lance and the Shield*, 287.

181 Robert M. Utley, *The Lance and the Shield*, 287; Norman E. Matteoni, *Prairie Man*, 257.

182 James McLaughlin, *My Friend the Indian*, 200; Robert M. Utley, *The Lance and the Shield*, 287.

183 Rex Alan Smith, *Moon of the Popping Trees*, 116; Robert M. Utley, *The Lance and the Shield*, 289.

184 James McLaughlin, *My Friend the Indian*, 201.

185 James McLaughlin, *My Friend the Indian*, 201, 202.

186 James McLaughlin, *My Friend the Indian*, 202–03.

187 James McLaughlin, *My Friend the Indian*, 204.

188 Ibid.

189 James McLaughlin, *My Friend the Indian*, 205, 206.

190 James McLaughlin, *My Friend the Indian*, 206.

191 James McLaughlin, *My Friend the Indian*, 207.

192 Ibid.

193 Ibid.

194 Ibid.

195 Stanley Vestal, *Sitting Bull: Champion of the Sioux*, 273.

196 Stanley Vestal, *Sitting Bull: Champion of the Sioux*, 274.

197 Norman E. Matteoni, *Prairie Man*, 263, 264; Robert M. Utley, *The Lance and the Shield*, 293.

198 Robert M. Utley, *The Lance and the Shield*, 289, 293; Norman E. Matteoni, *Prairie Man*, 263.

199 James McLaughlin, *My Friend the Indian*, 208, 209.

200 Robert M. Utley, *The Lance and the Shield*, 292; Stanley Vestal, *New Sources of Indian History*, 7–8.

201 Robert M. Utley, *The Lance and the Shield*, 289; Norman E. Matteoni, *Prairie Man*, 261.

202 Stanley Vestal, *Sitting Bull: Champion of the Sioux*, 278–79.

203 Norman E. Matteoni, *Prairie Man*, 266.

204 Bobby Bridger, *Buffalo Bill and Sitting Bull*, 378.

205 Bobby Bridger, *Buffalo Bill and Sitting Bull*, 361–64.

206 Bobby Bridger, *Buffalo Bill and Sitting Bull*, 378–79.

207 Bobby Bridger, *Buffalo Bill and Sitting Bull*, 379, 380.

208 Bobby Bridger, *Buffalo Bill and Sitting Bull*, 380.

209 Bobby Bridger, *Buffalo Bill and Sitting Bull*, 380; James McLaughlin, *My Friend the Indian*, 210.

210 Bobby Bridger, *Buffalo Bill and Sitting Bull*, 381; Stanley Vestal, *Sitting Bull: Champion of the Sioux*, 280–81.

211 Bobby Bridger, *Buffalo Bill and Sitting Bull*, 381; Norman E. Matteoni, *Prairie Man*, 268.

212 Bobby Bridger, *Buffalo Bill and Sitting Bull*, 381.

213 Bobby Bridger, *Buffalo Bill and Sitting Bull*, 381; Stanley Vestal, *Sitting Bull: Champion of the Sioux*, 281.

214 Bobby Bridger, *Buffalo Bill and Sitting Bull*, 381; James McLaughlin, *My Friend the Indian*, 211.

215 Stanley Vestal, *Sitting Bull: Champion of the Sioux*, 281; Stanley Vestal, *New Sources of Indian History*, 2.

216 Stanley Vestal, *New Sources of Indian History*, 67, 68.

217 Stanley Vestal, *New Sources of Indian History*, 68.

218 Ibid.

219 Ibid.

220 Stanley Vestal, *New Sources of Indian History*, 69.

221 Stanley Vestal, *New Sources of Indian History*, 70.

222 James McLaughlin, *My Friend the Indian*, 211–12.

223 Robert M. Utley, *The Lance and the Shield*, 295; James McLaughlin, *My Friend the Indian*, 212.

224 Rex Alan Smith, *Moon of the Popping Trees*, 149.

225 Norman E. Matteoni, *Prairie Man*, 270.

226 Rex Alan Smith, *Moon of the Popping Trees*, 149; Stanley Vestal, *Sitting Bull: Champion of the Sioux*, 282.

227 James McLaughlin, *My Friend the Indian*, 216.

228 Norman E. Matteoni, *Prairie Man*, 271.

229 Norman E. Matteoni, *Prairie Man*, 271, 272; Rex Alan Smith, *Moon of the Popping Trees*, 151.

230 Rex Alan Smith, *Moon of the Popping Trees*, 149–50; Robert M. Utley, *The Lance and the Shield*, 296; Stanley Vestal, *Sitting Bull: Champion of the Sioux*, 285.

231 Robert M. Utley, *The Lance and the Shield*, 296.

232 Robert M. Utley, *The Lance and the Shield*, 296; Stanley Vestal, *Sitting Bull: Champion of the Sioux*, 288.

233 Robert M. Utley, *The Lance and the Shield*, 296, 297.

234 Robert M. Utley, *The Lance and the Shield*, 297.

235 Rex Alan Smith, *Moon of the Popping Trees*, 153; Robert M. Utley, *The Lance and the Shield*, 297; James McLaughlin, *My Friend the Indian*, 216–17.

236 Rex Alan Smith, *Moon of the Popping Trees*, 153.

237 James McLaughlin, *My Friend the Indian*, 218.

238 Rex Alan Smith, *Moon of the Popping Trees*, 153, 155, 156.

239 Rex Alan Smith, *Moon of the Popping Trees*, 154.

240 Rex Alan Smith, *Moon of the Popping Trees*, 155.

241 Rex Alan Smith, *Moon of the Popping Trees*, 156.

242 Rex Alan Smith, *Moon of the Popping Trees*, 157.

243 Stanley Vestal, *Sitting Bull: Champion of the Sioux*, 289.

244 Stanley Vestal, *Sitting Bull: Champion of the Sioux*, 278.

SIDEBAR: THE GHOST DANCE

245 Rex Alan Smith, *Moon of the Popping Trees*, 65–67.

246 Rex Alan Smith, *Moon of the Popping Trees*, 66.

247 Roger L. Di Silvestro, *In the Shadow of Wounded Knee*, 64; Rex Alan Smith, *Moon of the Popping Trees*, 68.

248 Rex Alan Smith, *Moon of the Popping Trees*, 68.

249 Rex Alan Smith, *Moon of the Popping Trees*, 68–69.

250 Rex Alan Smith, *Moon of the Popping Trees*, 70, 71.

251 Rex Alan Smith, *Moon of the Popping Trees*, 72–73, 75.

252 Roger L. Di Silvestro, *In the Shadow of Wounded Knee*, 67–68.

CHAPTER 13: THE KILLING OF SITTING BULL, DECEMBER 1890

1 Rex Alan Smith, *Moon of the Popping Trees*, 157; Stanley Vestal, *Sitting Bull: Champion of the Sioux*, 290.

2 Rex Alan Smith, *Moon of the Popping Trees*, 157.

3 Ibid.

4 Robert M. Utley, *The Lance and the Shield*, 299.

5 Stanley Vestal, *Sitting Bull: Champion of the Sioux*, 294.

6 Robert M. Utley, *The Lance and the Shield*, 300; Stanley Vestal, *Sitting Bull: Champion of the Sioux*, 295.
7 Robert M. Utley, *The Lance and the Shield*, 300; Stanley Vestal, *Sitting Bull: Champion of the Sioux*, 295, 296.
8 Stanley Vestal, *Sitting Bull: Champion of the Sioux*, 295–96; Robert M. Utley, *The Lance and the Shield*, 300.
9 Stanley Vestal, *Sitting Bull: Champion of the Sioux*, 297.
10 Ibid.
11 Stanley Vestal, *Sitting Bull: Champion of the Sioux*, 297–98.
12 Stanley Vestal, *Sitting Bull: Champion of the Sioux*, 298.
13 Stanley Vestal, *Sitting Bull: Champion of the Sioux*, 299.
14 Robert M. Utley, *The Lance and the Shield*, 301.
15 Ibid.
16 Robert M. Utley, *The Lance and the Shield*, 301, 302.
17 Stanley Vestal, *Sitting Bull: Champion of the Sioux*, 300.
18 Robert M. Utley, *The Lance and the Shield*, 302.
19 Ibid.
20 Ibid.
21 Stanley Vestal, *New Sources of Indian History*, 28–29, 30; Robert M. Utley, *The Lance and the Shield*, 302; Stanley Vestal, *Sitting Bull: Champion of the Sioux*, 302–03.
22 Robert M. Utley, *The Lance and the Shield*, 303; Stanley Vestal, *New Sources of Indian History*, 29–30.
23 Robert M. Utley, *The Lance and the Shield*, 303; Stanley Vestal, *Sitting Bull: Champion of the Sioux*, 305.
24 Robert M. Utley, *The Lance and the Shield*, 304; Stanley Vestal, *Sitting Bull: Champion of the Sioux*, 304.
25 Robert M. Utley, *The Lance and the Shield*, 304; Stanley Vestal, *New Sources of Indian History*, 31.
26 Robert M. Utley, *The Lance and the Shield*, 304; Stanley Vestal, *Sitting Bull: Champion of the Sioux*, 306–07.

SIDEBAR: SITTING BULL'S GRAVES

27 Rob De Wall, *The Saga of Sitting Bull's Bones* (Crazy Horse, SD: Korczak's Heritage, Inc., 1984), 63; Bill Markley, "Sitting Bull Rests, But Is He at Peace?" *Wild West Magazine* (June 2008); Robert M. Utley, *The Lance and the Shield*, 305.
28 James McLaughlin, *My Friend the Indian*, 222; Rob De Wall, *The Saga of Sitting Bull's Bones*, 124.
29 Stanley Vestal, *Sitting Bull: Champion of the Sioux*, 310–11; Bill Markley, "Sitting Bull Rests, But Is He at Peace?"
30 Rob De Wall, *The Saga of Sitting Bull's Bones*, 64.
31 Rob De Wall, *The Saga of Sitting Bull's Bones*, 64; Bill Markley, "Sitting Bull Rests, But Is He at Peace?"
32 Rob De Wall, *The Saga of Sitting Bull's Bones*, 36, 38–39, 42, 43, 65.

33 Rob De Wall, *The Saga of Sitting Bull's Bones*, 47.

34 Bill Markley, "Sitting Bull Rests, But Is He at Peace?"

35 Rob De Wall, *The Saga of Sitting Bull's Bones*, 83–104; Bill Markley, "Sitting Bull Rests, But Is He at Peace?"

36 Rob De Wall, *The Saga of Sitting Bull's Bones*, 104–11; Bill Markley, "Sitting Bull Rests, But Is He at Peace?"

37 Rob De Wall, *The Saga of Sitting Bull's Bones*, 113–14.

38 Rob De Wall, *The Saga of Sitting Bull's Bones*, 138, 262; Bill Markley, "Sitting Bull Rests, But Is He at Peace?"

39 Rob De Wall, *The Saga of Sitting Bull's Bones*, 117, 127; Bill Markley, "Sitting Bull Rests, But Is He at Peace?"

40 Rob De Wall, *The Saga of Sitting Bull's Bones*, 272; Bill Markley, "Sitting Bull Rests, But Is He at Peace?"

CHAPTER 14: THE LIFE AND DEATH OF GERONIMO, 1890–FEBRUARY 17, 1909

1 Robert M. Utley, *Geronimo*, 242.

2 W. Michael Farmer, *Geronimo: Prisoner of Lies*, 99, 118; Robert M. Utley, *Geronimo*, 242–45.

3 W. Michael Farmer, *Geronimo: Prisoner of Lies*, 99; Robert M. Utley, *Geronimo*, 245.

4 W. Michael Farmer, *Geronimo: Prisoner of Lies*, 99, 100–101, 102; Robert M. Utley, *Geronimo*, 245, 246.

5 W. Michael Farmer, *Geronimo: Prisoner of Lies*, 107–08, 150.

6 Bob Boze Bell, *The Illustrated Life and Times of Geronimo*, 85.

7 Eve Ball, *Indeh: An Apache Odyssey*, 159; Robert M. Utley, *Geronimo*, 247.

8 W. Michael Farmer, *Geronimo: Prisoner of Lies*, 110–11.

9 Forty-five children remained at Carlisle Indian School in Pennsylvania (W. Michael Farmer, *Geronimo: Prisoner of Lies*, 111).

10 W. Michael Farmer, *Geronimo: Prisoner of Lies*, 111; Angie Debo, *Geronimo*, 363–64.

11 W. Michael Farmer, *Geronimo: Prisoner of Lies*, 111; Robert M. Utley, *Geronimo*, 249.

12 W. Michael Farmer, *Geronimo: Prisoner of Lies*, 109, 111.

13 Robert M. Utley, *Geronimo*, 250–51.

14 W. Michael Farmer, *Geronimo: Prisoner of Lies*, 113.

15 W. Michael Farmer, *Geronimo: Prisoner of Lies*, 112, 115; Robert M. Utley, *Geronimo*, 250, 252; Bob Boze Bell, *The Illustrated Life and Times of Geronimo*, 90–91.

16 W. Michael Farmer, *Geronimo: Prisoner of Lies*, 114–15; Robert M. Utley, *Geronimo*, 250–51, 253.

17 W. Michael Farmer, *Geronimo: Prisoner of Lies*, 115; Robert M. Utley, *Geronimo*, 251.

18 Robert M. Utley, *Geronimo*, 252.

19 Robert M. Utley, *Geronimo*, 251.

20 W. Michael Farmer, *Geronimo: Prisoner of Lies*, 121–22; Robert M. Utley, *Geronimo*, 253.

21 W. Michael Farmer, *Geronimo: Prisoner of Lies*, 124.

22 W. Michael Farmer, *Geronimo: Prisoner of Lies*, 125.

23 Ibid.

24 Robert M. Utley, *Geronimo*, 253.

25 W. Michael Farmer, *Geronimo: Prisoner of Lies*, 127.

26 W. Michael Farmer, *Geronimo: Prisoner of Lies*, 127, 128, 129.

27 Robert M. Utley, *Geronimo*, 254.

28 Robert M. Utley, *Geronimo*, 255.

29 W. Michael Farmer, *Geronimo: Prisoner of Lies*, 135.

30 Robert M. Utley, *Geronimo*, 255.

31 Woodworth Clum, *Apache Agent*, 287–88.

32 "Spoken by President," *St. Joseph Herald* (St. Joseph, Missouri), October 13, 1898, page 1, Newspapers.com, accessed March 23, 2020, https://www.newspapers.com/image/230222451/?terms=Trans-Mississippi%2Band%2BInternational%2BExposition%2C%2BGeronimo%2C%2BNelson%2BMiles.

33 Bonnie M. Miller, "The Incoherencies of Empire: The 'Imperial' Image of the Indian at the Omaha World's Fairs of 1898–99," *American Studies*, vol. 49, nos. 3/4 (Fall/Winter 2008), Lawrence, KS: Mid-America American Studies Association, University of Kansas, 39–40, accessed March 24, 2020, file:///C:/Users/WCN%20Customer/Downloads/4010-Article%20Text-5470-1-10-20100830%20(1).pdf.

34 Woodworth Clum, *Apache Agent*, 289–90.

35 W. Michael Farmer, *Geronimo: Prisoner of Lies*, 136; "William McKinley," Wikipedia, accessed March 20, 2020, https://en.wikipedia.org/wiki/William_McKinley.

36 Angie Debo, *Geronimo*, 407–08, 425.

37 W. Michael Farmer, *Geronimo: Prisoner of Lies*, 136.

38 Angie Debo, *Geronimo*, 355, 430, 431.

39 Angie Debo, *Geronimo*, 432.

40 Angie Debo, *Geronimo*, 433; S. M. Barrett, ed., *Geronimo*, 181.

41 W. Michael Farmer, *Geronimo: Prisoner of Lies*, 137; Bob Boze Bell, *The Illustrated Life and Times of Geronimo*, 89; Robert M. Utley, *Geronimo*, 256.

42 W. Michael Farmer, *Geronimo: Prisoner of Lies*, 137, 152.

43 W. Michael Farmer, *Geronimo: Prisoner of Lies*, 141–42.

44 Bob Boze Bell, *The Illustrated Life and Times of Geronimo*, 97. Robert M. Utley, *Geronimo*, 257.

45 Ibid.

46 Walter Edward Harris, "The Inauguration of Roosevelt and Fairbanks," *Times Dispatch* (Richmond, Virginia), March 5, 1905, page 13, Newspapers.com, accessed March 23, 2020, https://www.newspapers.com/image/145499311; Woodworth Clum, *Apache Agent*, 291.

47 Woodworth Clum, *Apache Agent*, 291–92.

48 "From Washington," *Alexandria Gazette* (Alexandria, Virginia), March 9, 1905, page 2, Newspapers.com, accessed March 23, 2020, https://www.newspapers.com/image/44228329.

49 S. M. Barrett, ed., *Geronimo*, 49.

50 S. M. Barrett, ed., *Geronimo*, 50–51.

51 S. M. Barrett, ed., *Geronimo*, 51; Robert M. Utley, *Geronimo*, 260.

52 Angie Debo, *Geronimo*, 288; W. Michael Farmer, *Geronimo: Prisoner of Lies*, 173; Eve Ball, *Indeh: An Apache Odyssey*, 173.

53 S. M. Barrett, ed., *Geronimo*, 52; Eve Ball, *Indeh: An Apache Odyssey*, 174.

54 Eve Ball, *Indeh: An Apache Odyssey*, 174; W. Michael Farmer, *Geronimo: Prisoner of Lies*, 173–74.

55 S. M. Barrett, ed., *Geronimo*, 53.

56 S. M. Barrett, ed., *Geronimo*, 54.

57 S. M. Barrett, ed., *Geronimo*, 54–56.

58 Eve Ball, *Indeh: An Apache Odyssey*, 174; W. Michael Farmer, *Geronimo: Prisoner of Lies*, 175; Robert M. Utley, *Geronimo*, 261. I have used Geronimo's autobiography throughout this book.

59 S. M. Barrett, ed., *Geronimo*, 125–26.

60 S. M. Barrett, ed., *Geronimo*, 183–84.

61 W. Michael Farmer, *Geronimo: Prisoner of Lies*, 68–69.

62 Eve Ball, *Indeh: An Apache Odyssey*, 46–47.

63 W. Michael Farmer, *Geronimo: Prisoner of Lies*, 66, 70.

64 Angie Debo, *Geronimo*, 437; W. Michael Farmer, *Geronimo: Prisoner of Lies*, 176, 178.

65 Jason Betzinez, *I Fought with Geronimo*, 197.

66 Angie Debo, *Geronimo*, 439–40; Eve Ball, *Indeh: An Apache Odyssey*, 179.

67 Angie Debo, *Geronimo*, 440.

68 Ibid. Eugene Chihuahua tells a different story, reporting that he and Geronimo slept on the ground under blankets through the night. The next morning, he found Geronimo feverish and took him to the Apache hospital (Eve Ball, *Indeh: An Apache Odyssey*, 179).

69 Angie Debo, *Geronimo*, 440.

70 Angie Debo, *Geronimo*, 441; Eve Ball, *Indeh: An Apache Odyssey*, 181.

71 Angie Debo, *Geronimo*, 441.

72 Eve Ball, *Indeh: An Apache Odyssey*, 181.

73 Angie Debo, *Geronimo*, 441; Eve Ball, *Indeh: An Apache Odyssey*, 181.

SIDEBAR: GERONIMO'S SKULL

74 W. Michael Farmer, *Geronimo: Prisoner of Lies*, 185–86, 187; Sharon S. Magee, *Geronimo! Stories of an American Legend* (Phoenix: Arizona Highways Books, 2002), 136, 138.

75 W. Michael Farmer, *Geronimo: Prisoner of Lies*, 186; Sharon S. Magee, *Geronimo! Stories of an American Legend*, 138; Eve Ball, *Indeh: An Apache Odyssey*, 182.

76 Eve Ball, *Indeh: An Apache Odyssey*, 182.

77 Ibid.

78 Angie Debo, *Geronimo*, 443–44; W. Michael Farmer, *Geronimo: Prisoner of Lies*, 187.

79 Ross Goldberg, "Letter Fuels Speculation that Skulls Have Geronimo's Skull," *Yale News* (May 2006), accessed January 10, 2020, https://yaledailynews.com/

blog/2006/05/09/letter-fuels-speculation-that-skulls-have-geronimos-skull/; W. Michael Farmer, *Geronimo: Prisoner of Lies*, 187.

80 Leo W. Banks, "The Strange Saga of Geronimo's Skull: A Century After His Death, the Apache Leader's Remains Continue to Make News," *Santa Fe Reporter*, June 30, 2009, accessed January 10, 2020, https://www.sfreporter.com/news/coverstories/2009/07/01/the-strange-saga-of-geronimos-skull/.

81 Leo W. Banks, "The Strange Saga of Geronimo's Skull."

82 Ross Goldberg, "Letter Fuels Speculation that Skulls Have Geronimo's Skull."

83 Martha Neil, "Yale Secret Society Skull and Bones Wins Lawsuit Over Geronimo's Remains," *American Bar Association Journal* (August 2010), accessed January 10, 2020, http://www.abajournal.com/news/article/yale_secrety_society_skull_bones_wins_lawsuit_over_geronimos_remains.

84 Marc Wortman, "The Bin Laden of His Day? A New Biography of Geronimo," *The Daily Beast* (July 2017), accessed January 10, 2020, https://www.thedailybeast.com/the-bin-laden-of-his-day-a-new-biography-of-geronimo?ref=author; Leo W. Banks, "The Strange Saga of Geronimo's Skull."

CHAPTER 15: THE END OF THE TRAIL

1 James Crutchfield et al., *The Settlement of America*, vol. 2, 508–09.

2 Ernie LaPointe, *Sitting Bull*, 113, 114.

3 Angie Debo, *Geronimo*, 447, 448.

4 Angie Debo, *Geronimo*, 445.

5 W. Michael Farmer, *Geronimo: Prisoner of Lies*, 153.

6 Fletcher Johnson, *Life of Sitting Bull and History of the Indian War of 1890–'91* (Philadelphia, PA: Edgewood Publishing Company, 1891), 189–90.

7 James McLaughlin, *My Friend the Indian*, 180.

8 Hamlin Garland, *The Book of the American Indian* (Lincoln: University of Nebraska Press, 2002), xxiv.

9 Hamlin Garland, *The Book of the American Indian*, xxx, xxxi, 2.

10 Robert M. Utley, *The Lance and the Shield*, xvi.

11 *Sitting Bull—The Hostile Sioux Indian Chief* (1914), Turner Classic Movies, accessed March 29, 2020, http://www.tcm.turner.com/tcmdb/title/552515/Sitting-Bull-The-Hostile-Sioux-Indian-Chief/.

12 "Sitting Bull," Wikipedia, accessed March 29, 2020, https://en.wikipedia.org/wiki/Sitting_Bull#cite_note-64.

13 Irwin Porges, *Edgar Rice Burroughs: The Man Who Created Tarzan* (Provo, UT: Brigham Young University Press,1975), 54, 57–60, 423, 791, 792.

14 Woodworth Clum, *Apache Agent*, 292.

15 Robert M. Utley, *Geronimo*, 256.

16 "*Geronimo* (1939 film)," Wikipedia, accessed March 29, 2020, https://en.wikipedia.org/wiki/Geronimo_(1939_film.

17 "*Broken Arrow* (1950 film)," Wikipedia, accessed April 1, 2020, https://en.wikipedia.org/wiki/Broken_Arrow_(1950_film).

18 "*Geronimo: An American Legend*," Wikipedia, accessed March 29, 2020, https://en.wikipedia.org/wiki/Geronimo:_An_American_Legend; "*Geronimo* (1993

film)," Wikipedia, accessed March 29, 2020, https://en.wikipedia.org/wiki/Geronimo_(1993_film).

19 William H. Goetzmann and William N. Goetzmann, *The West of the Imagination* (Norman: University of Oklahoma Press, 2009), 529.

20 Bob Boze Bell, *The Illustrated Life and Times of Geronimo*, 116.

21 S. M. Barrett, ed., *Geronimo*, 183.

22 Stanley Vestal, *Sitting Bull: Champion of the Sioux*, 244–45.

BIBLIOGRAPHY

Abrams, Mac H. *Sioux War Dispatches: Reports from the Field, 1876–1877.* Yardley, PA: Westholme Publishing, 2012.

Ambrose, Stephen E. *Nothing Like It in the World: The Men Who Built the Transcontinental Railroad, 1863–1869.* New York: Simon & Schuster, 2000.

Athearn, Robert G. *Forts of the Upper Missouri.* Lincoln: University of Nebraska Press, 1967.

Ball, Eve. *In the Days of Victorio: Recollections of a Warm Springs Apache.* Tucson: University of Arizona Press, 1970.

———. *An Apache Odyssey Indeh.* Norman: University of Oklahoma Press, 1980.

Barrett, S. M., ed. *Geronimo: His Own Story.* New York: Ballantine Books, 1970.

Bell, Bob Boze. *The Illustrated Life and Times of Geronimo.* Cave Creek, AZ: Two Roads West, 2020.

Bergemann, Kurt D. *Brackett's Battalion: Minnesota Cavalry in the Civil War and Dakota War.* St. Paul: Minnesota Historical Society Press, 2004.

Betzinez, Jason. *I Fought with Geronimo.* Lincoln: University of Nebraska Press, 1959.

Borneman, Walter R. *Rival Rails: The Race to Build America's Greatest Transcontinental Railroad.* New York: Random House, 2010.

Bourke, John G. *On the Border with Crook.* New York: Skyhorse Publishing, 2014.

Brady, Cyrus Townsend. *Indian Fights and Fighters.* Lincoln: University of Nebraska Press, 1971.

Bridger, Bobby. *Buffalo Bill and Sitting Bull: Inventing the West.* Austin: University of Texas Press, 2002.

Brown, Dee. *Bury My Heart at Wounded Knee: An Indian History of the American West.* New York: Henry Holt and Company, 1970.

Chaky, Doreen. *Terrible Justice: Sioux Chiefs and U.S. Soldiers on the Upper Missouri, 1854–1868.* Norman: University of Oklahoma Press, 2012.

Clow, Richmond L. *Spotted Tail: Warrior and Statesman.* Pierre: South Dakota Historical Society Press, 2019.

Clum, Woodworth. *Apache Agent: The Story of John P. Clum.* Lincoln: University of Nebraska Press, 1963.

Cody, William F. *Buffalo Bill's Life Story: An Autobiography.* New York: Cosmopolitan Book Corporation, 1920.

Cooper, Courtney Ryley. *Annie Oakley: Woman at Arms.* New York: Konecky & Konecky, 1927.

Crawford, Lewis F. *Rekindling Camp Fires.* Bismarck, ND: Capital Books, 1926.

Cremony, John C. *Life Among the Apaches.* San Francisco: A. Roman & Company, 1868.

Crummett, Michael. *Tataka-Iyotanka: A Biography of Sitting Bull.* Tucson, AZ: Western National Parks Association, 2002.

Crutchfield, James, Candy Moulton, and Terry Del Bene, eds. *The Settlement of America: Encyclopedia of Western Expansion from Jamestown to the Closing of the Frontier*, vols. 1 and 2. Armonk, NY: M. E. Sharp, Inc., 2011.

Custer, Elizabeth B. *"Boots and Saddles," or, Life in Dakota with General Custer*. Norman: University of Oklahoma Press, 1961.

Davis, Britton. *The Truth About Geronimo*. Lincoln: University of Nebraska Press, 1929.

De Barthe, Joe. *The Life and Adventures of Frank Grouard*. St. Joseph, MO: Combe Printing Company, 1894.

Debo, Angie. *Geronimo: The Man, His Time, His Place*. Norman: University of Oklahoma Press, 1976.

Deloria Jr., Vine. *The World We Used to Live In: Remembering the Powers of the Medicine Men*. Golden, CO: Fulcrum Publishing, 2006.

DeMallie, Raymond J., volume editor. *Plains*, Handbook of North American Indians, vol. 13, parts 1 and 2. Washington, DC: Smithsonian Institution, 2001.

De Wall, Rob. *The Saga of Sitting Bull's Bones*. Crazy Horse, SD: Korczak's Heritage, Inc., 1984.

Di Silvestro, Roger L. *In the Shadow of Wounded Knee: The Untold Final Story of the Indian Wars*. New York: Walker & Company, 2007.

Donovan, James. *A Terrible Glory: Custer and the Little Bighorn: The Last Great Battle of the American West*. New York: Little, Brown & Company, 2008.

Editors of Time-Life Books. *The Spirit World*, The American Indians Series. Alexandria, VA: Time-Life Books, 1992.

———. *The Buffalo Hunters*, The American Indians Series. Alexandria, VA: Time-Life Books, 1993.

Farmer, W. Michael. *Apacheria: True Stories of the Apache Culture 1860–1920*. Guilford, CT: TwoDot, 2017.

———. *Geronimo: Prisoner of Lies: Twenty-Three Years as a Prisoner of War, 1886–1909*, Guilford, CT: TwoDot, 2019.

Friesen, Steve. *Buffalo Bill: Scout, Showman, Visionary*. Golden, CO: Fulcrum Publishing, Inc., 2010.

Garland, Hamlin. *The Book of the American Indian*. Lincoln: University of Nebraska Press, 2002.

Goetzmann, William H., and William N. Goetzmann. *The West of the Imagination*. Norman: University of Oklahoma Press, 2009.

Green, Jerome A. *Slim Buttes, 1876: An Episode of the Great Sioux War*. Norman: University of Oklahoma Press, 1982.

Hämäläinen, Pekka. *Lakota America: A New History of Indigenous Power*. New Haven: Yale University Press, 2019.

Hedren, Paul L. *First Scalp for Custer*. Lincoln: Nebraska State Historical Society, 2005.

———. *Ho! For the Black Hills: Captain Jack Crawford Reports the Black Hills Gold Rush and the Great Sioux War*. Pierre: South Dakota State Historical Society Press, 2011.

———. *Rosebud, June 17, 1876: Prelude to the Little Big Horn*. Norman: University of Oklahoma Press, 2019.

Hocking, Doug. *Tom Jeffords, Friend of Cochise*. Guilford, CT: TwoDot, 2017.

———. *The Black Legend: George Bascom, Cochise, and the Start of the Apache Wars*. Guilford, CT: TwoDot, 2019.

Horn, Tom. *Life of Tom Horn, Government Scout and Interpreter*. Scotts Valley, CA: CreateSpace, 2016.

Horsted, Paul, and Ernest Grafe. *Exploring with Custer: The 1874 Black Hills Expedition*. Custer, SD: Golden Valley Press, 2002.

Horsted, Paul, Ernest Grafe, and Jon Nelson. *Crossing the Plains with Custer*. Custer, SD: Golden Valley Press, 2009.

Howard, Oliver Otis. *My life and Experiences Among Our Hostile Indians*. Hartford, CT: A. D. Worthington & Company, 1907.

———. *Famous Indian Chiefs I Have Known*. New York: The Century Co., 1908.

Hunkins, Ralph V., and John Clark Lindsey. *South Dakota: Its Past, Present, and Future*. New York: Macmillan, 1932.

Hutton, Paul Andrew. *Phil Sheridan and His Army*. Norman: University of Oklahoma Press, 1985.

———. *The Apache Wars: The Hunt for Geronimo, the Apache Kid, and the Captive Boy Who Started the Longest War in American History*. New York: Broadway Books, 2016.

Jennewein, J. Leonard, and Jane Boorman, eds. *Dakota Panorama*. Freeman, SD: Brevet Press, 1973.

Johnson, Fletcher. *Life of Sitting Bull and History of the Indian War of 1890–'91*. Philadelphia, PA: Edgewood Publishing Company, 1891.

Kelly, Fanny. *Narrative of My Captivity Among the Sioux Indians*. New York: Barnes & Noble, 1994.

Knight, Oliver. *Following the Indian Wars: The Story of the Newspaper Correspondents Among the Indian Campaigners*. Norman: University of Oklahoma Press, 1960.

Kraft, Louis, ed. *Lt. Charles Gatewood & His Apache Wars Memoir*. Lincoln: University of Nebraska Press, 2005.

Krause, Herbert, and Gary D. Olson. *Prelude to Glory: A Newspaper Accounting of Custer's 1874 Expedition to the Black Hills*. Sioux Falls, SD: Brevet Press, 1974.

Kühn, Berndt. *Chronicles of War: Apache and Yavapai Resistance in the Southwestern United States and Northern Mexico, 1821–1937*. Tucson: Arizona Historical Society, 2014.

Lane, Jack C., ed. *Chasing Geronimo: The Journal of Leonard Wood, May–September 1886*. Lincoln: University of Lincoln Press, 1970.

LaPointe, Ernie. *Sitting Bull: His Life and Legacy*. Layton, UT: Gibbs Smith, 2009.

Larson, Robert W. *Red Cloud: Warrior-Statesman of the Lakota Sioux*. Norman: University of Oklahoma Press, 1997.

———. *Gall: Lakota War Chief*. Norman: University of Oklahoma Press, 2007.

Lubetkin, M. John. *Custer and the 1873 Yellowstone Survey: A Documentary History*. Norman: University of Oklahoma Press, 2013.

———. *Before Custer: Surveying the Yellowstone, 1872*. Norman: University of Oklahoma Press, 2015.

———. *Road to War: The 1871 Yellowstone Surveys*. Norman: University of Oklahoma Press, 2016.

Magee, Sharon S. *Geronimo! Stories of an American Legend*. Phoenix: Arizona Highways Books, 2002.

Markley, Bill, and Kellen Cutsforth. *Old West Showdown: Two Authors Wrangle over the Truth about the Mythic Old West*. Guilford, CT: TwoDot, 2018.

Markstrom, Carol A. *Empowerment of North American Indian Girls: Ritual Expressions at Puberty*. Lincoln: University of Nebraska Press, 2008.

Marshall III, Joseph M. *The Journey of Crazy Horse: A Lakota History*. New York: Penguin Books, 2004.

———. *The Power of Four: Leadership Lessons of Crazy Horse*. New York: Sterling Publishing Company, Inc., 2009.

Matteoni, Norman E. *Prairie Man: The Struggle Between Sitting Bull and Indian Agent James McLaughlin*. Guilford, CT: TwoDot, 2015.

McChristian, Douglas. *Fort Laramie: Military Bastion of the High Plains*. Norman: University of Oklahoma Press, 2008.

McDermott, John D. *Red Cloud's War: The Bozeman Trail, 1866–1868*, vol. 2. Norman: University of Oklahoma Press, 2010.

McLaughlin, James. *My Friend the Indian*. Lincoln: University of Nebraska Press, 1989.

Michno, Gregory F. *Lakota Noon: The Indian Narrative of Custer's Defeat*. Missoula, MT: Mountain Press Publishing Company, 1997.

Miles, Nelson Appleton. *Personal Recollections and Observations of General Nelson A. Miles*. Chicago: Werner, 1896.

Miller, David Humphreys. *Custer's Fall: The Indian Side of the Story*. Lincoln: University of Nebraska Press, 1957.

Neihardt, John G. *Black Elk Speaks: Being the Life Story of a Holy Man of the Oglala Sioux*. Lincoln: University of Nebraska Press, 1932.

Nelson, Mark J. *White Hat: The Military Career of Captain William Philo Clark*. Norman: University of Oklahoma Press, 2018.

Opler, Morris Edward. *An Apache Life-Way: The Economic, Social, and Religious Institutions of the Chiricahua Indians*. Lincoln: University of Nebraska Press, 1941.

———. *Myths and Tales of the Chiricahua Apache Indians*. Lincoln: University of Nebraska Press, 1942.

Ortiz, Alfonzo, volume editor. *Southwest*, Handbook of North American Indians, vol. 10. Washington, DC: Smithsonian Institution, 1983.

Paul, R. Eli, ed. *The Frontier Army: Episodes from Dakota and the West*. Pierre: South Dakota Historical Society Press, 2019.

Pollack, Eileen. *Woman Walking Ahead: In Search of Catherine Weldon and Sitting Bull*. Albuquerque: University of New Mexico Press, 2002.

Pope, Dennis C. *Sitting Bull, Prisoner of War*. Pierre: South Dakota State Historical Society Press, 2010.

Porges, Irwin. *Edgar Rice Burroughs: The Man Who Created Tarzan*. Provo, UT: Brigham Young University Press, 1975.

Powers, Thomas. *The Killing of Crazy Horse*. New York: Alfred A. Knopf, 2010.

Roberts, David. *Once They Moved Like the Wind: Cochise, Geronimo, and the Apache Wars*. New York: Simon & Schuster, 1993.

Robinson, Sherry. *Apache Voices: Their Stories of Survival as Told to Eve Ball*. Albuquerque: University of New Mexico Press, 2000.

St. John, Rachel. *Line in the Sand: A History of the Western U.S.–Mexico Border*. Princeton, NJ: Princeton University Press, 2012.

Schubert, Frank N. *Vanguard of Expansion: Army Engineers in the Trans-Mississippi West, 1819–1879*. Washington, DC: Office of the Chief of Engineers, 1980.

Schuler, Harold H. *Fort Pierre Chouteau*. Vermillion: University of South Dakota Press, 1990.

———. *Fort Sully: Guns at Sunset*. Vermillion: University of South Dakota Press, 1992.

Smith, Rex Alan. *Moon of the Popping Trees: The Tragedy at Wounded Knee and the End of the Indian Wars*. Lincoln: University of Nebraska Press, 1975.

Sprague, Donovin Arleigh. *Images of America Standing Rock*. Charleston, SC: Arcadia Publishing, 2004.

Standing Bear, Luther. *My People the Sioux*. Lincoln: University of Nebraska Press, 1975.

Stillman, Deanne. *Blood Brothers: The Story of the Strange Friendship Between Sitting Bull and Buffalo Bill*. New York: Simon & Schuster, 2017.

Stirling, M. W. *Three Pictographic Autobiographies of Sitting Bull*, Smithsonian Miscellaneous Collection, vol. 97, no. 5. Washington, DC: Smithsonian Institution, 1938.

Sweeney, Edwin R. *Cochise, Chiricahua Apache Chief*. Norman: University of Oklahoma Press, 1991.

———. *Mangas Coloradas: Chief of the Chiricahua Apaches*. Norman: University of Oklahoma Press, 1998.

———. *From Cochise to Geronimo: The Chiricahua Apaches, 1874–1886*. Norman: University of Oklahoma Press, 2010.

Terry, Alfred H. *The Field Diary of General Alfred H. Terry: The Yellowstone Expedition—1876*, 2nd ed. Bellevue, NE: Old Army Press, 1970.

Thrapp, Dan L. *The Conquest of Apacheria*. Norman: University of Oklahoma Press, 1967.

Trimble, Marshall. *Roadside History of Arizona*. Missoula, MT: Mountain Press Publishing Company, 2004.

Utley, Robert M. *Frontiersmen in Blue: The United States Army and the Indian, 1848–1865*. Lincoln: University of Nebraska Press, 1967.

———. *The Lance and the Shield: The Life and Times of Sitting Bull*. New York: Ballantine Books, 1994.

———. *Geronimo*. New Haven: Yale University Press, 2012.

Vestal, Stanley. *Sitting Bull: Champion of the Sioux*. Norman: University of Oklahoma Press, 1932.

————. *New Sources of Indian History 1850–1891: The Ghost Dance, the Prairie Sioux, a Miscellany*. Norman: University of Oklahoma Press, 1934.

Waggoner, Josephine. *Witness: A Hunkpapha Historian's Strong-Heart Song of the Lakotas*. Lincoln: University of Nebraska Press, 2013.

Warren, Louis S. *Buffalo Bill's America: William Cody and the Wild West Show*. New York: Random House, 2005.

Wert, Jeffery D. *Custer: The Controversial Life of George Armstrong Custer*. New York: Simon & Schuster, 1996.

Wheeler, Keith. *The Railroaders*. New York: Time-Life Books, 1973.

PERIODICALS

Dakota Wind (Goodhouse). "The Apple Creek Conflict, 150 Years Later," *Bismarck Tribune*, August 18, 2013, accessed August 22, 2019. bismarcktribune.com/news/local/bismarck/the-apple-creek-conflict-years-later/article_56cc0e3e-0687-11e3-9bf7-001a4bcf887a.html.

Gray, John S. "What Made Johnnie Bruguier Run?" *Montana: The Magazine of Western History*, vol. 14, no. 2 (Spring 1964).

Hughes, Fred G. "Geronimo: Some Facts Concerning the Wily Old Apache Chief," *Arizona Daily Star*, March 8, 1890.

Lee, Jesse M. "The Capture and Death of an Indian Chieftain," *Journal of the Military Service Institution of the United States* (May–June 1914).

Markley, Bill, "Sitting Bull Rests, But Is He at Peace?" *Wild West Magazine*, June 2008.

————. "Fort Dilts and Fanny's Bid for Freedom," *Wild West Magazine*, April 2014.

————. "Custer's Gold," *True West Magazine*, April 2018.

McCarty, Kieran, and C. L. Sonnichsen. "Trini Verdin and the Truth of History," *Journal of Arizona History*, vol. 14, no. 2 (Summer 1973).

Sweeney, Edwin R. " 'I had lost all': Geronimo and the Carrasco Massacre of 1851," *Journal of Arizona History*, vol. 27, no. 1. (Spring 1986).

INTERNET RESOURCES

Banks, Leo W., "The Strange Saga of Geronimo's Skull: A Century after His Death, the Apache Leader's Remains Continue to Make News," *Santa Fe Reporter*, June 30, 2009, accessed January 10, 2020. https://www.sfreporter.com/news/coverstories/2009/07/01/the-strange-saga-of-geronimos-skull/.

"*Broken Arrow* (1950 film)," Wikipedia, accessed April 1, 2020. https://en.wikipedia.org/wiki/Broken_Arrow_(1950_film).

"From Washington," *Alexandria Gazette* (Alexandria, Virginia, March 9, 1905), Newspapers.com, accessed March 23, 2020. https://www.newspapers.com/image/44228329.

"Gadsden Purchase," Wikipedia, accessed January 4, 2020. https://en.wikipedia.org/wiki/Gadsden_Purchase.

Geronimo (1939 film)," Wikipedia, accessed March 29, 2020. https://en.wikipedia.org/wiki/Geronimo_(1939_film).

Geronimo (1993 film)," Wikipedia, accessed March 29, 2020. https://en.wikipedia.org/wiki/Geronimo_(1993_film).

"*Geronimo: An American Legend*," Wikipedia, accessed March 29, 2020. https://en.wikipedia.org/wiki/Geronimo:_An_American_Legend.

Goldberg, Ross, "Letter Fuels Speculation that Skulls Have Geronimo's Skull," *Yale News*, May 2006, accessed January 10, 2020. https://yaledailynews.com/blog/2006/05/09/letter-fuels-speculation-that-skulls-have-geronimos-skull/.

Goodwin, Grenville, "Experiences of an Indian Scout: Excerpts from the Life of John Rope, an Old-Timer of the White Mountain Apaches," part 2, *Arizona Historical Review*, vol. 7 (April 1936), accessed December 10, 2019. https://repository.arizona.edu/bitstream/handle/10150/623772/azu_h9791_a72_h6_07_02_art4_w.pdf?sequence=1&isAllowed=y.

Harris, Walter Edward, "The Inauguration of Roosevelt and Fairbanks," *Times Dispatch* (Richmond, Virginia, March 5, 1905), Newspapers.com, accessed March 23, 2020. https://www.newspapers.com/image/145499311.

"Major Crimes Act," *Wikipedia*, accessed December 14, 2019. https://en.wikipedia.org/wiki/Major_Crimes_Act.

Mary Collins Collection, South Dakota State Historical Society, Manuscript Collection, accessed February 5, 2020. https:// history.sd.gov/archives/manuscripts.aspx.

Miller, Bonnie M., "The Incoherencies of Empire: The 'Imperial' Image of the Indian at the Omaha World's Fairs of 1898–99," *American Studies*, vol. 49, no. 3/4 (Fall/Winter 2008), Lawrence, KS: Mid-America American Studies Association, University of Kansas, accessed March 24, 2020. file:///C:/Users/WCN%20Customer/Downloads/4010-Article%20Text-5470-1-10-20100830%20(1).pdf.

Neil, Martha, "Yale Secret Society Skull and Bones Wins Lawsuit Over Geronimo's Remains," *American Bar Association Journal* (August 2010), accessed January 10, 2020. http://www.abajournal.com/news/article/yale_secrety_society_skull_bones_wins_lawsuit_over_geronimos_remains.

"She Loves Sitting Bull," *Bismarck Weekly Tribune* (Bismarck, North Dakota: July 5, 1889), page 7, Newspapers.com, accessed February 7, 2020. www.newspapers.com/image/81382767/?terms=Bismarck%2BTribune%2BSitting%2BBull.

"Sitting Bull," Wikipedia, accessed March 29, 2020. https://en.wikipedia.org/wiki/Sitting_Bull#cite_note-64.

Sitting Bull—The Hostile Sioux Indian Chief (1914), Turner Classic Movies, accessed March 29, 2020. http://www.tcm.turner.com/tcmdb/title/552515/Sitting-Bull-The-Hostile-Sioux-Indian-Chief/.

"Spoken by President," *St. Joseph Herald* (St. Joseph, Missouri, October 13, 1898), page 1, Newspapers.com, accessed March 23, 2020. https://www.newspapers.com/image/230222451/?terms=Trans-Mississippi%2Band%2BInternational%2BExposition%2C%2BGeronimo%2C%2BNelson%2BMiles.

"Transcript of Treaty of Fort Laramie (1868)," Our Documents, accessed August 25, 2019. https://www.ourdocuments.gov/doc.php?flash=false&doc=42&page =transcript.

US Commissioners and Delegations of Sioux Chiefs Visiting Washington, October 15, 1888, Photograph, US Library of Congress, accessed February 5, 2020. www.loc.gov/item/93514650.

"William McKinley," Wikipedia, accessed March 20, 2020. https://en.wikipedia. org/wiki/William_McKinley.

Wortman, Marc, "The Bin Laden of His Day? A New Biography of Geronimo," *Daily Beast*, July 2017, accessed January 10, 2020. https://www.thedailybeast. com/the-bin-laden-of-his-day-a-new-biography-of-geronimo?ref=author.

PRIMARY RESOURCES

Hocking, Doug, personal communication, November 22, 2019.

INDEX

Acknowledgments

First, thank you to Geronimo and Sitting Bull for living such extraordinary lives; it's been an honor to explore and write about them. Thanks to all the folks who remembered and spoke about the lives of these two leaders, and to those who recorded those memories, as well as those who recorded and preserved the events that took place during Geronimo and Sitting Bull's lifetimes.

To Erin Turner, Lynn Zelem, Melissa Hayes, and the folks at TwoDot and Rowman & Littlefield, thank you for giving me the opportunity to write this book and working with me to make it a reality. Jim Hatzell, thank you for your outstanding illustrations; it's always great to work with you. Donovin Sprague, thank you for your insight into the creation of several of those illustrations. Thank you to freelance wordsmith Barry Keith Williams for polishing the manuscript and fact checking.

To George Gilland, aka *Tatanka Owichakuya* (Brings Back Buffalo), and Sharon Rasmussen, thank you for your guidance and review of the Sitting Bull and Lakota portions of this book. Kellen Cutsforth, thanks for the Buffalo Bill Cody leads. Mike Pellerzi, as always, thanks for providing your cowboy point of view.

An extra special thanks to Doug Hocking, who has reviewed and provided insight on all the Apache portions of this book. Additional thanks to Doug for taking me on Arizona field trips to such places as Dragoon Springs, Sulphur Springs, the Chiricahua Mountains (with a hike to Fort Bowie), the John Slaughter Ranch, Cottonwood Canyon, Stein's Peak, and the ruins of Old San Carlos. These trips were of extreme benefit to me as I told Geronimo's story. Thanks to all the people who accompanied us on those field trips: Guy Brunt, Bernd Brand, Carol and Rick Markstrom, Gene Baker, and Ron Olson. Thank you, Carol Markstrom, for reviewing the Apache Sunrise Ceremony sidebar.

A big thank-you to my wife, Liz, for putting up with my long hours in the basement plunking away on the computer keyboard, helping with the occasional spelling of a word, and traveling with me to New Mexico's Silver City, Pinos Altos, and beyond, into the Gila National Forest, as well as obscure places on my research trips. Thanks to my entire family for their continued support. Most of all, thanks to the Lord for giving me this opportunity and for the ability to think and write.

About the Author

BILL MARKLEY is a member of Western Writers of America (WWA) and a staff writer for WWA's *Roundup* magazine. He also writes for *True West*, *Wild West*, and *South Dakota* magazines.

Bill's first book in the Legendary West series, *Wyatt Earp and Bat Masterson: Lawmen of the Legendary West*, examines the lives of those two well-known Old West characters. His second book in the series, *Billy the Kid and Jesse James: Outlaws of the Legendary West*, delves into the lives of the two famous desperados. Both books were 2020 Will Rogers Medallion Award finalists in nonfiction.

His book, written with coauthor Kellen Cutsforth, *Old West Showdown: Two Authors Wrangle over the Truth about the Mythic Old West*, explores differing viewpoints on ten Old West characters and events, and was a 2019 Will Rogers Medallion Award finalist in nonfiction.

Bill has written three additional nonfiction books: *Dakota Epic: Experiences of a Reenactor during the Filming of* Dances with Wolves; *Up the Missouri River with Lewis and Clark*; and *American Pilgrim: A Post–September 11th Bus Trip and Other Tales of the Road*. His first historical novel, *Deadwood Dead Men*, was selected by Western Fictioneers as a finalist for its 2014 Peacemaker Award in the category Best First Western Novel. Bill also wrote the "Military Establishment" chapter and thirty entries for the *Encyclopedia of Western Expansion*.

Bill earned a bachelor's degree in biology and a master's degree in environmental sciences and engineering at Virginia Tech. In 1972 and 1973, he participated in two Antarctic field teams in association with Virginia Tech. He worked as an engineer and administrator for forty years with the South Dakota Department of Environment and Natural Resources and was a member of Toastmasters International for twenty years. Raised on a farm near Valley Forge, Pennsylvania, Bill has always loved history. He has reenacted Civil War infantry and frontier cavalry and has participated in the films *Dances with Wolves*, *Son of the Morning Star*, *Far and Away*, *Gettysburg*, and *Crazy Horse*. Bill and his wife Liz live in Pierre, South Dakota, where they raised two children and currently have two grandchildren.

ABOUT THE ILLUSTRATOR

JIM HATZELL is a graduate of the American Academy of Art in Chicago, Illinois, with a degree in Advertising and Design and in Illustration. He has a strong background in acrylic painting, pen-and-ink illustrations, and photography, and from time to time volunteers to teach art. Jim was a photographer for *Down Country Roads* magazine, and Books In Motion has used his artwork for more than one hundred book covers. Jim has been in the motion picture business since 1989, when he and Bill Markley first met on the set of *Dances with Wolves*. Jim drew quick sketches during the filming, and some illustrate Bill's book, *Dakota Epic*. Since *Dances with Wolves*, Jim has been involved in many films, including *Far and Away*, *Gettysburg*, *Geronimo*, *Crazy Horse*, *Rough Riders*, *Ride with the Devil*, *Skins*, *Comanche Warriors*, *National Treasure 2*, and, recently, *Black Wood*. He is a stagehand, and member of International Alliance of Theatrical Stage Employees Local 731. During two summer seasons, he worked as a park ranger and historic interpreter at the Little Bighorn Battlefield National Monument. Jim created the illustrations for Bill's books *Wyatt Earp and Bat Masterson: Lawmen of the Legendary West* and *Billy the Kid and Jesse James: Outlaws of the Legendary West*. Jim and his wife Jacqui make their home in Rapid City, South Dakota.